David Darot

# MASTERING THE ART OF ASSET ALLOCATION

## Comprehensive Approaches to Managing Risk and Optimizing Returns

**DAVID M. DARST**

McGraw-Hill

New York    Chicago    San Francisco    Lisbon    London
Madrid    Mexico City    Milan    New Delhi    San Juan
Seoul    Singapore    Sydney    Toronto

2 3 4 5 6 7 8 9 0 DOC/DOC 0 9 8 7

ISBN-13: 978-0-07-146334-8
ISBN-10: 0-07-146334-8

Library of Congress Cataloging-in-Publication Data
Darst, David M.
    Mastering the art of asset allocation : comprehensive approaches to managing risk and optimizing returns / by David M. Darst. -- 1st ed.
        p.      cm.
    ISBN 0-07-146334-8 (hardcover : alk. paper)   1. Asset allocation.   I. Title.
    HG4529.5.D373   2006
    332.67--dc22

                                        2005031149

This book is printed on acid-free paper.

# CONTENTS

## CHAPTER 6

## Correlations of Returns between Asset Classes    159

## SECTION 4

## FINANCIAL MARKETS ANALYSIS AND
## INVESTMENT INSIGHTS

## CHAPTER 7

## Recognizing Cyclical and Secular Turning Points    311

*This book is dedicated*

*To those who have gone before*

*Guy Bewley Darst*
*James McGinnis Darst*
*Susan McGinnis Darst*
*Kimberly Lawrence Netter*
*Eleanor Humphrey Wassman*

*and*

*To those who are going forward*

*David Martin Darst, Jr.*
*Elizabeth Mathews Darst*
*Diane Wassman Darst*

# FOREWORD

For any serious investor—whether individual or institutional—their single most important decision is how to frame the asset allocation process. The title of David Darst's book, *Mastering the Art of Asset Allocation*, is well chosen, because allocation is indeed an art. And it is an art deserving of far more thought and ongoing attention than it typically receives. All too often, portfolio allocations devolve into peer-like copycats or entrenched legacy structures.

Ideally, the allocation process should begin with a frank assessment of the investor's special circumstances—their liabilities, liquidity needs, relevant time horizons, risk tolerance (as a function of the investor's *ability* and *willingness* to assume risk), alternative resources, level of flexibility, available effort and resources for investment management and monitoring, comparative informational advantages (and disadvantages), and access to various asset classes, as well as the temperament and level of oversight of other interested parties such as an investment committee—or a spouse.

Integrating all these considerations can indeed be a complex task and a daunting challenge. This challenge should be tempered by the recognition that there is no single perfect solution, but rather the idea is to shape a balanced allocation that reasonably reflects what we know (and what we don't know) about markets and the investor's specific situation as it may evolve over time.

And like all artistic endeavors, there is significant value to be garnered from the effort, even if complete perfection always remains beyond one's grasp.

But also, like art, one can attain a higher level of skill and gratification by acquiring some basic techniques, and by studying past masters (and, in this case, past follies as well). David Darst's highly readable book is a vast reservoir of invaluable information and insights for developing more comprehensive allocation strategies that can help investors move down the path toward their financial goals.

**Martin L. Leibowitz**

# PREFACE

*Mastering the Art of Asset Allocation* is completely distinct and different from its sibling, *The Art of Asset Allocation*. Figure P.1 highlights the important differences and linkages between these two works.

As set forth in the three perimeter arrows representing *Mastering the Art of Asset Allocation*, this book builds upon and expands the building blocks of *The Art of Asset Allocation*, represented by the three inner arrows in the center of Figure P.1.

*Mastering the Art of Asset Allocation* integrates investor needs, market principles, and asset characteristics to help investors construct, conduct, and correct approaches to managing risk and optimizing returns in every type of economic and financial market environment.

The book you now have in your hands is filled with practical information to help investors allocate their assets, manage risk, and optimize returns in any set of financial market circumstances. As shown in Figure P.2, *Mastering the Art of Asset Allocation* contains tools, charts, illustrations, data information sources, and practical guidance designed to illuminate: (i) asset allocation insights; (ii) the underpinnings of asset allocation; (iii) asset class attributes; (iv) financial markets analysis and investment insights; (v) implementation tactics and strategies; and (vi) a comprehensive review of and approach to key information sources.

*Mastering the Art of Asset Allocation* has been specifically designed to enhance the financial thinking and actions of individual investors across the wealth spectrum, ranging from: (i) the *84 million U.S. households* with $100,000 or less in discretionary financial assets totaling $3.4 trillion; (ii) the *16 million U.S. households* with between $100,000 and $1 million in discretionary financial assets totaling $5.6 trillion; (iii) the *2.2 U.S. million households* with between $1 million and $10 million in discretionary financial assets totaling $6.0 trillion; and (iv) the *100,000 U.S. households* with greater than $10 million in discretionary financial assets totaling $2.2 trillion.

Many other investors, intermediaries, issuers, regulators, educators, and students will also benefit from this book, including profes-

## F I G U R E  P.1

How *Mastering the Art of Asset Allocation* Builds upon and Relates to
The Art of Asset Allocation

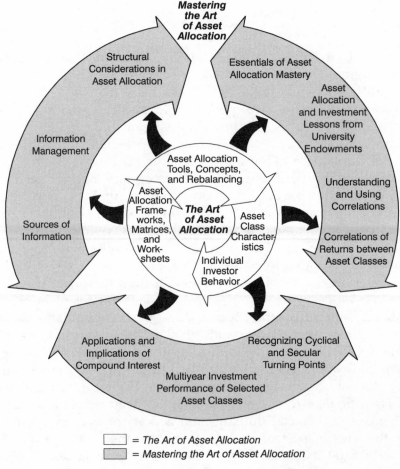

☐ = *The Art of Asset Allocation*
▨ = *Mastering the Art of Asset Allocation*

Source: The author.

sional investors, non-U.S. investors, corporate and governmental
financial officers, and supervisory authorities. Owing to its depth of
treatment and range of coverage, this book may be considered to be
unique in the realm of financial literature.

While many investors may prefer to read this book in chapter sequence from cover to cover, a number of other investors may wish to
begin with the four core chapters and fill in as they go along. Figure

**F I G U R E  P.2**

Important Themes of *Mastering the Art of Asset Allocation*

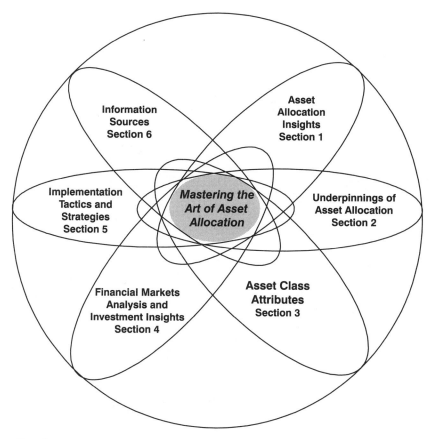

Source: The author.

P.3 sets forth one efficient method for using *Mastering the Art of Asset Allocation*.

In Figure P.3, four core chapters of this book, Chapters 1, 3, 7, and 2, are grouped together to offer the investor a quick yet thorough treatment of the most important asset allocation topics and approaches. Having read these chapters, the investor could then: (i) apply this learning to the process of asset allocation; (ii) continue reading chapters 8, 4, 5, 6, 9, and 10 (in clockwise sequence around the outside of the five core chapters shown in Figure P.3), before pursuing the process of asset allocation and investment strategy; or (iii) execute (i) and (ii) simultaneously.

One Approach to Reading *Mastering the Art of Asset Allocation*

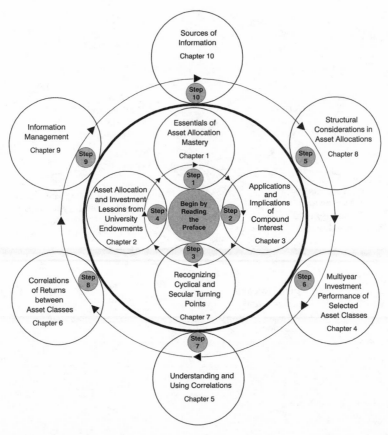

Source: The author.

Figure P.4 shows 10 special features, where to find them in this book, and why they are of use, relevance, and value to the investor. These special features include: (i) essentials of asset allocation mastery; (ii) how compound interest works; (iii) recognizing turning points; (iv) lessons from successful asset allocators; (v) structural considerations in asset allocation; (vi) asset class investment performance; (vii) understanding and using correlations; (viii) correlations of returns between asset classes; (ix) information management techniques; and (x) accessing and judging information sources.

In writing this book, I have been fortunate to be able to draw upon the wisdom and insight of a great many members of the professional,

## F I G U R E  P.4

Special Features of *The Art of Asset Allocation*

| Chapter in Which to Find the Features | Features to Be Found | Why the Features Are of Use, Relevance, and Value to the Investor |
|---|---|---|
| 1 | Essentials of asset allocation mastery | Describes the meanings, elements, and foundations of asset allocation mastery. |
| 3 | How compound interest works | Examines the inner workings and important investment applications of interest and dividend compounding. |
| 7 | Recognizing turning points | Explores how to recognize when asset prices may be reaching cyclical or secular high points or low points. |
| 2 | Lessons from successful asset allocators | Summarizes and critically assesses the approaches, advantages, and drawbacks of selected practitioners of asset allocation. |
| 8 | Structural considerations in asset allocation | Reviews financial planning, personal trusts, life insurance, annuities, tax management, and liability management in an asset allocation context. |
| 4 | Asset class investment performance | Furnishes important perspective on the returns and standard deviations of returns of 44 asset classes. |
| 5 | Understanding and using correlations | Employs several analytical constructs to help investors assess the efficacy, advantages, and caveats associated with mainstream and specialized correlations measures. |
| 6 | Correlations of returns between asset classes | Calculates and graphs the period-to-period progression of returns correlations between major asset pairs. |
| 9 | Information management techniques | Classifies information sources by topic, by channel, and by objective, and provides guidance on how to optimize conventional and internet-based information. |
| 10 | Accessing and judging information sources | Evaluates and provides pathways to 14 media-based and 9 subject-based information resources related to asset allocation and investing. |

Source: The author.

managerial, and support resources of Morgan Stanley and several other outstanding financial organizations. For reasons of space, I deeply regret that I am not able to cite each valued colleague by name; my debt is great to the asset managers, economists, portfolio managers, quantitative strategists, financial advisors, investment representatives, research analysts, legal and compliance personnel, human resources and marketing officers, investment bankers, institutional sales and trading professionals, graphics and creative services staff members, operations and technology specialists, branch managers, and the highly capable assistants, administrators, and staff members who so ably support these individuals. Many of my helpful colleagues are previously cited in the Preface to *The Art of Asset Allocation*.

In addition to these individuals, of particular value have been the advice and counsel provided by: *Charmaine Abad, Serra Abbasoglu, Helen Abe, Jon Abrahamovich, Eden Abrahams, David Abrams, Buck Adams, Jeffery Adams, Jere Sue Adams, Greg Adamson, Haroun Adamu, Daniel Aegerter, Randy Agley, Michelle Ahn, Patricia Ahn, Frank Albergo, Mark Albers, Ted Alfond, Majid Bin Ibrahim Al-Ibrahim, John Alkire, Gary Allen, Robert Allison, Tatiana Alonso, Ahmed Al-Saleh, Mohammed Mubarak Al-Sulaity, Jocelyn Altman, Arthur Altschul, Takuma Amano, Jay Ambrose, Laura Ambroseno, Bruce Amman, Kheiry Amr, Constantine Anagnostopoulos, Jill Andre-Mannix, Robert Anestis, V. Lee Archer, Jon Ardrey, George Argyros, Maxine Armstrong, Michael Armstrong, Sigurdur Arngrimsson, Robert Arnott, Anne Arras, Karen Arras, Rob Arras, Ruth Arras, Mike Arundel, Diana Aschettino, Stephen Ashley, Tabitha Aspling, Suzy Assaad, William Auriemma, Arlene Avidon, Mark Axelowitz, Miguel Bacal, Eunice Baek, Pavlos Bailas, John Bailey, Ed Baird, Scott Baker, Charlie Banta, Michael Bapis, Nicholas Bapis, Walter Bareiss, Kenneth Barrett, Lourdes Bartolome-Chuidian, Ray Basile, Jeffery Bates, Tom Batson, Keith Baum, Alison Beard, Anson Beard, Linda Beck, Morgan Becker, George Behrakis, Robert Belfer, Beverly Bell, Jonathan Bell, Molly Evans Bell, Martin Belz, Claire Benenson, Bob Benne, Amanda Bennett, J. Anthony Bennett, Bruce Bensley, Eran Ben-Zour, Laurence Bergreen, Marie-Claude Bernal, Richard Berner, Ian Bernstein, Peter Bernstein, Tom Bernstein, Steven Berstler, Walter Berukoff, Scott Bessent, Marci Bettinger, Sonja Beutler, Paul Bevin, Charlotte Beyer, Lucinda Bhavsar, Anne Bianchi, Andrea Bici, Douglas Bielefeld, Tony Bienstock, Jennifer Bier, Michael Bills, Kathy Birk, Martin Bisang, Karen Bisgeir, Jonathan Blau, Courtney Smith Blondel, Susan Boccardi, Mimi Bock, Leslie Bocskor, Kathy Boger, Michelle Bogner, Candace Bond, Sheldon Bonovitz, Sara Boonin, Gog Boonswang, Stephen Booth, Walter Bopp, Sue Bordash, Ruggero Borletti, Jorge Born, Benjamin Bornstein, Ivan Borriello, Debra Bosniak, Jean-Baptiste Bosson, Anthony Bova, Denis Bovin, Robert Bowers, Amanda Bowker, Brian Boyd, Patrick Brady, Lawrence Braitman, Richard Braitman, Sabine Brandt, Josh Bratt, Neil Braverman, Steve Braverman, Lee Brewington, Louis Brill, Peggy Brill, Felipe Brillembourg, Michel Brogard, Rita Brogley, Diana Brooks, Yolanda Brooks, Frank Brosens, Bill Brown, Noelle Brussard, Brian Buckley, Dasi Budhrani, Lois Budman, Mary Lou Budman-Labe, Allan Bufferd, Georgia Bullitt, Autumn Buracker, Franz Burda, Granville Burgess, Michael Burke, Mira Burke, Robert Burke, Matt Burkhard, Alex Burlingame, Jim Burns, Bruce Burrow, James Burton, Martin Bussmann, Erin Byboth, Brenda Bynum, Carlton Byrd, Conrad*

Cafritz, Julia Cahill, Don Callahan, Bob Capazzo, Janet Carlson, Andrew Carter, Brother Brian Carty, Joan Caspi, Dwight Cass, Rose Castrignano, Jerry Castro, Wayland Cato, Neil Cavuto, Daniel Cedro, Paul Cejas, Geoff Centner, Dorothea Cernera, Walid Chammah, Simon Chaput, Rajiv Chaudhri, David Chazen, Elizabeth Chen, Duen-Chian Cheng, Nicole Cheslock, William Child, Tim Childe, Silas Chou, Alexandra Christiansen, Tom Chubet, Laura Ciminera, Liz Claman, Mitzi Clawson, Tom Clephane, Coco Close, John Close, Kelly Close, Fred Clough, Putnam Coes, Orly Cogan, Doug Cohen, Gwen Cohen, Keith Colburn, Chris Cole, Bob Coleman, Mike Collins, Rob Colvin, Stephen Comiskey, Michael Commaroto, Catherine Compere, Pete Coneway, Casey Considine, Andrew Conti, Michael Conway, Richard Coons, Thea Cooper, Peter Coors, John Copeland, Dewey Corley, Robert Cornie, Richard Corriere, Nick Corso, Mario Corti, Cynthia Coulson, James Cramer, George Crapple, Carl Crego, L. Russell Crow, Bill Crowley, Cristina Cruz, Michele Cubic, Germaine Cuff, Simon Cundey, Stephen Cunningham, Karen Cuozzo, Sean Cusack, Robert Cushman, Andrea Da Rif, Douglas Da Rif, Gerda Da Rif, Linda Daines, Allen Damon, David W. Darst, Bernard Darty, Marius Daugirdas, Claudia Dave, Hemang Dave, Lindsay Davenport, Johnson David, Frank Davidson, Thomas Davin, Christopher Davis, Charles Davis, Henry Davison, William Davison, Marguerite Day, Sean Day, Carlos de Almeida, Gabriel de Bobadilla, Guy de Chazal, Andrea de Cholnoky, Guillaume de Dalmas, Frank De Luca, Joao Marcos Cabral De Menezes, Matteo de Nora, Patrick de Piccioto, Vivian de Picciotto, Gael de Roquefeuil, Nathaniel de Rothschild, Robert de Rothschild, Stephanie Dedes, Christel DeHaan, Rick Della Vedova, Michael Dellinger, Susan Delmonico, Alex Denner, Jasmina Denner, Steven Denning, Ken DeRegt, Matt DeSalvo, Rich DeSalvo, Desh Deshpande, Jacques Desmidt, Maryellen Dever, Beth DeWoody, Anthony Di Iorio, Steve Dixon, Tanja Djurdjevic, Randy Domikis, Alexis Donnelly-Glick, Daniel Donohue, Christine Dooley, Mark Douglass, Laura Dox, Teun Draaisma, Sean Drewniak, Devon Driscoll, Harley DuBois, Lou Duff, Phillip Duff, Joseph Dumars, Robert Dwyer, John Dyment, Glenn Earle, Jackie Eastwick, Matt Eastwick, Marilyn Ebbitt, Claire Eckert, Fred Eckert, Argie Economou, Christi Edwards, Florence Eid, Nancy Eklund, Winthrop Eldredge, George Elinsky, Debbie Ellen, Jennifer Emanuelson, Okechukwu Enelamah, Kathy Entwistle, Pamela Erlanger, Christopher Errico, Stephen Errico, Doug Everson, Marc Faber, Charles Fago, Maya Faivre, Mike Fascitelli, Deb Fay, Joseph Field, Mark Fisher, Mariana Fitzpatrick, Andrew Fitzsimmons, Ed Fitzsimmons, Fred Fleisher, Gene Flood, Lars Forsberg, Oscar Forsberg, Chris Forster, Ami Forte, Katherine Foster, Carl Fragapane, Rose Fragapane, Richard Frank, Robert Frank, David Frankfort, Anne Fredericks, Deborah Friant, Ed Friedman, Scott Frost,

*Ming-Xia Fu, Ben Fujihara, Patrice Fujimoto, Michael Fung, Ben Funnell, Lorraine Gallard, Maryann Gallivan, Sam Gallucci, Pablo Gana, Juan Gandarias, Bill Garbarino, Victor Garber, Peter Garrison, Diane Gartner, Robert Gauntt, Mark Gherity, Mac Gibbons, Sabrina Gibbs, Paul Gigot, Bruce Gilardi, Michelle Gilardi, Valerie Gilson,* and *Nick Giovanniello.*

Major encouragement, insight, and support have been unremittingly and faithfully rendered by: *Tina Giovanniello, Jolyon Gissell, Judy Glaser, Ed Glassmeyer, Alan Glatt, Richard Gledhill, Susan Glusica, Peter Goddard, Bob Goergen, Pam Goergen, Alan Goldberg, Mickey Goldberg, Lloyd Goldfarb, Paul Goldschmidt, Edward Goldstein, Marian Goodell, Jerry Goodman, James Gorman, Karene Grad, Joan Granlund, Robert Granovsky, Irina Grant, George Grattan, Harry Gray, Rachel Gray, Mark Green, Helen Greiner, Troy Griepp, Donald Gries, Steven Grossman, Devin Grosz, David Grumhaus, Jennifer Grumhaus, Shubie Gulati, Gilman Gunn, Randy Gunnip, Mark Habley, Lynn Haffner, Luc Hafner, Judith Halabrin, Reed Halladay, Paige Hallsted, Randall Halvorsen, Curt Hammond, Emily Hanlon, Jeff Hanlon, Jessica Hann, Erv Hanson, Carla Harris, Jonathan Harris, Ray Harris, Trevor Harris, Griff Harsh, Rodes Hart, Aubrey Harwell, Lloyd Hascoe, Bill Haslam, Daria Hassner, Bob Hatala, Eileen Hatala, Gus Hauser, Rita Hauser, Jennifer Hausler, Sandy Haviland, Drew Hawkins, Katie Hay, Rick Haynes, Suzn Head, Steve Hefter, Doug Heidt, Angela Hejdak, Katherine Hennessey, Mary Herms, Sue Herrera, James Herring, Mami Hidaka, Barry Hines, Jonathan Hirtle, Lucy Hochberg, Noelle Holly, Gina Holzman, Lucie Honosutomo, Catherine Hooper, Elie Horn, Charles Hostetler, Cynthia Hostetler, John Houlihan, Sheila Houlihan, Charles Huebner, Jeff Huebner, Bill Huffman, Dan Hughes, Will Huthnance, Julie Iarossi, Roger Ibbotson, Barbara Iler, Tyler Iller, Allison Ilsley, Richard Ilsley, Ron Insana, Frederick Ip, Honsum Ip, Tom Ireland, Audrey Irmas, Andrea Iten, John Jaber, Rupa Jack, Ashawnta Jackson, Jess Jackson, Martin Jacobson, Manoj Jain, O. Aldon James, David Jarach, Guillermo Jasson, Robert Jeffrey, Daniel Jick, Michelle Johns, Brenda Johnson, Lucy Baines Johnson, Howard Johnson, Jamie Johnston, Ellis Jones, Louise Jones, Anne Juge, David Juge, Derek Junck, Matt Kabot, Daniel Kahneman, Mark Kammert, Henry Kaplan, Ajay Kapur, Karn Karuhadej, Eric Kayne, Musa Kazdal, Mark Kelly, Sean Kelly, Jack Kemp, Jimmy Kemp, Bernard Kennedy, George Kennedy, Tracy Kennedy, Doug Ketterer, Aditya Khanna, Mary Kidder, Jane Kim, Rick Kimball, James Kimmel, Lillian King, Pen King, Chew-Mee Foo Kirtland, Petr Kocourek, Elizabeth Kolleeny, Hayedeh Kosrovani, Aaron Kozmetsky, Greg Kozmetsky, Jeffrey Krames, Harby Kreeger, Dick Kreitler, Holly Kreuter, Lenny Kreutner, Philipp Kreuzer, Rocky Kroeger, Roxanne Kuba, Adam Kudelka, Jason Kudelka, Tom Kuhns, Elian Kulukundis, Abhisek Kumar, Richa Kumar, Mary Kurish, Didi Kurniawan, Yumi Kuwana,*

*Cammie Kwok, Raymond Kwok, Audra Lalley, James Lane, Brian Lange, Patrick Langone, Bob Lanigan, Tom Lanter, Elizabeth Lasco, Tracy Lavery, Druscilla Lawton, Brian Leach, Steven Leatherman, Sara LeBlanc, Bob Lee, Paul Lehrman, Marty Leibowitz, Jorge Paulo Lemann, Brook Lenfest, Sarah Leopold, Andre Levy, Dominique Levy, Kurt Lewin, Mike Lewittes, Charlie Leykum, Lucy Leykum, Rosalie Leykum, Howard Liberman, Laura Libretti, Carla Lien, David Lifschultz, Derek Limbocker, Susan Lin, Carrie Lincourt, Bill Link, Jay Link, Joanne Lipman, Linda Litner, Jacques Littlefield, Carol Liucci, Joe Lizzio, Katharine Lo, Todd Locicero, Jim Lockhart, Dahlia Loeb, Svetlana Lokhova, Diane Lotti, Jonathan Lourie, Beverly Love, John Lowden, Linda Ludeke, Iver Lyche, Todd Lyon, Paul Lyons, Consuelo Mack, Ranger Mack, Walter Mack, Elizabeth Madigan, Bob Magel, Londa Maher, Charles Mak, Shazia Makhdumi, Matt Maloney, Steve Mandel, Kirk Mandlin, Allison Maner, Robert Mann, Mary Jane Maounis, Alvaro Marangoni, Ezra Marcos, Joanne Marini, Andrea Markezin, Jack Markwalter, Juanita Markwalter, Clay Marquardt, Mona Marquardt, Tom Marsico, Dick Marston, Jane Martinez, Del Marting, Laurel Martin-Harris, Raul Mas, Eric Maskin, Carol Massar, Olga Massov, Ed Mathias, Bob Matschullat, Karen Matte, Cecile Mattei, Cecilia Mattingly, James Mattingly, Mary Mattingly, Monica Mattingly, Geoffrey Mavar, Jacqueline Mazzilli, Ann Olivarius McAllister, Jef McAllister, Brian McAuliffe, Mac McCabe, Jean McCann, Giselle McCrea, Kathy McDonough, Pat McDonough, Dagen McDowell, Leslie McElwreath, Peter McGeough, Mike McGrath, John McIntyre, Bill McKenna, Ken McKenzie, James McLaren, Tim McLaughlin, Neil McLeish, Bill McMahon, Steve McMenamin, Susan McNealy, John McNulty, Henry McVey, Mike McVicker, Mathew Mead, Alan Meckler, Michael Melignano, Tom Melly, Hermann Memmer, Les Menkes, Julia Menocal, David Merage, Greg Merage, Lin Merage, Paul Merage, Richard Merage, Cory Mervis, Shawn Mesaros, Chrissy Mesia, Brett Messing, Angelos Metaxa, Michael Michael, Sharon Milligan, Eric Mindich, Francesca Minerva, Lisa Moavero, Ken Moffett, Jennifer Mogck, David Molotsky, Michelle Money, Tarek Mooro, Garrett Moran, Kevin Morano, Christina Morin, Amanda Morris, Helen Morris, Wistar Morris, Alasdair Morrison, Julie Morrone, Mike Moses, Sig Mosley, Melinda Mount, Vreni Mueller, Sophie Muir, Cynthia Muller, Steve Munger, Barry Munitz, Mariana Munoz, Aviva Murphy, Lisa Murphy, Gregg Nabhan, Girish Nadkarny, Patricia Nadosy, Peter Nadosy, Parviz Nafissian, Mike Nahass, Andrea Nasher, Ray Nasher, Marcel Nauer, David Neeleman, David Neibart, Roger Nekton, Brad Nelson, Don Nelson, Jo Nelson, Karen Nelson, Marcus Nelson, Steve Nelson, John Nemelka, Matt Nesto, Joe Neubauer, Anita Nichols, Chris Niehaus, Ed Nolan, Carly Noland, Sharri Northcut, Craig Norton, Cynthia Norville, Sam Nunn, Paul Nuti, Colleen O'Brien, Joe O'Brien,*

*Anna-Marie O'Connor, Stephanie Oesch, Ellen Oetjen, Dan Offit, Karim Ojjeh, Pilar O'Leary, Bill O'Leary, Valerie O'Neill, Jeff Opdyke, Virginia Oregui, Scott Orr, Sev Ortale, Kathy Osborne, Jim O'Shaughnessy, Bill O'Shaughnessy,* and *Larry Oshin.*

Of great help have been: *Marc Oster, Donna Ziegler O'Sullivan, Erinch Ozada, Gary Pacarro, Gwen Pacarro, Noel Pacarro, Cynthia Pachikara, Steve Page, Mary Palladino, Richard Palladino, Peter Palmedo, Dick Palmer, William Pao, Diane Paolilli, Kyri Papadopoulos, Leonora Papadopoulos, Rosalie Papadopoulos, Diane Papaleonardos, Steve Papermaster, Kathleen Paprocki, Jeffrey Parker, Pierluigi Parmeggiani, Bill Parrott, Chuck Patton, Richard Patton, Stan Pauley, Jeff Paulsen, Doug Pavese, Nick Pavle, Riccardo Pavoncelli, Bo Peabody, Harry Peden, Paula Penn, Sharon Perhac, Donald Perlyn, Marilyn Perlyn, Andre Perold, Richard Perry, Keley Petersen, Brian Pfeifler, Brian Phillips, Courtney Phillips, James Phillips, Joseph Phillips, Robert Philpott, Pansy Phua, Aviva Pinto, David Piotrowski, Christine Plappart-Leenheer, Erica Platt, Karen Plitt, Jennifer Poff, Beth Pollack, Jeff Polner, Paul Pomfret, Sue Ponce, Steve Pond, Richard Portogallo, Wiet Pot, Greg Powell, Malcolm Pray, Seth Price, Marilyn Prince, Leslie Pritchett, Morris Propp, Wayne Provost, Betsy Quick, Bard Quku, Stuart Rabin, Rich Radke, Lily Rafii, Mitra Rafii, Tina Rafii, Zia Rafii, Gautam Ramchandani, Sandy Randt, Roz Ratchford, Pramathesh Rath, Dewitt Reel, Guy Reel, Ronald Reel, Willard Reel, Rich Reynolds, Peter Ricchiuti, Hanako Ricciardi, Kevin Richardson, Kristin Richardson, Laura Richardson, Tim Richardson, Matthew Ridnouer, Linda Riefler, George Rieger, Lynn Riehl, Bob Riley, Dennis Roach, Sid Roberson, Rich Roberts, Adam Robison, Lori Roethenmund, Clarence Rogers, Joe Rogers, Vreni Rohrer, Kristen Rolfes, Kevin Rollins, Michael Rome, Joan Ronayne, Jada Rosenberg, Steve Rosenberg, Howard Rosenbloom, Keith Rosenbloom, Harold Rossen, Steve Rossi, Evan Roth, Kay Rothman, Olivier Roussel, Dave Rozek, Jami Rubin, Andrew Rudd, Paul Ruddleston, Glenn Ruffenach, Gene Ruiz, Regina Rule, Lisa Rumore, Karl Ruppert, Cherie Ryan, Diana Ryan, Rick Ryan, Thomas Ryan, Troy Ryder, Mark Rzepczynski, Karl Safft, Cinzia Sala, Ugo Sala, Joan Saltzman, Jeff Salzman, Tarik Abu Samra, David Samson, Rick Sanchez, Mark Sandbach, Steven Sansom, Linda Santacroce, Bob Santora, Brad Saunders, Eric Savolainen, John Schaefer, David Schaeffer, Steven Schaeffer, Gene Schatz, Robert Scherer, Eric Schiffer, Walter Schindler, Michael Schneickert, Elizabeth Schoellkopf, Todd Schrock, Jim Schwab, Samuel Schwab, Tom Schwartz, Steve Schwarzman, Rosanna Scimeca, Andrea Scola, Bob Scott, Daniel Sears, Kate Seelye, Ilana Seidel, Stefan Selig, Molly Sell, Frank Seminara, Raffaella Serventi, Severn T. Severn, Myra Shankin, Alfred Shasha, Dennis Shasha, Robert Shasha, Neal Shear, Chuck Sheedy, Melissa*

*Sheer, Jim Sheerin, Thad Shelly, Bing Shen, Mark Shenkman, Orrin Sherman, Richard Sherman, Steve Sherrill, Virgil Sherrill, James Sherrin, Robert Shiller, Judith Shipley, Karen Shore, Mary Jo Shotting, Rick Shubart, Linda Shwab, Carlos Sicupira, Herb Siegel, Jeremy Siegel, Peter Sigal, Matthew Sigel, Said Signor, Ron Silver, Shira Simon, Elizabeth Simpson, Alison Singer, Maxine Singer, Stephanie Singer, Atinant Sirivadhanabhakdi, Linda Sittenfeld, Bing Sizemore, Ole Skaarup, Damaris Skouras, Amy Slack, Andrea Slattery, Jeri Slavin, Andrew Slimmon, Ray Smesko, Ben Smith, Chet Smith, David Smith, Janet Marie Smith, Menlo Smith, Roger Smith, John Smyth, Cori Snyder, John Snyder, Nickolas Sophinos, Bernardo Soriano, Paul Sortal, Larry Spears, Bettina Spiller, Marga Spiller, Jeff Springer, Kristin Sprows, Manganam Srinivasan, Bob Stafford, Susan Steele, Fred Stein, Joan Steinberg, Paul Steinborn, Carolyn Stewart, Chuck Stewart, Milt Stewart, Rebecca Stilwell, Mariela Stochetti, Erich Stöckli, Tom Stokes, Hans Stoll, Wendy Strauss, Bill Strong, Michael Struckman, Bill Stutt, Ram Subramaniam, Keith Suenholz, Carroll Suggs, Ed Sullivan, Lawrence Summers, Troy Sumrall, Stuart Sundlun, Jennifer Suri, Aldo Svaldi, Bill Svoboda, Kendra Swanson, David Swartz, Jeff Swartz, David Swensen, Andy Szabo, Bill Szilasi, Renee Tabben, Geoff Tabin, Ashley Tagatac, Dean Takahashi, Su-Shan Tan, Tap Taplin, Ben Tarantino, Ron Taylor, Ron Thacker, Todd Thedinga, Ann Thivierge, David Thomas, Jacquelyn Thomas, Lisa Thomas, Matt Thomas, John Townsend, Steve Townsend, Leah Trabich, Vince Travagliato, Marcia Tucker, Peter Tufano, Bill Tugurian, Peter Tung, Matthew Turnbull, Greg Turner, Ian Turpin, Chris Umscheid, Kara Underwood, Sarah Urbanovsky, Salima Vahabzadeh, Kara Valentine, Chris van Aeken, Jim Van De Ven, Valentina van der Dys, Laura Van Orden, Karin Van Petten, Bill Van Scoyoc, Heath Vanrenen, Donna Varbaro, Romny Vasquez, Greg Vaughan, Bridget Venus, Peter Veruki, Leo Villareal, Matias Villarroel, Daniel Vock, Bill Vogel, Ted Vogt, Tatiana Von Der Pahlen, Jon von Planta, Ellyn von Schilling, Alexandra Vovolini-Laskaridis, Chris Wadner, Jack Wadsworth, Peggy Gries Wager, Robert Waggoner, David Walker, Ira Walker, Stephen Walker, David Wallace, Jean Wallace, W. Gardner Wallace, Ken Wallace, Nicole Warin, Sandy Warner, Casey Wasserman, Brian Weber, John Westerfield, Bianca Watts, Caleb Watts, Cynthia Watts, John Wauters, Sue Weinberg, Carrie Wenger, Susanna Thomas Weston, Marcus Wheeler, Mike Wheeler, Steve Wheeler, James Whitehead, John Whitney, Fred Whittemore, Laurence Whittemore, Byron Wien, Benjamin Williams, Mark Williamson, Sarah Wilmer, Mindy Wilson, Daniel Wimsatt, Thomas Windler, Jennifer Winn, Greg Winner, Amelia Wolfe, Ken Wolfe, Tom Wolfe, Mark Wolfson, Jerry Wood, Mike Wood, Edward Woolner, Erin Wright, Doug Wuerl, Todd Yannuzzi, Alex Yearsley, Susan York, Robin Yoshimura,*

*Heather Young, Joan Young, William Zabel, Frank Zafran, Drew Zager, Gerald Zang, Sulaika Zarrouk, Dean Zikria, C.J. Zilveti, Gregory Zorthian, Bobby Zrike, Barbara Zuckerberg, Dina Zuckerberg, Lloyd Zuckerberg,* and *Roy Zuckerberg.*

Particular energy, creativity, and diligence have characterized all the input from my teammates: *Annie Chang, Frances Drake, Liya Eijvertinya, Dave El Helou, Nick Greenough, Allison Kotzin, Elaine Lavin,* and *Eric Perlyn.* Words cannot express the depth of my gratitude to several of my partners in this work. In many ways, this book could not have become a reality without their affirmation, persistence, patience, intelligence, enthusiasm, guidance, character, perspective, diligence, dedication, clarity of thinking, pragmatism, and high ideals. I want to thank: *Regina Maher, Sarah Nelson, Jennifer Polner, Barbara Reinhard, Josephine Rosenberg, Annie Rusher, Michael Strong,* and *Stephanie Whittier.*

It gives me great joy to here salute, love, and appreciate my family, who have unfailingly cheered me and cheered me on. In respectful homage this book is presented with my embrace to: my wife, *Diane Darst,* our children, *Elizabeth Darst* and *David Darst,* my brothers, *Guy Darst, Chuck Darst,* and *Dan Darst,* as well as *Kitty Darst, Josie Darst, Mary Darst, Jackson Darst, Elaine Woodall, Allison Eden, Jim Eden, Tom Woodall, Valerie Belmont, Debra Lanman, Jonathan Lanman, J.T. Lanman, Nell Lanman, Donald Netter, Bob Wassman, Bobby Wassman, Robert Wassman,* and *Susan Wassman.*

The word "mastering" can be traced through the word "mastery" to the Old English word "maegester" meaning "one having control or authority," to the Latin word "magister," meaning "chief, head, director, or teacher," which derives from the Latin "magnus," meaning "great." "Mastering," or "mastery" appears in familiar usage in such expressions as an International Grandmaster in chess, a Life Master in bridge, the Grand Master of the Order of Malta, the Gandalf Grand Master Award for life achievement in fantasy writing, the Masters Golf Tournament held each year in Augusta, Georgia, and not least, in the work of the hip-hop impresario Grandmaster Flash.

Among our numerous modern-day dictionary definitions of mastery are: (i) great skillfulness and knowledge of some subject or activity; (ii) command, possession, reliance, perseverance, or tenacity; and (iii) dexterity, address, adroitness, expertness, proficiency, competence, craft, facility, excellence, or success. I hereby wish investors much success in all market environments with the help of these pages.

**David Martin Darst**

# SECTION 1

## ASSET ALLOCATION INSIGHTS

# CHAPTER 1

# ESSENTIALS OF ASSET ALLOCATION MASTERY

## OVERVIEW

The purpose of this chapter is to introduce the concept of mastering the art of asset allocation, to explain how, why, and when mastery of the discipline of asset allocation contributes to investment success, and to spell out some of the significant advantages of and hindrances to asset allocation mastery. Mastering a given subject or field of endeavor often requires: (i) fundamental knowledge of and exposure to pathways of practical usage; (ii) the development of insight, skill, and judgment; and (iii) curiosity about and openness to continued learning.

This chapter also explores and examines the meanings of mastering the art of asset allocation. Mastery of a discipline usually means approaching it with energy and enthusiasm, exploring its core and frontiers in novel ways, both on their own and via bridges to other experiences, and embracing the discipline with respect for historical understanding and with openness toward new approaches, tools, and concepts.

Mastering the art of asset allocation builds upon and extends *investor-related* successes and lessons, *market-related* principles and subtleties, and *asset-related* characteristics and performance parameters. In view of their potentially significant role within many portfolios, this chapter contains investment perspectives on alternative investments, which are often considered to be outside of the conventionally defined asset categories of equities, fixed-income securities, and cash. Alternative investments include: real estate and real estate investment trusts (REITs); real assets such as precious metals, commodities, oil and gas interests, and timber interests; private equity and venture capital; managed futures funds; hedge funds and funds of funds; and inflation-protected securities.

This chapter concludes with selected guidelines, considerations, and potential investment areas for exploration in an environment subject to crises and financial market dislocations.

## MEANINGS AND ELEMENTS OF MASTERY

True mastery of an activity frequently involves steady improvement through careful, patient, and reflective effort. Some of the fundamental meanings and elements of asset allocation are set forth in Figure 1.1.

For example, Tiger Woods and Michael Jordan, each a champion within their respective sports of golf and basketball, are reputed to have considerably augmented and extended their natural athletic powers by rigorous practice regimens, judicious adaptation of physiology, strength and conditioning techniques, and the engagement of candid, perceptive coaches and personal trainers. Similarly, attaining asset allocation mastery requires: (i) regular and structured scrutiny of the *actual* results of asset allocation and investment strategy relative to their *anticipated* outcomes, to discern the reasons for and causes of important investment successes or failures; (ii) searching out ways of improving the flow of relevant information regarding asset classes, capital-market conditions, and implementation vehicles (in the post-2000 era, a good example of such implementation vehicles is the substantial increase in the types and coverage of exchange-traded funds); and (iii) locating one or a small number of sources of wisdom, objectivity, acumen, and integrity who can opine on the reasonableness and potential efficacy of investment strategies and vehicles.

In the worlds of art, science, literature, government, religion, business, medicine, or investing, mastery of any vocation may be furthered by an ability to visualize the known (and unknown) world in innova-

**F I G U R E  1.1**

Fundamental Meanings of Asset Allocation Mastery

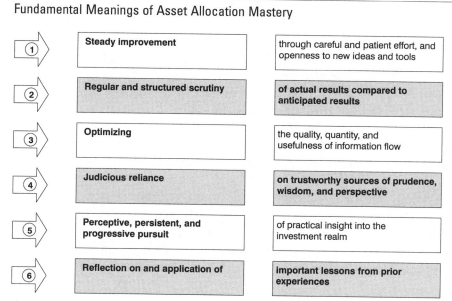

Note: The diagram above is intended to build upon and extend the approach set forth in Figure 1.2, "Fundamental Meanings of Asset Allocation," on page 6 of *The Art of Asset Allocation*.

Source: The author.

tive and welcoming ways. Just as Pablo Picasso could mentally see a bicycle seat and a set of handlebars juxtaposed to powerfully represent the head of a steer, so can certain investors perceive value or growth potential where consensus investor opinion sees none. Mastery of the art of asset allocation may derive from such talents as (i) recognizing the portfolio protection power of two or more specific asset classes acting in combination; (ii) identifying tax- and expense-efficient ways of increasing (or limiting) exposure to selected types of investments; or (iii) identifying cross-market and cross-border asset equivalencies that differ only in superficial ways.

Mastery of the challenges, tenets, nuances, and potential shortfalls of asset allocation is often associated with an ability to approach financial and real asset markets with perspective and sound judgment. Perspective can assist in the appraisal of an asset's intrinsic value relative to its price: (i) viewed in the light of recent market history; and (ii) compared to other kinds of similar and dissimilar assets. In an investment context, perspective also helps separate what is important from what is not important. In the realm of chess, one of the traits that separates a true grandmaster from an otherwise exceptionally skilled player is a tendency to consider only a limited set of elegant moves, rather than a larger number of suboptimal gambits. Similarly, mastering the art of asset allocation stems from focusing on, considering, and executing the right number of strategic and tactical shifts, at the right times, and for appropriate lengths of time. An equally crucial component of perspective is the facility to admit mistakes and unwind or reverse certain investment actions if they prove to be wrong.

Another important facet of asset allocation mastery comes from a longer-term understanding of the influences of geopolitics, economic and demographic trends, inter- and intraregional conflicts and alliances, the evolution of financial, fiscal, and currency market developments, technology and the Internet, taxation and regulatory norms, and other factors on the prices of stocks, bonds, cash, and alternative investments. For example, many financial-market participants considered cash-equivalent instruments to be *inexpensive* in 1980–1981, when U.S. dollar-denominated certificates of deposit and similar securities were yielding 15% or more. When considering the opportunity costs of rolling over such instruments (as they matured) into 12%, then 9%, then 6%, and then 3% securities, *while missing out on two of the most powerful bull markets in history* (as the S&P 500 index rose 15 times, from 100 in 1982 to more than 1,500 in early 2000, and 10-year U.S. Treasury bond yields declined from 15.7% in 1981 to 3.08% in June 2003), cash instruments in 1980 and 1981 were, in fact, *expensive*, rather than cheap. On the other hand, when short-term interest rates are quite low, a similar two-sided debate may be conducted about whether cash is expensive or cheap.

## FOUNDATIONS OF MASTERY

In the discipline and practice of asset allocation, the foundations of mastery derive from the meanings and elements of mastery and lay the groundwork for strategic portfolio construction and tactical portfolio rebalancing. Figure 1.2 spells out several important asset-related, market-related, and investor-related foundations of asset allocation mastery.

   ◆ **Asset-Related Foundations:** To master asset allocation and
      investment strategy, it is important to understand and be able
      to apply the principles of dividend and interest-income
      compounding to portfolio value preservation and growth.
      Chapter 3 describes these principles.

Foundations of Asset Allocation Mastery

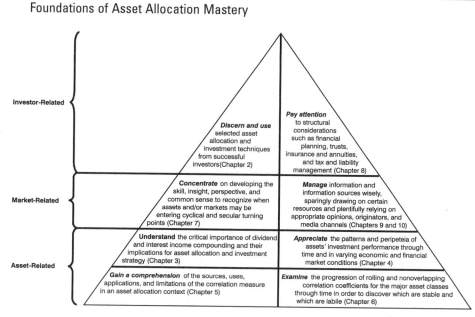

Note: The diagram above is intended to build upon and extend the approach delineated in Figure 1.3, "Foundations of Asset Allocation," on page 8 of *The Art of Asset Allocation*.

Source: The author.

Another fundamental component of asset allocation mastery is having comprehension and perspective about the patterns, amplitudes, durations, and reversals of assets' returns, standard deviations of returns, and correlations of returns in varying economic and financial market conditions. Chapter 4 presents these crucially significant details of assets' investment performance.

By quantifying the ways in which assets' returns tend to move in concert with or in contrast to the returns of other assets, correlations can exert meaningful influence on the investment success or failure of a portfolio as a whole. Chapter 5 explores the sources, uses, applications and limitations of the correlation measure in an asset allocation context, and Chapter 6 examines the specific progression through time of rolling and nonoverlapping correlation coefficients for the major asset classes in order to discover which are stable and which are likely to change.

- ◆ **Market-Related Foundations:** It is very difficult to master asset allocation without being able to recognize when different kinds of asset classes are approaching, at, or past cyclical and secular turning points in their pricing and valuation. Through analysis of the fundamental, valuation, and psychological/technical/liquidity factors affecting the prices of selected asset classes, Chapter 7 sets forth some of the essential constituents needed to develop the skill, insight, perspective, and common sense that can help identify primary short- and long-term asset-price inflection points.

In many respects, asset allocation mastery is also an exercise in effective and efficient information management. Chapters 9 and 10 provide guidance in the location and usage of information sources and equally importantly, in the evaluation of appropriate opinions, originators, and media channels.

- ◆ **Investor-Related Foundations:** True mastery of any calling often rests upon an ability to perceive and apply some of the methods, reasoning, and skill sets of other successful practitioners. Chapter 2 helps recognize and individually shape selected asset allocation and investment techniques from certain investors who have compiled exemplary records of investment performance under highly diverse sets of global asset-market conditions.

Because *how* investors own assets can be as indispensable as *what* assets they own, it is useful to pay attention to structural considerations such as taxes and liability management. Chapter 8 focuses on structural considerations in asset allocation.

## ADVANTAGES AND DRAWBACKS OF MASTERY

### Advantages

- ◆ **Deepened understanding** of how and why specific investment results have been achieved in the past (or might be achieved in the future), and whether such results should be considered rare or ordinary.
- ◆ **Improved risk identification, risk quantification, and risk management** in portfolio construction and portfolio adjustment. Understanding the primacy of income compounding to wealth creation and the criticality of correlation coefficients to the management of portfolio standard deviations can fortify and augment investment results through time.

◆ **Augmented likelihood of achieving sustained satisfactory investment results.** The chances of favorable consequences may be increased through appreciation of investments' past and projected return, risk, and correlation characteristics, knowledge and application of appropriate investment techniques, judicious structural considerations, efficacious information management, and clear-seeing cyclical and secular investment perspective.

## Drawbacks

◆ **A specious sense of investment accomplishment due to fallacious linkages** between portfolio allocations and results. At times, positive outcomes may have been due to fortune and chance instead of skill and science. It is important, yet sometimes difficult, to distinguish luck-engendered returns from deliberately produced returns.

◆ **Incomplete and/or inaccurate ideas** as to how and why assets' investment performance may differ from past results. Erroneous expectations and substandard outcomes may follow from faulty assumptions, linear extrapolations, and unawareness of just how far removed from normality certain returns, standard deviations of returns, and correlations of returns might be.

◆ **Adoption of a static, inflexible, one-size-fits-all approach** with insufficient regard for global asset market conditions and input from impartial sources of discernment, understanding, and insight.

## INVESTING PERSPECTIVES ON ALTERNATIVE INVESTMENTS

### Choices and Considerations

Alternative assets should only be considered for qualified investors of appropriate financial means, investment experience, time horizon, tax status, and risk profile. Alternative assets include: (i) real estate and real estate investment trusts (REITs); (ii) private equity and venture capital; (iii) managed futures; (iv) hedge funds and funds of funds; (v) real assets (such as commodities, precious metals, oil and gas interests, and timber interests); and (vi) inflation-indexed securities.

The key drivers of returns, standard deviations of returns, and correlations of returns for alternative asset classes tend to be different from those affecting conventional asset classes such as stocks, bonds, and cash. Such factors include: (i) manager skill and proprietary trading methodologies; (ii) the use of leverage, derivatives, and short-selling; (iii) exploitable inefficiencies in the underlying asset markets; and (iv) supply-demand influences, and/or store-of-value forces, rather than the capitalization of income flows, as important determinants of alternative assets' prices.

Due to the relatively wide dispersions of returns among active asset managers within the alternative investments space between first quartile investment performance (25th best out of a population of 100 managers) and third quartile investment performance (75th best out of a population of 100 managers), several categories of alternative assets may offer the opportunity to capture significant alpha (returns in excess of benchmark returns). It is important to keep in mind that different types of alternative assets may differ significantly from each other as well as from conventional assets.

Certain kinds of alternative assets may help enhance an investor's portfolio performance in unusual economic and financial conditions, including: (i) extremely volatile, or unusually stable, stock, bond, or currency environments; (ii) highly inflationary, deflationary, or stagflationary eras; (iii) periods of significant imbalances in global supply-demand relationships for certain kinds of assets, goods, or materials; and (iv) instances of extraordinary levels of investor capital inflows or outflows to or from specific kinds of assets.

## Assessing Alternative Investments

Given their heterogeneous and frequently differentiated nature, alternative investments possess a number of advantages and disadvantages, which Table 1.1 lists.

## Advantages

- **Improved overall risk-reward profile** of investors' portfolios, owing to special patterns of returns, standard deviations of returns, and correlations of returns of many alternative investments.
- **New implementation vehicles, analytical techniques, research resources, asset-class breadth, and forms of regulatory and third-party oversight** have brought substantial

**T A B L E  1.1**

Selected Advantages and Disadvantages of Alternative Investments

| Advantages | Disadvantages |
|---|---|
| ❏ Alternative investments may improve the risk-reward profile of portfolios | ❏ Several kinds of alternative investments may exhibit: (i) reduced liquidity; (ii) low information transparency; (iii) tax inefficiency; (iv) sizeable fee structures; and (v) unpredictable patterns of capital inflow and outflow |
| ❏ Recent years have witnessed new implementation vehicles, analytical techniques, research resources, asset class breadth, and forms of oversight for alternative investments | ❏ Some alternative investments may actually have higher-than-claimed standard deviations of returns and correlations of returns, resulting in lower-than-claimed Sharpe ratios and suboptimal allocations to such assets |
| ❏ The types of assets underlying many kinds of alternative investments may offer skilled managers the opportunity to establish and maintain a meaningful performance advantage through time | ❏ A not inconsiderable number of alternative investments may reflect a wide range of investment practices, new sources and uses of capital, and untested asset managers |

Source: The author.

growth in the universe of investors in alternative investments and the supply and forms of alternative investments from the 1980s through the 1990s and the post-2000 era.

◆ **A meaningful investment-performance advantage** that skilled managers may be able to establish and maintain in certain alternative investments, due to inefficiencies in many kinds of alternative investments' underlying markets.

## Disadvantages

◆ **Light regulation, relative illiquidity,** and a somewhat lacking flow of transparent information.

◆ **Tax inefficiency** for taxable investors.

◆ **High minimum investment amounts** and/or sizeable management fees and incentive compensation structures.

◆ **Unpredictable patterns** of capital investment and return.

◆ **Understated volatility and correlation measures** of many types of alternative investments and overstated Sharpe Ratios, due to illiquid investment strategies, infrequent and/or eccentric valuation methodologies, and the nonnormally distributed nature of their risks and returns may understate the volatility and correlation measures of alternative investments. This could result in potentially erroneous and thus financially injurious overallocations in many of the generally used mean-variance optimization programs.

◆ **A wide range of investment paradigms and practices,** as new suppliers and users of capital, and in some cases, untested asset managers, operate in this relatively newly defined and somewhat inchoate asset supercategory.

## Alternative Investment Guidelines

Investors need to carefully and thoughtfully evaluate whether or not to invest in alternative investments, and pay particular attention to: (i) the aggregate amounts of their investable funds; (ii) their liquidity and income needs; (iii) their overall asset and liability structure; and (iv) their time horizon, investment temperament, and risk profile.

In recent years, several new, conventionally based investment vehicles have begun providing lower-cost, more closely regulated, and more liquid means of gaining exposure to the returns, volatility, and correlations patterns of alternative investments. Such investments include a number of closed-end and open-end mutual funds, structured products, derivatives, exchange-traded funds (ETFs), and various kinds of common, preferred, and fixed-income securities focused on real estate, timber, oil and gas, precious metals, inflation-indexed securities, hedge funds, private equity, and venture capital. Investors should pay special attention to: (i) the explicit costs; (ii) the implicit costs (such as potentially reduced financial flexibility and foregone investment opportunities associated with capital lockup periods); and (iii) the tax-efficiency of portfolio allocations to alternative investments.

Due to the costs and difficulty of quickly implementing tactical asset allocation shifts within the alternative-investments universe, investors need to proceed cautiously and deliberately in: (i) establishing strategic asset allocation commitments; (ii) making tactical asset allocation moves; and (iii) portfolio rebalancing activity in response to changing valuations through time.

Manager selection can be a critically important determinant of success, or lack of success, in alternative investments. Extra levels of questioning, testing, probing, due diligence, insight, and judgment are called for in connection with manager choice, which is a relatively challenging endeavor for many individual investors to carry out on their own in the alternative-investments space.

## INVESTING IN AN ENVIRONMENT SUBJECT TO CRISES AND GLOBAL ASSET MARKET DISLOCATIONS

### General Guidelines

Mastery of the art of asset allocation entails broad consideration of so-called "tail events," also sometimes referred to as "bolts from the blue." Within an investment context, tail events are generally considered to be low-probability occurrences that could affect portfolio values in a meaningfully negative (or positive) way if they should come to pass.

Thinking beforehand about the scenarios, ramifications, and implications associated with tragic events, crises, and market dislocations in no way mitigates the physical and emotional suffering that may be associated with such events and their aftermath. Investors should consider the strategies and investment vehicles reviewed in this section in light of their own profile, objectives, and investment outlook. Market participants may also want to consider the likely effects of a number of different scenarios on the short- and long-term price behavior of equities, fixed-income securities, cash, currencies, and various types of alternative investments. Some examples of possible shocks that could materially affect global asset markets are described in Table 1.2.

A possible shock or serious market crisis may have a low probability of occurrence, while the base case of conventional economic developments may be considered to be the most likely outcome. Nevertheless, some cautious investors may want to evaluate whether it is advisable to adopt a defensive stance and invest a portion of their portfolio assets in anticipation of an potential crisis scenario. Such a defensive posture could have unfavorable effects on the portfolio in the event that crises or financial market dislocations do not in fact occur or unfold in a different way than anticipated.

It is also important to recognize that a portfolio that has been planned and structured *before* a crisis or global asset market dislocation will tend to differ in important respects from portfolio structuring activity that is undertaken *after* a crisis event takes place. Investors should think about how much risk they are willing to live with and protect themselves against: a 30-year flood event, versus a 50-to-70 year

## T A B L E  1.2

Examples of Possible Shocks That Could Materially Affect Global
Asset Markets

| Events External to Global Asset Markets | Internal Imbalances Within Global Asset Markets |
|---|---|
| ◆ Debt rescheduling talks are initiated and/or default is declared by a major sovereign borrower. | ◆ Large-scale losses are revealed in the lending and/or derivatives markets. |
| ◆ Non-U.S. investors execute substantial, market-moving sales of U.S. dollar-denominated financial assets. | ◆ One or more large financial institutions and/or industrial enterprises declares insolvency. |
| ◆ A serious terrorist act is perpetrated in a major urban center, involving conventional or unconventional weapons, or possibly biological, chemical, or nuclear agents, thus affecting a substantial number of people, systems, communications channels, and/or transportation hubs. | ◆ Highly valued asset classes experience significant and sustained price declines. |
| | ◆ Economic growth falls sharply in selected economies. |
| | ◆ External debt burdens and/or non-performing financial loans lead to a banking crisis within a major economy. |
| ◆ Tensions escalate toward widened armed conflict in troubled regions. | ◆ The creation or dissipation of price and valuation bubbles in goods and/or asset markets leads to disorder and turmoil in investor behavior, asset markets, and/or the real economy. |
| ◆ Confrontation spreads between governments and financial markets. | |
| ◆ Trade-affecting measures, possibly including tariffs, quotas, and/or currency policies are pursued by one or more major economic powers. | **Policy Errors Affecting the Financial Markets** |
| ◆ Significant operational and/or financial problems within or between large securities custodians or payments networks prevent the timely clearing and settlement of a material number of transactions. | ◆ Excessive monetary liquidity is injected (or suddenly withdrawn) worldwide, leading to significant asset price inflation (or deflation), and/or general inflation (or deflation). |
| ◆ Hackers and virus-writers effectively disrupt or disable a significant part of a nation's or the globe's computer-reliant utility, financial, telecommunications, air traffic control, defense, or other infrastructures. | ◆ Major currency instability develops in the yen, euro, U.S. dollar, and/or other major currencies. |
| | ◆ Governments adopt protectionist policies restricting the free flow of goods, services, capital, intellectual property, or people. |

Note: The diagram above is intended to build upon and update the shocks described in Figure 8.3, "Scenarios with Potentially Serious Consequences," on page 306 of *The Art of Asset Allocation*.

Source: The author.

flood event, versus a 100-year flood event. Such outcomes and portfolio protection activities are outlined in Figure 6.25 on page 253 of *The Art of Asset Allocation*.

Several types of activities or events can induce financial-market dislocations with varying degrees of actual and psychological damage over the short and long term, and with a wide range of effects on different kinds of financial and physical assets. Among investors' greatest counter-defenses against financial market dislocations can be: (i) keeping things in proper perspective; (ii) not getting paralyzed or caught off guard by events; and (iii) realizing that human beings and markets are resilient and "people will live to fight another day."

Shocks to global asset markets or to selected kinds of assets may offer opportunities to enter certain investments at attractive prices. In words attributed to Baron Rothschild during the Napoleonic wars: "Investors should buy with the sound of cannons firing [in modern-day terms, when people are fixated on watching CNN], and sell when the trumpets of victory sound [in modern-day terms, when people are fixated on watching CNBC]."

## Comments on Specific Asset Classes

If investors wish to plan for the possibility of a crisis of the type that results in global asset market dislocations, it may make sense to have higher-than-normal levels of cash and short- to intermediate-maturity, high-quality fixed-income instruments to take advantage of lower asset prices that generally tend to be found in the wake of crises or global asset market dislocations. Under such circumstances, investors should seek to invest with a margin of safety and allow for some margin of error.

During a period of crisis, highly liquid investments such as selected equities, bonds, or cash instruments, may offer an added degree of portfolio flexibility, allowing for tactical rebalancing in appropriate asset classes. It may be a good idea to seek diversification, not only across asset classes, but within asset classes, including: (i) diversification across sectors, styles, and industry groups; and (ii) diversification across geographies (not only across countries, but also across regions within a country, for location-specific assets such as state and local government bonds, utility securities, residential and commercial real estate, REITS, and companies highly focused on supply from or marketing activity to one or more geographic areas).

To establish the time frame, level of protection, and cost of financial "insurance," investors may consider the purchase of put options on asset class indices and on specific kinds of investments. It may be worthwhile to consider selected asset classes that have tended to perform well during periods of previous global asset market dislocations. Such asset classes may include precious metals, managed futures, real assets, and various kinds of high-quality fixed-income instruments.

*Before a shock* associated with a crisis or global asset market dislocation, investors may wish to: (i) have a lower-than-normal degree of

## T A B L E  1.3

Representative Investments for an Environment Subject to Crises and Global Asset Market Dislocations

- **High-Quality Cash and Fixed-Income Instruments:** Diversified exposure to high-quality cash and fixed-income securities may offer some degree of portfolio protection during turbulent global asset market environments.

- **Defense and Aerospace Companies:** During a crisis or global asset market dislocation affecting national security, investors may wish to consider increasing their portfolio exposure to appropriate companies in the defense and aerospace sectors.

- **Technological Security:** Several companies in the technological security sector focus on creating secure and reliable networks, and preventing the spread of computer viruses, identity theft, technological piracy, and other forms of technology-related attacks.

- **Pharmaceutical and Generic Drug Companies:** Certain pharmaceutical and generic drug firms aim to ensure that the right antibiotic and vaccine treatments are available in sufficient quantities on a timely basis to respond to widespread disease outbreaks or biological attacks if the need arises.

- **Diagnostic Testing:** Diagnostic testing seeks to improve the ability to diagnose critical diseases and health conditions that may occasion global asset market dislocations.

- **Biometric:** A heightened global security environment tends to increase usage of biometric products and services, which measure an individual's unique physical or behavioral characteristics to recognize and verify claimed identity.

- **Precious Metals and Real Assets:** During and after crises and global asset market dislocations, investors have sometimes increased exposure to precious metals and, in some cases, to certain kinds of real assets such as timber, oil and gas, and/or real estate.

- **Managed Futures:** Partly owing to their ability to sell short and to pursue strategies in a wide variety of commodity and financial futures markets, some commodity trading advisors (CTAs) active in the managed futures arena may have the ability to perform well in a wide variety of financial and economic environments.

- **Derivatives-Based Strategies:** Where appropriate, investors may wish to consider certain kinds of put and call option strategies, structured notes, credit derivatives, and convertible bonds.

Source: The author.

exposure to sectors such as transportation and insurance companies, high-profile multinational companies, and assets that depend on positive consumer psychology, including theme parks, retailers, tourism enterprises, restaurant chains, certain hotel REITs, hotels, and gaming companies; (ii) have a higher-than-normal degree of exposure to conventional and technological security, defense, biotech, pharmaceutical, and generic drug companies; and (iii) avoid risky and/or contingent investments such as leverage, the sale of put options, and similar strategies, as well as financial and operating constructs that may involve long periods of time until realization.

*After a shock* that has resulted in significant price depreciation, investors may wish to: (i) consider building positions in price-disrupted but attractively valued transportation and insurance companies, high-profile multinational companies, and other assets that depend on positive consumer psychology; and (ii) look for opportunities to gain a sound degree of asset exposure to companies, sectors, or asset classes that may have suffered significant, but not enduring, declines due to the effects of a crisis or global asset market dislocation.

Representative investments for an environment subject to crises and global asset market dislocations are highlighted in Table 1.3.

# CHAPTER 2

# ASSET ALLOCATION AND INVESTMENT LESSONS FROM UNIVERSITY ENDOWMENTS

## OVERVIEW

Investors of all types can gain valuable perspective on asset allocation and investment strategy by studying the organization, investment-policy implementation, successes, risks, and shortcomings of leading college and university endowments. Several of these institutions of higher learning have devoted rigorous thought and analysis to the process of investing in multiple asset classes, and a number of these schools have been willing to describe in some detail the evolution of their distinctive investment approaches through time.

This chapter seeks to shed light on the distinguishing financial and other characteristics of college and university endowments, to discover which successful endowments' experiences can be applied to

other investors. Some of these practices, which any investor can emu-
late, include: (i) understanding the nature of each asset class; (ii) knowing how to invest in each asset class; (iii) concentrating on developing
and rebalancing to an appropriate asset allocation; and (iv) thinking
about risk in a rigorous and realistic fashion. This chapter also takes
care to describe aspects of college and university endowments' activities that are likely to hold less relevance to other institutional and individual investors.

We examine here in some detail the historical investment performance, asset allocation through time, and asset class-by-asset class implementation strategies of Harvard University and Yale University,
two of America's largest endowments, with special emphasis on the
distinctive approaches each school follows, and their potential applications to other investors.

## SPECIAL FEATURES OF COLLEGE AND UNIVERSITY ENDOWMENTS

In the aggregate, the assets of American college and university endowments amounted to approximately $267 billion, $231.5 billion, and $316
billion as of December 31, in 2004, 2003, and 2002 respectively. Table
2.1 shows the 25 largest endowments as of their fiscal year-ends.

As the table indicates, at the end of June 2004, the 25 largest college and university endowments accounted for $135.2 billion, about
50.6% of the nation's total endowment funds. The 10 largest college
and university endowments held $89.1 billion, about 33.4%, of the na-
tion's total endowment funds. Harvard University had the largest endowment ($22.1 billion), followed by Yale University ($12.7 billion), the
University of Texas System ($10.3 billion), Princeton University ($9.9
billion), Stanford University ($9.9 billion), Massachusetts Institute of
Technology ($5.9 billion), the University of California ($4.8 billion),
Emory University ($4.5 billion), Columbia University ($4.5 billion),
Texas A&M University System ($4.4 billion), and the University of
Michigan ($4.2 billion).

During the last three decades of the twentieth century, college and
university endowments of all sizes tended to increase the proportion of
U.S.—and to a lesser degree, foreign—equities in their portfolios, while
reducing the percentages they invested in fixed-income securities.
Keeping in mind that not all schools disclose the strategies, tactics, and
results of their investment activities in the same degree of detail (or even
in the same format from year to year, in some cases), larger endowments

## T A B L E   2.1

### Endowment Assets of Colleges and Universities

| School | Endowment Size ($ Billions) | | | | | University Web Sites |
|---|---|---|---|---|---|---|
| | 2000[1] | 2001[1] | 2002[1] | 2003[1] | 2004[1] | |
| Harvard University | 18.8 | 18.0 | 17.2 | 18.8 | 22.1 | www.harvard.edu |
| Yale University | 10.1 | 10.7 | 10.5 | 11.0 | 12.7 | www.yale.edu |
| University of Texas System[2] | 10.0 | 9.4 | 8.6 | 8.7 | 10.3 | www.utsystem.edu |
| Princeton University | 8.4 | 8.4 | 8.3 | 8.7 | 9.9 | www.princeton.edu |
| Stanford University[3] | 8.6 | 8.2 | 7.6 | 8.6 | 9.9 | www.stanford.edu |
| Massachusetts Institute of Technology | 6.5 | 6.1 | 5.4 | 5.1 | 5.9 | www.mit.edu |
| University of California | 4.8 | 4.7 | 4.2 | 4.4 | 4.8 | www.ucop.edu |
| Emory University[4] | 5.0 | 4.3 | 4.6 | 4.0 | 4.5 | www.emory.edu |
| Columbia University | 4.3 | 4.3 | 4.2 | 4.4 | 4.5 | www.columbia.edu |
| Texas A&M University System | 4.2 | 4.0 | 3.7 | 3.8 | 4.4 | www.tamu.edu |
| University of Michigan | 3.5 | 3.6 | 3.4 | 3.5 | 4.2 | www.mich.edu |
| University of Pennsylvania | 3.2 | 3.4 | 3.4 | 3.5 | 4.0 | www.upenn.edu |
| Washington University | 4.2 | 4.0 | 3.5 | 3.5 | 4.0 | www.wustl.edu |
| Northwestern University | 3.4 | 3.3 | 3.0 | 3.1 | 3.7 | www.nwu.edu |
| University of Chicago | 3.8 | 3.5 | 3.3 | 3.2 | 3.6 | www.uchicago.edu |
| Duke University | 3.2 | 3.1 | 2.9 | 3.0 | 3.3 | www.duke.edu |
| Rice University | 3.4 | 3.2 | 2.9 | 2.9 | 3.3 | www.rice.edu |
| Cornell University | 3.4 | 3.2 | 2.8 | 2.9 | 3.2 | www.cornell.edu |
| University of Notre Dame | 3.1 | 2.8 | 2.6 | 2.6 | 3.1 | www.nd.edu. |
| University of Virginia | 1.7 | 1.7 | 1.7 | 1.8 | 2.8 | www.virginia.edu |
| Dartmouth College | 2.5 | 2.4 | 2.2 | 2.1 | 2.5 | www.dartmouth.edu |
| University of Southern California | 2.2 | 2.1 | 2.1 | 2.1 | 2.4 | www.usc.edu |
| Vanderbilt University | 2.3 | 2.2 | 2.0 | 2.0 | 2.3 | www.vanderbilt.edu |
| Johns Hopkins University | 1.8 | 1.8 | 1.7 | 1.7 | 2.1 | www.jhu.edu |
| Brown University | 1.4 | 1.4 | 1.4 | 1.5 | 1.6 | www.brown.edu |
| Total | $123.8 | $119.8 | $113.2 | $116.9 | $135.1 | |

[1]For the fiscal year ending June 30, except for Stanford University and the University of Texas System, which use a fiscal year ending August 31.

[2]The University of Texas system is the beneficiary of an 1876 state grant of 2 million acres of land in West Texas, which have been found to contain significant oil and gas reserves. Of the public portion of this endowment, consisting of the land grant itself and securities and other investments purchased with petroleum royalties from the land, two-thirds is for the benefit of the University of Texas and one-third is for the benefit of Texas A&M University.

[3]Included in the Stanford University endowment is more than 8,000 acres of land given by Jane and Leland Stanford to the university, with the restriction that it can never be sold. The real estate portion of the endowment reflects the market value of Stanford properties that have been commercially developed, such as the Stanford Shopping Center and Stanford Research Park, but does not reflect what the university's land would be worth if it had the potential to be sold.

[4]A significant portion of the Emory University endowment represents shares in the Coca-Cola Company that were donated to the university in 1979 (with a then-current value of $105 million) by Robert and George Woodruff.

Source: *Fiscal 2004 Endowment Study* of the National Association of College and University Business Officers (NACUBO).

demonstrated several other trends. First, many schools' investment offices have devoted considerable thought to: (i) asset allocation; (ii) portfolio diversification; (iii) risk management techniques; (iv) appropriate spending policies to help support annual operating budgets; and (v) when and how to use and compensate internal investment staff, outside consultants, and external asset managers.

Second, in contrast to the concentration of smaller endowments' portfolios in *conventional* marketable equities and fixed-income securities, a growing number of the larger endowments have invested in less liquid, less efficient, and sometimes more volatile *alternative* asset classes in an effort to access noncorrelated assets, capture higher investment returns, and/or improve the overall risk-reward profile of their portfolios. These asset classes include private equity, venture capital, commodities, precious metals, real estate, oil and gas interests, timberland, and managed futures funds. In the late 1980s, Yale University and other schools defined and began to give focus to a new asset class, called "absolute return" investments, such as: various forms of event-driven, relative value, and global macro investment styles; arbitrage-based strategies, encompassing merger, convertible, equity, bond, and statistical arbitrage techniques; and hedge funds, and hedge-fund funds of funds, employing hedging, leverage, long and short strategies, securities borrowing and lending, and derivatives operations.

Before attempting to identify aspects of endowments' asset allocation and investment strategy processes that are potentially worth emulating by other individual and institutional investors, it is worthwhile to keep in mind several special characteristics affecting the investment activities of colleges and universities. These attributes include:

- ◆ **Time Horizon and Purpose:** Colleges and universities exist to deepen understanding, to advance learning, and to expand the intellectual and reasoning power of society, generally with a multigenerational or even a multicentury time horizon. As a result, investment managers at these schools' endowments usually focus on preserving the long-term purchasing power of their assets.

- ◆ **Tax Status:** The tax-exempt nature of educational institutions imposes certain investment restrictions under Section 501(c)(3) and other parts of the Internal Revenue Code, while also allowing colleges and universities to consider the full range of taxable investments. This permits them to consider vehicles such as hedge funds that may otherwise generate significant tax liabilities for taxpaying investors.

- ◆ **Management and Governance:** Usually, college and university endowments are subject to the oversight of financial and investment officers, who report to an investment or finance committee that is subject to prudent investor legal precedents and is ultimately responsible to the school's board of trustees. As a consequence, this system creates checks and balances; in many cases, the power-sharing occurs at the cost of group normative psychology and considerable organizational inertia.

◆ **Relationship with Constituencies:** Colleges and universities operate very much in the public eye and must take account of the wishes of numerous groups of stakeholders, including faculty, students, alumni, donors, the administration, nonteaching employees, suppliers, local host communities, other educational institutions, and society at large. Many of these and other groups may have strong opinions about how the school's endowment should and should not be invested.

◆ **Money Inflows:** In contrast to many other types of investors, college and university endowments may be beneficiaries of donations to annual appeals and/or to capital campaigns. Economic and financial conditions and givers' overall level of satisfaction with the institution affect the success and absolute level of these money-raising efforts. During multiyear periods encompassing a variety of economic and financial environments, most colleges and universities maintain endowment inflows of individual gifts, bequests, and other gifts, of between 3% and 6% per annum. Many schools' endowments are in fact composed of numerous individual donor-established pools of capital. In many cases, a donor may establish restrictions on how the income and/or principal of his or her gift may be *spent,* even though no restrictions are usually placed on how the funds are *invested.*

◆ **Money Outflows:** In general, institutions of higher learning spend funds from their endowments for a variety of purposes, including additions to physical plants, library acquisition, faculty chairs, student scholarships and loan subsidies, athletic programs, and other academic initiatives. Most colleges and universities have a *spending rule,* which seeks to balance the school's need to fund its current operations reliably against the objective of preserving and expanding the purchasing power of its capital assets. A number of schools have developed spending rule formulas that use a multiyear rolling average of the endowment value to smooth out extreme oscillations in annual spending levels as a result of capital-market fluctuations. Many colleges and universities distribute between 4% and 6% of the endowment's market value each year to help fund school operations. Some schools are higher and some are lower than this range.

- **Size:** As the absolute value of an endowment increases in size, the complexity, range, and scope of its investment activities may expand to include: more in-house resources for internal asset management and/or external manager selection; and consideration of a broader range of asset classes, managers, and structures.

- **Nature of Liabilities:** Over the long term, an imperative to replace and add to physical facilities and the need to competitively compensate school faculty and other personnel determine the nature of colleges' and universities' liabilities. Unlike some investors—such as insurance companies and defined benefit pension plans that must meet some guaranteed level of benefits in the future—endowments may enjoy a somewhat greater degree of flexibility in the types of assets and investment approaches they choose to offset their future obligations. Depending on the absolute size of the school's portfolio, the cyclical and secular financial market outlook, and other factors, endowments may be in a position to weight their portfolios more heavily toward various forms of equities and equity-like products having various degrees of liquidity.

- **Prior Investment Experience:** During the 1970s, when inflation soared and financial markets generated lackluster returns, the inflation-adjusted value of several large endowment portfolios declined by 40%, 50%, or more. Partially in response, during the latter part of the 1980s and through the 1990s, many colleges and universities shifted more toward equity instruments than fixed-income securities, to protect their portfolios primarily against the long-term erosive power of *inflation, rather than deflation,* on real asset values.

## APPLICATIONS OF SUCCESSFUL ENDOWMENTS' EXPERIENCES TO OTHER INVESTORS

After making allowance for their own risk tolerance, time horizon, income needs, market outlook, and other important differentiating factors, investors of all types can learn from the experiences and approaches of successful endowments. Several of these precepts and guidelines are set forth below:

- **Understand the Nature of Each Asset Class:** Investors should seek to understand the key liquidity, risk, and return characteristics of each major asset class, including: (i) the principal determinants of value, primary price drivers, and factors that can cause prices to diverge significantly from prices for any meaningful period of time; (ii) how the asset class behaves in combination with other asset classes; and (iii) how the asset class tends to respond to *anticipated inflation, unanticipated inflation, anticipated deflation,* and *unanticipated deflation.* In brief, investors should aim to comprehend what the asset can and cannot do within a portfolio over the short, intermediate, and long term.

- **Know How to Invest in Each Asset Class:** It is a good idea for investors to recognize the differing *methods* (such as managing the assets internally versus hiring an external manager), *styles* (such as active or passive management), *structures* (such as outright ownership, separate or commingled accounts, partnerships, unit trusts, and structured instruments), *tax treatment,* and *ongoing ownership costs* of the various ways of investing in each asset class. The best way of owning one asset may or may not be the best way of owning another asset.

- **Concentrate on Getting the Asset Allocation Right:** Many investors do not spend enough time thinking about an appropriate asset allocation during various time frames and financial market environments. Instead, they devote excessive attention to industry, sector, and specific investment selection; manager selection; market timing decisions; and other concerns. Successful endowments, and successful investors in other fields, focus on finding a specific, diversified blend of assets to which they can adhere through time and that best reflects their own circumstances, goals, objectives, and expectations about investments and the investment process. Getting the asset allocation right also implies taking a considered, fresh look at the long-term asset mix on at least an annual or bi-annual basis, questioning assumptions, assessing change, and making adjustments if they are called for.

- **Rebalance the Portfolio to the Strategic Policy Allocation:** Chapter 4 in *The Art of Asset Allocation* describes in some detail the pros, cons, and means of asset allocation rebalancing. After

assets' prices have drifted with the passage of a suitable
amount of time, and/or when major shifts in asset prices call
for a tactical response, successful endowments carefully evaluate their investment performance compared to appropriate
benchmarks, and then rebalance their portfolios to their strategic policy allocation. Judgment, flexibility, and conviction may
naturally influence the timing and degree of rebalancing decisions, but investors must face such points of determination actively and thoughtfully rather than in a disorganized way or
not at all.

◆ **Think About Risk in a Rigorous and Realistic Fashion:**
Investors need to approach every aspect of asset allocation
with caution and a healthy questioning attitude, so they can
assess the various forms of risk associated with investing in
general and with their own portfolios in particular. Hedging,
volatility control, scenario analysis, and other means help
them develop an essential understanding of how to anticipate, measure, and possibly offset risk. Many successful endowments place great emphasis on the means and results of
their risk management activities, and take almost as much
pride in reducing their risk as they do in increasing the
return on their investment portfolios.

◆ **Devote Special Attention to Monitoring Any Alternative Investments:** Alternative investments include managed futures
funds, inflation-indexed securities, commodities, precious metals, timber- and oil and gas-related interests, private equity,
venture capital, real estate, hedge funds, and hedge-fund
funds of funds. By their very nature, alternative assets may
generally be less liquid, more complex, and considerably more
(in some cases, less) volatile than conventional asset classes.
Investors should treat alternative investments with special care
and diligence, considering these other features of many alternative assets: (i) partnership structures involving reliance upon
one or a small group of general partners to make investment
decisions; (ii) high minimum investment requirements,
capital-call features and/or lockup periods, time restrictions
on capital withdrawal, and nonstandard forms and times for
capital distributions; (iii) high annual management fees and
performance-based incentive-fee arrangements; (iv) nonuni-
form reporting conventions; (v) in some cases, the use of

leverage, short-selling, derivatives, arbitrage, and other investment techniques; (vi) wide variations between the performance of outstanding, mediocre, and subpar investment managers; and (vii) specialized and frequently complicated tax reporting procedures.

Successful endowments dedicate considerable time and resources to the evaluation, selection, monitoring, and dismissal of: alternative asset managers and/or firms that select alternative asset managers. Investors without the means and organizational infrastructure to establish a robust supervisory capability for the surveillance of alternative assets must exercise an appropriately high degree of vigilance in selecting managers or their overseers.

◆ **Pay Attention to Spending Patterns:** Investors of all types can benefit from the thoughtful way successful endowments manage spending flows. Depending on assumptions as to the time horizon, forms and amounts of annual income, and the actual long-term growth rates of underlying assets, a given amount of capital withdrawn for current spending may effectively translate into a much larger amount of forgone future capital values. Many schools determine spending by applying a prespecified percentage, ranging from 4% to 6%, of the total endowment value at the beginning of each fiscal year. Many colleges and universities utilize a formula that determines annual spending based on a set percentage of the moving average of the endowment's market value. Some spend a certain percentage of the endowment's current yield, some decide on an appropriate rate each year, and others follow highly customized spending rules. Regardless of the method employed, investors need to consider the effects that taxes and other annual spending outflows can have on future values of their assets. Seemingly small positive or negative increments in annual growth rates due to increased or decreased spending can produce relatively large additions to or subtractions from final projected asset values. For example, during a 20-year period, $1.00 invested at 10% per annum produces an ending value of $6.70, at 7.5% per annum, $4.25, and at 12.5% per annum, $10.55. In this case, a 25% *reduction* in the annual growth rate (from 10% to 7.5%) produces a 36.6% reduction in the final value (= $4.25 divided by $6.70), while a 25% *increase*

in the annual growth rate (from 10% to 12.5%) produces a
57.5% increase in the final value (= $10.55 divided by $6.70).

◆ **Use Common Sense in Applying Others' Methods:** Depending
on their own characteristics and mentality, investors may use
some broad approaches that successful colleges and universities
follow in managing their endowments. At the same time, keep
in mind that while some of these approaches may be applicable
*and* feasible, others may be applicable *but not* feasible, feasible
*but not* applicable, or *neither* applicable nor feasible. Some
schools have full-time internal staffs and sophisticated analytical
tools at their disposal to allocate assets, manage portfolios,
and/or evaluate external money managers. Many individual
and institutional investors do not have the capability to carry
out these important functions on their own, and must rely on
third-party sources. In all cases, investors would do well to use
pragmatism, alertness, prudence, and circumspection in steering
an appropriate course between emulating, partially adapting, or
eschewing altogether some or all of the asset management processes that successful endowments employ.

◆ **Keep Up-to-Date on Developments in Endowment Asset
Management:** Many colleges and universities allocate capital
across a range of asset classes, and report yearly on the results
of these activities to their stakeholders. Investors can gain valuable perspective on the asset allocation process by reading the
annual reports of successful endowments. Table 2.1 presents a
partial list of the Web sites of the 25 largest educational endowments in the U.S. An annual endowment study conducted by
the National Association of College and University Business Officers (NACUBO) presents additional information on the historical cumulative and annual investment performance, investment
management policies and practices, asset allocation, spending
characteristics, management expenses, and the external asset
managers and investment custodians of more than 741 public
and private college and university endowments. NACUBO
(*nacubo.org*) was founded in 1962 and represents the chief administrative officers at more than 2,500 colleges and universities.

Relevant books on endowment management include:

◆ *Pioneering Portfolio Management: An Unconventional Approach to
Institutional Investment,* by David F. Swensen.

- ◆ *Asset Management for Endowments and Foundations*, by William Schneider, Robert DiMeo, and D. Robinson Cluck.
- ◆ *Selecting and Evaluating an Investment Manager*, by the staff of NACUBO.

## IMPORTANT DISTINCTIONS BETWEEN ENDOWMENTS AND OTHER INVESTORS

While investors can glean valuable lessons and insights from careful observation of successful endowments, they also need to understand several important distinctions between endowments and other kinds of investors that may limit or even preclude their broad application. Several of these distinctions include:

- ◆ **Resource Constraints:** Many individual investors and some institutional investors do not have the human, technological, and other resources needed to manage in-house money in a highly sophisticated fashion across an extensive set of asset classes, nor to select and monitor external asset managers operating in specialized fields. In such cases, investors need to exercise caution not only in the selection of asset categories and implementation strategies within these asset classes, but also in the selection of any third parties who are charged with engaging and supervising outside managers.
- ◆ **Rebalancing Alternative Assets:** Due to the less-liquid, longer-horizon nature of several types of alternative assets, such as private equity, venture capital, private real estate, and various hedge funds, it is often not easy or practicable to rebalance these assets with the same frequency or divisibility as conventional assets. Some colleges and universities can generally make allowances for the greater position inertia of alternative assets. This is often due to the overall size of these schools' portfolios and in many cases, due to liquidity-providing flows of capital from: interest, dividends, capital gains, and returns of capital from their holdings of conventional asset classes; and ongoing donations of funds to the school's endowment.
- ◆ **External Manager Sourcing and Terms Negotiation:** External asset managers specializing in specific asset classes frequently court successful endowments. If a school wants to gain exposure to a highly focused asset subclass, geographic region, or investment approach, it may actively approach and perhaps

even provide initial funding for an investment fund run by a talented asset manager. In these and many other circumstances, the college or university may be able to utilize its size, reputation, and potential follow-on funds flows to obtain fee arrangements, capital inflow and exit conditions, and additional special terms not normally available to other investors.

◆ **Preserving Influence over Alternative Assets:** Because of their size and full-time professional staffing, several successful endowments are able to assertively voice their opinions and exercise some degree of influence over their investments in alternative asset partnerships and other structures. It is important for nonendowment investors to recognize that alternative assets often do not easily afford them early exit opportunities for all or part of their position (such as can be done by selling off portions of their equity or bond holdings in conventional asset classes) if developments are not proceeding as anticipated.

◆ **Obtaining Superior Alternative Asset Managers:** Owing to their experience, networking abilities, and an unwillingness to tolerate subpar performance for extended periods, successful endowments may be able to increase the odds of finding top-quality alternative investment managers. Figure 2.1 shows that the difference between first-quartile and third-quartile investment results widens dramatically as the investor ventures from conventional into alternative asset classes.

It is possible to rank the investment results of active managers in 13 asset classes for the 10 years ending December 31, 1999 using data contained in the *Pensions and Investments Performance Evaluation Report* (PIPER) for Managed Accounts, data on real estate from the National Council of Real Estate Investment Funds (NCREIF), and data appearing in *Venture Economics* on leveraged buyout and venture capital funds formed between 1990 and 1994. During this time period, the spread between first-quartile and third-quartile performance was 100 basis points (1.00%) for U.S. fixed-income securities, 420 basis points (4.2%) for large-capitalization U.S. equities, 670 basis points (6.7%) for small-capitalization U.S. equities, 270 basis points (2.7%) for international equities, 750 basis points (7.5%) for emerging-markets equities, and 740 basis points (7.4%) for real estate.

By contrast, in two of the less efficient, less liquid alternative asset classes for which data are available, the differential between first-quartile and third-quartile performance widens considerably, to 2,460 basis

## FIGURE 2.1

### Dispersion of Active Management Returns

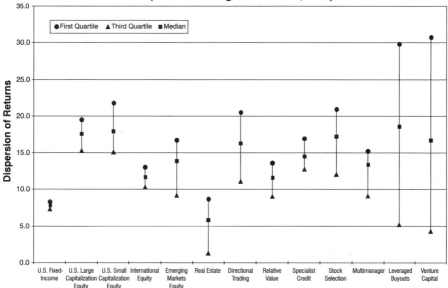

**Asset Returns by Quartile
(10 Years Ending December 31, 1999)**

| Asset Class | First Quartile | Median | Third Quartile | Range |
|---|---|---|---|---|
| U.S. Fixed-Income | 8.3% | 7.8% | 7.3% | 1.0% |
| U.S. Large Capitalization Equity | 19.5 | 17.6 | 15.3 | 4.2 |
| U.S. Small Capitalization Equity | 21.8 | 17.9 | 15.1 | 6.7 |
| International Equity | 13.0 | 11.7 | 10.3 | 2.7 |
| Emerging Markets Equity | 16.7 | 13.9 | 9.2 | 7.5 |
| Real Estate | 8.7 | 5.8 | 1.3 | 7.4 |
| Directional Trading Hedge Funds[1] | 20.5 | 16.3 | 11.1 | 9.4 |
| Relative Value Hedge Funds [1] | 13.6 | 11.6 | 9.0 | 4.6 |
| Specialist Credit Hedge Funds[1] | 16.9 | 14.5 | 12.7 | 4.2 |
| Stock Selection Hedge Funds[1] | 20.9 | 17.2 | 12.0 | 8.9 |
| Multimanager Hedge Funds [1] | 15.2 | 13.4 | 9.1 | 6.1 |
| Leveraged Buyouts | 29.8 | 18.6 | 5.2 | 24.6 |
| Venture Capital | 30.7 | 16.7 | 4.3 | 26.4 |

Sources: *Report of the Yale Endowment 2000,* Yale University Investments Office. Data for the marketable securities are from the *PIPER Managed Accounts Report* of December 31, 1999. The venture capital and leveraged buyouts data are from *Venture Economics.* Venture capital and leveraged buyouts data represent returns on funds formed between 1990 and 1994, excluding more recent funds so that immature investments will not influence reported results. Real Estate data are from NCREIF.

points (24.6%) for leveraged buyouts (29.8% versus 5.2%) and to 2,640 basis points (26.4%) for venture capital (30.7% versus 4.3%). In fact, an investor who ended up receiving the 10-year *median* results in venture capital (16.7%) and in leveraged buyouts (18.6%) would have assumed greater volatility in returns, less liquidity, and higher fee structures, but would have fared essentially the same as an investor who obtained the 10-year *median* returns for large-capitalization U.S. equities (17.6%) and for small-capitalization U.S. equities (17.9%). If the investor contemplates allocating funds to alternative assets, he or she must leave no stone unturned in the search for superior asset managers. This is a considerable challenge for successful endowments, and perhaps even more so for other individual and institutional investors.

## SIMILARITIES IN APPROACH BY HARVARD AND YALE UNIVERSITY ENDOWMENTS

As of June 30, 2004, the two largest university endowments in the United States were Harvard University, with $22.1 billion, and Yale University, with $12.7 billion. During several decades, and with deepened emphasis during the 1990s, the investment and financial officers of both Harvard and Yale devoted considerable thought and attention to asset allocation, the implementation of their investment strategy and tactics, and internal and external manager selection, evaluation, and incentivization. While each school investment arm has successfully executed its investment mandate in specific and differentiated ways, a number of similarities are worth noting:

- ◆ **Equity Emphasis:** To meet their objective of preserving long-term purchasing power, both Harvard and Yale have elected to emphasize in their asset mix equities, equity-like assets, and other types of inflation-protecting assets.
- ◆ **Alternative Investments and Absolute-Return Strategies:** Believing that higher expected returns and attractive risk and correlation characteristics outweigh any liquidity and fee issues, Harvard and Yale have significant exposure to alternative asset classes and absolute-return strategies.
- ◆ **Fixed-Income De-emphasis:** Neither Harvard nor Yale allocates a meaningful proportion of its overall assets to fixed-income securities that are neither unhedged nor enhanced with an alpha-transfer strategy. Both institutions tend to hold bonds and cash-equivalent instruments primarily for deflation protection and for liquidity management expenses.
- ◆ **Risk Management:** Harvard and Yale devote considerable resources to understanding, monitoring, measuring, and hedging the various market, credit, liquidity, interest rate, sovereign, currency, legal, operational, systemic, and other

forms of risk associated with their portfolios. During the 1990s, each institution was able to achieve a 10-year standard deviation of returns of around 10%, with some of the more volatile asset classes' volatilities offset partially by hedging activity and partially by less variation in the values of certain alternative asset classes.

◆ **Rigorous Analysis:** Harvard and Yale apply a blend of quantitative and qualitative methods to their asset allocation and portfolio management processes. Each institution's approach may be characterized by intensive analytical methods, balanced with discipline and human judgment.

◆ **Access to Top-Quality Alternative Asset Managers:** Several factors—including many years of experience, the intensive effort and focus devoted to their efforts, the quality and quantity of their networking and evaluative resources, and their reputation and prestige as potential clients—have enabled Harvard and Yale to identify and gain entree to many of the best asset managers in the alternative assets asset class. For many other investors, such know-how and experience are often difficult to replicate and keep up-to-date.

◆ **Diversification with Overlays:** Harvard and Yale have both sought to allocate their portfolios among a sufficiently broad array of asset classes, investment styles, regions, and structures, many of which have essentially different underlying characteristics and responsiveness to various kinds of economic and financial conditions. At the same time, to protect certain large investments and/or take advantage of favorable investment opportunities in a cost-effective fashion, both schools utilize from time to time a variety of overlay techniques involving short- and long-dated options, futures, borrowing, swap agreements, and other instruments.

◆ **Attention to Implementation Methodology:** In its own way, each school seeks to tailor the means it uses to invest in selected groups of assets. They often use passive, index-following approaches for highly efficient, well-researched investment categories, and often apply active management methods in sectors and asset classes they deem less efficient and thus able to reward the intensity, creativity, and quality of their investigation and analysis. Harvard and Yale rely on internal managers in instances where they feel they can develop and take advantage of a distinctive investment skill. On the other hand, both schools are willing to engage properly and provide incentives for outside managers who have demonstrable, consistent, and specialized financial knowledge that they can apply to asset types that reward ingenuity and enterprise.

◆ **Strategic Thinking and Portfolio Rebalancing:** Harvard and Yale devote considerable thought to the strategic positioning and long-term policy mix of their assets. They develop these asset allocation guidelines, and allowable deviations from the guidelines, with internal and external sources of wise counsel in a thorough, periodic vetting of the university's financial health and needs, the investment outlook, and price-value relationships for specific assets, risk-reward relationships, and other factors. As asset prices and financial conditions change over time, both schools regularly consider rebalancing their portfolios to their strategic policy allocations.

## HARVARD UNIVERSITY

Throughout much of its history since its founding in 1636 as America's oldest institution of higher learning, Harvard University has paid careful attention to the financial and endowment resources that underpin its renown and destiny. Since 1974, Harvard's own separately incorporated, not-for-profit subsidiary, the Harvard Management Company (HMC), has carried out its investment activities. The HMC reports to its Board of Directors, who are appointed by Harvard's board of governors, officially known as the President and Fellows of Harvard College, or the Harvard Corporation.

The HMC is situated in the financial district of Boston, some distance from Harvard University's administration and main campus in Cambridge. With about a few dozen in-house investment professionals and a few hundred total employees, the HMC has the resources and mindset to pursue a quantitatively and analytically intensive approach to monitoring financial and real asset classes and global capital and derivatives markets, in search of attractive price-value alignments, mispricing opportunities, and proprietary trading, investment, and arbitrage strategies. As of mid-2002, approximately two-thirds of HMC's assets were managed internally, and one-third through external asset managers. Table 2.2 shows Harvard's total endowment value and net investment returns for selected fiscal years from 1986 through 2004.

## T A B L E  2.2

### Harvard University Endowment Value and Investment Returns

| Fiscal Year (Ending June 30) | Endowment Value ($ Millions)[1] | Total Investment Returns | | |
|---|---|---|---|---|
| | | Harvard General Investment Account[2] | Harvard Benchmark Composite Index[3] | TUCS Median[4] |
| 1985 | – | 26.8% | 30.5% | – |
| 1986 | – | 31.3 | 30.3 | – |
| 1987 | – | 19.9 | 17.9 | – |
| 1988 | – | 5.7 | –1.1 | – |
| 1989 | $4,572 | 12.8 | 17.7 | – |
| 1990 | $4,760 | 7.5 | 13.3 | – |
| 1991 | $4,708 | 1.1 | 8.6 | – |
| 1992 | $5,118 | 11.8 | 10.3 | 13.1 |
| 1993 | $5,778 | 16.7 | 12.7 | 14.1 |
| 1994 | $6,201 | 9.8 | 6.8 | 3.6 |
| 1995 | $7,391 | 16.8 | 17.2 | 16.1 |
| 1996 | $9,059 | 26.0 | 22.3 | 17.6 |
| 1997 | | 25.8 | 20.0 | 20.3 |
| 1998 | $13,279 | 20.5 | 17.1 | 17.9 |
| 1999 | $14,756 | 12.2 | 18.9 | 11.2 |
| 2000 | $19,148 | 32.2 | 18.6 | 10.4 |
| 2001 | $18,259 | –2.7 | –9.8 | –5.7 |
| 2002 | $17,518 | –0.5 | –4.5 | –5.9 |
| 2003 | $19,300 | 12.5 | 8.3 | 4.0 |
| 2004 | $22,600 | 21.1 | 16.4 | 16.2 |
| 2005 | $25,900 | 19.2 | 14.2 | 10.5 |
| 5-Year Annual Rate of Growth (2000–2004) | | 11.8% | 5.2% | 3.8% |
| 10-Year Annual Rate of Growth (1995–2004) | | 15.9% | 11.9% | 10.1% |
| 10-Year Standard Deviation of Annual Returns | | 11.3% | 11.0% | 9.7% |

[1]Changes in the endowment value over time are a function of distributed and undistributed dividend and interest income, realized and unrealized capital gains or losses, donor gifts and pledges for capital, funds distributions to support university operations, and other transfers and adjustments.

[2]Net of all fees and expenses; all but a small fraction of the Harvard endowment is invested in the Harvard Pooled General Investment Account.

[3]The Harvard Benchmark Composite Index represents a weighted average of the performance of specific benchmark indices for each of the 12 asset classes in the Harvard Management Company Policy Allocation, with weights equal to the percentage that each asset class represents as part of the overall Harvard Policy Portfolio.

[4]The Trust Universe Comparison Service (TUCS) Median is a universe of over 100 investment funds, each with assets of $1 billion or more.

Source: 1998–1999, 1999–2000, 2000–2001, 2001–2002, 2002–2003, 2003–2004, and 2004–2005 issues of the *Annual Report of the Harvard Management Company*.

As of June 30, 2004, the total value of the Harvard endowment amounted to $22.6 billion, compared with $18.3 billion at the end of fiscal 2001, $7.4 billion at the end of fiscal 1995, and $4.7 billion at the end of fiscal 1990. For the 5 fiscal years from 2000 through 2004, the Harvard General Investment Account's net compound annual growth rate was 11.8%, compared with 15.9% for the 10 fiscal years from 1995 through 2004, with a 10-year standard deviation of annual returns equal to 11.3%. These investment returns substantially exceeded the performance of the Harvard Benchmark Composite Index, which for the 5 fiscal years ending in June 2004 generated returns of 5.2%, versus 11.9% for the 10 fiscal years ending in June 2002, with a 10-year standard deviation of 10.1%. The Harvard Benchmark Composite Index represents a weighted average of the performance of the chosen benchmark indices for each of the 12 asset classes in the Harvard Management Company Policy Allocation, with specific weights equal to the percentage of each asset class in the overall Harvard Policy Portfolio.

On a 5-year and a 10-year basis, Harvard also outperformed the Trust Universe Comparison Service (TUCS) Median, a universe of more than 100 investment funds, each with assets of $1 billion or more. For the 5 fiscal years ending in June 2004, the TUCS Median had returns of 3.8%, compared with 10.1% for the 10 fiscal years ending in June 2004, with a 10-year standard deviation of 9.7%.

For a number of years prior to 1980, Harvard's asset allocation policy generally called for weightings of 60% in equities, 30% in fixed-income securities, and 10% in cash equivalents. In the mid- to late 1980s, Harvard moved approximately 20% of the endowment into investments in venture capital, real estate, and oil and gas interests. Beginning in the early 1990s, Harvard began to devote increasing attention to a broader program of asset diversification, risk control, and asset allocation policy. As of June 30, 2004, Harvard University's strategic asset allocation—also known as the Harvard Management Company Policy Portfolio—was invested in 12 separate asset classes, as shown in Table 2.3. While the board of the HMC determines the Policy Portfolio, its management is permitted to make short-run tactical asset allocation adjustments within maximum and minimum guidelines without prior consultation with the HMC Board.

The HMC Policy Portfolio presented in Table 2.3 represents an early twenty-first-century version of Harvard's desired long-term asset mix, which HMC developed through: (i) quantitative inputs, modeling, and analysis; (ii) consideration and discussion of the University's return goals balanced against an appropriate level of

**T A B L E   2.3**

Harvard Management Company Policy Portfolio

| HMC Policy Allocation | Asset Allocation | | | | | | |
|---|---|---|---|---|---|---|---|
| | June 30, 1995 | June 30, 1999 | June 30, 2000 | June 30, 2001 | June 30, 2002 | June 30, 2003 | June 30, 2004 |
| Domestic Equities | 38% | 32% | 22% | 21% | 15% | 15% | 15% |
| Absolute Return | 0 | 4 | 5 | 6 | 12 | 12 | 12 |
| Foreign Equities | 15 | 15 | 15 | 14 | 10 | 10 | 10 |
| Emerging Markets | 5 | 9 | 9 | 7 | 5 | 5 | 5 |
| High-Yield Securities | 2 | 2 | 3 | 3 | 5 | 5 | 5 |
| Commodities | 6 | 5 | 6 | 9 | 13 | 13 | 13 |
| Real Estate | 7 | 7 | 7 | 7 | 10 | 10 | 10 |
| Private Equities | 12 | 15 | 15 | 15 | 13 | 13 | 13 |
| Domestic Bonds | 15 | 11 | 10 | 10 | 11 | 11 | 11 |
| Foreign Bonds | 5 | 5 | 4 | 4 | 5 | 5 | 5 |
| Inflation-Indexed Bonds | 0 | 0 | 7 | 7 | 6 | 6 | 6 |
| Cash | −5 | −5 | −3 | −3 | −5 | −5 | −5 |
| **Total** | **100%** | **100%** | **100%** | **100%** | **100%** | **100%** | **100%** |

Source: 1994–1995, 1998–1999, 1999–2000, 2000–2001, 2001–2002, 2002–2003, 2003–2004, and 2004–2005 issues of the *Annual Report of the Harvard Management Company*.

risk; (iii) qualitative judgments affected by prior experiences with and new knowledge about asset classes, financial markets, and changing circumstances; and (iv) recognition that the Policy Portfolio is deemed to be the central long-term strategy around which HMC evaluates and undertakes shorter-term, tactical moves.

Relative to many other large endowments, the HMC Policy Portfolio has had generally more asset classes, generally higher allocations to foreign securities and commodities, and a generally lower allocation to domestic fixed-income securities. The HMC has the flexibility to vary on a tactical basis the short- and intermediate-term percentages, within certain prescribed but undisclosed boundaries, that it invests in the respective asset classes. Beginning in the early 1900s, Harvard has been among a small group employing alpha-transfer techniques, in which a significant portion of the HMC Policy portfolio is invested in asset class-based index funds, and internally managed hedge funds are used to generate *incremental returns over the benchmark* (known as *alpha*). With the passage of time, most of these groups of talented managers have left HMC and founded independent hedge funds in which Harvard has invested such as Highfields, Sowood, and Convexity Capital.

The HMC usually does not carry out tactical moves above or below the strategic allocation weightings in the Policy Portfolio unless it can make a very strong case that prices are significantly out of line with values for an asset class, and thus highly likely to revert to their true

## T A B L E  2.4

### Harvard Management Company Multiyear Investment Performance

| HMC Policy Allocation | 2001 Returns[1] | | 2002 Returns[1] | | 2003 Returns[1] | | 2004 Returns[1] | |
|---|---|---|---|---|---|---|---|---|
| | HMC | Benchmark | HMC | Benchmark | HMC | Benchmark | HMC | Benchmark |
| Domestic Equities | −4.6% | −10.9% | −12.2% | −15.3% | 1.7% | −0.2% | 22.8% | 21.5% |
| Absolute Return | 26.9 | −8.4 | 10.2 | −4.0 | 9.4 | 8.3 | 15.7 | 9.9 |
| Foreign Equities | −16.9 | −23.3 | −6.5 | −8.7 | −3.8 | −5.4 | 36.1 | 34.0 |
| Emerging Markets | 3.0 | −14.2 | 7.5 | 1.9 | 10.8 | 7.3 | 36.6 | 33.9 |
| High-Yield Securities | −3.3 | −4.2 | 0.5 | 0.5 | 31.1 | 32.9 | 12.4 | 15.3 |
| Commodities | 4.2 | −0.3 | 1.6 | −5.4 | 12.3 | 11.3 | 19.7 | 12.9 |
| Real Estate | 10.2 | 11.2 | −1.0 | 4.8 | 6.3 | 11.9 | 16.0 | 16.8 |
| Private Equities | −25.2 | −22.6 | −19.7 | −20.2 | −5.2 | −8.5 | 20.8 | 20.3 |
| Domestic Bonds | 19.1 | 10.2 | 14.8 | 9.2 | 29.9 | 17.3 | 9.2 | −3.4 |
| Foreign Bonds | 13.2 | −7.3 | 32.4 | 15.6 | 52.4 | 18.0 | 17.4 | 7.6 |
| Inflation-Indexed Bonds | 13.3 | 13.4 | 9.2 | 9.1 | 15.9 | 16.5 | 4.2 | 3.9 |
| Cash | – | – | – | – | – | – | – | – |
| Total | −2.7% | −9.8%[3] | −0.5% | −4.5%[3] | 12.5% | 8.3%[3] | 21.1% | 16.4%[3] |

| HMC Policy Allocation | 5-Year Performance[2] | | 10-Year Performance[2] | |
|---|---|---|---|---|
| | HMC | Benchmark | HMC | Benchmark |
| Domestic Equities | 3.9% | 0.4% | 17.8% | 12.7% |
| Absolute Return | 16.6 | 3.6 | N/A | N/A |
| Foreign Equities | 5.1 | 0.7 | 8.5 | 5.2 |
| Emerging Markets | 13.8 | 7.6 | 9.7 | 5.7 |
| High-Yield Securities | 8.0 | 4.4 | 9.7 | 6.1 |
| Commodities | 16.4 | 10.0 | 10.9 | 7.9 |
| Real Estate | 9.5 | 11.5 | 15.0 | 13.1 |
| Private Equities | 28.7 | 0.7 | 31.5 | 16.1 |
| Domestic Bonds | 17.1 | 7.6 | 14.9 | 7.9 |
| Foreign Bonds | 23.1 | 6.7 | 16.9 | 6.4 |
| Inflation-Indexed Bonds | 9.9 | 10.0 | N/A | N/A |
| Cash | – | – | – | – |
| Total | 11.8% | 5.2%[3] | 15.9% | 11.9%[3] |

[1]For the fiscal years ending in June.
[2]For the 5-year and 10-year fiscal periods ending June 2004.
[3]A weighted average of the performance of the specific benchmark indices for each of the 12 asset classes in the HMC Policy Allocation, with weights equal to the percentage that each asset class represents as part of the overall Harvard Policy Portfolio.

Source: 1998–1999, 1999–2000, 2000–2001, 2001–2002, 2002–2003, 2003–2004, and 2004–2005 issues of the *Annual Report of the Harvard Management Company*.

underlying valuations. The investment results of the HMC can underperform or outperform the Benchmark Composite Index (shown in Table 2.4) of the HMC Policy Portfolio as a result of two factors: (i) the HMC may have implemented correct or incorrect tactical asset allocation decisions from time to time to vary the percentages invested in selected asset classes relative to their strategic weightings; and/or (ii) internal or external investment managers within a given asset class may have fared better or worse than the performance of the index used as a benchmark for that specific asset class.

The following paragraphs set forth the investment implementation methods and strategic portfolio weightings as of June 30, 2004, for each of the 12 asset classes in the HMC Policy Portfolio (in several instances these paragraphs may quote from or paraphrase the Harvard Management Company *Annual Report*):

- **Domestic Equities:** Harvard employs two strategies in its domestic-equity program. In the first, focusing on stock selection, a team of analysts and portfolio managers attempts to identify, through fundamental analysis, companies within an industry sector that are over- or undervalued. Because Harvard keeps industry weightings close to the relevant benchmarks, the returns the stock selection process generates can be isolated. A second strategy involves arbitrage strategies, including merger arbitrage, warrant and convertible securities arbitrage, pairs trading, and occasionally substantial offsetting long and short positions in individual securities, futures, options, and/or specially structured instruments. Four external managers also invest in portfolios of small capitalization equities. Domestic equities represented 15% of the HMC Policy Portfolio as of June 30, 2004, versus 38% as of June 30, 1995.

- **Absolute Return:** Harvard's absolute-return strategy aims to achieve positive returns without regard to a specific security index. It typically focuses on merger arbitrage, warrant and convertible arbitrage, synthetic security arbitrage, pairs trading, and hedged balance sheet or cross-ownership arbitrage, with an admixture of absolute value trades. Ideally, the portfolio should be sufficiently hedged to generate positive returns in either up or down markets. Absolute return investments accounted for 12% of the HMC Policy Portfolio as of June 30, 2004, up from 0% as of June 30, 1995.

- **Foreign Equities:** One portion of Harvard's managed foreign-equities portfolio focuses on arbitrage possibilities. A second segment is indexed to the EAFE Index, with lending securities earning incremental returns. Two external managers also invest in foreign equities. Foreign equities represented 10% of the HMC Policy Portfolio as of June 30, 2004, down from 15% as of June 30, 1995.

- **Emerging Markets:** The HMC uses four strategies to manage assets in the emerging-markets sector. The first employs an internal group that focuses on closed-end funds selling at sharp discounts to net asset values. A second tranche employs an index-based strategy. Third, a small portion of commitments to emerging markets is in the form of private-equity funds. Fourth, through 2005, a meaningful portion of this asset class was invested in emerging-markets debt. Emerging-markets investments accounted for 5% of the HMC Policy Portfolio as of June 30, 2004, unchanged since June 30, 1995.

- **High-Yield Securities:** A small number of external firms manage Harvard's high-yield funds, emphasizing situations in which debt securities appear to be incorrectly valued. High-yield securities represented 5% of the HMC Policy Portfolio as of June 30, 2004, versus 2% as of June 30, 1995.

- **Commodities:** The primary strategy in Harvard's commodities portfolio is to discover and exploit mispricings within a broadly diversified pool of commodities, timber, and their related derivative securities. Commodities accounted for 13% of the HMC Policy Portfolio as of June 30, 2004, up from 6% as of June 30, 1995.

- **Real Estate:** The real estate portfolio, most of which is internally managed, includes direct equity investments in specific income-producing properties, diversified across office buildings, residential properties, hotels, and retail projects. Harvard supplements its internal portfolio with several externally managed real estate funds. Real estate investments comprised 10% of the HMC Policy Portfolio as of June 30, 2004, up from 7% as of June 30, 1995.

- **Private Equities:** Harvard's private-equities portfolio consists of roughly 60 externally managed private equity partnerships that invest in: venture-capital opportunities such as start-ups and early round financings in new companies; private-equity opportunities such as leveraged buyouts; and on rare occasions, outright purchases of mature companies that possess skills complementary to those employed by the Harvard Management Company. Private equities accounted for 13% of the HMC Policy Portfolio as of June 30, 2004, up slightly from 12% as of June 30, 1995.

- **Domestic Bonds:** The entire domestic-bonds portfolio is managed internally, with a primary emphasis on finding opportunities to buy relatively cheap securities and simultaneously sell overvalued securities with similar characteristics. These include long and short positions in fixed-income securities, futures, and swap arrangements. Such strategies attempt to arbitrage various aspects of the fixed-income market that are subject to mispricing, including credit risk, yield-curve shape, call features, option characteristics, or combinations of these and other features. Domestic bonds represented 11% of the HMC Policy Portfolio as of June 30, 2004, down from 15% as of June 30, 1995.

◆ **Foreign Bonds:** As with domestic bonds, Harvard's emphasis in foreign bonds is on arbitrage, with substantial and partially offsetting long and short positions in foreign fixed-income securities and derivatives based on these markets. Duration and country allocation tend not to vary substantially from the benchmark. Foreign bonds accounted for 5% of the HMC Policy Portfolio as of June 30, 2004, unchanged from June 30, 1995.

◆ **Inflation-Indexed Bonds:** These securities, first issued by the U.S. Treasury in January 1997, provide a guaranteed rate of return over the CPI inflation rate. They were initially added to the Harvard Policy Portfolio during fiscal 2000. Inflation-indexed bonds represented 6% of the HMC Policy Portfolio as of June 30, 2004 versus 0% as of June 30, 2000.

◆ **Cash:** Harvard does not generally target cash as an asset class in its Policy Portfolio. In fact, in the course of its investing, hedging, and arbitrage activities, Harvard has often targeted a strategic *borrowing* position (shown as negative cash) representing from 3% to 5% of its total endowment assets in the fiscal years from 1995 through 2004.

For many years in the 1990s, Harvard has produced some of the best investment returns in the academic world, consistently ranking in the top few percentiles among the endowments tracked by the National Association of College and University Business Officers (NACUBO). As part of its performance measurement and monitoring activity, Harvard explicitly compares its own investment results in each asset class against the returns of a benchmark it has chosen to represent that specific type of asset. Table 2.4 contains these comparisons for fiscal 2001 through 2004, as well as for the 5- and 10-year periods ending June 30, 2004.

In fiscal 2004, the Harvard Management Company exceeded the benchmark returns in nine asset classes. For the portfolio as a whole, the Harvard endowment increased 21.1% versus a gain of 16.4 % for its weighted benchmark. The top four performing asset classes for Harvard were: emerging markets, +36.6%; foreign equities, +36.1%; domestic equities, +22.8%; and private equities, +20.8%. For the portfolio as a whole in 2003, the Harvard endowment increased 12.5%, versus an increase of 8.3% for its weighted benchmark. The top four performing asset classes for Harvard in fiscal 2003 were: foreign bonds, +52.4%; high-yield securities, +31.1%; domestic bonds, +29.9%; and inflation-indexed bonds, +15.9%.

For the 5- and 10-year fiscal years ending June 30, 2004, the Harvard endowment earned compounded returns of: 28.7% and 31.5%, respectively in private equities; 23.1% and 16.9%, respectively, in foreign bonds; and 17.1% and 14.9%, respectively, in domestic bonds.

The Harvard Management Company has developed and implemented an incentive-compensation system that has allowed certain of its internal asset managers to earn significant bonuses if they meaningfully outperform appropriate benchmarks over extended periods. In response to commentary about the level of such reward packages compared with tenured faculty members' and others' compensation, the HMC has pointed out that: (i) incentive-based compensation with substantial upside potential is necessary to attract the highly talented and motivated asset managers who help produce successful investment performance; (ii) on an all-in basis, the total annual operating costs of the HMC are approximately 50 basis points (0.005 of the total market value of the Harvard Endowment), of which 33 basis points represent base fees and 17 basis points represent incentive compensation; (iii) the amounts it pays to successful internal managers are a relatively small percentage of the overall profits those managers produce for Harvard; and, (iv) colleges and universities that externally manage a significant portion of their endowment assets in many cases also pay high performance-based fees to *outside* asset managers, but these compensation packages are generally much less widely disclosed than the rewards earned by *inside* investment managers.

A special aspect of HMC's approach to asset allocation and investment strategy involves the use of several diversified arbitrage strategies intended to enhance portfolio returns without changing the portfolio's risk profile. Only a relatively small number of investors have the mentality, the internal analytical and trading resources, and the strong credit rating of HMC to undertake such activity.

In essence, Harvard's return enhancement strategies attempt to find market anomalies in the form of specific financial instruments that are mispriced relative to other similar instruments. After these mispricings have been discovered, HMC implements a number of long and short transactions in the underlying investments and in such off-balance-sheet products as forwards, futures, options, swaps, and over-the-counter exchange agreements, often in large size. These transactions tend to remain neutral to changes in the value of the specific asset class while attempting to capture the differentials between similar instruments if and when their prices converge to expected normal relationships. From time to time, Harvard may also use methods and instruments that protect its core positions, such as by shorting equity-related futures and/or by purchasing equity-related put options as a way of hedging its equity exposures. The HMC may also make tactical adjustments to its core asset allocation in a cost-effective, timely, and nondisruptive manner.

Table 2.5 summarizes the year-to-year changes in Harvard's arbitrage, hedging, and tactical adjustment overlays relative to its core market exposure in equity-related, fixed-income-related, and other asset classes for the fiscal years 1995 through 2004. The data presented in Table 2.5 are net to the core market exposure of Harvard's aggregate portfolio, which in turn agrees with the asset allocation in the *Annual Report of the Harvard Management Company* and which approximates the market exposure of the Policy Portfolio.

As of June 30, 1995, the Harvard endowment's equity-related classes consisted of $6.167 billion in total long positions, $1.639 billion in total short positions, and total net-adjusted market exposure of $4.528 billion. The endowment's fixed-income-related asset classes included total long positions of $17.128 billion, total short positions of $15.580 billion, and total net-adjusted market exposure of $1.548 billion. Other asset classes were comprised of total long positions of $2.061 billion, total short positions of $210 million, and total net-adjusted market exposure of $1.851 billion. The portfolio as a whole consisted of total long positions of $25.356 billion, total short positions of $17.429 billion, total gross positions of $42.785 billion, and total net-adjusted market exposure of $7.927 billion.

As of June 30, 2004, the Harvard endowment's equity-related classes included total long positions of $14.551 billion, total short positions of $1.852 billion, and total net-adjusted market exposure of $12.699 billion. Its fixed-income-related asset classes consisted of total long positions of $56.287 billion, total short positions of $42.940 billion, and total net-adjusted market exposure of $13.347 billion. Other asset classes included total long positions of $7.522 billion, total short positions of

## T A B L E  2.5

Harvard Management Company Gross and Net Adjusted Market Exposure

| | (Amounts in $ Millions) | | | | | |
|---|---|---|---|---|---|---|
| | Equity-Related Asset Classes[2] | | | Fixed-Income-Related Asset Classes[3] | | |
| Year[1] | Long | Short | Net Adjusted Market Exposure[6] | Long | Short | Net Adjusted Market Exposure[6] |
| 1995 | 6,167 | (1,639) | 4,528 | 17,128 | (15,580) | 1,548 |
| 1996 | 7,718 | (2,165) | 5,553 | 16,152 | (14,494) | 1,658 |
| 1997 | 10,533 | (3,291) | 7,242 | 26,049 | (24,014) | 2,035 |
| 1998 | 12,489 | (4,435) | 8,054 | 42,721 | (40,337) | 2,384 |
| 1999 | 14,055 | (5,875) | 8,180 | 57,204 | (54,591) | 2,613 |
| 2000 | 17,385 | (7,757) | 9,628 | 47,231 | (42,836) | 4,395 |
| 2001 | 14,120 | (3,479) | 10,641 | 35,497 | (30,004) | 5,493 |
| 2002 | 11,553 | (1,996) | 9,537 | 49,703 | (39,262) | 10,441 |
| 2003 | 11,872 | (1,976) | 9,896 | 66,356 | (53,827) | 12,529 |
| 2004 | 14,551 | (1,852) | 12,699 | 56,287 | (42,940) | 13,347 |

[1] For fiscal years ending June 30.

[2] Includes Domestic Equity, Foreign Equity, Emerging Markets Equity and Fixed-Income Securities, and Arbitrage Accounts.

[3] Includes Domestic Fixed-Income, Foreign Fixed-Income, High Yield Fixed-Income, Inflation-Indexed Fixed-Income, and Arbitrage Accounts.

[4] Includes Private Equity, Real Estate, Core Commodities, and Commodities Arbitrage Accounts.

[5] Excludes cash and cash equivalents, collateral advanced on borrows, collateral held on loans, accounts payable, market exposure adjustment, option premium, and the cash side of off-balance-sheet positions.

$0.849 billion, and total net-adjusted market exposure of $6.673 billion. The portfolio consisted of total long positions of $78.360 billion, total short positions of $45.641 billion, total gross positions of $124.001 billion, and total net-adjusted market exposure of $32.719 billion.

At the end of fiscal 1995, the ratio of Harvard's gross positions to its net adjusted market exposure was 5.4 times (equal to $42.785 billion divided by $7.927 billion). By the end of fiscal 1999, the ratio of Harvard's gross positions to its net adjusted market exposure had grown to 9.2 times (equal to $137.836 billion divided by $14.966 billion), before contracting in fiscal 2000 to 6.2 times, and then again in 2001 to a ratio of 4.3 times (equal to $90.778 billion divided by $21.158 billion). The ratio expanded in 2002 and 2003 to 4.4 times and 5.1 times, respectively. In 2004, the ratio contracted to 3.8 times, the lowest level of any of the fiscal years from 1995 through 2004.

Table 2.5 illustrates that a significant proportion of the HMB's total gross positions established during fiscal years 1995 through 2004 involve fixed-income-related asset classes. For example, as of June 30,

| (Amounts in $ Millions) | | | | | | | |
| Other Asset Classes[4] | | | Total[5] | | | | Ratio of Gross |
| Long | Short | Net Adjusted Market Exposure[6] | Long | Short | Gross Positions | Net Adjusted Market Exposure | Positions to Net Adjusted Market Exposure |
|---|---|---|---|---|---|---|---|
| 2,061 | (210) | 1,851 | 25,356 | (17,429) | 42,785 | 7,927 | 5.4x |
| 2,751 | (424) | 2,327 | 26,621 | (17,083) | 43,704 | 9,538 | 4.6x |
| 2,866 | (517) | 2,349 | 39,448 | (27,822) | 67,270 | 11,626 | 5.8x |
| 3,944 | (647) | 3,297 | 59,154 | (45,419) | 104,573 | 13,735 | 7.6x |
| 5,143 | (970) | 4,173 | 76,402 | (61,436) | 137,838 | 4,966 | 9.2x |
| 7,705 | (1,469) | 6,236 | 72,321 | (52,062) | 124,383 | 20,259 | 6.1x |
| 6,351 | (1,327) | 5,024 | 55,968 | (34,810) | 90,778 | 21,158 | 4.3x |
| 6,022 | (1,093) | 4,929 | 67,258 | (42,351) | 109,609 | 24,907 | 4.4x |
| 5,446 | (366) | 5,080 | 83,674 | (56,169) | 139,843 | 27,505 | 5.1x |
| 7,522 | (849) | 6,673 | 78,360 | (45,641) | 124,001 | 32,719 | 3.8x |

[6]Numbers presented in this column net to the core market exposure of Harvard's aggregate portfolio, which agrees with the Asset Allocation in the Annual Report of the Harvard Management Company and which approximates the market exposure of the HMC Policy Portfolio.

Source: Supplemental information section on pooled general investments in the *Financial Report to the Board of Overseers of Harvard College* for the fiscal years 1994–1995 through 2003–2004.

1995, 76.4% of the $42.785 billion in total gross positions surrounding the Harvard portfolio ($32.708 billion divided by $42.785 billion) was associated with fixed-income-related asset classes. As of June 30, 2001, 72.2% of the Harvard portfolio ($65.501 billion divided by $90.778 billion in total gross positions) was associated with fixed-income-related asset classes. As of June 30, 2004, 80.0% of the $124.001 billion in total gross positions surrounding the Harvard portfolio ($99.227 billion divided by $124.001 billion) was associated with fixed-income-related asset classes.

In a significant part of its fixed-income hedging and arbitrage activities, Harvard uses its triple-A credit rating, the margining potential of its own portfolio, and standby borrowing facilities it has paid for and arranged with banks to borrow substantial amounts of funds. This capital is then used to *buy* at relatively *lower prices* (higher yields) various combinations of fixed-income securities (such as zero-coupon U.S. Treasury issues plus high-coupon U.S. Treasury bonds) and *sell short* a package of U.S. Treasury bonds and/or other fixed-income securities that simultaneously trade in the marketplace at *higher prices* (lower yields). If this tactic works out as planned, the prices of the purchased securities should rise, and/or the prices of the securities sold short should decline, yielding a profit on the transaction.

The securities that Harvard has deemed to offset each other may not always prove to be virtually equal to one another. In other instances, systemic risk, technical or fundamental factors, or other events such as short-squeeze activity, may cause prices to move *down* on the *long* side, and/or prices to move *up* on the *short* side of such a transaction, resulting in a loss. In view of the complexity, high leverage, position sizes, and monitoring requirements associated with such trades, most investors should not contemplate directly undertaking the type of arbitrage and hedging activity that Harvard employs. Investors need to appreciate the risks as well as the rewards of these transactions in light of their own resources and risk tolerance.

## YALE UNIVERSITY

Founded in 1701, Yale University is the third oldest institution of higher learning in the United States. From 1985 through the beginning of the twenty-first century, the Yale University Investments Office (YUIO) has managed the Yale Endowment in a thoughtful, disciplined, and innovative manner that has added to the body of practical knowledge about asset allocation, investment strategy, and university spending policies. In the process, the Yale Endowment has delivered impressive investment performance. For the 10 fiscal years ending June 30, 2004, Yale's actual investment returns added an estimated $5.4 billion to the portfolio relative to the university's composite benchmark, and an estimated $5.6 billion relative to the mean return of a broad universe of colleges and universities.

Consisting of a small number of professionals plus support staff, the YUIO is located near the main Yale campus in New Haven, Connecticut. The Investments Office reports to and interacts regularly with an Investment Committee, composed primarily of prominent alumni and others with knowledge about and experience in specialized areas of conventional and alternative asset classes. The Investments Office also reports to the Treasurer of Yale University and, ultimately, to the university's governing body, the Yale Corporation. A significant part of the YUIO's mandate is to frame, recommend, and carry out the asset allocation, strategic and tactical investment implementation, and spending policy for the Yale Endowment. Another highly important mission of the Investments Office is to identify, evaluate, select, negotiate terms with, monitor, and either add funds to or withdraw funds from, external managers in each of its main asset classes.

Table 2.6 shows the annual investment returns for the Yale Endowment for the fiscal years 1980 through 2004.

As of June 30, 2004, the total value of the Yale endowment was $12.747 billion, compared with $11.035 billion at the end of fiscal 2003, $3.982 billion at the end of fiscal 1995, $2.570 billion at the end of fiscal 1990, and $1.319 billion at the end of fiscal 1985.

For the 10 fiscal years 1995 through 2004, the Yale Endowment generated a compound investment return, net of fees, of 16.8% per annum, exceeding calendar year benchmark returns for the same years of 7.6% for equities (the S&P 500 index) and 12.1% for bonds (the Lehman Brothers Aggregate index). For the five fiscal years from 2000 through 2004, the Yale Endowment generated a compound investment return, net of fees, of 13.6% per annum, versus calendar year returns of –2.3% per annum for the S&P 500 index and 7.7% per annum for the Lehman Brothers Aggregate index. During the 1995–2004 time frame, the standard deviation of annual returns for the Yale Endowment was 11.1 %, well below the 21.1% standard deviation of annual returns for U.S. equities as measured by the S&P 500 index.

The multiyear success of the Yale Endowment derives from several factors, including: (i) a disciplined approach to, and an appreciation of, the benefits and limitations of asset allocation and a clearly defined investment policy; (ii) emphasis on a diversified portfolio, with a bias toward equities and asset classes having equitylike characteristics, in an attempt to achieve high returns and protect against the university's long-term vulnerability to inflation; (iii) a willingness to seek investment opportunities in less-efficient markets, investment styles, and asset classes; (iv) painstaking care in the due-diligence process associated with the selection and cultivation of long-term relationships with high-quality asset managers who receive appropriate incentives to align their interests with those of the Yale Endowment; and (v) close and hands-on monitoring of these managers' investment activities.

In broad terms, since the late 1980s and early 1990s the Yale University Investments Office has significantly reduced the Yale Endowment's exposure to domestic marketable securities and cash investments. As late as 1989, 70% of the total portfolio was invested in such traditional asset classes as U.S. equities, U.S. fixed-income securities, and

## T A B L E  2.6

Yale Endowment Portfolio Returns versus Selected Benchmarks

| Fiscal Year (Ending June 30) | Endowment Value ($ Millions)[1] | Yale Endowment | S&P 500[2] | Lehman Brothers Aggregate[2] |
|---|---|---|---|---|
| 1980 | $676.4 | 18.7% | 32.4% | NA |
| 1981 | 799.0 | 22.7 | −4.9 | NA |
| 1982 | 746.8 | −4.3 | 21.4 | 32.6 |
| 1983 | 1,098.0 | 50.1 | 22.5 | 8.4 |
| 1984 | 1,068.6 | −0.2 | 6.3 | 15.2 |
| 1985 | 1,318.6 | 25.8 | 32.2 | 22.1 |
| 1986 | 1,750.7 | 36.0 | 18.5 | 15.3 |
| 1987 | 2,111.1 | 22.8 | 5.2 | 2.8 |
| 1988 | 2,055.8 | −0.2 | 16.8 | 7.9 |
| 1989 | 2,342.1 | 17.3 | 31.5 | 14.5 |
| 1990 | 2,571.0 | 13.1 | −3.2 | 9.0 |
| 1991 | 2,591.1 | 2.0 | 30.5 | 16.0 |
| 1992 | 2,845.7 | 13.2 | 7.6 | 7.4 |
| 1993 | 3,243.7 | 17.3 | 10.1 | 9.7 |
| 1994 | 3,549.3 | 12.0 | 1.3 | −2.9 |
| 1995 | 3,981.8 | 15.7 | 37.5 | 18.5 |
| 1996 | 4,860.5 | 25.7 | 22.9 | 3.6 |
| 1997 | 5,794.1 | 21.8 | 33.4 | 9.7 |
| 1998 | 6,597.9 | 18.0 | 28.6 | 8.7 |
| 1999 | 7,185.6 | 12.2 | 21.0 | −0.8 |
| 2000 | 10,084.9 | 41.0 | −9.1 | 11.6 |
| 2001 | 10,725.1 | 9.2 | −11.9 | 8.4 |
| 2002 | 10,523.6 | 0.7 | −22.1 | 10.3 |
| 2003 | 11,034.6 | 8.8 | 28.7 | 4.1 |
| 2004 | 12,747.2 | 19.4 | 10.9 | 4.3 |
| 5-Year Annual Rate of Growth (2000–2004) | | 13.6% | −2.3% | 7.7% |
| 10-Year Annual Rate of Growth (1995–2004) | | 16.8% | 7.6% | 12.1% |
| Standard Deviation of Annual Returns | | | | |
| 20-Year (1985–2004) | | 11.2% | 17.0% | 6.3% |
| 10-Year (1995–2004) | | 11.1% | 21.1% | 5.3% |

[1]Changes in endowment values over time are a function of distributed and undistributed dividend and interest income, realized and unrealized capital gains or losses, donor gifts and pledges for capital, funds distributions to support university operations, and other transfers and adjustments.

[2]Year ending December 31.

Sources: *Yale University Investments Office*, Harvard Business School Case No. 9-201-048, by Professor Josh Lerner, November 17, 2000; and *The Yale Endowment 2000 through 2004*.

cash. At the end of fiscal 2002, the YUIO had heavily reallocated assets toward nontraditional asset classes, with 75% of the university's total portfolio invested in private equity, absolute-return strategies, real assets, and foreign equity. Table 2.7 presents the actual asset allocations of the Yale Endowment for the fiscal years 1995 through 2004, and the 10-year compound annual rate of growth for each asset class and its relevant benchmark.

The YUIO's compound annual rate of growth for the 10 fiscal years ending in 2004 outperformed its relevant benchmarks: in domestic equity, 17.0 % versus 11.5%; in foreign equity, 10.1% versus 4.2%; in fixed-income, 7.8% versus 7.1%; in real assets, 16.8% versus 14.7%; in private equity, 37.6% versus 22.9%; and in absolute-return strategies, 12.2% versus 11.0%.

In addition to its emphasis on external asset managers for a large part of the University endowment, the Yale Investments Office executes its mandate differently than the Harvard Management Company in a number of other ways. Yale focuses on fewer asset classes than Harvard, eschewing investment in or separate classification of high-yield bonds, inflation-indexed bonds, foreign bonds, and commodities, due to minimal exposure to those asset classes. Yale's exposure to selected alternative-asset classes is higher than Harvard's in absolute return (26% for Yale versus 12% for Harvard), in private equity (15% for Yale versus 13% for Harvard), and in real assets/real estate (19% for Yale versus 10% for Harvard). Yale tends to view its portfolio holdings as opportunities to earn potentially high returns, offered by equity-oriented and alternative-asset positions even at a cost of reduced liquidity, higher incentives paid to external managers, and in some cases, greater volatility in returns. By contrast, Harvard has to varying degrees employed a significant portion of its portfolio as core assets, around which significant arbitrage, hedging, leveraging, short-selling, borrowing, and lending activities can be conducted using options, futures, swaps, and other derivative instruments.

While Yale's asset allocation, investment policies, and performance results have many important implications for investors, how the YUIO invests in specific asset classes can provide equally important insights. The following paragraphs describe the investment implementation methods and strategic portfolio weightings as of June 30, 2004, for each of the seven asset classes in the Yale Endowment portfolio (in several instances, these paragraphs may quote from or paraphrase the *Annual* Report of the Yale University Investments Office):

T A B L E  2.7

Yale Endowment Investment Portfolio

| Asset Class | Asset Allocation[1] | | | | | | |
|---|---|---|---|---|---|---|---|
| | 1995 | 1999 | 2000 | 2001 | 2002 | 2003 | 2004 |
| Domestic Equity | 22% | 15% | 14% | 16% | 15% | 15% | 15% |
| Absolute Return | 21 | 22 | 20 | 23 | 27 | 25 | 26 |
| Foreign Equity | 13 | 11 | 9 | 11 | 13 | 15 | 15 |
| Private Equity[3] | 17 | 23 | 25 | 18 | 14 | 15 | 15 |
| Real Assets[3] | 14 | 18 | 15 | 17 | 21 | 21 | 19 |
| Fixed-Income | 14 | 10 | 9 | 10 | 10 | 7 | 7 |
| Cash | 0 | 2 | 8 | 6 | 6 | 2 | 4 |
| Total | 100% | 100% | 100% | 100% | 100% | 100% | 100% |

[1]For fiscal years ending June 30; totals may not add due to rounding.
[2]Year ending December 31.
[3]Prior to 1999, oil and gas and timber were classified as private equity rather than real assets.
Source: *The Yale Endowment 2000 through 2004*, Yale University Investments Office.

- ◆ **Domestic Equity:** Yale uses bottom-up, fundamental research-intensive active managers of concentrated portfolios across an array of market sectors and strategies, typically with a bias toward value and small-capitalization stocks. In certain circumstances, the university has been willing to respond to attractive valuations by taking significant positions in out-of-favor investment styles, sectors, and securities. Domestic equity represented 15% of the Yale Endowment portfolio as of June 30, 2004, versus 22% as of June 30, 1995.

- ◆ **Absolute Return:** In October 1989, Yale became the first institutional investor to define absolute-return strategies as an asset class, beginning with an allocation of 4.5%. Yale's absolute-return portfolio is composed primarily of event-driven, value-driven, and opportunistic value strategies managed by 14 external managers in search of risk-controlled, noncorrelated returns largely independent of overall market movements. In many cases, absolute-return strategies often consist of marketable securities hedged against broad market moves and also focus on the exploitation of market inefficien-

**Compound Annual Rate of Growth**
**1994–2004**

| Yale University Investments Office | Benchmark[2] | Benchmark Description |
|---|---|---|
| 17.0% | 11.5% | Wilshire 5000 Index |
| 12.2 | 11.0 | 1-yr constant maturity Treasury plus 6 percent |
| 10.1 | 4.2 | MSCI EAFE/MSCI EMF[2] |
| 37.6 | 22.9 | University inflation plus 10 percent |
| 16.8 | 14.7 | University inflation plus 6 percent |
| 7.8 | 7.1 | Lehman Brothers U.S. Treasury Index |
| NA | 0.0 | |
| 16.8% | NA | |

cies, financially distressed securities, and arbitrage strategies. Absolute-return investments accounted for 26% of the Yale Endowment portfolio as of June 30, 2004, up from 21% of the portfolio on June 30, 1995.

◆ **Foreign Equity:** Relying on disciplined (and in some instances, quantitatively driven) external managers with a bias toward bottom-up fundamental research in value and small capitalization equities, Yale also occasionally responds to extreme valuations by over- or underweighting specific foreign equity markets on a tactical or rebalancing basis. Approximately one-half of the foreign-equity portfolio is allocated to emerging markets. Foreign equity represented 15% of the Yale Endowment portfolio on June 30, 2004, up from 13% of total assets in June 30, 1995.

◆ **Private Equity:** The Yale Endowment invests in a number of private-equity partnerships through the development of long-term relationships with leading venture capital and leveraged buyout firms that seek to exploit market inefficiencies. In its private-equity investments, the Yale University Investments

Office has sought to develop long-term relationships with a limited number of top-quality organizations that are committed to helping Yale build a deep understanding of the deal flow, deal structuring, governance, management evaluation, information networking, and exit-strategy skills involved in the private-equity investment process. Unlike many investors, Yale has paid attention to the differences between the venture-capital and the leveraged-buyout subsectors of this asset class, as well as its international forms. Within the leveraged buyout area, Yale has concentrated on finding managers who emphasize a value-added, operationally intensive approach to investing, rather than focusing on a financial engineering approach. Yale has further differentiated its approach to private equity through exposure to international private equity, through the judicious application of short sales, and through the use of derivative instruments to hedge its underlying exposure to specific investments that it considers to be overvalued. Private equity accounted for 15% of the Yale Endowment portfolio on June 30, 2004, down from 17% as of June 30, 1995.

◆ **Real Assets:** For portfolio diversification, cash-flow generation, and inflation-hedging purposes, Yale invests through partnerships with external managers in: (i) real estate, with a focus on purchasing properties at discounts to replacement cost; (ii) oil and gas, with a focus on the acquisition and restructuring of existing oil and gas fields; and (iii) timberland, with a focus on acquiring forests at discounts to standing timber value. In real assets, the YUIO seeks to take advantage of the inefficient pricing and purchasing-power protection characteristics of this asset class, while seeking asset managers with a competitive edge in their field, strong track records, and impeccable reputations. Further, Yale has sought to work with real-asset managers employing potentially contrarian approaches and appropriate investment structures that reflect the business practices and realities of the chief subsectors of this asset class. Real assets represented 19% of the Yale Endowment portfolio on June 30, 2004, an increase from 14% as of June 30, 1995.

◆ **Fixed-Income:** Utilizing an internal manager, the Yale Endowment seeks to meet crisis-protection and deflation-hedging objectives, to retain the portfolio-protection characteristics of high-quality fixed-income instruments, and to add incremental returns through creative, patient portfolio-management techniques and by identifying overlooked, illiquid securities. The fixed-income portfolio is invested primarily in high-quality, noncallable instruments backed by the full faith and credit of the U.S. government. Fixed-income accounted for 7% of the Yale Endowment portfolio on June 30, 2004, down from 14% as of June 30, 1995.

◆ **Cash:** The Yale Endowment tends to utilize cash more as an asset for tactical purposes than for strategic purposes. In the fiscal years 1985 through 1988, the Yale Endowment allocated 10%, 5%, 2%, and 2%, respectively, to cash. From fiscal 1990 through 1998, 0% was allocated to cash; in fiscal 1999 through 2004, 2%, 8%, 6%, 6%, 2% and 4%, respectively, were allocated to cash.

The target asset allocation of the Yale Endowment is shown in Table 2.8.

In Table 2.8, it is possible to discern the degree of Yale's *underweighting* of *conventional asset classes* and its *overweighting of alternative asset classes* versus the holdings other colleges and universities as measured by the Educational Institution Mean in the *2004 Endowment*

## T A B L E  2.8

Yale Endowment Target Asset Allocation

| Asset Class | Yale Target Allocation[2,3] | Educational Institution Mean[2,4] |
|---|---|---|
| Domestic Equity | 15% | 37% |
| Absolute Return | 25 | 15 |
| Foreign Equity | 15 | 16 |
| Private Equity | 18 | 6 |
| Real Assets[1] | 20 | 6 |
| Fixed-Income | 8 | 18 |
| Cash | 0 | 3 |
| Total | 100% | 100% |

[1]Prior to 1999, oil and gas and timber were classified as private equity rather than real assets.

[2]Totals may not add due to rounding.

[3]As of June 30, 2004.

[4]Based on data contained in the *2004 Endowment Study of the National Association of College and University Business Officers (NACUBO)*.

Source: *The Yale Endowment 2004*, Yale University Investments Office.

*Study* of the National Association of College and University Business Officers. In *conventional* asset classes. Yale's target asset allocation underweightings compared to the Educational Institution Mean were 15% versus 37% in domestic equity, 15% versus 16% in foreign equity, 8% versus 18% in fixed-income, and 0% versus 3% in cash. In *alternative* asset classes, Yale's target asset allocation overweightings compared to the Educational Institutional Mean were 25% versus 15% in absolute-return strategies, 18% versus 6% in private equity, and 20% versus 6% in real assets.

The reasons Yale's investment activity emphasizes alternative rather than conventional asset classes include: (i) the higher expected returns of alternative assets, even though such returns are associated with higher expected standard deviations of returns; (ii) the low expected correlations of many types of alternative assets, both with conventional assets and with other types of alternative assets; and (iii) the significantly wider spreads between the returns that can be achieved by top-performing investment managers compared with those produced by median and poorly performing investment managers. Table 2.9 sets forth the expectations of the Yale University Investments Office as of June 30, 2004 for the real annual returns and the standard deviations of annual returns for the seven major asset classes in which Yale invests.

Table 2.9 demonstrates that the YUIO expects private equity to produce real annual returns (equal to the expected nominal return less some generally accepted measure of the long-term inflation rate) of 11.4%, with a standard deviation of annual returns of 29.1%. The YUIO expects absolute-return strategies to produce real annual returns of 6.0%, with a standard deviation of annual returns of 15.0%; and real assets to produce relatively uncorrelated real annual returns of 6.0%, with a standard deviation of annual returns of 15.0%.

Among conventional asset classes, the YUIO expects both domestic equity and foreign equity (in developed markets) to produce real annual returns of 6.0%, with a standard deviation of annual returns of 20.0%. It also expects emerging-markets foreign equity to produce real annual returns of 8.0%, with a standard deviation of annual returns of 25.0%; and fixed-income to produce real annual returns of 2.0%, with a standard deviation of annual returns of 10.0%.

The laudable post-1985 record of the YUIO in overseeing the Yale Endowment has several implications and lessons for many investors. First, it is important to think deeply, skeptically, and realisti-

**T A B L E 2.9**

Yale's Expected Risk and Return for Selected Asset Classes

| Asset Class | Expected Real Annual Return[2] | Expected Standard Deviation of Annual Returns |
|---|---|---|
| Domestic Equity | 6.0% | 20.0% |
| Absolute Return | 6.0 | 15.0 |
| Foreign Equity | 6.0[3] | 20.0[3] |
| Private Equity[1] | 11.4 | 29.1 |
| Real Assets[1] | 6.0 | 15.0 |
| Fixed-Income | 2.0 | 10.0 |
| Cash | NA | NA |
| Total | 6.2 | 11.7 |

[1]Prior to 1999, oil and gas and timber were classified as private equity rather than real assets.

[2]The expected real returns are equal to the expected nominal return less some generally accepted measure of the long-term inflation rate.

[3]Expected real return and expected standard deviation data are for developed markets equities. For emerging markets equities, the expected real return is 8.0% and the expected standard deviation is 25.0%.

Source: *The Yale Endowment 2004*, Yale University Investments Office.

cally about: (i) the inherent characteristics, implications, advantages, and disadvantages of asset classes; (ii) how each asset class fits with all the other asset classes; (iii) what various asset classes are capable of doing and not doing in different kinds of market environments and through financial-market cycles; and (iv) how the asset class meets or does not meet the investor's own biases and investment constraints. Second, investors should identify areas of internal versus external investment emphasis, focus, and activity based on a frank assessment of their own financial aptitudes and attitudes. Finally, investors should devote considerable resources and relentless energy to finding superior-quality asset managers for the externally run portions of the investment portfolio, particularly in the more inefficient asset categories.

# SECTION 2

# UNDERPINNINGS OF ASSET ALLOCATION

# CHAPTER 3

# APPLICATIONS AND IMPLICATIONS OF COMPOUND INTEREST

## OVERVIEW

Compound interest lies at the heart of wealth creation, preservation, distribution, and dissipation, yet few investors understand the manifold ways in which the compounding of investment returns can shape the outcomes of asset allocation and investment activity. After describing compound interest in the context of interest rates as used in banking, finance, and capital budgeting, and yields as used in debt capital markets, this chapter describes several practical applications of compound interest, including: (i) how much of an asset's total increase in value occurs within each part of an investment holding period; (ii) the equivalency of certain growth rates and capital-multiplication factors over various time horizons; (iii) distinctions between time-weighted annual returns and internal rates of return; and (iv) the various patterns of compound growth rates that can produce the same ending investment values.

This chapter then discusses the after-tax merits of earning investment returns in the form of capital gains versus annual income, favorable and unfavorable year-to-year financial market environments for investors who make periodic capital contributions as compared with investors who make periodic capital withdrawals, and the relative attractiveness of spending versus reinvesting portfolio income flows over time.

This chapter also treats several critical aspects of *coupon reinvestment* in fixed-income securities as well as equally crucial aspects of *dividend reinvestment* in equities. After demonstrating how important reinvesting interim-interest or dividend-income flows are to achieving projected long-term rates of return for these asset classes, the chapter concludes with an illustration of how incremental years' returns affect multiyear compound growth rates.

## SELECTED INSIGHTS INTO COMPOUND INTEREST

Some of the most overlooked yet crucial elements of asset allocation and investment strategy revolve around the concept and practical utilization of compound interest. Investors can benefit from learning and thinking about the form, timing, amounts, and periodic reproducibility of returns their investments generate. Because compound interest, and the compounding of returns, have a crucially determinative effect on what happens to investment assets, such patterns influence which assets investors should chose, in what form and for how long they should hold them, and what their ultimate disposition should be.

Investors need to evaluate rationally and objectively the magnitude and sequence of the positive and negative returns from their investments, the degree of ease or difficulty in reinvesting these returns at favorable rates, and the range of potential outcomes associated with various allocations of assets and investment strategies. To this end, Figure 3.1 displays a number of applications associated with interest rates, yield, and compound interest.

Professionals in the worlds of banking, finance, and corporate capital budgeting use with great frequency many of the primary notions relating to interest rates, which Figure 3.1 show in the upper-left circle. These fundamental concepts include, but are not limited to: (i) simple and compound interest; (ii) the present value of a single sum and/or a stream of payments; (iii) the future value of a single sum

**F I G U R E   3.1**

Selected Economic, Statistical, and Financial Concepts
Affecting Asset Allocation

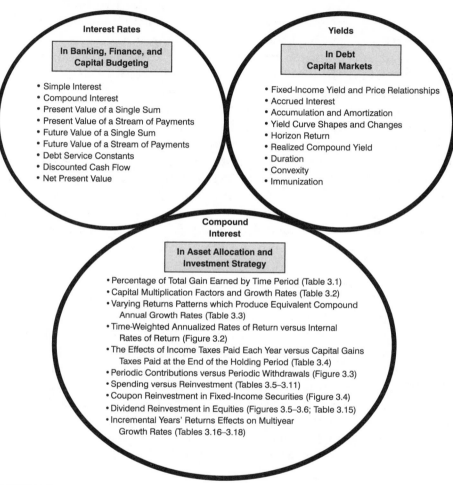

Source: The author.

and/or a stream of payments; (iv) debt-service constants, defined as
the constant amount of annual interest and principal repayments required to pay off a loan, mortgage, or certain other types of debt during a specified time period; and (v) discounted cash flow and net
present value techniques for evaluating the monetary inflows and outflows associated with capital budgeting. These ideas and terms are defined and explained in many introductory financial texts and

handbooks, two of which include *The Desktop Guide to Money, Time, Interest and Yields,* by Charles J. Woelfel, and *Mathematics of Finance,* by Robert Cissell, Helen Cissell, and Daniel C. Flaspohler.

Beginning in the last three decades of the twentieth century, rapid advances in computing power and the vastly increased size and complexity of the fixed-income investment universe led to more widespread and rigorous treatment of the subject of yields in debt capital markets. The right-hand circle of Figure 3.1 lists several key yield-related analytical constructs that have become more widespread in modern times. These important intellectual and practical frameworks include, but are not limited to: (i) yield and price relationships in fixed-income securities markets; (ii) accrued interest, the accumulation of bond price discounts from par value, and the amortization of bond price premiums from par; (iii) the analysis of yield-curve shapes and changes; (iv) horizon return and realized-compound yield, which take into account a specified holding period for a bond investment, the bond's quoted yield-to-maturity adjusted for the actual reinvestment rates of its coupons, and the actual sale price of the bond if sold prior to maturity; (v) duration, commonly defined as the present-value weighted-average life of a bond's cash-flow stream (another frequently used definition of duration is the percentage change in a bond's price for a 100 basis point change in interest rates); (vi) convexity, a measure of the curvature of a bond's price-yield relationship; and (viii) immunization, a term that describes the process of matching the present value of fixed-income investment cash flows with the present value of the future liabilities that the fixed-income investment has been purchased to satisfy. Among the wide variety of books that discuss these topics are *Inside the Yield Book,* by Sidney Homer and Martin L. Leibowitz, *Yield Curve Analysis,* by Livingston A. Douglas, and *Bond Markets, Analysis and Strategies,* by Frank J. Fabozzi and T. Dessa Fabozzi.

Many of the intrinsic properties—some manifest, some subtle—of compound interest can play a decisive role in the success or failure of asset allocation and investment strategy. The ellipse in the bottom part of Figure 3.1 highlights several of these applications, including: (i) the percentage of an investment's total gain that is earned by time period; (ii) capital-multiplication factors that various compound annual growth rates generate; (iii) varying returns patterns that produce equivalent compound annual growth rates and final investment values; (iv) time-weighted returns compared with internal rates of return; (v) the effects of paying income taxes on the annual returns of an investment versus paying capital gains taxes at the end of an investment's holding period; (vi) the consequences of varying returns patterns on a series of periodic investment *contributions* compared with a series of periodic investment *withdrawals;* (vii) spending versus investing the income flows from an investment; (viii) coupon reinvestment in fixed-income securities; (ix) dividend reinvestment in equities; and (x) the effect of incremental years' returns on multiyear compound annual growth rates.

For an investment horizon of 20 years, and compound annual rates of return ranging from 1% to 20%, Table 3.1 shows the percentage of the *total gain* from an investment that it earns in each of the four 5-year holding periods.

Table 3.2 shows that with increasing compound annual rates of return, more and more of the aggregate increase from a compounding investment occurs in the final portion of the investor's holding period. For example, a $1.00 initial investment that generates a compound annual growth rate of 10% increases in value to $6.73 at the end of 20 years, a total gain of $5.73. After 15 years, the total value is $4.18, a total gain of $3.18. Therefore, the difference between $5.73 and $3.18, or $2.55, is earned in the final 5-year period of the 20-year investment

## T A B L E 3.1

Percentage of Total Gain Earned by Time Period

| Period Ending | Compound Annual Rate of Return | | | | | | |
|---|---|---|---|---|---|---|---|
| | 1 Percent | 5 Percent | 8 Percent | 10 Percent | 12 Percent | 15 Percent | 20 Percent |
| **First 5 Years** (Year 1 through Year 5) | 23% | 17% | 13% | 11% | 9% | 7% | 4% |
| **Second 5 Years** (Year 6 through Year 10) | 24% | 21% | 19% | 17% | 16% | 13% | 10% |
| **Third 5 Years** (Year 11 through Year 15) | 26% | 27% | 28% | 28% | 27% | 27% | 25% |
| **Fourth 5 Years** (Year 16 through Year 20) | 27% | 35% | 41% | **45%** | 48% | 54% | 61% |
| **Total Gain** (Year 1 through Year 20) | 100% | 100% | 100% | 100% | 100% | 100% | 100% |

**The miracle of compound interest depends on the passage of time. For instance, of the increase in the value of a 10% compounding investment held for 20 years, 45% of the total gain occurs in the final five years.**

Source: The author.

horizon. Dividing $2.55 by the total gain, $5.73, shows that the fourth 5-year segment of the investor's 20-year holding period generates 45% of the *total gain*.

Table 3.2 shows the amount by which the investor's initial capital is multiplied, for compound annual growth rates between 5% and 25%, and investment time horizons between 5 years and 30 years.

An investor who is able to achieve a compound annual growth rate of 10% would have multiplied his or her capital 4.18 times at the end of 15 years. In other words, an initial investment of $1.00 would be worth $4.18 at the end of 15 years at a 10% compound annual growth rate, generating a *total gain* of $3.18 on the investor's original investment of $1.00. If, on the other hand, the investor had been able to achieve a 15% compound annual rate of growth for 10 years, an initial investment of $1.00 would be worth $4.05. A compound rate of growth of 15% over 10 years thus produces approximately the same increase in the investor's original capital as a compound rate of growth of 10% over 15 years (4.05 times versus 4.18 times). When combined with compound annual rates of growth, capital multiplication factors are a useful way of evaluating investment results, particularly in asset classes such as private equity, real estate, and venture capital, where the timing and magnitude of the interim and final cash flows associated with an investment may be unpredictable.

**T A B L E   3.2**

Capital Multiplication Factors and Growth Rates for Selected Time Periods

| Compound Annual Growth Rate | Investment Time Horizon | | | | |
|---|---|---|---|---|---|
| | 5 Years | 10 Years | 15 Years | 20 Years | 30 Years |
| 5.0% | 1.28 x | 1.63 x | 2.08 x | 2.65 x | 4.32 x |
| 10.0% | 1.61 x | 2.59 x | 4.18 x | 6.73 x | 17.45 x |
| 15.0% | 2.01 x | 4.05 x | 8.14 x | 16.37 x | 66.21 x |
| 20.0% | 2.49 x | 6.19 x | 15.41 x | 38.34 x | 237.38 x |
| 25.0% | 3.05 x | 9.31 x | 28.42 x | 86.74 x | 807.79 x |

Source: The author.

Another important aspect of compound interest that investors should know relates to the varying patterns of year-to-year returns that effectively produce equivalent compound annual growth rates. In a somewhat simplified form, Table 3.3 depicts several of these relationships.

In the second panel of Table 3.3, four different year-to-year returns patterns are shown, all of which involve an initial investment of $1.00 and a final value after three years of $1.33, which represents a 10% compound annual growth rate. In the first row of the second panel, a $1.00 initial investment grows by 10% in year one, to a value of $1.10; by another 10% in year two, to a value of $1.21; and by 10% in year three, to a value of $1.33.

In the second row of the second panel, a $1.00 initial investment grows by 10%, to a value of $1.10 at the end of year one, before declining by 10% in year two, to a value of $0.99. For this investment to achieve a final value of $1.33 at the end of the third year, it has to grow by $0.34, or 34% of the end-of-year-two value of $0.99. After a second year in which an investment declines by a percentage amount equal to its percentage gain in the first year, the magnitude of the percentage catch-up needed to achieve a given final value increases meaningfully, the higher the targeted compound annual rate of growth. The second row of the third panel shows that if an investment grows by 15% in the first year and then declines by 15% in the second year, it must grow by 56% in the third year to produce the same outcome, a $1.52 final value, as an investment that grows by a constant 20% per year in each of the three years.

In the third row of the second panel, a $1.00 initial investment grows by 10% in year one before exhibiting zero growth in the second year. To reach a final value of $1.33, this investment must grow by $0.23, or 21%, in the third year. In the fourth row of the second panel, a $1.00 initial investment grows by 10% in year one, and then experiences growth at double the first year's growth rate, or 20%, to a value of $1.32 at the end of the second year. To attain a final value of $1.33, this investment only needs to grow by $0.01, or 1%, in the third year. Investors should realize that they would need high rates of return to overcome the effects of negative or zero returns in a given investment period. Such catch-up rates of return are even higher if the investor experiences multiple years of zero or negative returns.

Investors may benefit from understanding the difference between: (i) the *compound annual growth rate* of an investment, which assumes that each year's returns compound at the same positive or negative

**T A B L E  3.3**

Varying Year-to-Year Returns Patterns That Produce Equivalent Compound Annual Growth Rates

| | Initial Investment | Final Values of $1.00 Initial Investment at the End of | | |
| --- | --- | --- | --- | --- |
| | | Year 1 | Year 2 | Year 3 |
| **Variations on 5% Annual Growth Rates: Three-year final value of $1.00; initial investment is $1.16.** | | | | |
| | $1.00 | $1.05 | $1.10 | **$1.16** |
| *Stable Annual Percentage Changes* | | *5%* | *5%* | *5%* |
| | $1.00 | 1.05 | 1.00 | **1.16** |
| *2nd Year's % Decline Is Equal to 1st Year's % Gain* | | *5%* | *–5%* | *16%* |
| | $1.00 | 1.05 | 1.05 | **1.16** |
| *Zero % Change in 2nd Year after 1st Year's Gain* | | *5%* | *0%* | *10%* |
| | $1.00 | 1.05 | 1.16 | **1.16** |
| *2nd Year's % Gain Is Double the 1st Year's % Gain* | | *5%* | *10%* | *0%* |
| **Variations on 10% Annual Growth Rates: Three-year final value of $1.00; initial investment is $1.33.** | | | | |
| | $1.00 | $1.10 | $1.21 | **$1.33** |
| *Stable Annual Percentage Changes* | | *10%* | *10%* | *10%* |
| | $1.00 | 1.10 | 0.99 | **1.33** |
| *2nd Year's % Decline Is Equal to 1st Year's % Gain* | | *10%* | *–10%* | *34%* |
| | $1.00 | 1.10 | 1.10 | **1.33** |
| *Zero % Change in 2nd Year after 1st Year's Gain* | | *10%* | *0%* | *21%* |
| | $1.00 | 1.10 | 1.32 | **1.33** |
| *2nd Year's % Gain Is Double the 1st Year's % Gain* | | *10%* | *20%* | *1%* |
| **Variations on 15% Annual Growth Rates: Three-year final value of $1.00; initial investment is $1.52.** | | | | |
| | $1.00 | $1.15 | $1.32 | **$1.52** |
| *Stable Annual Percentage Changes* | | *15%* | *15%* | *15%* |
| | $1.00 | 1.15 | 0.98 | **1.52** |
| *2nd Year's % Decline Is Equal to 1st Year's % Gain* | | *15%* | *–15%* | *56%* |
| | $1.00 | 1.15 | 1.15 | **1.52** |
| *Zero % Change in 2nd Year after 1st Year's Gain* | | *15%* | *0%* | *32%* |
| | $1.00 | 1.15 | 1.50 | **1.52** |
| *2nd Year's % Gain Is Double the 1st Year's % Gain* | | *15%* | *30%* | *2%* |
| **Variations on 20% Annual Growth Rates: Three-year final value of $1.00; initial investment is $1.73.** | | | | |
| | $1.00 | $1.20 | $1.44 | **$1.73** |
| *Stable Annual Percentage Changes* | | *20%* | *20%* | *20%* |
| | $1.00 | 1.20 | 0.96 | **1.73** |
| *2nd Year's % Decline Is Equal to 1st Year's % Gain* | | *20%* | *–20%* | *80%* |
| | $1.00 | 1.20 | 1.20 | **1.73** |
| *Zero % Change in 2nd Year after 1st Year's Gain* | | *20%* | *0%* | *44%* |
| | $1.00 | 1.20 | 1.68 | **1.73** |
| *2nd Year's % Gain Is Double the 1st Year's % Gain* | | *20%* | *40%* | *3%* |

Source: The author.

growth rate; and (ii) the *internal rate of return* of an investment, which explicitly takes account of any differences in the timing and magnitude of each year's positive or negative returns. In mathematical terms, the internal rate of return is defined as that constant annual rate of return that happens to equate the *present value* of each of an investment's *periodic cash flows* with the *initial capital value* of the investment. Compound annual growth rates usually assume the reinvestment of each year's returns, while the internal rate of return does not usually assume the reinvestment of each year's returns. As a result, the internal rate of return of a given series of cash flows will generally differ from the internal rate of return of the same cash flows arranged in a different sequence. Figure 3.2 differentiates between: (i) the compound annual growth rate of an investment, also known as its time-weighted annualized rate of return; and (ii) the internal rate of return of an investment.

The top part of Figure 3.2 assumes that a $1.00 investment that generates a compound annual growth rate, or time-weighted annualized rate of return, of 12.9% grows by a smooth 12.9% and is reinvested at 12.9% each year for 10 years, reaching a final value of $3.37 at the end of the tenth year. In practice, many investments generate a series of varying positive or negative annual returns, the cash component of which may or may not be reinvested at some rate of return. The middle and bottom parts of Figure 3.2 show how the sequence and absolute amounts of each individual year's positive and negative returns can influence the calculation of an investment's internal rate of return.

The middle part of Figure 3.2 shows the year-by-year sequence of annual returns of the Standard & Poor's 500 Index from 1992 through 2001 as: +7.67%; +9.99%, +1.31%; +37.43%; +23.07%; +33.36%; +28.58%; +21.04%; –9.11%; and –11.89%, respectively. Assuming that each year's total return flows are not reinvested, the *internal rate of return* of this pattern of returns is 7.7%. The *compound annual rate of growth* of this pattern of returns is still 12.9%, since an initial investment of $1.00 in the S&P 500 Index at the beginning of 1992 would have grown to a final value of $3.37 at the end of 2001.

The bottom part of Figure 3.2 places the year-by-year unreinvested sequence of annual returns of the Standard & Poor's 500 Index from 1992 through 2001 *in reverse order*, as: –11.89%; –9.11%; +21.04%; +28.58%; +33.36%; +23.07%; +37.43%; +1.31%; +9.99%; and +7.67%, respectively. Due to the unfavorable affects of having the two negative-returns years at the beginning of the 10-year sequence, the *internal rate of return* of this reverse-order pattern of returns is 5.7%. The *compound annual rate of growth* of this pattern of returns is 12.9%, since

## Time-Weighted Annualized Rates of Return versus Internal Rates of Return

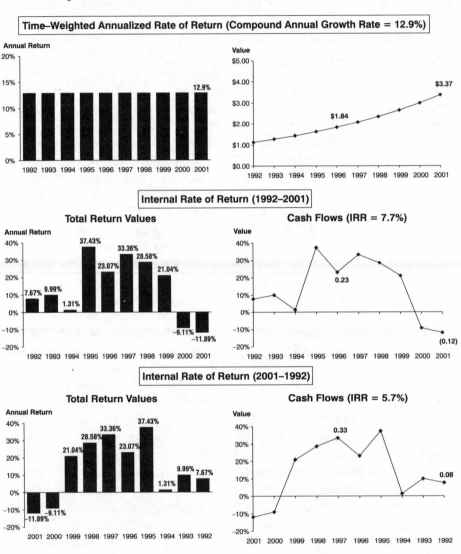

Source: The author.

an initial investment of $1.00 in the S&P 500 Index in reverse-order sequence would also have produced a final value of $3.37 at the end of this reversed 10-year pattern of returns. Many practitioners in the real estate, leveraged buyout, and venture capital sectors utilize the internal rate of return as a measure of the success of an investment in these asset classes because the internal rate of return inherently captures important information about when and how much money an investment gains or loses each year, and generally assumes that returns flows are not reinvested into the original investment.

## RETURNS IN THE FORM OF INCOME VERSUS CAPITAL GAINS

Many investors ponder whether it is more beneficial to earn a given compound annual rate of return *completely in the form of capital gains each year* and defer the payment of capital taxes until they sell the investment at the end of the holding period; or to earn a given compound annual rate of return *completely in the form of income each year*, paying annual taxes on the income and no capital gains at the end of the holding period. For example, the investor may wish to compare the after-tax attractiveness during a 10-year holding period of a non-dividend-paying equity security (which may increase in price at a 10% compound annual rate of growth) with a bond or a preferred stock that provides a 10% income return each year during a 10-year holding period.

For capital gains-based compound annual growth rates versus income-based annual returns of 5%, 10%, 15%, and 20%, and investment holding periods of 5, 10, 20, and 30 years, Table 3.4 shows the aftertax effects of paying income taxes on each year's income-based return versus paying capital-gains taxes at the end of the investment holding period. For the purposes of these calculations, Table 3.4 assumes that the investor is able each year to invest the full amount of the principal and all of the previous year's income, after paying income taxes at the income-based rate of annual return.

As the gray-shaded section of Table 3.4 shows, an investor who purchases an asset that generates a 10% compound annual rate of capital growth would see his or her investment grow to $2.59 during a 10-year holding period, for a total gain of $1.59. After the sale of this investment and the payment of 20% capital gains taxes on the amount of the gain (20% times $1.59, or $0.318), the investor would have a total of $2.27 (equal to $2.59 minus $0.32). The total gain after payment of 20% capital gains taxes thus amounts to $1.27.

On the other hand, if the same investor earns a 10% income-based annual return and pays 20% income taxes each year during the 10-year holding period, the total amount of the investment would be $2.16, for a total gain of $1.16. After paying taxes at a 20% rate on income and a

**T A B L E   3.4**

The Effects of Income Taxes Paid Each Year versus Capital Gains Taxes Paid at the End of Multiyear Holding Periods

| | Ending Value of a $1.00 Investment After | | | | | |
| --- | --- | --- | --- | --- | --- | --- |
| | At the End of 5 Years | | | At the End of 10 Years | | |
| | Ending Value | $ Gain | % Reduction in Income-Based Gain After Taxes versus Capital-Gains-Based Gain After Taxes | Ending Value | $ Gain | % Reduction in Income-Based Gain After Taxes versus Capital-Gains-Based Gain After Taxes |
| **At a 5.0% Capital-Gains–Based Compound Annual Growth Rate versus a 5% Income-Based Annual Return:** | | | | | | |
| Value before capital-gains taxes | $1.28 | $0.28 | | $1.63 | $0.63 | |
| Value after payment of 20% capital-gains taxes at the end of the holding period | 1.22 | 0.22 | | 1.50 | 0.50 | |
| Value if **20%** income taxes are paid from each year's annual return | 1.22 | 0.22 | −2.0% | 1.48 | 0.48 | −4.5% |
| Value if **40%** income taxes are paid from each year's annual return | 1.16 | 0.16 | −27.9% | 1.34 | 0.34 | −31.6% |
| **At a 10.0% Capital-Gains–Based Compound Annual Growth Rate versus a 10% Income–Based Annual Return:** | | | | | | |
| Value before capital-gains taxes | $1.61 | $0.61 | | $2.59 | 1.59 | |
| Value after payment of 20% capital-gains taxes at the end of the holding period | 1.49 | 0.49 | | 2.27 | 1.27 | |
| Value if **20%** income taxes are paid fro each year's annual return | 1.47 | 0.47 | −3.9% | 2.16 | 1.16 | −9.1% |
| Value if **40%** income taxes are paid from each year's annual return | 1.34 | 0.34 | −30.7% | 1.79 | 0.79 | −38.0% |
| **At a 15.0% Capital-Gains–Based Compound Annual Growth Rate versus a 15% Income–Based Annual Return:** | | | | | | |
| Value before capital-gains taxes | $2.01 | $1.01 | | $4.05 | $3.05 | |
| Value ater payment of 20% capital-gains taxes at the end of the holding period | 1.81 | 0.81 | | 3.44 | 2.44 | |
| Value if **20%** income taxes are paid from each year's annual return | 1.76 | 0.76 | −5.8% | 3.11 | 2.11 | −13.6% |
| Value if **40%** income taxes are paid from each year's annual return | 1.54 | 0.54 | −33.4% | 2.37 | 1.37 | −43.9% |
| **At a 20.0% Capital-Gains–Based Compound Annual Growth Rate versus a 20% Income–Based Annual Return:** | | | | | | |
| Value before capital-gains taxes | $2.49 | $1.49 | | $6.19 | 5.19 | |
| Value after payment of 20% capital-gains taxes at the end of the holding period | 2.19 | 1.19 | | 5.15 | 4.15 | |
| Value if **20%** income taxes are paid from each year's annual return | 2.10 | 1.10 | −7.6% | 4.41 | 3.41 | −17.9% |
| Value if **40%** income taxes are paid from each year's annual return | 1.76 | 0.76 | −36.0% | 3.11 | 2.11 | −49.3% |

Source: The author.

## Paying Income Taxes or Capital-Gains Taxes

| | At the End of 20 Years | | | At the End of 30 Years | |
| --- | --- | --- | --- | --- | --- |
| Ending Value | $ Gain | % Reduction in Income-Based Gain After Taxes versus Capital-Gains-Based Gain After Taxes | Ending Value | $ Gain | % Reduction in Income-Based Gain After Taxes versus Capital-Gains-Based Gain After Taxes |
| $2.65 | $1.65 | | $4.32 | $3.32 | |
| 2.32 | 1.32 | | 3.66 | 2.66 | |
| 2.19 | 1.19 | -9.9% | 3.24 | 2.24 | -15.6% |
| 1.81 | 0.81 | -39.1% | 2.43 | 1.43 | -46.3% |
| $6.73 | $5.73 | | $17.45 | $16.45 | |
| 5.58 | 4.58 | | 14.16 | 15.16 | |
| 4.66 | 3.66 | -20.1% | 10.06 | 9.06 | -31.1% |
| 3.21 | 2.21 | -51.8% | 5.74 | 4.74 | -64.0% |
| $16.37 | $15.37 | | $66.21 | $65.21 | |
| 13.29 | 12.29 | | 53.17 | 52.17 | |
| 9.65 | 8.65 | -29.7% | 29.96 | 28.96 | -44.5% |
| 5.60 | 4.60 | -62.5% | 13.27 | 12.27 | -76.5% |
| $38.34 | $37.34 | | $237.38 | $236.38 | |
| 30.87 | 29.87 | | 190.10 | 189.10 | |
| 19.46 | 18.46 | -38.2% | 85.85 | 84.85 | -55.1% |
| 9.65 | 8.65 | -71.1% | 29.96 | 28.96 | -84.7% |

10-year holding period, an investor whose gains were income based would have generated a gain that was 9.1% less ($1.16 divided by $1.27) than the investor whose gains were capital gains based. The use of a 20% annual income tax rate in Table 3.4 serves two purposes: (i) it facilitates comparison with the 20% capital gains tax rate applied to the increase in the capital value of the investment at the end of the holding period; and (ii) it allows the investor to compare the results of selling the investment (assuming its returns were in the form of 10% annual capital gains rather than in the form of 10% annual income) at the end of 10 consecutive 1-year holding periods and paying 20% capital-gains taxes at the end of each year.

In many countries and state and local tax jurisdictions, ordinary income is not taxed at the same rate as capital gains. As a practical matter during a reasonably long multiyear investment holding period, tax rates on income and on capital gains may be raised or lowered by legislative action in response to economic developments and fiscal conditions. Individual investors may be subject to a range of maximum income tax rates based on their filing status, the applicability of any alternative minimum tax calculations, the investor's place of legal residence, and other factors.

To take account of the potentially wide differential between the top tax rate on ordinary income and the capital-gains tax rate, Table 3.4 also shows the aftertax effects of paying income taxes at a rate *of 40% on each year's income-based return* versus paying capital gains taxes at a rate of *20% at the end of the investment holding period*. Referring again to the upper gray-shaded section of Table 3.4, if the investor earns a 10% income-based return and pays 40% income taxes each year during the 10-year holding period, the total amount of the investment would amount to $1.79, for a total gain of $0.79. After the payment of income taxes at a 40% rate and a 10-year holding period, an investor whose gains were income based would have generated a gain that was 38% less ($0.79 divided by $1.27) than the investor whose gains were capital gains based.

As a corner-to-corner review of Table 3.4 illustrates, the effects of delaying the payment of taxes to the end of the investment period rather than annually, and paying them on capital gains rather than on income, increase in significance: (i) the longer the holding period; (ii) the higher the capital-gains-based compound annual growth rate and the income-based annual return; and (iii) the greater the difference between the (higher) income-tax rate and the (lower) capital-gains tax rate. For example, the upper left portion of Table 3.4 shows that during a five-year investment period, an investor would experience a 27.9% reduction in the gain generated by a 5% annual income return after paying 40% income taxes each year, versus the gain generated by a 5% capital-gains-based compound annual growth rate after paying a 20% capital-gains tax at the end of the holding period. By contrast, the lower right portion of Table 3.4 shows that over a 30-year investment period, an investor would experience an 84.9% reduction in the gain generated by a 20% annual income return after paying 40% income taxes each year, versus the gain generated by a 20% capital-gains-based compound annual growth rate after paying a 20% capital-gains tax at the end of the holding period.

The work of Robert H. Jeffrey contains several important insights on the importance of unrealized gains, the tax consequences of various levels of portfolio turnover and the length of an investment's holding period, and deferred taxes. Mr. Jeffrey's writings include: (i) "The Folly of Stock Market Timing," in the July-August 1984 issue of *Harvard Business Review*; (ii) "Is Your Alpha Big Enough to Cover Its Taxes?" in the Spring 1993 issue of *The Journal of Portfolio Management*; (iii) "Reflections on Portfolio Management After 25 Years," in the Spring 2001 issue of *The Journal of Investing*; and (iv) "Tax-Efficient Investing Is Easier Said Than Done," in the Summer 2001 issue of *The Journal of Wealth Management*.

## PERIODIC CONTRIBUTIONS AND PERIODIC WITHDRAWALS

For many investors, one of the primary purposes of investing is to accumulate sufficient assets during a given time frame to meet future objectives, such as: (i) funding annual expenses during retirement years; (ii) purchasing one or more homes; (iii) launching or buying a business; (iv) making a significant philanthropic donation and/or a bequest to one's heirs; or (v) meeting a projected series of outlays, such as educational or medical expenses. In some cases at the outset of the *capital-accumulation* phase, the investor may be able to set aside and invest a substantial lump sum to attempt to pay for future spending. In other cases, the investor may make *periodic contributions* of funds to his or her investment portfolio during the capital-accumulation years.

At some point in the future, the investor may decide to make withdrawals from his or her accumulated capital. Depending on the nature of the investor's spending needs, these withdrawals may be concentrated into one large sum or a number of periodic payments spaced out over a series of years. A retired investor who meets annual expenses by drawing regularly from an invested pool of capital is one common example of a series of capital withdrawals.

Whether they are in a capital-accumulation phase (making periodic contributions to build up a lump sum) or in a capital-depletion phase (making periodic withdrawals from an existing lump sum), investors need to be especially mindful of the sequence and magnitude of annual investment returns during their investment time frame and their contribution/withdrawal horizon. The annual returns can significantly affect: (i) whether *periodically contributing investors* are able to amass sufficient money to accomplish their projected goals and objectives; and (ii) whether *periodically withdrawing investors* are able to avoid exhausting their capital resources before the end of their projected withdrawal period.

For a hypothetical 10-year time horizon, Figure 3.3 depicts: (i) a series of *periodic contributions* (panel A); (ii) a representative favorable investment environment for making periodic contributions (panel B); (iii) a series of *periodic withdrawals* (panel C); and (iv) a representative favorable investment environment for making periodic withdrawals (panel D). A similar analysis could be conducted for longer or shorter time periods than the years shown in Figure 3.3.

In panel A of Figure 3.3, an investor makes periodic contributions in years 1 through 10. Each of these periodic contributions experiences the series of positive or negative annual returns for every year beginning with its year of contribution and continuing through year 10, when the investor intends to have accumulated a specific final lump sum. In a somewhat simplified fashion, the total capital set aside by a periodically contributing investor is symbolized by the series of three gradually increasing circles in the background of panel A. For the purposes of Figure 3.3, each of the periodic contributions is a fixed amount of capital. In practice, the investor's periodic contributions may follow other patterns, such as a specified percentage of the previous year's total accumulated lump sum, or it may be allowed to change in accordance with fluctuations in a broadly accepted price index.

Panel B of Figure 3.3 shows a schematic version of a representative favorable environment for making periodic contributions. In such an environment, it is better for the periodically contributing investor to experience relatively higher investment returns in the latter part of the investment time horizon, after he or she has already put regular sums of money into the portfolio, which is thus in a position to benefit from

## F I G U R E  3.3

### Periodic Contributions versus Periodic Withdrawals

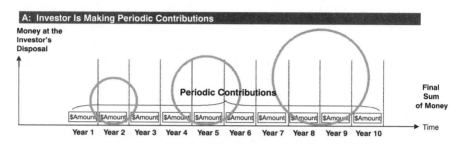

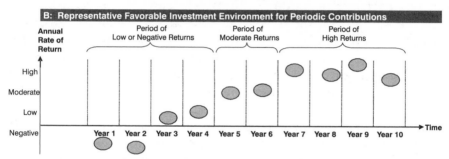

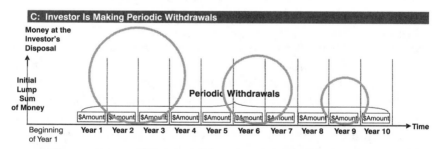

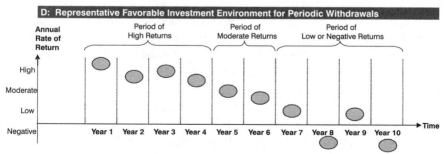

Source: The author.

higher investment returns. Periodically contributing investors whose long contributions time horizons (of 10 to 25 years or more) concluded with a number of consecutive years of high returns, such in the late 1960s, the late 1990s, or the late 1950s, saw the investment-adjusted sum of their earlier contributions compound at favorable rates. By contrast, periodically contributing investors whose contribution rates were too low and whose contribution time horizons ended in the 1970s or in the mid 1980s may have found that their final investment lump sums fell far short of their originally projected targets.

Panel C of Figure 3.3 shows an investor who makes periodic withdrawals in years one through 10. The initial lump sum of assets, reduced by each year's capital withdrawals, earns a series of positive or negative annual returns for every year through year 10, when the investor intends to have used up most or all of the initial assets. Also in a somewhat simplified fashion, a periodically withdrawing investor who draws upon the total capital is symbolized by the series of three gradually decreasing circles in the background of panel C. For the purposes of Figure 3.3, each of the periodic withdrawals is a fixed amount of capital. In practice, the investor's periodic withdrawals may also follow other patterns, such as withdrawals of a specified percentage of the previous year's remaining accumulated lump sum, or changing withdrawals in accordance with changes in a broadly accepted price index.

Panel D of Figure 3.3 shows a schematic version of a representative favorable environment for making periodic withdrawals. In such an environment, the periodically withdrawing investor will experience relatively higher investment returns in the earlier part of the investment time horizon, when a large proportion of the initial lump sum still remains in the portfolio so he or she can benefit from higher investment returns. Periodically withdrawing investors whose long withdrawing time horizons (of 10 to 25 years or more) began with a number of years of consecutive high returns, such as eras commencing with the decade of the 1950s, the 1960s, or the 1990s, benefited from having the bulk of the remaining values of their initial lump sums compound at favorable rates. By contrast, periodically withdrawing investors whose withdrawal rates were too high and whose long withdrawal time horizons began in the 1970s or in the mid-1980s may have prematurely spent all of their investment capital long before they intended to.

In fact, a considerable number of investors may embark upon a program of periodic contributions to amass a quantity of investment capital that allows them later to carry out a program of periodic withdrawals. Individuals who put money aside on a multiyear basis in anticipation of their retirement, followed by the year-to-year withdrawing of funds from their retirement capital, represent a commonly encountered example of periodic contributions for a specified time period, followed by periodic withdrawals for some other specified time period.

To help the investor examine the range of outcomes associated with periodic contributions or periodic withdrawals, it is useful to set up a simple spreadsheet showing the annual contributions (or withdrawals) that will be made, and the projected annual rates of investment return that will apply to the buildup or drawdown of the investor's capital. As an initial step, the investor might use two or three constant rates of annual return in his or her simple spreadsheet model. A more realistic refinement of this process might use several multiyear periods from past history that corresponds to the investor's contemplated contribution or withdrawal time frame and to favorable and unfavorable returns environments.

Keeping in mind that market structures, asset classes, and investment patterns may shift over time, and that history tends not to repeat itself, investors may vary the sequence of returns outcomes for a given periodic contributions or periodic withdrawals schedule by: (i) applying any prior periods' returns in reverse or in jumbled sequence; and/or (ii) drawing upon so-called Monte Carlo methods to simulate several sets of possible outcomes. Monte Carlo simulation techniques, used for centuries, earned their name in the early 1940s to describe the use of a sizeable number of randomly generated outcomes to assess the potential success or failure of a process or series of outcomes. *Monte Carlo Methods in Finance*, by Peter Jaeckel, and *Monte Carlo Statistical Methods*, by Christian P. Robert and George Casella, offer a fundamental introduction to Monte Carlo methods. The Web site *vanguardsw.com* provides Decision Pro, a useful Monte Carlo software simulation tool.

## SPENDING VERSUS REINVESTING INCOME FLOWS

A frequent and crucial asset allocation question revolves around the investor's decision to spend versus reinvest some or all of an investment's annual returns. The answer is shaped in part by the investor's preferences and the timing of his or her required capital flows, and in part by the level, pattern, and longevity of returns from a given asset class.

Consciously or unconsciously, investors often evaluate whether to spend now or in the future not only in financially quantifiable terms, but also according to hard-to-define measures such as utility, pleasure, or enjoyment. In doing so, investors need to take account of the effects of compounding, inflation and deflation in the general price level, and not least, psychological and highly individual attitudes about current and postponed gratification.

It is worthwhile to analyze the effects that spending annual investment returns immediately after they have been earned, versus reinvesting them at some given interest rate, will have on investment-generated cash flows—including income generated during an investment or a portfolio's life and its terminal value. The annual investment returns can take the form of dividend or interest income accrued or received, realized or unrealized capital gains, or some combination thereof.

## The Effects of Spending versus Reinvesting as a Function of the Rate of Return

◆ **Twenty-Year Investment Horizon, 20% Annual Returns:**
 Table 3.5 shows the effects of spending versus reinvesting varying proportions of annual returns for a $1,000 initial investment held for 20 years with annual returns of 20%.

Only a very small number of investors in certain asset categories have been able to achieve 20% returns for 20 years. It is an extraordinary accomplishment. Rarely do investments generate such rates of return for so long, even for performance-oriented investors in equities or fixed-income securities, much less for asset managers in less efficient markets such as absolute-return strategies, private equity, or venture capital. The two immediately following sections present a similar analysis for 20-year investment horizons using annual returns of 10% and 5%, respectively.

Several simplifying assumptions help highlight some of the important principles this analysis derives. For example, Tables 3.5, 3.6, and 3.7 make the highly unlikely assumption that the investor can reinvest annual returns from his or her investments at exactly the same rate as the investment's original rate of return—20% in Table 3.5, 10% in Table 3.6, and 5% in Table 3.7. In addition, for simplicity we do not consider here income taxes, capital-gains taxes, inflation and defla-

**T A B L E   3.5**

The Effects of Spending versus Reinvesting at 20% Annual Rates of Return

$1,000 Investment, 20-Year Horizon, 20% Annual Returns

| | (1) Repayment of Principal | (2) Total Annual Payments Received and Reinvested | (3) Total Composed Interest Earned on Annual Payments Received and Reinvested | (4) = (1) + (2) + (3) Total Invested Funds Received and Reinvested Plus Principal Repayment | (5) Total Annual Payments That Were Spent | (6) = (5) + (4) Grand Total Received Plus Spent Funds |
|---|---|---|---|---|---|---|
| 0% ($0) of Annual Return Reinvested, 100% of Annual Return ($200) Spent | | | | | | |
| | $1,000 | $0 | $0 | $1,000 | $4,000 | $5,000 |
| % of Grand Total | 20% | 0% | 0% | | 80% | 100% |
| | | | | | | |
| 25% ($50) of Annual Return Reinvested, 75% of Annual Return ($150) Spent | | | | | | |
| | 1,000 | 1,000 | 8,334 | 10,334 | 3,000 | 13,334 |
| % of Grand Total | 7% | 7% | 64% | | 22% | 100% |
| | | | | | | |
| 50% ($100) of Annual Return Reinvested, 50% of Annual Return ($100) Spent | | | | | | |
| | 1,000 | 2,000 | 16,669 | 19,669 | 2,000 | 21,669 |
| % of Grand Total | 5% | 9% | 77% | | 9% | 100% |
| | | | | | | |
| 75% ($150) of Annual Return Reinvested, 25% of Annual Return ($50) Spent | | | | | | |
| | 1,000 | 3,000 | 25,003 | 29,003 | 1,000 | 30,003 |
| % of Grand Total | 3% | 10% | 84% | | 3% | 100% |
| | | | | | | |
| 100% ($200) of Annual Return Reinvested, 0% of Annual Return ($0) Spent | | | | | | |
| | 1,000 | 4,000 | 33,338 | 38,338 | 0 | 38,338 |
| % of Grand Total | 3% | 10% | 87% | | 0% | 100% |

Source: The author.

tion, or transactions costs. Any one of these factors can meaningfully change the outcomes.

Table 3.5 shows the total flows of funds accruing to the investor that are generated by: (i) repaying the original $1,000 investment (column 1); (ii) reinvesting 0%, 25%, 50%, 75%, and 100%, respectively, of the investment's annual returns (column 2); and (iii) reinvesting the total compound interest earned on annual payments received (column 3). The sum of these respective amounts equals the total invested funds received and reinvested plus principal payment (column 4). Column 5 accounts for the portion of the total annual returns that was spent, not reinvested. Column 6 shows the grand total of invested funds that the investor received (column 4) and spent (column 5) each year and during the life of the investment.

**T A B L E  3.6**

The Effects of Spending versus Reinvesting at 10% Annual Rates of Return

$1,000 Investment, 20-Year Horizon, 10% Annual Returns

| | (1) Repayment of Principal | (2) Total Annual Payments Received and Reinvested | (3) Total Compound Interest Earned on Annual Payments Received and Reinvested | (4) = (1) + (2) + (3) Total Invested Funds Received and Reinvested Plus Principal Repayment | (5) Total Annual Payments That Were Spent | (6) = (5) + (4) Grand Total of Invested Funds Received Plus Spent Funds |
|---|---|---|---|---|---|---|
| **0% ($0) of Annual Return Reinvested, 100% of Annual Return ($100) Spent** | | | | | | |
| | $1,000 | $0 | $0 | $1,000 | $2,000 | $3,000 |
| % of Grand Total | 33% | 0% | 0% | | 67% | 100% |
| **25% ($25) of Annual Return Reinvested, 75% of Annual Return ($75) Spent** | | | | | | |
| | 1,000 | 500 | 932 | 2,432 | 1,500 | 3,932 |
| % of Grand Total | 25% | 13% | 24% | | 38% | 100% |
| **50% ($50) of Annual Return Reinvested, 50% of Annual Return ($50) Spent** | | | | | | |
| | 1,000 | 1,000 | 1,864 | 3,864 | 1,000 | 4,864 |
| % of Grand Total | 21% | 21% | 37% | | 21% | 100% |
| **75% ($75) of Annual Return Reinvested, 25% of Annual Return ($25) Spent** | | | | | | |
| | 1,000 | 1,500 | 2,796 | 5,296 | 500 | 5,796 |
| % of Grand Total | 17% | 26% | 48% | | 9% | 100% |
| **100% ($100) of Annual Return Reinvested, 0% of Annual Return ($0) Spent** | | | | | | |
| | 1,000 | 2,000 | 3,727 | 6,727 | 0 | 6,727 |
| % of Grand Total | 15% | 30% | 55% | | 0% | 100% |

Source: The author.

The first row of Table 3.5 shows that at the end of 20 years, if the investor spends *all of the annual return,* and reinvests none, the investor will possess the original $1,000 plus fond memories during 20 years generated by the spending of the 20% annual return ($200) each year, or $4,000 in all. The sum of these two amounts equals $5,000.

At the other end of the spectrum, the bottom row of Table 3.5 shows that when an investor spends *none of the annual return* and reinvests it all, 20 years of 20% compound annual returns results in a reasonably austere two decades of no spending, but generates a grand total of $38,338. This is more than 7.5 times the grand total the investor who spent each year's returns accumulates. Put another way, foregoing spending of $200 each year for 20 years ($4,000) produces an additional $33,338 after 20 years.

**T A B L E  3.7**

The Effects of Spending versus Reinvesting at 5% Annual Rates of Return

**$1,000 Investment, 20-Year Horizon, 5% Annual Returns**

| | (1) Repayment of Principal | (2) Total Annual Payments Received and Reinvested | (3) Total Compound Interest Earned on Annual Payments Received and Reinvested | (4) = (1) + (2) + (3) Total Invested Funds Received and Reinvested Plus Principal Repayment | (5) Total Annual Payments That Were Spent | (6) = (5) + (4) Grand Total of Invested Funds Received Plus Spent Funds |
|---|---|---|---|---|---|---|
| **0% ($0) of Annual Return Reinvested, 100% of Annual Return ($50) Spent** | | | | | | |
| | $1,000 | $0 | $0 | $1,000 | $2,000 | $2,000 |
| % of Grand Total | 50% | 0% | 0% | | 50% | 100% |
| **25% ($12.50) of Annual Return Reinvested, 75% of Annual Return ($37.50) Spent** | | | | | | |
| | 1,000 | 250 | 163 | 1,413 | 750 | 2,163 |
| % of Grand Total | 45% | 12% | 8% | | 35% | 100% |
| **50% ($25) of Annual Return Reinvested, 50% of Annual Return ($25) Spent** | | | | | | |
| | 1,000 | 500 | 327 | 1,827 | 500 | 2,327 |
| % of Grand Total | 43% | 21% | 15% | | 21% | 100% |
| **75% ($37.50) of Annual Return Reinvested, 25% of Annual Return ($12.50) Spent** | | | | | | |
| | 1,000 | 750 | 490 | 2,240 | 250 | 2,490 |
| % of Grand Total | 40% | 30% | 20% | | 10% | 100% |
| **100% ($50) of Annual Return Reinvested, 0% of Annual Return ($0) Spent** | | | | | | |
| | 1,000 | 2,000 | 653 | 2,653 | 0 | 2,653 |
| % of Grand Total | 38% | 38% | 24% | | 0% | 100% |

Source: The author.

The middle three rows of Table 3.5 demonstrates that if the investor had been able to reinvest 25%, 50%, or 75% of the 20% annual returns at 20% for 20 years, he or she would have accumulated $13,334, $21,669, or $30,003, respectively.

◆ **Twenty-Year Investment Horizon, 10% Annual Returns:** Table 3.6 illustrates the effects of spending versus reinvesting varying proportions of annual returns for a $1,000 investment, held for a period of 20 years, with annual returns of 10%.

During the past several decades, some investors have found it possible to generate 10% nominal returns for 20 years. In fact, a number of investors in certain time periods have frequently targeted a 10% rate of return on their investments. Extended periods of sub-10% returns have persisted in various disinflationary or deflationary eras, however, and it bears repeating that just because certain investors have targeted a 10% annual rate of return has not necessarily increased the likelihood of their achieving 10% per year for 20 years. The first row of Table 3.6 shows that after 20 years of 10% annual returns, the investor who reinvested *nothing* and spent *all* of his or her $100 annual return (that the $1,000 initial investment generated) would accrue a grand total of $3,000. At the other extreme, the last row of Table 3.6 shows that the investor who reinvested *everything* and spent *nothing* would end up with $6,727—more than 2.2 *times* the grand total that the investor who spent each year's returns accumulated.

The second, third, and fourth rows of Table 3.6 show that if the investor had been able to reinvest 25%, 50%, and 75% of the 10% annual returns at 10% for 20 years, he or she would have ended up with terminal accumulated monetary values of $3,932, $4,864, and $5,796, respectively.

◆ Twenty-Year Investment Horizon, 5% Annual Returns: Table 3.7 depicts the effects of spending versus reinvesting varying proportions of annual returns for a $1,000 investment held for 20 years, with annual returns of 5%.

While 5% returns during any given two-decade time frame are by no means a certainty, they have been achievable for such time horizons in a number of broad classes of investments, including equities, long-term government bonds, and long-term corporate bonds.

The first row of Table 3.7 shows that an investor who earned 5% annual returns on a $1,000 initial investment, who reinvested *nothing* and spent *all* of his or her $50 annual return, would end up with a grand total of $2,000 at the end of 20 years. On the contrary, the last row points out that the investor who reinvested *everything* and spent *nothing* would have garnered $2,653, approximately 1.3 *times* the grand total at the disposal of an investor who spent each year's returns.

Rows two, three, and four of Table 3.7 show that if the investor had actually reinvested 25%, 50%, and 75% of the 5% annual returns at 5% for 20 years, he or she would have ended up with $2,163, $2,327, and $2,490, respectively.

## The Effects of Spending versus Reinvesting as a Function of the Investment Time Horizon

Table 3.8 shows the effects of spending versus reinvesting varying proportions of annual returns for a $1,000 investment, held for 10 years rather than 20 years, with annual returns of 20%.

It is worth repeating that 20% annual returns are extraordinarily high, and achieving such investment performance is rare, even if the time period during which such gains are generated extends only for one decade, not two.

At the end of 10 years with 20% annual returns, Table 3.8 shows that the investor who reinvested *nothing* and spent *all* of his or her $200 annual return would have earned a grand total of $3,000. The investor who reinvested *everything* and spent *nothing* would own $6,192. This is a little more than *two times* the grand total an investor who spent each year's returns would have accrued.

Rows two, three, and four of Table 3.8 show that if the investor had reinvested 25%, 50%, and 75% of the 20% annual returns at 20% for *10 years*, he or she would have ended up with $3,798, $4,596, and $5,394, respectively.

## Implications of Spending versus Reinvesting

To illuminate some of the broad implications of the spending versus reinvesting decision, Table 3.9 draws data from Tables 3.5, 3.6 and 3.7, relating to 20-year investments with 20%, 10%, and 5% annual returns, and compares that with data from Table 3.8, relating to a *10-year* investment with 20% annual returns.

One important implication of the spending versus reinvesting decision is that the final accumulated effects of postponing spending are dramatically higher *the higher the reinvestment rate*. For example, given a 20-year investment horizon, 100% of annual returns reinvested leads to final accumulated monetary value of $38,338 at 20% annual returns, $6,727 at 10% annual returns, and $2,653 at 5% annual returns (Box A in Table 3.9).

Similarly, the effects of postponing spending are significantly higher *the longer the investment horizon*. For instance, assuming 20% annual returns, with 50% of the annual returns reinvested, the investor will have amassed $21,669 at the end of 20 years, more than 4.7 times the $4,596 accumulated at the end of 10 years (Box B in Table 3.9).

## T A B L E  3.8

### The Effects of Spending versus Reinvesting at 20% Annual Rates of Return

**$1,000 Investment, 10-Year Horizon, 20% Annual Returns**

| | (1) Repayment of Principal | (2) Total Annual Payments Received and Reinvested | (3) Total Compound Interest Earned on Annual Payments Received and Reinvested | (4) = (1) + (2) + (3) Total Invested Funds Received and Reinvested Plus Principal Repayment | (5) Total Annual Payments That Were Spent | (6) = (5) + (4) Grand Total of Invested Funds Received Plus Spent Funds |
|---|---|---|---|---|---|---|
| **0% ($0) of Annual Return Reinvested, 100% of Annual Return ($200) Spent** | | | | | | |
| | $1,000 | $0 | $0 | $1,000 | $2,000 | $3,000 |
| % of Grand Total | 33% | 0% | 0% | | 67% | 100% |
| **25% ($50.00) of Annual Return Reinvested, 75% of Annual Return ($150) Spent** | | | | | | |
| | 1,000 | 500 | 798 | 2,298 | 1,500 | 3,798 |
| % of Grand Total | 26% | 13% | 22% | | 39% | 100% |
| **50% ($100) of Annual Return Reinvested, 50% of Annual Return ($100) Spent** | | | | | | |
| | 1,000 | 1,000 | 1,596 | 3,596 | 1,000 | 4,596 |
| % of Grand Total | 22% | 22% | 34% | | 22% | 100% |
| **75% ($150) of Annual Return Reinvested, 25% of Annual Return ($50) Spent** | | | | | | |
| | 1,000 | 1,500 | 2,394 | 4,894 | 500 | 5,394 |
| % of Grand Total | 19% | 28% | 44% | | 9% | 100% |
| **100% ($200) of Annual Return Reinvested, 0% of Annual Return ($0) Spent** | | | | | | |
| | 1,000 | 2,000 | 3,192 | 6,192 | 0 | 6,192 |
| % of Grand Total | 16% | 32% | 52% | | 0% | 100% |

Source: The author.

A third implication of the spending versus reinvesting decision is that at sufficiently low rates of return (and for short- to intermediate-term investment horizons of 10 years or less), postponing spending has no significant effects. For instance, 20 years of reinvesting all of 20% annual returns produces 7.7 times (Box C in Table 3.9) as much as reinvesting 0%, with the absolute dollar difference between these two paths amounting to $38,338 minus $5,000, or $33,338. In contrast, reinvesting 100% of 5% annual returns for 20 years produces 1.3 times higher annual returns than reinvesting 0% (Box D in Table 3.9), with

**T A B L E  3.9**

Ending Accumulated Monetary Values for a $1,000 Initial Investment

| % of Annual Returns Reinvested | 10-Year Investment Horizon | Annual Rate of Return and Reinvestment Rate | | |
|---|---|---|---|---|
| | | 20-Year Investment Horizon | | |
| | **20%** | **20%** | **10%** | **5%** |
| 0% | $3,000 | $5,000 | $3,000 | $2,000 |
| 25% | 3,798 | 13,334 | 3,932 | 2,163 |
| 50% | 4,596 | 21,669 (B) | 4,864 | 2,327 |
| 75% | 5,394 | 30,003 | 5,796 | 2,490 |
| 100% | 6,192 | 38,338 | 6,727 | 2,653 (A) |
| **Ratio of 100% Reinvestment Rate to 0% Reinvestment Rate** | 2.1x | 7.7x (C) | 2.2x | 1.3x (D) |

Source: The author.

the absolute dollar difference between these two alternatives amounting to $2,653 minus $2,000, or $653.

## Realized Compound Yield Tradeoffs of Spending versus Reinvesting

Table 3.10 sheds light on an additional important implication of the spending versus reinvesting decision, relating to the *realized compound yield* of total investment funds received (as distinct from any monies that were *spent* rather than reinvested). As was mentioned at the beginning of this chapter, realized compound yield takes into account: (i) a specified holding period for a given investment; (ii) the reinvestment rates of intervening income flows generated by the investment; and (iii) the actual sale price of the investment at the end of the investor's holding period.

As shown in Table 3.10, merely reinvesting *some* of the annual returns into the original asset class can raise the realized compound yield to a meaningful percentage of the realized compound yield that

**T A B L E  3.10**

## Realized Compound Yield Tradeoffs of Spending versus Reinvestment

| Percentage Share of Annual Return | | Realized Compound Yield (RCY) of Total Investment Funds Received and Reinvested Plus Principal Payment[1] | Realized Compound Yield as a Percentage of RCY If 100% of Annual Payments Had Been Reinvested |
|---|---|---|---|
| Reinvested | Spent | | |
| **20-Year Horizon, 20% Annual Returns (Table 3.5)** | | | |
| 0% | 100% | 0.0% | 0% |
| 25% | 75% | E  12.4% | A  62% |
| 50% | 50% | 16.1% | 80% |
| 75% | 25% | 18.3% | 92% |
| 100% | 0% | 20.0% | 100% |
| **20-Year Horizon, 10% Annual Returns (Table 3.6)** | | | |
| 0% | 100% | 0.0% | 0% |
| 25% | 75% | 4.5% | B  45% |
| 50% | 50% | 7.0% | 70% |
| 75% | 25% | 8.7% | 87% |
| 100% | 0% | 10.0% | 100% |
| **20-Year Horizon, 5% Annual Returns (Table 3.7)** | | | |
| 0% | 100% | 0.0% | 0% |
| 25% | 75% | 1.7% | C  34% |
| 50% | 50% | 3.1% | 62% |
| 75% | 25% | 4.1% | 82% |
| 100% | 0% | 5.0% | 100% |
| **10-Year Horizon, 20% Annual Returns (Table 3.8)** | | | |
| 0% | 100% | 0.0% | 0% |
| 25% | 75% | 8.7% | D  43% |
| 50% | 50% | 13.7% | 68% |
| 75% | 25% | 17.2% | 86% |
| 100% | 0% | 20.0% | 100% |

[1]The realized compound yield (RCY) is the compound annual growth rate of a $1,000 initial investment which produces a given final value for the total investment funds received and reinvested plus principal payment. For example, referring to Table 3.5 of this chapter, a $1,000 initial investment whose $200 annual returns are 25% reinvested and 75% spent generates $13,334 in Total investment funds received and reinvested plus principal payment over a 20-year horizon, and results in a realized compound yield of 12.4% (shown as Box E above), which is equal to 62% of the 20% realized compound yield if 100% of the annual returns had been invested.

Source: The author.

would have been achieved if 100% of the annual payments had been reinvested.

For example, if 25% of a 20%-annual-return-producing investment were reinvested for 20 years, the proportion of full-investment realized compound yield that would be achieved at 20% annual returns would be 62% (Box A in Table 3.10); at 10% annual returns, 45% (Box B in Table 3.10); and at 5% annual returns, 34% (Box C in Table 3.10). If 25% of a 20%-annual-return-producing investment were reinvested for 10 years, the proportion of the full-investment realized compound yield that would be achieved at 20% annual returns would be 43% (Box D in Table 3.10).

## COUPON REINVESTMENT IN FIXED-INCOME SECURITIES

One of the most important, yet least appreciated, aspects of investing in equity- and fixed-income-related asset classes is the concept of *interest and dividend reinvestment*. For compounding to work its highly beneficial effects on portfolio values over time, investors must pay attention to the necessity, the consequences, and the challenges of investing coupon payments or dividends at sufficiently high rates of return. Spending such income flows, using them to pay taxes, or reinvesting them at low returns can significantly reduce the investment's realized compound yield and thus the total long-term asset value of a portfolio.

For individual and professional investors, the reinvestment of coupon and dividend payments, in the most tax-advantaged manner possible, is of vital importance in actually achieving the long-term quoted returns that investors associate with the ownership of debt or equity securities. This is particularly true the longer the investment holding period and the higher the expected compound annual rate of return.

The proportion of a fixed-income security's total return represented by the reinvestment of interest coupons *increases*: (i) the higher the coupon; (ii) the higher the initial and anticipated yield to maturity; and (iii) the longer the maturity of the instrument. For sufficiently long holding periods, and sufficiently high-coupon, long-maturity bonds, purchased at sufficiently high initial and anticipated yields to maturity, the assumed reinvestment of interest coupons, assumed to be *at that same high initial yield to maturity*, can account for a dramatically large share of the total funds received from an investment.

Figure 3.4 shows that a $1,000 par-value, 30-year, 10% annual cou-pon bond, purchased at a 10% yield to maturity, will produce total funds of $17,449.40 during the bond's life.

Of the total funds received over the life of the bond, $1,000, or 5.7%, represents the repayment of principal; $3,000, or 17.2%, repre-sents the 30 annual coupon payments of $100; and $13,449.40, or 77.1%,

## F I G U R E  3.4

Periodic Contributions versus Periodic Withdrawals

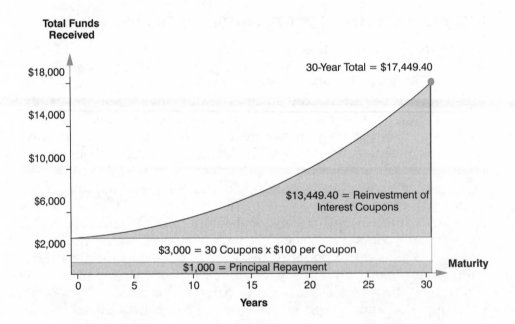

| Source of Funds | Amount | Dollars Received Percent of Total |
|---|---|---|
| Principal | $1,000.00 | 5.7% |
| Coupons | $3,000.00 | 17.2% |
| Coupon Reinvestment | $13,449.40 | 77.1% |
| Total | $17,449.40 | 100.0% |

Source: The author.

**T A B L E   3.11**

Coupon Reinvestment as a Percentage of Total Funds Received

**10% and 5% Annual Coupon Bonds, 5-, 10-, 20-, and 30-Year Maturities**

| | | | Percentage of Total Funds Received | | | |
|---|---|---|---|---|---|---|
| Coupon | Initial Yield to Maturity | Years to Maturity | Repayment of Principal | Interest Coupons | Reinvestment of Interest Coupons | Total Funds Received |
| 10% | 10% | 5 | 62.1% | 31.0% | 6.9% | $1,610.51 |
| 10% | 10% | 10 | 38.6% | 38.6% | 22.8% | 2,593.74 |
| 10% | 10% | 20 | 14.9% | 29.7% | 55.4% | 6,727.50 |
| 10% | 10% | 30 | 5.7% | 17.2% | 77.1% | 17,449.40 |
| 5% | 5% | 5 | 78.3% | 19.6% | 2.1% | $1,276.28 |
| 5% | 5% | 10 | 61.4% | 30.7% | 7.9% | 1,628.89 |
| 5% | 5% | 20 | 37.7% | 37.7% | 24.6% | 2,653.30 |
| 5% | 5% | 30 | 23.1% | 34.7% | 42.2% | 4,321.94 |

Source: The author.

represents the aggregate total produced by reinvesting each $100 annual coupon[1] at an interest rate of *exactly* 10%.

For coupons and initial yields to maturity of 10% and 5%, respectively, Table 3.11 shows, for bonds of 5-, 10-, 20-, and 30-year maturities, the percentage of total funds received that is represented by the repayment of principal; the interest coupons; and the reinvestment of the interest coupons.

As a percent of the total funds received from a 10% annual-coupon bond purchased at a beginning yield level of 10%, the importance of coupon reinvestment, also known as *interest on interest,* ranges from 77.1% on a 30-year bond, to 55.4% on a 20-year bond, to 22.8% on a 10-year bond, to 6.9% on a 5-year bond.

---

[1] For the sake of simplicity, annual, rather than semiannual, coupons are used in this analysis. For a $1,000 par value, 10% bond, with 60 *semiannual* coupons of 5%, the total funds received amount to $18,679.19, of which $14,679.19, or 78.6%, represents the reinvestment of semi-annual interest coupons at an assumed rate of 10%.

Table 3.11 also demonstrates the diminished relative importance of coupon reinvestment for long-maturity bonds at lower coupon rates and initial yield levels. For instance, for a 30-year, 5% annual coupon bond, purchased at a 5% initial and anticipated yield to maturity, the reinvestment of interest coupons represents 42.2%, or $1,821.94, of the $4,321.94 in total funds received by the investor.

For short-maturity bonds, the importance of coupon reinvestment is modest, regardless of coupon and beginning yield level. For five-year, 10% coupon bonds, purchased at a 10% yield to maturity, the reinvestment of interest coupons represents 6.9% of the total funds received, and for five-year, 5% coupon bonds, purchased at a 5% yield to maturity, the reinvestment of interest coupons represents only 2.1% of the total funds received.

In practice, interest rates do not remain stable for the life of a 30-year bond, much less a bond of 20-, 10-, or even 5-year maturities. Investors are thus subject to one key form of *reinvestment risk*, or the chance that they will not be able to invest coupons (or principal) at a rate equal to the bond's original yield to maturity. A further complication for many individual and some professional investors stems from the annual taxability of interest and dividend income, which effectively reduces the amount of the coupon income they can reinvest.

Taking account of such tax considerations, many taxable investors have sought, whenever possible, to own any securities that have a meaningful degree of reinvestment risk within tax-advantaged structures, such as a foundation, an individual retirement account (IRA), or a 401(k) plan. Having a tax-advantaged ownership structure is equally important in the case of zero-coupon bonds, which otherwise incur taxes on the phantom interest income that is not paid in cash but which the tax authorities consider to *accrete* each year.

## Zero-Coupon Bonds

Zero-coupon bonds (also known as zeros) eliminate coupon reinvestment risk by means of the annual internal compounding of capital values, to a final value for the bond (usually its $1,000 par value). Zeros have been popular with low-tax or tax-advantaged investors seeking to lock in a specific compounding rate of interest at the time of the bond's purchase. In addition, some investors seek zero-coupon bonds due to their high degree of capital-value responsiveness in reaction to interest rate changes.

**T A B L E  3.12**

Accretion Percentage to Par Value for Zero-Coupon Bond

**10% and 5% Initial Yields to Maturity, 5-, 10-, 20-, and 30-Year Maturities**

| | | Percentage of Total Funds Received | | |
| Initial Yield to Maturity | Years to Investment | Initial Investment | Total Accretion to Par Value | Final Par Value |
| --- | --- | --- | --- | --- |
| 10% | 5 | 62.1% | 37.9% | $1,000.00 |
| 10% | 10 | 38.6% | 61.4% | 1,000.00 |
| 10% | 20 | 14.9% | 85.1% | 1,000.00 |
| 10% | 30 | 5.7% | 94.3% | 1,000.00 |
| 5% | 5 | 78.4% | 21.6% | 1,000.00 |
| 5% | 10 | 61.4% | 38.6% | 1,000.00 |
| 5% | 20 | 37.7% | 62.3% | 1,000.00 |
| 5% | 30 | 23.1% | 76.9% | 1,000.00 |

Source: The author.

Without a coupon that requires annual reinvestment exactly at the yield to maturity prevailing at the time of purchase, zero-coupon bonds derive a meaningful proportion of their total funds received from the internal compounding, or accretion, of their initial investment value to final par value. Table 3.12 illustrates how this proportion varies by the bond's initial yield to maturity and its total number of years to maturity.

Table 3.12 shows that for zero-coupon bonds purchased at a 10% yield to maturity, the percentage of total funds received represented by internal compounding, or accretion, ranges from 37.9% for a 5-year bond, to 94.3% for a 30-year bond. For zero-coupon bonds purchased at a 5% yield to maturity, the percentage of total funds received represented by internal compounding, or accretion, ranges from 21.6% for a 5-year bond, to 76.9% for a 30-year bond.

## The Effects of Not Reinvesting Coupons

For coupon-bearing bonds, investors can further glean the importance of coupon reinvestment by calculating the actual realized compound yield resulting from spending rather than reinvesting a bond's annual coupon payments. Table 3.13 outlines how not reinvesting coupons affects realized compound yields.

For 10% coupon bonds, purchased at a 10% yield to maturity, not reinvesting the coupons lowers the effective realized compound yield from 10% to 8.45% for a five-year bond, and from 10% to 4.73% for a 30-year bond. For 5% coupon bonds, purchased at a 5% yield to maturity, not reinvesting the coupons lowers the effective realized compound yield from 5% to 4.56% for a five-year bond, and from 5% to 3.10% for a 30-year bond.

The proportion of realized compound yield represented by the reinvestment of interest coupons increases with higher coupon rates, higher yield levels, and longer maturities. Table 3.14 compares *the proportion of total funds* received from reinvestment of interest coupons to the *proportion of total realized compound yield* from the reinvestment of interest coupons.

For 10% bonds, purchased at a 10% yield to maturity, the proportion of total realized compound yield accounted for by the reinvestment of interest coupons ranges from 15.5% for a 5-year bond, to 52.7% for a 30-year bond. This compares to 6.9% of the total funds received for a 5-year, 10% coupon bond, and 77.1% of the total funds received for a 30-year, 10% coupon bond. For 5% bonds, purchased at a 5% yield

**T A B L E  3.13**

Realized Compound Yields When Coupons Are Not Reinvested

**10% and 5% Coupon, 5-, 10-, 20-, and 30-Year Maturities**

| | | | Total Funds Received | | Realized Compound Yield Without Coupons Reinvested |
|---|---|---|---|---|---|
| Coupon | Initial Yield to Maturity | Years to Maturity | With Coupons Reinvested | Without Coupons Reinvested | |
| 10% | 10% | 5 | $1,610.51 | $1,500.00 | 8.45% |
| 10% | 10% | 10 | 2,593.74 | 2,000.00 | 7.18% |
| 10% | 10% | 20 | 6,727.50 | 3,000.00 | 5.65% |
| 10% | 10% | 30 | 17,449.40 | 4,000.00 | 4.73% |
| 5% | 5% | 5 | $1,276.28 | $1,250.00 | 4.56% |
| 5% | 5% | 10 | 1,628.89 | 1,500.00 | 4.14% |
| 5% | 5% | 20 | 2,653.30 | 2,000.00 | 3.53% |
| 5% | 5% | 30 | 4,321.94 | 2,500.00 | 3.10% |

Source: The author.

**T A B L E  3.14**

Coupon Reinvestment as a Proportion of Total Funds Received and Realized
Compound Yield

**10% and 5% Coupon, 5-, 10-, 20-, and 30-Year Maturities**

| | | | Reinvestment of Interest Coupons | |
|---|---|---|---|---|
| Coupon | Initial Yield to Maturity | Years to Maturity | Proportion of Total Funds Received | Proportion of Total Realized Compound Yield |
| 10% | 10% | 5 | 6.9% | 15.5% |
| 10% | 10% | 10 | 22.8% | 28.2% |
| 10% | 10% | 20 | 55.4% | 43.5% |
| 10% | 10% | 30 | 77.1% | 52.7% |
| 5% | 5% | 5 | 2.1% | 8.8% |
| 5% | 5% | 10 | 7.9% | 17.2% |
| 5% | 5% | 20 | 24.6% | 29.4% |
| 5% | 5% | 30 | 42.2% | 38.0% |

Source: The author.

to maturity, the proportion of total realized compound yield accounted for by the reinvestment of interest coupons ranges from 8.8% for a 5-year bond, to 38.0% for a 30-year bond. This compares to 2.1% of the total funds received for a 5-year, 5% coupon bond, and 42.2% of the total funds received for a 30-year, 5% coupon bond.

## DIVIDEND REINVESTMENT IN EQUITIES

*Dividend reinvestment* affects long-term results from investing in *equities* as much as coupon reinvestment affects fixed-income investing. In many instances, investors, regulators, tax authorities, and corporations often pay insufficient attention to this important component of equity investing and asset allocation. Cash dividends are not deductible from corporations' income taxes. During the last quarter of the twentieth century, an increasing number of companies lowered their dividend payout ratios (the ratio of after-tax profits to dividends), or elected not to pay cash dividends, asserting that they could put their profits and retained earnings to better use by reinvesting in their own businesses

**F I G U R E   3.5**

The Growth of $1.00 Invested in the Standard & Poor's 500 Index

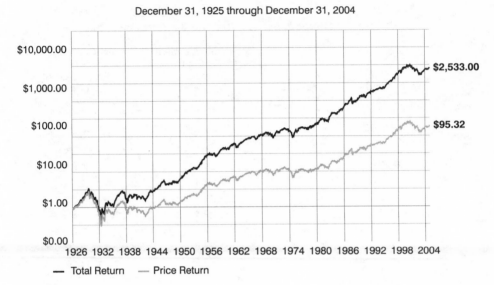

December 31, 1925 through December 31, 2004

Source: Ibbotson Associates.

or by repurchasing their own shares. In the years after 2000, this trend began gradually to reverse. Cash dividends are generally taxed as ordinary income to individual investors. As a result, investors may wish to hold dividend-paying equities in tax-advantaged and/or tax-deferring structures whenever possible, to maximize the amount of cash dividends they can reinvest.

The effects of dividend reinvestment become even more pronounced over a long time frame. Figure 3.5 shows the multidecade growth of $1.00 originally invested in the Standard & Poor's 500 Index[2] on December 31, 1925.

At the end of 2004, a $1.00 investment in the Standard & Poor's 500 Index with dividends reinvested and without taking taxes into account, had grown to $2,533.00, representing a 10.3% compound annual rate of growth during this 80-year period.

---

[2] The Standard & Poor's 500 Index was originally the Standard & Poor's 90 Index; it became the Standard & Poor's 500 Index on March 4, 1957.

## The Effects of Not Reinvesting Dividends

If dividends were not reinvested each year[3], the $1.00 original investment would have grown to $95.32 before taxes, a 80-year compound rate of growth of 5.9%. The three key determinants of the difference between these two growth rates are the compound rate of return for equities, the amount of the dividend to be reinvested into equities each year, and the length of the reinvestment period.

Table 3.15 shows the percentage shortfalls from various ending portfolio values, as a result of not reinvesting dividends.

A $1.00 initial equity investment held for five years, at a compound annual growth rate of 12%, will grow to a final value of $1.76. If 2% of the 12% compound growth rate represents dividends that should have been reinvested, but were not, the portfolio's final value ends up 9% below $1.76, at $1.61. If 5% of the 12% compound growth rate represents dividends that should have been reinvested but were not, the portfolio's five-year final value ends up 20% below $1.76, at $1.40.

For long periods, the percentage and absolute-dollar contributions from reinvested dividends are even more dramatic. A $1.00 equity initial investment, held for 70 years at a compound annual growth rate of 12%, will grow to a final portfolio value of $2,787.80. If 2% of the 12% compound growth rate represents dividends that should have been reinvested but were not, the portfolio's final value ends up 72% below $2,787.80, at $789.75, for a dollar shortfall of $1,998.05. If 5% of the 12% compound annual growth rate represents dividends that should have been reinvested but were not, the portfolio's 70-year final value ends up 96% below $2,787.80, at $113.99, for a dollar shortfall of $2,673.81.

The actual percentage dividend rate reinvested back into the investor's underlying equity assets depends on the portfolio companies' cash flow, earnings, dividend payout policies, and subsequent equity-price performance throughout the investor's holding period. For a series of 20 decades beginning with 1802–1809 and ending with 1990–1999, the bottom panel of Table 3.15 shows the importance of dividends received and reinvested to the total returns generated by investing in equities. In 13 of the 20 decades, the returns from the receipt of dividends and their reinvestment exceed the returns from the capital gains, and in the last half of the twentieth century, the percentage of each decade's total equity return that is represented by the return from

---

[3] For purposes of simplicity, the dividends (which for most companies are paid on a quarterly basis in the United States) are assumed to be reinvested annually; quarterly reinvestment for 308 quarters would produce a 10.2% compound annual rate of growth for 77 years.

## T A B L E  3.15

## Dividends' Contribution to Equity Investment Returns

| Percentage Shortfall in Investment Values from Neglecting Dividend Reinvestment |

*Based on 12% and 9% Compound Annual Equity Returns*

| Compound Annual Equity Return | Of Which Annual Dividend Reinvestment Component | For a $1.00 Initial Investment, Final Portfolio Value After | | | | |
|---|---|---|---|---|---|---|
| | | 5 Years | 10 Years | 20 Years | 40 Years | 70 Years |
| 12% → | All Dividends Reinvested → | $1.76 | $3.11 | $9.65 | $93.05 | $2,787.80 |
| | Uninvested Annual Dividends | Percentage Shortfall Due to Not Reinvesting Dividends | | | | |
| 12% | 2% | 9% | 17% | 30% | 51% | 72% |
| 12% | 3% | 12% | 24% | 42% | 66% | 85% |
| 12% | 4% | 16% | 31% | 52% | 77% | 92% |
| 12% | 5% | 20% | 37% | 60% | 84% | 96% |
| | | 5 Years | 10 Years | 20 Years | 40 Years | 70 Years |
| 9% → | All Dividends Reinvested → | $1.54 | $2.37 | $5.60 | $31.41 | $416.73 |
| | Uninvested Annual Dividends | Percentage Shortfall Due to Not Reinvesting Dividends | | | | |
| 9% | 2% | 9% | 17% | 31% | 52% | 73% |
| 9% | 3% | 13% | 24% | 43% | 67% | 86% |
| 9% | 4% | 17% | 31% | 53% | 83% | 93% |
| 9% | 5% | 21% | 38% | 61% | 85% | 96% |

| Dividend Receipt and Reinvestment Compared to Capital Change |

$$\textcircled{C} = \textcircled{A} + \textcircled{B}$$

$$\textcircled{D} = \textcircled{C} \div \textcircled{B}$$

| Decade | (A) Return from Capital Gains | (B) Return from Dividend Receipt and Reinvestment | (C) Total Equity Return Including Dividend Reinvestment | (D) Percent of Total Equity Return Represented by Return from Dividend Receipt and Reinvestment |
|---|---|---|---|---|
| 1802–1809 | −0.26% | 5.03% | 4.77% | 105.50% |
| 1810–1819 | −2.44 | 5.12 | 2.68 | 191.00 |
| 1820–1829 | 0.05 | 5.26 | 5.31 | 99.10 |
| 1830–1839 | −0.69 | 5.23 | 4.53 | 115.50 |
| 1840–1849 | 1.24 | 5.49 | 6.73 | 81.60 |
| 1850–1859 | −4.59 | 5.05 | 0.45 | 1,122.20 |
| 1860–1869 | 10.74 | 5.00 | 15.73 | 31.80 |
| 1870–1879 | 1.61 | 5.97 | 7.58 | 78.80 |
| 1880–1889 | 0.78 | 5.94 | 6.72 | 88.40 |
| 1890–1899 | 1.24 | 4.21 | 5.45 | 77.30 |
| 1900–1909 | 5.52 | 4.11 | 9.62 | 42.30 |
| 1910–1919 | −1.65 | 6.34 | 4.69 | 135.20 |
| 1920–1929 | 9.42 | 4.44 | 13.86 | 32.00 |
| 1930–1939 | −5.26 | 5.09 | −0.17 | 2,994.10 |
| 1940–1949 | 2.98 | 6.59 | 9.57 | 68.90 |
| 1950–1959 | 13.58 | 4.65 | 18.23 | 25.50 |
| 1960–1969 | 4.39 | 3.78 | 8.17 | 46.30 |
| 1970–1979 | 1.60 | 5.14 | 6.75 | 76.20 |
| 1980–1989 | 12.59 | 4.04 | 16.64 | 24.30 |
| 1990–1999 | 15.89 | 2.93 | 18.82 | 15.60 |

Note: Dividends and returns data for 1802–1970 are from "Indexes of U.S. Stock Prices from 1802 to 1987," by G. William Schwert in Volume 63, Number 3 of the University of Chicago *Journal of Business,* and for 1970–1999, the Wilshire Performance Index as calculated by Wilshire Associates.

Source: Global Financial Data, and "Speaking of Dividends," *Barron's,* March 4, 2002.

**F I G U R E  3.6**

Dividend Yields on the Standard & Poor's 500 Index

## December 31, 1925 through December 31, 2004

**Dividend Yield
in Percent**

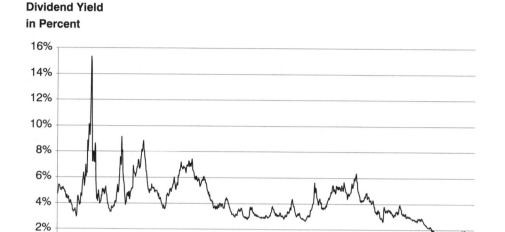

**Month-End**

Source: Standard & Poor's.

dividend receipt and reinvestment has ranged from 15.60% in the 1990s to 76.20% in the 1970s.

As Figure 3.6 illustrates, equity dividend yields vary over time, depending on corporations' earnings, cash flow, dividend policies, and the overall level of stock prices.

## MULTIYEAR RATES OF RETURN

Investors would be wise to appreciate the year-to-year returns patterns that comprise a multiyear investment period. The addition or subtraction of gain or loss years to a series of investment results may affect compound annual rates of growth and ending investment values in profound ways that may not be immediately or intuitively obvious. If investors can gain some degree of understanding of how positive or negative results influence investment outcomes, they may more thoughtfully structure their asset allocations and investing activity.

**T A B L E  3.16**

Dividends' Contribution to Equity Investment Returns

| | Year 1990 | Year 1991 | Year 1992 | Year 1993 | Year 1994 | Year 1995 |
|---|---|---|---|---|---|---|
| **YEAR →** | 1 | 2 | 3 | 4 | 5 | 6 |
| Annual Ending Value of $1.00 Initial Investment | −3.17% | 30.55% | 7.67% | 9.99% | 1.31% | 37.43% |
| | $1.00   0.97 | 1.26 | 1.36 | 1.50 | 1.52 | 2.08 |

| | | Year 1990 | Year 1991 | Year 1992 | Year 1993 | Year 1994 |
|---|---|---|---|---|---|---|
| **YEAR →** | | 1 | 2 | 3 | 4 | 5 |
| Annual Ending Value of $1.00 Initial Investment | | | 30.55% | 7.67% | 9.99% | 1.31% | 37.43% |
| | | $1.00 | 1.31 | 1.41 | 1.55 | 1.57 | 2.15 |

| | | | Year 1992 | Year 1993 | Year 1994 | Year 1995 |
|---|---|---|---|---|---|---|
| **YEAR →** | | | 1 | 2 | 3 | 4 |
| Annual Ending Value of $1.00 Initial Investment | | | | 7.67% | 9.99% | 1.31% | 37.43% |
| | | | $1.00 | 1.08 | 1.18 | 1.20 | 1.65 |

Source: The author.

As an example of how meaningfully investment growth rates and ending values can change in response to apparently modest shifts in annual returns, Table 3.16 shows the investment returns for the Standard & Poor's 500 Index during three consecutive rolling 10-year periods, 1990 through 1999, 1991 through 2000, and 1992 through 2001.

In the top part of Table 3.16, an investor who invested $1.00 in the Standard & Poor's 500 Index at the beginning of 1990, and reinvested all gains, losses, or dividends, would have seen his or her initial investment grow to $5.32 by the end of 1999, an 18.2% compound annual rate of growth.

| Year 1996 | Year 1997 | Year 1998 | Year 1999 | Year 2000 | Year 2001 | Value of $1.00 (compounded annually) | |
|---|---|---|---|---|---|---|---|
| | | | | | | 10-Year | |
| | | | | | | Ending Value | Compound Annual Growth Rate |
| _7_ | _8_ | _9_ | _10_ | | | | |
| 23.07% | 33.36% | 28.58% | 21.04% | | | *(1990–1999)* | 18.2% |
| 2.57 | 3.42 | 4.40 | 5.32 | | | $5.32 | |
| _6_ | _7_ | _8_ | _9_ | _10_ | | | |
| 23.07% | 33.36% | 28.58% | 21.04% | −9.11% | | *(1991–2000)* | 17.5% |
| 2.65 | 3.53 | 4.54 | 5.50 | 5.00 | | $5.00 | |
| _5_ | _6_ | _7_ | _8_ | _9_ | _10_ | | |
| 23.07% | 33.36% | 28.58% | 21.04% | −9.11% | −11.88% | *(1992–2001)* | 12.9% |
| 2.03 | 2.71 | 3.48 | 4.21 | 3.83 | 3.37 | 3.37 | |

The middle part of Table 3.16 shows the investment results for an investor who initially invested $1.00 at the beginning of 1991 (thereby *avoiding* the negative 3.17% S&P 500 return for 1990), followed by the 10 years of S&P 500 total returns ending in 2000 (which *includes* a negative return of 9.11% in 2000). Such an investor would have fared similarly to the investor whose 10-year time frame extended from 1990 through 1999, amassing $5.00 as an ending portfolio value at the end of 2000, a 17.5% compound annual rate of growth.

The bottom part of Table 3.16 depicts an investor who placed $1.00 into the S&P 500 Index at the beginning of 1992 (thereby avoiding the negative 3.17% S&P 500 return for 1990, but also missing out on the positive 30.55% S&P 500 return for 1991), and reinvested all gains, losses, or dividends for the 10 years including 2000 and 2001 (which produced negative returns of 9.11% and 11.88%, respectively). This investor would have seen his or her initial investment grow to $3.37 at the end of 2001, a compound annual growth rate of 12.9%. An investor who *excluded* the slightly negative investment results of 1990 and robust positive results of 1991, and *included* the two moderately negative return years of 2000 and 2001, would have suffered a surprisingly large 38% reduction in his or her ending portfolio value (from $5.32 to $3.37), and a 30% reduction in his or her effective compound annual growth rate (from 18.2% to 12.9%). The effects of different incremental returns years on effective compound annual growth rates and final investment values are further explored below.

For 5-year, 10-year, and 15-year holding periods, and for initial compound annual growth rates of 10%, 15%, and 20%, Table 3.17 shows what happens to effective compound annual growth rates and final investment values if the last 1, 2, or 3 years of the holding periods produce negative compound returns.

In the two middle vertical panels of Table 3.17, an investor whose 10-year holding period included 8 years of 10% compound returns, followed by 2 back-to-back years of negative 15% compound returns, would experience a sharp decline in the effective 10-year compound annual rate of growth, from a 10% original compound annual rate of growth to a 4.5% effective compound annual rate of growth (depicted by the dashed box within the top middle panel). At such a lowered growth rate, the final value of a $1.00 initial investment would be $1.55 (depicted by the dashed box within the bottom middle panel), 40% less than the final value of $2.59 which would have resulted from 10 full years at a 10% compound annual growth rate.

As might be expected, the reduction in effective compound annual growth rates and in final values *within fixed-length investment periods* is greater: (i) the more years of negative returns (i.e., 3 years of negative compound annual returns are relatively more detrimental than 1 year of negative returns); (ii) the higher the absolute amount of negative annual returns (i.e., substituted rates of return of negative 20% are relatively more detrimental than substituted rates of return of negative 5%); (iii) the lower the initial compound annual growth rate (i.e., negative substituted rates of return have a relatively more detrimental effect on 10% initial compound annual growth rates than on 20% initial com-

pound annual growth rates); and (iv) the shorter the original investment time period (i.e., negative substituted rates of return have a
relatively more detrimental effect if they take place within a 5-year
holding period than a 20-year holding period).

By adding 1, 2, and 3 years of negative investment returns onto
the end of 5-, 10-, and 20-year holding periods, (producing holding periods of: (i) 6, 7, and 8 years; (ii) 11, 12, and 13 years; and (iii) 21, 22, and
23 years), Table 3.18 pursues a slightly different tack of analysis than
Table 3.17, with its fixed 5-, 10-, and 20-year holding periods that *substituted negative return years for positive return years*. Table 3.18 shows
what happens to effective compound annual growth rates and final investment values by extending the original holding periods by 1, 2, or 3
years of negative compound returns.

The two left-hand vertical panels of Table 3.18 shows that an investor whose original five-year holding period was extended to seven
years, with the latter two years producing negative returns of 5% per
year, would experience a significant decline in the effective compound annual rate of growth, from 15% compounded annually
through the end of five years to 8.9% compounded annually through
the end of seven years (depicted by the dashed box within the top left
panel). At such a lowered growth rate, the final value of a $1.00 initial
investment would be $1.82 (depicted by the dashed box within the
bottom left panel), 32% less than the final value of $2.66 which would
have resulted from seven full years at a 15% compound annual
growth rate.

As might be expected, the reduction in effective compound annual
growth rates and in final values for *incrementally extendible-length investment periods* is greater: (i) the more years of negative returns (i.e., 3
add-on years of negative compound annual returns are relatively more
detrimental than only 1 add-on year of negative returns); (ii) the higher
the absolute amount of negative annual returns (i.e., incremental rates
of return of negative 15% are relatively more detrimental than incremental rates of return of negative 10%); (iii) the lower the initial compound annual growth rate (i.e., negative incremental rates of return
have a relatively more detrimental effect on 10% initial compound annual growth rates than on 20% initial compound annual growth rates);
and (iv) the shorter the original investment time period (i.e., negative
incremental rates of return have a relatively more detrimental effect if
they are added onto a 5-year initial holding period than a 20-year initial holding period).

**T A B L E  3.17**

The Effect of Negative Substituted Rates of Return Within Selected Multiyear Holding Periods

| Initial Compound Annual Growth Rate | Substituted Rate of Return for *Each Year* for 1 Year, 2 Years, or 3 Years | Effective 5-Year Compound Annual Growth Rate | | |
|---|---|---|---|---|
| | | With the Last 1 Year a Declining Year | With the Last 2 Years as Declining Years | With the Last 3 Years as Declining Years |
| 10% | –5% | 6.8% | 3.7% | 0.7% |
| 10% | –10% | 5.7% | 1.5% | –2.5% |
| 10% | –15% | 4.5% | –0.8% | –5.8% |
| 10% | –20% | 3.2% | –3.2% | –9.1% |
| 15% | –5% | 10.7% | 6.5% | 2.5% |
| 15% | –10% | 9.5% | 4.3% | –0.7% |
| 15% | –15% | 8.3% | 1.9% | –4.1% |
| 15% | –20% | 6.9% | –0.5% | –7.5% |
| 20% | –5% | 14.5% | 9.3% | 4.3% |
| 20% | –10% | 13.3% | 7.0% | 1.0% |
| 20% | –15% | 12.0% | 4.5% | –2.4% |
| 20% | –20% | 10.7% | 2.0% | –5.9% |

| Initial Compound Annual Growth Rate | Substituted Rate of Return for *Each Year* for 1 Year, 2 Years, or 3 Years | Final Value of $1.00 Initial Investment At the End of 5 Years | | |
|---|---|---|---|---|
| | | With the Last Year a Declining Year | With the Last 2 Years as Declining Years | With the Last 3 Years as Declining Years |
| 10% | –5% | 1.39 | 1.20 | 1.04 |
| 10% | –10% | 1.32 | 1.08 | 0.88 |
| 10% | –15% | 1.24 | 0.96 | 0.74 |
| 10% | –20% | 1.17 | 0.85 | 0.62 |
| 15% | –5% | 1.66 | 1.37 | 1.13 |
| 15% | –10% | 1.57 | 1.23 | 0.96 |
| 15% | –15% | 1.49 | 1.10 | 0.81 |
| 15% | –20% | 1.40 | 0.97 | 0.68 |
| 20% | –5% | 1.97 | 1.56 | 1.23 |
| 20% | –10% | 1.87 | 1.40 | 1.05 |
| 20% | –15% | 1.76 | 1.25 | 0.88 |
| 20% | –20% | 1.66 | 1.11 | 0.74 |

[1]The 10-year compound annual growth rate (CAGR) of an initial investment of $1.00 which produces a value of $1.55 at the end of the tenth year is 4.5%. The year-by-year calculation of these values is set forth below.

Initial Investment Value: $1.00
Year 1:  At a CAGR of 10.0%— $1.00 times 1.10 = $1.10
Year 2:  At a CAGR of 10.0%— $1.10 times 1.10 = $1.21
Year 3:  At a CAGR of 10.0%— $1.21 times 1.10 = $1.33

Source: The author.

| Effective 10-Year Compound Annual Growth Rate | | |
|---|---|---|
| With the Last 1 Year a Declining Year | With the Last 2 Years as Declining Years | With the Last 3 Years as Declining Years |
| 8.4% | 6.8% | 5.3% |
| 7.8% | 5.7% | 3.6% |
| 7.2% | 4.5%[1] | 1.8% |
| 6.6% | 3.2% | 0.0% |
| 12.8% | 10.7% | 8.6% |
| 12.2% | 9.5% | 6.8% |
| 11.6% | 8.3% | 5.0% |
| 10.9% | 6.9% | 3.1% |
| 17.2% | 14.5% | 11.9% |
| 16.6% | 13.3% | 10.1% |
| 15.9% | 12.0% | 8.2% |
| 15.2% | 10.7% | 6.3% |

| Effective 20-Year Compound Annual Growth Rate | | |
|---|---|---|
| With the Last 1 Year a Declining Year | With the Last 2 Years as Declining Years | With the Last 3 Years as Declining Years |
| 9.2% | 8.4% | 7.6% |
| 8.9% | 7.8% | 6.7% |
| 8.6% | 7.2% | 5.8% |
| 8.3% | 6.6% | 4.9% |
| 13.9% | 12.8% | 11.8% |
| 13.6% | 12.2% | 10.8% |
| 13.3% | 11.6% | 9.9% |
| 12.9% | 10.9% | 8.9% |
| 18.6% | 17.2% | 15.9% |
| 18.3% | 16.6% | 14.9% |
| 17.9% | 15.9% | 14.0% |
| 17.6% | 15.2% | 12.9% |

| Final Value of $1.00 Initial Investment At the End of 10 Years | | |
|---|---|---|
| With the Last 1 Year a Declining Year | With the Last 2 Years as Declining Years | With the Last 3 Years as Declining Years |
| 2.24 | 1.93 | 1.67 |
| 2.12 | 1.74 | 1.42 |
| 2.00 | 1.55[1] | 1.20 |
| 1.89 | 1.37 | 1.00 |
| 3.34 | 2.76 | 2.28 |
| 3.17 | 2.48 | 1.94 |
| 2.99 | 2.21 | 1.63 |
| 2.81 | 1.96 | 1.36 |
| 4.90 | 3.88 | 3.07 |
| 4.64 | 3.48 | 2.61 |
| 4.39 | 3.11 | 2.20 |
| 4.13 | 2.75 | 1.83 |

| Final Value of $1.00 Initial Investment At the End of 20 Years | | |
|---|---|---|
| With the Last 1 Year a Declining Year | With the Last 2 Years as Declining Years | With the Last 3 Years as Declining Years |
| 5.81 | 5.02 | 4.33 |
| 5.50 | 4.50 | 3.68 |
| 5.20 | 4.02 | 3.10 |
| 4.89 | 3.56 | 2.59 |
| 13.52 | 11.17 | 9.23 |
| 12.81 | 10.02 | 7.84 |
| 12.10 | 8.94 | 6.61 |
| 11.39 | 7.92 | 5.51 |
| 30.35 | 24.03 | 19.02 |
| 28.75 | 21.56 | 16.17 |
| 27.16 | 19.24 | 13.63 |
| 25.56 | 17.04 | 11.36 |

Year 4:  At a CAGR of  10.0%— $1.33 times 1.10 = $1.46
Year 5:  At a CAGR of  10.0%— $1.46 times 1.10 = $1.61
Year 6:  At a CAGR of  10.0%— $1.61 times 1.10 = $1.77
Year 7:  At a CAGR of  10.0%— $1.77 times 1.10 = $1.94
Year 8:  At a CAGR of  10.0%— $1.94 times 1.10 = $2.14
Year 9:  At a CAGR of −15.0%— $2.14 times 0.85 = $1.82
Year 10: At a CAGR of −15.0%— $1.82 times 0.85 = $1.55

## T A B L E  3.18

### The Effect of Negative Incremental Rates of Return Added Onto the End of Selected Multiyear Holding Periods

| | | Effective Compound Annual Growth Rate | | | |
|---|---|---|---|---|---|
| Compound Annual Growth Rate Through End of Initial Multiyear Period | Incremental Rate of Return for *Each Year* for 1 Year, 2 Years, or 3 Years | Through Year 5 | Through Year 6 (includes 1 Year of Negative Return) | Through Year 7 (includes 2 Years of Negative Return) | Through Year 8 (includes 3 Years of Negative Return) |
| 10% | −5% | 10.0% | 7.3% | 5.5% | 4.1% |
| 10% | −10% | 10.0% | 6.4% | 3.9% | 2.0% |
| 10% | −15% | 10.0% | 5.4% | 2.2% | −0.1% |
| 10% | −20% | 10.0% | 4.3% | 0.4% | −2.4% |
| 15% | −5% | 15.0% | 11.4% | 8.9%[1] | 7.0% |
| 15% | −10% | 15.0% | 10.4% | 7.2% | 4.9% |
| 15% | −15% | 15.0% | 9.3% | 5.5% | 2.7% |
| 15% | −20% | 15.0% | 8.3% | 3.7% | 0.4% |
| 20% | −5% | 20.0% | 15.4% | 12.3% | 9.9% |
| 20% | −10% | 20.0% | 14.4% | 10.5% | 7.7% |
| 20% | −15% | 20.0% | 13.3% | 8.7% | 5.4% |
| 20% | −20% | 20.0% | 12.2% | 6.9% | 3.1% |

| | | Final Value of $1.00 Initial Investment at End of Year 5, Year 6, Year 7, and Year 8 | | | |
|---|---|---|---|---|---|
| Compound Annual Growth Rate Through end of Initial Multiyear Period | Incremental Rate of Return for *Each Year* for 1 Year, 2 Years, or 3 Years | At End of Year 5 | Year 6 (includes 1 Year of Negative Return) | Year 7 (includes 2 Years of Negative Returns) | Year 8 (includes 3 Years of Negative Returns) |
| 10% | −5% | 1.61 | 1.53 | 1.45 | 1.38 |
| 10% | −10% | 1.61 | 1.45 | 1.30 | 1.17 |
| 10% | −15% | 1.61 | 1.37 | 1.16 | 0.99 |
| 10% | −20% | 1.61 | 1.29 | 1.03 | 0.82 |
| 15% | −5% | 2.01 | 1.91 | 1.82[1] | 1.72 |
| 15% | −10% | 2.01 | 1.81 | 1.63 | 1.47 |
| 15% | −15% | 2.01 | 1.71 | 1.45 | 1.24 |
| 15% | −20% | 2.01 | 1.61 | 1.29 | 1.03 |
| 20% | −5% | 2.49 | 2.36 | 2.25 | 2.13 |
| 20% | −10% | 2.49 | 2.24 | 2.02 | 1.81 |
| 20% | −15% | 2.49 | 2.12 | 1.80 | 1.53 |
| 20% | −20% | 2.49 | 1.99 | 1.59 | 1.27 |

[1]The 7-year compound annual growth rate (CAGR) of an initial investment of $1.00 which produces a value of $1.55 at the end of the tenth year is 8.9%. The year-by-year calculation of these values is set forth below.

Year 1:  At a CAGR of 15.0% — $1.00 times 1.15 = $1.15
Year 2:  At a CAGR of 15.0% — $1.15 times 1.15 = $1.32

Source: The author.

| Effective Compound Annual Growth Rate | | | |
| --- | --- | --- | --- |
| Through Year 10 | Through Year 11 (includes 1 Year of Negative Return) | Through Year 12 (includes 2 Years of Negative Return) | Through Year 13 (includes 3 Years of Negative Return) |
| 10.0% | 8.5% | 7.3% | 6.3% |
| 10.0% | 8.0% | 6.4% | 5.0% |
| 10.0% | 7.5% | 5.4% | 3.6% |
| 10.0% | 6.9% | 4.3% | 2.2% |
| 15.0% | 13.0% | 11.4% | 10.0% |
| 15.0% | 12.5% | 10.4% | 8.7% |
| 15.0% | 11.9% | 9.3% | 7.3% |
| 15.0% | 11.3% | 8.3% | 5.8% |
| 20.0% | 17.5% | 15.4% | 13.7% |
| 20.0% | 16.9% | 14.4% | 12.3% |
| 20.0% | 16.3% | 13.3% | 10.8% |
| 20.0% | 15.7% | 12.2% | 9.3% |

| Effective Compound Annual Growth Rate | | | |
| --- | --- | --- | --- |
| Through Year 20 | Year 21 (includes 1 Year of Negative Return) | Year 22 (includes 2 Years of Negative Returns) | Year 23 (includes 3 Years of Negative Returns) |
| 10.0% | 9.2% | 8.5% | 7.9% |
| 10.0% | 9.0% | 8.0% | 7.2% |
| 10.0% | 8.7% | 7.5% | 6.4% |
| 10.0% | 8.3% | 6.9% | 5.5% |
| 15.0% | 14.0% | 13.0% | 12.2% |
| 15.0% | 13.7% | 12.5% | 11.4% |
| 15.0% | 13.4% | 11.9% | 10.6% |
| 15.0% | 13.0% | 11.3% | 9.7% |
| 20.0% | 18.7% | 17.5% | 16.4% |
| 20.0% | 18.4% | 16.9% | 15.6% |
| 20.0% | 18.0% | 16.3% | 14.7% |
| 20.0% | 17.7% | 15.7% | 13.8% |

| Final Value of $1.00 Initial Investment at End of Year 10, Year 11, Year 12, and Year 13 | | | |
| --- | --- | --- | --- |
| At End of Year 10 | Year 11 (includes 1 Year of Negative Return) | Year 12 (includes 2 Years of Negative Returns) | Year 13 (includes 3 Years of Negative Returns) |
| 2.59 | 2.46 | 2.34 | 2.22 |
| 2.59 | 2.33 | 2.10 | 1.89 |
| 2.59 | 2.20 | 1.87 | 1.59 |
| 2.59 | 2.07 | 1.66 | 1.33 |
| 4.05 | 3.84 | 3.65 | 3.47 |
| 4.05 | 3.64 | 3.28 | 2.95 |
| 4.05 | 3.44 | 2.92 | 2.48 |
| 4.05 | 3.24 | 2.59 | 2.07 |
| 6.19 | 5.88 | 5.59 | 5.31 |
| 6.19 | 5.57 | 5.02 | 4.51 |
| 6.19 | 5.26 | 4.47 | 3.80 |
| 6.19 | 4.95 | 3.96 | 3.17 |

| Final Value of $1.00 Initial Investment at End of Year 20, Year 21, Year 22, and Year 23 | | | |
| --- | --- | --- | --- |
| At End of Year 20 | Year 21 (includes 1 Year of Negative Return) | Year 22 (includes 2 Years of Negative Returns) | Year 23 (includes 3 Years of Negative Returns) |
| 6.73 | 6.39 | 6.07 | 5.77 |
| 6.73 | 6.05 | 5.45 | 4.90 |
| 6.73 | 5.72 | 4.86 | 4.13 |
| 6.73 | 5.38 | 4.31 | 3.44 |
| 16.37 | 15.55 | 14.77 | 14.03 |
| 16.37 | 14.73 | 13.26 | 11.93 |
| 16.37 | 13.91 | 11.82 | 10.05 |
| 16.37 | 13.09 | 10.47 | 8.38 |
| 38.34 | 36.42 | 34.60 | 32.87 |
| 38.34 | 34.50 | 31.05 | 27.95 |
| 38.34 | 32.59 | 27.70 | 23.54 |
| 38.34 | 30.67 | 24.54 | 19.63 |

Year 3: At a CAGR of 15.0% — $1.32 times 1.15 = $1.52
Year 4: At a CAGR of 15.0% — $1.52 times 1.15 = $1.75
Year 5: At a CAGR of 15.0% — $1.75 times 1.15 = $2.01
Year 6: At a CAGR of −5.0% — $2.01 times 0.95 = $1.91
Year 7: At a CAGR of −5.0% — $1.91 times 0.95 = $1.82

SECTION 3

# ASSET CLASS ATTRIBUTES

C H A P T E R

# MULTIYEAR INVESTMENT PERFORMANCE OF SELECTED ASSET CLASSES

## OVERVIEW

Investors can develop meaningful perspective and insight into the nature and usefulness of various asset classes by carefully analyzing their multiyear investment performance. Two frequently cited measures of an asset's investment performance are its compound annual growth rate (CAGR) and its standard deviation of annual returns.

By studying, reflecting upon, and judiciously projecting these measures into the future, financial-market participants may: (i) track historical patterns of returns and standard deviations of returns for a variety of asset categories, subcategories, and specific investments; (ii) compare and contrast the year-by-year investment behavior of different kinds of assets under varying financial-market conditions; (iii) assess the short- and intermediate-term likelihood of an asset's deviation

from or reversion to its long-term mean returns and standard deviations characteristics; and (iv) hypothesize potential ranges for future
investment-performance data as part of portfolio construction and asset allocation rebalancing activity.

## INVESTMENT PERFORMANCE PARAMETERS

In thinking about the multiyear performance of asset classes, investors
can choose from a variety of important alternatives that may tighten or
broaden their analytical focus. Table 4.1 presents a number of these
choices, with the specific parameters selected for this chapter denoted
by shading.

In Table 4.1, *benchmark coverage* refers to the desired degree of rep-
resentativeness for an asset class. For example, investors might choose
the Standard & Poor's 500 Composite Index as a proxy for large-
capitalization U.S. equities, or the Dow Jones Utility Index of 15 stocks
as a proxy for U.S.-based utility companies. *Volatility measure* describes
whether the standard deviation is calculated based on: (i) annual returns, which do not reflect week-to-week or month-to-month volatility;
(ii) monthly returns; or (iii) returns for some other length of time. The
*length of analysis period* covers the multiperiod groupings of investment
performance, ranging from as short an interval as 1 to 2 years, to time
frames of 10 years or longer.

*Interperiod relationship* refers to whether the time periods under
analysis consist of: (i) *rolling returns,* in which successive intervals are
*added* to the multiyear analysis period, with the appropriate number of
earlier intervals *excluded* from consideration; or (ii) *nonoverlapping returns,* which separate groups of analysis periods from one another to
isolate each interval's investment performance from that of other intervals. *Reference currency* describes the investor's customary unit of monetary account, and may include U.S. dollars, euros, Japanese yen, or
other currencies. *Treatment of taxes* and *expenses* refers to whether taxes
and expenses are included or excluded from the analysis of assets'
multiyear investment performance.

Although this chapter does not consider taxes and expenses, taxable investors should factor in the effects such factors may have on
multiyear compounding of returns. Which investment performance parameter is brought to bear in a specific investment context often depends on the investor's financial goals. The factors influencing the
choice of an investment parameter include: (i) the investor's tax status

**T A B L E  4.1**

Representative Choices Among Investment Performance Parameters

| Investment Performance Parameter | Representative Choices | | |
|---|---|:---:|---|
| Benchmark Coverage | Broad-Based | ↔ | Narrow-Based |
| Volatility Measure | Standard Deviation of Annual Returns | ↔ | Standard Deviation of Monthly Returns |
| Length of Analysis Period | 10 Years | ↔ | 3 Years |
| Interperiod Relationship | Rolling Returns | ↔ | Nonoverlapping Returns |
| Reference Currency | U.S. Dollar | ↔ | Other Currencies |
| Treatment of Taxes and Expenses | Not Taken Into Account | ↔ | Taken into Account |

Source: The author.

and time horizon; (ii) the desired degree of international portfolio exposure; (iii) the kinds of assets considered; (iv) the frequency, comparability, and reliability of performance data; and (v) the volatility characteristics of the underlying assets.

## MULTIYEAR INVESTMENT PERFORMANCE DATA

For four rolling 10-year periods from 1986–1995, 1987–1996, 1988–1997, 1989–1998, 1990–1999, respectively, Table 4.2 presents values for CAGRs and standard deviations of annual returns for 44 asset classes and for the U.S. Consumer Price Index (CPI). Table 4.3 contains similar measures for four rolling 10-year periods, from 1991–2000, 1992–2001, 1993–2002, 1994–2003, and 1995–2004.

For each of the 15 calendar years from 1990 through 2004, Table 4.4 displays the annual rates of return for the 44 asset classes and the CPI inflation rate contained in Table 4.3. Similarly, for each of the 10 calendar years from 1980 through 1989, Table 4.5 displays the annual rates of return for the 43 asset classes and the CPI contained in Table 4.2.

For example, Table 4.4 and Table 4.5 show that the Lehman Brothers Aggregate Taxable Bond Index (consisting of more than 7,000 SEC-registered, taxable, U.S. dollar-denominated bond issues in the government, corporate, mortgage passthrough, and asset-backed securities sectors) experienced only two years of negative total returns during the 1980 through 2004 time interval: –2.9% in 1994, and –0.8% in 1999.

**T A B L E  4.2**

## Rolling 10-Year Investment Performance
## (Value of $1.00 Compounded Annually for Selected Asset Classes, 1986–1995 through 1990–1999)

| Percentage Total Returns Expressed in U.S. Dollars (% Compounded Annually) | Value of $1.00 on 12/31/95 | | Value of $1.00 on 12/31/96 | | Value of $1.00 on 12/31/97 | | Value of $1.00 on 12/31/98 | | Value of $1.00 on 12/31/99 | |
|---|---|---|---|---|---|---|---|---|---|---|
| | 10 Years (1986–1995) | | 10 Years (1987–1996) | | 10 Years (1988–1997) | | 10 Years (1989–1998) | | 10 Years (1990–1999) | |
| Asset Class Indices | CAGR | Std. Dev | CAGR | Std. Dev | CAGR | Std. Dev | CAGR | Std. Dev | CAGR | Std. Dev |
| **U.S. Equity Indices** | | | | | | | | | | |
| S&P 500 Index | 14.9 | 13.8 | 15.3 | 14.0 | 18.0 | 14.4 | 19.2 | 14.7 | 18.2 | 14.1 |
| S&P 400 Mid-Cap Index | 12.1 | 18.1 | 12.4 | 18.1 | 15.9 | 17.3 | 15.7 | 17.3 | 17.3 | 16.6 |
| S&P 600 Small-Cap Index | – | – | – | – | – | – | – | – | 12.2 | 20.2 |
| NASDAQ Composite (Price Return) | 12.5 | 21.7 | 14.0 | 21.7 | 16.9 | 20.5 | 19.1 | 21.5 | 24.5 | 29.6 |
| Russell 2000 Index (Smaller Cap of 3000 Index) | 8.4 | 19.3 | 9.4 | 19.2 | 12.7 | 17.5 | 9.9 | 18.3 | 13.4 | 18.4 |
| Russell 1000—Growth | 11.4 | 16.2 | 12.1 | 16.4 | 14.6 | 16.4 | 17.1 | 17.2 | 20.3 | 17.0 |
| Russell 1000—Value | 10.6 | 14.4 | 10.8 | 14.5 | 14.1 | 14.7 | 13.4 | 14.6 | 15.6 | 14.8 |
| Russell 2000—Growth | 6.9 | 20.3 | 7.7 | 20.1 | 10.2 | 18.4 | 8.3 | 18.8 | 13.5 | 21.0 |
| Russell 2000—Value | 9.6 | 19.7 | 10.9 | 19.7 | 14.9 | 18.5 | 11.2 | 19.8 | 12.5 | 20.5 |
| Wilshire 5000 | 14.2 | 14.6 | 14.7 | 14.8 | 17.6 | 14.7 | 18.1 | 14.8 | 17.6 | 14.5 |
| **Non-U.S. Equity Indices** | | | | | | | | | | |
| MSCI World Free Gross | – | – | – | – | 11.0 | 13.2 | 11.1 | 13.3 | 11.8 | 13.9 |
| MSCI World ex-U.S. Gross | – | – | – | – | – | – | – | – | – | – |
| MSCI U.S. Net | 13.7 | 13.8 | 14.4 | 14.1 | 17.4 | 14.4 | 18.9 | 14.8 | 18.1 | 14.4 |
| MSCI EAFE Net | 13.6 | 25.5 | 8.4 | 17.3 | 6.2 | 16.6 | 5.5 | 15.6 | 7.0 | 16.9 |
| MSCI Europe Free Net | 14.0 | 16.0 | 12.0 | 12.7 | 14.0 | 12.7 | 15.2 | 13.4 | 14.0 | 12.7 |
| MSCI Japan Net | 12.7 | 37.7 | 3.4 | 25.6 | (2.9) | 23.6 | (5.3) | 20.2 | -0.9 | 28.9 |
| MSCI Far East Free ex -Japan Gross | – | – | – | – | – | – | – | – | – | – |
| MSCI Emerging Global Free Latin America Gross | – | – | – | – | – | – | – | – | 19.1 | 51.8 |
| MSCI Emerging Markets Free Gross | – | – | – | – | 18.2 | 34.3 | 10.9 | 36.6 | 11.0 | 36.8 |
| **U.S. and Non-U.S. Fixed-Income Indices** | | | | | | | | | | |
| Lehman Brothers Aggregate (Taxable) [1] | 9.6 | 6.6 | 8.5 | 6.5 | 9.2 | 6.2 | 9.3 | 6.2 | 7.7 | 6.6 |
| Lehman Brothers 7-Year Municipal Bond Index | 9.4 | 9.1 | 7.2 | 6.8 | 8.6 | 5.1 | 8.1 | 5.1 | 6.6 | 5.2 |
| High Yield (CSFB Upper/Middle Tier) | – | – | 11.6 | 14.0 | 12.3 | 13.9 | 11.1 | 14.3 | 11.5 | 14.0 |
| 10-Year U.S. Treasury Note | 9.3 | 10.0 | 7.4 | 9.8 | 8.9 | 9.0 | 9.5 | 9.0 | 6.9 | 10.4 |
| International (J.P. Morgan Non-U.S. Bond) | 15.0 | 11.1 | 12.8 | 10.6 | 9.0 | 8.2 | 10.6 | 8.2 | 8.5 | 9.3 |
| Global (J.P. Morgan Global Government Bond) | – | – | 8.7 | 6.1 | 8.7 | 6.2 | 9.5 | 6.5 | 7.5 | 7.7 |
| Emerging Markets Bond Index (J.P. Morgan EMBI+) [2] | – | – | – | – | – | – | – | – | – | – |
| Morgan Stanley U.S. 225 Convertible Index [3] | – | – | – | – | – | – | – | – | – | – |

Continued

All indices are expressed in total return terms unless noted in the description. "Gross" denotes total returns inclusive of gross dividends; "Net" denotes total returns inclusive of dividends net of foreign withholding taxes; "Price Return" indicates that dividends are not included in the percentage returns data; and "Free" denotes that portion of the relevant underlying market whose securities are freely tradeable by international investors.

[1] The Lehman Brothers Aggregate Index represents securities that are U.S. domestic, taxable, and dollar denominated, and which covers the U.S. investment-grade, fixed-rate bond market. As of December 2001, the components of the index included approximately: 61% government and corporate credit; 35% mortgage-backed securities; 2% asset-backed securities; and 2% ERISA (Eligible Commercial Mortgage-Backed Securities).

[2] The EMBI+ Index is used from 1994 to the present; the EMBI Index is used for prior periods.

[3] For 1999–2002, returns are based on the Morgan Stanley U.S. 225 "Daily" Convertible Index; for 1991–1998, returns are based on the Morgan Stanley U.S. 225 "Monthly" Convertible Index.

**T A B L E 4.2**

Rolling 10-Year Investment Performance
(Value of $1.00 Compounded Annually for Selected Asset Classes,
1986–1995 through 1990–1999) (Concluded)

| Percentage Total Returns Expressed in U.S. Dollars (% Compounded Annually) | Value of $1.00 on 12/31/95 | | Value of $1.00 on 12/31/96 | | Value of $1.00 on 12/31/97 | | Value of $1.00 on 12/31/98 | | Value of $1.00 on 12/31/99 | |
|---|---|---|---|---|---|---|---|---|---|---|
| | 10 Years (1986–1995) | | 10 Years (1987–1996) | | 10 Years (1988–1997) | | 10 Years (1989–1998) | | 10 Years (1990–1999) | |
| Asset Class Indices | CAGR | Std. Dev | CAGR | Std. Dev | CAGR | Std. Dev | CAGR | Std. Dev | CAGR | Std. Dev |
| **Alternative Assets Indices** | | | | | | | | | | |
| NAREIT (Real Estate Investment Trusts) | 10.3 | 14.0 | 11.7 | 15.8 | 14.2 | 14.9 | 10.6 | 18.1 | 9.2 | 18.9 |
| NCREIF Property Index (Commercial Real Estate) | 4.0 | 5.5 | 4.2 | 5.7 | 4.8 | 6.4 | 5.4 | 7.2 | 5.7 | 7.4 |
| National Assn. of Realtors (Residential Housing) | 4.0 | 3.0 | 3.8 | 2.8 | 3.8 | 2.8 | 3.8 | 2.8 | 4.0 | 2.7 |
| NCREIF Farmland Index (U.S. Farmland) | 2.1 | 10.6 | 4.9 | 8.4 | 7.8 | 1.4 | 8.1 | 0.9 | 7.9 | 1.1 |
| Cambridge Associates Private Equity Funds Index | 11.3 | 7.8 | 13.8 | 8.2 | 16.5 | 8.7 | 16.8 | 8.6 | 19.0 | 9.6 |
| Cambridge Associates Venture Funds Index | 14.1 | 13.9 | 17.3 | 15.9 | 20.3 | 16.4 | 22.8 | 15.1 | 39.3 | 80.6 |
| Venture Economics All Private Equity Fund Index | 12.1 | 14.8 | 15.3 | 15.5 | 17.8 | 15.2 | 18.7 | 14.8 | 29.6 | 43.7 |
| HFRI Fund Weighted Composite Hedge Fund Index | – | – | – | – | – | – | – | – | 18.3 | 11.3 |
| HFRI Fund of Funds Index | – | – | – | – | – | – | – | – | 12.6 | 10.5 |
| MSCI Hedge Fund Composite Index[4] | | | | | | | | | | |
| Commodity Research Bureau Total Return Index | 5.9 | 7.6 | 7.2 | 7.4 | 5.8 | 6.3 | 1.9 | 9.6 | 1.7 | 9.5 |
| Barclay CTA Index (Commodity Trading Advisor) | 12.1 | 17.6 | 12.7 | 17.4 | 8.8 | 8.2 | 7.4 | 6.9 | 7.1 | 7.2 |
| Handy & Harmon Spot Gold Price | 1.6 | 13.0 | (0.7) | 11.5 | (5.1) | 10.5 | (3.5) | 9.9 | (3.2) | 10.0 |
| Handy & Harmon Spot Silver Price | (1.3) | 18.1 | (1.3) | 18.1 | (1.2) | 18.2 | (1.7) | 18.6 | 0.4 | 18.1 |
| Lehman Brothers TIPS Index/Bridgewater[5] | 8.3 | 2.5 | 8.3 | 2.5 | 7.8 | 3.1 | 7.3 | 3.3 | 6.4 | 3.4 |
| Mei Moses Fine Art Index | 9.6 | 28.6 | 10.9 | 28.1 | 5.3 | 27.4 | 2.2 | 21.1 | 1.0 | 20.0 |
| **U.S. Cash Equivalent Indices** | | | | | | | | | | |
| Citigroup 90-Day U.S. Treasury Bill Index | 5.8 | 1.8 | 5.7 | 1.8 | 5.6 | 1.8 | 5.5 | 1.7 | 5.1 | 1.3 |
| Inflation (CPI-U) | 3.5 | 1.4 | 3.7 | 1.2 | 3.4 | 1.3 | 3.1 | 1.3 | 2.9 | 1.2 |

[4]The MSCI Hedge Fund Composite Index is equal weighted. The index was launched in 2002 and back calculated to 1994.

[5]The synthetically constructed Bridgewater Strategic Benchmark U.S. TIPS 8-year Duration Index is used for the January 1971 through February 1997 time period; the Lehman Brothers TIPS Index is used after February 1997.

Sources: Morgan Stanley Investment Management; Hedge Fund Research; Morgan Stanley IIG Asset Allocation Group.

Past performance is not a guarantee of future results.

To show how the 10-year rolling returns are calculated for each asset class, Table 4.6 displays 1990 through 2004 total returns data for the Standard & Poor's 500 Index, with boxes to denote each succeeding 10-year investment interval.

One dollar invested in the Standard & Poor's 500 Index on January 1, 1990 would have grown to a final value of $5.33 on December, 31, 1999, a 10-year CAGR of 18.2%. The 1990 through 1999 CAGR of 18.2%, representing the *geometric mean return* for this 10-year interval, differs from its *arithmetic mean return* of 19.0% (calculated by adding

# T A B L E  4.3

## Rolling 10-Year Investment Performance
## (Value of $1.00 Compounded Annually for Selected Asset Classes, 1991–2000 through 1995–2004)

| Percentage Total Returns Expressed in U.S. Dollars (% Compounded Annually) | Value of $1.00 on 12/31/00 | | Value of $1.00 on 12/31/01 | | Value of $1.00 on 12/31/02 | | Value of $1.00 on 12/31/03 | | Value of $1.00 on 12/31/04 | |
|---|---|---|---|---|---|---|---|---|---|---|
| | 10 Years (1991–2000) | | 10 Years (1992–2001) | | 10 Years (1993–2002) | | 10 Years (1994–2003) | | 10 Years (1995–2004) | |
| Asset Class Indices | CAGR | Std. Dev | CAGR | Std. Dev | CAGR | Std. Dev | CAGR | Std. Dev | CAGR | Std. Dev |
| **U.S. Equity Indices** | | | | | | | | | | |
| S&P 500 Index | 17.5 | 15.3 | 12.9 | 17.3 | 9.3 | 20.7 | 11.1 | 21.5 | 12.1 | 21.1 |
| S&P 400 Mid-Cap Index | 19.8 | 14.4 | 15.0 | 11.5 | 12.0 | 14.9 | 13.9 | 16.6 | 16.1 | 15.2 |
| S&P 600 Small-Cap Index | 16.9 | 14.9 | 13.2 | 11.4 | 9.5 | 14.2 | 11.3 | 16.8 | 14.3 | 15.7 |
| NASDAQ Composite (Price Return) | 20.8 | 33.8 | 12.8 | 34.7 | 7.0 | 38.0 | 9.9 | 39.8 | 11.2 | 39.3 |
| Russell 2000 Index (Smaller Cap of 3000 Index) | 15.5 | 15.5 | 11.5 | 12.0 | 7.2 | 15.5 | 9.5 | 19.7 | 11.5 | 19.3 |
| Russell 1000—Growth | 17.3 | 21.1 | 10.8 | 22.9 | 6.7 | 26.3 | 9.2 | 26.8 | 9.6 | 26.7 |
| Russell 1000—Value | 17.3 | 12.6 | 14.1 | 14.3 | 10.8 | 17.3 | 11.9 | 18.1 | 13.8 | 17.3 |
| Russell 2000—Growth | 12.8 | 21.9 | 7.2 | 18.9 | 2.6 | 22.5 | 5.4 | 26.4 | 7.1 | 26.2 |
| Russell 2000—Value | 17.6 | 16.2 | 15.1 | 14.0 | 10.9 | 15.6 | 12.7 | 18.7 | 15.2 | 18.0 |
| Wilshire 5000 | 17.0 | 15.4 | 12.3 | 16.7 | 8.7 | 19.9 | 10.5 | 20.9 | 11.8 | 20.5 |
| **Non-U.S. Equity Indices** | | | | | | | | | | |
| MSCI World Free Gross | 12.3 | 13.1 | 8.4 | 15.8 | 6.5 | 17.9 | 7.4 | 19.1 | 8.4 | 19.2 |
| MSCI World ex-U.S. Gross | 8.6 | 15.0 | 4.9 | 17.8 | 4.4 | 18.2 | 5.0 | 19.5 | 6.2 | 20.1 |
| MSCI U.S. Net | 16.9 | 16.3 | 12.3 | 18.2 | 8.8 | 21.6 | 10.5 | 22.3 | 11.5 | 21.9 |
| MSCI EAFE Net | 8.2 | 15.2 | 4.5 | 17.9 | 4.0 | 18.3 | 4.5 | 19.4 | 5.6 | 19.9 |
| MSCI Europe Free Net | 13.5 | 13.5 | 9.6 | 17.3 | 8.0 | 19.1 | 8.7 | 20.4 | 10.5 | 20.4 |
| MSCI Japan Net | 0.3 | 27.8 | (4.0) | 29.5 | (2.7) | 28.8 | (1.9) | 30.0 | (2.3) | 29.6 |
| MSCI Far East Free ex-Japan Gross | 5.4 | 45.0 | 2.4 | 44.8 | (0.6) | 44.9 | (3.9) | 33.3 | (0.3) | 32.8 |
| MSCI Emerging Global Free Latin America Gross | 18.3 | 52.3 | 8.0 | 31.5 | 3.7 | 33.2 | 5.1 | 36.9 | 8.6 | 37.8 |
| MSCI Emerging Markets Free Gross | 8.3 | 38.9 | 3.1 | 35.6 | 1.3 | 35.8 | 0.2 | 32.1 | 3.3 | 32.5 |
| **U.S. and Non-U.S. Fixed-Income Indices** | | | | | | | | | | |
| Lehman Brothers Aggregate (Taxable) [1] | 8.0 | 6.7 | 7.2 | 6.2 | 7.5 | 6.2 | 7.0 | 6.3 | 7.7 | 5.3 |
| Lehman Brothers 7-Year Municipal Bond Index | 6.8 | 5.2 | 6.1 | 4.9 | 6.3 | 5.1 | 5.9 | 4.9 | 6.5 | 4.0 |
| High Yield (CSFB Upper/Middle Tier) | 11.7 | 13.7 | 8.3 | 8.3 | 7.0 | 7.9 | 7.8 | 9.7 | 9.1 | 9.2 |
| 10-Year U.S. Treasury Note | 7.7 | 10.6 | 6.4 | 10.2 | 7.2 | 10.4 | 6.1 | 10.5 | 7.5 | 9.3 |
| International (J.P. Morgan Non-U.S. Bond) | 6.7 | 9.6 | 4.7 | 9.6 | 5.8 | 9.8 | 6.2 | 10.3 | 6.9 | 10.4 |
| Global (J.P. Morgan Global Government Bond) | 6.9 | 7.9 | 5.3 | 7.7 | 6.7 | 8.8 | 6.9 | 9.0 | 7.8 | 8.8 |
| Emerging Markets Bond Index (J.P. Morgan EMBI+) [2] | 15.8 | 21.8 | 11.9 | 21.1 | 12.7 | 21.0 | 11.4 | 19.1 | 15.0 | 15.5 |
| Morgan Stanley U.S. 225 Convertible Index [3] | 15.3 | 18.3 | 11.4 | 18.5 | 8.5 | 19.5 | 8.8 | 19.8 | 10.1 | 19.1 |

Continued

All indices are expressed in total return terms unless noted in the description. "Gross" denotes total returns inclusive of gross dividends; "Net" denotes total returns inclusive of dividends net of foreign withholding taxes; "Price Return" indicates that dividends are not included in the percentage returns data; and "Free" denotes that portion of the relevant underlying market whose securities are freely tradeable by international investors.

[1] The Lehman Brothers Aggregate Index represents securities that are U.S. domestic, taxable, and dollar denominated, and which covers the U.S. investment-grade, fixed-rate bond market. As of December 2001, the components of the index included approximately: 61% government and corporate credit; 35% mortgage-backed securities; 2% asset-backed securities; and 2% ERISA (Eligible Commercial Mortgage-Backed Securities).

[2] The EMBI+ Index is used from 1994 to the present; the EMBI Index is used for prior periods.

[3] For 1999–2004, returns are based on the Morgan Stanley U.S. 225 "Daily" Convertible Index; for 1991–1998, returns are based on the Morgan Stanley U.S. 225 "Monthly" Convertible Index.

[4] The MSCI Hedge Fund Composite Index is equal weighted. The index was launched in 2002 and back calculated to 1994.

[5] The synthetically constructed Bridgewater Strategic Benchmark U.S. TIPS 8-Year Duration Index is used for the January 1971 through February 1997 time period; the Lehman Brothers TIPS Index is used after February 1997.

**T A B L E  4.3**

Rolling 10-Year Investment Performance
(Value of $1.00 Compounded Annually for Selected Asset Classes,
1991–2000 through 1995–2004) (Concluded)

| Percentage Total Returns Expressed in U.S. Dollars (% Compounded Annually) | Value of $1.00 on 12/31/00 10 Years (1991–2000) | | Value of $1.00 on 12/31/01 10 Years (1992–2001) | | Value of $1.00 on 12/31/02 10 Years (1993–2002) | | Value of $1.00 on 12/31/03 10 Years (1994–2003) | | Value of $1.00 on 12/31/04 10 Years (1995–2004) | |
|---|---|---|---|---|---|---|---|---|---|---|
| Asset Class Indices | CAGR | Std. Dev | CAGR | Std. Dev | CAGR | Std. Dev | CAGR | Std. Dev | CAGR | Std. Dev |
| **Alternative Assets Indices** | | | | | | | | | | |
| NAREIT (Real Estate Investment Trusts) | 13.6 | 17.0 | 11.7 | 15.3 | 10.6 | 15.6 | 12.1 | 17.4 | 14.8 | 17.9 |
| NCREIF Property Index (Commercial Real Estate) | 6.7 | 7.5 | 8.1 | 6.1 | 9.3 | 4.3 | 10.0 | 3.3 | 10.9 | 3.3 |
| National Assn. of Realtors (Residential Housing) | 4.6 | 2.0 | 4.5 | 1.7 | 4.8 | 1.6 | 5.4 | 2.3 | 6.1 | 2.3 |
| NCREIF Farmland Index (U.S. Farmland) | 7.5 | 1.5 | 6.7 | 2.5 | 5.9 | 3.7 | 6.0 | 3.8 | 7.0 | 5.7 |
| Cambridge Associates Private Equity Funds Index | 18.7 | 10.2 | 16.3 | 13.8 | 13.7 | 16.1 | 13.6 | 16.0 | 14.4 | 16.1 |
| Cambridge Associates Venture Funds Index | 41.8 | 79.5 | 32.1 | 84.4 | 27.0 | 86.7 | 23.6 | 88.1 | 23.8 | 86.5 |
| Venture Economics All Private Equity Fund Index | 32.9 | 41.8 | 27.3 | 45.5 | 24.5 | 47.4 | 23.2 | 47.5 | 24.2 | 47.1 |
| HFRI Fund Weighted Composite Hedge Fund Index | 18.2 | 11.4 | 15.4 | 11.1 | 13.1 | 12.2 | 11.8 | 10.7 | 12.6 | 10.5 |
| HFRI Fund of Funds Index | 11.2 | 10.7 | 10.0 | 11.0 | 8.8 | 11.4 | 7.5 | 9.8 | 8.6 | 9.0 |
| MSCI Hedge Fund Composite Index[4] | – | – | – | – | – | – | – | – | 13.9 | 8.1 |
| Commodity Research Bureau Total Return Index | 2.5 | 10.3 | 1.0 | 12.0 | 3.1 | 12.9 | 3.6 | 13.1 | 3.8 | 13.2 |
| Barclay CTA Index (Commodity Trading Advisor) | 5.9 | 5.4 | 5.6 | 5.6 | 6.9 | 5.4 | 6.7 | 5.3 | 7.2 | 4.9 |
| Handy & Harmon Spot Gold Price | (3.6) | 10.0 | (2.4) | 9.8 | 0.3 | 12.8 | 0.6 | 13.3 | 1.3 | 13.3 |
| Handy & Harmon Spot Silver Price | 1.0 | 17.5 | 1.9 | 17.2 | 2.6 | 17.0 | 1.6 | 14.5 | 3.5 | 14.7 |
| Lehman Brothers TIPS Index/Bridgewater[5] | 6.7 | 3.8 | 6.7 | 3.8 | 7.1 | 4.1 | 7.1 | 4.1 | 7.7 | 3.9 |
| Mei Moses Fine Art Index | 1.6 | 20.3 | 6.4 | 14.9 | 4.2 | 14.9 | 7.2 | 15.0 | – | – |
| **U.S. Cash Equivalent Indices** | | | | | | | | | | |
| Citigroup 90-Day U.S. Treasury Bill Index | 4.9 | 1.0 | 4.7 | 1.0 | 4.9 | 1.3 | 4.2 | 1.7 | 3.8 | 1.9 |
| Inflation (CPI-U) | 2.7 | 0.6 | 2.5 | 0.6 | 2.8 | 0.6 | 2.2 | 0.6 | 2.0 | 0.6 |

Sources: Morgan Stanley Investment Management; Hedge Fund Research; Morgan Stanley IIG Asset Allocation Group.
Past performance is not a guarantee of future results.

together each year's investment return for 1990 through 1999 and dividing the sum by 10).

The 1991 through 2000 period excludes the –3.1% total return for 1990 from the calculation interval and includes the –9.1% total return for 2000. An investment of $1.00 in the S&P 500 Index on January 1, 1991 would have grown to a final value of $5.00 on December 31, 2000, a 10-year CAGR of 17.5%, compared to an arithmetic mean return of 18.4% during the same period.

The 1992 through 2001 period excludes the 30.5% total return for 1991 from the calculation interval and includes the –11.9% total return for 2001. An investment of $1.00 in the S&P 500 Index on January 1, 1992 would have grown to a final value of $3.37 on December 31, 2001,

## T A B L E  4.4

### Assets' Annual Rates of Return by Year, 1990–2004

**Percentage Total Returns
Expressed in U.S. Dollars**

| Asset Class Indices | 1990 | 1991 | 1992 | 1993 | 1994 |
|---|---|---|---|---|---|
| **U.S. Equity Indices** | | | | | |
| S&P 500 Index | (3.1)% | 30.5% | 7.7% | 10.0% | 1.3% |
| S&P 400 Mid-Cap Index | (5.1) | 50.1 | 11.9 | 13.9 | (3.6) |
| S&P 600 Small-Cap Index | (25.4) | 45.9 | 19.4 | 17.6 | (5.7) |
| NASDAQ Composite (Price Return) | (17.8) | 56.8 | 15.5 | 14.8 | (3.2) |
| Russell 2000 Index (Smaller Cap of 3000 Index) | (19.5) | 46.0 | 18.4 | 18.9 | (1.8) |
| Russell 1000—Growth | (0.3) | 41.3 | 5.0 | 2.9 | 2.6 |
| Russell 1000—Value | (8.1) | 24.6 | 13.6 | 18.1 | (2.0) |
| Russell 2000—Growth | (17.4) | 51.2 | 7.8 | 13.4 | (2.4) |
| Russell 2000—Value | (21.8) | 41.7 | 29.1 | 23.8 | (1.5) |
| Wilshire 5000 | (6.2) | 34.2 | 9.0 | 11.3 | (0.1) |
| **Non-U.S. Equity Indices** | | | | | |
| MSCI World Free Gross | (16.5)% | 19.1% | (4.6)% | 23.2% | 5.1% |
| MSCI World ex-U.S. Gross | – | 12.4 | (11.9) | 32.6 | 7.3 |
| MSCI U.S. Net | (3.2) | 30.1 | 6.4 | 9.1 | 1.1 |
| MSCI EAFE Net | (23.5) | 12.1 | (12.2) | 32.6 | 7.8 |
| MSCI Europe Free Net | (3.9) | 13.1 | (4.7) | 29.3 | 2.3 |
| MSCI Japan Net | (36.1) | 8.9 | (21.5) | 25.5 | 21.4 |
| MSCI Far East Free ex-Japan Gross | – | 31.0 | 21.8 | 103.4 | (19.0) |
| MSCI Emerging Global Free Latin America Gross | (7.8) | 146.2 | 17.0 | 52.3 | 0.6 |
| MSCI Emerging Markets Free Gross | (10.6) | 59.9 | 11.4 | 74.8 | (7.3) |
| **U.S. and Non-U.S. Fixed-Income Indices** | | | | | |
| Lehman Brothers Aggregate (Taxable) [1] | 9.0% | 16.0% | 7.4% | 9.8% | (2.9)% |
| Lehman Brothers 7-Year Municipal Bond Index | 7.4 | 11.7 | 8.1 | 10.4 | (2.8) |
| High Yield (CSFB Upper/Middle Tier) | (6.4) | 43.8 | 16.6 | 18.9 | (0.4) |
| 10-Year U.S. Treasury Note | 6.8 | 17.2 | 6.5 | 11.8 | (7.9) |
| International (J.P. Morgan Non-U.S. Bond) | 15.6 | 15.9 | 1.6 | 14.5 | 4.9 |
| Global (J.P. Morgan Global Government Bond) | 8.6 | 15.5 | 4.6 | 12.3 | 1.3 |
| Emerging Markets Bond Index (J.P. Morgan EMBI+) [2] | – | 38.8 | 6.9 | 44.2 | (18.9) |
| Morgan Stanley U.S. 225 Convertible Index [3] | – | 32.8 | 18.8 | 19.3 | (4.7) |

| Year | | | | | | | | | Full Year 2004 |
| 1995 | 1996 | 1997 | 1998 | 1999 | 2000 | 2001 | 2002 | 2003 | |
|---|---|---|---|---|---|---|---|---|---|
| 37.4% | 23.1% | 33.4% | 28.6% | 21.0% | (9.1)% | (11.9)% | (22.1)% | 28.7% | 10.9% |
| 30.9 | 19.2 | 32.3 | 19.1 | 14.7 | 17.5 | (0.6) | (14.5) | 35.6 | 16.5 |
| 30.0 | 21.3 | 25.6 | (1.3) | 12.4 | 11.8 | 6.6 | (14.6) | 38.8 | 22.6 |
| 39.9 | 22.7 | 21.6 | 39.6 | 85.6 | (39.3) | (21.1) | (31.5) | 50.0 | 8.6 |
| 28.5 | 16.5 | 22.4 | (2.6) | 21.3 | (3.0) | 2.5 | (20.5) | 47.3 | 18.3 |
| 37.2 | 23.1 | 30.5 | 38.7 | 33.2 | (22.4) | (20.4) | (27.9) | 29.8 | 6.3 |
| 38.4 | 21.6 | 35.2 | 15.6 | 7.4 | 7.0 | (5.6) | (15.5) | 30.0 | 16.5 |
| 31.0 | 11.3 | 13.0 | 1.2 | 43.1 | (22.4) | (9.2) | (30.3) | 48.5 | 14.3 |
| 25.8 | 21.4 | 31.8 | (6.5) | (1.5) | 22.8 | 14.0 | (11.4) | 46.0 | 22.3 |
| 36.5 | 21.0 | 31.3 | 23.4 | 23.6 | (10.9) | (11.0) | (20.9) | 30.6 | 12.6 |
| | | | | | | | | | |
| 20.7% | 13.5% | 16.2% | 24.8% | 25.2% | (12.9)% | (16.5)% | (19.5)% | 33.8% | 15.3% |
| 11.8 | 6.9 | 2.6 | 19.1 | 28.3 | (13.2) | (21.2) | (15.5) | 40.0 | 20.8 |
| 37.1 | 23.2 | 33.4 | 30.1 | 21.9 | (12.8) | (12.4) | (23.1) | 28.4 | 10.1 |
| 11.2 | 6.0 | 1.8 | 20.0 | 27.0 | (14.2) | (21.4) | (15.9) | 38.6 | 20.3 |
| 21.6 | 21.1 | 23.8 | 28.5 | 15.9 | (8.4) | (19.9) | (18.4) | 38.5 | 20.9 |
| 0.7 | (15.5) | (23.7) | 5.1 | 61.5 | (28.2) | (29.4) | (10.3) | 35.9 | 15.9 |
| 8.8 | 11.1 | (45.5) | (4.8) | 62.1 | (36.8) | (2.1) | (9.2) | 45.0 | 14.2 |
| (15.8) | 18.9 | 31.7 | (35.3) | 65.5 | (14.0) | (0.4) | (22.5) | 73.7 | 39.6 |
| (5.2) | 6.0 | (11.6) | (25.3) | 66.4 | (30.6) | (2.4) | (6.0) | 56.3 | 26.0 |
| | | | | | | | | | |
| 18.5% | 3.6% | 9.7% | 8.7% | (0.8)% | 11.6% | 8.4% | 10.3% | 4.1% | 4.3% |
| 14.1 | 4.4 | 7.7 | 6.2 | (0.1) | 9.1 | 5.2 | 10.4 | 5.4 | 3.2 |
| 17.8 | 13.0 | 13.0 | 1.9 | 3.9 | (4.2) | 5.8 | 3.1 | 27.9 | 12.0 |
| 23.7 | 0.1 | 11.3 | 12.9 | (8.4) | 14.5 | 4.0 | 14.7 | 1.3 | 4.9 |
| 21.1 | 5.3 | (3.8) | 18.3 | (4.5) | (2.5) | (3.6) | 12.7 | 18.8 | 12.1 |
| 19.3 | 4.4 | 1.4 | 15.3 | (5.1) | 2.3 | (0.8) | 19.4 | 14.5 | 10.1 |
| 26.8 | 39.3 | 13.0 | (14.4) | 26.0 | 15.7 | (0.8) | 14.2 | 28.8 | 11.8 |
| 24.7 | 15.1 | 18.5 | 6.7 | 49.7 | (15.1) | (5.8) | (8.8) | 23.4 | 7.1 |

Continued

**T A B L E  4.4**

Assets' Annual Rates of Return by Year, 1990–Present (Concluded)

**Percentage Total Returns
Expressed in U.S. Dollars**

| Asset Class Indices | 1990 | 1991 | 1992 | 1993 | 1994 |
|---|---|---|---|---|---|
| **Alternative Assets Indices** | | | | | |
| NAREIT (Real Estate Investment Trusts) | (15.4)% | 35.7% | 14.6% | 19.7% | 3.2% |
| NCREIF Property Index (Commercial Real Estate) | 2.3 | (5.6) | (4.3) | 1.4 | 6.4 |
| National Assn. of Realtors (Residential Housing) | (1.1) | 9.4 | 2.4 | 4.9 | 2.5 |
| NCREIF Farmland Index (U.S. Farmland) | 8.2 | 8.9 | 6.3 | 8.2 | 8.7 |
| Cambridge Associates Private Equity Funds Index | 4.4 | 8.6 | 14.4 | 24.5 | 12.0 |
| Cambridge Associates Venture Funds Index | 2.3 | 24.1 | 11.5 | 19.9 | 17.8 |
| Venture Economics All Private Equity Fund Index | (5.0) | 22.4 | 14.0 | 28.5 | 7.4 |
| HFRI Fund Weighted Composite Hedge Fund Index | 5.8 | 32.2 | 21.2 | 30.9 | 4.1 |
| HFRI Fund of Funds Index | 17.5 | 14.5 | 12.3 | 26.3 | (3.5) |
| MSCI Hedge Fund Composite Index[4] | – | – | – | – | – |
| Commodity Research Bureau Total Return Index | 5.1 | (4.0) | (3.2) | 6.1 | 10.2 |
| Barclay CTA Index (Commodity Trading Advisor) | 21.0 | 3.7 | (0.9) | 10.4 | (0.7) |
| Handy & Harmon Spot Gold Price | (2.5) | (10.1) | (5.6) | 17.5 | (2.4) |
| Handy & Harmon Spot Silver Price | (19.3) | (7.9) | (4.7) | 38.4 | (4.1) |
| Lehman Brothers TIPS Index/Bridgewater[5] | 10.8 | 7.8 | 7.3 | 9.2 | 3.2 |
| Mei Moses Fine Art Index | 9.5 | (36.2) | 17.1 | (8.1) | (9.6) |
| **U.S. Cash Equivalent Indices** | | | | | |
| Citicorp 90-Day U.S. Treasury Bill Index | 7.9% | 5.8% | 3.6% | 3.1% | 4.2% |
| Inflation (CPI-U) | 6.1 | 3.0 | 3.0 | 2.8 | 2.6 |

All indices are expressed in total return terms unless noted in the description. "Gross" denotes total returns inclusive of gross dividends; "Net" denotes total returns inclusive of dividends net of foreign withholding taxes; "Price Return" indicates that dividends are not included in the percentage returns data; and "Free" denotes that portion of the relevant underlying market whose securities are freely tradeable by international investors.

[1]The Lehman Brothers Aggregate Index represents securities that are U.S. domestic, taxable, and dollar denominated, and which covers the U.S. investment-grade, fixed-rate bond market. As of December 2001, the components of the index included approximately: 61% government and corporate credit; 35% mortgage-backed securities; 2% asset-backed securities; and 2% ERISA (Eligible Commercial Mortgage-Backed Securities).

[2]The EMBI+ Index is used from 1994 to the present; the EMBI Index is used for prior periods.

[3]For 1999–2004, returns are based on the Morgan Stanley U.S. 225 "Daily" Convertible Index; for 1991–1998, returns are based on the Morgan Stanley U.S. 225 "Monthly" Convertible Index.

a 10-year CAGR of 12.9%, compared to an arithmetic mean return of 14.2% during the same period.

The 1993 through 2002 period excludes the 7.7% total return for 1992 from the calculation interval and includes the –22.1% total return

| | Year | | | | | | | | Full Year 2004 |
|---|---|---|---|---|---|---|---|---|---|
| 1995 | 1996 | 1997 | 1998 | 1999 | 2000 | 2001 | 2002 | 2003 | |
| 15.3% | 35.3% | 20.3% | (17.5)% | (4.6)% | 26.4% | 13.9% | 3.8% | 37.1% | 31.6% |
| 7.5 | 10.3 | 13.9 | 16.3 | 11.4 | 12.3 | 7.4 | 6.7 | 8.7 | 14.5 |
| 4.2 | 4.7 | 6.0 | 3.7 | 4.0 | 4.5 | 9.6 | 6.1 | 8.9 | 9.3 |
| 8.9 | 9.0 | 7.7 | 7.2 | 5.9 | 4.8 | 0.9 | (1.8) | 9.7 | 18.1 |
| 23.2 | 26.8 | 29.9 | 15.4 | 32.4 | 0.1 | (11.9) | (7.9) | 23.2 | 23.5 |
| 48.3 | 42.3 | 37.3 | 27.5 | 271.0 | 29.9 | (39.0) | (31.2) | (1.8) | 15.4 |
| 44.0 | 33.6 | 28.5 | 17.5 | 152.4 | 22.1 | (20.4) | (11.0) | 18.3 | 16.4 |
| 21.5 | 21.1 | 16.8 | 2.6 | 31.3 | 5.0 | 4.6 | (1.5) | 17.5 | 9.0 |
| 11.1 | 14.4 | 16.2 | (5.1) | 26.5 | 4.1 | 2.8 | 1.0 | 11.3 | 6.9 |
| 26.0 | 17.9 | 18.0 | 7.6 | 26.3 | 14.9 | 7.5 | 2.7 | 14.7 | 6.5 |
| 8.9 | 12.0 | 4.4 | (20.5) | 2.1 | 14.3 | (17.2) | 18.4 | 11.2 | 12.5 |
| 13.6 | 9.1 | 10.9 | 7.0 | (1.2) | 7.9 | 0.8 | 12.2 | 8.7 | 3.3 |
| 1.2 | (4.6) | (22.2) | 0.6 | 0.5 | (6.7) | 2.1 | 24.7 | 20.9 | 4.5 |
| 4.9 | (7.4) | 25.8 | (15.1) | 6.9 | (14.8) | 1.1 | 1.6 | 26.1 | 15.0 |
| 11.2 | 6.9 | 2.1 | 3.9 | 2.4 | 13.2 | 7.9 | 11.8 | 9.4 | 8.5 |
| 32.5 | 8.5 | (14.6) | 18.6 | 11.8 | 16.2 | 0.8 | (4.9) | 21.7 | 13.0 |
| | | | | | | | | | |
| 5.8% | 5.3% | 5.3% | 5.1% | 4.7% | 6.0% | 4.1% | 1.7% | 1.1% | 1.2% |
| 2.6 | 3.2 | 1.7 | 1.6 | 2.7 | 3.4 | 1.8 | 2.7 | 1.8 | 2.3 |

[4]Data are through September 30, 2004.

[5]Data are through November 30, 2004.

[6]Data are through June 30, 2004.

[7]The MSCI Hedge Fund Composite Index is equal weighted. The index was launched in 2002 and back calculated to 1994.

[8]The synthetically constructed Bridgewater Strategic Benchmark U.S. TIPS 8-Year Duration Index is used for the January 1971 through February 1997 time period; the Lehman Brothers TIPS Index is used after February 1997.

Sources: Morgan Stanley Investment Management; Hedge Fund Research; Morgan Stanley IIG Asset Allocation Group.

Past performance is not a guarantee of future results.

for 2002. An investment of $1.00 in the S&P 500 Index on January 1, 1993 would have grown to a final value of $2.44 on December 31, 2002, a 10-year CAGR of 9.3%, compared to an *arithmetic mean return* of 11.2% during the same period.

## T A B L E 4.5

### Assets' Annual Rates of Return by Year, 1980–1989

| Percentage Total Returns Expressed in U.S. Dollars | | Year | |
| --- | --- | --- | --- |
| Asset Class Indices | 1980 | 1981 | 1982 |
| **U.S. Equity Indices** | | | |
| S&P 500 Index | 32.5% | (4.9)% | 21.5% |
| S&P 400 Mid-Cap Index | – | – | 22.7 |
| S&P 600 Small-Cap Index | – | – | – |
| NASDAQ Composite (Price Return) | 33.9 | (3.2) | 18.7 |
| Russell 2000 Index (Smaller Cap of 3000 Index) | (38.6) | 2.0 | 25.0 |
| Russell 1000 – Growth | (39.6) | (11.3) | 20.5 |
| Russell 1000 – Value | (24.4) | 1.3 | 20.0 |
| Russell 2000 – Growth | (52.3) | (9.2) | 21.0 |
| Russell 2000 – Value | (25.4) | 14.9 | 28.5 |
| Wilshire 5000 | 33.7 | (3.8) | 18.7 |
| **Non-U.S. Equity Indices** | | | |
| MSCI World Free Gross | – | – | – |
| MSCI World ex-U.S. Gross | – | – | – |
| MSCI U.S. Net | – | (5.7) | 20.0 |
| MSCI EAFE Net | 22.6 | (2.3) | (1.9) |
| MSCI Europe Free Net | 11.9 | (12.5) | 4.0 |
| MSCI Japan Net | 29.7 | 15.5 | (0.9) |
| MSCI Far East Free ex-Japan Gross | – | – | – |
| MSCI Emerging Global Free Latin America Gross | – | – | – |
| MSCI Emerging Markets Free Gross | – | – | – |
| **U.S. and Non-U.S. Fixed-Income Indices** | | | |
| Lehman Brothers Aggregate (Taxable)[1] | 2.7% | 6.3% | 32.6% |
| Lehman Brothers 7-Year Municipal Bond Index | (17.6) | (15.5) | 47.9 |
| High Yield (First Boston Upper/Middle Tier) | – | – | – |
| 10-Year U.S. Treasury Note | (0.1) | 5.4 | 33.5 |
| International (J.P. Morgan Non-U.S. Bond) | – | – | – |
| Global (J.P. Morgan Global Government Bond) | – | – | – |
| Emerging Markets Bond Index (J.P. Morgan EMBI+)[2] | – | – | – |
| Morgan Stanley U.S. 225 Convertible Index[3] | – | – | – |

| | | | Year | | | |
|---|---|---|---|---|---|---|
| **1983** | **1984** | **1985** | **1986** | **1987** | **1988** | **1989** |
| 22.6% | 6.3% | 31.7% | 18.7% | 5.3% | 16.6% | 31.7% |
| 26.1 | 1.2 | 35.6 | 16.2 | (2.0) | 20.9 | 35.5 |
| – | – | – | – | – | – | – |
| 19.9 | (11.2) | 31.4 | 7.4 | (5.3) | 15.4 | 19.3 |
| 29.1 | (7.3) | 31.1 | 5.7 | (8.8) | 25.0 | 16.3 |
| 16.0 | (1.0) | 32.9 | 15.4 | 5.3 | 11.3 | 35.9 |
| 28.3 | 10.1 | 31.5 | 20.0 | 0.5 | 23.2 | 25.2 |
| 20.1 | (15.8) | 31.0 | 3.6 | (10.5) | 20.4 | 20.2 |
| 38.6 | 2.3 | 31.0 | 7.4 | (7.1) | 29.5 | 12.4 |
| 23.5 | 3.0 | 32.6 | 16.1 | 2.3 | 17.9 | 29.2 |
| | | | | | | |
| – | – | – | – | – | 23.9% | 17.2% |
| – | – | – | – | – | – | – |
| 20.4 | 4.5 | 31.1 | 16.3 | 2.9 | 14.6 | 30.0 |
| 23.7 | 7.4 | 56.2 | 69.4 | 24.6 | 28.3 | 10.5 |
| 21.0 | 0.6 | 78.9 | 43.9 | 3.7 | 15.8 | 28.5 |
| 24.5 | `16.9 | 43.1 | 99.4 | 43.0 | 35.4 | 1.7 |
| – | – | – | – | – | – | – |
| – | – | – | – | – | – | – |
| – | – | – | – | – | 40.4 | 65.0 |
| | | | | | | |
| 8.4% | 15.2% | 22.1% | 15.3% | 2.8% | 7.9% | 14.5% |
| 3.3 | 8.4 | 24.0 | 27.3 | (5.1) | 11.5 | 14.6 |
| – | – | – | – | 6.5 | 13.7 | 0.4 |
| 2.9 | 14.3 | 27.3 | 19.7 | (3.2) | 6.4 | 16.4 |
| – | – | – | 28.1 | 36.1 | 1.8 | 15.6 |
| – | – | – | – | 2.2 | 6.8 | 14.0 |
| – | – | – | – | – | – | – |
| – | – | – | – | – | – | – |

Continued

## T A B L E   4.5

### Assets' Annual Rates of Return by Year, 1980–1989 (Concluded)

| Percentage Total Returns Expressed in U.S. Dollars | Year | | |
|---|---|---|---|
| **Asset Class Indices** | **1980** | **1981** | **1982** |
| **Alternative Assets Indices** | | | |
| NAREIT (Real Estate Investment Trusts) | 24.4% | 6.0% | 21.6% |
| NCREIF Property Index (Commercial Real Estate) | 18.1 | 16.6 | 9.4 |
| National Assn. of Realtors (Residential Housing) | 11.5 | 5.7 | 1.8 |
| NCREIF Farmland Index (U.S. Farmland) | – | – | (3.1) |
| Cambridge Associates Private Equity Funds Index | – | – | – |
| Cambridge Associates Venture Funds Index | – | 18.1 | 5.3 |
| Venture Economics All Private Equity Fund Index | 77.4 | (13.1) | 27.4 |
| HFRI Fund Weighted Composite Hedge Fund Index | – | – | – |
| HFRI Fund of Funds Index | – | – | – |
| Commodity Research Bureau Total Return Index | – | – | 12.9 |
| Barclay Commodity Advisors Index | 63.7 | 23.9 | 16.7 |
| Handy & Harmon Spot Gold Price | 14.5 | (31.9) | 13.9 |
| Handy & Harmon Spot Silver Price | (44.1) | (47.3) | 32.1 |
| Lehman Brothers TIPS Index/Bridgewater[4] | 13.7 | 9.4 | 13.2 |
| Mei/Moses Fine Art Index | 40.9 | 9.8 | (4.3) |
| **U.S. Cash Equivalent Indices** | | | |
| Citigroup 90-Day U.S. Treasury Bill Index | 15.5% | 15.0% | 11.3% |
| Inflation (CPI-U) | 12.5 | 8.9 | 3.8 |

All indices are expressed in total return terms unless noted in the description. "Gross" denotes total returns inclusive of gross dividends; "Net" denotes total returns inclusive of dividends net of foreign withholding taxes; and "Price Return" indicates that dividends are not included in the percentage returns data. "Free" denotes that portion of the relevant underlying market whose securities are freely tradable by international investors.

[1]The Lehman Brothers Aggregate Index represents securities that are U.S. domestic, taxable, and dollar denominated, and which covers the U.S. investment-grade, fixed-rate bond market. As of September 2005, the components of the index included approximately: 61% government and corporate credit; 34% mortgage-backed securities; 4% (ERISA Eligible Commercial Mortgage-Backed Securities); and 1% asset-backed securities.

The 1994 through 2003 period excludes the 10.0% total return for 1993 from the calculation interval and includes the 28.7% total return for 2003. An investment of $1.00 in the S&P 500 Index on January 1, 1994 would have grown to a final value of $2.86 on December 31, 2003,

| | | | Year | | | |
|---|---|---|---|---|---|---|
| **1983** | **1984** | **1985** | **1986** | **1987** | **1988** | **1989** |
| 30.6% | 20.9% | 19.1% | 19.2% | (3.6)% | 13.5% | 8.8% |
| 13.1 | 13.8 | 11.2 | 8.3 | 8.0 | 9.6 | 7.8 |
| 3.1 | 3.1 | 4.7 | 7.0 | 5.7 | 3.9 | 1.5 |
| 2.1 | (4.9) | (4.1) | (16.3) | (18.4) | 4.7 | 7.7 |
| – | – | – | 1.2 | 3.5 | 12.7 | 10.4 |
| 18.1 | (1.2) | 2.0 | 7.3 | 6.7 | 3.1 | 6.6 |
| 43.7 | (6.6) | 9.0 | 0.9 | 2.9 | 9.3 | 4.5 |
| – | – | – | – | – | – | – |
| – | – | – | – | – | – | – |
| (9.1) | 4.9 | (1.2) | 18.7 | 16.0 | 4.6 | 5.1 |
| 23.8 | 8.7 | 25.5 | 3.8 | 57.3 | 21.8 | 1.8 |
| (16.5) | (19.2) | 6.9 | 20.4 | 21.9 | (15.1) | (1.9) |
| (17.9) | (28.9) | (8.3) | (7.9) | 24.8 | (10.1) | (14.0) |
| 3.5 | 7.8 | 12.4 | 6.9 | 7.1 | 8.7 | 11.1 |
| 11.3 | 17.8 | 41.5 | (3.9) | 43.5 | 60.0 | 25.5 |
| 8.9% | 10.0% | 7.8% | 6.2% | 5.9% | 6.8% | 8.6% |
| 3.8 | 4.0 | 3.8 | 1.1 | 4.4 | 4.4 | 4.7 |

[2]The EMBI+ Index is used from 1994 to the present; the EMBI Index is used for prior periods.

[3]For 1999–2004, returns are based on the Morgan Stanley U.S. 225 "Daily" Convertible Index; for 1991–1998, returns are based on the Morgan Stanley U.S. 225 "Monthly" Convertible Index.

[4]The synthetically constructed Bridgewater Strategic Benchmark U.S. TIPS 8-Year Duration Index is used for the January 1971 through February 1997 time period; the Lehman Brothers TIPS 6.41-year duration index is used after February 1997.

Sources: Morgan Stanley Investment Management; Hedge Fund Research; Morgan Stanley IIG Asset Allocation Group.

Past performance is not a guarantee of future results.

a 10-year CAGR of 11.1%, compared to an arithmetic mean return of 13.0% during the same period.

The 1995 through 2004 period excludes the 1.3% total return for 1994 from the calculation interval and includes the 10.9% total return

**T A B L E  4.6**

Calculation of Rolling 10-Year Returns for the S&P 500 Composite Index

| 10-Year Time Period | Calendar Year Total Returns (Price Change Plus Dividend) | | | | | | | |
| | 1990 | 1991 | 1992 | 1993 | 1994 | 1995 | 1996 | 1997 |
|---|---|---|---|---|---|---|---|---|
| 1990–1999 | (3.1)% | 30.5% | 7.7% | 10.0% | 1.3% | 37.4% | 23.1% | 33.4% |
| 1991–2000 | (3.1) | 30.5 | 7.7 | 10.0 | 1.3 | 37.4 | 23.1 | 33.4 |
| 1992–2001 | (3.1) | 30.5 | 7.7 | 10.0 | 1.3 | 37.4 | 23.1 | 33.4 |
| 1993–2002 | (3.1) | 30.5 | 7.7 | 10.0 | 1.3 | 37.4 | 23.1 | 33.4 |
| 1994–2003 | (3.1) | 30.5 | 7.7 | 10.0 | 1.3 | 37.4 | 23.1 | 33.4 |
| 1995–2004 | (3.1) | 30.5 | 7.7 | 10.0 | 1.3 | 37.4 | 23.1 | 33.4 |

Source: The author.

for 2004. An investment of $1.00 in the S&P 500 Index on January 1, 1995 would have grown to a final value of $3.13 on December 31, 2004, a 10-year CAGR of 12.1%, compared to an arithmetic mean return of 14.0% during the same period.

Working through these four examples may shed some light on the sequential, cascading, order-based nature of compound interest and serve as a precaution on the use of "rule-of-thumb" calculation short-cuts when multiyear compounding is involved. For example, in comparing the CAGR of the 1990 through 1999 and the 1993 through 2002 periods, an investor may observe that the 1990 through 1999 period includes the –3.1%, 30.5%, and 7.7% investment results for 1990, 1991 and 1992 respectively, while excluding the –9.1%, –11.9%, and –22.1% investment results for 2000, 2001, and 2002, respectively. Conversely, an investor may observe that the 1993 through 2002 period excludes the –3.1%, 30.5%, and 7.7% investment results for 1990, 1991, and 1992, respectively, while including the –9.1%, –11.9% and –22.1% investment results for 2000, 2001, and 2002, respectively.

As a result, to estimate the CAGR of the 1993 through 2002 series of returns from the 1990 through 1999 CAGR and the subsequent returns

| Calendar Year Total Returns (Price Change Plus Dividend) | | | | | | | Selected 10-Year | |
|---|---|---|---|---|---|---|---|---|
| 1998 | 1999 | 2000 | 2001 | 2002 | 2003 | 2004 | Final Value of $1.00 Investment | CAGR |
| 28.6% | 21.0% | (9.1)% | (11.9)% | (22.1)% | 28.7% | 10.9% | $5.33 | 18.2% |
| 28.6 | 21.0 | (9.1) | (11.9) | (22.1) | 28.7 | 10.9 | 5.00 | 17.5 |
| 28.6 | 21.0 | (9.1) | (11.9) | (22.1) | 28.7 | 10.9 | 3.37 | 12.9 |
| 28.6 | 21.0 | (9.1) | (11.9) | (22.1) | 28.7 | 10.9 | 2.44 | 9.3 |
| 28.6 | 21.0 | (9.1) | (11.9) | (22.1) | 28.7% | 10.9% | 2.86 | 11.1 |
| 28.6 | 21.0 | (9.1) | (11.9) | (22.1) | 28.7% | 10.9% | 3.13 | 12.1 |

for 2000, 2001, 2002, it is usually not sufficient to: (i) add together the 1990 through 1992 returns (the sum of −3.1%, 30.5% and 7.7%, which comes to 35.1%); (ii) add together the 2000 through 2002 returns (the sum of −9.1%, −11.9%, and −22.1%, which comes to −43.1%); (iii) net out the sum of the dropped years' returns against the added years' returns (+35.1% and −43.1%, or −8.0%); and (iv) divide the net result by the number of years that were dropped from the one interval or added to the other interval (−8.0% divided by three years, or −2.7%). Such a procedure would lead the investor to estimate that the 1993 through 2002 CAGR for the Standard & Poor's 500 Index might be approximated by subtracting 2.7% in compound annual returns from the original 1990 through 1999 CAGR of 18.2% to produce a rough estimate of 15.5% as a CAGR for the 1993 through 2002 interval. As Table 4.4 shows, because the annual returns affect the entire prior accumulated value of the portfolio, their cumulative force is *geometrically multiplicative* and cannot be accurately estimated through arithmetic shortcuts. Consequently, when considering the multiyear investment performance of specific asset classes, investors need to pay attention to the interplay of the *sequencing* and the *magnitude* of year-to-year investment returns patterns.

## CAVEATS IN MULTIYEAR INVESTMENT PERFORMANCE ANALYSIS

Before exploring the multiyear investment performance of selected asset classes, it is worthwhile to enumerate some caveats. First, past patterns of and rates of change in assets' total returns and past levels of standard deviations in assets' returns do not guarantee a continuation of these results in the future. At any point in time, numerous fundamental, valuation, and psychological/technical/liquidity forces may continue, intensify, weaken, or reverse trends in the returns, standard deviations of returns, and/or correlations of returns for specific investments.

Second, as mentioned in connection with Table 4.1, the multiyear investment performance of an asset class may demonstrate similar or different results according to factors such as: (i) the length of the multiyear analysis period; (ii) whether the returns are expressed as rolling returns or as nonoverlapping returns; (iii) the reference currency used; (iv) the treatment of taxes and expenses; and (v) whether the standard deviations are calculated as standard deviations of annual, quarterly, monthly, or some other interval's returns.

Third, the length of the multiyear period chosen for analysis may be longer or shorter than a complete investment returns cycle for a given asset. For example, the calculation of a rolling multiyear investment performance may or may not include a sustained period, lasting more than the length of the multiyear interval, of consistently rising, falling, or essentially unchanged investment returns, standard deviations of returns, and/or correlations of returns. Similarly, a multiyear time interval may completely contain within itself two, three, or more offsetting cycles that are obscured when observing the beginning-to-end CAGR, the standard deviation of returns, and/or correlations of returns for the period as a whole.

Fourth, the standard deviation measure may overstate or understate the true attractiveness of an asset because of the methodology used to compute standard deviations of returns involving the: (i) squaring of each period's positive or negative deviation from its periodic arithmetic mean; (ii) the summing of these squared values; and (iii) the calculation of the square root of the arithmetic average of (ii). For example, the standard deviation of annual returns is 49%, which many market participants consider high for an asset held for five years whose annual returns remained unchanged in years one, three, and five and whose annual return doubled in years two and four.

Fifth, it is important to consider the composition and calculation conventions for the benchmark representing the investment performance of a specific asset class. In some cases, the index (such as a broadly based fine art price index) may or may not reflect the investment performance of a subcategory of the asset class (such as twentieth-century sculpture).

Sixth, analysis of the multiyear investment performance of selected asset classes should include a healthy admixture of perspective and judgment. For example, a series of three or four consecutive rolling multiyear periods characterized by consistently attractive patterns of investment returns for *that kind of asset* and apparently reasonable standard deviations of returns and correlations of returns for *that kind of asset* may indicate: (i) the long-term appeal of investing in such an asset class; or (ii) the formation of an important cyclical (or perhaps secular) topping-out in the attractiveness of the asset class. It is worth repeating that close and appropriately broad scrutiny of the multiyear investment performance of selected asset classes can furnish some degree of insight, perspective, and realism, but *does not* promise clairvoyance or success in indicating whether to buy, hold, or sell an asset at a given point in time.

## OBSERVATIONS ON ASSET CLASSES' INVESTMENT PERFORMANCE

The following paragraphs offer several observations in reference to the boxed data in Table 4.2 and to Table 4.4, about the investment performance for the rolling 10-year periods from 1990 through 1999, 1991 through 2000, 1992 through 2001, 1993 through 2002, 1994 through 2003, and 1995 through 2004. Similar scrutiny of Tables 4.3 and 4.5 can furnish perspective about the investment performance for the rolling 10-year periods from 1986 through 1995, 1987 through 1996, 1988 through 1997, and 1989 through 1998.

- ◆ **U.S. Equity Indices:** Comparing the 1990 through 1999 period with the 1995 through 2004 period, the Standard & Poor's 500 Index experienced a significant *decline* in its 10-year CAGR (from 18.2% compounded annually to 12.1% compounded annually) and a significant *increase* in its standard deviation of annual returns (from 14.1% to 21.1%). Comparing 1990 through 1999 with 1995 through 2004, the Nasdaq Composite Price Return Index underwent a similar shift, with a *decline* in its 10-year CAGR, from 24.5% to 11.2%, and an *increase* in its standard deviation of annual returns, from 29.6% to 39.3%.

The Russell 1000 Growth Index generated a 10-year CAGR of 20.3% over the 1990–1999 time period, but the CAGR for this index fell to 6.7% over the 1993–2002 time span and moved up to 9.2% and 9.6% in the 1994–2003 and 1995–2004 time spans. The Russell 2000 Value Index showed relatively consistent rolling 10-year returns and standard deviations of returns for each of the six 10-year periods; 12.5% and 20.5%, 17.6% and 16.2%, 15.1% and 14.0%, 10.9% and 15.6%, 12.7% and 18.7%, and 15.2% and 18.0% for the 1990 through 1999, 1991 through 2000, 1992 through 2001, 1993 through 2002, 1994 through 2003, and 1995 through 2004 10-year intervals, respectively.

◆ **Non-U.S. Equity Indices:** Because the non-U.S. assets' total returns in Tables 4.2, 4.3, 4.4, and 4.5 are expressed in U.S. dollars, net *appreciation* of their local currencies versus the U.S. dollar should *add* to their U.S. dollar-expressed returns, and net *depreciation* of their local currencies versus the U.S. dollar should *detract* from their U.S. dollar-expressed returns. As a result, year-to-year fluctuations in non-U.S. currency values may have the effect of increasing the standard deviation of their U.S. dollar expressed annual returns.

For the six rolling 10-year periods shown in Table 4.2, 1990 through 1999, 1991 through 2000, 1992 through 2001, 1993 through 2002, 1994 through 2003, and 1995 through 2004, the MSCI Japan Net Index ("Net" indicates that the asset's total returns are inclusive of dividends net of foreign withholding taxes) exhibited negative or very low CAGRs and relatively high standard deviations of annual returns: –0.9% and 28.9%; 0.3% and 27.8%; –4.0% and 29.5%; –2.7% and 28.8%; –1.9% and 30.0%; and –2.3% and 29.6%, respectively.

From the 1990 through 1999 period to the 1993 through 2002 period, the MSCI Emerging Markets Free Latin America Gross Index ("Free" indicates that portion of the relevant underlying markets whose securities are freely tradable by international investors, and "Gross" indicates that the asset's total returns include gross dividends *before* deduction of foreign withholding taxes) declined from a CAGR of 19.1% to 3.7%, with a concomitant decline in the standard deviation of annual returns, from 51.8% in the earlier interval to a still-high 33.2% in the later time frame. During the 1994 to 2003 and 1995 to 2004 10-year periods, the CAGR and standard deviation of annual returns moved upward to 5.1% and 36.9, and 8.6% and 37.8%, respectively.

Similarly, the MSCI Emerging Markets Free Gross Index generated declining CAGRs and relatively high standard deviations of annual returns over the 1990 through 1999, 1991 through 2000, 1992 through 2001, 1993 through 2002, 1994 through 2003, and 1995 through 2004 10-year time periods: 11.0% and 36.8%; 8.3% and 38.9%; 3.1% and 35.6%; 1.3% and 35.8%; 0.2% and 32.1%; and 3.3% and 32.5%, respectively.

◆ **U.S. and Non-U.S. Fixed-Income Indices:** For the six rolling 10-year periods shown in Table 4.2, 1990 through 1999, 1991 through 2000, 1992 through 2001, 1993 through 2002, 1994 through 2003, and 1995 through 2004, the Lehman Brothers Aggregate Bond Index of taxable bonds exhibited relatively steady CAGRs and relatively low standard deviations of annual returns: 7.7% and 6.6%; 8.0% and 6.7%; 7.2% and 6.2%; 7.5% and 6.2%; 7.0% and 6.3%; and 7.7% and 5.3%, respectively. During the same six rolling 10-year periods, the Lehman Brothers 7-Year Municipal Bond Index generated similar CAGRs and even lower standard deviations of annual returns: 6.6% and 5.2%; 6.8% and 5.2%; 6.1% and 4.9%; 6.3% and 5.1%; 5.9% and 4.9%; and 6.5% and 4.0%, respectively.

From the 1990 through 1999 period to the 1993 through 2002 period, the First Boston Upper/Middle Tier High Yield Index declined from a CAGR of 11.5% to 7.0%, with a concomitant decline in the standard deviation of annual returns from 14.0% in the earlier interval to 7.9% in the later time frame. With annual currency fluctuations versus the U.S. dollar adding somewhat to their U.S. dollar-expressed standard deviation of annual returns, from the 1990 through 1999 period to the 1993 through 2002 period, the J.P. Morgan Non-U.S. Bond International Bond Index declined from an 8.5% to a 5.8% CAGR, with a slight increase, from 9.3% to 9.8%, in the standard deviation of annual returns.

◆ **Alternative Investments Indices:** The alternative investments category contains a number of asset classes whose returns drivers, returns patterns, and standard deviations of annual returns are distinctly different from those of equities, fixed-income securities, and cash equivalents. For the six rolling 10-year periods shown in Table 4.2, 1990 through 1999, 1991 through 2000, 1992 through 2001, 1993 through 2002, 1994 through 2003, and 1995 through 2004, the NAREIT Real Estate Investment Trusts Index exhibited relatively high CAGRs and mid-teens standard deviations of annual returns: 9.2% and 18.9%; 13.6% and 17.0%; 11.7% and 15.3%; 10.6% and 15.6%; 12.1% and 17.4%; and 14.8 and 17.9%, respectively.

In part due to appraisal-based valuation systems and the relatively infrequent pricing of properties, the NCREIF Commercial Real Estate Property Index, the National Association of Realtors Residential Housing Index, and the NCREIF U.S. Farmland Index tended to exhibit single-digit (and in several cases, low single-digit) standard deviations of annual returns during the 1990 through 1999, 1991 through 2000, 1992 through 2001, 1993 through 2002, 1994 through 2003, and 1995 through 2004 periods: from 1.1% to 7.4%, 1.5% to 7.5%, 1.7% to 6.1%, 1.6% to 4.3%, 2.3% to 3.8%, and 2.3% to 5.9%, respectively.

For the 10-year rolling periods 1990 through 1999, 1991 through 2000, 1992 through 2001, 1993 through 2002, 1994 through 2003, and 1995 through 2004, the highest CAGRs, and by far the highest standard deviations of annual returns, were generated by the Cambridge Associates Venture Funds Index: 39.3% and 80.6%, 41.8% and 79.5%, 32.1% and 84.4%, 27.0% and 86.7%, 23.6% and 88.1%, and 23.8% and 86.5%, respectively. For the same 10-year rolling periods, the HFRI Fund Weighted Composite Hedge Fund Index produced gradually declining CAGRs and relatively stable standard deviations of annual returns: 18.3% and 11.3%; 18.2% and 11.4%; 15.4% and 11.1%; 13.1% and 12.2%; 11.8% and 10.7%; and 12.6% and 10.5%, respectively.

For the 10-year rolling periods 1990 through 1999, 1991 through 2000, 1992 through 2001, 1993 through 2002, 1994 through 2003, and 1995 through 2004, the Commodity Research Bureau Total Return Index produced low positive returns and relatively stable standard deviations of annual returns: 1.7% and 9.5%; 2.5% and 10.3%; 1.0% and 12.0%; 3.1% and 12.9%; 3.6% and 13.1%; and 3.8% and 13.2%, respectively. By contrast, the Barclay Commodity Advisors Index of Commodity Trading Advisors (CTAs) generated higher CAGRs and lower standard deviations of annual returns during the same rolling 10-year periods: 7.1% and 7.2%; 5.9% and 5.4%; 5.6% and 5.6%; 6.9% and 5.4%; 6.7% and 5.3%; and 7.2% and 4.9%, respectively.

For the 10-year rolling periods 1990 through 1999, 1991 through 2000, 1992 through 2001, 1993 through 2002, 1994 through 2003, and 1995 through 2004, the Handy & Harmon Spot Gold Price and the

Handy & Harmon Spot Silver Price produced very low positive or small negative CAGRs, together with relatively stable standard deviations of annual returns. For gold: –3.2% and 10.0%; –3.6% and 10.0%; –2.4% and 9.8%; 0.3% and 12.8%; 0.6% and 13.3%; and 1.3% and 13.3%, respectively. For silver: 0.4% and 18.1%; 1.0% and 17.5%; 1.9% and 17.2%; 2.6% and 17.0%; 1.6% and 14.5%; and 3.5% and 14.7%, respectively.

During the 10-year rolling periods 1990 through 1999, 1991 through 2000, 1992 through 2001, 1993 through 2002, 1994 through 2003, and 1995 through 2004, the Lehman Brothers/Bridgewater Index of Treasury Inflation Protected Securities (TIPS) generated mid-single digit CAGRs and low single-digit standard deviations of annual returns: 6.4% and 3.4%; 6.7% and 3.8%; 6.7% and 3.8%; 7.1% and 4.1%; and 7.7% and 3.9%, respectively. During the same rolling 10-year time periods, the Mei/Moses Fine Art Index exhibited relatively low positive CAGRs and equity-like standard deviations of annual returns: 1.0% and 20.0%; 1.6% and 20.3%; 6.4% and 14.9%; 4.2% and 14.9%; 7.2% and 15.0%; and 9.6% and 13.7%, respectively.

**U.S. Cash Equivalent Indices:** As might be expected, during the 10-year rolling periods 1990 through 1999, 1991 through 2000, 1992 through 2001, 1993 through 2002, 1994 through 2003, and 1995 through 2004, the Citigroup 90-day U.S. Treasury Bill Index yielded low positive CAGRs, combined with the lowest sustained standard deviations of annual returns for any of the 43 asset classes listed in Table 4.2: 5.1% and 1.3%; 4.9% and 1.0%; 4.7% and 1.0%; 4.9% and 1.3%; 4.2% and 1.7%; and 3.8% and 1.9%, respectively.

C H A P T E R

# UNDERSTANDING AND USING CORRELATIONS

## OVERVIEW

### Understanding and Using Correlations

Successful mastery of asset allocation requires a basic comprehension of the crucial role that assets' returns correlations play in reducing portfolio volatility. Even though more and more investors have come to appreciate the significance of standard deviations of returns as an important measure of an asset's risk, many market participants remain only faintly aware of what correlations are, how they are calculated in a portfolio context, and the ways in which correlations influence multiasset investment outcomes.

After defining the correlation measure and describing its development in the late 1880s by Sir Francis Galton and Karl Pearson, this chapter examines closely allied concepts such as covariance and $R^2$, also known as the coefficient of determination. This chapter then discusses several caveats related to correlations, including the reliability and distribution of the underlying performance data, the effects of varying correlations through time, and the influence of data outliers and restrictions on correlations calculations.

This chapter also addresses the important distinctions between correlation and causation, examines various types of correlation coefficients, and furnishes some rule-of-thumb guidelines for interpreting absolute and relative correlations values.

The chapter concludes with a detailed analysis of how correlations inform investment performance by affecting portfolio standard deviation, and by such agency, correlations' contribution to the workings of mainstream mean-variance optimization models.

## DEFINITIONS OF CORRELATION

In asset allocation and investment strategy, the concept of correlation is employed to examine: (i) whether or not two assets are related; and (ii) the degree of any existing relationship between two assets. Another way of describing correlations, known as correlation coefficients, is as an indicator of the *association*, or the *degree of linear relationship, between a pair of variables*. Financial experts frequently describe this relationship in terms of the investment performance of two assets. Depending on the context in which it is discussed, the investment performance of an asset during a specified time period may be described as: (i) its price change, or (ii) its total return, which is comprised of its dividend or interest income, the reinvestment of such interim dividend or interest flows from the asset, plus or minus its price change.

Some financial market participants may erroneously equate correlation with *regression analysis*, but these two measures differ from one another. Correlation emphasizes the nature of the *two-way, nondirectional* relationship between two variables, whereas regression analysis focuses on the *one-way, predictive, directional* relationship between one variable, identified as the predictor, and the other variable, identified as the predicted value.

Correlation measures the strength and direction of a series of values that each of two different variables generate. In financial markets, these variables are frequently considered to be the specific investment performance of two assets. One can compare two stocks, two industry groups, two fixed-income sectors, or two different kinds of assets, such as stocks and bonds. Saying that two assets are highly positively or highly negatively correlated implies that the investment performance of one asset can yield insight about the investment performance of the

**F I G U R E  5.1**

Formula for Calculating Correlation

$$\text{Correlation} = \frac{\text{Covariance between Asset A and Asset B}}{\left(\begin{array}{c}\text{Standard}\\\text{Deviation}\\\text{of Asset A}\end{array}\right) \times \left(\begin{array}{c}\text{Standard}\\\text{Deviation}\\\text{of Asset B}\end{array}\right)}$$

Source: The author.

other asset with which it is positively or negatively correlated. Correlation coefficients are also used to analyze the risk of several different trading or investment positions, to structure hedges between various kinds of assets, and to determine the pricing and valuation of many derivative instruments.

From a computational standpoint, the correlation coefficient between two assets, designated as Asset A and Asset B, may be expressed as the covariance between the two assets, divided by the standard deviation of Asset A times the standard deviation of Asset B. The formula for calculating correlation is shown in Figure 5.1.

The formula depicted in Figure 5.2 standardizes the covariance measure between the investment performance of Asset A and Asset B by making each of the two assets' investment performances comparable in magnitude and dispersion. The formula accomplishes this by: (i) subtracting the mean from each asset's investment performance; and (ii) dividing by its standard deviation, effectively giving each asset's investment performance a mean value of zero and a standard deviation value of one.

The *covariance* between two assets is defined as the *cross product* of the two assets' *variances* from their respective means, as Figure 5.2 illustrates.

Figure 5.2 shows that the covariance measure is often used to measure the degree of similarity in how much each of two assets' investment performances deviate from their respective mean investment performance.

## DEVELOPMENT OF THE CORRELATION MEASURE

Two British researchers in the field of genetics, Sir Francis Galton and Karl Pearson, originally developed the correlation coefficient in the late

## F I G U R E  5.2

Formula for Calculating Covariance

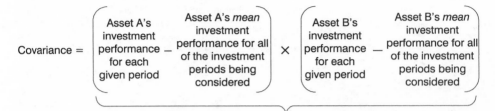

Multiplied and summed over the total number of periods for
which the assets' investment performances are being
compared, and then divided by the number of periods

Source: The author.

1880s as a quantitative tool for measuring relationships between various kinds of human dimensions, such as hand length, hip height, head
size, and length of forefinger, among other physical characteristics.

There are three important properties of Pearson's and Galton's
methodology for calculating correlations: (i) because both the numerator and the denominator of the correlation formula are expressed as
products of quantities that are less than one, their quotient must also,
by definition, range in value between –1.0 and +1.0; (ii) because the
units of the numerator and the units of the denominator are expressed
in the same terms, their quotient effectively produces a unitless quantity; and (iii) correlation coefficients are symmetric, in that the correlation between Asset A and Asset B is equivalent to the correlation
between Asset B and Asset A. As a result, investors can compare correlation coefficients regardless of any linear transformations of the underlying investment performance data and regardless of the specific
scale used to calculate investment performance. Providing that the
transformation of values for either variable in a correlation is linear in
nature, changing the numerical scale of either variable does not change
the overall value of the correlation coefficient.

While several different measures have been developed to compute
correlation, the most commonly used measure in asset allocation and
investment activity is known as the *Pearson product-moment correlation
coefficient*, which may take on any value in the numerical range between –1.0 and +1.0. When the correlation coefficient has a *positive* sign,

this means that: (i) as the value of one variable increases, the value of the other variable also increases; or (ii) as the value of one variable decreases, the value of the other variable also decreases. On the other hand, when the correlation coefficient has a *negative* sign, this means that: (i) as the value of one variable increases, the value of other variable decreases; or (ii) as the value of one variable decreases, the value of the other variable increases.

The term "product" indicates that a key element of the correlation coefficient derives from summation during the number of periods for which the two assets' investment performance is being compared, of the cross-multiplication, or cross-product, between each of the two assets' investment performance and their respective means. The term "moment" refers to an arithmetic technique that describes certain kinds of averages.

In many contexts, the letter "r" has become accepted as a symbol for correlation, perhaps to denote the fact that correlations are a measure of the *relationship* between two variables. The correlation coefficient has achieved fairly broad usage relative to the usage of covariance as a means of assessing whether and to what extent two assets' investment performances are related. This is partly because: (i) the *covariance* between two variables is *not* limited to values between –1.0 and +1.0; and (ii) the covariance between two variables *does* depend upon the specific scale of the variables being compared.

A correlation coefficient between two assets of –1.0 indicates that the investment performance of one asset behaves in a fashion *completely opposite to* the investment performance of an asset with which it is being compared. A correlation coefficient between two assets of +1.0 indicates that the investment performance of one asset behaves in a fashion *completely similar* to the investment performance of an asset with which it is being compared. A correlation coefficient between two assets of zero indicates that the investment performance of one asset provides *no degree of predictability* about the investment performance of the asset with which it is being compared.

## R-SQUARED MEASURE, OR COEFFICIENT OF DETERMINATION

Financial market participants may assess the *strength* of the relationship between two assets through the *R-squared measure*, also known as the *coefficient of determination*. They compute R-squared by squaring the value of the correlation between two assets' investment performance. In other words, the R-squared measure shows the percentage of variance in the investment returns of Asset A that is *associated with* or *related to* the investment return of Asset B, or vice-versa. For example, two assets with a correlation of 0.80 have an R-squared measure of $(0.80)^2$, or 64%, indicating that 64% of the variation in the investment performance of either asset would be associated with the investment performance of the other asset, with 36% of the relative movement in the two assets' investment performances associated with other factors. The R-squared measure captures the proportion or percentage variance in one asset that can be accounted for by knowing the investment performance of the asset with which it is correlated.

Another way of thinking about the R-squared measure relates to its insight into the *degree of accuracy* with which the investment performance of one asset can be predicted by knowing the investment performance of the asset with which it is being compared. For example, for two assets with a correlation coefficient of 0.70, their R-squared measure of $(0.70)^2 = 0.49$ indicates the percentage, 49%, by which investors have improved their ability to predict the investment performance of either asset by knowing the investment performance of the other asset with which it is being compared.

## CAVEATS TO CORRELATIONS

While correlations can furnish profound insights about the relationship between two assets' investment performance, it is important to be mindful of several of the limitations associated with this measure. Table 5.1 summarizes some of these important caveats, which are described in more detail in the following paragraphs.

First, the reliability of correlations data depends on the quality and time period of the data being analyzed. For example, the correlation between two assets using data covering a period as long as 15 to 20 years may be substantially more reliable than correlations between two assets using data covering a period as short as 2 to 3 years.

Second, correlations can give misleading indications about the degree of association between two assets if the relationship between the two assets is *nonlinear* and/or if the relationship *varies* depending on the value of one asset's investment performance. The statistical term for this condition, i.e., the nonconstancy of the variance of a measure over the range of the factor under study, is 18 letters long and is called *heteroscedasticity* (from "hetero," the Greek word for "different," and "skedastikos," the Greek word for "able to scatter"). The opposite of heteroscedasticity, *homoscedasticity*, refers to a uniform degree of associ-

## T A B L E  5.1

Important Caveats Related to Correlations

| Correlations Caveat | Nature of Caveat |
| --- | --- |
| Quality of underlying data | The reliability of correlations data depends on the quality and time period of the data being analyzed. |
| Nonlinear associations | Nonlinear relationships and/or investment performance-affected relationships may give misleading indications about the degree of association between two assets. |
| Nonnormal distributions | An asset's investment performance may follow a nonnormal pattern of distributions. |
| Instability of correlations | Correlations data may vary greatly in response to different kinds of financial market conditions. |
| Effects of data outliers | One or more large outlying values can significantly affect correlations. |
| Effects of data restrictions | Restrictions placed on the underlying data may influence correlations results. |

Source: The author.

ation in the relationship between the two assets at any point along their linear relationship.

Third, correlation calculations between two assets are based on the assumption that the underlying distributions of investment performance are similar for each asset. Financial market experts assume that for many (but by no means all) assets, investment performance follows a normal, bell-curve shaped distribution pattern, with *continuous* and *symmetrical* data that are *centered on their mean*. Certain kinds of assets may have nonnormal distributions of investment returns due to: (i) nonstandard, managed, "stale," or inconsistent valuation conventions for the asset; (ii) pricing anomalies for the asset due to illiquidity, lockup provisions, incentive-performance fees, survivorship bias, back-fill bias, reporting bias, kurtosis, and positive or negative skew; (iii) the use of options or optionlike investment stratagems associated with the asset; (iv) the employment of short-selling, margin-based, or securities-lending techniques connected with the asset; or (v) convexity or concavity in the shape of the asset's investment returns under certain kinds of financial-market conditions. Correlations may also be affected by highly serially correlated data (described later in the section on se-rial correlation).

Fourth, correlations data can also vary greatly in response to dif-ferent kinds of financial-market conditions. For example, *negative* corre-lations may occur between equities and fixed-income securities prices when positive (or negative) changes in the economic and earnings out-look are sufficiently meaningful to *override* the *offsetting* effects of rising (or falling) bond yields. *Positive* correlations may occur between equi-ties and fixed-income securities prices when positive (or negative) changes in the economic and earnings outlook are *reinforced* by falling (or rising) bond yields. In periods of financial-market instability, the correlations *within* asset classes and frequently *between* asset classes may tend to rise as prices move dramatically in the same direction.

Correlations between many pairs of assets tend not to be fixed over time, but instead can vary to a meaningful degree. For example, Figure 5.3 shows, for the period from 1926 through 2005, the rolling two-year correlations of monthly returns for: U.S. equities (as mea-sured by the Standard & Poor's 500 Composite Index) with U.S. bonds (as measured by 10-year U.S. Treasury bonds).

As Figure 5.3 shows, during the 77 years from 1926 through 2005, U.S. equities–U.S. bond correlations exhibited a substantial degree of variation, ranging from high correlation values of over 0.60 in two sep-arate years to low correlation values of below -0.40 in two separate years. The rolling 10-year correlations of monthly returns for U.S. equi-ties and U.S. bonds have been positive for much, but not all, of the time between 1926 and 2005, although these correlations were negative in the late 1920s and early 1930s, from the mid-1950s through the late 1960s, and during the 2000–2005 period.

In sum, over a period of investment intervals, correlations be-tween different pairs of assets may demonstrate a reasonably high de-gree of constancy, undergo gradual change, or exhibit sudden changes. Various relatively specialized algorithms take account of conditional correlations that are influenced by market volatility or by preceding values, correlations which are mean reverting, and other types of nonstationary correlations that tend to change through time. Some of these dynamic conditional correlation models use exponential smooth-ing and other types of decay rates, some use moving-average values, some use scalar, diagonal, and orthogonal variance targeting, and some use an approach known as complex multivariate Generalized Autoregressive Conditional Heteroskedasticy (GARCH) procedures. The GARCH methodology relates current standard deviations of re-

**F I G U R E   5.3**

Correlation between U.S. Equities and U.S. Bonds, 1926–2005

Note: Correlations are based on monthly total returns of the S&P 500 Composite Index and 10-year U.S. Treasury bonds. They employ an exponentially weighted time series, giving greater weightings to more recent months and approximate rolling 2-year holding periods, with an 18-month half-life.

Source: Morgan Stanley Research.

turns to earlier standard deviations of returns and squared current and earlier returns.

Factors that may cause correlations between one or more asset pairs to increase include: (i) shifts in the underlying assets' market structures; (ii) adoption of similar trading, hedging, valuation, financing, and settlement practices; or (iii) shocks affecting the suppliers, investors, intermediaries, and marketplace of one asset that could potentially carry over to the suppliers, investors, intermediaries, and marketplace of another asset. Because time intervals with high correlations of returns between assets frequently may coincide with increased volatility of those returns, enlightened investors find it useful to estimate correlations under historically normal circumstances as well as during heightened volatility.

Fifth, because covariance and standard deviation calculations ultimately depend on mean or average values, correlations which are derived from those calculations can be significantly affected by any large outlying values that substantially raise or lower the mean or average of a set of investment performance data. As a result, when correlation coefficients appear too high or too low in relation to nearby periods' results or in relation to the investor's judicious instincts, it is wise to examine carefully the values, range, and sample size of the underlying investment performance data to ascertain whether large outlying values may be unduly influencing the computations.

Sixth, restrictions placed on the underlying data can also influence correlations results. For example, correlations between one index used as the performance benchmark of Asset A and another index used as the performance benchmark of Asset B may omit important descriptive data that more completely characterize the true investment performance of each asset. As a result, the calculated correlation coefficient between Asset A and Asset B may not capture the true degree of the relationship between the assets. Similarly, the chosen level of analysis can greatly influence correlation calculations. For instance, the correlation of monthly investment performance between two assets for a given 3-year interval may be computed as zero, implying no correlation between the two assets' monthly investment performance. Similarly, investigation of the correlation of monthly investment performance for the same two assets in each of three adjacent 3-year intervals may yield the same results, with no measurable degree of correlation between the two assets. However, when investors examine the two assets' investment performance during the entire 12-year time frame captured by the four separate 3-year intervals, the assets' investment returns may turn out, in fact, to show a meaningful degree of positive or negative correlation. Stated another way, on a 3-year basis, the assets' investment returns may not have demonstrated any correlation, whereas on a 12-year basis, the assets' investment returns may have exhibited significant correlation.

## CORRELATION AND CAUSATION

Correlation does not imply causation. Even though two assets may be highly correlated, the investment performance of one asset may not be *caused* by the investment performance of the other asset. For example, if 10-year U.S. Treasury bond prices and 10-year Eurozone sovereign bond prices tend to move in the same direction and exhibit a high degree of correlation, it is erroneous to assume that movements in 10-year U.S. Treasury bond prices *cause* movements in 10-year Eurozone sovereign bond prices, or vice versa. It is more likely that each of these two asset types are reacting to external factors (such as global monetary policies or inflationary/deflationary expectations) that cause them both to move in the same direction during the same period.

To take another example, a high correlation coefficient between U.S. equities and U.K. equities does not mean that if U.S. equities' investment performance moves in a specified pattern, U.K. equities' investment performance will be *controlled* by such movement and of necessity follow a similar pattern of investment performance. From a standpoint of *causation*, it is possible that U.S. equities' investment performance and U.K. equities' investment performance may have tended to move together during a certain time period (and thus have demonstrated a high degree of correlation) due to similar patterns of economic growth and trends in corporate profitability in both countries during that interval. As a result, U.S. equities' investment performance and U.K. equities' investment performance may have been relatively highly correlated with *each other* because *each separate* equity market's investment performance was correlated with the outlook for the economy and corporate profitability in the U.S. and in the U.K. Correlation may also not be an appropriate indicator of the nature of the relationship between two assets' investment performance when they involve interactive feedback processes in which the value of one asset's investment performance may actually *affect* another asset's investment performance through time.

Clive W. J. Granger and Robert F. Engle have developed statistical techniques to analyze standard deviations of returns that tend to vary through time, and to assess the *degree of causality* embedded in the correlation between two variables. In the investment world, their work, for which they were awarded the Nobel Prize for Economic Sciences in 2003, can help determine whether the correlation between two assets' investment performances implies that one asset's investment performance plausibly causes the other, or that each asset's return merely happens to be moving in the same direction as the other asset's return. The latter technique, known as the *Granger causality test*, involves: (i) computing the autocorrelation, or serial correlation of an asset's investment performance as a so-called *stationary series;* then (ii) introducing another asset's investment performance to determine whether it has an effect as a correlating variable with the first asset's investment performance in its stationary condition; and in appropriate cases, (iii) recomputing the stationary series of the second asset's investment performance and introducing the investment performance of the first asset to test for possible *reverse causality*.

## ABSOLUTE AND RELATIVE VALUES OF CORRELATION

The degree of strength of a correlation coefficient is dependent to some extent on the context in which it is being considered. For instance, correlations in the range of +0.70 to +0.90 and higher, or correlations of –0.70 to –0.90 and lower, may indicate relatively *high* degrees of positive or negative correlation between two assets. Correlations in the range of +0.30 to +0.70, or correlations in the range of –0.30 to –0.70, may indicate relatively *moderate* degrees of positive or negative correlation. Correlations in the range of 0.00 to +0.30, or correlations of 0.00 to –0.30, may indicate relatively *low* degrees of positive or negative correlation. At the same time, a correlation coefficient of 0.35 between two assets may be very significant if the correlation has moved up from a level such as –0.35 or from 0.00, or down from 0.50 or above, or if the correlation is with an asset whose absolute investment performance is highly positive or highly negative. Instead of relying on absolute values of correlation coefficients to guide their asset allocation activity, investors would be wise to consider correlations in the light of the circumstances in which they have been measured, the purposes for which they are being used, and comparisons with historical values, recent trends, and the actual underlying investment performance of the assets being examined.

## SELECTED TYPES OF CORRELATION COEFFICIENTS

Several specialized measures of correlation coefficients have been developed to deal with: (i) different kinds of relationships between two variables; (ii) different ways of describing the data being analyzed; or (iii) combinations of (i) and (ii). Table 5.2 describes several types of correlation coefficients. Selected statistics textbooks and Web sites dealing with statistical concepts detail their calculation methodologies.

Some of the correlation types in Table 5.2 include: (i) *partial correlation*, which measures the degree of association of one variable with another, while taking account of one or more additional variables; and (ii) *multiple correlation*, which measures the degree of association of one dependent variable with multiple independent variables.

The tau measure of correlation, also known as Kendall's Tau, calculates correlation when the values of the two variables are expressed in relative rank order for each specific variable instead of in absolute terms.

**T A B L E  5.2**

Types of Correlation Coefficients

| Correlation Type | Brief Description of Correlation Type |
|---|---|
| Partial correlation | Measures the degree of association of one variable with another, while taking account of one or more additional variables. |
| Multiple correlation | Measures the degree of association of one dependent variable with multiple independent variables. |
| Tau measure | Calculates correlation when the values of the two variables are expressed not in absolute terms but instead in relative rank order for each specific variable. |
| Lambda measure | Quantifies correlation when the values of each of the two variables are not expressed in numerical terms but instead in terms of categories. |
| Gamma measure | Computes correlation when the values of the two variables are quantitatively ranked into groupings such as quartiles, quintiles, deciles, or percentiles. |
| Spearman's rho | Uses ranked or ordered data to avoid an undue degree of weight to outlying values. |
| Polyserial correlation | Helps coordinate one set of data that is measured along an interval with another set of data that is expressed on a ranked (ordinal) basis. |
| Polychoric correlation | Measures correlation between two sets of data that are expressed on a ranked (ordinal) basis. |
| Phi measure | Computes correlation between two sets of data that are expressed on an "either/or," or dichotomous, basis. |
| Point-biserial correlation | Calculates correlation when only one set of data is expressed on an "either/or," or dichotomous, basis. |

Source: The author.

The *lambda measure* of correlation is sometimes used to calculate correlation when the values of the two variables are not expressed in numerical terms but instead are expressed in terms of *categories*. For example, the investment performance of each of two assets may have been categorized into qualitative ratings such as "outstanding," "good," "average," "below average," and "poor." The *gamma measure* can calculate correlation when the classification categories are quantitatively ranked into groupings such as quartiles, quintiles, deciles, or percentiles.

The *Spearman's rho* correlation coefficient also relies on the ranking or ordering of data and may avoid giving an undue degree of weight to outlying values. Spearman's rho is one type of *polyserial correlation*, in which one asset's investment performance is measured along an interval and the other is expressed on a ranked (ordinal) basis. A *polychoric* correlation may be used when *both* assets' investment performances are expressed on a ranked (ordinal) basis. The *phi measure* correlation coefficient, a form of so-called *tetrachoric* correlation calculation, may be used when the investment performance of *both* Asset A and Asset B is measured on an "either/or," or so-called *dichotomous*, basis. For example, the investment performance of Asset A and of Asset B during a given time interval may have been judged as "acceptable" or "unacceptable." When *only one* of the two assets' investment performances is classified on an "either/or" basis (dichotomously), the *point-biserial* correlation may be utilized. If the investment performance data of the "either/or" asset are in fact continuous in distribution and have been somewhat "forced" into an "either/or" classification scheme, a *biserial* correlation coefficient may be calculated in an attempt to assess correlation more accurately.

## THE EFFECTS OF CORRELATIONS ON PORTFOLIO INVESTMENT PERFORMANCE

One of the primary ways in which correlations affect the investment performance of a multiple-asset portfolio is through their influence on the weighted-average standard deviation of the portfolio as a whole. It is worth recalling that the *standard deviation* of an asset (or of a portfolio of assets) is a measure of the degree of dispersion around the arithmetic mean, or average, of the asset's (or the portfolio's) investment performance. Figure 5.4 shows how to calculate the weighted-average standard deviation of a *two-asset* portfolio by employing a multistep process that uses: (i) the percentage portfolio weightings for each of the two assets; (ii) their respective standard deviations of returns; and (iii) the correlations of returns between the two assets. These inputs then determine a set of 4 values for a two-asset portfolio ($2^2=4$), which are then summed before taking the square root of the sum to compute the portfolio's weighted-average standard deviation. A three-asset portfolio calculates a total of 9 values ($3^2=9$), sums them, and takes their square root. A four-asset portfolio utilizes 16 values ($4^2=16$). In other

Calculation of the Weighted-Average Standard Deviation of a Two-Asset Portfolio

**Step 1:** Determine: (i) the percentage portfolio weightings of Asset A and of Asset B; (ii) the standard deviations of returns of Asset A and of Asset B; and (iii) the correlation of returns of Asset A and Asset B.

**Step 2:** Using a matrix format similar to the one shown below:

| Asset | A | B |
|---|---|---|
| A | Value (i) | Value (ii) |
| B | Value (iii) | Value (iv) |

Calculate the following four values for the matrix:

Value (i)   = (Std. dev. of A) (A's portfolio wt.) (Std. dev. of A) (A's portfolio wt.) (Correlation of Asset A with Asset A)
Value (ii)  = (Std. dev. of A) (A's portfolio wt.) (Std. dev. of B) (B's portfolio wt.) (Correlation of Asset A with Asset B)
Value (iii) = (Std. dev. of B) (B's portfolio wt.) (Std. dev. of A) (A's portfolio wt.) (Correlation of Asset B with Asset A)
Value (iv)  = (Std. dev. of B) (B's portfolio wt.) (Std. dev. of B) (B's portfolio wt.) (Correlation of Asset B with Asset B)

It should be noted that: (i) the correlation of an asset with itself is equal to 1.0, and the correlation of Asset A's investment performance with Asset B's investment performance is *equivalent* to the correlation of Asset B's investment performance with Asset A's investment performance.

**Step 3:** Take the square root of the *sum* of Values (i), (ii), (iii), and (iv), which is equal to the weighted-average standard deviation of a two-asset portfolio.

Source: The author.

words, the number of additional values rises as a function of the square of the number of assets in the portfolio.

Figure 5.5, using actual data to calculate the weighted-average standard deviation of a two-asset portfolio, demonstrates that a portfolio's weighted-average standard deviation is determined by: (i) the weighting of each asset; (ii) the standard deviation of returns of each asset; and (iii) the correlations of returns between each set of asset pairs in the portfolio. The two-asset portfolio in Figure 5.5, with a weighting of 60% in Asset A and 40% in Asset B, standard deviations of returns of 20% for Asset A and 10% for Asset B, and a correlation of returns between Asset A and Asset B of 0.40, produces a weighted-average standard deviation of the portfolio of 14.1%.

Figure 5.5 also contains a rudimentary sensitivity analysis to show how a two-asset portfolio's weighted-average standard deviation would change if its asset weightings and each asset's standard deviations were held constant, while varying the correlation of returns between the two assets. In such cases, if the correlation of returns between Asset A and Asset B *increases,* from 0.40 to 0.70, the portfolio's weighted-average standard deviation of returns *increases,* from 14.1% to 15.1%. If the correlation of returns between Asset A and Asset B *decreases,* from 0.40 to -0.30, the portfolio's weighted-average standard deviation of return *decreases,* from 14.1% to 11.5%.

## F I G U R E   5.5

Numerical Example of the Calculation of a Two-Asset Portfolio's
Weighted-Average Standard Deviation

**Example:** For a portfolio which has: (i) a weighting of 60% in Asset A and 40% in Asset B;
(ii) standard deviations of returns of 20% for Asset A and 10% for Asset B; and
(iii) a correlation of returns between Asset A and Asset B (which is also equivalent
to the correlation of returns between Asset B and Asset A) of 0.40, calculate
values (i), (ii), (iii), and (iv) as defined in Step 2 of Figure 5.4.

**Calculation:** Value (i)   = 0.014400;
Value (ii)  = 0.001920;
Value (iii) = 0.001920; and
Value (iv) = 0.001600

**Weighted Average** $= \sqrt{\text{Value (i)} + \text{Value (ii)} + \text{Value (iii)} + \text{Value (iv)}}$

**Standard Deviation
of Portfolio:** $= 0.1409 = 14.1\%$

**Sensitivity Analysis:** With a correlation of returns between Asset A and Asset B of 0.70, the weighted-
average standard deviation of the portfolio becomes 15.1%, and with a correlation
of returns between Asset A and Asset B of –0.30, the weighted-average standard
deviation of returns of the portfolio becomes 11.5%.

Source: The author.

## CORRELATIONS AS A DETERMINANT OF PORTFOLIO INVESTMENT PERFORMANCE

Using the specific inputs contained in Figure 5.5 to calculate a two-asset portfolio's weighted-average standard deviation illustrates many of the important determinants of the investment performance of a given asset allocation. Table 5.3 lists many of these inputs, and briefly describes how these asset characteristics and portfolio characteristics may vary in practice.

In Table 5.3, selected asset characteristics or portfolio characteristics that can exert a meaningful degree of influence on a portfolio's investment performance include: (i) the absolute value of assets' returns, standard deviations of returns, and correlations of returns; (ii) the number of assets in the portfolio and the percentage weightings for each asset; (iii) the length and grouping of returns time periods; (iv) the length of the overall investment interval, also known as the investment horizon; (v) the magnitude, direction, and time required for returns, standard deviations of returns, and correlations of re-

**T A B L E  5.3**

Selected Determinants of a Portfolio's Investment Performance

| Asset Characteristic or Portfolio Characteristic | Range of Ways in Which the Characteristic May Vary |
|---|---|
| Absolute Value of Assets' Returns | Low Returns to High Returns |
| Absolute Value of Assets' Standard Deviations of Returns | Low Standard Deviations to High Standard Deviations of Returns |
| Absolute Value of Correlations of Returns Between Asset Pairs | Low Correlations to High Correlations Between Asset Pairs |
| Number of Assets in Portfolio | Few Assets to Many Assets in Portfolio |
| Percentage Weightings of Each Asset | Low Weightings to High Weightings |
| Length of Returns Time Periods | Hourly, Daily, Weekly, Monthly, Quarterly, Semiannual, Annual, or Multiannual Periods |
| Grouping of Returns Time Periods | Rolling Overlapping Periods versus Nonoverlapping Periods |
| Length of Overall Investment Interval | Shorter Intervals (e.g., One Year or Less) to Longer Intervals (e.g., Five Years to Ten Years or Longer) |
| Magnitude of Returns, Standard Deviations, and Correlations Change | Small Degree of Change to Large Degree of Change |
| Direction of Returns, Standard Deviations, and Correlations Change | Returns, Standard Deviations, and Correlations Decrease to Returns, Standard Deviations, and Correlations Increase |
| Time Required for Returns, Standard Deviations, and Correlations to Change | Short Time (e.g., One Day) to Long Time (e.g., Several Years) |
| Duration of Change in Returns, Standard Deviations, and Correlations | Short Duration (e.g., Less than One Month) to Long Duration (e.g., Several Years or Longer) |
| Degree of Homogeneity in Change of Returns, Standard Deviations, and Correlations | Movement in the Same Direction to Movement in Different Directions |

Source: The author.

turns to change, and the duration of such change; and (vi) the degree of homogeneity in the change of returns, standard deviations of returns, and correlations of returns.

# CORRELATIONS DYNAMICS IN MULTIASSET PORTFOLIOS

As the number of distinct assets rises in a portfolio, the number of asset pairs rises as well. In order to determine the standard deviation of the portfolio as a whole, it is important to compute the correlation coefficient between each asset pair. For portfolios consisting of two, three, four, five, and six distinct assets, Table 5.4 depicts: (i) the correlations matrices; (ii) the total number of correlation values; (iii) the total number of asset *pairings* (defined as two-way symmetrical relationships, such as between Asset A and Asset B, or between Asset B and Asset A, in the investment performance of two assets); and (iv) the total number of asset *pairs* (defined as individual one-way relationships, such as between Asset A and Asset B, and between Asset B and Asset A, in the investment performance of two assets).

# SERIAL CORRELATIONS

As Figure 5.2 and Table 5.1 showed earlier, together with each asset's standard deviation of returns and its percentage portfolio weighting, all of the values in a correlations matrix are used in calculating the weighted-average standard deviation of a portfolio. These values include the so-called autocorrelation of an asset's investment performance with itself, which has a value of 1.0.

If the total *number of assets* in a portfolio is designated as n, then the total number of *asset correlations* (including autocorrelations) in that portfolio can be expressed as n x n, or $n^2$. The number of *one-way* pairs of individual assets with other assets in the portfolio, exclusive of autocorrelations, can therefore be expressed as $n^2-n$. For example, for an 8-asset portfolio, the number of one-way pairs of one asset with another asset would be equal to: $8^2-8=56$, and for a 10-asset portfolio, the number of one-way pairs of one asset with another asset would be equal to: $10^2-10=90$.

The number of *two-way, symmetrical pairings* (e.g., Asset A with Asset B, and Asset B with Asset A) can be expressed as $(n^2-n)/2$. As shown in Table 5.4, the number of two-way, symmetrical asset pairings for a 4-asset portfolio is equal to $(4^2-4)/2=6$, and for a 5-asset portfolio, $(5^2-5)/2=10$. Because correlations coefficients between two assets are expressed as two-way, symmetrical relationships, the number of correlations coefficients that need to be calculated for a multiasset portfolio is also $(n^2-n)/2$. For an 8-asset portfolio, the number of two-way, symmetrical correlations coefficients is equal to $(8^2-8)/2=28$, and for a 10-asset portfolio, the number of two-way, symmetrical correlations coefficients is equal to $(10^2-10)/2=45$.

The potential for one correlations coefficient, or a group of correlations coefficients, to influence the investment performance of an entire portfolio depends on an interplay of factors, including: (i) the standard deviation of returns of each asset in the portfolio; (ii) the percentage weighting of each asset in the portfolio; (iii) the number of assets in the portfolio; and (iv) the magnitude of the correlations coefficient for each asset pairing contained in the portfolio.

At this point, it may be wise to reflect upon: (i) the underlying drivers affecting the correlations between pairs of assets; (ii) the contribution that correlations make to portfolio diversification; (iii) the arithmetic and computational pathways through which low or negative correlations tend to lower the weighted-average standard deviation of a portfolio; and (iv) whether and how correlations might or might not shift in response either to slowly evolving influences or to swiftly moving forces. For example, in times of unusual turbulence in financial markets, the normally low correlations between certain kinds of assets may experience a sudden and simultaneous increase. Such a short-term spike in correlations may be traceable not only to factors acting on the assets themselves, but in certain cases also to powerful forces operating on the *holders* of these assets during a given period of time.

Serial correlation measures the correlation in an asset's investment performance *with its own investment performance in consecutive time periods*. The serial correlation thus indicates the extent to which an asset's investment performance in a given period is nonrandom and is related to its investment performance in a prior time period. A highly positive serial correlation (for example, ranging between +0.5 and +1.0) may indicate that an asset's investment performance in a certain time period is relatively strongly positively associated with its own investment performance in the immediately preceding time period.

On the other hand, a highly negative serial correlation (for example, ranging between –0.5 and –1.0) may indicate that an asset's investment performance is relatively strongly negatively associated with its own investment performance in the immediately preceding time period. A very low serial correlation (clustering in the neighborhood of 0.0) may indicate that an asset's investment performance is essentially uncorrelated with its own investment performance in consecutive time periods.

A number of assets exhibit only a small degree, if any, of serial correlations in their investment performance. Some assets (particularly alternative investments such as certain kinds of real estate, art,

**T A B L E  5.4**

## Correlations Values for Two-, Three-, Four-, Five-, and Six-Asset Portfolios

| Number of Assets in Portfolio | 2 | 3 | 4 |
|---|---|---|---|
| Asset Descriptions | A,B, | A,B,C, | A,B,C,D |

**Correlations Matrix**

| Asset | A | B |
|---|---|---|
| A | 1.0 | V |
| B | V | 1.0 |

| Asset | A | B | C |
|---|---|---|---|
| A | 1.0 | V | V |
| B | V | 1.0 | V |
| C | V | V | 1.0 |

| Asset | A | B | C | D |
|---|---|---|---|---|
| A | 1.0 | V | V | V |
| B | V | 1.0 | V | V |
| C | V | V | 1.0 | V |
| D | V | V | V | 1.0 |

1.0 = The correlation coefficient of an asset's investment performance with itself is equal to 1.0.

$V$ = Value of the correlation of returns between a given pair of assets (from $-1.0$ to $+1.0$).

| Total Number of Matrix Correlation Values | $2^2=4$ | $3^2=9$ | $4^2=16$ |
|---|---|---|---|
| **Asset Pairings** | A +B | A +B | A +B |
| | | A +C | A +C |
| | | | A +D |
| | | B +C | B +C |
| | | | B +D |
| | | | C +D |
| **Total Number of Asset Pairings** | 1 | 3 | 6 |
| **Total Number of Asset Pairs** | 2 | 6 | 12 |

Source: The author.

|   | 5 | | | | 6 | | | | | |
|---|---|---|---|---|---|---|---|---|---|---|

| A,B,C,D,E | | | | | A,B,C,D,E,F | | | | | |
|---|---|---|---|---|---|---|---|---|---|---|

| Asset | A | B | C | D | E | Asset | A | B | C | D | E | F |
|---|---|---|---|---|---|---|---|---|---|---|---|---|
| A | 1.0 | $V$ | $V$ | $V$ | $V$ | A | 1.0 | $V$ | $V$ | $V$ | $V$ | $V$ |
| B | $V$ | 1.0 | $V$ | $V$ | $V$ | B | $V$ | 1.0 | $V$ | $V$ | $V$ | $V$ |
| C | $V$ | $V$ | 1.0 | $V$ | $V$ | C | $V$ | $V$ | 1.0 | $V$ | $V$ | $V$ |
| D | $V$ | $V$ | $V$ | 1.0 | $V$ | D | $V$ | $V$ | $V$ | 1.0 | $V$ | $V$ |
| E | $V$ | $V$ | $V$ | $V$ | 1.0 | E | $V$ | $V$ | $V$ | $V$ | 1.0 | $V$ |
|   |   |   |   |   |   | F | $V$ | $V$ | $V$ | $V$ | $V$ | 1.0 |

$5^2 = 25$ $\qquad\qquad\qquad$ $6^2 = 36$

| | |
|---|---|
| A + B | A + B |
| A + C | A + C |
| A + D | A + D |
| A + E | A + E |
|  | A + F |
| B + C | B + C |
| B + D | B + D |
| B + E | B + E |
| B + F | B + F |
| C + D | C + D |
| C + E | C + E |
|  | C + F |
| D + E | D + E |
|  | D + F |
|  | E + F |

**10** $\qquad\qquad\qquad\qquad$ **15**

**20** $\qquad\qquad\qquad\qquad$ **30**

restricted securities, hedge fund strategies, private equity, and venture capital) may display a meaningful degree of serial correlation in their period-to-period investment performance due in part to: (i) infrequent or nonexistent transactions in the asset within or between performance-measurement periods; and/or (ii) appraisal-, smoothing-, linear-extrapolated-, or estimate-based pricing and valuation methodologies for the asset.

When an asset's investment performance exhibits an artificially high degree of serial correlation, some degree of downward bias may seep into its standard deviation of returns and the correlation of the asset's performance with the performance of other assets. Stale pricing of relatively illiquid assets may thus significantly understate the volatility of returns data and the true degree of correlation between conventional asset classes and several kinds of alternative assets. As a result, investors should pay special attention to the underlying system of investment performance measurement for assets whose correlations of performance with other assets' performance may appear to be counterintuitively low.

## HOW CORRELATIONS WORK IN MEAN-VARIANCE OPTIMIZATION MODELS

Optimization is a powerful process in the field of applied mathematics for describing the maximization (or minimization) of a specific *objective function* of a number of *decision variables* given certain *functional constraints*. Table 5.5 shows how to apply the mathematical concepts related to optimization to asset allocation.

Special classification systems and optimization algorithms have been developed to address optimization problems that are: (i) either constrained or unconstrained; (ii) discrete or continuous; (iii) linear, quadratic, or conic; and (iv) stochastic or robust. Table 5.5 shows that investors think of the *decision variable* as how much of each asset to have in the portfolio, the *objective function* as maximizing the portfolio's return or minimizing the portfolio's standard deviation of returns, and the *functional constraint* as any restriction placed on how much or how little of any given asset may be included in the portfolio.

In the early- to mid-1950s, Harry Markowitz formally applied optimization to portfolio selection and asset allocation. Markowitz, who was awarded the 1990 Nobel Prize for Economic Sciences, developed the *theory of portfolio choice*, which analyzes how investors can optimally allocate financial assets that differ in their expected return

**T A B L E   5.5**

The Application of Optimization to Asset Allocation

| Optimization in a Mathematical Context | Financial Application of Optimization in a Mean-Variance Optimization Context |
| --- | --- |
| Objective Function to be Maximized or Minimized | Maximize the Portfolio's Return or Minimize the Portfolio's Standard Deviation of Returns |
| Decision Variable | How much in Percentage Weighting-Terms of Each Asset to Have in the Portfolio |
| Functional Constraint | Percentage Restrictions or Limits on How Much or How Little of Each Asset Can Be Invested in the Portfolio |

Source: The author.

and risk, under uncertainty. An associated tool, Markowitz's *mean-variance optimization technique,* helps investors find so-called *efficient portfolios* of assets that have either: (i) the *maximum expected return* among all portfolios with the same standard deviation; or (ii) the *minimum standard deviation* among all portfolios with the same expected return. The collection of efficient portfolios forms the *efficient frontier* of the portfolio universe. Later refinements and modifications to these mathematical optimization methods have extended their application to risk and asset-liability management.

Markowitz's mean-variance optimization approach relies on a *quadratic optimization* methodology that uses linear constraints to optimize a quadratic objective and that in its most common format seeks to maximize return (or minimize standard deviation) given certain constraints. These constraints include: (i) the total of the decision variables—i.e., the specific percentage weights of each asset in the portfolio (including possible negative percentages reflecting short sales)—should sum to 100%; (ii) the expected return of the portfolio should be greater than a certain target value, or the standard deviation of the portfolio should be below a certain target value; and (iii) the percentage of certain specified assets may be limited as to their upper and/or lower weightings by factors such as regulation or investor-driven preferences.

The expected return and standard deviation of returns from asset allocation activity are considered to be the two primary measures of investor satisfaction or utility from various portfolios of assets. Because the expected return of an asset is known as its *mean*, and the standard deviation of an asset's returns is defined as the square root of its *variance* about its mean return, finding optimal asset mixes has come to be known as *mean-variance optimization* (MVO). As stated earlier, optimization refers to the search for and selection of specific mixes of assets that provide the highest possible expected return for a given standard deviation, or the lowest possible standard deviation for a given expected return. Some investors erroneously perceive mean-variance optimization to be a highly accurate numerical computation tool, while in fact it is a statistical estimation process subject to significant sampling error.

MVO may be carried out for a single period or several periods, in which the portfolio is rebalanced to a specified asset allocation at the end of each relevant time interval. As mentioned above, *single-period* MVO is usually carried out via a quadratic programming algorithm. In many cases in *single-period MVO*, it is possible to reduce the overall standard deviation of the portfolio to a level below that of the asset with the lowest standard deviation of returns, but it is mathematically impossible to increase the overall return of the portfolio to a level above that of the asset with the highest investment return. In *multiperiod MVO*, the distinction between assets' arithmetic and geometric mean returns data may produce projected portfolio returns that differ from the actual returns generated by a rebalanced portfolio. As well, multiperiod MVO, through portfolio rebalancing, may possibly produce overall geometric mean portfolio returns that are higher than the geometric mean return of the best-performing asset in the portfolio.

Correlations affect the MVO process primarily by influencing the overall standard deviation of the portfolio. Whereas the *expected return* of an asset allocation is computed as the weighted average of the expected returns of the asset classes represented in the portfolio, the *expected standard deviation* of that same asset allocation is computed as the square root of the sum of the matrix multiplication values of each asset's standard deviation and its correlation with itself and all the other pairs of assets in the portfolio. This process is described in more detail and illustrated in Figures 5.1 and 5.2 earlier in this chapter.

When viewed purely from the standpoint of optimizing the asset allocation of a portfolio, a reduction in the correlation coefficients between pairs of assets leads to a reduction in portfolio risk, as defined as the weighted-average standard deviation of the portfolio. As a result, the portfolio may: (i) exhibit a higher overall return without increasing its standard deviation; (ii) exhibit a lower standard deviation without a reduction in overall return; or (iii) some combination of (i) and (ii). When viewed from the standpoint of optimizing the *surplus* of a portfolio (the value of the portfolio's assets less the value of the portfolio's liabilities) an increase in the correlation coefficients between those asset classes that are projected to match with the portfolio's liabilities may improve the portfolio's chances of meeting or immunizing these liabilities.

During turbulent and stressful financial market conditions, many assets' returns exhibit higher-than-normal standard deviations and correlations of returns between asset pairs. These values may be referred to as outlier values. As a result, some MVO techniques seek to identify values that may be unusual for one or more reasons to compute standard deviations, correlations of returns, and optimal portfolios using both the full-sample and the outlier-sample investment performance for each asset.

MVO programs have several potential drawbacks. First, the asset allocation outputs of MVO programs are generally highly sensitive to relatively small changes in the input data. For example, since the optimization algorithm tends to assign high portfolio weights to assets with high projected returns, even a small increase in the projected return for a given asset may lead the MVO program to overallocate that asset relative to the other assets in the optimized portfolio output. Second, given the tendency of many assets' returns to revert to their mean over time, reliance on historical data may lead to: (i) overestimation of certain assets' returns, with a consequent *overweighting* of these assets in the MVO portfolio output relative to their likely future investment *underperformance;* and (ii) underestimation of certain other assets' returns, with a consequent *underweighting* of these assets in the MVO portfolio output relative to their likely future investment *outperformance.*

Third, because the arithmetic mean return for an asset is by definition greater than its geometric mean, the return predicted by many arithmetic-mean-driven MVO programs may differ from the actual return generated by the investor's actual multiperiod portfolio rebalancing activity. The advantages of rebalancing tend to increase for portfolios containing meaningful weightings in asset classes with high standard deviations and low correlations of returns.

In sum, many MVO software packages assume that assets' standard deviations and correlations of returns are stable through time (sometimes referred to as *unconditional* correlations). They also may assume that assets' returns follow a normally shaped distribution curve, without a meaningful number of leptokurtic, or fat-tailed, events two or more standard deviations below or above the asset's expected mean return. MVO software also tends to be highly sensitive even to relatively small changes in estimates of assets' returns and/or standard deviations of returns. In fact, assets' returns and volatilities of returns may frequently influence assets' standard deviations and correlations of returns and thus they may vary through time. As well, many assets' returns do not follow a normal distribution pattern. Last, it is frequently difficult to forecast projected returns and standard deviations of returns with accuracy.

The Web sites of Efficient Solutions Inc. (*effisols.com*), Risk Metrics (*riskmetrics.com*), Ibbotson Associates (*ibbotson.com*), Frontier Analytics (*sungard.com*), and Wagner Inc. (*mathfinance.wagner.com*) offer further insights into MVO software packages.

CHAPTER 6

# CORRELATIONS OF RETURNS
# BETWEEN ASSET CLASSES

## OVERVIEW

Examining how correlations of returns between asset classes move through time can elicit powerful insights into investment performance. Such understanding can be highly useful in strategic and tactical portfolio construction, in evaluating various hedging and risk-reduction maneuvers, and in determining how often and to what degree asset allocations should be rebalanced.

Because correlations computations are based on the returns generated by specific assets or collections of assets, it is important to verify the quality of the investments' underlying data sources. These data may be judged according to such criteria as: (i) the frequency of price reporting; (ii) the reliability and accuracy of data collection methods; (iii) idiosyncratic or special valuation considerations associated with certain kinds of assets; (iv) index calculation methodologies; and (v) the degree to which the chosen benchmark appropriately represents a proxy for a specific asset class.

Additional decisions involve the calculation of the returns correlations themselves. Among these choices are parameters such as: (i) the *investment holding period*, which refers to the investment-measurement interval and which commonly describes annual, monthly, or quarterly returns, although in some contexts the investment holding period may be as long two, three, or five years or as short as monthly, weekly, daily, or even hourly; (ii) the *investment horizon*, which consists of the total time frame during which the performance of the asset is being scrutinized, generally expressed in 3-to-10 years or longer time frames; and (iii) whether the returns on which the correlations are based are calculated as a series of *rolling multiperiod returns* or *nonoverlapping multiperiod returns*.

Table 6.1 contains selected benchmark indices and their associated Web site addresses for 17 asset classes within the equity fixed-income and alternative investments asset-class subcategories.

When comparing correlations data among pairs of asset classes, the correlations of returns calculations must utilize a consistent investment-holding period, investment-horizon, and type of multiperiod returns. It is also worthwhile to consider whether or not any unusual episodes of price appreciation, price weakness, or price stability for a given asset class are wholly or partially contained within the interval(s) under scrutiny.

## SUMMARY OF 10-YEAR OVERLAPPING CORRELATIONS

This analysis focuses on the multiyear progression of correlations of returns between several different asset-class benchmark pairs over the long term. The *investment holding period*, or the investment measurement interval employed, is the *annual return* for 17 individual asset classes. The *investment horizon*, or the total time frame of the analysis, covers 26 *intervals of 10-year periods* beginning in 1970 and ending in 2004[1]. The correlations of returns are calculated as a series of rolling multiperiod returns. The benchmarks that represent the returns for each asset class have been selected based on the underlying data.

Within three of the major supercategories of assets—equities, fixed-income securities, and alternative investments—brief comments focus on: (i) the *absolute amount* of positive or negative correlations of returns; (ii) the *range* of fluctuation in correlations of returns; (iii) how the correlations have *moved* during the 1970–2004 time frame; and (iv) whether the correlations have tended to *cluster* around or between specified values during the multiyear intervals.

---

[1] Investors may choose to calculate correlations over shorter or longer multiyear time frames, generally ranging upward from three-year intervals.

**T A B L E  6.1**

Benchmark Indices for Selected Asset Classes

| Asset Class | Index | Web Site Address or Index Provider |
|---|---|---|
| U.S. Large-Cap Equities | Standard & Poor's 500 Composite | *standardandpoors.com* |
| U.S. Unlisted Equities | Nasdaq Composite | *nasdaq.com* |
| U.S. Equities | Wilshire 5000 | *wilshire.com* |
| Europe, Australasia, Far East Equities | MSCI EAFE | *msci.com* |
| European Equities | MSCI Europe Free Net[1] | *msci.com* |
| Japanese Equities | MSCI Japan Net [1] | *msci.com* |
| Intermediate-Maturity Tax-Exempt Bonds | Lehman Brothers 7-Year Municipal Bond | *lehman.com, bloomberg.com* |
| Intermediate-Maturity U.S. Treasury Bonds | U.S. Treasury 10-Year Note | *treasury.gov, bloomberg.com* |
| Real Estate Investment Trusts | NAREIT | *nareit.com* |
| Residential Real Estate | National Association of Realtors Median Home Price | *realtor.org* |
| Private Equity | Venture Economics All Private Equity Fund | *ventureeconomics.com* |
| Real Assets—Precious Metals: Gold | Handy & Harmon Spot Gold Price | Handy & Harmon, *bloomberg.com* |
| Real Assets—Precious Metals: Silver | Handy & Harmon Spot Silver Price | Handy & Harmon, *bloomberg.com* |
| Inflation-Indexed Securities | Lehman Brothers/Bridgewater TIPS | *lehman.com/bwater.com* |
| Fine Art | Mei Moses Fine Art | *meimosesfineartindex.com* |
| U.S. Taxable Fixed-Income Securities | Lehman Brothers Aggregate Bond | *lehman.com, bloomberg.com* |
| Hedge Funds | HFRI Fund Weighted Composite Hedge Fund | *hedgefundresearch.com* |

[1]"Net" denotes total returns inclusive of dividends net of foreign withholding taxes; "Free" denotes that portion of the relevant underlying market whose securities are freely tradable by international investors.

Source: The author.

## HISTORICAL PERSPECTIVE ON 10-YEAR OVERLAPPING CORRELATIONS BETWEEN EQUITY ASSET CLASSES

For the time period from 1970 through 2004, Table 6.2, on pages 164–165, shows the median and mean correlation values, the range of correlations, the number of 10-year rolling periods, and the degree of correlation, whether there is any evidence of clustering of 10-year annual correlations of returns of the Standard & Poor's 500 Index with 16 asset classes. The U.S. equity asset class, represented by the **S&P 500 Composite Index** benchmark, displays generally *highly positive* correlations with the **Nasdaq Composite Index** (a median correlation value of 0.83, a *mean* correlation value of 0.84, and an overall range of 0.66 to 0.99) during 26 10-year periods. The correlation of annual returns of the S&P 500

Composite Index with the returns of the **Wilshire 5000 Index** has a *median* and *mean* correlation value of 0.99 and an overall range of 0.97 to 0.99 during 24 10-year periods. The correlation of annual returns of the S&P 500 Composite Index with the returns of the **MSCI Europe Free Net Index** has a *median* correlation value of 0.67, a *mean* correlation value of 0.66, and a value range of 0.36 to 0.94 during 26 10-year periods.

The U.S. equity asset class, represented by the **S&P 500 Composite Index** benchmark, displays generally *moderately positive* correlations with the **MSCI EAFE Net** index (a *median* correlation value of 0.44, a *mean* correlation value of 0.49, and an overall range of 0.26 to 0.75) during 25 10-year time periods. The correlation of annual returns of the S&P 500 Composite Index with the returns of the **Lehman Brothers 7-Year Municipal Bond Index** has a *median* correlation value of 0.33, a *mean* correlation value of 0.38, and an overall range of 0.06 to 0.67 during 26 10-year periods. The correlation of annual returns of the S&P 500 Composite Index with the returns of the **U.S. Treasury 10-Year Note** has a *median* correlation value of 0.35, a *mean* correlation value of 0.40, and an overall range of 0.06 to 0.80 during 26 10-year periods. The correlation of annual returns of the S&P 500 Composite Index with the returns of the **NAREIT Index** has a *median* correlation value of 0.61, a *mean* correlation value of 0.47, and an overall range of –0.17 to 0.77 during 24 10-year periods. The correlation of annual returns of the S&P 500 Composite index with the returns of the **Venture Economics All Private Equity Fund Index** has a *median* correlation value of 0.58, a *mean* correlation value of 0.55, and an overall range of 0.20 to 0.88 during 26 10-year periods. The correlation of annual returns of the S&P 500 Composite Index with the returns of the **Lehman Brothers Aggregate Bond Index** has a *median* correlation value of 0.39, a *mean* correlation value of 0.45, and an overall range of 0.07 to 0.81 during 20 10-year periods. The correlation of annual returns of the S&P 500 Composite Index with the returns of the **HFRI Fund Weighted Composite Hedge Fund Index** has a *median* correlation value of 0.36, a *mean* correlation value of 0.51, and a value range of 0.32 to 0.69 during six 10-year periods.

The U.S. equity asset class, represented by the S&P 500 Composite Index benchmark, displays generally *low positive* correlations with the **MSCI Japan Net Index** (a *median* and *mean* correlation value of 0.21, and an overall range of –0.03 to 0.45) during 26 10-year periods. The correlation of annual returns of the S&P 500 Composite Index with the returns of the **National Association of Realtors Median Home Price** has a *median* correlation of 0.03, a *mean* correlation value of 0.12, and an overall range of –0.31 to 0.71, with some clustering of the negative values, during 26 10-year periods. The correlation of annual returns of the S&P 500 Composite Index with the returns of the **Handy & Harmon Spot Silver Price** has a *median* correlation value of 0.07, and a *mean* correlation value of 0.08, and an overall range of –0.25 to 0.39, with some clustering of negative values, during a period of 25 10-year periods. The correlation of annual returns of the S&P 500 Composite Index with the returns of the **Mei Moses Fine Art Index** has a *median* correlation value of 0.11, a *mean* correlation value of 0.15, and a value range of –0.19 to 0.59 during 26 10-year periods.

The U.S. equity asset class, represented by the S&P 500 Composite Index benchmark, displays *very low positive* correlations or *negative* correlations with the **Handy & Harmon Spot Gold Price** (a *median* correlation value of –0.22, a *mean* correlation value of –0.13, and an overall range of –0.52 to 0.45, with some clustering of negative values) during 26 10-year periods. The correlation of annual returns of the S&P 500 Composite index with the returns of the **Lehman Brothers/Bridgewater TIPS Index** has a *median* correlation value of 0.12, a *mean* correlation value of –0.02, and an overall range of –0.61 to 0.46, with some clustering of negative values, during 26 10-year periods.

## SUMMARY OF HISTORICAL PERSPECTIVE ON 10-YEAR OVERLAPPING CORRELATIONS BETWEEN FIXED-INCOME ASSET CLASSES

For the time period from 1970 through 2004, Table 6.3 on pages 166–167 shows the median and mean correlation values, the range of correlations, the number of 10-year rolling periods, the degree of correlation, and whether there is any evidence of clustering of 10-year annual correlations of returns of the **U.S. Treasury 10-Year Note** with 16 asset classes. The fixed-income securities asset class, represented by the **U.S. Treasury 10-Year Note**, displays generally *high positive correlations* with the **Lehman Brothers 7-Year Municipal Bond Index** (a *median* correlation value of 0.89, a *mean* correlation value of 0.92, and an overall range of 0.53 to 0.96) during 26 10-year periods. The correlation of annual returns of the U.S. Treasury 10-Year Note with the returns of the **Lehman Brothers Aggregate Bond Index** has a *median* and *mean* correlation value of 0.98, an overall range of 0.97 to 0.98, and some clustering of absolute values during 20 10-year periods.

The fixed-income securities asset class, represented by the U.S. Treasury 10-Year Note, displays generally *moderately positive* correlations

## T A B L E   6.2

Equity Correlation Summary—1970 through 2004
(Represented by the S&P 500 Composite Index)

| 10-Year Rolling Correlations of Annual Returns with: | Median Correlation | Mean Correlation |
|---|---|---|
| Nasdaq Composite | 0.83 | 0.84 |
| Wilshire 5000 | 0.99 | 0.99 |
| MSCI Europe Free Net | 0.67 | 0.66 |
| | | |
| MSCI EAFE Net | 0.44 | 0.49 |
| Lehman Brothers 7-Year Municipal Bond | 0.33 | 0.38 |
| U.S. Treasury 10-Year Note | 0.35 | 0.40 |
| NAREIT | 0.61 | 0.47 |
| Venture Economics All Private Equity Fund | 0.58 | 0.55 |
| Lehman Brothers Aggregate Bond | 0.39 | 0.45 |
| HFRI Fund Weighted Composite Hedge Fund | 0.36 | 0.51 |
| | | |
| MSCI Japan Net | 0.21 | 0.21 |
| National Assn. of Realtors Median Home Price | 0.03 | 0.12 |
| Handy & Harmon Spot Silver Price | 0.07 | 0.08 |
| MEI/Moses Fine Art | 0.11 | 0.15 |
| | | |
| Handy & Harmon Spot Gold Price | −0.22 | −0.13 |
| Lehman Brothers/Bridgewater TIPS | 0.12 | −0.02 |

Source: The author.

with the **S&P 500 Composite Index** (a *median* correlation value of 0.34, a *mean* correlation value of 0.40, and an overall range of 0.06 to 0.80) during 26 10-year time periods. The correlation of annual returns of the U.S. Treasury 10-Year Note with the returns of the **Lehman Brothers/Bridgewater TIPS Index** has a *median* correlation value of 0.54, a *mean* correlation value of 0.34, an overall range of −0.36 to 0.80, and some clustering of negative values, during 26 10-year periods.

The fixed-income securities asset class, represented by the U.S. Treasury 10-Year Note, displays generally *low positive* correlations with the **Nasdaq Composite Index** (a *median* correlation value of 0.13, a *mean* correlation value of 0.20, and an overall range of −0.30 to 0.68, with some clustering of negative values) during 24 10-year periods. The correlation of annual returns of the U.S. Treasury 10-Year Note with the returns of the **Wilshire 5000 Index** has a *median* correlation value of 0.26, a *mean* correlation value of 0.36, and an overall range of −0.03 to 0.79, during 25 10-year periods. The correlation of annual returns of the U.S. Treasury 10-Year Note with the returns of the **MSCI EAFE Net Index** has a *median* correlation value of 0.01, a *mean* correla-

| Range of Correlations | Number of 10-Year Periods | Degree of Correlation | Evidence of Clustering |
|:---:|:---:|:---:|:---:|
| 0.66 to 0.99 | 26 out of 26 | High Positive | — |
| 0.97 to 0.99 | 24 out of 26 | High Positive | — |
| 0.36 to 0.94 | 26 out of 26 | High Positive | — |
| | | | |
| 0.26 to 0.75 | 25 out of 26 | Moderately Positive | — |
| 0.06 to 0.67 | 26 out of 26 | Moderately Positive | — |
| 0.06 to 0.80 | 26 out of 26 | Moderately Positive | — |
| −0.17 to 0.77 | 24 out of 26 | Moderately Positive | — |
| 0.20 to 0.88 | 26 out of 26 | Moderately Positive | — |
| 0.07 to 0.81 | 20 out of 26 | Moderately Positive | — |
| 0.32 to 0.69 | 6 out of 26 | Moderately Positive | — |
| | | | |
| −0.03 to 0.45 | 26 out of 26 | Low Positive | — |
| −0.31 to 0.71 | 26 out of 26 | Low Positive | of Negative Values |
| −0.25 to 0.39 | 25 out of 26 | Low Positive | of Negative Values |
| −0.19 to 0.59 | 26 out of 26 | Low Positive | — |
| | | | |
| −0.52 to 0.45 | 26 out of 26 | Low Negative | of Negative Values |
| −0.61 to 0.46 | 26 out of 26 | Very Low Positive | of Negative Values |

tion value of 0.02, an overall range of −0.61 to 0.51, and some clustering of negative values, during 26 10-year periods. The correlation of annual returns of the U.S. Treasury 10-Year Note with the returns of the **MSCI Europe Free Net Index** has a *median* correlation value of 0.36, a *mean* correlation value of 0.24, and an overall range of −0.45 to 0.80, during 26 10-year periods. The correlation of annual returns of the U.S. Treasury 10-Year Note with the returns of the **NAREIT Index** has a *median* correlation value of 0.23, a *mean* correlation value of 0.25, and an overall range of −0.11 to 0.59, during 24 10-year periods.

The fixed-income securities asset class, represented by the U.S. Treasury 10-Year Note, displays *very low positive* correlations or *negative* correlations with the **MSCI Japan Net Index** (a *median* correlation value of −0.05, a *mean* correlation value of −0.10, an overall range of −0.57 to 0.31, and some clustering of negative values) during 26 10-year periods. The correlation of annual returns of the U.S. Treasury 10-Year Note with the returns of the **National Association of Realtors Median Home Price** has a *median* correlation value of 0.10, a *mean* correlation value of −0.15, an overall range of −0.82 to 0.44, and some clustering of

**T A B L E   6.3**

Fixed-Income Correlation Summary —1970 through 2004
(Represented by the U.S. Treasury 10-Year Note)

| 10-Year Rolling Correlations of Annual Returns with: | Median Correlation | Mean Correlation |
|---|---|---|
| Lehman Brothers 7-Year Municipal Bond | 0.89 | 0.92 |
| Lehman Brothers Aggregate Bond | 0.98 | 0.98 |
| | | |
| S&P 500 Composite | 0.34 | 0.40 |
| Lehman Brothers/Bridgewater TIPS | 0.54 | 0.34 |
| | | |
| Nasdaq | 0.13 | 0.20 |
| Wilshire 5000 | 0.26 | 0.36 |
| MSCI EAFE Net | 0.01 | 0.02 |
| MSCI Europe Free Net | 0.36 | 0.24 |
| NAREIT | 0.23 | 0.25 |
| | | |
| MSCI Japan Net | −0.05 | −0.10 |
| National Assn. of Realtors Median Home Price | 0.10 | −0.15 |
| Venture Economics All Private Equity Fund | −0.19 | −0.08 |
| Handy & Harmon Spot Gold Price | −0.02 | −0.08 |
| Handy & Harmon Spot Silver Price | −0.14 | −0.05 |
| HFRI Fund Weighted Composite Hedge Fund | −0.06 | −0.10 |
| MEI/Moses Fine Art | −0.06 | −0.03 |

Source: The author.

negative values) during 26 10-year periods. The correlation of annual returns of the U.S. Treasury 10-Year Note with the returns of the **Venture Economics All Private Equity Fund Index** has a *median* correlation value of –0.19, a *mean* correlation value of –0.08, an overall range of –0.52 to 0.48, and some clustering of negative values, during 26 10-year periods. The correlation of annual returns of the U.S. Treasury 10-Year Note with the returns of the **Handy & Harmon Spot Gold Price** has a *median* correlation value of –0.02, a *mean* correlation value of –0.08, an overall range of –0.56 to 0.35, and some clustering of negative values, during 26 10-year periods. The correlation of annual returns of the U.S. Treasury 10-Year Note with the returns of the **Handy & Harmon Spot Silver Price** has a *median* correlation value of –0.14, a *mean* correlation value of –0.05, an overall range of –0.38 to 0.39, and some clustering of negative values, during 25 10-year periods. The correlation of annual returns of the U.S. Treasury 10-Year Note with the returns of the **HFRI Fund Weighted Composite Hedge Fund Index** had a *median* correlation value of –0.06, a *mean* correlation value of –0.10, and an overall

| Range of Correlations | Number of 10-Year Periods | Degree of Correlation | Evidence of Clustering |
|---|---|---|---|
| 0.53 to 0.96 | 26 out of 26 | High Positive | — |
| 0.97 to 0.98 | 20 out of 26 | High Positive | of Absolute Values |
| 0.06 to 0.80 | 26 out of 26 | Moderately Positive | — |
| −0.36 to 0.80 | 26 out of 26 | Moderately Positive | of Negative Values |
| −0.30 to 0.68 | 24 out of 26 | Low Positive | of Negative Values |
| −0.03 to 0.79 | 25 out of 26 | Low Positive | — |
| −0.61 to 0.51 | 26 out of 26 | Low Positive | of Negative Values |
| −0.45 to 0.80 | 26 out of 26 | Low Positive | — |
| −0.11 to 0.59 | 24 out of 26 | Low Positive | — |
| −0.57 to 0.31 | 26 out of 26 | Low Negative | of Negative Values |
| −0.82 to 0.44 | 26 out of 26 | Very Low Positive | of Negative Values |
| −0.52 to 0.48 | 26 out of 26 | Low Negative | of Negative Values |
| −0.56 to 0.35 | 26 out of 26 | Low Negative | of Negative Values |
| −0.38 to 0.39 | 25 out of 26 | Low Negative | of Negative Values |
| −0.28 to 0.14 | 6 out of 26 | Low Negative | — |
| −0.45 to 0.42 | 26 out of 26 | Low Negative | — |

range of −0.28 to 0.14, during six 10-year periods. The correlation of annual returns of the U.S. Treasury 10-Year Note with the returns of the **Mei Moses Fine Art Index** has a *median* correlation value of −0.06, a *mean* correlation value of −0.03, an overall range of −0.45 to 0.42, and some clustering of negative values, during 26 10-year periods.

## SUMMARY OF HISTORICAL PERSPECTIVE ON 10-YEAR OVERLAPPING CORRELATIONS BETWEEN ALTERNATIVE INVESTMENTS ASSET CLASSES

The alternative investments asset class, summarized in Table 6.4 on pages 170–171 and represented by the **NAREIT Index**, displays essentially *no high degree of positive* correlation with any of the other 16 asset classes. This is due in part to the fact that the returns from real estate are largely driven by asset-specific supply and demand considerations.

The alternative investments asset class, represented by the NAREIT Index, displays *moderately positive* correlations with the **S&P 500 Composite**

**Index** (a median correlation value of 0.60, a mean correlation value of 0.47, and an overall range of –0.17 to 0.77) during 24 10-year time periods. The correlation of annual returns of the NAREIT Index with the returns of the **Nasdaq Composite Index** has a *median* correlation value of 0.63, a *mean* correlation value of 0.47, and an overall range of –0.48 to 0.91 during 24 10-year periods. The correlation of annual returns of the NAREIT Index with the returns of the **Wilshire 5000 Index** has a *median* correlation value of 0.64, a *mean* correlation value of 0.52, and an overall range of –0.16 to 0.83 during 24 10-year periods. The correlation of annual returns of the NAREIT Index with the returns of the **National Association of Realtors Median Home Price** has a *median* correlation value of 0.31, a *mean* correlation value of 0.38, and an overall range of –0.15 to 0.87 during 24 10-year periods. The correlation of annual returns of the NAREIT index with the returns of the **Venture Economics All Private Equity Fund Index** has a *median* correlation value of 0.58, a *mean* correlation value of 0.38, an overall range of –0.30 to 0.74, and some clustering of negative values, during 24 10-year periods.

The alternative investments asset class, represented by the NAREIT Index, displays generally *low positive* correlations with the **MSCI EAFE Net Index** (a *median* correlation value of 0.16, a *mean* correlation value of 0.14, an overall range of –0.40 to 0.49, and some clustering of negative values) during 24 10-year time periods. The correlation of annual returns of the NAREIT Index with the returns of the **MSCI Europe Free Net Index** has a *median* correlation value of 0.22 and a *mean* correlation value of 0.23 and an overall range of –0.18 to 0.53 during 24 10-year periods. The correlation of annual returns of the NAREIT Index with the returns of the **Lehman Brothers 7-Year Municipal Bond Index** has a *median* correlation value of 0.31, a *mean* correlation value of 0.31, and an overall range of 0.13 to 0.52 during 24 10-year periods. The correlation of annual returns of the NAREIT Index with the returns of the **U.S. Treasury 10-Year Note** has a *median* correlation value of 0.23, a *mean* correlation value of 0.25, and an overall range of –0.11 to 0.59 during 24 10-year periods. The correlation of annual returns of the NAREIT Index with the returns of the **Handy & Harmon Spot Silver Price** has a *median* correlation value of 0.21, a *mean* correlation value of 0.20, and an overall range of –0.27 to 0.59 during 24 10-year periods. The correlation of annual returns of the NAREIT Index with the returns of the **Lehman Brothers Aggregate Bond Index** has a median and mean correlation value of 0.28, and an overall range of –0.05 to 0.56 during 20 10-year periods. The correlation of annual returns of the NAREIT index with the returns of the **HFRI Fund Weighted Composite Hedge Fund Index** has a *median* correlation value of 0.27, a *mean* correlation value of 0.33, and an overall range of 0.22 to 0.63 during 6 10-year periods.

The alternative investments asset class, as represented by the NAREIT Index, displays *very low* correlations or *negative* correlations with the **MSCI Japan Net Index** (a *median* correlation value of 0.01, a *mean* correlation value of –0.02, an overall range of –0.55 to 0.43, and some clustering of negative values) during 24 10-year time periods. The correlation of annual returns of the NAREIT Index with the returns of the **Handy & Harmon Spot Gold Price** has a *median* correlation value of –0.19, a *mean* correlation value of –0.06, an overall range of –0.39 to 0.54, and some clustering of negative values, during 24 10-year periods. The correlation of annual returns of the NAREIT Index with the returns of the **Lehman Brothers/Bridgewater TIPS Index** has a *median* and *mean* correlation value of 0.00, an overall range of –0.45 to 0.54, and some clustering of negative values, during 24 10-year periods. The correlation of annual returns of the NAREIT Index with the returns of the **Mei Moses Fine Art Index** has a *median* correlation value of –0.31, a *mean* correlation value of –0.14, an overall range of –0.46 to 0.62, and some clustering of negative values, during 24 10-year periods.

## Comments on Multiyear Correlations Data

The following sections of this chapter review in detail the *rolling 10-year* correlations of annual returns for 17 separate indices, representing the asset classes shown in Table 6.1.

For each of these 17 asset classes, the *rolling 10-year* correlations of annual returns calculations cover 26 periods, beginning with the 1970–1979 decade and ending with the 1995–2004 decade. It is possible to construct a wide variety of correlations data with different holding periods, investment horizons, beginning and ending dates, and rolling versus nonoverlapping interval definitions.

Analyzing the year-to-year evaluation of multiperiod correlations data can shed light on: (i) the *absolute value* of positive or negative correlations between pairs of asset classes for specific periods or groups of periods; (ii) the range within which these correlations have fluctuated; (iii) how the correlations have moved through time; and (iv) the degree to which the correlations have tended to cluster between specified values for several multiyear intervals of time.

**T A B L E  6.4**

Alternative Investments Correlation Summary—1970 through 2004
(Represented by the NAREIT)

| 10-Year Rolling Correlations of Annual Returns with: | Median Correlation | Mean Correlation |
|---|---|---|
| S&P 500 Composite | 0.60 | 0.47 |
| Nasdaq Composite | 0.63 | 0.47 |
| Wilshire 5000 | 0.64 | 0.52 |
| National Assn. of Realtors Median Home Price | 0.31 | 0.38 |
| Venture Economics All Private Equity Fund | 0.58 | 0.38 |
| MSCI EAFE Net | 0.16 | 0.14 |
| MSCI Europe Free Net | 0.22 | 0.23 |
| Lehman Brothers 7-Year Municipal Bond | 0.31 | 0.31 |
| U.S. Treasury 10-Year Note | 0.23 | 0.25 |
| Handy & Harmon Spot Silver Price | 0.21 | 0.20 |
| Lehman Brothers Aggregate Bond | 0.28 | 0.28 |
| HFRI Fund Weighted Composite Hedge Fund | 0.27 | 0.33 |
| MSCI Japan Net | 0.01 | −0.02 |
| Handy & Harmon Spot Gold Price | −0.19 | −0.06 |
| Lehman Brothers/Bridgewater TIPS | 0.00 | 0.00 |
| MEI/Moses Fine Art | −0.31 | −0.14 |

Source: The author.

## ROLLING 10-YEAR CORRELATIONS OF ANNUAL RETURNS

Based on the annual returns for each year from 1970 through 2004, rolling 10-year correlations calculations cover 26 periods, presented in a series of tables and figures with 17 asset classes beginning with the Standard & Poor's 500 Composite Index representing U.S. large-cap equities and ending with the HFRI Fund Weighted Composite Hedge Fund Index representing hedge funds. Rolling 10-year correlations data are not shown for any assets and periods for which the underlying annual returns have not been reported by the index creator. In each exhibit, the progression of correlations on a multiyear period-to-period basis for 4 of the 17 asset classes has been identified by a box around the data.

Without drawing any conclusions about possible causality or the underlying asset price conditions affecting each of the four asset pairs chosen for commentary, the following sections offer brief observations about the frequency of 10-year correlations of annual returns within selected correlation ranges. Accompanying tables and figures display the progression of correlations for the four selected asset pairs.

| Range of Correlations | Number of 10-Year Periods | Degree of Correlation | Evidence of Clustering |
|---|---|---|---|
| –0.17 to 0.77 | 24 out of 26 | Moderately Positive | — |
| –0.48 to 0.91 | 24 out of 26 | Moderately Positive | — |
| –0.16 to 0.83 | 24 out of 26 | Moderately Positive | — |
| –0.15 to 0.87 | 24 out of 26 | Moderately Positive | — |
| –0.30 to 0.74 | 24 out of 26 | Moderately Positive | — |
| –0.40 to 0.49 | 24 out of 26 | Low Positive | of Negative Values |
| –0.18 to 0.53 | 24 out of 26 | Low Positive | — |
| 0.13 to 0.52 | 24 out of 26 | Low Positive | — |
| –0.11 to 0.59 | 24 out of 26 | Low Positive | — |
| –0.27 to 0.59 | 24 out of 26 | Low Positive | — |
| –0.05 to 0.56 | 20 out of 26 | Low Positive | — |
| 0.22 to 0.63 | 6 out of 26 | Low Positive | — |
| –0.55 to 0.43 | 24 out of 26 | Very Low Positive | of Negative Values |
| –0.39 to 0.54 | 24 out of 26 | Low Negative | — |
| –0.45 to 0.54 | 24 out of 26 | Zero | of Negative Values |
| –0.46 to 0.62 | 24 out of 26 | Low Negative | of Negative Values |

Wherever possible, asset pairs have been chosen for commentary based on: (i) potentially interesting asset *affinities within* the major supercategories of asset classes, such as between various kinds of equities, between various kinds of fixed-income securities, or between various kinds of alternative investments; or (ii) potentially interesting asset *contrasts between* major supercategories of assets, such as correlation pairings between equities and fixed-income securities or alternative investments, between fixed-income securities and equities or alternative investments, or between alternative investments and equities or fixed-income securities.

It is worth recalling that the correlation of returns between Asset A and Asset B is definitionally *the same* as the correlations of returns between Asset B and Asset A. As a result, the figures and tables note where applicable the location of additional observations about the frequency and range of correlations of returns between an identified asset and another asset.

**T A B L E  6.5**

## U.S. Large Cap Equities: Correlations of the Standard & Poor's 500 Composite Index[1]

| | S&P 500 Composite Index for 10-Year Periods from: | S&P 500 Composite Index | Nasdaq Composite Index | Wilshire 5000 Index | MSCI EAFE Net Index | MSCI Europe Free Net Index | MSCI Japan Net Index | Lehman Brothers 7-Year Municipal Bond Index |
|---|---|---|---|---|---|---|---|---|
| | | 1 | 2 | 3 | 4 | 5 | 6 | 7 |
| 1 | 1995–2004 | 1.00 | 0.81 | 0.99 | 0.72 | 0.92 | 0.33 | 0.07 |
| 2 | 1994–2003 | 1.00 | 0.81 | 0.99 | 0.75 | 0.94 | 0.34 | 0.06 |
| 3 | 1993–2002 | 1.00 | 0.80 | 0.99 | 0.65 | 0.89 | 0.25 | 0.07 |
| 4 | 1992–2001 | 1.00 | 0.75 | 0.99 | 0.56 | 0.84 | 0.24 | 0.26 |
| 5 | 1991–2000 | 1.00 | 0.72 | 0.99 | 0.39 | 0.73 | 0.09 | 0.33 |
| 6 | 1990–1999 | 1.00 | 0.66 | 0.98 | 0.40 | 0.69 | 0.09 | 0.43 |
| 7 | 1989–1998 | 1.00 | 0.82 | 0.98 | 0.42 | 0.72 | 0.09 | 0.57 |
| 8 | 1988–1997 | 1.00 | 0.82 | 0.99 | 0.32 | 0.70 | 0.03 | 0.59 |
| 9 | 1987–1996 | 1.00 | 0.86 | 0.99 | 0.28 | 0.70 | 0.01 | 0.66 |
| 10 | 1986–1995 | 1.00 | 0.85 | 0.99 | 0.26 | 0.58 | 0.10 | 0.57 |
| 11 | 1985–1994 | 1.00 | 0.83 | 0.99 | 0.49 | 0.69 | 0.29 | 0.67 |
| 12 | 1984–1993 | 1.00 | 0.83 | 0.99 | 0.49 | 0.69 | 0.31 | 0.61 |
| 13 | 1983–1992 | 1.00 | 0.84 | 0.99 | 0.52 | 0.71 | 0.32 | 0.53 |
| 14 | 1982–1991 | 1.00 | 0.88 | 0.99 | 0.42 | 0.64 | 0.21 | 0.40 |
| 15 | 1981–1990 | 1.00 | 0.91 | 0.99 | 0.55 | 0.78 | 0.29 | 0.62 |
| 16 | 1980–1989 | 1.00 | 0.90 | 0.99 | 0.36 | 0.66 | 0.00 | 0.33 |
| 17 | 1979–1988 | 1.00 | 0.89 | 0.97 | 0.44 | 0.66 | 0.11 | 0.32 |
| 18 | 1978–1987 | 1.00 | 0.86 | 0.97 | 0.39 | 0.62 | 0.04 | 0.35 |
| 19 | 1977–1986 | 1.00 | 0.79 | 0.97 | 0.39 | 0.49 | 0.15 | 0.30 |
| 20 | 1976–1985 | 1.00 | 0.83 | 0.98 | 0.35 | 0.38 | 0.13 | 0.30 |
| 21 | 1975–1984 | 1.00 | 0.82 | 0.98 | 0.31 | 0.36 | (0.03) | 0.23 |
| 22 | 1974–1983 | 1.00 | 0.94 | 0.99 | 0.61 | 0.60 | 0.34 | 0.36 |
| 23 | 1973–1982 | 1.00 | 0.93 | 0.99 | 0.66 | 0.62 | 0.45 | 0.33 |
| 24 | 1972–1981 | 1.00 | 0.93 | 0.99 | 0.71 | 0.65 | 0.41 | 0.29 |
| 25 | 1971–1980 | 1.00 | 0.99 | – | 0.69 | 0.62 | 0.41 | 0.23 |
| 26 | 1970–1979 | 1.00 | 0.67 | – | – | 0.65 | 0.44 | 0.51 |

[1]Rolling 10-year correlations of annual returns of the Standard & Poor's 500 Composite Index with selected asset classes during 26 10-year periods beginning with 1970–1979 and ending with 1995–2004.

Source: The author.

| U.S. Treasury 10-Year Note | NAREIT Index | Nat'l Assn of Realtors Median Home Price | Venture Economics All Private Equity Fund Index | Handy & Harmon Spot Gold Price | Handy & Harmon Spot Silver Price | Lehman Brothers/ Bridgewater TIPS Index | Mel Moses Fine Art Index | Lehman Brothers Aggregate Bond Index | HFRI Fund Weighted Composite Hedge Fund Index |
|---|---|---|---|---|---|---|---|---|---|
| 8 | 9 | 10 | 11 | 12 | 13 | 14 | 15 | 16 | 17 |
| 0.06 | 0.08 | (0.28) | 0.45 | (0.34) | 0.37 | (0.41) | 0.41 | 0.07 | 0.69 |
| 0.06 | 0.09 | (0.18) | 0.41 | (0.34) | 0.39 | (0.41) | 0.42 | 0.07 | 0.69 |
| 0.10 | (0.04) | (0.31) | 0.45 | (0.52) | 0.20 | (0.56) | 0.36 | 0.11 | 0.58 |
| 0.30 | (0.17) | (0.20) | 0.41 | (0.22) | 0.23 | (0.34) | 0.24 | 0.24 | 0.41 |
| 0.35 | (0.04) | 0.44 | 0.20 | (0.22) | 0.17 | (0.30) | (0.06) | 0.39 | 0.36 |
| 0.54 | 0.37 | 0.71 | 0.30 | (0.33) | 0.18 | (0.15) | 0.02 | 0.52 | 0.32 |
| 0.70 | 0.37 | 0.57 | 0.61 | (0.32) | 0.09 | (0.01) | 0.11 | 0.65 | – |
| 0.69 | 0.61 | 0.59 | 0.63 | (0.31) | 0.17 | 0.06 | 0.01 | 0.67 | – |
| 0.74 | 0.64 | 0.45 | 0.64 | (0.28) | (0.14) | 0.43 | 0.02 | 0.73 | – |
| 0.80 | 0.65 | 0.44 | 0.58 | (0.19) | (0.13) | 0.45 | 0.01 | 0.81 | – |
| 0.80 | 0.71 | 0.49 | 0.26 | (0.13) | (0.25) | 0.46 | 0.02 | 0.81 | – |
| 0.72 | 0.61 | 0.47 | 0.34 | (0.05) | (0.14) | 0.34 | (0.09) | 0.70 | – |
| 0.62 | 0.66 | 0.47 | 0.46 | (0.04) | (0.07) | 0.16 | (0.16) | 0.64 | – |
| 0.54 | 0.69 | 0.40 | 0.51 | (0.03) | 0.04 | 0.16 | (0.19) | 0.47 | – |
| 0.57 | 0.61 | 0.03 | 0.58 | 0.34 | 0.33 | 0.17 | 0.15 | 0.54 | – |
| 0.33 | 0.51 | 0.07 | 0.61 | 0.45 | 0.08 | 0.44 | 0.17 | 0.29 | – |
| 0.29 | 0.60 | 0.24 | 0.71 | 0.26 | 0.07 | 0.35 | 0.17 | 0.26 | – |
| 0.34 | 0.63 | (0.01) | 0.52 | 0.21 | 0.07 | 0.28 | 0.21 | 0.32 | – |
| 0.35 | 0.47 | (0.26) | 0.31 | 0.17 | 0.09 | 0.28 | 0.47 | 0.35 | – |
| 0.36 | 0.49 | (0.23) | 0.41 | 0.13 | 0.08 | 0.31 | 0.59 | 0.37 | – |
| 0.11 | 0.45 | (0.09) | 0.73 | 0.00 | 0.07 | 0.12 | 0.03 | – | – |
| 0.22 | 0.73 | (0.24) | 0.84 | (0.27) | 0.03 | (0.38) | 0.35 | – | – |
| 0.26 | 0.77 | (0.13) | 0.88 | (0.33) | 0.03 | (0.40) | 0.11 | – | – |
| 0.15 | 0.74 | (0.01) | 0.88 | (0.28) | 0.04 | (0.44) | 0.18 | – | – |
| 0.20 | – | (0.20) | 0.87 | (0.45) | (0.03) | (0.52) | 0.17 | – | – |
| 0.23 | – | (0.14) | 0.85 | (0.38) | – | (0.61) | 0.09 | – | – |

## U.S. Large-Cap Equities

Table 6.5 displays the Standard & Poor's 500 Composite Index's rolling 10-year correlations of annual returns with 16 other asset classes for 26 time periods, beginning with the 1970–1979 decade and ending with the 1995–2004 decade.

The four boxed columns in Table 6.5 highlight the rolling 10-year correlations of annual returns between the Standard & Poor's 500 Composite Index and four asset classes: (i) European equities, as represented by the MSCI Europe Free Net Index; (ii) Japanese equities, as represented by the MSCI Japan Net Index; (iii) real estate investment trusts, as represented by the NAREIT Index; and (iv) U.S. taxable fixed-income securities, as represented by the Lehman Brothers Aggregate Bond Index.

For the 26 10-year periods between 1970–1979 and 1995–2004, the correlations of annual returns between the Standard & Poor's 500 Composite index and the:

- ◆ **MSCI Europe Net Index**: ranged between 0.58 and 0.94 for 23 of 26 10-year periods, and between 0.36 and 0.49 for 3 of 26 10-year periods;

- ◆ **MSCI Japan Net Index:** ranged between -0.03 and 0.34 for 22 of 26 10-year periods, and between 0.41 and 0.45 for 4 of 26 10-year periods;

- ◆ **NAREIT Index**: ranged between 0.45 and 0.77 for 17 out of 24 10-year periods, and between –0.17 and 0.37 for 7 out of 24 10-year periods; and

- ◆ **Lehman Brothers Aggregate Bond Index**: ranged between 0.52 and 0.81 in nine out of 20 10-year periods, and between 0.07 and 0.47 in 11 out of 20 10-year periods.

Figure 6.1 depicts the rolling 10-year correlations of annual returns between the Standard & Poor's 500 Composite Index and the MSCI Europe Free Net Index, the MSCI Japan Net Index, the NAREIT Index, and the Lehman Brothers Aggregate Bond Index.

For additional observations on the rolling 10-year correlations of annual returns between the Standard & Poor's 500 Composite Index and other asset classes, please refer to the tables and figures for the Nasdaq Composite Index, the Wilshire 5000 Index, the Lehman Brothers 7-Year Municipal Bond Index, the U.S. Treasury 10-Year Note, the National Association of Realtors Median Home Price, the Venture Economics All Private Equity Fund Index, the Handy & Harmon Spot Gold Price, the Lehman Brothers/Bridgewater TIPS Index, the Mei Moses Fine Art Index, and the HFRI Fund Weighted Composite Hedge Fund Index.

F I G U R E   6.1

U.S. Large-Cap Equities: Correlations of the Standard & Poor's 500
Composite Index

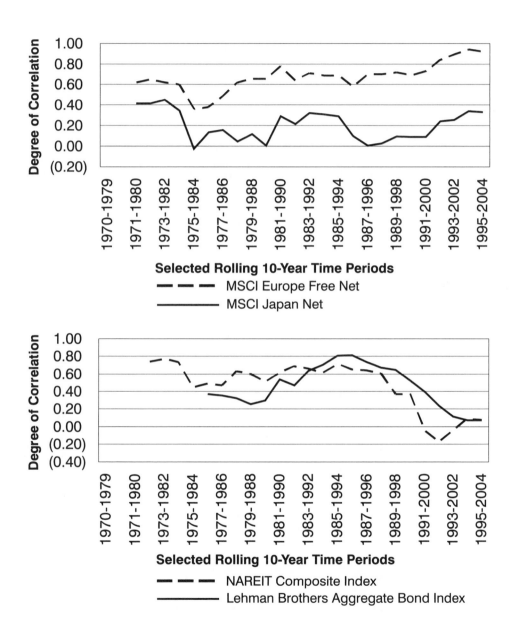

Source: The author.

**T A B L E  6.6**

## U.S. Unlisted Equities: Correlations of the Nasdaq Composite Index[1]

| Nasdaq Composite Index for 10-Year Periods from: | S&P 500 Composite Index | Nasdaq Composite Index | Wilshire 5000 Index | MSCI EAFE Net Index | MSCI Europe Free Net Index | MSCI Japan Net Index | Lehman Brothers 7-Year Municipal Bond Index |
|---|---|---|---|---|---|---|---|
| | 1 | 2 | 3 | 4 | 5 | 6 | 7 |
| 1  1995–2004 | 0.81 | 1.00 | 0.85 | 0.84 | 0.78 | 0.74 | (0.23) |
| 2  1994–2003 | 0.81 | 1.00 | 0.85 | 0.88 | 0.80 | 0.76 | (0.24) |
| 3  1993–2002 | 0.80 | 1.00 | 0.84 | 0.79 | 0.74 | 0.70 | (0.23) |
| 4  1992–2001 | 0.75 | 1.00 | 0.80 | 0.71 | 0.65 | 0.70 | (0.14) |
| 5  1991–2000 | 0.72 | 1.00 | 0.79 | 0.63 | 0.52 | 0.63 | (0.05) |
| 6  1990–1999 | 0.66 | 1.00 | 0.74 | 0.62 | 0.43 | 0.65 | 0.03 |
| 7  1989–1998 | 0.82 | 1.00 | 0.87 | 0.53 | 0.52 | 0.31 | 0.47 |
| 8  1988–1997 | 0.82 | 1.00 | 0.88 | 0.41 | 0.47 | 0.21 | 0.53 |
| 9  1987–1996 | 0.86 | 1.00 | 0.92 | 0.27 | 0.51 | 0.03 | 0.60 |
| 10  1986–1995 | 0.85 | 1.00 | 0.91 | 0.11 | 0.32 | (0.04) | 0.38 |
| 11  1985–1994 | 0.83 | 1.00 | 0.90 | 0.26 | 0.41 | 0.08 | 0.44 |
| 12  1984–1993 | 0.83 | 1.00 | 0.90 | 0.27 | 0.42 | 0.10 | 0.38 |
| 13  1983–1992 | 0.84 | 1.00 | 0.91 | 0.27 | 0.42 | 0.10 | 0.33 |
| 14  1982–1991 | 0.88 | 1.00 | 0.93 | 0.28 | 0.43 | 0.10 | 0.28 |
| 15  1981–1990 | 0.91 | 1.00 | 0.95 | 0.53 | 0.72 | 0.29 | 0.51 |
| 16  1980–1989 | 0.90 | 1.00 | 0.95 | 0.28 | 0.56 | (0.05) | 0.18 |
| 17  1979–1988 | 0.89 | 1.00 | 0.96 | 0.20 | 0.50 | (0.15) | 0.12 |
| 18  1978–1987 | 0.86 | 1.00 | 0.95 | 0.20 | 0.50 | (0.16) | 0.12 |
| 19  1977–1986 | 0.79 | 1.00 | 0.90 | 0.23 | 0.46 | (0.09) | 0.05 |
| 20  1976–1985 | 0.83 | 1.00 | 0.92 | 0.38 | 0.43 | 0.09 | 0.15 |
| 21  1975–1984 | 0.82 | 1.00 | 0.90 | 0.32 | 0.41 | (0.05) | 0.08 |
| 22  1974–1983 | 0.94 | 1.00 | 0.97 | 0.67 | 0.65 | 0.40 | 0.30 |
| 23  1973–1982 | 0.93 | 1.00 | 0.97 | 0.73 | 0.66 | 0.55 | 0.24 |
| 24  1972–1981 | 0.93 | 1.00 | 0.97 | 0.75 | 0.68 | 0.42 | 0.23 |
| 25  1971–1980 | – | – | – | – | – | – | – |
| 26  1970–1979 | – | – | – | – | – | – | – |

[1]Rolling 10-year correlations of annual returns of the Nasdaq Composite Index with selected asset classes during 24 10-year periods beginning with 1972–1981 and ending with 1995–2004.

Source: The author.

| U.S. Treasury 10-Year Note | NAREIT Index | Nat'l Assn of Realtors Median Home Price | Venture Economics All Private Equity Fund Index | Handy & Harmon Spot Gold Price | Handy & Harmon Spot Silver Price | Lehman Brothers/ Bridgewater TIPS Index | Mei Moses Fine Art Index | Lehman Brothers Aggregate Bond Index | HFRI Fund Weighted Composite Hedge Fund Index |
|---|---|---|---|---|---|---|---|---|---|
| 8 | 9 | 10 | 11 | 12 | 13 | 14 | 15 | 16 | 17 |
| (0.30) | (0.18) | (0.27) | 0.76 | (0.05) | 0.35 | (0.52) | 0.40 | (0.26) | 0.80 |
| (0.30) | (0.17) | (0.15) | 0.71 | (0.04) | 0.39 | (0.52) | 0.41 | (0.27) | 0.80) |
| (0.26) | (0.36) | (0.35) | 0.81 | (0.20) | 0.20 | (0.63) | 0.33 | (0.23) | 0.70 |
| (0.18) | (0.48) | (0.28) | 0.79 | 0.09 | 0.21 | (0.52) | 0.25 | (0.19) | 0.62 |
| (0.12) | (0.29) | 0.30 | 0.67 | 0.07 | 0.12 | (0.46) | (0.08) | (0.02) | 0.62 |
| 0.04 | 0.13 | 0.60 | 0.81 | (0.02) | 0.10 | (0.32) | 0.01 | 0.08 | 0.60 |
| 0.64 | 0.46 | 0.80 | 0.63 | (0.14) | 0.05 | (0.05) | (0.13) | 0.59 | – |
| 0.63 | 0.82 | 0.84 | 0.67 | (0.16) | 0.16 | 0.07 | (0.20) | 0.63 | – |
| 0.68 | 0.84 | 0.71 | 0.71 | (0.34) | (0.04) | 0.18 | (0.30) | 0.67 | – |
| 0.66 | 0.87 | 0.62 | 0.73 | (0.34) | 0.00 | 0.23 | (0.26) | 0.66 | – |
| 0.62 | 0.91 | 0.66 | 0.65 | (0.31) | (0.09) | 0.22 | (0.27) | 0.63 | – |
| 0.51 | 0.74 | 0.63 | 0.72 | (0.11) | 0.08 | 0.11 | (0.35) | 0.48 | – |
| 0.44 | 0.73 | 0.62 | 0.61 | (0.16) | 0.06 | 0.01 | (0.36) | 0.45 | – |
| 0.41 | 0.73 | 0.59 | 0.60 | (0.12) | 0.10 | 0.05 | (0.37) | 0.37 | – |
| 0.51 | 0.65 | 0.16 | 0.63 | 0.17 | 0.27 | 0.19 | 0.21 | 0.49 | – |
| 0.23 | 0.51 | 0.21 | 0.71 | 0.31 | (0.03) | 0.52 | 0.23 | 0.20 | – |
| 0.11 | 0.63 | 0.41 | 0.77 | 0.42 | 0.31 | 0.57 | 0.20 | 0.06 | – |
| 0.11 | 0.63 | 0.30 | 0.71 | 0.43 | 0.31 | 0.57 | 0.21 | 0.07 | – |
| 0.01 | 0.51 | 0.19 | 0.64 | 0.47 | 0.34 | 0.54 | 0.52 | 0.00 | – |
| 0.09 | 0.51 | 0.20 | 0.65 | 0.43 | 0.31 | 0.49 | 0.54 | 0.06 | – |
| (0.14) | 0.52 | 0.32 | 0.78 | 0.35 | 0.32 | 0.36 | 0.14 | – | – |
| 0.13 | 0.86 | (0.07) | 0.84 | (0.14) | 0.15 | (0.40) | 0.50 | – | – |
| 0.17 | 0.90 | 0.02 | 0.88 | (0.27) | 0.12 | (0.46) | 0.11 | – | – |
| 0.09 | 0.87 | 0.16 | 0.88 | (0.24) | 0.12 | (0.48) | 0.15 | – | – |
| – | – | – | – | – | – | – | – | – | – |
| – | – | – | – | – | – | – | – | – | – |

## U.S. Unlisted Equities

For the Nasdaq Composite Index for 24 time periods, Table 6.6 displays the rolling 10-year correlations of annual returns with 16 other asset classes, beginning with the 1972–1981 decade and ending with the 1995–2004 decade.

The four boxed columns in Table 6.6 highlight the rolling 10-year correlations of annual returns between the Nasdaq Composite Index and four asset classes: (i) large-cap equities, as represented by the Standard & Poor's 500 Composite Index; (ii) U.S. equities, as represented by the Wilshire 5000 Index; (iii) intermediate-maturity tax-exempt bonds, as represented by the Lehman Brothers 7-Year Municipal Bond Index; and (iv) private equity, as represented by the Venture Economics All Private Equity Fund Index.

For the 24 10-year periods between 1972–1981 and 1995–2004, the correlations of annual returns between the Nasdaq Composite Index and the:

- ◆ **Standard & Poor's 500 Composite Index**: ranged between 0.66 and 0.75 for 3 of 24 10-year periods, and between 0.80 and 0.94 for 21 of 24 10-year periods;
- ◆ **Wilshire 5000 Index**: ranged between 0.87 and 0.97 for 18 of 24 10-year periods, and between 0.74 and 0.85 for six of 24 10-year periods;
- ◆ **Lehman Brothers 7-Year Municipal Index**: ranged between 0.44 and 0.68 for 5 of 24 10-year periods, between 0.03 and 0.38 for 14 of 23 periods, and between –0.05 and –0.24 for 5 of 24 10-year periods; and
- ◆ **Venture Economics All Private Equity Fund Index**: ranged between 0.60 and 0.67 for 9 of 24 10-year periods, and between 0.71 and 0.88 for 15 of 24 10-year periods.

Figure 6.2 depicts the rolling 10-year correlations of annual returns between the Nasdaq Composite Index and the Standard & Poor's 500 Composite Index, the Wilshire 5000 Index, the Lehman Brothers 7-Year Municipal Bond Index, and the Venture Economics All Private Equity Fund Index.

For additional observations on the rolling 10-year correlations of annual returns between the Nasdaq Composite Index and other asset classes, please refer to the exhibits for the Wilshire 5000 Index, the MSCI EAFE Net Index, the MSCI Europe Free Net Index, the MSCI Japan Net Index, the U.S. Treasury 10-Year Note, and the Lehman Brothers Aggregate Bond Index.

F I G U R E  6.2

U.S. Unlisted Equities: Correlations of the Nasdaq Composite Index

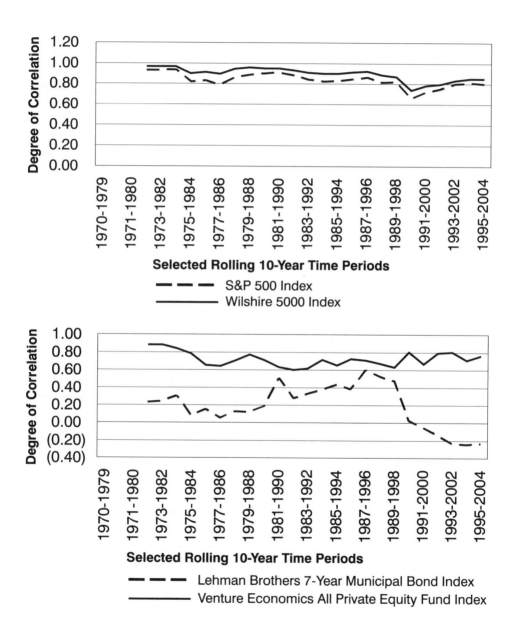

Source: The author.

**T A B L E   6.7**

## U.S. Equities: Correlations of the Wilshire 5000 Index[1]

| Wilshire 5000 Index for 10-Year Periods from: | S&P 500 Composite Index | Nasdaq Composite Index | Wilshire 5000 Index | MSCI EAFE Net Index | MSCI Europe Free Net Index | MSCI Japan Net Index | Lehman Brothers 7-Year Municipal Bond Index |
|---|---|---|---|---|---|---|---|
| | 1 | 2 | 3 | 4 | 5 | 6 | 7 |
| 1   1995–2004 | 0.99 | 0.85 | 1.00 | 0.76 | 0.93 | 0.39 | 0.05 |
| 2   1994–2003 | 0.99 | 0.85 | 1.00 | 0.78 | 0.94 | 0.40 | 0.05 |
| 3   1993–2002 | 0.99 | 0.84 | 1.00 | 0.67 | 0.89 | 0.31 | 0.07 |
| 4   1992–2001 | 0.99 | 0.80 | 1.00 | 0.58 | 0.83 | 0.30 | 0.26 |
| 5   1991–2000 | 0.99 | 0.79 | 1.00 | 0.41 | 0.69 | 0.16 | 0.34 |
| 6   1990–1999 | 0.98 | 0.74 | 1.00 | 0.45 | 0.65 | 0.18 | 0.45 |
| 7   1989–1998 | 0.98 | 0.87 | 1.00 | 0.44 | 0.67 | 0.14 | 0.61 |
| 8   1988–1997 | 0.99 | 0.88 | 1.00 | 0.39 | 0.68 | 0.10 | 0.62 |
| 9   1987–1996 | 0.99 | 0.92 | 1.00 | 0.31 | 0.68 | 0.04 | 0.69 |
| 10   1986–1995 | 0.99 | 0.91 | 1.00 | 0.24 | 0.54 | 0.07 | 0.55 |
| 11   1985–1994 | 0.99 | 0.90 | 1.00 | 0.45 | 0.65 | 0.25 | 0.64 |
| 12   1984–1993 | 0.99 | 0.90 | 1.00 | 0.45 | 0.65 | 0.26 | 0.58 |
| 13   1983–1992 | 0.99 | 0.91 | 1.00 | 0.48 | 0.66 | 0.27 | 0.49 |
| 14   1982–1991 | 0.99 | 0.93 | 1.00 | 0.42 | 0.62 | 0.20 | 0.33 |
| 15   1981–1990 | 0.99 | 0.95 | 1.00 | 0.57 | 0.79 | 0.30 | 0.55 |
| 16   1980–1989 | 0.99 | 0.95 | 1.00 | 0.36 | 0.65 | 0.00 | 0.25 |
| 17   1979–1988 | 0.97 | 0.96 | 1.00 | 0.36 | 0.62 | 0.00 | 0.20 |
| 18   1978–1987 | 0.97 | 0.95 | 1.00 | 0.33 | 0.60 | (0.05) | 0.22 |
| 19   1977–1986 | 0.97 | 0.90 | 1.00 | 0.35 | 0.50 | 0.07 | 0.17 |
| 20   1976–1985 | 0.98 | 0.92 | 1.00 | 0.37 | 0.40 | 0.11 | 0.21 |
| 21   1975–1984 | 0.98 | 0.90 | 1.00 | 0.35 | 0.41 | (0.05) | 0.15 |
| 22   1974–1983 | 0.99 | 0.97 | 1.00 | 0.64 | 0.63 | 0.35 | 0.31 |
| 23   1973–1982 | 0.99 | 0.97 | 1.00 | 0.69 | 0.65 | 0.48 | 0.28 |
| 24   1972–1981 | 0.99 | 0.97 | 1.00 | 0.71 | 0.67 | 0.38 | 0.29 |
| 25   1971–1980 | 0.99 | – | 1.00 | 0.70 | 0.65 | 0.38 | 0.24 |
| 26   1970–1979 | – | – | – | – | – | – | – |

[1]Rolling 10-year correlations of annual returns of the Wilshire 5000 Index with selected asset classes during 25 10-year periods beginning with 1971–1980 and ending with 1995–2004.

Source: The author.

| U.S. Treasury 10-Year Note | NAREIT Index | Nat'l Assn of Realtors Median Home Price | Venture Economics All Private Equity Fund Index | Handy & Harmon Spot Gold Price | Handy & Harmon Spot Silver Price | Lehman Brothers/ Bridgewater TIPS Index | Mei Moses Fine Art Index | Lehman Brothers Aggregate Bond Index | HFRI Fund Weighted Composite Hedge Fund Index |
|---|---|---|---|---|---|---|---|---|---|
| 8 | 9 | 10 | 11 | 12 | 13 | 14 | 15 | 16 | 17 |
| 0.02 | 0.11 | (0.23) | 0.49 | (0.29) | 0.44 | (0.40) | 0.42 | 0.04 | 0.75 |
| 0.02 | 0.12 | (0.13) | 0.45 | (0.29) | 0.46 | (0.40) | 0.43 | 0.04 | 0.74 |
| 0.08 | (0.03) | (0.29) | 0.51 | (0.48) | 0.26 | (0.56) | 0.34 | 0.10 | 0.64 |
| 0.26 | (0.16) | (0.19) | 0.47 | (0.18) | 0.30 | (0.34) | 0.23 | 0.22 | 0.51 |
| 0.33 | 0.02 | 0.51 | 0.26 | (0.20) | 0.22 | (0.28) | (0.13) | 0.40 | 0.50 |
| 0.52 | 0.46 | 0.79 | 0.37 | (0.31) | 0.24 | (0.13) | (0.06) | 0.53 | 0.48 |
| 0.72 | 0.49 | 0.67 | 0.65 | (0.30) | 0.15 | 0.02 | 0.01 | 0.69 | – |
| 0.71 | 0.67 | 0.67 | 0.65 | (0.30) | 0.19 | 0.06 | (0.02) | 0.69 | – |
| 0.76 | 0.71 | 0.52 | 0.66 | (0.32) | (0.11) | 0.39 | (0.04) | 0.75 | – |
| 0.79 | 0.74 | 0.49 | 0.63 | (0.26) | (0.10) | 0.41 | (0.04) | 0.79 | – |
| 0.78 | 0.79 | 0.53 | 0.38 | (0.20) | (0.22) | 0.43 | (0.02) | 0.79 | – |
| 0.69 | 0.67 | 0.52 | 0.46 | (0.08) | (0.08) | 0.31 | (0.13) | 0.67 | – |
| 0.58 | 0.71 | 0.50 | 0.54 | (0.11) | (0.06) | 0.11 | (0.18) | 0.60 | – |
| 0.47 | 0.72 | 0.46 | 0.55 | (0.11) | 0.00 | 0.10 | (0.20) | 0.41 | – |
| 0.52 | 0.64 | 0.07 | 0.60 | 0.24 | 0.26 | 0.14 | 0.21 | 0.49 | – |
| 0.27 | 0.53 | 0.12 | 0.65 | 0.37 | (0.01) | 0.44 | 0.23 | 0.22 | – |
| 0.16 | 0.67 | 0.36 | 0.76 | 0.38 | 0.23 | 0.46 | 0.21 | 0.11 | – |
| 0.21 | 0.70 | 0.15 | 0.62 | 0.35 | 0.23 | 0.41 | 0.23 | 0.17 | – |
| 0.19 | 0.55 | (0.10) | 0.44 | 0.33 | 0.24 | 0.39 | 0.54 | 0.19 | – |
| 0.23 | 0.56 | (0.07) | 0.50 | 0.28 | 0.22 | 0.38 | 0.63 | 0.22 | – |
| (0.03) | 0.51 | 0.06 | 0.78 | 0.14 | 0.20 | 0.20 | 0.07 | – | – |
| 0.14 | 0.78 | (0.16) | 0.86 | (0.21) | 0.11 | (0.38) | 0.40 | – | – |
| 0.19 | 0.83 | (0.05) | 0.90 | (0.28) | 0.10 | (0.41) | 0.11 | – | – |
| 0.14 | 0.80 | 0.04 | 0.89 | (0.25) | 0.11 | (0.44) | 0.16 | – | – |
| 0.19 | – | (0.13) | 0.89 | (0.42) | 0.03 | (0.51) | 0.16 | – | – |
| – | – | – | – | – | – | – | – | – | – |

## U.S. Equities

For the Wilshire 5000 Index for 25 time periods, Table 6.7 displays the rolling 10-year correlations of annual returns with 16 other asset classes, beginning with the 1971–1980 decade and ending with the 1995–2004 decade.

The four boxed columns in Table 6.7 highlight the rolling 10-year correlations of annual returns between the Wilshire 5000 Index and four asset classes: (i) U.S. large-cap equities, as represented by the Standard & Poor's 500 Composite Index; (ii) U.S. unlisted equities, as represented by the Nasdaq Composite Index; (iii) intermediate-maturity U.S. Treasury Bonds, as represented by the U.S. Treasury 10-year Note; and (iv) fine art, as represented by the Mei Moses Fine Art Index.

For the 25 10-year periods between 1971–1980 and 1995–2004, the correlations of annual returns between the Wilshire 5000 Index and the:

- **Standard & Poor's 500 Composite** Index ranged between 0.97 and 0.99 for 25 of 25 10-year periods;
- **Nasdaq Composite Index**: ranged between 0.74 and 0.85 for six of 24 10-year periods, and between 0.87 and 0.95 for 18 of 24 10-year periods;
- **U.S. Treasury 10-Year Note:** ranged between –0.03 and 0.33 for 15 out of 25 10-year periods, and between 0.47 and 0.79 for 10 out of 25 10-year periods; and
- **Mei Moses Fine Art Index**: ranged between –0.20 and 0.23 for 19 out of 25 10-year periods, and between 0.34 and 0.63 for 6 out of 25 10-year periods.

Figure 6.3 depicts the rolling 10-year correlations of annual returns between the Wilshire 5000 Index and the Standard & Poor's 500 Composite Index, the Nasdaq Composite Index, the U.S. Treasury 10-Year Note, and the Mei Moses Fine Art Index.

For additional observations on the rolling 10-Year correlations of annual returns between the Wilshire 5000 Index and other asset classes, please refer to the exhibits for the Nasdaq Composite Index, the NAREIT Index, the Handy & Harmon Spot Silver Price, and the Lehman Brothers Aggregate Bond Index.

## Europe, Australasia, Far East Equities

For the MSCI EAFE Net Index for 26 time periods, Table 6.8 displays the rolling 10-year correlations of annual returns with 16 other asset

**F I G U R E  6.3**

U.S. Equities: Correlations of the Wilshire 5000 Index

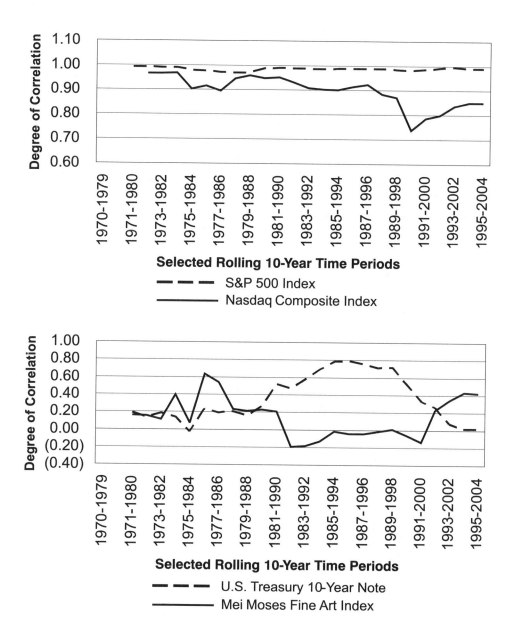

Source: The author.

**T A B L E  6.8**

Europe, Australasia, Far East Equities: Correlations of the MSCI EAFE Net Index[1]

| MSCI EAFE Net Index for 10-Year Periods from: | S&P 500 Composite Index | Nasdaq Composite Index | Wilshire 5000 Index | MSCI EAFE Net Index | MSCI Europe Free Net Index | MSCI Japan Net Index | Lehman Brothers 7-Year Municipal Bond Index |
|---|---|---|---|---|---|---|---|
| | 1 | 2 | 3 | 4 | 5 | 6 | 7 |
| 1  1995–2004 | 0.73 | 0.84 | 0.76 | 1.00 | 0.88 | 0.82 | (0.33) |
| 2  1994–2003 | 0.75 | 0.88 | 0.78 | 1.00 | 0.88 | 0.82 | (0.31) |
| 3  1993–2002 | 0.65 | 0.79 | 0.67 | 1.00 | 0.85 | 0.80 | (0.15) |
| 4  1992–2001 | 0.56 | 0.71 | 0.58 | 1.00 | 0.84 | 0.83 | (0.08) |
| 5  1991–2000 | 0.39 | 0.63 | 0.41 | 1.00 | 0.76 | 0.82 | (0.12) |
| 6  1990–1999 | 0.40 | 0.62 | 0.45 | 1.00 | 0.76 | 0.83 | (0.06) |
| 7  1989–1998 | 0.42 | 0.53 | 0.44 | 1.00 | 0.79 | 0.85 | 0.17 |
| 8  1988–1997 | 0.32 | 0.41 | 0.39 | 1.00 | 0.71 | 0.89 | 0.28 |
| 9  1987–1996 | 0.28 | 0.27 | 0.31 | 1.00 | 0.63 | 0.90 | (0.00) |
| 10  1986–1995 | 0.26 | 0.11 | 0.24 | 1.00 | 0.82 | 0.97 | 0.49 |
| 11  1985–1994 | 0.49 | 0.26 | 0.45 | 1.00 | 0.81 | 0.94 | 0.61 |
| 12  1984–1993 | 0.49 | 0.27 | 0.45 | 1.00 | 0.81 | 0.94 | 0.63 |
| 13  1983–1992 | 0.52 | 0.27 | 0.48 | 1.00 | 0.81 | 0.95 | 0.60 |
| 14  1982–1991 | 0.42 | 0.28 | 0.42 | 1.00 | 0.79 | 0.94 | 0.14 |
| 15  1981–1990 | 0.55 | 0.53 | 0.57 | 1.00 | 0.81 | 0.93 | 0.25 |
| 16  1980–1989 | 0.36 | 0.28 | 0.36 | 1.00 | 0.81 | 0.89 | 0.22 |
| 17  1979–1988 | 0.44 | 0.20 | 0.36 | 1.00 | 0.84 | 0.89 | 0.27 |
| 18  1978–1987 | 0.39 | 0.20 | 0.33 | 1.00 | 0.84 | 0.89 | 0.23 |
| 19  1977–1986 | 0.39 | 0.23 | 0.35 | 1.00 | 0.86 | 0.89 | 0.24 |
| 20  1976–1985 | 0.35 | 0.38 | 0.37 | 1.00 | 0.92 | 0.74 | (0.02) |
| 21  1975–1984 | 0.31 | 0.32 | 0.35 | 1.00 | 0.87 | 0.63 | (0.30) |
| 22  1974–1983 | 0.61 | 0.67 | 0.64 | 1.00 | 0.92 | 0.75 | (0.04) |
| 23  1973–1982 | 0.66 | 0.73 | 0.69 | 1.00 | 0.91 | 0.79 | (0.04) |
| 24  1972–1981 | 0.71 | 0.75 | 0.71 | 1.00 | 0.88 | 0.74 | 0.18 |
| 25  1971–1980 | 0.69 | – | 0.70 | 1.00 | 0.89 | 0.75 | 0.17 |
| 26  1970–1979 | 0.67 | – | – | 1.00 | 0.91 | 0.78 | 0.07 |

[1]Rolling 10-year correlations of annual returns of the MSCI EAFE Net Index with selected asset classes during 26 10-year periods beginning with 1970–1979 and ending with 1995–2004.

Source: The author.

| U.S. Treasury 10-Year Note | NAREIT Index | Nat'l Assn of Realtors Median Home Price | Venture Economics All Private Equity Fund Index | Handy & Harmon Spot Gold Price | Handy & Harmon Spot Silver Price | Lehman Brothers/ Bridgewater TIPS Index | Mel Moses Fine Art Index | Lehman Brothers Aggregate Bond Index | HFRI Fund Weighted Composite Hedge Fund Index |
|---|---|---|---|---|---|---|---|---|---|
| 8 | 9 | 10 | 11 | 12 | 13 | 14 | 15 | 16 | 17 |
| (0.34) | 0.03 | (0.21) | 0.51 | 0.15 | 0.40 | (0.35) | 0.46 | (0.39) | 0.58 |
| (0.34) | (0.05) | (0.16) | 0.47 | 0.14 | 0.37 | (0.39) | 0.45 | (0.37) | 0.59 |
| (0.18) | (0.29) | (0.56) | 0.60 | 0.06 | 0.40 | (0.49) | 0.12 | (0.23) | 0.72 |
| (0.08) | (0.40) | (0.32) | 0.58 | 0.48 | 0.44 | (0.33) | (0.06) | (0.18) | 0.54 |
| (0.13) | (0.38) | 0.16 | 0.45 | 0.63 | 0.47 | (0.31) | (0.17) | (0.13) | 0.43 |
| (0.00) | 0.12 | 0.54 | 0.54 | 0.50 | 0.52 | (0.28) | (0.12) | (0.06) | 0.45 |
| 0.28 | 0.25 | 0.54 | 0.50 | 0.50 | 0.48 | (0.10) | (0.16) | 0.16 | – |
| 0.18 | 0.47 | 0.51 | 0.38 | 0.25 | 0.46 | 0.05 | 0.13 | 0.12 | – |
| 0.05 | 0.33 | 0.60 | 0.29 | 0.36 | 0.64 | (0.08) | 0.19 | 0.02 | – |
| 0.28 | 0.43 | 0.65 | 0.02 | 0.57 | 0.32 | (0.22) | (0.03) | 0.21 | – |
| 0.51 | 0.47 | 0.61 | 0.09 | 0.56 | 0.23 | 0.08 | 0.14 | 0.46 | – |
| 0.50 | 0.41 | 0.61 | 0.14 | 0.55 | 0.27 | (0.02) | 0.09 | 0.43 | – |
| 0.47 | 0.39 | 0.59 | 0.08 | 0.49 | 0.22 | (0.05) | 0.14 | 0.43 | – |
| 0.15 | 0.35 | 0.61 | 0.01 | 0.36 | 0.00 | (0.25) | 0.21 | 0.00 | – |
| 0.22 | 0.49 | 0.73 | 0.15 | 0.42 | 0.15 | (0.27) | 0.23 | 0.09 | – |
| 0.14 | 0.16 | 0.34 | (0.01) | 0.48 | 0.09 | (0.17) | 0.14 | (0.00) | – |
| 0.23 | (0.05) | 0.08 | (0.11) | (0.05) | (0.25) | (0.28) | 0.16 | 0.10 | – |
| 0.19 | (0.07) | 0.16 | (0.04) | (0.01) | (0.24) | (0.24) | 0.14 | 0.07 | – |
| 0.22 | (0.08) | 0.11 | (0.05) | (0.02) | (0.24) | (0.23) | 0.17 | 0.09 | – |
| 0.01 | (0.22) | 0.17 | 0.14 | (0.00) | (0.20) | (0.01) | 0.45 | (0.06) | – |
| (0.61) | (0.21) | 0.51 | 0.73 | (0.09) | (0.21) | (0.26) | (0.20) | – | – |
| (0.35) | 0.40 | 0.27 | 0.85 | (0.32) | (0.18) | (0.60) | 0.18 | – | – |
| (0.26) | 0.49 | 0.45 | 0.89 | (0.36) | (0.16) | (0.61) | (0.04) | – | – |
| (0.25) | 0.43 | 0.34 | 0.79 | (0.30) | (0.15) | (0.67) | (0.07) | – | – |
| (0.10) | – | 0.18 | 0.77 | (0.49) | (0.26) | (0.78) | (0.00) | – | – |
| (0.27) | – | 0.37 | 0.78 | (0.31) | – | (0.74) | 0.12 | – | – |

classes, beginning with the 1970–1979 decade and ending with the 1995–2004 decade.

The four boxed columns in Table 6.8 highlight the rolling 10-year correlations of annual returns between the MSCI EAFE Net Index and four asset classes: (i) unlisted equities, as represented by the Nasdaq Index; (ii) European equities, as represented by the MSCI Europe Net Index; (iii) Japanese equities, as represented by the MSCI Japan Net Index; and (iv) inflation-indexed securities, as represented by the Lehman Brothers/Bridgewater TIPS Index.

For the 26 10-year periods between 1970–1979 and 1995–2004, the correlations of annual returns between the MSCI EAFE Net Index and the:

- ◆ **Nasdaq Composite Index:** ranged between 0.11 and 0.41 for 13 out of 24 10-year periods, and between 0.53 and 0.88 for 11 out of 24 10-year periods;

- ◆ **MSCI Europe Net Index:** ranged between 0.63 and 0.79 for six out of 26 10-year periods, and between 0.81 and 0.92 for 20 out of 26 10-year periods;

- ◆ **MSCI Japan Net Index:** ranged between 0.63 and 0.79 for seven out of 26 10-year periods, and between 0.80 and 0.97 for 19 out of 26 10-year periods;

- ◆ **Lehman Brothers/Bridgewater TIPS Index:** ranged between 0.05 and 0.08 for two out of 26 10-year periods, and between –0.78 and –0.01 for 24 out of 26 10-year periods.

Figure 6.4 depicts the rolling 10-year correlations of annual returns between the MSCI EAFE Net Index and the Nasdaq Composite Index, the MSCI Europe Net Index, the MSCI Japan Net Index, and the Lehman Brothers/Bridgewater TIPS Index.

For additional observations on the rolling 10-year correlations of annual returns between the MSCI EAFE Net Index and other asset classes, please refer to the exhibit for the Venture Economics All Private Equity Fund Index.

## European Equities

For the MSCI Europe Net Index for 26 time periods, Table 6.9 displays the rolling 10-year correlations of annual returns with 16 other asset classes, beginning with the 1970–1979 decade and ending with the 1995–2004 decade.

**F I G U R E   6.4**

Europe, Australasia, Far East Equities: Correlations of the MSCI EAFE Net Index

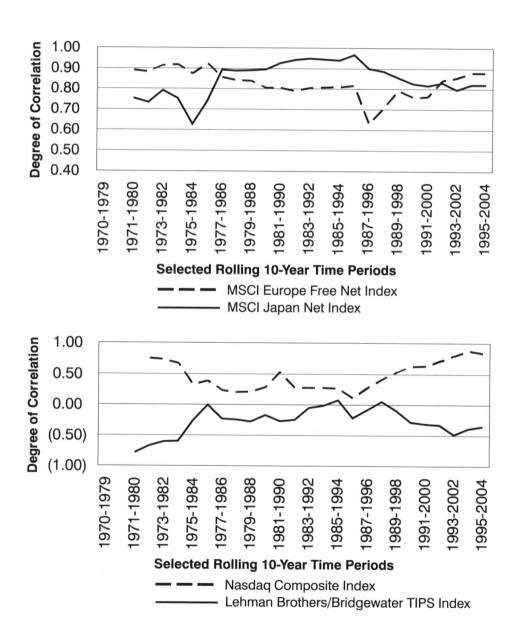

**T A B L E  6.9**

European Equities: Correlations of the MSCI Europe Net Index[1]

| | MSCI Europe Net Index for 10-Year Periods from: | S&P 500 Composite Index | Nasdaq Composite Index | Wilshire 5000 Index | MSCI EAFE Net Index | MSCI Europe Free Net Index | MSCI Japan Net Index | Lehman Brothers 7-Year Municipal Bond Index |
|---|---|---|---|---|---|---|---|---|
| | | 1 | 2 | 3 | 4 | 5 | 6 | 7 |
| 1 | 1995–2004 | 0.92 | 0.78 | 0.93 | 0.88 | 1.00 | 0.47 | (0.07) |
| 2 | 1994–2003 | 0.94 | 0.80 | 0.94 | 0.88 | 1.00 | 0.46 | (0.04) |
| 3 | 1993–2002 | 0.89 | 0.74 | 0.89 | 0.85 | 1.00 | 0.40 | 0.07 |
| 4 | 1992–2001 | 0.84 | 0.65 | 0.83 | 0.84 | 1.00 | 0.44 | 0.20 |
| 5 | 1991–2000 | 0.73 | 0.52 | 0.69 | 0.76 | 1.00 | 0.30 | 0.18 |
| 6 | 1990–1999 | 0.69 | 0.43 | 0.65 | 0.76 | 1.00 | 0.31 | 0.26 |
| 7 | 1989–1998 | 0.72 | 0.52 | 0.67 | 0.79 | 1.00 | 0.41 | 0.41 |
| 8 | 1988–1997 | 0.70 | 0.47 | 0.68 | 0.71 | 1.00 | 0.35 | 0.48 |
| 9 | 1987–1996 | 0.70 | 0.51 | 0.68 | 0.63 | 1.00 | 0.27 | 0.54 |
| 10 | 1986–1995 | 0.58 | 0.32 | 0.54 | 0.82 | 1.00 | 0.67 | 0.77 |
| 11 | 1985–1994 | 0.69 | 0.41 | 0.65 | 0.81 | 1.00 | 0.58 | 0.78 |
| 12 | 1984–1993 | 0.69 | 0.42 | 0.65 | 0.81 | 1.00 | 0.59 | 0.78 |
| 13 | 1983–1992 | 0.71 | 0.42 | 0.66 | 0.81 | 1.00 | 0.59 | 0.75 |
| 14 | 1982–1991 | 0.64 | 0.43 | 0.62 | 0.79 | 1.00 | 0.55 | 0.29 |
| 15 | 1981–1990 | 0.78 | 0.72 | 0.79 | 0.81 | 1.00 | 0.53 | 0.43 |
| 16 | 1980–1989 | 0.66 | 0.56 | 0.65 | 0.81 | 1.00 | 0.47 | 0.42 |
| 17 | 1979–1988 | 0.66 | 0.50 | 0.62 | 0.84 | 1.00 | 0.52 | 0.42 |
| 18 | 1978–1987 | 0.62 | 0.50 | 0.60 | 0.84 | 1.00 | 0.52 | 0.41 |
| 19 | 1977–1986 | 0.49 | 0.46 | 0.50 | 0.86 | 1.00 | 0.55 | 0.38 |
| 20 | 1976–1985 | 0.38 | 0.43 | 0.40 | 0.92 | 1.00 | 0.47 | 0.23 |
| 21 | 1975–1984 | 0.36 | 0.41 | 0.41 | 0.87 | 1.00 | 0.20 | (0.00) |
| 22 | 1974–1983 | 0.60 | 0.65 | 0.63 | 0.92 | 1.00 | 0.45 | 0.16 |
| 23 | 1973–1982 | 0.62 | 0.66 | 0.65 | 0.91 | 1.00 | 0.49 | 0.16 |
| 24 | 1972–1981 | 0.65 | 0.68 | 0.67 | 0.88 | 1.00 | 0.37 | 0.34 |
| 25 | 1971–1980 | 0.62 | – | 0.65 | 0.89 | 1.00 | 0.41 | 0.29 |
| 26 | 1970–1979 | 0.65 | – | – | 0.91 | 1.00 | 0.46 | 0.12 |

[1]Rolling 10-year correlations of annual returns of the MSCI Europe Net Index with selected asset classes during 26 10-year periods beginning with 1970–1979 and ending with 1995–2004.

Source: The author.

| | U.S. Treasury 10-Year Note | NAREIT Index | Nat'l Assn of Realtors Median Home Price | Venture Economics All Private Equity Fund Index | Handy & Harmon Spot Gold Price | Handy & Harmon Spot Silver Price | Lehman Brothers/ Bridgewater TIPS Index | Mei Moses Fine Art Index | Lehman Brothers Aggregate Bond Index | HFRI Fund Weighted Composite Hedge Fund Index |
|---|---|---|---|---|---|---|---|---|---|---|
| | 8 | 9 | 10 | 11 | 12 | 13 | 14 | 15 | 16 | 17 |
| | (0.07) | 0.18 | (0.21) | 0.36 | (0.14) | 0.42 | (0.35) | 0.43 | (0.12) | 0.59 |
| | (0.06) | 0.14 | (0.14) | 0.32 | (0.15) | 0.40 | (0.37) | 0.42 | (0.10) | 0.59 |
| | 0.08 | (0.04) | (0.43) | 0.42 | (0.28) | 0.37 | (0.51) | 0.17 | 0.03 | 0.66 |
| | 0.23 | (0.16) | (0.22) | 0.38 | 0.12 | 0.43 | (0.29) | (0.02) | 0.12 | 0.47 |
| | 0.20 | (0.18) | 0.27 | 0.17 | 0.28 | 0.51 | (0.29) | (0.09) | 0.17 | 0.30 |
| | 0.36 | 0.21 | 0.55 | 0.26 | 0.21 | 0.53 | (0.16) | (0.01) | 0.26 | 0.26 |
| | 0.49 | 0.20 | 0.40 | 0.53 | 0.21 | 0.40 | (0.01) | 0.10 | 0.38 | – |
| | 0.48 | 0.50 | 0.43 | 0.55 | 0.16 | 0.52 | 0.12 | 0.04 | 0.41 | – |
| | 0.52 | 0.53 | 0.31 | 0.56 | 0.11 | 0.28 | 0.41 | 0.02 | 0.47 | – |
| | 0.67 | 0.50 | 0.43 | 0.21 | 0.41 | 0.15 | 0.23 | (0.11) | 0.60 | – |
| | 0.80 | 0.44 | 0.32 | 0.08 | 0.34 | (0.02) | 0.52 | 0.18 | 0.77 | – |
| | 0.78 | 0.34 | 0.31 | 0.18 | 0.40 | 0.09 | 0.52 | 0.11 | 0.72 | – |
| | 0.74 | 0.31 | 0.30 | 0.09 | 0.36 | (0.00) | 0.38 | 0.15 | 0.72 | – |
| | 0.42 | 0.28 | 0.30 | 0.04 | 0.25 | (0.13) | 0.18 | 0.20 | 0.26 | – |
| | 0.48 | 0.41 | 0.30 | 0.22 | 0.40 | 0.12 | 0.14 | 0.23 | 0.35 | – |
| | 0.46 | 0.26 | 0.01 | 0.02 | 0.37 | 0.12 | 0.14 | 0.16 | 0.33 | – |
| | 0.46 | 0.22 | 0.00 | 0.01 | 0.09 | (0.05) | 0.04 | 0.16 | 0.33 | – |
| | 0.42 | 0.20 | 0.03 | 0.02 | 0.09 | (0.05) | 0.05 | 0.22 | 0.30 | – |
| | 0.36 | 0.09 | 0.02 | (0.02) | 0.10 | (0.06) | (0.01) | 0.35 | 0.25 | – |
| | 0.23 | (0.14) | 0.01 | (0.02) | 0.14 | (0.00) | 0.11 | 0.31 | 0.15 | – |
| | (0.45) | (0.12) | 0.40 | 0.75 | 0.12 | 0.08 | (0.16) | (0.51) | – | – |
| | (0.25) | 0.39 | 0.19 | 0.84 | (0.15) | 0.04 | (0.52) | (0.09) | – | – |
| | (0.19) | 0.43 | 0.35 | 0.86 | (0.18) | 0.06 | (0.52) | (0.20) | – | – |
| | (0.36) | 0.42 | 0.43 | 0.84 | (0.16) | 0.06 | (0.53) | (0.22) | – | – |
| | (0.18) | – | 0.21 | 0.81 | (0.42) | 0.09 | (0.70) | (0.15) | – | – |
| | (0.34) | – | 0.37 | 0.85 | (0.27) | – | (0.65) | 0.02 | – | – |

The four boxed columns in Table 6.9 highlight the rolling 10-year correlations of annual returns between the MSCI Europe Net Index and four asset classes: (i) unlisted securities, as represented by the Nasdaq Composite Index; (ii) Japanese equities, as represented by the MSCI Japan Net Index; (iii) intermediate-maturity U.S. Treasury Bonds, as represented by the U.S. Treasury 10-Year Note; and (iv) U.S. taxable fixed-income securities, as represented by the Lehman Brothers Aggregate Bond Index.

For the 26 10-year periods between 1970–1979 and 1995–2004, the correlations of annual returns between the MSCI Europe Net Index and the:

- **Nasdaq Composite Index**: ranged between 0.32 and 0.52 for 15 out of 24 10-year periods, and between 0.56 and 0.80 for 9 out of 24 10-year periods;

- **MSCI Japan Net Index:** ranged between 0.20 and 0.49 for 17 out of 26 10-year periods, and between 0.52 and 0.67 for 9 out of 26 10-year periods;

- **U.S. Treasury 10-Year Note:** ranged between –0.45 and 0.23 for 12 out of 26 10-year periods and between 0.36 and 0.80 for 14 out of 26 10-year periods; and

- **Lehman Brothers Aggregate Bond Index**: ranged between (0.12) and 0.35 for 13 out of 20 10-year periods, and between 0.38 and 0.77 for 7 out of 20 10-year periods.

Figure 6.5 depicts the rolling 10-year correlations of annual returns between the MSCI Europe Net Index and the Nasdaq Composite Index, the MSCI Japan Net Index, the U.S. Treasury 10-Year Note, and the Lehman Brothers Aggregate Bond Index.

For additional observations on the rolling 10-year correlations of annual returns between the MSCI Europe Free Net Index and other asset classes, please refer to the exhibits for the Standard & Poor's 500 Composite Index, the MSCI EAFE Net Index, and the National Association of Realtors Median Home Price.

## Japanese Equities

For the MSCI Japan Net Index for 26 time periods, Table 6.10 displays the rolling 10-year correlations of annual returns with 16 other asset classes, beginning with the 1970–1979 decade and ending with the 1995–2004 decade.

FIGURE 6.5

European Equities: Correlations of the MSCI Europe Net Index

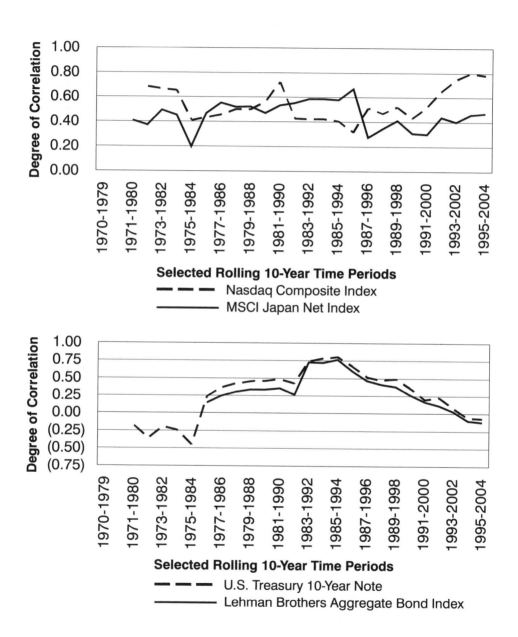

Source: The author.

**T A B L E  6.10**

Japanese Equities: Correlations of the MSCI Japan Net Index[1]

| MSCI Japan Net Index for 10-Year Periods from: | S&P 500 Composite Index | Nasdaq Composite Index | Wilshire 5000 Index | MSCI EAFE Net Index | MSCI Europe Free Net Index | MSCI Japan Net Index | Lehman Brothers 7-Year Municipal Bond Index |
|---|---|---|---|---|---|---|---|
|  | 1 | 2 | 3 | 4 | 5 | 6 | 7 |
| 1  1995–2004 | 0.33 | 0.74 | 0.39 | 0.82 | 0.47 | 1.00 | (0.54) |
| 2  1994–2003 | 0.34 | 0.76 | 0.40 | 0.82 | 0.46 | 1.00 | (0.53) |
| 3  1993–2002 | 0.25 | 0.70 | 0.31 | 0.80 | 0.40 | 1.00 | (0.43) |
| 4  1992–2001 | 0.24 | 0.70 | 0.30 | 0.83 | 0.44 | 1.00 | (0.43) |
| 5  1991–2000 | 0.09 | 0.63 | 0.16 | 0.82 | 0.30 | 1.00 | (0.44) |
| 6  1990–1999 | 0.09 | 0.65 | 0.18 | 0.83 | 0.31 | 1.00 | (0.39) |
| 7  1989–1998 | 0.09 | 0.31 | 0.14 | 0.85 | 0.41 | 1.00 | (0.05) |
| 8  1988–1997 | 0.03 | 0.21 | 0.10 | 0.89 | 0.35 | 1.00 | 0.08 |
| 9  1987–1996 | 0.01 | 0.03 | 0.04 | 0.90 | 0.27 | 1.00 | (0.29) |
| 10  1986–1995 | 0.10 | (0.04) | 0.07 | 0.97 | 0.67 | 1.00 | 0.35 |
| 11  1985–1994 | 0.29 | 0.08 | 0.25 | 0.94 | 0.58 | 1.00 | 0.42 |
| 12  1984–1993 | 0.31 | 0.10 | 0.26 | 0.94 | 0.59 | 1.00 | 0.48 |
| 13  1983–1992 | 0.32 | 0.10 | 0.27 | 0.95 | 0.59 | 1.00 | 0.45 |
| 14  1982–1991 | 0.21 | 0.10 | 0.20 | 0.94 | 0.55 | 1.00 | 0.09 |
| 15  1981–1990 | 0.29 | 0.29 | 0.30 | 0.93 | 0.53 | 1.00 | 0.11 |
| 16  1980–1989 | 0.00 | (0.05) | (0.00) | 0.89 | 0.47 | 1.00 | 0.06 |
| 17  1979–1988 | 0.11 | (0.15) | (0.00) | 0.89 | 0.52 | 1.00 | 0.15 |
| 18  1978–1987 | 0.04 | (0.16) | (0.05) | 0.89 | 0.52 | 1.00 | 0.10 |
| 19  1977–1986 | 0.15 | (0.09) | 0.07 | 0.89 | 0.55 | 1.00 | 0.13 |
| 20  1976–1985 | 0.13 | 0.09 | 0.11 | 0.74 | 0.47 | 1.00 | (0.22) |
| 21  1975–1984 | (0.03) | (0.05) | (0.05) | 0.63 | 0.20 | 1.00 | (0.40) |
| 22  1974–1983 | 0.34 | 0.40 | 0.35 | 0.75 | 0.45 | 1.00 | (0.18) |
| 23  1973–1982 | 0.45 | 0.55 | 0.48 | 0.79 | 0.49 | 1.00 | (0.17) |
| 24  1972–1981 | 0.41 | 0.42 | 0.38 | 0.74 | 0.37 | 1.00 | 0.05 |
| 25  1971–1980 | 0.41 | – | 0.38 | 0.75 | 0.41 | 1.00 | 0.09 |
| 26  1970–1979 | 0.44 | – | – | 0.78 | 0.46 | 1.00 | (0.05) |

[1]Rolling 10-year correlations of annual returns of the MSCI Japan Net Index with selected asset classes during 26 10-year periods beginning with 1970–1979 and ending with 1995–2004.

Source: The author.

| U.S. Treasury 10-Year Note | NAREIT Index | Nat'l Assn of Realtors Median Home Price | Venture Economics All Private Equity Fund Index | Handy & Harmon Spot Gold Price | Handy & Harmon Spot Silver Price | Lehman Brothers/ Bridgewater TIPS Index | Mel Moses Fine Art Index | Lehman Brothers Aggregate Bond Index | HFRI Fund Weighted Composite Hedge Fund Index |
|---|---|---|---|---|---|---|---|---|---|
| 8 | 9 | 10 | 11 | 12 | 13 | 14 | 15 | 16 | 17 |
| (0.57) | (0.24) | (0.26) | 0.66 | 0.34 | 0.29 | (0.36) | 0.27 | (0.60) | 0.50 |
| (0.57) | (0.30) | (0.22) | 0.62 | 0.33 | 0.26 | (0.38) | 0.26 | (0.59) | 0.51 |
| (0.48) | (0.52) | (0.56) | 0.74 | 0.27 | 0.25 | (0.40) | 0.05 | (0.51) | 0.55 |
| (0.45) | (0.55) | (0.37) | 0.74 | 0.49 | 0.27 | (0.41) | (0.04) | (0.48) | 0.49 |
| (0.47) | (0.49) | (0.03) | 0.69 | 0.54 | 0.26 | (0.39) | (0.12) | (0.42) | 0.40 |
| (0.37) | (0.11) | 0.29 | 0.74 | 0.47 | 0.30 | (0.37) | (0.09) | (0.37) | 0.42 |
| 0.04 | 0.13 | 0.37 | 0.20 | 0.56 | 0.30 | (0.06) | (0.24) | (0.04) | – |
| (0.04) | 0.21 | 0.32 | 0.06 | 0.25 | 0.19 | 0.04 | 0.17 | (0.07) | – |
| (0.20) | 0.03 | 0.51 | (0.03) | 0.38 | 0.58 | (0.31) | 0.24 | (0.21) | – |
| 0.08 | 0.30 | 0.61 | (0.15) | 0.57 | 0.25 | (0.41) | (0.01) | 0.02 | – |
| 0.25 | 0.34 | 0.62 | (0.05) | 0.58 | 0.23 | (0.21) | 0.09 | 0.20 | – |
| 0.31 | 0.34 | 0.63 | (0.02) | 0.54 | 0.23 | (0.28) | 0.09 | 0.24 | – |
| 0.28 | 0.32 | 0.63 | (0.01) | 0.52 | 0.29 | (0.23) | 0.11 | 0.24 | – |
| 0.03 | 0.30 | 0.63 | (0.06) | 0.41 | 0.09 | (0.39) | 0.16 | (0.09) | – |
| 0.06 | 0.43 | 0.88 | 0.02 | 0.37 | 0.12 | (0.42) | 0.11 | (0.05) | – |
| (0.05) | 0.01 | 0.48 | (0.12) | 0.44 | 0.04 | (0.34) | (0.01) | (0.18) | – |
| 0.13 | (0.32) | 0.01 | (0.29) | (0.26) | (0.46) | (0.51) | 0.03 | 0.03 | – |
| 0.06 | (0.36) | 0.18 | (0.15) | (0.20) | (0.45) | (0.44) | (0.01) | (0.05) | – |
| 0.14 | (0.37) | 0.12 | (0.14) | (0.22) | (0.44) | (0.38) | (0.04) | 0.03 | – |
| (0.09) | (0.31) | 0.26 | 0.21 | (0.39) | (0.59) | (0.23) | 0.51 | (0.14) | – |
| (0.37) | (0.28) | 0.40 | 0.27 | (0.39) | (0.60) | (0.31) | 0.31 | – | – |
| (0.23) | 0.26 | 0.27 | 0.53 | (0.51) | (0.52) | (0.55) | 0.48 | – | – |
| (0.14) | 0.42 | 0.39 | 0.64 | (0.56) | (0.47) | (0.60) | 0.16 | – | – |
| (0.02) | 0.16 | 0.03 | 0.28 | (0.22) | (0.25) | (0.61) | 0.08 | – | – |
| 0.07 | – | (0.07) | 0.28 | (0.31) | (0.31) | (0.67) | 0.14 | – | – |
| (0.11) | – | 0.15 | 0.34 | (0.19) | – | (0.64) | 0.25 | – | – |

The four boxed columns in Table 6.10 highlight the rolling 10-year correlations of annual returns between the MSCI Japan Net Index and four asset classes: (i) unlisted securities, as represented by the Nasdaq Composite Index; (ii) intermediate-maturity U.S. Treasury Bonds, as represented by the U.S. Treasury 10-Year Note; (iii) inflation-indexed securities, as represented by the Lehman Brothers/Bridgewater TIPS Index; and (iv) U.S. taxable fixed-income securities, as represented by the Lehman Brothers Aggregate Bond Index.

For the 26 10-year periods between 1970–1979 and 1995–2004, the correlations of annual returns between the MSCI Japan Net Index and the:

◆ **Nasdaq Composite Index:** ranged between –0.16 and 0.29 for 14 out of 24 10-year periods, and between 0.31 and 0.76 for 10 out of 24 10-year periods;

◆ **U.S. Treasury 10-Year Note:** ranged between –0.57 and 0.14 for 23 out of 26 10-year periods, and between 0.25 and 0.31 for 3 out of 26 10-year periods;

◆ **Lehman Brothers/Bridgewater TIPS Index**: ranged between –0.64 and –0.06 for 25 out of 26 10-year periods, and 0.04 for 1 out of 26 10-year periods; and

◆ **Lehman Brothers Aggregate Bond Index**: ranged between –0.60 and –0.04 for 14 out of 20 10-year periods, and between 0.02 and 0.24 for 6 out of 20 10-year periods.

Figure 6.6 depicts the rolling 10-year correlation of annual returns between the MSCI Japan Net Index and the Nasdaq Composite Index, the U.S. Treasury 10-Year Note, the Lehman Brothers/Bridgewater TIPS Index, and the Lehman Brothers Aggregate Bond Index.

For additional observations on the rolling 10-year correlations of annual returns between the MSCI Japan Net Index and other asset classes, please refer to the exhibits for the Standard & Poor's 500 Composite Index, the MSCI EAFE Net Index, and the MSCI Europe Free Net Index.

## Intermediate-Maturity Tax-Exempt Bonds

For the Lehman Brothers 7-Year Municipal Bond Index for 26 time periods, Table 6.11 displays the rolling 10-year correlations of annual returns with 16 other asset classes, beginning with the 1970–1979 decade and ending with the 1995–2004 decade.

F I G U R E   6.6

Japanese Equities: Correlations of the MSCI Japan Net Index

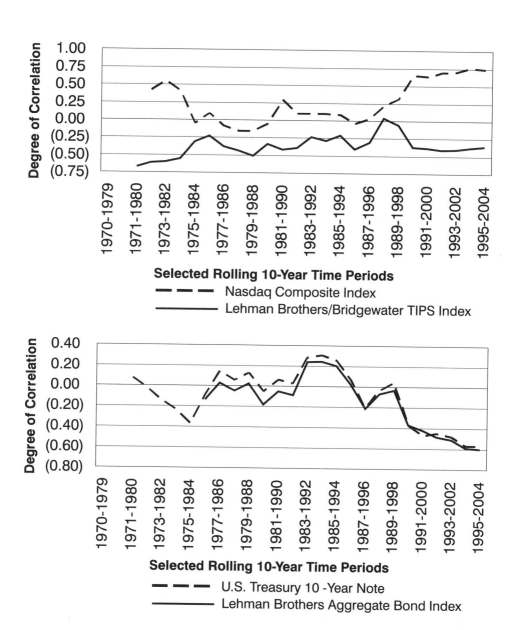

Source: The author.

**T A B L E   6.11**

Intermediate-Maturity Tax-Exempt Bonds: Correlations of the
Lehman Brothers 7-Year Municipal Bond Index[1]

| Lehman Brothers 7-Year Municipal Bond Index for 10-Year Periods from: | S&P 500 Composite Index | Nasdaq Composite Index | Wilshire 5000 Index | MSCI EAFE Net Index | MSCI Europe Free Net Index | MSCI Japan Net Index | Lehman Brothers 7-Year Municipal Bond Index |
|---|---|---|---|---|---|---|---|
| | 1 | 2 | 3 | 4 | 5 | 6 | 7 |
| 1  1995–2004 | 0.07 | (0.23) | 0.05 | (0.33) | (0.07) | (0.54) | 1.00 |
| 2  1994–2003 | 0.06 | (0.24) | 0.05 | (0.31) | (0.04) | (0.53) | 1.00 |
| 3  1993–2002 | 0.07 | (0.23) | 0.07 | (0.15) | 0.07 | (0.43) | 1.00 |
| 4  1992–2001 | 0.26 | (0.14) | 0.26 | (0.08) | 0.20 | (0.43) | 1.00 |
| 5  1991–2000 | 0.33 | (0.05) | 0.34 | (0.12) | 0.18 | (0.44) | 1.00 |
| 6  1990–1999 | 0.43 | 0.03 | 0.45 | (0.06) | 0.26 | (0.39) | 1.00 |
| 7  1989–1998 | 0.57 | 0.47 | 0.61 | 0.17 | 0.41 | (0.05) | 1.00 |
| 8  1988–1997 | 0.59 | 0.53 | 0.62 | 0.28 | 0.48 | 0.08 | 1.00 |
| 9  1987–1996 | 0.66 | 0.60 | 0.69 | (0.00) | 0.54 | (0.29) | 1.00 |
| 10  1986–1995 | 0.57 | 0.38 | 0.55 | 0.49 | 0.77 | 0.35 | 1.00 |
| 11  1985–1994 | 0.67 | 0.44 | 0.64 | 0.61 | 0.78 | 0.42 | 1.00 |
| 12  1984–1993 | 0.61 | 0.38 | 0.58 | 0.63 | 0.78 | 0.48 | 1.00 |
| 13  1983–1992 | 0.53 | 0.33 | 0.49 | 0.60 | 0.75 | 0.45 | 1.00 |
| 14  1982–1991 | 0.40 | 0.28 | 0.33 | 0.14 | 0.29 | 0.09 | 1.00 |
| 15  1981–1990 | 0.62 | 0.51 | 0.55 | 0.25 | 0.43 | 0.11 | 1.00 |
| 16  1980–1989 | 0.33 | 0.18 | 0.25 | 0.22 | 0.42 | 0.06 | 1.00 |
| 17  1979–1988 | 0.32 | 0.12 | 0.20 | 0.27 | 0.42 | 0.15 | 1.00 |
| 18  1978–1987 | 0.35 | 0.12 | 0.22 | 0.23 | 0.41 | 0.10 | 1.00 |
| 19  1977–1986 | 0.30 | 0.05 | 0.17 | 0.24 | 0.38 | 0.13 | 1.00 |
| 20  1976–1985 | 0.30 | 0.15 | 0.21 | (0.02) | 0.23 | (0.22) | 1.00 |
| 21  1975–1984 | 0.23 | 0.08 | 0.15 | (0.30) | (0.00) | (0.40) | 1.00 |
| 22  1974–1983 | 0.36 | 0.30 | 0.31 | (0.04) | 0.16 | (0.18) | 1.00 |
| 23  1973–1982 | 0.33 | 0.24 | 0.28 | (0.04) | 0.16 | (0.17) | 1.00 |
| 24  1972–1981 | 0.29 | 0.23 | 0.29 | 0.18 | 0.34 | 0.05 | 1.00 |
| 25  1971–1980 | 0.23 | – | 0.24 | 0.17 | 0.29 | 0.09 | 1.00 |
| 26  1970–1979 | 0.51 | – | – | 0.07 | 0.12 | (0.05) | 1.00 |

[1]Rolling 10-year correlations of annual returns of the Lehman Brothers 7-Year Municipal Bond Index with selected asset classes during 26 10-year periods beginning with 1970–1979 and ending with 1995–2004.

Source: The author.

| U.S. Treasury 10-Year Note | NAREIT Index | Nat'l Assn of Realtors Median Home Price | Venture Economics All Private Equity Fund Index | Handy & Harmon Spot Gold Price | Handy & Harmon Spot Silver Price | Lehman Brothers/ Bridgewater TIPS Index | Mei Moses Fine Art Index | Lehman Brothers Aggregate Bond Index | HFRI Fund Weighted Composite Hedge Fund Index |
|---|---|---|---|---|---|---|---|---|---|
| 8 | 9 | 10 | 11 | 12 | 13 | 14 | 15 | 16 | 17 |
| 0.95 | 0.15 | 0.16 | (0.27) | 0.11 | 0.00 | 0.65 | 0.37 | 0.97 | (0.10) |
| 0.96 | 0.22 | 0.21 | (0.28) | 0.12 | 0.05 | 0.69 | 0.39 | 0.97 | (0.12) |
| 0.96 | 0.31 | 0.29 | (0.27) | 0.27 | 0.26 | 0.69 | 0.31 | 0.96 | 0.04 |
| 0.94 | 0.38 | 0.18 | (0.23) | 0.10 | 0.25 | 0.69 | 0.41 | 0.96 | 0.20 |
| 0.95 | 0.47 | 0.47 | (0.31) | 0.03 | 0.17 | 0.69 | 0.06 | 0.97 | 0.29 |
| 0.95 | 0.37 | 0.33 | (0.30) | 0.05 | 0.19 | 0.70 | 0.03 | 0.97 | 0.35 |
| 0.92 | 0.22 | 0.19 | 0.26 | 0.12 | 0.12 | 0.69 | 0.25 | 0.95 | – |
| 0.91 | 0.17 | 0.18 | 0.21 | 0.06 | 0.05 | 0.70 | 0.34 | 0.92 | – |
| 0.90 | 0.36 | 0.00 | 0.36 | (0.43) | (0.25) | 0.75 | 0.00 | 0.87 | – |
| 0.86 | 0.51 | 0.25 | 0.14 | 0.04 | (0.31) | 0.40 | (0.15) | 0.81 | – |
| 0.92 | 0.52 | 0.25 | 0.01 | 0.09 | (0.35) | 0.52 | (0.01) | 0.87 | – |
| 0.88 | 0.45 | 0.21 | 0.04 | 0.09 | (0.32) | 0.32 | (0.17) | 0.80 | – |
| 0.89 | 0.30 | 0.23 | (0.19) | 0.21 | (0.33) | 0.43 | (0.16) | 0.81 | – |
| 0.92 | 0.31 | (0.06) | 0.18 | 0.37 | 0.39 | 0.62 | (0.30) | 0.92 | – |
| 0.88 | 0.41 | (0.18) | 0.39 | 0.56 | 0.58 | 0.50 | (0.29) | 0.90 | – |
| 0.90 | 0.27 | (0.57) | (0.18) | 0.34 | 0.66 | 0.19 | (0.39) | 0.92 | – |
| 0.89 | 0.18 | (0.55) | (0.20) | 0.03 | 0.01 | 0.05 | (0.38) | 0.90 | – |
| 0.90 | 0.23 | (0.53) | (0.25) | 0.01 | 0.02 | 0.02 | (0.51) | 0.91 | – |
| 0.89 | 0.13 | (0.54) | (0.33) | 0.01 | 0.02 | (0.03) | (0.44) | 0.89 | – |
| 0.89 | 0.23 | (0.53) | (0.18) | (0.02) | 0.05 | 0.08 | (0.22) | 0.91 | – |
| 0.86 | 0.27 | (0.48) | 0.02 | (0.03) | 0.07 | 0.01 | (0.40) | – | – |
| 0.87 | 0.37 | (0.51) | 0.21 | (0.11) | 0.08 | (0.15) | (0.22) | – | – |
| 0.87 | 0.32 | (0.59) | 0.18 | (0.10) | 0.08 | (0.18) | (0.19) | – | – |
| 0.53 | 0.40 | (0.01) | 0.36 | (0.01) | 0.19 | (0.36) | 0.06 | – | – |
| 0.73 | – | (0.47) | 0.28 | (0.33) | (0.00) | (0.60) | 0.13 | – | – |
| 0.84 | – | (0.70) | 0.32 | (0.66) | – | (0.59) | 0.07 | – | – |

The four boxed columns in Table 6.11 highlight the rolling 10-year correlations of annual returns between the Lehman Brothers 7-Year Municipal Bond Index and four asset classes: (i) large-cap equities, as represented by the Standard & Poor's 500 Composite Index; (ii) intermediate-maturity U.S. Treasury Bonds, as represented by the Treasury 10-Year Note; iii) real estate investment trusts, as represented by the NAREIT Index; and (iv) U.S. taxable fixed-income securities, as represented by the Lehman Brothers Aggregate Bond Index.

For the 26 10-year periods between 1970–1979 and 1995–2004, the correlations of annual returns between the Lehman Brothers 7-Year Municipal Bond Index and the:

- **Standard & Poor's 500 Composite Index**: ranged between 0.06 and 0.36 in 15 of 26 10-year periods, and between 0.40 and 0.67 in 11 of 26 10-year periods;
- **U.S. Treasury 10-Year Note:** ranged between 0.84 and 0.96 in 24 of 26 10-year periods, and between 0.53 and 0.73 in two of 26 10-year periods;
- **NAREIT Index**: ranged between 0.13 and 0.32 in 14 of 24 10-year periods, and between 0.36 and 0.52 in 10 of 24 10-year periods; and
- **Lehman Brothers Aggregate Bond Index**: ranged between 0.80 and 0.97 in 20 of 20 10-year periods.

Figure 6.7 depicts the rolling 10-year correlations of annual returns between the Lehman Brothers 7-Year Municipal Bond Index and the Standard & Poor's 500 Composite Index, the U.S. Treasury 10-Year Note, the NAREIT Index, and the Lehman Brothers Aggregate Bond Index.

For additional observations on the rolling 10-year correlations of annual returns between the Lehman Brothers 7-Year Municipal Bond Index and unlisted U.S. equities, please refer to the exhibit for the Nasdaq Composite Index.

## Intermediate-Maturity U.S. Treasury Bonds

For the U.S. Treasury 10-Year Note for 26 time periods, Table 6.12 displays the rolling 10-year correlations of annual returns with 16 other asset classes, beginning with the 1970–1979 decade and ending with the 1995–2004 decade.

**F I G U R E  6.7**

Intermediate-Maturity Tax-Exempt Bonds: Correlations of the
Lehman Brothers 7-Year Municipal Bond Index

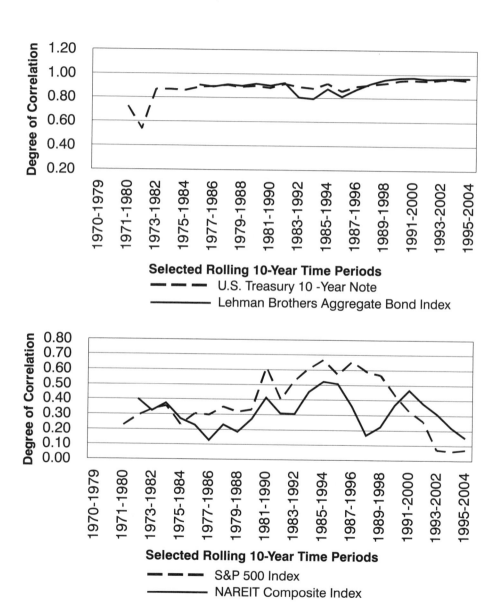

**Selected Rolling 10-Year Time Periods**

— — —  U.S. Treasury 10 -Year Note

————  Lehman Brothers Aggregate Bond Index

**Selected Rolling 10-Year Time Periods**

— — —  S&P 500 Index

————  NAREIT Composite Index

Source: The author.

**T A B L E  6.12**

## Intermediate-Maturity U.S. Treasury Bonds: Correlations of the U.S. Treasury 10-Year Note[1]

| Intermediate-Maturity U.S. Treasury Bonds for 10-Year Periods from: | S&P 500 Composite Index | Nasdaq Composite Index | Wilshire 5000 Index | MSCI EAFE Net Index | MSCI Europe Free Net Index | MSCI Japan Net Index | Lehman Brothers 7-Year Municipal Bond Index |
|---|---|---|---|---|---|---|---|
| | 1 | 2 | 3 | 4 | 5 | 6 | 7 |
| 1  1995–2004 | 0.06 | (0.30) | 0.02 | (0.34) | (0.07) | (0.57) | 0.95 |
| 2  1994–2003 | 0.06 | (0.30) | 0.02 | (0.34) | (0.06) | (0.57) | 0.96 |
| 3  1993–2002 | 0.10 | (0.26) | 0.08 | (0.18) | 0.08 | (0.48) | 0.96 |
| 4  1992–2001 | 0.30 | (0.18) | 0.26 | (0.08) | 0.23 | (0.45) | 0.94 |
| 5  1991–2000 | 0.35 | (0.12) | 0.33 | (0.13) | 0.20 | (0.47) | 0.95 |
| 6  1990–1999 | 0.54 | 0.04 | 0.52 | (0.00) | 0.36 | (0.37) | 0.95 |
| 7  1989–1998 | 0.70 | 0.64 | 0.72 | 0.28 | 0.49 | 0.04 | 0.92 |
| 8  1988–1997 | 0.69 | 0.63 | 0.71 | 0.18 | 0.48 | (0.04) | 0.91 |
| 9  1987–1996 | 0.74 | 0.68 | 0.76 | 0.05 | 0.52 | (0.20) | 0.90 |
| 10  1986–1995 | 0.80 | 0.66 | 0.79 | 0.28 | 0.67 | 0.08 | 0.86 |
| 11  1985–1994 | 0.80 | 0.62 | 0.78 | 0.51 | 0.80 | 0.25 | 0.92 |
| 12  1984–1993 | 0.72 | 0.51 | 0.69 | 0.50 | 0.78 | 0.31 | 0.88 |
| 13  1983–1992 | 0.62 | 0.44 | 0.58 | 0.47 | 0.74 | 0.28 | 0.89 |
| 14  1982–1991 | 0.54 | 0.41 | 0.47 | 0.15 | 0.42 | 0.03 | 0.92 |
| 15  1981–1990 | 0.57 | 0.51 | 0.52 | 0.22 | 0.48 | 0.06 | 0.88 |
| 16  1980–1989 | 0.33 | 0.23 | 0.27 | 0.14 | 0.46 | (0.05) | 0.90 |
| 17  1979–1988 | 0.29 | 0.11 | 0.16 | 0.23 | 0.46 | 0.13 | 0.89 |
| 18  1978–1987 | 0.34 | 0.11 | 0.21 | 0.19 | 0.42 | 0.06 | 0.90 |
| 19  1977–1986 | 0.35 | 0.01 | 0.19 | 0.22 | 0.36 | 0.14 | 0.89 |
| 20  1976–1985 | 0.36 | 0.09 | 0.23 | 0.01 | 0.23 | (0.09) | 0.89 |
| 21  1975–1984 | 0.11 | (0.14) | (0.03) | (0.61) | (0.45) | (0.37) | 0.86 |
| 22  1974–1983 | 0.22 | 0.13 | 0.14 | (0.35) | (0.25) | (0.23) | 0.87 |
| 23  1973–1982 | 0.26 | 0.17 | 0.19 | (0.26) | (0.19) | (0.14) | 0.87 |
| 24  1972–1981 | 0.15 | 0.09 | 0.14 | (0.25) | (0.36) | (0.02) | 0.53 |
| 25  1971–1980 | 0.20 | – | 0.19 | (0.10) | (0.18) | 0.07 | 0.73 |
| 26  1970–1979 | 0.23 | – | – | (0.27) | (0.34) | (0.11) | 0.84 |

[1]Rolling 10-year correlations of annual returns of Intermediate-Maturity U.S. Treasury Bonds with selected asset classes during 26 10-year periods beginning with 1970–1979 and ending with 1995–2004.

Source: The author.

| U.S. Treasury 10-Year Note | NAREIT Index | Nat'l Assn of Realtors Median Home Price | Venture Economics All Private Equity Fund Index | Handy & Harmon Spot Gold Price | Handy & Harmon Spot Silver Price | Lehman Brothers/ Bridgewater TIPS Index | Mei Moses Fine Art Index | Lehman Brothers Aggregate Bond Index | HFRI Fund Weighted Composite Hedge Fund Index |
|---|---|---|---|---|---|---|---|---|---|
| 8 | 9 | 10 | 11 | 12 | 13 | 14 | 15 | 16 | 17 |
| 1.00 | 0.01 | 0.07 | (0.35) | 0.00 | (0.11) | 0.57 | 0.33 | 0.97 | (0.28) |
| 1.00 | 0.03 | 0.04 | (0.33) | 0.01 | (0.10) | 0.58 | 0.34 | 0.97 | (0.28) |
| 1.00 | 0.15 | 0.19 | (0.36) | 0.16 | 0.10 | 0.62 | 0.36 | 0.97 | (0.15) |
| 1.00 | 0.20 | 0.15 | (0.32) | 0.02 | 0.12 | 0.61 | 0.42 | 0.97 | (0.06) |
| 1.00 | 0.31 | 0.44 | (0.41) | (0.04) | 0.05 | 0.63 | 0.08 | 0.98 | 0.04 |
| 1.00 | 0.25 | 0.35 | (0.37) | (0.02) | 0.13 | 0.57 | 0.03 | 0.98 | 0.14 |
| 1.00 | 0.09 | 0.31 | 0.38 | 0.06 | 0.14 | 0.49 | 0.22 | 0.98 | – |
| 1.00 | 0.20 | 0.31 | 0.40 | 0.08 | 0.19 | 0.56 | 0.07 | 0.99 | – |
| 1.00 | 0.31 | 0.18 | 0.46 | (0.16) | (0.05) | 0.80 | (0.06) | 0.99 | – |
| 1.00 | 0.56 | 0.31 | 0.48 | 0.00 | (0.14) | 0.65 | (0.15) | 0.99 | – |
| 1.00 | 0.58 | 0.33 | 0.17 | 0.08 | (0.25) | 0.69 | (0.06) | 0.99 | – |
| 1.00 | 0.59 | 0.26 | 0.10 | (0.05) | (0.35) | 0.46 | (0.29) | 0.98 | – |
| 1.00 | 0.40 | 0.28 | (0.19) | 0.08 | (0.38) | 0.54 | (0.26) | 0.98 | – |
| 1.00 | 0.41 | 0.04 | 0.10 | 0.24 | 0.21 | 0.67 | (0.36) | 0.97 | – |
| 1.00 | 0.44 | (0.10) | 0.16 | 0.35 | 0.30 | 0.67 | (0.34) | 0.97 | – |
| 1.00 | 0.29 | (0.46) | (0.22) | 0.22 | 0.39 | 0.44 | (0.45) | 0.97 | – |
| 1.00 | 0.12 | (0.52) | (0.27) | (0.16) | (0.19) | 0.13 | (0.41) | 0.97 | – |
| 1.00 | 0.17 | (0.59) | (0.37) | (0.23) | (0.20) | 0.06 | (0.41) | 0.98 | – |
| 1.00 | (0.11) | (0.70) | (0.52) | (0.24) | (0.20) | 0.01 | (0.22) | 0.98 | – |
| 1.00 | 0.05 | (0.68) | (0.40) | (0.27) | (0.18) | 0.08 | (0.02) | 0.98 | – |
| 1.00 | 0.16 | (0.68) | (0.30) | (0.22) | (0.14) | 0.05 | (0.15) | – | – |
| 1.00 | 0.23 | (0.67) | (0.08) | (0.22) | (0.10) | (0.01) | (0.08) | – | – |
| 1.00 | 0.27 | (0.82) | (0.03) | (0.28) | (0.13) | (0.12) | (0.12) | – | – |
| 1.00 | 0.39 | (0.53) | 0.03 | (0.40) | (0.22) | (0.29) | 0.30 | – | – |
| 1.00 | – | (0.60) | 0.10 | (0.42) | (0.24) | (0.36) | 0.41 | – | – |
| 1.00 | – | (0.77) | (0.04) | (0.56) | – | (0.29) | 0.09 | – | – |

The four boxed columns in Table 6.12 highlight the rolling 10-year correlations of annual returns between the U.S. Treasury 10-Year Note and four asset classes: (i) large-cap equities, as represented by the Standard & Poor's 500 Composite Index; (ii) unlisted securities, as represented by the Nasdaq Composite Index; (iii) fine art, as represented by the Mei Moses Fine Art Index; and (iv) U.S. taxable fixed-income securities, as represented by the Lehman Brothers Aggregate Bond Index.

For the 26 10-year periods between 1970–1979 and 1995–2004, the correlations of annual returns between the U.S. Treasury 10-year Note and the:

◆ **Standard & Poor's 500 Composite Index:** ranged between 0.06 and 0.36 in 16 of 26 10-year periods, and between 0.54 and 0.80 in 10 of 26 10-year periods;

◆ **Nasdaq Composite Index:** ranged between −0.30 and 0.17 in 14 of 24 10-year periods, and between 0.23 and 0.66 in 10 of 24 10-year periods;

◆ **Mei Moses Fine Art Index:** ranged between −0.45 and −0.02 in 15 of 26 10-year periods, and between 0.07 and 0.42 in 11 of 26 10-year periods; and

◆ **Lehman Brothers Aggregate Bond Index:** ranged between 0.97 and 0.99 in 20 of 20 10-year periods.

Figure 6.8 depicts the rolling 10-year correlation of annual returns between the U.S. Treasury 10-Year Note and the Standard & Poor's 500 Composite Index, the Nasdaq Composite Index, the Mei Moses Fine Art Index, and the Lehman Brothers Aggregate Bond Index.

For additional observations on the rolling 10-year correlations of annual returns between the U.S. Treasury 10-Year Note and other asset classes, please refer to the exhibits for the Wilshire 5000 Index, the MSCI Europe Free Net Index, the MSCI Japan Net Index, the Lehman Brothers 7-Year Municipal Bond Index, the Venture Economics All Private Equity Fund Index, and the Lehman Brothers/Bridgewater TIPS Index.

## Real Estate Investment Trusts

For the NAREIT Composite Index for 24 time periods, Table 6.13 displays the rolling 10-year correlations of annual returns with 16 other asset classes, beginning with the 1972–1981 decade and ending with the 1995–2004 decade.

Intermediate-Maturity U.S. Treasury Bonds: Correlations of the U.S. Treasury
10-Year Note

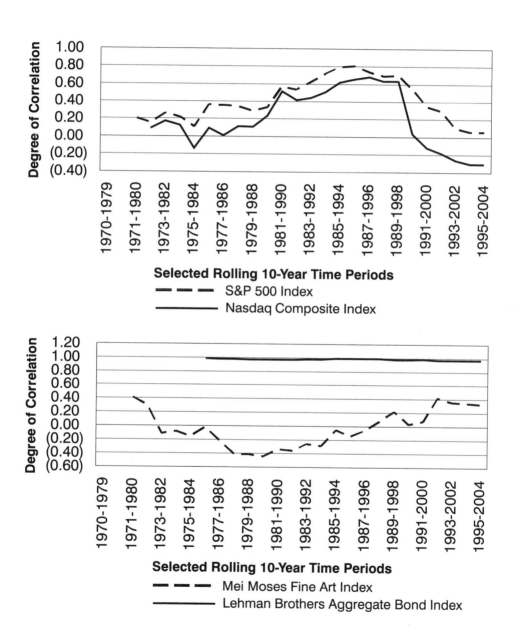

Source: The author.

**T A B L E  6.13**

Real Estate Investment Trusts: Correlations of the NAREIT Index[1]

| NAREIT Index for 10-Year Periods from: | S&P 500 Composite Index | Nasdaq Composite Index | Wilshire 5000 Index | MSCI EAFE Net Index | MSCI Europe Free Net Index | MSCI Japan Net Index | Lehman Brothers 7-Year Municipal Bond Index |
|---|---|---|---|---|---|---|---|
| | 1 | 2 | 3 | 4 | 5 | 6 | 7 |
| 1   1995–2004 | 0.08 | (0.18) | 0.11 | 0.03 | 0.18 | (0.24) | 0.15 |
| 2   1994–2003 | 0.09 | (0.17) | 0.12 | (0.05) | 0.14 | (0.30) | 0.22 |
| 3   1993–2002 | (0.04) | (0.36) | (0.03) | (0.29) | (0.04) | (0.52) | 0.31 |
| 4   1992–2001 | (0.17) | (0.48) | (0.16) | (0.40) | (0.16) | (0.55) | 0.38 |
| 5   1991–2000 | (0.04) | (0.29) | 0.02 | (0.38) | (0.18) | (0.49) | 0.47 |
| 6   1990–1999 | 0.37 | 0.13 | 0.46 | 0.12 | 0.21 | (0.11) | 0.37 |
| 7   1989–1998 | 0.37 | 0.46 | 0.49 | 0.25 | 0.20 | 0.13 | 0.22 |
| 8   1988–1997 | 0.61 | 0.82 | 0.67 | 0.47 | 0.50 | 0.21 | 0.17 |
| 9   1987–1996 | 0.64 | 0.84 | 0.71 | 0.33 | 0.53 | 0.03 | 0.36 |
| 10  1986–1995 | 0.65 | 0.87 | 0.74 | 0.43 | 0.50 | 0.30 | 0.51 |
| 11  1985–1994 | 0.71 | 0.91 | 0.79 | 0.47 | 0.44 | 0.34 | 0.52 |
| 12  1984–1993 | 0.61 | 0.74 | 0.67 | 0.41 | 0.34 | 0.34 | 0.45 |
| 13  1983–1992 | 0.66 | 0.73 | 0.71 | 0.39 | 0.31 | 0.32 | 0.30 |
| 14  1982–1991 | 0.69 | 0.73 | 0.72 | 0.35 | 0.28 | 0.30 | 0.31 |
| 15  1981–1990 | 0.61 | 0.65 | 0.64 | 0.49 | 0.41 | 0.43 | 0.41 |
| 16  1980–1989 | 0.51 | 0.51 | 0.53 | 0.16 | 0.26 | 0.01 | 0.27 |
| 17  1979–1988 | 0.60 | 0.63 | 0.67 | (0.05) | 0.22 | (0.32) | 0.18 |
| 18  1978–1987 | 0.63 | 0.63 | 0.70 | (0.07) | 0.20 | (0.36) | 0.23 |
| 19  1977–1986 | 0.47 | 0.51 | 0.55 | (0.08) | 0.09 | (0.37) | 0.13 |
| 20  1976–1985 | 0.49 | 0.51 | 0.56 | (0.22) | (0.14) | (0.31) | 0.23 |
| 21  1975–1984 | 0.45 | 0.52 | 0.51 | (0.21) | (0.12) | (0.28) | 0.27 |
| 22  1974–1983 | 0.73 | 0.86 | 0.78 | 0.40 | 0.39 | 0.26 | 0.37 |
| 23  1973–1982 | 0.77 | 0.90 | 0.83 | 0.49 | 0.43 | 0.42 | 0.32 |
| 24  1972–1981 | 0.74 | 0.87 | 0.80 | 0.43 | 0.42 | 0.16 | 0.40 |
| 25  1971–1980 | – | – | – | – | – | – | – |
| 26  1970–1979 | – | – | – | – | – | – | – |

[1]Rolling 10-year correlations of annual returns of the NAREIT Index with selected asset classes during 24 10-year periods beginning with 1972–1981 and ending with 1995–2004.

Source: The author.

| U.S. Treasury 10-Year Note | NAREIT Index | Nat'l Assn of Realtors Median Home Price | Venture Economics All Private Equity Fund Index | Handy & Harmon Spot Gold Price | Handy & Harmon Spot Silver Price | Lehman Brothers/ Bridgewater TIPS Index | Mei Moses Fine Art Index | Lehman Brothers Aggregate Bond Index | HFRI Fund Weighted Composite Hedge Fund Index |
|---|---|---|---|---|---|---|---|---|---|
| 8 | 9 | 10 | 11 | 12 | 13 | 14 | 15 | 16 | 17 |
| 0.01 | 1.00 | 0.44 | (0.22) | (0.01) | 0.42 | 0.44 | 0.13 | 0.06 | 0.24 |
| 0.03 | 1.00 | 0.44 | (0.25) | (0.04) | 0.36 | 0.43 | 0.10 | 0.12 | 0.26 |
| 0.15 | 1.00 | 0.31 | (0.20) | (0.25) | 0.21 | 0.32 | (0.12) | 0.24 | 0.27 |
| 0.20 | 1.00 | 0.28 | (0.26) | (0.19) | 0.20 | 0.54 | (0.15) | 0.28 | 0.22 |
| 0.31 | 1.00 | 0.57 | (0.30) | (0.27) | 0.09 | 0.52 | (0.39) | 0.40 | 0.38 |
| 0.25 | 1.00 | 0.71 | (0.08) | (0.22) | 0.35 | 0.17 | (0.46) | 0.30 | 0.63 |
| 0.09 | 1.00 | 0.72 | 0.62 | (0.20) | 0.40 | 0.03 | (0.44) | 0.18 | – |
| 0.20 | 1.00 | 0.87 | 0.71 | (0.14) | 0.30 | (0.24) | (0.31) | 0.19 | – |
| 0.31 | 1.00 | 0.71 | 0.74 | (0.30) | 0.06 | (0.12) | (0.38) | 0.28 | – |
| 0.56 | 1.00 | 0.77 | 0.58 | (0.13) | 0.12 | (0.07) | (0.42) | 0.53 | – |
| 0.58 | 1.00 | 0.77 | 0.73 | (0.10) | 0.08 | (0.00) | (0.37) | 0.54 | – |
| 0.59 | 1.00 | 0.72 | 0.55 | (0.21) | (0.02) | (0.24) | (0.44) | 0.56 | – |
| 0.40 | 1.00 | 0.62 | 0.63 | (0.39) | (0.27) | (0.42) | (0.42) | 0.46 | – |
| 0.41 | 1.00 | 0.57 | 0.64 | (0.32) | (0.09) | (0.28) | (0.44) | 0.42 | – |
| 0.44 | 1.00 | 0.31 | 0.61 | (0.11) | 0.02 | (0.25) | (0.16) | 0.47 | – |
| 0.29 | 1.00 | 0.05 | 0.59 | (0.06) | (0.23) | 0.01 | (0.31) | 0.32 | – |
| 0.12 | 1.00 | 0.26 | 0.62 | 0.45 | 0.47 | 0.37 | (0.31) | 0.10 | – |
| 0.17 | 1.00 | (0.00) | 0.44 | 0.38 | 0.45 | 0.30 | (0.26) | 0.15 | – |
| (0.11) | 1.00 | (0.06) | 0.39 | 0.54 | 0.59 | 0.14 | 0.07 | (0.05) | – |
| 0.05 | 1.00 | 0.01 | 0.48 | 0.28 | 0.37 | 0.04 | 0.37 | 0.08 | – |
| 0.16 | 1.00 | (0.03) | 0.21 | 0.30 | 0.37 | 0.09 | 0.46 | – | – |
| 0.23 | 1.00 | (0.15) | 0.59 | (0.09) | 0.24 | (0.44) | 0.62 | – | – |
| 0.27 | 1.00 | (0.02) | 0.70 | (0.19) | 0.21 | (0.45) | 0.25 | – | – |
| 0.39 | 1.00 | 0.11 | 0.71 | (0.19) | 0.22 | (0.39) | 0.29 | – | – |
| – | – | – | – | – | – | – | – | – | – |
| – | – | – | – | – | – | – | – | – | – |

The four boxed columns in Table 6.13 highlight the rolling 10-year correlations of annual returns between the NAREIT Composite Index and four asset classes: (i) U.S. equities, as represented by the Wilshire 5000 Index; (ii) residential real estate, as represented by the National Association of Realtors Median Home Price; (iii) inflation-indexed securities, as represented by the Lehman Brothers/Bridgewater TIPS Index; and (iv) U.S. taxable fixed-income securities, as represented by the Lehman Brothers Aggregate Bond Index.

For the 24 10-year periods between 1972–1981 and 1995–2004, the correlations of annual returns between the NAREIT Composite Index and the:

- **Wilshire 5000 Index**: ranged between −0.16 and 0.12 in 5 of 24 10-year periods, and between 0.46 and 0.83 in 19 of 24 10-year periods;
- **National Association of Realtors Median Home Price**: ranged between −0.15 and 0.44 in 14 of 24 10-year periods and between 0.57 and 0.87 in 10 of 24 10-year periods;
- **Lehman Brothers/Bridgewater TIPS Index**: ranged between −0.45 and 0.17 in 17 of 24 10-year periods, and between 0.30 and 0.54 in 7 of 24 10-year periods; and
- **Lehman Brothers Aggregate Bond Index**: ranged between −0.05 and 0.19 in 8 of 20 10-year periods, and between 0.24 and 0.56 in 12 of 20 10-year periods.

Figure 6.9 depicts the rolling 10-year correlations of annual returns between the NAREIT Composite Index and the Wilshire 5000 Index, the National Association of Realtors Median Home Price, the Lehman Brothers/Bridgewater TIPS Index, and the Lehman Brothers Aggregate Bond Index.

For additional observations on the rolling 10-year correlations of annual returns between the NAREIT Index and other asset classes, please refer to the exhibits for the Standard & Poor's 500 Composite Index, the Lehman Brothers 7-Year Municipal Bond Index, the Venture Economics All Private Equity Fund Index, the Handy & Harmon Spot Gold Price, the Mei Moses Fine Art Index, and the HFRI Fund Weighted Composite Hedge Fund Index.

## Residential Real Estate

For the National Association of Realtors Median Home Price for 26 time periods, Table 6.14 displays the rolling 10-year correlations of

## F I G U R E  6.9

Real Estate Investment Trusts: Correlations of the NAREIT Index

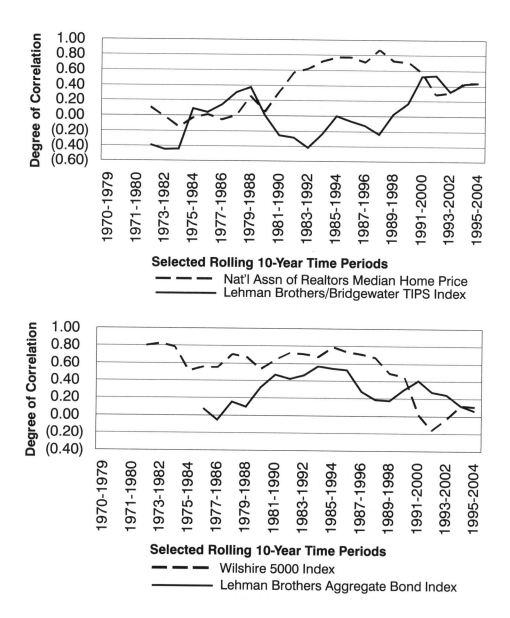

**T A B L E  6.14**

Residential Real Estate: Correlations of the National Association of Realtors Median Home Price[1]

| National Association of Realtors Median Home Price for 10-Year Periods from: | S&P 500 Composite Index | Nasdaq Composite Index | Wilshire 5000 Index | MSCI EAFE Net Index | MSCI Europe Free Net Index | MSCI Japan Net Index | Lehman Brothers 7-Year Municipal Bond Index |
|---|---|---|---|---|---|---|---|
| | 1 | 2 | 3 | 4 | 5 | 6 | 7 |
| 1   1995–2004 | (0.28) | (0.27) | (0.23) | (0.21) | (0.21) | (0.26) | 0.16 |
| 2   1994–2003 | (0.18) | (0.15) | (0.13) | (0.16) | (0.14) | (0.22) | 0.21 |
| 3   1993–2002 | (0.31) | (0.35) | (0.29) | (0.56) | (0.43) | (0.56) | 0.29 |
| 4   1992–2001 | (0.20) | (0.28) | (0.19) | (0.32) | (0.22) | (0.37) | 0.18 |
| 5   1991–2000 | 0.44 | 0.30 | 0.51 | 0.16 | 0.27 | (0.03) | 0.47 |
| 6   1990–1999 | 0.71 | 0.60 | 0.79 | 0.54 | 0.55 | 0.29 | 0.33 |
| 7   1989–1998 | 0.57 | 0.80 | 0.67 | 0.54 | 0.40 | 0.37 | 0.19 |
| 8   1988–1997 | 0.59 | 0.84 | 0.67 | 0.51 | 0.43 | 0.32 | 0.18 |
| 9   1987–1996 | 0.45 | 0.71 | 0.52 | 0.60 | 0.31 | 0.51 | 0.00 |
| 10   1986–1995 | 0.44 | 0.62 | 0.49 | 0.65 | 0.43 | 0.61 | 0.25 |
| 11   1985–1994 | 0.49 | 0.66 | 0.53 | 0.61 | 0.32 | 0.62 | 0.25 |
| 12   1984–1993 | 0.47 | 0.63 | 0.52 | 0.61 | 0.31 | 0.63 | 0.21 |
| 13   1983–1992 | 0.47 | 0.62 | 0.50 | 0.59 | 0.30 | 0.63 | 0.23 |
| 14   1982–1991 | 0.40 | 0.59 | 0.46 | 0.61 | 0.30 | 0.63 | (0.06) |
| 15   1981–1990 | 0.03 | 0.16 | 0.07 | 0.73 | 0.30 | 0.88 | (0.18) |
| 16   1980–1989 | 0.07 | 0.21 | 0.12 | 0.34 | 0.01 | 0.48 | (0.57) |
| 17   1979–1988 | 0.24 | 0.41 | 0.36 | 0.08 | 0.00 | 0.01 | (0.55) |
| 18   1978–1987 | (0.01) | 0.30 | 0.15 | 0.16 | 0.03 | 0.18 | (0.53) |
| 19   1977–1986 | (0.26) | 0.19 | (0.10) | 0.11 | 0.02 | 0.12 | (0.54) |
| 20   1976–1985 | (0.23) | 0.20 | (0.07) | 0.17 | 0.01 | 0.26 | (0.53) |
| 21   1975–1984 | (0.09) | 0.32 | 0.06 | 0.51 | 0.40 | 0.40 | (0.48) |
| 22   1974–1983 | (0.24) | (0.07) | (0.16) | 0.27 | 0.19 | 0.27 | (0.51) |
| 23   1973–1982 | (0.13) | 0.02 | (0.05) | 0.45 | 0.35 | 0.39 | (0.59) |
| 24   1972–1981 | (0.01) | 0.16 | 0.04 | 0.34 | 0.43 | 0.03 | (0.01) |
| 25   1971–1980 | (0.20) | – | (0.13) | 0.18 | 0.21 | (0.07) | (0.47) |
| 26   1970–1979 | (0.14) | – | – | 0.37 | 0.37 | 0.15 | (0.70) |

[1]Rolling 10-year correlations of annual returns of the National Association of Realtors Median Home Price with selected asset classes during 26 10-year periods beginning with 1970–1979 and ending with 1995–2004.

Source: The author.

| U.S. Treasury 10-Year Note | NAREIT Index | Nat'l Assn of Realtors Median Home Price | Venture Economics All Private Equity Fund Index | Handy & Harmon Spot Gold Price | Handy & Harmon Spot Silver Price | Lehman Brothers/ Bridgewater TIPS Index | Mei Moses Fine Art Index | Lehman Brothers Aggregate Bond Index | HFRI Fund Weighted Composite Hedge Fund Index |
|---|---|---|---|---|---|---|---|---|---|
| 8 | 9 | 10 | 11 | 12 | 13 | 14 | 15 | 16 | 17 |
| 0.07 | 0.44 | 1.00 | (0.41) | 0.31 | 0.48 | 0.30 | 0.09 | 0.15 | (0.16) |
| 0.04 | 0.44 | 1.00 | (0.44) | 0.36 | 0.52 | 0.29 | (0.04) | 0.16 | (0.08) |
| 0.19 | 0.31 | 1.00 | (0.36) | 0.02 | 0.26 | 0.21 | (0.25) | 0.33 | (0.11) |
| 0.15 | 0.28 | 1.00 | (0.24) | (0.01) | 0.31 | 0.12 | (0.30) | 0.29 | (0.12) |
| 0.44 | 0.57 | 1.00 | (0.03) | (0.31) | 0.12 | 0.12 | (0.69) | 0.54 | 0.48 |
| 0.35 | 0.71 | 1.00 | 0.19 | (0.24) | 0.35 | (0.19) | (0.60) | 0.37 | 0.62 |
| 0.31 | 0.72 | 1.00 | 0.65 | (0.24) | 0.40 | (0.30) | (0.64) | 0.30 | – |
| 0.31 | 0.87 | 1.00 | 0.64 | (0.23) | 0.41 | (0.32) | (0.49) | 0.29 | – |
| 0.18 | 0.71 | 1.00 | 0.50 | 0.09 | 0.39 | (0.24) | (0.31) | 0.20 | – |
| 0.31 | 0.77 | 1.00 | 0.35 | 0.26 | 0.33 | (0.28) | (0.36) | 0.32 | – |
| 0.33 | 0.77 | 1.00 | 0.49 | 0.27 | 0.32 | (0.22) | (0.33) | 0.32 | – |
| 0.26 | 0.72 | 1.00 | 0.49 | 0.28 | 0.33 | (0.47) | (0.40) | 0.24 | – |
| 0.28 | 0.62 | 1.00 | 0.24 | 0.28 | 0.41 | (0.29) | (0.38) | 0.27 | – |
| 0.04 | 0.57 | 1.00 | 0.15 | 0.17 | 0.14 | (0.40) | (0.30) | (0.05) | – |
| (0.10) | 0.31 | 1.00 | (0.15) | 0.15 | (0.01) | (0.38) | 0.15 | (0.20) | – |
| (0.46) | 0.05 | 1.00 | 0.48 | 0.34 | (0.43) | 0.20 | 0.23 | (0.55) | – |
| (0.52) | 0.26 | 1.00 | 0.52 | 0.64 | 0.47 | 0.55 | 0.17 | (0.63) | – |
| (0.59) | (0.00) | 1.00 | 0.62 | 0.56 | 0.33 | 0.52 | 0.28 | (0.69) | – |
| (0.70) | (0.06) | 1.00 | 0.62 | 0.53 | 0.28 | 0.38 | 0.23 | (0.77) | – |
| (0.68) | 0.01 | 1.00 | 0.63 | 0.51 | 0.27 | 0.38 | 0.24 | (0.75) | – |
| (0.68) | (0.03) | 1.00 | 0.47 | 0.47 | 0.24 | 0.39 | 0.25 | – | – |
| (0.67) | (0.15) | 1.00 | 0.19 | 0.44 | 0.19 | 0.35 | 0.20 | – | – |
| (0.82) | (0.02) | 1.00 | 0.22 | 0.32 | 0.13 | 0.07 | 0.17 | – | – |
| (0.53) | 0.11 | 1.00 | 0.29 | 0.32 | 0.15 | 0.21 | (0.05) | – | – |
| (0.60) | – | 1.00 | 0.12 | 0.08 | 0.02 | 0.16 | (0.21) | – | – |
| (0.77) | – | 1.00 | 0.26 | 0.30 | – | 0.13 | 0.17 | – | – |

annual returns with 16 other asset classes, beginning with the 1970–1979 decade and ending with the 1995–2004 decade.

The four boxed columns in Table 6.14 highlight the rolling 10-year correlations of annual returns between the National Association of Realtors Median Home Price and four asset classes: (i) U.S. large-cap equities, as represented by the Standard & Poor's 500 Composite Index; (ii) European equities, as represented by the MSCI Europe Net Index; (iii) fine art, as represented by the Mei Moses Fine Art Index; and (iv) U.S. taxable fixed-income securities, as represented by the Lehman Brothers Aggregate Bond Index.

For the 26 10-year periods between 1970–1979 and 1995–2004, the correlations of annual returns between the National Association of Realtors Median Home Price and the:

♦ **Standard & Poor's 500 Composite Index:** ranged between –0.31 and 0.07 in 15 of 26 10-year periods, and between 0.24 and 0.71 in 11 of 26 10-year periods;

♦ **MSCI Europe Net Index:** ranged between –0.43 and 0.27 in 12 of 26 10-year periods, and between 0.30 and 0.55 in 14 of 26 10-year periods;

♦ **Mei Moses Fine Art Index:** ranged between –0.64 and 0.21 in 21 of 26 10-year periods, and between 0.23 and 0.28 in 5 of 26 10-year periods; and

♦ **Lehman Brothers Aggregate Bond Index:** ranged between –0.77 and 0.30 in 15 of 20 10-year periods, and between 0.32 and 0.54 in 5 of 20 10-year periods.

Figure 6.10 depicts the rolling 10-year correlation of annual returns between the National Association of Realtors Median Home Price and the Standard & Poor's 500 Composite Index, the MSCI Europe Free Net Index, the Mei Moses Fine Art Index, and the Lehman Brothers Aggregate Bond Index.

For additional observations on the rolling 10-year correlations of annual returns between the National Association of Realtors Median Home Price and other asset classes, please refer to the exhibits for the NAREIT Index and the Handy & Harmon Spot Silver Price.

## Private Equity

For the Venture Economics All Private Equity Fund Index for 26 time periods, Table 6.15 displays the rolling 10-year correlations of annual

**F I G U R E   6.10**

Residential Real Estate: Correlations of the National Association of Realtors Median Home Price

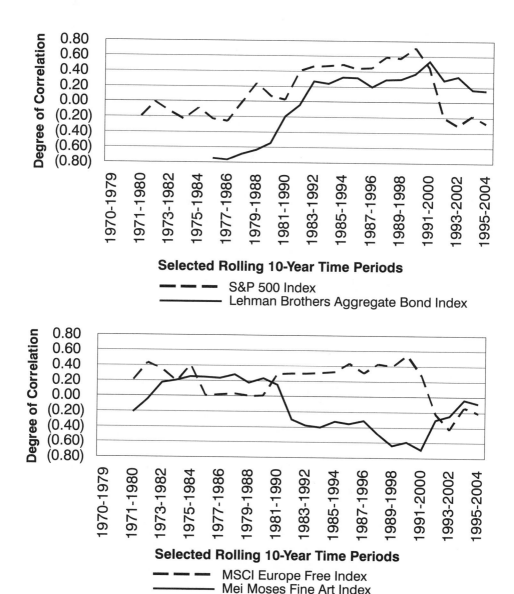

Source: The author.

**T A B L E   6.15**

Private Equity: Correlations of the Venture Economics All Private Equity Fund Index[1]

| | Venture Economics All Private Equity Fund Index for 10-Year Periods from: | S&P 500 Composite Index | Nasdaq Composite Index | Wilshire 5000 Index | MSCI EAFE Net Index | MSCI Europe Free Net Index | MSCI Japan Net Index | Lehman Brothers 7-Year Municipal Bond Index |
|---|---|---|---|---|---|---|---|---|
| | | 1 | 2 | 3 | 4 | 5 | 6 | 7 |
| 1 | 1995–2004 | 0.45 | 0.76 | 0.49 | 0.51 | 0.36 | 0.66 | (0.27) |
| 2 | 1994–2003 | 0.41 | 0.71 | 0.45 | 0.47 | 0.32 | 0.62 | (0.28) |
| 3 | 1993–2002 | 0.45 | 0.81 | 0.51 | 0.60 | 0.42 | 0.74 | (0.27) |
| 4 | 1992–2001 | 0.41 | 0.79 | 0.47 | 0.58 | 0.38 | 0.74 | (0.23) |
| 5 | 1991–2000 | 0.20 | 0.67 | 0.26 | 0.45 | 0.17 | 0.69 | (0.31) |
| 6 | 1990–1999 | 0.30 | 0.81 | 0.37 | 0.54 | 0.26 | 0.74 | (0.30) |
| 7 | 1989–1998 | 0.61 | 0.63 | 0.65 | 0.50 | 0.53 | 0.20 | 0.26 |
| 8 | 1988–1997 | 0.63 | 0.67 | 0.65 | 0.38 | 0.55 | 0.06 | 0.21 |
| 9 | 1987–1996 | 0.64 | 0.71 | 0.66 | 0.29 | 0.56 | (0.03) | 0.36 |
| 10 | 1986–1995 | 0.58 | 0.73 | 0.63 | 0.02 | 0.21 | (0.15) | 0.14 |
| 11 | 1985–1994 | 0.26 | 0.65 | 0.38 | 0.09 | 0.08 | (0.05) | 0.01 |
| 12 | 1984–1993 | 0.34 | 0.72 | 0.46 | 0.14 | 0.18 | (0.02) | 0.04 |
| 13 | 1983–1992 | 0.46 | 0.61 | 0.54 | 0.08 | 0.09 | (0.01) | (0.19) |
| 14 | 1982–1991 | 0.51 | 0.60 | 0.55 | 0.01 | 0.04 | (0.06) | 0.18 |
| 15 | 1981–1990 | 0.58 | 0.63 | 0.60 | 0.15 | 0.22 | 0.02 | 0.39 |
| 16 | 1980–1989 | 0.61 | 0.71 | 0.65 | (0.01) | 0.02 | (0.12) | (0.18) |
| 17 | 1979–1988 | 0.71 | 0.77 | 0.76 | (0.11) | 0.01 | (0.29) | (0.20) |
| 18 | 1978–1987 | 0.52 | 0.71 | 0.62 | (0.04) | 0.02 | (0.15) | (0.25) |
| 19 | 1977–1986 | 0.31 | 0.64 | 0.44 | (0.05) | (0.02) | (0.14) | (0.33) |
| 20 | 1976–1985 | 0.41 | 0.65 | 0.50 | 0.14 | (0.02) | 0.21 | (0.18) |
| 21 | 1975–1984 | 0.73 | 0.78 | 0.78 | 0.73 | 0.75 | 0.27 | 0.02 |
| 22 | 1974–1983 | 0.84 | 0.84 | 0.86 | 0.85 | 0.84 | 0.53 | 0.21 |
| 23 | 1973–1982 | 0.88 | 0.88 | 0.90 | 0.89 | 0.86 | 0.64 | 0.18 |
| 24 | 1972–1981 | 0.88 | 0.88 | 0.89 | 0.79 | 0.84 | 0.28 | 0.36 |
| 25 | 1971–1980 | 0.87 | – | 0.89 | 0.77 | 0.81 | 0.28 | 0.28 |
| 26 | 1970–1979 | 0.85 | – | – | 0.78 | 0.85 | 0.34 | 0.32 |

[1]Rolling 10-year correlations of annual returns of the Venture Economics All Private Equity Fund Index with selected asset classes during 26 10-year periods beginning with 1970–1979 and ending with 1995–2004.

Source: The author.

| U.S. Treasury 10-Year Note | NAREIT Index | Nat'l Assn of Realtors Median Home Price | Venture Economics All Private Equity Fund Index | Handy & Harmon Spot Gold Price | Handy & Harmon Spot Silver Price | Lehman Brothers/ Bridgewater TIPS Index | Mei Moses Fine Art Index | Lehman Brothers Aggregate Bond Index | HFRI Fund Weighted Composite Hedge Fund Index |
|---|---|---|---|---|---|---|---|---|---|
| 8 | 9 | 10 | 11 | 12 | 13 | 14 | 15 | 16 | 17 |
| (0.35) | (0.22) | (0.41) | 1.00 | (0.21) | 0.11 | (0.40) | 0.27 | (0.29) | 0.80 |
| (0.33) | (0.25) | (0.44) | 1.00 | (0.26) | 0.07 | (0.41) | 0.24 | (0.28) | 0.78 |
| (0.36) | (0.20) | (0.36) | 1.00 | (0.13) | 0.15 | (0.37) | 0.30 | (0.32) | 0.71 |
| (0.32) | (0.26) | (0.24) | 1.00 | 0.05 | 0.16 | (0.30) | 0.21 | (0.29) | 0.65 |
| (0.41) | (0.30) | (0.03) | 1.00 | 0.15 | 0.18 | (0.29) | 0.20 | (0.32) | 0.48 |
| (0.37) | (0.08) | 0.19 | 1.00 | 0.13 | 0.25 | (0.37) | 0.19 | (0.30) | 0.54 |
| 0.38 | 0.62 | 0.65 | 1.00 | 0.03 | 0.55 | (0.05) | (0.01) | 0.32 | – |
| 0.40 | 0.71 | 0.64 | 1.00 | 0.11 | 0.58 | (0.10) | (0.14) | 0.33 | – |
| 0.46 | 0.74 | 0.50 | 1.00 | 0.02 | 0.31 | 0.12 | (0.18) | 0.39 | – |
| 0.48 | 0.58 | 0.35 | 1.00 | (0.07) | 0.43 | 0.26 | (0.10) | 0.44 | – |
| 0.17 | 0.73 | 0.49 | 1.00 | (0.07) | 0.53 | (0.06) | (0.40) | 0.12 | – |
| 0.10 | 0.55 | 0.49 | 1.00 | 0.15 | 0.62 | (0.04) | (0.40) | (0.00) | – |
| (0.19) | 0.63 | 0.24 | 1.00 | (0.35) | (0.00) | (0.58) | (0.24) | (0.11) | – |
| 0.10 | 0.64 | 0.15 | 1.00 | (0.19) | 0.24 | (0.27) | (0.31) | 0.23 | – |
| 0.16 | 0.61 | (0.15) | 1.00 | 0.14 | 0.44 | (0.24) | (0.09) | 0.31 | – |
| (0.22) | 0.59 | 0.48 | 1.00 | 0.31 | (0.12) | 0.27 | 0.13 | (0.15) | – |
| (0.27) | 0.62 | 0.52 | 1.00 | 0.38 | 0.25 | 0.41 | 0.11 | (0.22) | – |
| (0.37) | 0.44 | 0.62 | 1.00 | 0.39 | 0.21 | 0.43 | 0.21 | (0.34) | – |
| (0.52) | 0.39 | 0.62 | 1.00 | 0.41 | 0.20 | 0.35 | 0.34 | (0.46) | – |
| (0.40) | 0.48 | 0.63 | 1.00 | 0.37 | 0.15 | 0.24 | 0.35 | (0.36) | – |
| (0.30) | 0.21 | 0.47 | 1.00 | 0.04 | 0.01 | 0.03 | (0.16) | – | – |
| (0.08) | 0.59 | 0.19 | 1.00 | (0.28) | (0.05) | (0.45) | 0.20 | – | – |
| (0.03) | 0.70 | 0.22 | 1.00 | (0.39) | (0.07) | (0.57) | (0.07) | – | – |
| 0.03 | 0.71 | 0.29 | 1.00 | (0.40) | (0.07) | (0.50) | (0.08) | – | – |
| 0.10 | – | 0.12 | 1.00 | (0.64) | (0.18) | (0.60) | (0.08) | – | – |
| (0.04) | – | 0.26 | 1.00 | (0.48) | – | (0.62) | (0.01) | – | – |

returns with 16 other asset classes, beginning with the 1970–1979 decade and ending with the 1995–2004 decade.

The four boxed columns in Table 6.15 highlight the rolling 10-year
correlations of annual returns between the Venture Economics All Private Equity Fund Index and four asset classes: (i) U.S. large-cap equities, as represented by the Standard & Poor's 500 Composite Index; (ii)
Europe, Australasia, Far East equities, as represented by the MSCI
EAFE Net Index; (iii) intermediate-maturity U.S. Treasury Bonds, as
represented by the U.S. Treasury 10-Year Note; and (iv) real estate investment trusts, as represented by the NAREIT Composite Index.

For the 26 10-year periods between 1970–1979 and 1995–2004, the
correlations of annual returns between the Venture Economics All Private Equity Fund Index and the:

- **Standard & Poor's 500 Composite Index:** ranged between 0.20
  and 0.46 for 11 of 26 10-year periods, and between 0.51 and
  0.88 for 15 of 26 10-year periods;

- **MSCI EAFE Net Index:** ranged between –0.11 and 0.47 for 15
  of 26 10-year periods, and between 0.50 and 0.89 for 11 of 26
  10-year periods;

- **U.S. Treasury 10-year Note:** ranged between –0.52 and 0.03 for
  17 of 26 10-year periods, and between 0.10 and 0.48 for 9 of 26
  10-year periods; and

- **NAREIT Index:** ranged between –0.30 and 0.21 for 7 of 24
  10-year periods, and between 0.39 and 0.74 for 17 of 24 10-year
  periods.

Figure 6.11 depicts the rolling 10-year correlations of annual returns between the Venture Economics All Private Equity Fund Index
and the Standard & Poor's 500 Composite Index, the MSCI EAFE Net
Index, the U.S. Treasury 10-Year Note, and the NAREIT Index.

For additional observations on the rolling 10-year correlations of
annual returns between the Venture Economics All Private Equity Fund
Index and other asset classes, please refer to the exhibits for the Nasdaq
Composite Index and the Lehman Brothers Aggregate Bond Index.

## Real Assets—Precious Metals—Gold

For the Handy & Harmon Spot Gold Price for 26 time periods, Table
6.16 displays the rolling 10-year correlations of annual returns with 16

**F I G U R E  6.11**

Private Equity: Correlations of the Venture Economics All Private Equity Fund

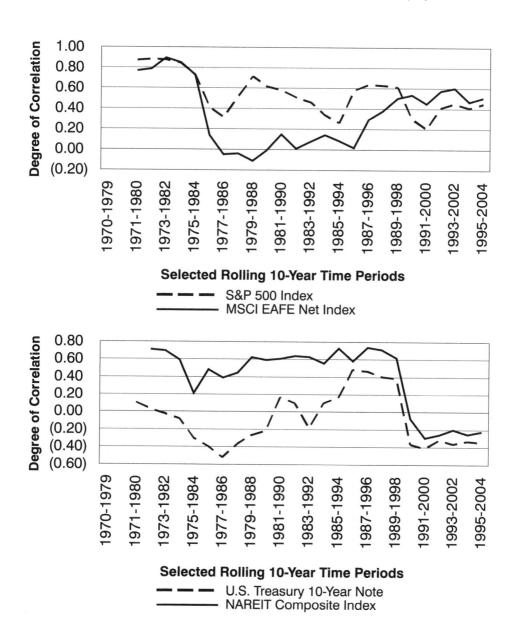

Source: The author.

**T A B L E   6.16**

Real Assets—Precious Metals—Gold:: Correlations of the Handy & Harmon Spot
Gold Price[1]

| Handy & Harmon Spot Gold Price for 10-Year Periods from: | S&P 500 Composite Index | Nasdaq Composite Index | Wilshire 5000 Index | MSCI EAFE Net Index | MSCI Europe Free Net Index | MSCI Japan Net Index | Lehman Brothers 7-Year Municipal Bond Index |
|---|---|---|---|---|---|---|---|
|  | 1 | 2 | 3 | 4 | 5 | 6 | 7 |
| 1  1995–2004 | (0.34) | (0.05) | (0.29) | 0.15 | (0.14) | 0.34 | 0.11 |
| 2  1994–2003 | (0.34) | (0.04) | (0.29) | 0.14 | (0.15) | 0.33 | 0.12 |
| 3  1993–2002 | (0.52) | (0.20) | (0.48) | 0.06 | (0.28) | 0.27 | 0.27 |
| 4  1992–2001 | (0.22) | 0.09 | (0.18) | 0.48 | 0.12 | 0.49 | 0.10 |
| 5  1991–2000 | (0.22) | 0.07 | (0.20) | 0.63 | 0.28 | 0.54 | 0.03 |
| 6  1990–1999 | (0.33) | (0.02) | (0.31) | 0.50 | 0.21 | 0.47 | 0.05 |
| 7  1989–1998 | (0.32) | (0.14) | (0.30) | 0.50 | 0.21 | 0.56 | 0.12 |
| 8  1988–1997 | (0.31) | (0.16) | (0.30) | 0.25 | 0.16 | 0.25 | 0.06 |
| 9  1987–1996 | (0.28) | (0.34) | (0.32) | 0.36 | 0.11 | 0.38 | (0.43) |
| 10  1986–1995 | (0.19) | (0.34) | (0.26) | 0.57 | 0.41 | 0.57 | 0.04 |
| 11  1985–1994 | (0.13) | (0.31) | (0.20) | 0.56 | 0.34 | 0.58 | 0.09 |
| 12  1984–1993 | (0.05) | (0.11) | (0.08) | 0.55 | 0.40 | 0.54 | 0.09 |
| 13  1983–1992 | (0.04) | (0.16) | (0.11) | 0.49 | 0.36 | 0.52 | 0.21 |
| 14  1982–1991 | (0.03) | (0.12) | (0.11) | 0.36 | 0.25 | 0.41 | 0.37 |
| 15  1981–1990 | 0.34 | 0.17 | 0.24 | 0.42 | 0.40 | 0.37 | 0.56 |
| 16  1980–1989 | 0.45 | 0.31 | 0.37 | 0.48 | 0.37 | 0.44 | 0.34 |
| 17  1979–1988 | 0.26 | 0.42 | 0.38 | (0.05) | 0.09 | (0.26) | 0.03 |
| 18  1978–1987 | 0.21 | 0.43 | 0.35 | (0.01) | 0.09 | (0.20) | 0.01 |
| 19  1977–1986 | 0.17 | 0.47 | 0.33 | (0.02) | 0.10 | (0.22) | 0.01 |
| 20  1976–1985 | 0.13 | 0.43 | 0.28 | (0.00) | 0.14 | (0.39) | (0.02) |
| 21  1975–1984 | 0.00 | 0.35 | 0.14 | (0.09) | 0.12 | (0.39) | (0.03) |
| 22  1974–1983 | (0.27) | (0.14) | (0.21) | (0.32) | (0.15) | (0.51) | (0.11) |
| 23  1973–1982 | (0.33) | (0.27) | (0.28) | (0.36) | (0.18) | (0.56) | (0.10) |
| 24  1972–1981 | (0.28) | (0.24) | (0.25) | (0.30) | (0.16) | (0.22) | (0.01) |
| 25  1971–1980 | (0.45) | – | (0.42) | (0.49) | (0.42) | (0.31) | (0.33) |
| 26  1970–1979 | (0.38) | – | – | (0.31) | (0.27) | (0.19) | (0.66) |

[1]Rolling 10-year correlations of annual returns of the Handy & Harmon Spot Gold Price with selected asset classes during 26 10-year periods beginning with 1970–1979 and ending with 1995–2004.

Source: The author.

| U.S. Treasury 10-Year Note | NAREIT Index | Nat'l Assn of Realtors Median Home Price | Venture Economics All Private Equity Fund Index | Handy & Harmon Spot Gold Price | Handy & Harmon Spot Silver Price | Lehman Brothers/ Bridgewater TIPS Index | Mei Moses Fine Art Index | Lehman Brothers Aggregate Bond Index | HFRI Fund Weighted Composite Hedge Fund Index |
|---|---|---|---|---|---|---|---|---|---|
| 8 | 9 | 10 | 11 | 12 | 13 | 14 | 15 | 16 | 17 |
| 0.00 | (0.01) | 0.31 | (0.21) | 1.00 | 0.09 | 0.50 | 0.27 | (0.03) | (0.21) |
| 0.01 | (0.04) | 0.36 | (0.26) | 1.00 | 0.07 | 0.50 | 0.26 | (0.02) | (0.24) |
| 0.16 | (0.25) | 0.02 | (0.13) | 1.00 | 0.13 | 0.59 | (0.04) | 0.12 | (0.07) |
| 0.02 | (0.19) | (0.01) | 0.05 | 1.00 | 0.22 | 0.33 | 0.12 | 0.03 | 0.28 |
| (0.04) | (0.27) | (0.31) | 0.15 | 1.00 | 0.27 | 0.29 | 0.27 | (0.08) | 0.21 |
| (0.02) | (0.22) | (0.24) | 0.13 | 1.00 | 0.22 | 0.41 | 0.30 | (0.06) | 0.16 |
| 0.06 | (0.20) | (0.24) | 0.03 | 1.00 | 0.19 | 0.48 | 0.29 | 0.01 | – |
| 0.08 | (0.14) | (0.23) | 0.11 | 1.00 | 0.29 | 0.50 | (0.05) | 0.04 | – |
| (0.16) | (0.30) | 0.09 | 0.02 | 1.00 | 0.86 | 0.02 | 0.05 | (0.17) | – |
| 0.00 | (0.13) | 0.26 | (0.07) | 1.00 | 0.66 | (0.11) | (0.07) | (0.04) | – |
| 0.08 | (0.10) | 0.27 | (0.07) | 1.00 | 0.64 | (0.03) | (0.02) | 0.04 | – |
| (0.05) | (0.21) | 0.28 | 0.15 | 1.00 | 0.72 | (0.06) | (0.06) | (0.15) | – |
| 0.08 | (0.39) | 0.28 | (0.35) | 1.00 | 0.71 | 0.16 | 0.09 | (0.02) | – |
| 0.24 | (0.32) | 0.17 | (0.19) | 1.00 | 0.72 | 0.29 | (0.00) | 0.22 | – |
| 0.35 | (0.11) | 0.15 | 0.14 | 1.00 | 0.82 | 0.20 | (0.06) | 0.35 | – |
| 0.22 | (0.06) | 0.34 | 0.31 | 1.00 | 0.59 | 0.31 | 0.02 | 0.21 | – |
| (0.16) | 0.45 | 0.64 | 0.38 | 1.00 | 0.94 | 0.68 | (0.06) | (0.22) | – |
| (0.23) | 0.38 | 0.56 | 0.39 | 1.00 | 0.93 | 0.69 | 0.08 | (0.29) | – |
| (0.24) | 0.54 | 0.53 | 0.41 | 1.00 | 0.93 | 0.70 | 0.06 | (0.29) | – |
| (0.27) | 0.28 | 0.51 | 0.37 | 1.00 | 0.93 | 0.75 | (0.00) | (0.32) | – |
| (0.22) | 0.30 | 0.47 | 0.04 | 1.00 | 0.92 | 0.78 | 0.19 | – | – |
| (0.22) | (0.09) | 0.44 | (0.28) | 1.00 | 0.86 | 0.78 | 0.02 | – | – |
| (0.28) | (0.19) | 0.32 | (0.39) | 1.00 | 0.83 | 0.80 | 0.17 | – | – |
| (0.40) | (0.19) | 0.32 | (0.40) | 1.00 | 0.83 | 0.70 | 0.14 | – | – |
| (0.42) | – | 0.08 | (0.64) | 1.00 | 0.83 | 0.70 | 0.04 | – | – |
| (0.56) | – | 0.30 | (0.48) | 1.00 | – | 0.71 | 0.23 | – | – |

other asset classes, beginning with the 1970–1979 decade and ending with the 1995–2004 decade.

The four boxed columns in Table 6.16 highlight the rolling 10-year correlations of annual returns between the Handy & Harmon Spot Gold Price and four asset classes: (i) U.S. large-cap equities, as represented by the Standard & Poor's 500 Composite Index; (ii) real estate investment trusts, as represented by the NAREIT Index; (iii) inflation-indexed securities, as represented by the Lehman Brothers/Bridgewater TIPS Index; and (iv) U.S. taxable fixed-income securities, as represented by the Lehman Brothers Aggregate Bond Index.

For the 26 10-year periods between 1970–1979 and 1995–2004, the correlations of annual returns between the Handy & Harmon Spot Gold Price and the:

◆ **Standard & Poor's 500 Composite Index**: ranged between –0.52 and –0.03 for 19 of 26 10-year periods, and between 0.00 and 0.45 in 7 of 26 10-year periods;

◆ **NAREIT Index**: ranged between –0.30 and 0.21 for 7 of 24 10-year periods, and between 0.39 and 0.74 for 17 of 24 10-year periods;

◆ **Lehman Brothers/Bridgewater TIPS Index**: ranged between –0.11 and 0.02 for 4 of 26 10-year periods, and between 0.16 and 0.80 for 22 of 26 10-year periods; and

◆ **Lehman Brothers Aggregate Bond Index**: ranged between –0.32 and –0.02 for 12 of 20 10-year periods, and between 0.01 and 0.35 for 8 of 20 10-year periods.

Figure 6.12 depicts the rolling 10-year correlations of annual returns between the Handy & Harmon Spot Gold Price and the Standard & Poor's 500 Composite Index, the NAREIT Index, the Lehman Brothers/Bridgewater TIPS Index and the Lehman Brothers Aggregate Bond Index.

For additional observations on the rolling 10-year correlations of annual returns between the Handy & Harmon Spot Gold Price and other asset classes, please refer to the exhibits for the Handy & Harmon Spot Silver Price, the Lehman Brothers/Bridgewater TIPS Index, and the HFRI Fund Weighted Composite Hedge Fund Index.

## Real Assets—Precious Metals—Silver

For the Handy & Harmon Spot Silver Price for 25 time periods, Table 6.17 displays the rolling 10-year correlations of annual returns with 16

F I G U R E   6.12

Real Assets—Precious Metals—Gold: Correlations of the Handy & Harmon Spot Gold Price

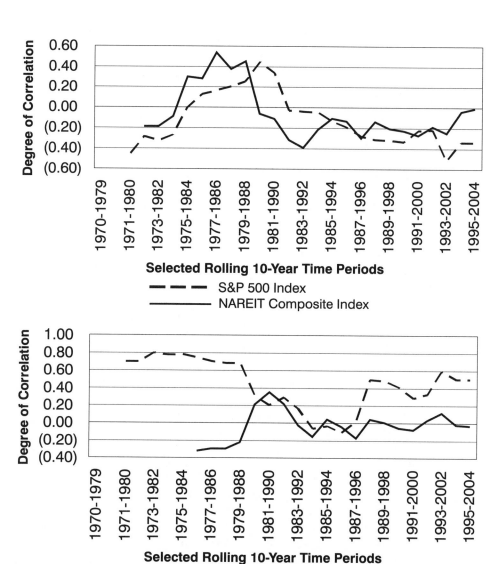

**T A B L E   6.17**

Real Assets—Precious Metals—Silver: Correlations of the Handy & Harmon Spot
Silver Price[1]

| Handy & Harmon Spot Silver Price for 10-Year Periods from: | S&P 500 Composite Index | Nasdaq Composite Index | Wilshire 5000 Index | MSCI EAFE Net Index | MSCI Europe Free Net Index | MSCI Japan Net Index | Lehman Brothers 7-Year Municipal Bond Index |
|---|---|---|---|---|---|---|---|
| | 1 | 2 | 3 | 4 | 5 | 6 | 7 |
| 1   1995–2004 | 0.37 | 0.35 | 0.44 | 0.40 | 0.42 | 0.29 | 0.00 |
| 2   1994–2003 | 0.39 | 0.39 | 0.46 | 0.37 | 0.40 | 0.26 | 0.05 |
| 3   1993–2002 | 0.20 | 0.20 | 0.26 | 0.40 | 0.37 | 0.25 | 0.26 |
| 4   1992–2001 | 0.23 | 0.21 | 0.30 | 0.44 | 0.43 | 0.27 | 0.25 |
| 5   1991–2000 | 0.17 | 0.12 | 0.22 | 0.47 | 0.51 | 0.26 | 0.17 |
| 6   1990–1999 | 0.18 | 0.10 | 0.24 | 0.52 | 0.53 | 0.30 | 0.19 |
| 7   1989–1998 | 0.09 | 0.05 | 0.15 | 0.48 | 0.40 | 0.30 | 0.12 |
| 8   1988–1997 | 0.17 | 0.16 | 0.19 | 0.46 | 0.52 | 0.19 | 0.05 |
| 9   1987–1996 | (0.14) | (0.04) | (0.11) | 0.64 | 0.28 | 0.58 | (0.25) |
| 10  1986–1995 | (0.13) | (0.00) | (0.10) | 0.32 | 0.15 | 0.25 | (0.31) |
| 11  1985–1994 | (0.25) | (0.09) | (0.22) | 0.23 | (0.02) | 0.23 | (0.35) |
| 12  1984–1993 | (0.14) | 0.08 | (0.08) | 0.27 | 0.09 | 0.23 | (0.32) |
| 13  1983–1992 | (0.07) | 0.06 | (0.06) | 0.22 | (0.00) | 0.29 | (0.33) |
| 14  1982–1991 | 0.04 | 0.10 | (0.00) | 0.00 | (0.13) | 0.09 | 0.39 |
| 15  1981–1990 | 0.33 | 0.27 | 0.26 | 0.15 | 0.12 | 0.12 | 0.58 |
| 16  1980–1989 | 0.08 | (0.03) | (0.01) | 0.09 | 0.12 | 0.04 | 0.66 |
| 17  1979–1988 | 0.07 | 0.31 | 0.23 | (0.25) | (0.05) | (0.46) | 0.01 |
| 18  1978–1987 | 0.07 | 0.31 | 0.23 | (0.24) | (0.05) | (0.45) | 0.02 |
| 19  1977–1986 | 0.09 | 0.34 | 0.24 | (0.24) | (0.06) | (0.44) | 0.02 |
| 20  1976–1985 | 0.08 | 0.31 | 0.22 | (0.20) | (0.00) | (0.59) | 0.05 |
| 21  1975–1984 | 0.07 | 0.32 | 0.20 | (0.21) | 0.08 | (0.60) | 0.07 |
| 22  1974–1983 | 0.03 | 0.15 | 0.11 | (0.18) | 0.04 | (0.52) | 0.08 |
| 23  1973–1982 | 0.03 | 0.12 | 0.10 | (0.16) | 0.06 | (0.47) | 0.08 |
| 24  1972–1981 | 0.04 | 0.12 | 0.11 | (0.15) | 0.06 | (0.25) | 0.19 |
| 25  1971–1980 | (0.03) | – | 0.03 | (0.26) | (0.09) | (0.31) | (0.00) |
| 26  1970–1979 | – | – | – | – | – | – | – |

[1]Rolling 10-year correlations of annual returns of the Handy & Harmon Spot Silver Price with selected asset classes during 25 10-year periods beginning with 1971–1980 and ending with 1995–2004.

Source: The author.

| U.S. Treasury 10-Year Note | NAREIT Index | Nat'l Assn of Realtors Median Home Price | Venture Economics All Private Equity Fund Index | Handy & Harmon Spot Gold Price | Handy & Harmon Spot Silver Price | Lehman Brothers/ Bridgewater TIPS Index | Mei Moses Fine Art Index | Lehman Brothers Aggregate Bond Index | HFRI Fund Weighted Composite Hedge Fund Index |
|---|---|---|---|---|---|---|---|---|---|
| 8 | 9 | 10 | 11 | 12 | 13 | 14 | 15 | 16 | 17 |
| (0.11) | 0.42 | 0.48 | 0.11 | 0.09 | 1.00 | (0.15) | (0.13) | (0.07) | 0.43 |
| (0.10) | 0.36 | 0.52 | 0.07 | 0.07 | 1.00 | (0.19) | (0.16) | (0.03) | 0.45 |
| 0.10 | 0.21 | 0.26 | 0.15 | 0.13 | 1.00 | (0.12) | (0.52) | 0.14 | 0.62 |
| 0.12 | 0.20 | 0.31 | 0.16 | 0.22 | 1.00 | (0.13) | (0.56) | 0.15 | 0.62 |
| 0.05 | 0.09 | 0.12 | 0.18 | 0.27 | 1.00 | (0.14) | (0.27) | 0.05 | 0.49 |
| 0.13 | 0.35 | 0.35 | 0.25 | 0.22 | 1.00 | (0.11) | (0.24) | 0.09 | 0.51 |
| 0.14 | 0.40 | 0.40 | 0.55 | 0.19 | 1.00 | (0.17) | (0.33) | 0.06 | – |
| 0.19 | 0.30 | 0.41 | 0.58 | 0.29 | 1.00 | (0.31) | (0.34) | 0.07 | – |
| (0.05) | 0.06 | 0.39 | 0.31 | 0.86 | 1.00 | (0.08) | (0.01) | (0.09) | – |
| (0.14) | 0.12 | 0.33 | 0.43 | 0.66 | 1.00 | (0.08) | 0.01 | (0.18) | – |
| (0.25) | 0.08 | 0.32 | 0.53 | 0.64 | 1.00 | (0.18) | (0.06) | (0.28) | – |
| (0.35) | (0.02) | 0.33 | 0.62 | 0.72 | 1.00 | (0.18) | (0.07) | (0.45) | – |
| (0.38) | (0.27) | 0.41 | (0.00) | 0.71 | 1.00 | (0.10) | 0.25 | (0.45) | – |
| 0.21 | (0.09) | 0.14 | 0.24 | 0.72 | 1.00 | 0.30 | (0.00) | 0.32 | – |
| 0.30 | 0.02 | (0.01) | 0.44 | 0.82 | 1.00 | 0.23 | 0.08 | 0.42 | – |
| 0.39 | (0.23) | (0.43) | (0.12) | 0.59 | 1.00 | 0.00 | (0.08) | 0.50 | – |
| (0.19) | 0.47 | 0.47 | 0.25 | 0.94 | 1.00 | 0.63 | (0.09) | (0.23) | – |
| (0.20) | 0.45 | 0.33 | 0.21 | 0.93 | 1.00 | 0.61 | (0.04) | (0.23) | – |
| (0.20) | 0.59 | 0.28 | 0.20 | 0.93 | 1.00 | 0.63 | (0.02) | (0.22) | – |
| (0.18) | 0.37 | 0.27 | 0.15 | 0.93 | 1.00 | 0.63 | (0.10) | (0.22) | – |
| (0.14) | 0.37 | 0.24 | 0.01 | 0.92 | 1.00 | 0.66 | 0.02 | – | – |
| (0.10) | 0.24 | 0.19 | (0.05) | 0.86 | 1.00 | 0.50 | 0.03 | – | – |
| (0.13) | 0.21 | 0.13 | (0.07) | 0.83 | 1.00 | 0.51 | 0.05 | – | – |
| (0.22) | 0.22 | 0.15 | (0.07) | 0.83 | 1.00 | 0.47 | 0.04 | – | – |
| (0.24) | – | 0.02 | (0.18) | 0.83 | 1.00 | 0.47 | (0.06) | – | – |
| – | – | – | – | – | – | – | – | – | – |

other asset classes, beginning with the 1971–1979 decade and ending with the 1995–2004 decade.

The four boxed columns in Table 6.17 highlight the rolling 10-year correlations of annual returns between the Handy & Harmon Spot Silver Price and four asset classes: (i) U.S. equities, as represented by the Wilshire 5000 Index; (ii) residential real estate, as represented by the National Association of Realtors Median Home Price; (iii) real assets—precious metals—gold, as represented by the Handy & Harmon Spot Gold Price; and (iv) fine art, as represented by the Mei Moses Fine Art Index.

For the 25 10-year periods between 1971–1980 and 1995–2004, the correlations of annual returns between the Handy & Harmon Spot Silver Price and the:

◆ **Wilshire 5000 Index**: ranged between −0.22 and 0.11 for 11 of 25 10-year periods, and between 0.15 and 0.46 for 14 of 25 10-year periods;

◆ **National Association of Realtors Median Home Price:** ranged between −0.43 and 0.15 for 7 of 25 10-year periods, and between 0.19 and 0.56 for 18 of 25 10-year periods;

◆ **Handy & Harmon Spot Gold Price:** ranged between 0.07 and 0.29 for 8 of 25 10-year periods, and between 0.59 and 0.94 for 17 of 25 10-year periods; and

◆ **Mei Moses Fine Art Index**: ranged between −0.52 and −0.01 for 17 of 25 10-year periods, and between 0.00 and 0.25 for eight of 25 10-year periods.

Figure 6.13 depicts the rolling 10-year correlations of annual returns between the Handy & Harmon Spot Silver Price and the Wilshire 5000 Index, the National Association of Realtors Median Home Price, the Handy & Harmon Spot Gold Price, and the Mei Moses Fine Art Index.

For additional observations on the rolling 10-year correlations of annual returns between the Handy & Harmon Spot Silver Price and other asset classes, please refer to the exhibits for the Lehman Brothers Aggregate Bond Index.

## Inflation-Indexed Securities

For the Lehman Brothers/Bridgewater TIPS Index for 26 time periods, Table 6.18 displays the rolling 10-year correlations of annual returns with 16 other asset classes, beginning with the 1970–1979 decade and ending with the 1995–2004 decade.

**F I G U R E   6.13**

Real Assets—Precious Metals—Silver: Correlations of the Handy & Harmon Spot Silver Price

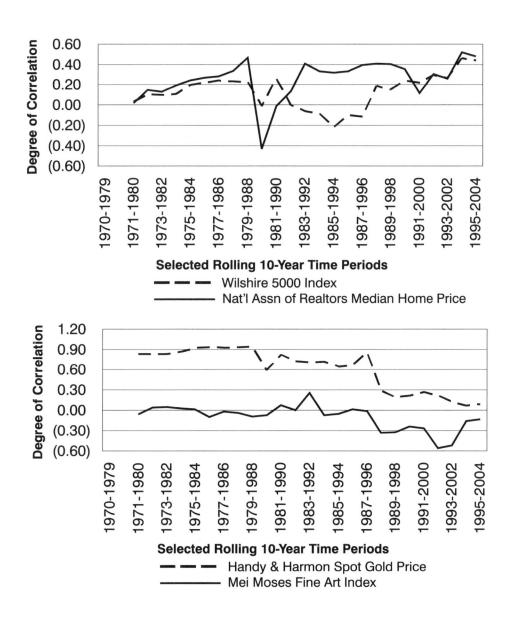

**T A B L E  6.18**

## Inflation-Indexed Securities: Correlations of the Lehman Brothers/Bridgewater TIPS Index[1]

| Lehman Brothers/ Bridgewater TIPS Index for 10-Year Periods from: | S&P 500 Composite Index | Nasdaq Composite Index | Wilshire 5000 Index | MSCI EAFE Net Index | MSCI Europe Free Net Index | MSCI Japan Net Index | Lehman Brothers 7-Year Municipal Bond Index |
|---|---|---|---|---|---|---|---|
| | 1 | 2 | 3 | 4 | 5 | 6 | 7 |
| 1   1995–2004 | (0.41) | (0.52) | (0.40) | (0.35) | (0.35) | (0.36) | 0.65 |
| 2   1994–2003 | (0.41) | (0.52) | (0.40) | (0.39) | (0.37) | (0.38) | 0.69 |
| 3   1993–2002 | (0.56) | (0.63) | (0.56) | (0.49) | (0.51) | (0.40) | 0.69 |
| 4   1992–2001 | (0.34) | (0.52) | (0.34) | (0.33) | (0.29) | (0.41) | 0.69 |
| 5   1991–2000 | (0.30) | (0.46) | (0.28) | (0.31) | (0.29) | (0.39) | 0.69 |
| 6   1990–1999 | (0.15) | (0.32) | (0.13) | (0.28) | (0.16) | (0.37) | 0.70 |
| 7   1989–1998 | (0.01) | (0.05) | 0.02 | (0.10) | (0.01) | (0.06) | 0.69 |
| 8   1988–1997 | 0.06 | 0.07 | 0.06 | 0.05 | 0.12 | 0.04 | 0.70 |
| 9   1987–1996 | 0.43 | 0.18 | 0.39 | (0.08) | 0.41 | (0.31) | 0.75 |
| 10  1986–1995 | 0.45 | 0.23 | 0.41 | (0.22) | 0.23 | (0.41) | 0.40 |
| 11  1985–1994 | 0.46 | 0.22 | 0.43 | 0.08 | 0.52 | (0.21) | 0.52 |
| 12  1984–1993 | 0.34 | 0.11 | 0.31 | (0.02) | 0.52 | (0.28) | 0.32 |
| 13  1983–1992 | 0.16 | 0.01 | 0.11 | (0.05) | 0.38 | (0.23) | 0.43 |
| 14  1982–1991 | 0.16 | 0.05 | 0.10 | (0.25) | 0.18 | (0.39) | 0.62 |
| 15  1981–1990 | 0.17 | 0.19 | 0.14 | (0.27) | 0.14 | (0.42) | 0.50 |
| 16  1980–1989 | 0.44 | 0.52 | 0.44 | (0.17) | 0.14 | (0.34) | 0.19 |
| 17  1979–1988 | 0.35 | 0.57 | 0.46 | (0.28) | 0.04 | (0.51) | 0.05 |
| 18  1978–1987 | 0.28 | 0.57 | 0.41 | (0.24) | 0.05 | (0.44) | 0.02 |
| 19  1977–1986 | 0.28 | 0.54 | 0.39 | (0.23) | (0.01) | (0.38) | (0.03) |
| 20  1976–1985 | 0.31 | 0.49 | 0.38 | (0.01) | 0.11 | (0.23) | 0.08 |
| 21  1975–1984 | 0.12 | 0.36 | 0.20 | (0.26) | (0.16) | (0.31) | 0.01 |
| 22  1974–1983 | (0.38) | (0.40) | (0.38) | (0.60) | (0.52) | (0.55) | (0.15) |
| 23  1973–1982 | (0.40) | (0.46) | (0.41) | (0.61) | (0.52) | (0.60) | (0.18) |
| 24  1972–1981 | (0.44) | (0.48) | (0.44) | (0.67) | (0.53) | (0.61) | (0.36) |
| 25  1971–1980 | (0.52) | – | (0.51) | (0.78) | (0.70) | (0.67) | (0.60) |
| 26  1970–1979 | (0.61) | – | – | (0.74) | (0.65) | (0.64) | (0.59) |

[1]Rolling 10-year correlations of annual returns of the Lehman Brothers/Bridgewater TIPS Index with selected asset classes during 26 10-year periods beginning with 1970–1979 and ending with 1995–2004.

Source: The author.

| U.S. Treasury 10-Year Note | NAREIT Index | Nat'l Assn of Realtors Median Home Price | Venture Economics All Private Equity Fund Index | Handy & Harmon Spot Gold Price | Handy & Harmon Spot Silver Price | Lehman Brothers/ Bridgewater TIPS Index | Mei Moses Fine Art Index | Lehman Brothers Aggregate Bond Index | HFRI Fund Weighted Composite Hedge Fund Index |
|---|---|---|---|---|---|---|---|---|---|
| 8 | 9 | 10 | 11 | 12 | 13 | 14 | 15 | 16 | 17 |
| 0.57 | 0.44 | 0.30 | (0.40) | 0.50 | (0.15) | 1.00 | 0.45 | 0.58 | (0.29) |
| 0.58 | 0.43 | 0.29 | (0.41) | 0.50 | (0.19) | 1.00 | 0.44 | 0.61 | (0.29) |
| 0.62 | 0.32 | 0.21 | (0.37) | 0.59 | (0.12) | 1.00 | 0.23 | 0.62 | (0.28) |
| 0.61 | 0.54 | 0.12 | (0.30) | 0.33 | (0.13) | 1.00 | 0.47 | 0.67 | (0.03) |
| 0.63 | 0.52 | 0.12 | (0.29) | 0.29 | (0.14) | 1.00 | 0.29 | 0.65 | 0.05 |
| 0.57 | 0.17 | (0.19) | (0.37) | 0.41 | (0.11) | 1.00 | 0.23 | 0.64 | 0.16 |
| 0.49 | 0.03 | (0.30) | (0.05) | 0.48 | (0.17) | 1.00 | 0.42 | 0.60 | – |
| 0.56 | (0.24) | (0.32) | (0.10) | 0.50 | (0.31) | 1.00 | 0.48 | 0.61 | – |
| 0.80 | (0.12) | (0.24) | 0.12 | 0.02 | (0.08) | 1.00 | 0.30 | 0.82 | – |
| 0.65 | (0.07) | (0.28) | 0.26 | (0.11) | (0.08) | 1.00 | 0.32 | 0.69 | – |
| 0.69 | (0.00) | (0.22) | (0.06) | (0.03) | (0.18) | 1.00 | 0.37 | 0.74 | – |
| 0.46 | (0.24) | (0.47) | (0.04) | (0.06) | (0.18) | 1.00 | 0.25 | 0.47 | – |
| 0.54 | (0.42) | (0.29) | (0.58) | 0.16 | (0.10) | 1.00 | 0.28 | 0.50 | – |
| 0.67 | (0.28) | (0.40) | (0.27) | 0.29 | 0.30 | 1.00 | 0.09 | 0.66 | – |
| 0.67 | (0.25) | (0.38) | (0.24) | 0.20 | 0.23 | 1.00 | 0.00 | 0.64 | – |
| 0.44 | 0.01 | 0.20 | 0.27 | 0.31 | 0.00 | 1.00 | 0.16 | 0.39 | – |
| 0.13 | 0.37 | 0.55 | 0.41 | 0.68 | 0.63 | 1.00 | 0.08 | 0.06 | – |
| 0.06 | 0.30 | 0.52 | 0.43 | 0.69 | 0.61 | 1.00 | 0.18 | (0.01) | – |
| 0.01 | 0.14 | 0.38 | 0.35 | 0.70 | 0.63 | 1.00 | 0.40 | (0.04) | – |
| 0.08 | 0.04 | 0.38 | 0.24 | 0.75 | 0.63 | 1.00 | 0.23 | (0.00) | – |
| 0.05 | 0.09 | 0.39 | 0.03 | 0.78 | 0.66 | 1.00 | 0.28 | – | – |
| (0.01) | (0.44) | 0.35 | (0.45) | 0.78 | 0.50 | 1.00 | (0.08) | – | – |
| (0.12) | (0.45) | 0.07 | (0.57) | 0.80 | 0.51 | 1.00 | 0.02 | – | – |
| (0.29) | (0.39) | 0.21 | (0.50) | 0.70 | 0.47 | 1.00 | 0.02 | – | – |
| (0.36) | – | 0.16 | (0.60) | 0.70 | 0.47 | 1.00 | (0.12) | – | – |
| (0.29) | – | 0.13 | (0.62) | 0.71 | – | 1.00 | (0.13) | – | – |

The four boxed columns in Table 6.18 highlight the rolling 10-year correlations of annual returns between the Lehman Brothers/ Bridgewater TIPS Index and four asset classes: (i) U.S. large-cap equities, as represented by the Standard & Poor's 500 Composite Index; (ii) intermediate-maturity U.S. Treasury Bonds, as represented by the U.S. Treasury 10-Year Treasury Note; (iii) real assets—precious metals—gold, as represented by the Handy & Harmon Spot Gold Price; and (iv) U.S. taxable fixed-income securities, as represented by the Lehman Brothers Aggregate Bond Index.

For the 26 10-year periods between 1970–1979 and 1995–2004, the correlations of annual returns between the Lehman Brothers/ Bridgewater TIPS Index and the:

◆ **Standard & Poor's 500 Composite Index**: ranged between –0.56 and –0.01 in 12 of 26 10-year periods, and between 0.06 and 0.46 in 14 of 26 10-year periods;

◆ **U.S. Treasury 10-Year Note:** ranged between –0.29 and 0.08 in 9 of 26 10-year periods, and between 0.13 and 0.80 in 17 of 26 10-year periods;

◆ **Handy & Harmon Spot Gold Price:** ranged between –0.11 and 0.20 in 6 of 26 10-year periods, and between 0.29 and 0.80 in 20 of 26 10-year periods; and

◆ **Lehman Brothers Aggregate Bond Index**: ranged between –0.04 and 0.06 in 4 of 20 10-year periods, and between 0.39 and 0.82 in 16 of 20 10-year periods.

Figure 6.14 depicts the rolling 10-year correlations of annual returns between the Lehman Brothers/Bridgewater TIPS Index and the Standard & Poor's 500 Composite Index, the U.S. Treasury 10-Year Note, the Handy & Harmon Spot Gold Price, and the Lehman Brothers Aggregate Bond Index.

For additional observations on the rolling 10-year correlations of annual returns between the Lehman Brothers/Bridgewater TIPS Index and other asset classes, please refer to the exhibits for the MSCI EAFE Net Index, the MSCI Japan Net Index, the NAREIT Index, the Handy & Harmon Spot Gold Price, and the Mei Moses Fine Art Index.

## Fine Art

For the Mei Moses Fine Art Index for 26 time periods, Table 6.19 displays the rolling 10-year correlations of annual returns with 16 other

**F I G U R E   6.14**

Inflation-Indexed Securities: Correlations of the Lehman Brothers/Bridgewater TIPS Index

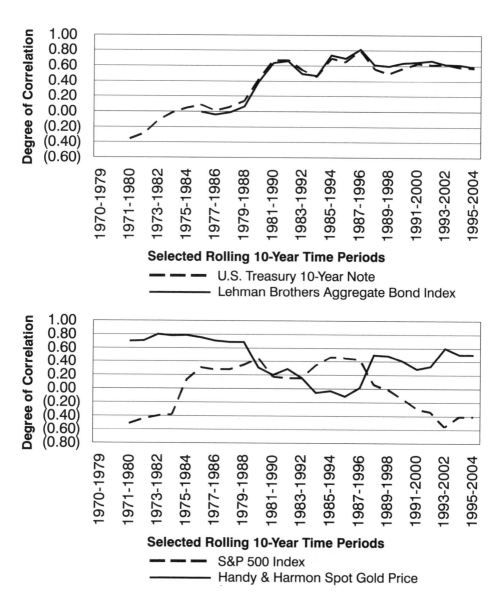

**T A B L E   6.19**

Fine Art: Correlations of the Mei/Moses Fine Art Index[1]

| | Mei Moses Fine Art Index for 10-Year Periods from: | S&P 500 Composite Index | Nasdaq Composite Index | Wilshire 5000 Index | MSCI EAFE Net Index | MSCI Europe Free Net Index | MSCI Japan Net Index | Lehman Brothers 7-Year Municipal Bond Index |
|---|---|---|---|---|---|---|---|---|
| | | 1 | 2 | 3 | 4 | 5 | 6 | 7 |
| 1 | 1995–2004 | 0.41 | 0.40 | 0.42 | 0.46 | 0.43 | 0.27 | 0.37 |
| 2 | 1994–2003 | 0.42 | 0.41 | 0.43 | 0.45 | 0.42 | 0.26 | 0.39 |
| 3 | 1993–2002 | 0.36 | 0.33 | 0.34 | 0.12 | 0.17 | 0.05 | 0.31 |
| 4 | 1992–2001 | 0.24 | 0.25 | 0.23 | (0.06) | (0.02) | (0.04) | 0.41 |
| 5 | 1991–2000 | (0.06) | (0.08) | (0.13) | (0.17) | (0.09) | (0.12) | 0.06 |
| 6 | 1990–1999 | 0.02 | 0.01 | (0.06) | (0.12) | (0.01) | (0.09) | 0.03 |
| 7 | 1989–1998 | 0.11 | (0.13) | 0.01 | (0.16) | 0.10 | (0.24) | 0.25 |
| 8 | 1988–1997 | 0.01 | (0.20) | (0.02) | 0.13 | 0.04 | 0.17 | 0.34 |
| 9 | 1987–1996 | 0.02 | (0.30) | (0.04) | 0.19 | 0.02 | 0.24 | 0.00 |
| 10 | 1986–1995 | 0.01 | (0.26) | (0.04) | (0.03) | (0.11) | (0.01) | (0.15) |
| 11 | 1985–1994 | 0.02 | (0.27) | (0.02) | 0.14 | 0.18 | 0.09 | (0.01) |
| 12 | 1984–1993 | (0.09) | (0.35) | (0.13) | 0.09 | 0.11 | 0.09 | (0.17) |
| 13 | 1983–1992 | (0.16) | (0.36) | (0.18) | 0.14 | 0.15 | 0.11 | (0.16) |
| 14 | 1982–1991 | (0.19) | (0.37) | (0.20) | 0.21 | 0.20 | 0.16 | (0.30) |
| 15 | 1981–1990 | 0.15 | 0.21 | 0.21 | 0.23 | 0.23 | 0.11 | (0.29) |
| 16 | 1980–1989 | 0.17 | 0.23 | 0.23 | 0.14 | 0.16 | (0.01) | (0.39) |
| 17 | 1979–1988 | 0.17 | 0.20 | 0.21 | 0.16 | 0.16 | 0.03 | (0.38) |
| 18 | 1978–1987 | 0.21 | 0.21 | 0.23 | 0.14 | 0.22 | (0.01) | (0.51) |
| 19 | 1977–1986 | 0.47 | 0.52 | 0.54 | 0.17 | 0.35 | (0.04) | (0.44) |
| 20 | 1976–1985 | 0.59 | 0.54 | 0.63 | 0.45 | 0.31 | 0.51 | (0.22) |
| 21 | 1975–1984 | 0.03 | 0.14 | 0.07 | (0.20) | (0.51) | 0.31 | (0.40) |
| 22 | 1974–1983 | 0.35 | 0.50 | 0.40 | 0.18 | (0.09) | 0.48 | (0.22) |
| 23 | 1973–1982 | 0.11 | 0.11 | 0.11 | (0.04) | (0.20) | 0.16 | (0.19) |
| 24 | 1972–1981 | 0.18 | 0.15 | 0.16 | (0.07) | (0.22) | 0.08 | 0.06 |
| 25 | 1971–1980 | 0.17 | – | 0.16 | (0.00) | (0.15) | 0.14 | 0.13 |
| 26 | 1970–1979 | 0.09 | – | – | 0.12 | 0.02 | 0.25 | 0.07 |

[1]Rolling 10-year correlations of annual returns of the Mei Moses Fine Art Index with selected asset classes during 26 10-year periods beginning with 1970–1979 and ending with 1995–2004.

Source: The author.

| U.S. Treasury 10-Year Note | NAREIT Index | Nat'l Assn of Realtors Median Home Price | Venture Economics All Private Equity Fund Index | Handy & Harmon Spot Gold Price | Handy & Harmon Spot Silver Price | Lehman Brothers/ Bridgewater TIPS Index | Mei Moses Fine Art Index | Lehman Brothers Aggregate Bond Index | HFRI Fund Weighted Composite Hedge Fund Index |
|---|---|---|---|---|---|---|---|---|---|
| 8 | 9 | 10 | 11 | 12 | 13 | 14 | 15 | 16 | 17 |
| 0.33 | 0.13 | 0.09 | 0.27 | 0.27 | (0.13) | 0.45 | 1.00 | 0.37 | 0.34 |
| 0.34 | 0.10 | (0.04) | 0.24 | 0.26 | (0.16) | 0.44 | 1.00 | 0.39 | 0.34 |
| 0.36 | (0.12) | (0.25) | 0.30 | (0.04) | (0.52) | 0.23 | 1.00 | 0.41 | 0.09 |
| 0.42 | (0.15) | (0.30) | 0.21 | 0.12 | (0.56) | 0.47 | 1.00 | 0.45 | 0.03 |
| 0.08 | (0.39) | (0.69) | 0.20 | 0.27 | (0.27) | 0.29 | 1.00 | 0.02 | (0.31) |
| 0.03 | (0.46) | (0.60) | 0.19 | 0.30 | (0.24) | 0.23 | 1.00 | (0.01) | (0.27) |
| 0.22 | (0.44) | (0.64) | (0.01) | 0.29 | (0.33) | 0.42 | 1.00 | 0.17 | – |
| 0.07 | (0.31) | (0.49) | (0.14) | (0.05) | (0.34) | 0.48 | 1.00 | 0.08 | – |
| (0.06) | (0.38) | (0.31) | (0.18) | 0.05 | (0.01) | 0.30 | 1.00 | (0.04) | – |
| (0.15) | (0.42) | (0.36) | (0.10) | (0.07) | 0.01 | 0.32 | 1.00 | (0.12) | – |
| (0.06) | (0.37) | (0.33) | (0.40) | (0.02) | (0.06) | 0.37 | 1.00 | (0.01) | – |
| (0.29) | (0.44) | (0.40) | (0.40) | (0.06) | (0.07) | 0.25 | 1.00 | (0.25) | – |
| (0.26) | (0.42) | (0.38) | (0.24) | 0.09 | 0.25 | 0.28 | 1.00 | (0.28) | – |
| (0.36) | (0.44) | (0.30) | (0.31) | (0.00) | (0.00) | 0.09 | 1.00 | (0.38) | – |
| (0.34) | (0.16) | 0.15 | (0.09) | (0.06) | 0.08 | 0.00 | 1.00 | (0.37) | – |
| (0.45) | (0.31) | 0.23 | 0.13 | 0.02 | (0.08) | 0.16 | 1.00 | (0.48) | – |
| (0.41) | (0.31) | 0.17 | 0.11 | (0.06) | (0.09) | 0.08 | 1.00 | (0.43) | – |
| (0.41) | (0.26) | 0.28 | 0.21 | 0.08 | (0.04) | 0.18 | 1.00 | (0.42) | – |
| (0.22) | 0.07 | 0.23 | 0.34 | 0.06 | (0.02) | 0.40 | 1.00 | (0.26) | – |
| (0.02) | 0.37 | 0.24 | 0.35 | (0.00) | (0.10) | 0.23 | 1.00 | (0.10) | – |
| (0.15) | 0.46 | 0.25 | (0.16) | 0.19 | 0.02 | 0.28 | 1.00 | – | – |
| (0.08) | 0.62 | 0.20 | 0.20 | 0.02 | 0.03 | (0.08) | 1.00 | – | – |
| (0.12) | 0.25 | 0.17 | (0.07) | 0.17 | 0.05 | 0.02 | 1.00 | – | – |
| 0.30 | 0.29 | (0.05) | (0.08) | 0.14 | 0.04 | 0.02 | 1.00 | – | – |
| 0.41 | – | (0.21) | (0.08) | 0.04 | (0.06) | (0.12) | 1.00 | – | – |
| 0.09 | – | 0.17 | (0.01) | 0.23 | – | (0.13) | 1.00 | – | – |

asset classes, beginning with the 1970–1979 decade and ending with the 1995–2004 decade.

The four boxed columns in Table 6.19 highlight the rolling 10-year correlations of annual returns between the Mei Moses Fine Art Index and four asset classes: (i) U.S. large-cap equities, as represented by the Standard & Poor's 500 Composite Index; (ii) real estate investment trusts, as represented by the NAREIT Index; (iii) inflation-indexed securities, as represented by Lehman Brothers/Bridgewater TIPS Index; and (iv) U.S. taxable fixed-income securities, as represented by the Lehman Brothers Aggregate Bond Index.

For the 26 10-year periods between 1970–1979 and 1995–2004, the correlations of annual returns between the Mei Moses Fine Art Index and the:

♦ **Standard & Poor's 500 Composite Index:** ranged between –0.19 and 0.21 in 19 of 26 10-year periods, and between 0.24 and 0.59 in 7 of 26 10-year periods;

♦ **NAREIT Index**: ranged between –0.46 and 0.13 in 19 of 24 10-year periods, and between 0.25 and 0.62 in 5 of 24 10-year periods;

♦ **Lehman Brothers/Bridgewater TIPS Index**: ranged between –0.08 and 0.18 in 10 of 26 10-year periods, and between 0.23 and 0.47 in 16 of 26 10-year periods; and

♦ **Lehman Brothers Aggregate Bond Index**: ranged between –0.48 and –0.01 in 13 of 20 10-year periods, and between 0.02 and 0.45 in 7 of 20 10-year periods.

Figure 6.15 depicts the rolling 10-year correlations of annual returns between the Mei Moses Fine Art Index and the Standard & Poor's 500 Composite Index, the NAREIT Index, the Lehman Brothers/Bridgewater TIPS Index, and the Lehman Brothers Aggregate Bond Index.

For additional observations on the rolling 10-year correlations of annual returns between the Mei Moses Fine Art Index and other asset classes, please refer to the exhibits for the Wilshire 5000 Index, the U.S. Treasury 10-Year Note, the National Association of Realtors Median Home Price, and the Handy & Harmon Spot Silver Price.

## U.S. Taxable Fixed-Income Securities

For the Lehman Brothers Aggregate Bond Index for 20 time periods, Table 6.20 displays the rolling 10-year correlations of annual returns

**F I G U R E  6.15**

Fine Art: Correlations of the Mei/Moses Fine Art Index

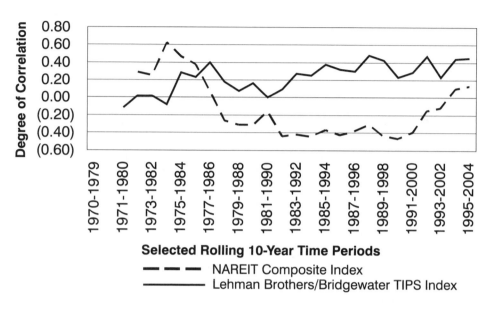

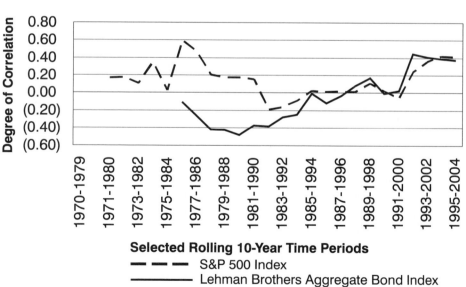

**T A B L E  6.20**

## U.S. Taxable Fixed-Income Securities: Correlations of the Lehman Brothers Aggregate Bond Index[1]

| Lehman Brothers Aggregate Bond Index for 10-Year Periods from: | S&P 500 Composite Index | Nasdaq Composite Index | Wilshire 5000 Index | MSCI EAFE Net Index | MSCI Europe Free Net Index | MSCI Japan Net Index | Lehman Brothers 7-Year Municipal Bond Index |
|---|---|---|---|---|---|---|---|
| | 1 | 2 | 3 | 4 | 5 | 6 | 7 |
| 1   1995–2004 | 0.07 | (0.26) | 0.04 | (0.39) | (0.12) | (0.60) | 0.97 |
| 2   1994–2003 | 0.07 | (0.27) | 0.04 | (0.37) | (0.10) | (0.59) | 0.97 |
| 3   1993–2002 | 0.11 | (0.23) | 0.10 | (0.23) | 0.03 | (0.51) | 0.96 |
| 4   1992–2001 | 0.24 | (0.19) | 0.22 | (0.18) | 0.12 | (0.48) | 0.96 |
| 5   1991–2000 | 0.39 | (0.02) | 0.40 | (0.13) | 0.17 | (0.42) | 0.97 |
| 6   1990–1999 | 0.52 | 0.08 | 0.53 | (0.06) | 0.26 | (0.37) | 0.97 |
| 7   1989–1998 | 0.65 | 0.59 | 0.69 | 0.16 | 0.38 | (0.04) | 0.95 |
| 8   1988–1997 | 0.67 | 0.63 | 0.69 | 0.12 | 0.41 | (0.07) | 0.92 |
| 9   1987–1996 | 0.73 | 0.67 | 0.75 | 0.02 | 0.47 | (0.21) | 0.87 |
| 10  1986–1995 | 0.81 | 0.66 | 0.79 | 0.21 | 0.60 | 0.02 | 0.81 |
| 11  1985–1994 | 0.81 | 0.63 | 0.79 | 0.46 | 0.77 | 0.20 | 0.87 |
| 12  1984–1993 | 0.70 | 0.48 | 0.67 | 0.43 | 0.72 | 0.24 | 0.80 |
| 13  1983–1992 | 0.64 | 0.45 | 0.60 | 0.43 | 0.72 | 0.24 | 0.81 |
| 14  1982–1991 | 0.47 | 0.37 | 0.41 | 0.00 | 0.26 | (0.09) | 0.92 |
| 15  1981–1990 | 0.54 | 0.49 | 0.49 | 0.09 | 0.35 | (0.05) | 0.90 |
| 16  1980–1989 | 0.29 | 0.20 | 0.22 | (0.00) | 0.33 | (0.18) | 0.92 |
| 17  1979–1988 | 0.26 | 0.06 | 0.11 | 0.10 | 0.33 | 0.03 | 0.90 |
| 18  1978–1987 | 0.32 | 0.07 | 0.17 | 0.07 | 0.30 | (0.05) | 0.91 |
| 19  1977–1986 | 0.35 | 0.00 | 0.19 | 0.09 | 0.25 | 0.03 | 0.89 |
| 20  1976–1985 | 0.37 | 0.06 | 0.22 | (0.06) | 0.15 | (0.14) | 0.91 |
| 21  1975–1984 | – | – | – | – | – | – | – |
| 22  1974–1983 | – | – | – | – | – | – | – |
| 23  1973–1982 | – | – | – | – | – | – | – |
| 24  1972–1981 | – | – | – | – | – | – | – |
| 25  1971–1980 | – | – | – | – | – | – | – |
| 26  1970–1979 | – | – | – | – | – | – | – |

[1]Rolling 10-year correlations of annual returns of the Lehman Brothers Aggregate Bond Index with selected asset classes during 20 10-year periods beginning with 1976–1985 and ending with 1995–2004.

Source: The author.

| U.S. Treasury 10-Year Note | NAREIT Index | Nat'l Assn of Realtors Median Home Price | Venture Economics All Private Equity Fund Index | Handy & Harmon Spot Gold Price | Handy & Harmon Spot Silver Price | Lehman Brothers/ Bridgewater TIPS Index | Mei Moses Fine Art Index | Lehman Brothers Aggregate Bond Index | HFRI Fund Weighted Composite Hedge Fund Index |
|---|---|---|---|---|---|---|---|---|---|
| 8 | 9 | 10 | 11 | 12 | 13 | 14 | 15 | 16 | 17 |
| 0.97 | 0.06 | 0.15 | (0.29) | (0.03) | (0.07) | 0.58 | 0.37 | 1.00 | (0.16) |
| 0.97 | 0.12 | 0.16 | (0.28) | (0.02) | (0.03) | 0.61 | 0.39 | 1.00 | (0.17) |
| 0.97 | 0.24 | 0.33 | (0.32) | 0.12 | 0.14 | 0.62 | 0.41 | 1.00 | (0.06) |
| 0.97 | 0.28 | 0.29 | (0.29) | 0.03 | 0.15 | 0.67 | 0.45 | 1.00 | 0.00 |
| 0.98 | 0.40 | 0.54 | (0.32) | (0.08) | 0.05 | 0.65 | 0.02 | 1.00 | 0.19 |
| 0.98 | 0.30 | 0.37 | (0.30) | (0.06) | 0.09 | 0.64 | (0.01) | 1.00 | 0.25 |
| 0.98 | 0.18 | 0.30 | 0.32 | 0.01 | 0.06 | 0.60 | 0.17 | 1.00 | – |
| 0.99 | 0.19 | 0.29 | 0.33 | 0.04 | 0.07 | 0.61 | 0.08 | 1.00 | – |
| 0.99 | 0.28 | 0.20 | 0.39 | (0.17) | (0.09) | 0.82 | (0.04) | 1.00 | – |
| 0.99 | 0.53 | 0.32 | 0.44 | (0.04) | (0.18) | 0.69 | (0.12) | 1.00 | – |
| 0.99 | 0.54 | 0.32 | 0.12 | 0.04 | (0.28) | 0.74 | (0.01) | 1.00 | – |
| 0.98 | 0.56 | 0.24 | (0.00) | (0.15) | (0.45) | 0.47 | (0.25) | 1.00 | – |
| 0.98 | 0.46 | 0.27 | (0.11) | (0.02) | (0.45) | 0.50 | (0.28) | 1.00 | – |
| 0.97 | 0.42 | (0.05) | 0.23 | 0.22 | 0.32 | 0.66 | (0.38) | 1.00 | – |
| 0.97 | 0.47 | (0.20) | 0.31 | 0.35 | 0.42 | 0.64 | (0.37) | 1.00 | – |
| 0.97 | 0.32 | (0.55) | (0.15) | 0.21 | 0.50 | 0.39 | (0.48) | 1.00 | – |
| 0.97 | 0.10 | (0.63) | (0.22) | (0.22) | (0.23) | 0.06 | (0.43) | 1.00 | – |
| 0.98 | 0.15 | (0.69) | (0.34) | (0.29) | (0.23) | (0.01) | (0.42) | 1.00 | – |
| 0.98 | (0.05) | (0.77) | (0.46) | (0.29) | (0.22) | (0.04) | (0.26) | 1.00 | – |
| 0.98 | 0.08 | (0.75) | (0.36) | (0.32) | (0.22) | (0.00) | (0.10) | 1.00 | – |
| – | – | – | – | – | – | – | – | – | – |
| – | – | – | – | – | – | – | – | – | – |
| – | – | – | – | – | – | – | – | – | – |
| – | – | – | – | – | – | – | – | – | – |
| – | – | – | – | – | – | – | – | – | – |
| – | – | – | – | – | – | – | – | – | – |

with 16 other asset classes, beginning with the 1976–1985 decade and ending with the 1995–2004 decade.

The four boxed columns in Table 6.20 highlight the rolling 10-year correlations of annual returns between the Lehman Brothers Aggregate Bond Index and four asset classes: (i) U.S. unlisted equities, as represented by the Nasdaq Composite Index; (ii) U.S. equities, as represented by the Wilshire 5000 Index; (iii) private equity, as represented by the Venture Economics All Private Equity Fund Index; and (iv) real assets—precious metals—silver, as represented by the Handy & Harmon Spot Silver Price.

For the 20 10-year periods between 1976–1985 and 1995–2004, the correlations of annual returns between the Lehman Brothers Aggregate Bond Index and the:

- **Nasdaq Composite Index**: ranged between –0.27 and 0.20 in 11 of 20 10-year periods, and between 0.37 and 0.67 in 9 of 20 10-year periods;

- **Wilshire 5000 Index**: ranged between 0.04 and 0.22 in 9 of 20 10-year periods, and between 0.40 and 0.79 in 11 of 20 10-year periods;

- **Venture Economics All Private Equity Fund Index**: ranged between –0.46 and 0.00 for 12 of 20 10-year periods, and between 0.12 and 0.44 for 8 of 20 10-year periods; and

- **Handy & Harmon Spot Silver Price**: ranged between –0.45 and –0.03 for 11 of 20 10-year periods, and between 0.05 and 0.50 for 9 of 20 10-year periods.

Figure 6.16 depicts the rolling 10-year correlations of annual returns between the Lehman Brothers Aggregate Bond Index and the Nasdaq Composite Index, the Wilshire 5000 Index, the Venture Economics All Private Equity Fund Index, and the Handy & Harmon Spot Silver Price.

For additional observations on the rolling 10-year correlations of annual returns between the Lehman Brothers Aggregate Bond Index and other asset classes, please refer to the exhibits for the Standard & Poor's 500 Composite Index, the MSCI Europe Free Net Index, the MSCI Japan Net Index, the Lehman Brothers 7-Year Municipal Bond Index, the U.S. Treasury 10-Year Note, the NAREIT Index, the National Association of Realtors Median Home Price, the Handy & Harmon Spot Gold Price, the Lehman Brothers/Bridgewater TIPS Index, and the Mei Moses Fine Art Index.

**F I G U R E  6.16**

U.S. Taxable Fixed-Income Securities: Correlations of the Lehman Brothers
Aggregate Bond Index

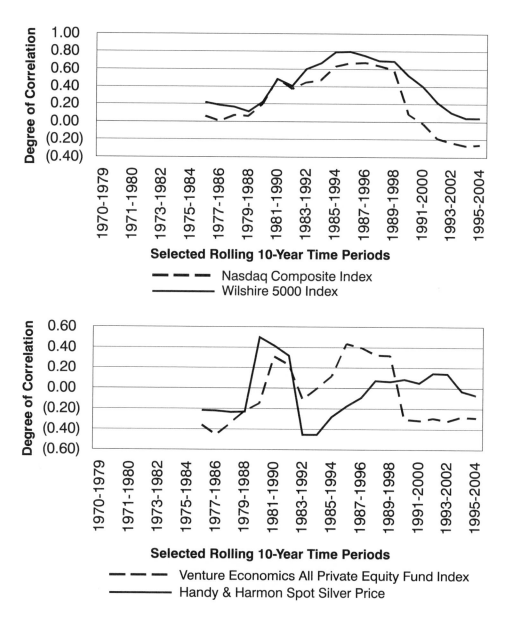

Source: The author.

**T A B L E  6.21**

Hedge Funds: Correlations of the HFRI Fund Weighted Composite Hedge Fund Index[1]

| HFRI Fund Weighted Composite Hedge Fund Index for 10-Year Periods from: | S&P 500 Composite Index | Nasdaq Composite Index | Wilshire 5000 Index | MSCI EAFE Net Index | MSCI Europe Free Net Index | MSCI Japan Net Index | Lehman Brothers 7-Year Municipal Bond Index |
|---|---|---|---|---|---|---|---|
| | 1 | 2 | 3 | 4 | 5 | 6 | 7 |
| 1　1995–2004 | 0.69 | 0.81 | 0.75 | 0.58 | 0.59 | 0.50 | (0.10) |
| 2　1994–2003 | 0.69 | 0.80 | 0.74 | 0.59 | 0.59 | 0.51 | (0.12) |
| 3　1993–2002 | 0.58 | 0.70 | 0.64 | 0.72 | 0.66 | 0.55 | 0.04 |
| 4　1992–2001 | 0.41 | 0.62 | 0.51 | 0.54 | 0.47 | 0.49 | 0.20 |
| 5　1991–2000 | 0.36 | 0.62 | 0.50 | 0.43 | 0.30 | 0.40 | 0.29 |
| 6　1990–1999 | 0.32 | 0.60 | 0.48 | 0.45 | 0.26 | 0.42 | 0.35 |
| 7　1989–1998 | – | – | – | – | – | – | – |
| 8　1988–1997 | – | – | – | – | – | – | – |
| 9　1987–1996 | – | – | – | – | – | – | – |
| 10　1986–1995 | – | – | – | – | – | – | – |
| 11　1985–1994 | – | – | – | – | – | – | – |
| 12　1984–1993 | – | – | – | – | – | – | – |
| 13　1983–1992 | – | – | – | – | – | – | – |
| 14　1982–1991 | – | – | – | – | – | – | – |
| 15　1981–1990 | – | – | – | – | – | – | – |
| 16　1980–1989 | – | – | – | – | – | – | – |
| 17　1979–1988 | – | – | – | – | – | – | – |
| 18　1978–1987 | – | – | – | – | – | – | – |
| 19　1977–1986 | – | – | – | – | – | – | – |
| 20　1976–1985 | – | – | – | – | – | – | – |
| 21　1975–1984 | – | – | – | – | – | – | – |
| 22　1974–1983 | – | – | – | – | – | – | – |
| 23　1973–1982 | – | – | – | – | – | – | – |
| 24　1972–1981 | – | – | – | – | – | – | – |
| 25　1971–1980 | – | – | – | – | – | – | – |
| 26　1970–1979 | – | – | – | – | – | – | – |

[1]Rolling 10-year correlations of annual returns of HFRI Fund Weighted Composite Hedge Fund Index with selected asset classes during six 10-year periods beginning with 1990–1999 and ending with 1995–2004.

Source: The author.

| U.S. Treasury 10-Year Note | NAREIT Index | Nat'l Assn of Realtors Median Home Price | Venture Economics All Private Equity Fund Index | Handy & Harmon Spot Gold Price | Handy & Harmon Spot Silver Price | Lehman Brothers/ Bridgewater TIPS Index | Mei Moses Fine Art Index | Lehman Brothers Aggregate Bond Index | HFRI Fund Weighted Composite Hedge Fund Index |
|---|---|---|---|---|---|---|---|---|---|
| 8 | 9 | 10 | 11 | 12 | 13 | 14 | 15 | 16 | 17 |
| (0.28) | 0.24 | (0.16) | 0.80 | (0.21) | 0.43 | (0.29) | 0.34 | (0.16) | 1.00 |
| (0.28) | 0.26 | (0.08) | 0.78 | (0.24) | 0.45 | (0.29) | 0.34 | (0.17) | 1.00 |
| (0.15) | 0.27 | (0.11) | 0.71 | (0.07) | 0.62 | (0.28) | 0.09 | (0.06) | 1.00 |
| (0.06) | 0.22 | (0.12) | 0.65 | 0.28 | 0.62 | (0.03) | 0.03 | 0.00 | 1.00 |
| 0.04 | 0.38 | 0.48 | 0.48 | 0.21 | 0.49 | 0.05 | (0.31) | 0.19 | 1.00 |
| 0.14 | 0.63 | 0.62 | 0.54 | 0.16 | 0.51 | 0.16 | (0.27) | 0.25 | 1.00 |
| – | – | – | – | – | – | – | – | – | – |
| – | – | – | – | – | – | – | – | – | – |
| – | – | – | – | – | – | – | – | – | – |
| – | – | – | – | – | – | – | – | – | – |
| – | – | – | – | – | – | – | – | – | – |
| – | – | – | – | – | – | – | – | – | – |
| – | – | – | – | – | – | – | – | – | – |
| – | – | – | – | – | – | – | – | – | – |
| – | – | – | – | – | – | – | – | – | – |
| – | – | – | – | – | – | – | – | – | – |
| – | – | – | – | – | – | – | – | – | – |
| – | – | – | – | – | – | – | – | – | – |
| – | – | – | – | – | – | – | – | – | – |

## Hedge Funds

For the HFRI Fund Weighted Composite Hedge Fund Index for six time periods, Table 6.21 displays the rolling 10-year correlations of annual returns with 16 other asset classes, beginning with the 1990–1999 decade and ending with the 1995–2004 decade.

The four boxed columns in Table 6.21 highlight the rolling 10-year correlations of annual returns between the HFRI Fund Weighted Composite Hedge Fund Index and four asset classes: (i) U.S. large-cap equities, as represented by the Standard & Poor's 500 Composite Index; (ii) real estate investment trusts, as represented by the NAREIT Index; (iii) real assets—precious metals—gold, as represented by the Handy & Harmon Spot Gold Price; and (iv) U.S. taxable fixed-income securities, as represented by the Lehman Brothers Aggregate Bon Index.

For the six 10-year periods between 1990–1999 and 1994–2003, the correlations of annual returns between the HFRI Fund Weighted Composite Hedge Fund Index and the:

- **Standard & Poor's 500 Composite** Index: rose from 0.32, to 0.36, to 0.41, to 0.58, to 0.69, for the six 10-year intervals from 1990–1999 through 1995–2004, respectively;

- **NAREIT Index**: declined from 0.63 to 0.38, to 0.22, before rising to 0.27, 0.26, and 0.24 for the six 10-year intervals from 1990–1999 through 1995–2004, respectively;

- **Handy & Harmon Spot Gold Price:** ranged between –0.21 and 0.28 for the six 10-year intervals from 1990–1999 through 1995–2004, respectively; and

- **Lehman Brothers Aggregate Bond** Index: declined from 0.25, to 0.19, to 0.00, to –0.06, to –0.16, and finally to –0.15 for the six 10-year intervals from 1990–1999 through 1995–2004, respectively.

Figure 6.17 depicts the rolling 10-year correlations of annual returns between the HFRI Fund Weighted Composite Hedge Fund Index and the Standard & Poor's 500 Composite Index, the NAREIT Index, the Handy & Harmon Spot Gold Price, and the Lehman Brothers Aggregate Bond Index.

**F I G U R E  6.17**

Hedge Funds: Correlations of the HFRI Fund Weighted Composite Hedge Fund Index

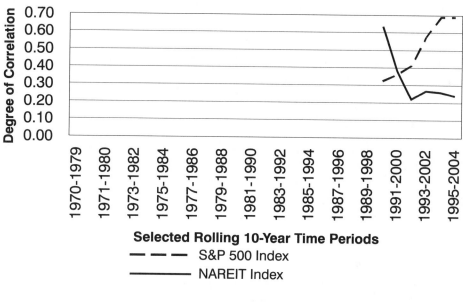

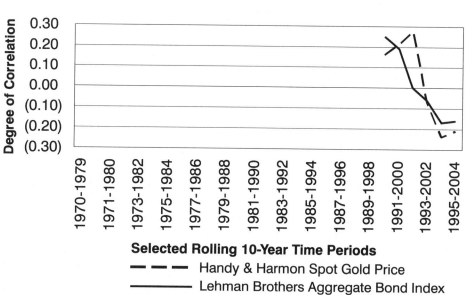

## OVERVIEW—THREE-YEAR NONOVERLAPPING CORRELATIONS

This analysis focuses on the progression through time of correlations between several different asset-class benchmark pairs over the short term, based on monthly returns. The *investment holding period*, or the investment measurement interval employed, is the *monthly return* for 15 individual asset classes. The *investment horizon*, or the total time frame of the analysis, covers nine *intervals of three-year periods* beginning in 1982 and ending in 2004.[2] The correlations of returns are calculated as a series of *nonoverlapping* three-year periods. The benchmarks that represent the returns for each asset class have been selected based on the availability of reliable underlying data.

Within three of the major supercategories of assets—equities, fixed-income securities, and alternative investments—comments focus on: (i) the *absolute amount* of positive or negative correlations of returns; (ii) the *range* of fluctuation in correlations of returns; (iii) how the correlations have *moved* during the 1982–2004 time frame; and (iv) whether the correlations have tended to *cluster* around or between specified values during the multiyear intervals.

## SUMMARY OF HISTORICAL PERSPECTIVE ON CORRELATIONS BETWEEN ASSET CLASSES—EQUITY

Table 6.22 contains a summary of three-year nonoverlapping correlations of monthly returns from 1982 through 2004, between U.S. Equities (as represented by the Standard & Poor's 500 Composite Index) and 14 asset classes.

The U.S. equity asset class, represented by the **Standard & Poor's 500 Composite Index** benchmark, displays generally *highly positive* correlations with the **Wilshire 5000 Index** (a *median* and *mean* correlation value of 0.99, and an overall range of 0.97 to 1.00) during nine three-year periods. The correlation of annual returns of the Standard & Poor's 500 Composite Index with the returns of the **Nasdaq Composite Index** has a *median* and *mean* correlation value of 0.85 and an overall range of 0.74 to 0.94 during nine three-year periods. The correlation of annual returns of the Standard & Poor's 500 Composite Index with the returns of the **MSCI Europe Free Net Index** has a *median* correlation value of 0.68, a *mean* correlation value of 0.71, and a value range of 0.55 to 0.91 during nine three-year periods. The correlation of annual re-

---

[2] Investors may choose to calculate monthly correlations of returns over shorter or longer multiyear time frames, generally ranging upward from three-year intervals.

**T A B L E   6.22**

Equity Correlation Summary—1982 through 2004
(Represented by the Standard & Poor's 500 Composite Index)

| 3-Year Nonoverlapping Correlations of Monthly Returns with: | Median Correlation | Mean Correlation | Range of Correlations | Number of 10-Year Periods | Degree of Correlation | Description of Range of Values |
|---|---|---|---|---|---|---|
| Wilshire 5000 | 0.99 | 0.99 | 0.97 to 1.00 | 9 out of 9 | High Positive | Tight Range |
| Nasdaq Composite | 0.85 | 0.85 | 0.74 to 0.94 | 9 out of 9 | High Positive | Moderate Range |
| MSCI Europe Free Net | 0.68 | 0.71 | 0.55 to 0.91 | 9 out of 9 | High Positive | |
| HFRI Fund Weighted Composite Hedge Fund | 0.67 | 0.70 | 0.55 to 0.85 | 7 out of 9 | High Positive | Moderate Range |
| MSCI EAFE Net | 0.56 | 0.63 | 0.39 to 0.89 | 9 out of 9 | Moderately Positive | Moderate Range |
| NAREIT | 0.43 | 0.47 | 0.19 to 0.74 | 9 out of 9 | Moderately Positive | Moderate Range |
| MSCI Japan Net | 0.31 | 0.34 | 0.19 to 0.50 | 9 out of 9 | Moderately Positive | Somewhat Tight |
| Lehman Brothers Aggregate Bond | 0.19 | 0.15 | −0.41 to 0.62 | 9 out of 9 | Low Positive | Wide Range |
| Lehman Brothers/ Bridgewater TIPS | 0.12 | 0.10 | −0.32 to 0.52 | 9 out of 9 | Low Positive | Wide Range |
| U.S. Treasury 10-Year Note | 0.12 | 0.08 | −0.54 to 0.62 | 9 out of 9 | Low Positive | Wide Range |
| Lehman Brothers 7-Year Municipal Bond | 0.09 | 0.05 | −0.42 to 0.65 | 7 out of 9 | Low Positive | Wide Range |
| National Assn. of Realtors Median Home Price | 0.09 | 0.09 | −0.21 to 0.47 | 9 out of 9 | Low Positive | Moderate Range |
| Handy & Harmon Spot Silver Price | 0.07 | 0.05 | −0.37 to 0.40 | 9 out of 9 | Low Positive | Wide Range |
| Handy & Harmon Spot Gold Price | −0.11 | −0.06 | −0.44 to 0.46 | 9 out of 9 | Negative | Wide Range |

Source: The author.

turns of the Standard & Poor's 500 Composite Index with the returns of the **HFRI Fund Weighted Composite Hedge Fund Index** has a *median* correlation value of 0.67, a *mean* correlation value of 0.70, and a value range of 0.55 to 0.85 during seven three-year periods.

The U.S. equity asset class, represented by the **Standard & Poor's 500 Composite** Index benchmark, displays generally *moderately positive* correlations with the **MSCI EAFE Net Index** (a *median* correlation value of 0.56, a *mean* correlation value of 0.63, and an overall range of 0.39 to 0.89) during nine three-year time periods. The correlation of annual returns of the Standard & Poor's 500 Composite Index with the returns of the **NAREIT Index** has a *median* correlation value of 0.43, a *mean* correlation value of 0.47, and an overall range of 0.19 to 0.74 during nine three-year periods. The correlation of annual returns of the Standard & Poor's 500 Composite Index with the returns of the **MSCI Japan Net Index** has a *median* correlation value of 0.31, a *mean* correlation value of 0.34, and an overall range of 0.19 to 0.50 during nine three-year periods.

The U.S. equity asset class, represented by the **Standard & Poor's 500 Composite Index** benchmark, displays generally *low positive* correlations with the **Lehman Brothers Aggregate Bond Index** (a *median* correlation value of 0.19, a *mean* correlation value of 0.15, and an overall range of –0.41 to 0.62) during nine three-year periods. The correlation of annual returns of the Standard & Poor's 500 Composite Index with the returns of the **Lehman Brothers/Bridgewater TIPS Index** has a *median* correlation of 0.12, a *mean* correlation value of 0.10, and an overall range of –0.32 to 0.52, during nine 13-year periods. The correlation of annual returns of the Standard & Poor's 500 Composite Index with the returns of the **U.S. Treasury 10-Year Note** has a *median* correlation value of 0.12, and a *mean* correlation value of 0.08, and an overall range of –0.54 to 0.62, during a period of nine three-year periods. The correlation of annual returns of the Standard & Poor's 500 Composite Index with the returns of the **Lehman Brothers 7-Year Municipal Bond** Index has a *median* correlation value of 0.09, a *mean* correlation value of 0.05, and a value range of –0.42 to 0.65 during seven three-year periods. The correlation of annual returns of the Standard & Poor 500 Composite Index with the returns of the **National Association of Realtors Median Home Price** has a *median* and *mean* correlation value of 0.09, and a value range of –0.21 to 0.47 during nine three-year periods. The correlation of annual returns of the Standard & Poor's 500 Composite Index with the returns of the **Handy & Harmon Spot Silver Price** has a *median* correlation value of 0.07, a *mean* correlation value of 0.05, and a value range of –0.37 to 0.40 during nine three-year periods.

The U.S. equity asset class, represented by the **Standard & Poor's 500 Composite** Index benchmark, displays *negative* correlations with the **Handy & Harmon Spot Gold Price** (a *median* correlation value of –0.11, a *mean* correlation value of –0.06, and an overall range of –0.44 to 0.46) during nine three-year periods.

## SUMMARY OF HISTORICAL PERSPECTIVE ON CORRELATIONS BETWEEN ASSET CLASSES—FIXED-INCOME SECURITIES

Table 6.23 contains a summary of three-year nonoverlapping correlations of monthly returns from 1982 through 2004 between U.S. fixed income securities (as represented by the U.S. Treasury 10-Year Note).

**T A B L E  6.23**

Fixed-Income Correlation Summary—1982 through 2004
(Represented by the U.S. Treasury 10-Year Note)

| 3-Year Nonoverlapping Correlations of Monthly Returns with: | Median Correlation | Mean Correlation | Range of Correlations | Number of 10-Year Periods | Degree of Correlation | Description of Range of Values |
|---|---|---|---|---|---|---|
| Lehman Brothers Aggregate Bond | 0.97 | 0.96 | 0.91 to 0.99 | 9 out of 9 | High Positive | Tight Range |
| Lehman Brothers/ Bridgewater TIPS | 0.87 | 0.81 | 0.84 to 0.88 | 9 out of 9 | High Positive | Somewhat Tight |
| Lehman Brothers 7-Year Municipal Bond | 0.82 | 0.75 | 0.36 to 0.93 | 7 out of 9 | High Positive | Moderate Range |
| MSCI Europe Free Net | 0.22 | 0.01 | −0.42 to 0.33 | 9 out of 9 | Low Positive | Wide Range |
| NAREIT | 0.15 | 0.10 | −0.38 to 0.47 | 9 out of 9 | Low Positive | Moderate Range |
| Standard & Poor's 500 Composite | 0.12 | 0.08 | −0.54 to 0.62 | 9 out of 9 | Low Positive | Moderate Range |
| Wilshire 5000 | 0.11 | 0.05 | −0.55 to 0.58 | 9 out of 9 | Low Positive | Wide Range |
| MSCI EAFE Net | 0.10 | −0.04 | −0.42 to 0.33 | 9 out of 9 | Low Positive | Wide Range |
| Handy & Harmon Spot Gold Price | 0.05 | 0.00 | −0.25 to 0.24 | 9 out of 9 | Low Positive | Wide Range |
| Nasdaq | 0.04 | −0.02 | −0.50 to 0.46 | 9 out of 9 | Low Positive | Wide Range |
| MSCI Japan Net | −0.01 | 0.01 | −0.19 to 0.24 | 9 out of 9 | Negative | Wide Range |
| National Assn. of Realtors Median Home Price | −0.12 | −0.15 | −0.44 to 0.05 | 9 out of 9 | Negative | Moderate Range |
| HFRI Fund Weighted Composite Hedge Fund | −0.20 | −0.06 | −0.38 to 0.32 | 7 out of 9 | Negative | Wide Range |
| Handy & Harmon Spot Silver Price | −0.21 | −0.20 | −0.36 to 0.01 | 9 out of 9 | Negative | Moderate Range |

Source: The author.

The fixed-income securities asset class, represented by the **U.S. Treasury 10-Year Note**, displays generally *high positive correlations* with the **Lehman Brothers Aggregate Bond Index** (a *median* correlation value of 0.97, a *mean* correlation value of 0.96, and an overall range of 0.91 to 0.99) during nine three-year periods. The correlation of annual returns of the U.S. Treasury 10-Year Note with the returns of the **Lehman Brothers/Bridgewater TIPS Index** has a *median* correlation value of 0.87, a *mean* correlation value of 0.81, and an overall range of 0.84 to 0.88) during nine three-year periods The correlation of annual returns of the U.S. Treasury 10-Year Note with the returns of the **Lehman Brothers 7-Year Municipal Bond Index** has a *median* correlation value of 0.82, a *mean* correlation value of 0.75, and an overall range of 0.36 to 0.93 during seven three-year periods.

The fixed-income securities asset class, represented by the **U.S. Treasury 10-Year Note**, displays generally *low positive* correlations with the **MSCI Europe Free Net Index** (a *median* correlation value of 0.22, a *mean* correlation value of 0.01, and an overall range of –0.42 to 0.33) during nine three-year time periods. The correlation of annual returns of the U.S. Treasury 10-Year Note with the returns of the **NAREIT Index** has a *median* correlation value of 0.15, a *mean* correlation value of 0.10, and an overall range of –0.38 to 0.47 during nine three-year periods. The correlation of annual returns of the U.S. Treasury 10-Year Note with the returns of the **Standard & Poor's 500 Composite Index** has a *median* correlation value of 0.12, a *mean* correlation value of 0.08, and an overall range of –0.54 to 0.62, during nine three-year periods. The correlation of annual returns of the U.S. Treasury 10-Year Note with the returns of the **Wilshire 5000 Index** has a *median* correlation value of 0.11, a *mean* correlation value of 0.05, and an overall range of –0.55 to 0.58 during nine three-year periods. The correlation of annual returns of the U.S. Treasury 10-Year Note with the returns of the **MSCI EAFE Net Index** has a *median* correlation value of 0.10, a *mean* correlation value of –0.04, and an overall range of –0.42 to 0.33 during nine three-year periods. The correlation of annual returns of the U.S. Treasury 10-Year Note with the returns of the **Handy & Harmon Spot Gold Price** has a *median* correlation value of 0.05, a *mean* correlation value of 0.00, and an overall range of –0.25 to 0.24 during nine three-year periods. The correlation of annual returns of the U.S. Treasury 10-Year Note with the returns of the **Nasdaq Composite Index** has a *median* correlation value of 0.04, a *mean* correlation value of –0.02, and an overall range of –0.50 to 0.46 during nine three-year periods.

The fixed-income securities asset class, represented by the **U.S. Treasury 10-Year Note**, displays *negative* correlations with the **MSCI Japan Net Index** (a *median* correlation value of –0.01, a *mean* correlation value of 0.01, and an overall range of –0.19 to 0.24) during nine three-year periods. The correlation of annual returns of the U.S. Treasury 10-Year Note with the returns of the **National Association of Realtors Median Home Price** has a *median* correlation value of –0.12, a *mean* correlation value of –0.15, and an overall range of –0.44 to 0.05 during nine three-year periods. The correlation of annual returns of the U.S. Treasury 10-Year Note with the returns of the **HFRI Fund Weighted Composite Hedge Fund Index** has a *median* correlation value of –0.20, a *mean* correlation value of –0.06, and an overall range of –0.38 to 0.32 during seven three-year periods. The correlation of annual returns of the U.S. Treasury 10-Year Note with the returns of the **Handy & Harmon Spot Silver Price** has a *median* correlation value of –0.21, a *mean* correlation value of –0.20, and an overall range of –0.36 to 0.01 during nine three-year periods.

## SUMMARY OF HISTORICAL PERSPECTIVE ON CORRELATIONS BETWEEN ASSET CLASSES—ALTERNATIVE INVESTMENTS

Table 6.24 contains a summary of three-year nonoverlapping correlations of monthly returns from 1982 through 2004 between real estate investment trusts (as represented by the NAREIT Index) and 14 asset classes.

The alternative investments asset class, partly represented by the **NAREIT Index,** displays essentially *no high degree of positive* correlation with any of the other 14 asset classes. This is due in part to the fact that the returns from real estate tend to be largely driven by asset-specific supply and demand considerations.

The alternative investments asset class, partly represented by the **NAREIT Index,** displays *moderately positive* correlations with the **HFRI Fund Weighted Composite Hedge Fund Index** (a median correlation value of 0.52, a mean correlation value of 0.40, and an overall range of 0.13 to 0.58) during seven three-year time periods. The correlation of

**T A B L E   6.24**

Alternative Investments Correlation Summary—1982 through 2004 (Represented by the NAREIT Index)

| 3-Year Nonoverlapping Correlations of Monthly Returns with: | Median Correlation | Mean Correlation | Range of Correlations | Number of 10-Year Periods | Degree of Correlation | Evidence of Clustering |
|---|---|---|---|---|---|---|
| HFRI Fund Weighted Composite Hedge Fund | 0.52 | 0.44 | 0.13 to 0.58 | 7 out of 9 | Moderately Positive | Moderate Range |
| Wilshire 5000 | 0.51 | 0.51 | 0.19 to 0.80 | 9 out of 9 | Moderately Positive | Moderate Range |
| Standard & Poor's 500 Composite | 0.43 | 0.47 | 0.19 to 0.74 | 9 out of 9 | Moderately Positive | Moderate Range |
| Nasdaq Composite | 0.40 | 0.46 | 0.04 to 0.84 | 9 out of 9 | Moderately Positive | Moderate Range |
| MSCI Europe Free Net | 0.39 | 0.40 | 0.19 to 0.62 | 9 out of 9 | Moderately Positive | Moderate Range |
| MSCI EAFE Net | 0.34 | 0.37 | 0.19 to 0.55 | 9 out of 9 | Moderately Positive | Moderate Range |
| National Assn. of Realtors Median Home Price | 0.28 | 0.24 | −0.32 to 0.54 | 9 out of 9 | Low Positive | Wide Range |
| MSCI Japan Net | 0.25 | 0.23 | 0.00 to 0.50 | 9 out of 9 | Low Positive | Moderate Range |
| Lehman Brothers Aggregate Bond | 0.17 | 0.13 | −0.36 to 0.48 | 9 out of 9 | Low Positive | Wide Range |
| U.S. Treasury 10-Year Note | 0.15 | 0.10 | −0.38 to 0.47 | 9 out of 9 | Low Positive | Wide Range |
| Lehman Brothers 7-Year Municipal Bond | 0.14 | 0.11 | −0.16 to 0.32 | 7 out of 9 | Low Positive | Moderate Range |
| Lehman Brothers/ Bridgewater TIPS | 0.11 | 0.12 | −0.18 to 0.35 | 9 out of 9 | Low Positive | Moderate Range |
| Handy & Harmon Spot Silver Price | 0.09 | 0.13 | −0.25 to 0.53 | 9 out of 9 | Low Positive | Wide Range |
| Handy & Harmon Spot Gold Price | −0.01 | −0.02 | −0.41 to 0.37 | 9 out of 9 | Negative | Wide Range |

Source: The author.

annual returns of the NAREIT **Index** with the returns of the **Wilshire 5000 Index** has a *median* and *mean* correlation value of 0.63 and an overall range of 0.19 to 0.80 during nine three-year periods. The correlation of annual returns of the NAREIT **Index** with the returns of the **Standard & Poor's 500 Composite Index** has a *median* correlation value of 0.43, a *mean* correlation value of 0.47, and an overall range of 0.19 to 0.74 during nine three-year periods. The correlation of annual returns of the NAREIT **Index** with the returns of the **Nasdaq Composite Index** has a *median* correlation value of 0.40, a *mean* correlation value of 0.46, and an overall range of 0.04 to 0.84 during nine three-year periods. The correlation of annual returns of the NAREIT **Index** with the returns of the **MSCI Europe Free Net Index** has a *median* correlation value of 0.39, a *mean* correlation value of 0.40, and an overall range of 0.19 to 0.62 during nine three-year periods. The correlation of annual returns of the NAREIT **Index** with the returns of the **MSCI EAFE Net Index** has a *median* correlation value of 0.34, a *mean* correlation value of 0.37, and an overall range of 0.19 to 0.55 during nine three-year periods.

The alternative asset class, partly represented by the **NAREIT Index**, displays generally *low positive* correlations with the **National Association of Realtors Median Home Price** (a *median* correlation value of 0.28, a *mean* correlation value of 0.24, and an overall range of –0.32 to 0.54) during nine three-year time periods. The correlation of annual returns of the NAREIT Index with the returns of the **MSCI Japan Net Index** has a *median* correlation value of 0.25, a *mean* correlation value of 0.23, and an overall range of 0.00 to 0.50 during nine three-year periods. The correlation of annual returns of the NAREIT Index with the returns of the **Lehman Brothers Aggregate Bond Index** has a *median* correlation value of 0.17, a *mean* correlation value of 0.13, and an overall range of –0.36 to 0.48 during nine three-year periods. The correlation of annual returns of the NAREIT Index with the returns of the **U.S. Treasury 10-Year Note** has a *median* correlation value of 0.15, a *mean* correlation value of 0.10, and an overall range of –0.38 to 0.47 during nine three-year periods. The correlation of annual returns of the NAREIT Index with the returns of the **Lehman Brothers 7-Year Municipal Bond Index** has a *median* correlation value of 0.14, a *mean* correlation value of 0.11, and an overall range of –0.16 to 0.32 during seven three-year periods. The correlation of annual returns of the NAREIT Index with the returns of the **Lehman Brothers/Bridgewater TIPS Index** has a *median* correlation value of 0.11, a *mean* correlation value of 0.12, and an overall range of –0.18 to 0.35 during nine three-year periods. The correlation of annual returns of the NAREIT Index with the returns of the **Handy & Harmon Spot Silver Price** has a *median* correlation value of 0.09, a *mean* correlation value of 0.13, and an overall range of –0.25 to 0.53 during nine three-year periods.

The alternative investments asset class, as partly represented by the NAREIT Index, displays *negative* correlations with the **Handy & Harmon Spot Gold Price** (a *median* correlation value of –0.01, a *mean* correlation value of –0.02, and an overall range of –0.41 to 0.37) during nine three-year time periods.

## NONOVERLAPPING THREE-YEAR CORRELATIONS OF MONTHLY RETURNS

Using the monthly returns for each of the months from 1982 through 2004, *nonoverlapping three-year correlations* (with the exception of the 2001 through 2003 and 2002 through 2004 periods, which do entail some overlap) have been calculated for nine periods and presented as a series of tables for 15 asset classes, beginning with the Standard & Poor's 500 Composite Index representing U.S. large-cap equities and ending with the HFRI Fund Weighted Composite Hedge Fund Index representing hedge funds. Monthly returns data are generally not available for many indices in the private-equity and fine-art classes.

In each table, the progression of correlations on a multimonth, period-to-period basis for four asset classes has been identified by a box around the data. Without attempting to form any inferences about possible causality or the underlying asset price conditions affecting each of the four asset pairs chosen for commentary, brief observations describe the frequency of three-year nonoverlapping correlations of monthly returns within selected correlation ranges. The multiperiod progression of correlations for the four chosen asset pairs is graphically displayed in accompanying figures.

Wherever possible, asset pairs have been chosen for commentary based on: (i) potentially interesting asset *affinities within* the major supercategories of asset classes, such as between various kinds of equities, various kinds of fixed-income securities, or various kinds of alternative investments; or (ii) potentially interesting asset *contrasts between* major supercategories of assets, such as correlation pairings between equities and fixed-income securities or alternative investments, between fixed-income securities and equities or alternative investments, or between alternative investments and equities or fixed-income securities.

**T A B L E   6.25**

U.S. Large Cap Equities: Correlations of the Standard & Poor's 500
Composite Index[1, 2]

| S&P 500 Composite Index for 3-Year Periods from: | S&P 500 Composite Index | Nasdaq Composite Index | Wilshire 5000 Index | MSCI EAFE Net Index | MSCI Europe Free Net Index | MSCI Japan Net Index | Lehman Brothers 7-Year Municipal Bond Index |
|---|---|---|---|---|---|---|---|
| | 1 | 2 | 3 | 4 | 5 | 6 | 7 |
| 1  2002–2004 [2] | 1.00 | 0.92 | 0.99 | 0.89 | 0.91 | 0.31 | (0.39) |
| 2  2001–2003 [2] | 1.00 | 0.91 | 0.99 | 0.88 | 0.90 | 0.44 | (0.42) |
| 3  2000–2002 | 1.00 | 0.77 | 0.97 | 0.84 | 0.81 | 0.50 | (0.32) |
| 4  1997–1999 | 1.00 | 0.82 | 0.99 | 0.71 | 0.72 | 0.43 | 0.07 |
| 5  1994–1996 | 1.00 | 0.74 | 0.97 | 0.56 | 0.68 | 0.26 | 0.65 |
| 6  1991–1993 | 1.00 | 0.78 | 0.98 | 0.39 | 0.58 | 0.19 | 0.41 |
| 7  1988–1990 | 1.00 | 0.88 | 0.99 | 0.42 | 0.56 | 0.29 | 0.33 |
| 8  1985–1987 | 1.00 | 0.94 | 1.00 | 0.48 | 0.65 | 0.19 | – |
| 9  1982–1984 | 1.00 | 0.85 | 0.99 | 0.52 | 0.55 | 0.42 | – |

[1]Nonoverlapping three-year correlations of monthly returns of the Standard & Poor's 500 Composite Index with selected asset classes during nine three-year periods beginning with 1982–1984 and ending with 2002–2004.

[2]Strictly speaking, the years 2003–2005 represent the logical progression of nonoverlapping three-year periods which extends from 1982–1984 to 2000–2002; to furnish additional perspective, data have also been compiled for the 2001–2003 and 2002–2004 time periods.

Source: The author.

It is worth remembering that the correlation of returns between asset H and asset Y is *the same* as the correlation of returns between asset Y and asset H. As a result, when additional observations have been made among the tables on the frequency and range of correlations of returns between an identified asset and another asset, the location of such comments is so noted.

| U.S. Treasury 10-Year Note | NAREIT Index | Nat'l Assn of Realtors Median Home Price | Venture Economics All Private Equity Fund Index | Handy & Harmon Spot Gold Price | Handy & Harmon Spot Silver Price | Lehman Brothers/ Bridgewater TIPS Index | Mei/Moses Fine Art Index | Lehman Brothers Aggregate Bond Index | HFRI Fund Weighted Composite Hedge Fund Index |
|---|---|---|---|---|---|---|---|---|---|
| 8 | 9 | 10 | 11 | 12 | 13 | 14 | 15 | 16 | 17 |
| (0.45) | 0.36 | 0.16 | – | (0.02) | 0.10 | (0.26) | – | (0.34) | 0.80 |
| (0.54) | 0.43 | 0.11 | – | (0.11) | 0.15 | (0.31) | – | (0.41) | 0.85 |
| (0.49) | 0.19 | 0.09 | – | (0.24) | 0.07 | (0.32) | – | (0.33) | 0.65 |
| 0.08 | 0.51 | 0.09 | – | 0.04 | 0.32 | 0.09 | – | 0.19 | 0.76 |
| 0.62 | 0.24 | (0.01) | – | (0.28) | (0.15) | 0.52 | – | 0.62 | 0.67 |
| 0.39 | 0.43 | 0.09 | – | (0.28) | (0.37) | 0.26 | – | 0.41 | 0.59 |
| 0.60 | 0.74 | 0.04 | – | (0.44) | (0.11) | 0.31 | – | 0.61 | 0.55 |
| 0.12 | 0.74 | 0.47 | – | (0.31) | 0.00 | 0.12 | – | 0.15 | – |
| 0.40 | 0.63 | (0.21) | – | 0.46 | 0.40 | 0.45 | – | 0.46 | – |

## U.S. Large-Cap Equities

For the Standard & Poor's 500 Composite Index for nine time periods, Table 6.25 displays the predominantly nonoverlapping three-year correlations of monthly returns with 14 other asset classes, beginning with the 1982 through 1984 triennium and ending with the 2002 through 2004 triennium.

The four boxed columns in Table 6.25 highlight the predominantly nonoverlapping three-year correlations of monthly returns between the Standard & Poor's 500 Composite Index and four asset classes: (i) European equities, as represented by the MSCI Europe Free Net Index; (ii) Japanese equities, as represented by the MSCI Japan Net Index; (iii) real estate investment trusts, as represented by the NAREIT Index; and (iv) U.S. taxable fixed-income securities, as represented by the Lehman Brothers Aggregate Bond Index.

For the nine predominantly nonoverlapping three-year periods between 1982 through 1984 and 2002 through 2004, the correlations of monthly returns between the Standard & Poor's 500 Composite Index and the:

- **MSCI Europe Free Net Index** ranged between 0.55 and 0.90;
- **MSCI Japan Net Index** ranged between 0.19 and 0.50;
- **NAREIT Index** ranged between 0.19 and 0.74; and
- **Lehman Brothers Aggregate Bond Index** ranged between −0.41 and 0.62.

Figure 6.18 graphically depicts the predominantly nonoverlapping three-year correlations of monthly returns between the Standard & Poor's 500 Composite Index and the MSCI Europe Free Net Index, the MSCI Japan Net Index, the NAREIT Index, and the Lehman Brothers Aggregate Bond Index.

For additional observations on the predominantly nonoverlapping three-year correlations of monthly returns between the Standard & Poor's 500 Composite Index and other asset classes, please refer to the tables for the Nasdaq Composite Index, the Wilshire 5000 Index, the Lehman Brothers 7-Year Municipal Bond Index, the U.S. Treasury 10-Year Note, the National Association of Realtors Median Home Price, the Handy & Harmon Spot Gold Price, the Lehman Brothers/Bridgewater TIPS Index, and the HFRI Fund Weighted Composite Hedge Fund Index.

**F I G U R E  6.18**

U.S. Large-Cap Equities: Correlations of the Standard & Poor's 500
Composite Index

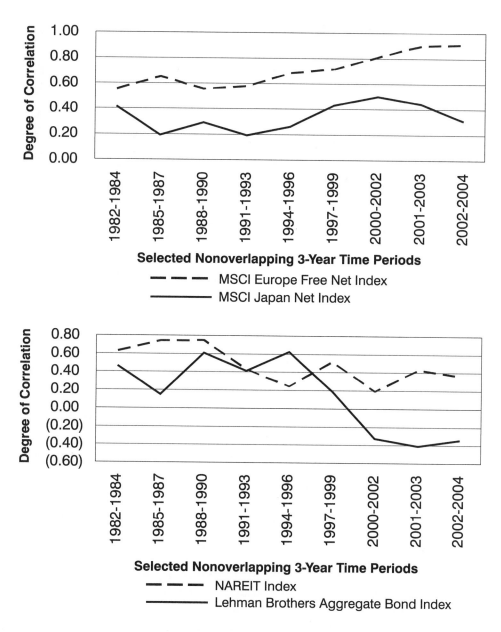

Source: The author.

**T A B L E   6.26**

U.S. Unlisted Equities: Correlations of the Nasdaq Composite Index[1, 2]

| Nasdaq Composite Index for 3-Year Periods from: | S&P 500 Composite Index | Nasdaq Composite Index | Wilshire 5000 Index | MSCI EAFE Net Index | MSCI Europe Free Net Index | MSCI Japan Net Index | Lehman Brothers 7-Year Municipal Bond Index |
|---|---|---|---|---|---|---|---|
| | 1 | 2 | 3 | 4 | 5 | 6 | 7 |
| 1   2002–2004 [2] | 0.92 | 1.00 | 0.93 | 0.76 | 0.78 | 0.26 | (0.47) |
| 2   2001–2003 [2] | 0.91 | 1.00 | 0.93 | 0.76 | 0.76 | 0.38 | (0.38) |
| 3   2000–2002 | 0.77 | 1.00 | 0.88 | 0.73 | 0.69 | 0.44 | (0.19) |
| 4   1997–1999 | 0.82 | 1.00 | 0.87 | 0.63 | 0.59 | 0.44 | 0.02 |
| 5   1994–1996 | 0.74 | 1.00 | 0.86 | 0.42 | 0.49 | 0.20 | 0.30 |
| 6   1991–1993 | 0.78 | 1.00 | 0.88 | 0.30 | 0.40 | 0.18 | 0.24 |
| 7   1988–1990 | 0.88 | 1.00 | 0.93 | 0.30 | 0.40 | 0.20 | 0.28 |
| 8   1985–1987 | 0.94 | 1.00 | 0.97 | 0.47 | 0.64 | 0.16 | – |
| 9   1982–1984 | 0.85 | 1.00 | 0.91 | 0.49 | 0.54 | 0.39 | – |

[1]Nonoverlapping three-year correlations of monthly returns of the Nasdaq Composite Index with selected asset classes during nine three-year periods beginning with 1982–1984 and ending with 2002–2004.

[2]Strictly speaking, the years 2003–2005 represent the logical progression of nonoverlapping three-year periods which extends from 1982–1984 to 2000–2002; to furnish additional perspective, data have also been compiled for the 2001–2003 and 2002–2004 time periods.

Source: The author.

## U.S. Unlisted Equities

For the Nasdaq Composite Index for nine time periods, Table 6.26 displays the predominantly nonoverlapping three-year correlations of monthly returns with 14 other asset classes, beginning with the 1982 through 1984 triennium and ending with the 2002 through 2004 triennium.

| U.S. Treasury 10-Year Note | NAREIT Index | Nat'l Assn of Realtors Median Home Price | Venture Economics All Private Equity Fund Index | Handy & Harmon Spot Gold Price | Handy & Harmon Spot Silver Price | Lehman Brothers/ Bridgewater TIPS Index | Mei/Moses Fine Art Index | Lehman Brothers Aggregate Bond Index | HFRI Fund Weighted Composite Hedge Fund Index |
|---|---|---|---|---|---|---|---|---|---|
| 8 | 9 | 10 | 11 | 12 | 13 | 14 | 15 | 16 | 17 |
| (0.50) | 0.34 | 0.12 | – | (0.05) | 0.03 | (0.30) | – | (0.43) | 0.79 |
| (0.50) | 0.38 | 0.04 | – | (0.20) | 0.04 | (0.28) | – | (0.39) | 0.86 |
| (0.40) | 0.04 | 0.07 | – | (0.06) | (0.01) | (0.31) | – | (0.19) | 0.89 |
| 0.04 | 0.40 | 0.13 | – | 0.14 | 0.29 | 0.10 | – | 0.12 | 0.85 |
| 0.20 | 0.21 | (0.01) | – | (0.20) | (0.05) | 0.15 | – | 0.23 | 0.82 |
| 0.17 | 0.56 | 0.14 | – | (0.29) | (0.26) | 0.11 | – | 0.18 | 0.80 |
| 0.46 | 0.84 | 0.15 | – | (0.46) | (0.02) | 0.16 | – | 0.47 | 0.60 |
| 0.04 | 0.79 | 0.50 | – | (0.28) | (0.03) | 0.05 | – | 0.07 | – |
| 0.32 | 0.60 | (0.17) | – | 0.37 | 0.44 | 0.35 | – | 0.38 | – |

The three boxed columns in Table 6.26 highlight the predominantly nonoverlapping three-year correlations of monthly returns between the Nasdaq Composite Index and three asset classes: (i) U.S. large-cap equities, as represented by the Standard & Poor's 500 Composite Index; (ii) U.S. equities, as represented by the Wilshire 5000 Index; and (iii) intermediate-maturity tax-exempt bonds, as represented by the Lehman Brothers 7-Year Municipal Bond Index.

For the nine predominantly nonoverlapping three-year periods between 1982 through 1984, and 2002 through 2004, the correlations of monthly returns between the Nasdaq Composite Index and the:

- **Standard & Poor's 500 Composite Index** ranged between 0.74 and 0.94;

- **Wilshire 5000 Index** ranged between 0.86 and 0.97; and

- **Lehman Brothers 7-Year Municipal Bond Index** ranged between –0.38 and 0.30 during six of the three-year periods.

Figure 6.19 graphically depicts the predominantly nonoverlapping three-year correlations of monthly returns between the Nasdaq Composite Index and the Standard & Poor's 500 Composite Index, the Wilshire 5000 Index, and the Lehman Brothers 7-Year Municipal Bond Index.

For additional observations on the predominantly nonoverlapping three-year correlations of monthly returns between the Nasdaq Composite Index and other asset classes, please refer to the tables for the Wilshire 5000 Index, the MSCI EAFE Net Index, the MSCI Europe Free Net Index, the MSCI Japan Net Index, the U.S. Treasury 10-Year Note, and the Lehman Brothers Aggregate Bond Index.

F I G U R E   6.19

**F I G U R E   6.19**

U.S. Unlisted Equities: Correlations of the Nasdaq Composite Index

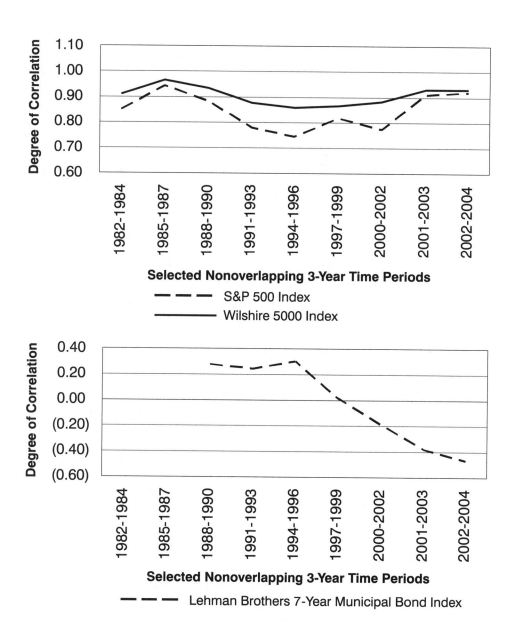

Source: The author.

**T A B L E  6.27**

U.S. Equities: Correlations of the Wilshire 5000 Index[1, 2]

| Wilshire 5000 Index for 3-Year Periods from: | S&P 500 Composite Index | Nasdaq Composite Index | Wilshire 5000 Index | MSCI EAFE Net Index | MSCI Europe Free Net Index | MSCI Japan Net Index | Lehman Brothers 7-Year Municipal Bond Index |
|---|---|---|---|---|---|---|---|
| | 1 | 2 | 3 | 4 | 5 | 6 | 7 |
| 1  2002–2004 [2] | 0.99 | 0.93 | 1.00 | 0.90 | 0.91 | 0.35 | (0.39) |
| 2  2001–2003 [2] | 0.99 | 0.93 | 1.00 | 0.89 | 0.89 | 0.46 | (0.41) |
| 3  2000–2002 | 0.97 | 0.88 | 1.00 | 0.87 | 0.83 | 0.52 | (0.28) |
| 4  1997–1999 | 0.99 | 0.87 | 1.00 | 0.73 | 0.73 | 0.44 | 0.04 |
| 5  1994–1996 | 0.97 | 0.86 | 1.00 | 0.56 | 0.67 | 0.27 | 0.58 |
| 6  1991–1993 | 0.98 | 0.88 | 1.00 | 0.40 | 0.55 | 0.22 | 0.38 |
| 7  1988–1990 | 0.99 | 0.93 | 1.00 | 0.39 | 0.52 | 0.27 | 0.32 |
| 8  1985–1987 | 1.00 | 0.97 | 1.00 | 0.48 | 0.65 | 0.19 | – |
| 9  1982–1984 | 0.99 | 0.91 | 1.00 | 0.52 | 0.55 | 0.42 | – |

[1]Nonoverlapping three-year correlations of monthly returns of the Wilshire 5000 Index with selected asset classes during nine three-year periods beginning with 1982–1984 and ending with 2002–2004.

[2]Strictly speaking, the years 2003–2005 represent the logical progression of nonoverlapping three-year periods which extends from 1982–1984 to 2000–2002; to furnish additional perspective, data have also been compiled for the 2001–2003 and 2002–2004 time periods.

Source: The author.

## U.S. Equities

For the Wilshire 5000 Index for nine time periods, Table 6.27 displays the predominantly nonoverlapping three-year correlations of monthly returns with 14 other asset classes, beginning with the 1982 through 1984 triennium and ending with the 2002 through 2004 triennium.

| U.S. Treasury 10-Year Note | NAREIT Index | Nat'l Assn of Realtors Median Home Price | Venture Economics All Private Equity Fund Index | Handy & Harmon Spot Gold Price | Handy & Harmon Spot Silver Price | Lehman Brothers/ Bridgewater TIPS Index | Mei/Moses Fine Art Index | Lehman Brothers Aggregate Bond Index | HFRI Fund Weighted Composite Hedge Fund Index |
|---|---|---|---|---|---|---|---|---|---|
| 8 | 9 | 10 | 11 | 12 | 13 | 14 | 15 | 16 | 17 |
| (0.45) | 0.41 | 0.16 | – | 0.02 | 0.11 | 0.24 | – | (0.34) | 0.84 |
| (0.55) | 0.47 | 0.12 | – | (0.10) | 0.14 | (0.30) | – | (0.42) | 0.88 |
| (0.49) | 0.19 | 0.11 | – | (0.15) | 0.07 | (0.34) | – | (0.30) | 0.80 |
| 0.04 | 0.56 | 0.10 | – | 0.07 | 0.34 | 0.06 | – | 0.15 | 0.84 |
| 0.51 | 0.28 | 0.00 | – | (0.27) | (0.14) | 0.41 | – | 0.52 | 0.77 |
| 0.34 | 0.49 | 0.09 | – | (0.28) | (0.34) | 0.24 | – | 0.36 | 0.69 |
| 0.58 | 0.80 | 0.07 | – | (0.45) | (0.09) | 0.28 | – | 0.59 | 0.57 |
| 0.11 | 0.77 | 0.48 | – | (0.30) | 0.00 | 0.11 | – | 0.14 | – |
| 0.38 | 0.62 | (0.20) | – | 0.45 | 0.43 | 0.43 | – | 0.45 | – |

The four boxed columns in Table 6.27 highlight the predominantly nonoverlapping three-year correlations of monthly returns between the Wilshire 5000 Index and (i) large-cap equities, as represented by the S&P 500 Composite Index; (ii) Europe, Australasia, Far East equities, as represented by the MSCI EAFE Net Index; (iii) intermediate-maturity U.S. Treasury Bonds, as represented by the U.S. Treasury 10-Year Note;

and (iv) U.S. taxable fixed-income securities, as represented by the Lehman Brothers Aggregate Bond Index.

For the nine predominantly nonoverlapping three-year periods between 1982 through 1984 and 2002 through 2004, the correlations of monthly returns between the Wilshire 5000 Index and the:

◆ **Standard & Poor's 500 Composite Index** ranged between 0.97 and 1.00;

◆ **MSCI EAFE Net Index** ranged between 0.39 and 0.89;

◆ **U.S. Treasury 10-Year Note** ranged between –0.55 and 0.58; and

◆ **Lehman Brothers Aggregate Bond Index** ranged between –0.42 and 0.59.

Figure 6.20 graphically depicts the predominantly nonoverlapping three-year correlations of monthly returns between the Wilshire 5000 Index and the Standard & Poor's 500 Composite Index, the MSCI EAFE Net Index, the U.S. Treasury 10-Year Note, and the Lehman Brothers Aggregate Bond Index.

For additional observations on the predominantly nonoverlapping three-year correlations of monthly returns between the Wilshire 5000 Index and other asset classes, please refer to the tables for the Nasdaq Composite Index, the NAREIT Index, the Handy & Harmon Spot Silver Price, and the Lehman Brothers Aggregate Bond Index.

F I G U R E   6.20

U.S. Equities: Correlations of the Wilshire 5000 Index

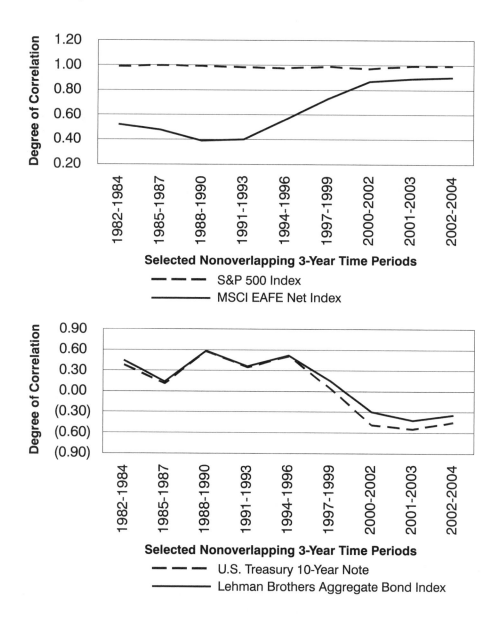

**T A B L E  6.28**

Europe, Australasia, Far East Equities: Correlations of the MSCI EAFE Net Index[1, 2]

| MSCI EAFE Net Index for 3-Year Periods from: | S&P 500 Composite Index | Nasdaq Composite Index | Wilshire 5000 Index | MSCI EAFE Net Index | MSCI Europe Free Net Index | MSCI Japan Net Index | Lehman Brothers 7-Year Municipal Bond Index |
|---|---|---|---|---|---|---|---|
| | 1 | 2 | 3 | 4 | 5 | 6 | 7 |
| 1  2002–2004[2] | 0.89 | 0.76 | 0.90 | 1.00 | 0.96 | 0.56 | (0.26) |
| 2  2001–2003[2] | 0.88 | 0.76 | 0.89 | 1.00 | 0.98 | 0.66 | (0.29) |
| 3  2000–2002 | 0.84 | 0.73 | 0.87 | 1.00 | 0.96 | 0.64 | (0.25) |
| 4  1997–1999 | 0.71 | 0.63 | 0.73 | 1.00 | 0.91 | 0.78 | (0.07) |
| 5  1994–1996 | 0.56 | 0.42 | 0.56 | 1.00 | 0.76 | 0.87 | 0.24 |
| 6  1991–1993 | 0.39 | 0.30 | 0.40 | 1.00 | 0.80 | 0.91 | 0.21 |
| 7  1988–1990 | 0.42 | 0.30 | 0.39 | 1.00 | 0.80 | 0.96 | 0.31 |
| 8  1985–1987 | 0.48 | 0.47 | 0.48 | 1.00 | 0.76 | 0.87 | – |
| 9  1982–1984 | 0.52 | 0.49 | 0.52 | 1.00 | 0.84 | 0.93 | – |

[1]Nonoverlapping three-year correlations of monthly returns of MSCI EAFE Net Index with selected asset classes during nine three-year periods beginning with 1982–1984 and ending with 2002–2004.

[2]Strictly speaking, the years 2003–2005 represent the logical progression of nonoverlapping three-year periods which extends from 1982–1984 to 2000–2002; to furnish additional perspective, data have also been compiled for the 2001–2003 and 2002–2004 time periods.

Source: The author.

## Europe, Australasia, Far East Equities

For the MSCI EAFE Net Index for nine time periods, Table 6.28 displays the predominantly nonoverlapping three-year correlations of monthly returns with 14 other asset classes, beginning with the 1982 through 1984 triennium and ending with the 2002 through 2004 triennium.

| U.S. Treasury 10-Year Note | NAREIT Index | Nat'l Assn of Realtors Median Home Price | Venture Economics All Private Equity Fund Index | Handy & Harmon Spot Gold Price | Handy & Harmon Spot Silver Price | Lehman Brothers/ Bridgewater TIPS Index | Mei/Moses Fine Art Index | Lehman Brothers Aggregate Bond Index | HFRI Fund Weighted Composite Hedge Fund Index |
|---|---|---|---|---|---|---|---|---|---|
| 8 | 9 | 10 | 11 | 12 | 13 | 14 | 15 | 16 | 17 |
| (0.33) | 0.49 | 0.22 | – | 0.16 | 0.24 | (0.11) | – | (0.21) | 0.84 |
| (0.41) | 0.55 | 0.18 | – | 0.03 | 0.22 | (0.16) | – | (0.29) | 0.83 |
| (0.38) | 0.28 | 0.21 | – | 0.00 | 0.10 | (0.22) | – | (0.20) | 0.71 |
| (0.18) | 0.34 | 0.07 | – | 0.23 | 0.22 | (0.29) | – | (0.10) | 0.71 |
| 0.10 | 0.19 | 0.08 | – | (0.13) | (0.02) | (0.04) | – | 0.12 | 0.48 |
| 0.30 | 0.24 | (0.03) | – | 0.09 | 0.12 | 0.15 | – | 0.38 | 0.36 |
| 0.20 | 0.23 | (0.12) | – | (0.06) | 0.03 | 0.01 | – | 0.22 | 0.20 |
| 0.19 | 0.52 | 0.17 | – | 0.19 | 0.18 | 0.05 | – | 0.13 | – |
| 0.15 | 0.46 | (0.16) | – | 0.22 | 0.12 | 0.17 | – | 0.15 | – |

The four boxed columns in Table 6.28 highlight the predominantly nonoverlapping three-year correlations of monthly returns between the MSCI EAFE Net Index and four asset classes: (i) unlisted securities, as represented by the Nasdaq Composite Index; (ii) European equities, as represented by the MSCI Europe Free Net Index; (iii) Japanese equities, as represented by the MSCI Japan Net Index; and (iv) inflation-indexed securities, as represented by the Lehman Brothers/Bridgewater TIPS Index.

For the nine predominantly nonoverlapping three-year periods between 1982 through 1984 and 2002 through 2004, the correlations of monthly returns between the MSCI EAFE Net Index and the:

- **Nasdaq Composite Index** ranged between 0.30 and 0.76;
- **MSCI Europe Free Net Index** ranged between 0.76 and 0.98;
- **MSCI Japan Net Index** ranged between 0.64 and 0.96; and
- **Lehman Brothers/Bridgewater TIPS Index** ranged between −0.29 and 0.17.

Figure 6.21 graphically depicts the predominantly nonoverlapping three-year correlations of monthly returns between the MSCI EAFE Net Index and the Nasdaq Composite Index, the MSCI Europe Free Net Index, the MSCI Japan Net Index, the NAREIT Index, and the Lehman Brothers/Bridgewater TIPS Index.

**F I G U R E   6.21**

Europe, Australasia, Far East Equities: Correlations of the MSCI EAFE Net Index

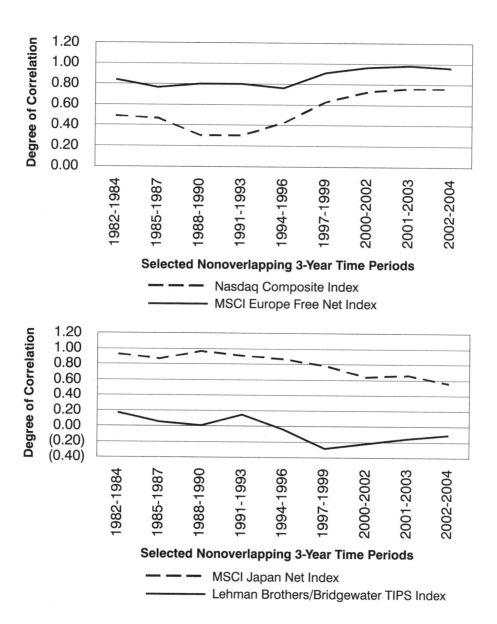

Source: The author.

**T A B L E   6.29**

European Equities: Correlations of the MSCI Europe Net Index[1,2]

| MSCI Europe Net Index for 3-Year Periods from: | S&P 500 Composite Index | Nasdaq Composite Index | Wilshire 5000 Index | MSCI EAFE Net Index | MSCI Europe Free Net Index | MSCI Japan Net Index | Lehman Brothers 7-Year Municipal Bond Index |
|---|---|---|---|---|---|---|---|
| | 1 | 2 | 3 | 4 | 5 | 6 | 7 |
| 1  2002–2004 [2] | 0.91 | 0.78 | 0.91 | 0.96 | 1.00 | 0.32 | (0.28) |
| 2  2001–2003 [2] | 0.90 | 0.76 | 0.89 | 0.98 | 1.00 | 0.48 | (0.32) |
| 3  2000–2002 | 0.81 | 0.69 | 0.83 | 0.96 | 1.00 | 0.40 | (0.31) |
| 4  1997–1999 | 0.72 | 0.59 | 0.73 | 0.91 | 1.00 | 0.47 | (0.04) |
| 5  1994–1996 | 0.68 | 0.49 | 0.67 | 0.76 | 1.00 | 0.36 | 0.43 |
| 6  1991–1993 | 0.58 | 0.40 | 0.55 | 0.80 | 1.00 | 0.49 | 0.31 |
| 7  1988–1990 | 0.56 | 0.40 | 0.52 | 0.80 | 1.00 | 0.62 | 0.34 |
| 8  1985–1987 | 0.65 | 0.64 | 0.65 | 0.76 | 1.00 | 0.36 | – |
| 9  1982–1984 | 0.55 | 0.54 | 0.55 | 0.84 | 1.00 | 0.60 | – |

[1]Nonoverlapping three-year correlations of monthly returns of the MSCI Europe Net Index with selected asset classes during nine three-year periods beginning with 1982–1984 and ending with 2002–2004.

[2]Strictly speaking, the years 2003–2005 represent the logical progression of nonoverlapping three-year periods which extends from 1982–1984 to 2000–2002; to furnish additional perspective, data have also been compiled for the 2001–2003 and 2002–2004 time periods.

Source: The author.

## European Equities

For the MSCI Europe Free Net Index for nine time periods, Table 6.29 displays the predominantly nonoverlapping three-year correlations of monthly returns with 14 other asset classes, beginning with the 1982 through 1984 triennium and ending with the 2002 through 2004 triennium.

| U.S. Treasury 10-Year Note | NAREIT Index | Nat'l Assn of Realtors Median Home Price | Venture Economics All Private Equity Fund Index | Handy & Harmon Spot Gold Price | Handy & Harmon Spot Silver Price | Lehman Brothers/Bridgewater TIPS Index | Mei/Moses Fine Art Index | Lehman Brothers Aggregate Bond Index | HFRI Fund Weighted Composite Hedge Fund Index |
|---|---|---|---|---|---|---|---|---|---|
| 8 | 9 | 10 | 11 | 12 | 13 | 14 | 15 | 16 | 17 |
| (0.38) | 0.39 | 0.19 | – | 0.05 | 0.15 | (0.19) | – | (0.26 | 0.77 |
| (0.42) | 0.50 | 0.19 | – | (0.02) | 0.21 | (0.22) | – | (0.29) | 0.78 |
| (0.42) | 0.29 | 0.23 | – | (0.08) | 0.06 | (0.32) | – | (0.24) | 0.65 |
| (0.16) | 0.44 | 0.09 | – | 0.11 | 0.24 | (0.36) | – | (0.06) | 0.70 |
| 0.32 | 0.25 | 0.04 | – | (0.26) | (0.20) | 0.24 | – | 0.35 | 0.45 |
| 0.33 | 0.19 | (0.06) | – | (0.11) | (0.14) | 0.20 | – | 0.40 | 0.37 |
| 0.22 | 0.39 | (0.01) | – | (0.15) | (0.07) | 0.05 | – | 0.24 | 0.40 |
| 0.31 | 0.62 | 0.21 | – | 0.08 | 0.16 | 0.15 | – | 0.29 | – |
| 0.25 | 0.55 | (0.25) | – | 0.20 | 0.22 | 0.24 | – | 0.28 | – |

The four boxed columns in Table 6.29 highlight the predominantly nonoverlapping three-year correlations of monthly returns between the MSCI Europe Free Net Index and four asset classes: (i) unlisted securities, as represented by the Nasdaq Composite Index; (ii) Japanese equities, as represented by the MSCI Japan Net Index; (iii) intermediate-maturity U.S. Treasury Bonds, as represented by the U.S.

Treasury 10-Year Note; and (iv) U.S. taxable fixed-income securities, as represented by the Lehman Brothers Aggregate Bond Index.

For the nine predominantly nonoverlapping three-year periods between 1982 through 1984 and 2002 through 2004, the correlations of monthly returns between the MSCI Europe Free Net Index and the:

◆ **Nasdaq Composite Index** ranged between 0.40 and 0.76;
◆ **MSCI Japan Net Index** ranged between 0.36 and 0.62;
◆ **U.S. Treasury 10-Year Note** ranged between –0.42 and 0.33; and
◆ **Lehman Brothers Aggregate Bond Index** ranged between –0.29 and 0.40.

Figure 6.22 graphically depicts the predominantly nonoverlapping three-year correlations of monthly returns between the MSCI Europe Free Net Index and the Nasdaq Composite Index, the MSCI Japan Net Index, the U.S. Treasury 10-Year Note, and the Lehman Brothers Aggregate Bond Index.

For additional observations on the predominantly nonoverlapping three-year correlations of monthly returns between the MSCI Europe Free Net Index and other asset classes, please refer to the tables for the Standard & Poor's 500 Composite Index, the MSCI EAFE Net Index, and the National Association of Realtors Median Home Price.

F I G U R E  6.22

European Equities: Correlations of the MSCI Europe Net Index

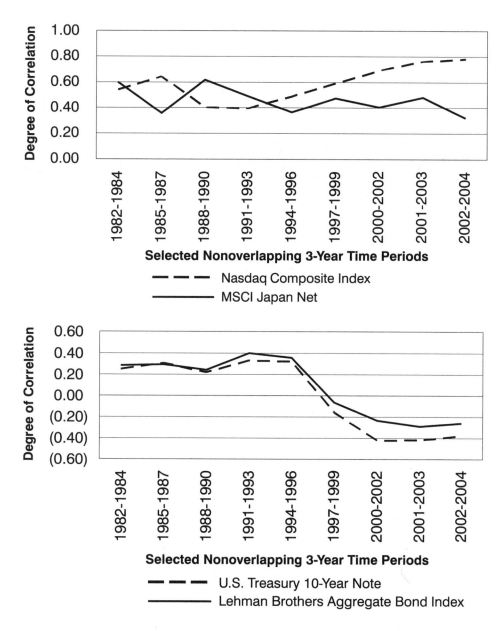

**T A B L E  6.30**

Japanese Equities: Correlations of the MSCI Japan Net Index[1, 2]

| MSCI Japan Net Index for 3-Year Periods from: | S&P 500 Composite Index | Nasdaq Composite Index | Wilshire 5000 Index | MSCI EAFE Net Index | MSCI Europe Free Net Index | MSCI Japan Net Index | Lehman Brothers 7-Year Municipal Bond Index |
|---|---|---|---|---|---|---|---|
| | 1 | 2 | 3 | 4 | 5 | 6 | 7 |
| 1  2002–2004[2] | 0.31 | 0.26 | 0.35 | 0.56 | 0.32 | 1.00 | (0.07) |
| 2  2001–2003[2] | 0.44 | 0.38 | 0.46 | 0.66 | 0.48 | 1.00 | (0.07) |
| 3  2000–2002 | 0.50 | 0.44 | 0.52 | 0.64 | 0.40 | 1.00 | 0.03 |
| 4  1997–1999 | 0.43 | 0.44 | 0.44 | 0.78 | 0.47 | 1.00 | (0.10) |
| 5  1994–1996 | 0.26 | 0.20 | 0.27 | 0.87 | 0.36 | 1.00 | (0.01) |
| 6  1991–1993 | 0.19 | 0.18 | 0.22 | 0.91 | 0.49 | 1.00 | 0.07 |
| 7  1988–1990 | 0.29 | 0.20 | 0.27 | 0.96 | 0.62 | 1.00 | 0.26 |
| 8  1985–1987 | 0.19 | 0.16 | 0.19 | 0.87 | 0.36 | 1.00 | – |
| 9  1982–1984 | 0.42 | 0.39 | 0.42 | 0.93 | 0.60 | 1.00 | – |

[1]Nonoverlapping three-year correlations of monthly returns of the MSCI Japan Net Index with selected asset classes during nine three-year periods beginning with 1982–1984 and ending with 2002–2004.

[2]Strictly speaking, the years 2003–2005 represent the logical progression of nonoverlapping three-year periods which extends from 1982–1984 to 2000–2002; to furnish additional perspective, data have also been compiled for the 2001–2003 and 2002–2004 time periods.

Source: The author.

## Japanese Equities

For the MSCI Japan Net Index for nine time periods, Table 6.30 displays the predominantly nonoverlapping three-year correlations of monthly returns with 14 other asset classes, beginning with the 1982 through 1984 triennium and ending with the 2002 through 2004 triennium.

| U.S. Treasury 10-Year Note | NAREIT Index | Nat'l Assn of Realtors Median Home Price | Venture Economics All Private Equity Fund Index | Handy & Harmon Spot Gold Price | Handy & Harmon Spot Silver Price | Lehman Brothers/ Bridgewater TIPS Index | Mei/Moses Fine Art Index | Lehman Brothers Aggregate Bond Index | HFRI Fund Weighted Composite Hedge Fund Index |
|---|---|---|---|---|---|---|---|---|---|
| 8 | 9 | 10 | 11 | 12 | 13 | 14 | 15 | 16 | 17 |
| (0.01) | 0.50 | 0.27 | – | 0.37 | 0.38 | 0.17 | – | 0.03 | 0.54 |
| (0.19) | 0.49 | 0.10 | – | 0.22 | 0.19 | 0.11 | – | (0.15) | 0.56 |
| (0.09) | 0.11 | 0.06 | – | 0.21 | 0.16 | 0.18 | – | (0.01) | 0.50 |
| (0.13) | 0.04 | 0.03 | – | 0.33 | 0.08 | (0.12) | – | (0.11) | 0.44 |
| (0.10) | 0.00 | 0.08 | – | (0.02) | 0.09 | (0.24) | – | (0.09) | 0.29 |
| 0.24 | 0.25 | 0.00 | – | 0.13 | 0.19 | 0.13 | – | 0.31 | 0.24 |
| 0.17 | 0.10 | (0.18) | – | (0.04) | 0.03 | 0.01 | – | 0.18 | 0.08 |
| 0.12 | 0.27 | 0.08 | – | 0.19 | 0.10 | 0.02 | – | 0.03 | – |
| 0.07 | 0.32 | (0.07) | – | 0.19 | 0.04 | 0.10 | – | 0.05 | – |

The four boxed columns in Table 6.30 highlight the predominantly nonoverlapping three-year correlations of monthly returns between the MSCI Japan Net Index and four asset classes: (i) unlisted securities, as represented by the Nasdaq Composite Index; (ii) intermediate-maturity U.S. Treasury Bonds, as represented by the U.S. Treasury 10-Year Note; (iii) inflation-indexed securities, as represented by the Lehman Brothers/Bridgewater TIPS Index; and (iv) U.S.

taxable fixed-income securities, as represented by the Lehman Brothers Aggregate Bond Index.

For the nine predominantly nonoverlapping three-year periods between 1982 through 1984 and 2002 through 2004, the correlations of monthly returns between the MSCI Japan Net Index and the:

- **Nasdaq Composite Index** ranged between 0.16 and 0.44;

- **U.S. Treasury 10-Year Note** ranged between –0.19 and 0.24;

- **Lehman Brothers/Bridgewater TIPS Index** ranged between –0.24 and 0.18; and

- **Lehman Brothers Aggregate Bond Index** ranged between –0.15 and 0.31.

Figure 6.23 graphically depicts the predominantly nonoverlapping three-year correlations of monthly returns between the MSCI Japan Net Index and the Nasdaq Composite Index, the U.S. Treasury 10-Year Note, the Lehman Brothers/Bridgewater TIPS Index, and the Lehman Brothers Aggregate Bond Index.

For additional observations on the predominantly nonoverlapping three-year correlations of monthly returns between the MSCI Japan Net Index and other asset classes, please see the tables for the Standard & Poor's 500 Composite Index, the MSCI EAFE Net Index, and the MSCI Europe Free Net Index.

Japanese Equities: Correlations of the MSCI Japan Net Index

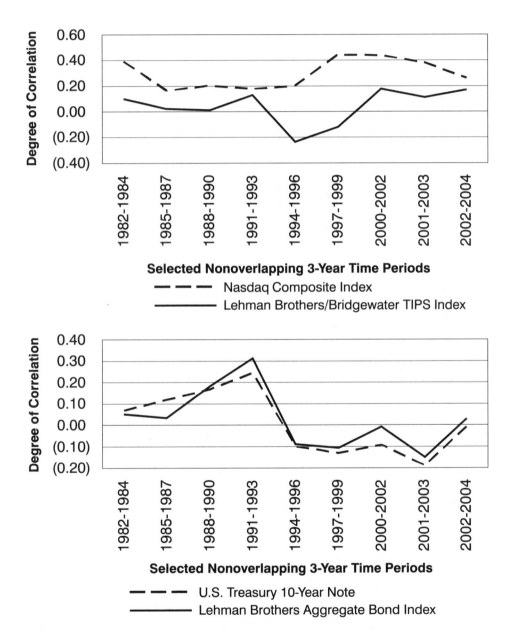

Source: The author.

## T A B L E  6.31

Intermediate-Maturity Tax-Exempt Bonds: Correlations of the Lehman Brothers 7-Year Municipal Bond Index[1, 2]

| Lehman Brothers 7-Year Municipal Bond Index for 3-Year Periods from: | S&P 500 Composite Index | Nasdaq Composite Index | Wilshire 5000 Index | MSCI EAFE Net Index | MSCI Europe Free Net Index | MSCI Japan Net Index | Lehman Brothers 7-Year Municipal Bond Index |
|---|---|---|---|---|---|---|---|
| | 1 | 2 | 3 | 4 | 5 | 6 | 7 |
| 1  2002–2004[2] | (0.39) | (0.47) | (0.39) | (0.26) | (0.28) | (0.07) | 1.00 |
| 2  2001–2003[2] | (0.42) | (0.38) | (0.41) | (0.29) | (0.32) | (0.07) | 1.00 |
| 3  2000–2002 | (0.32) | (0.19) | (0.28) | (0.25) | (0.31) | 0.03 | 1.00 |
| 4  1997–1999 | 0.07 | 0.02 | 0.04 | (0.07) | (0.04) | (0.10) | 1.00 |
| 5  1994–1996 | 0.65 | 0.30 | 0.58 | 0.24 | 0.43 | (0.01) | 1.00 |
| 6  1991–1993 | 0.41 | 0.24 | 0.38 | 0.21 | 0.31 | 0.07 | 1.00 |
| 7  1988–1990 | 0.33 | 0.28 | 0.32 | 0.31 | 0.34 | 0.26 | 1.00 |
| 8  1985–1987 | – | – | – | – | – | – | – |
| 9  1982–1984 | – | – | – | – | – | – | – |

[1]Nonoverlapping three-year correlations of monthly returns of the Lehman Brothers 7-Year Municipal Bond Index with selected asset classes during seven three-year periods beginning with 1988–1990 and ending with 2002–2004.

[2]Strictly speaking, the years 2003–2005 represent the logical progression of nonoverlapping three-year periods which extends from 1982–1984 to 2000–2002; to furnish additional perspective, data have also been compiled for the 2001–2003 and 2002–2004 time periods.

Source: The author.

## Intermediate-Maturity Tax Exempt Bonds

For the Lehman Brothers 7-Year Municipal Bond Index for seven time periods, Table 6.31 displays the predominantly nonoverlapping three-year correlations of monthly returns with 14 other asset classes, beginning with the 1988 through 1990 triennium and ending with the 2002 through 2004 triennium.

| U.S. Treasury 10-Year Note | NAREIT Index | Nat'l Assn of Realtors Median Home Price | Venture Economics All Private Equity Fund Index | Handy & Harmon Spot Gold Price | Handy & Harmon Spot Silver Price | Lehman Brothers/ Bridgewater TIPS Index | Mei/Moses Fine Art Index | Lehman Brothers Aggregate Bond Index | HFRI Fund Weighted Composite Hedge Fund Index |
|---|---|---|---|---|---|---|---|---|---|
| 8 | 9 | 10 | 11 | 12 | 13 | 14 | 15 | 16 | 17 |
| 0.93 | 0.14 | (0.35) | – | 0.23 | (0.08) | 0.85 | – | 0.95 | (0.14) |
| 0.90 | (0.16) | (0.25) | – | 0.17 | (0.36) | 0.84 | – | 0.92 | (0.17) |
| 0.82 | (0.13) | (0.16) | – | 0.16 | (0.18) | 0.72 | – | 0.87 | 0.00 |
| 0.74 | 0.14 | (0.17) | – | 0.03 | (0.05) | 0.52 | – | 0.77 | (0.10) |
| 0.82 | 0.31 | 0.00 | – | (0.24) | (0.31) | 0.72 | – | 0.83 | 0.30 |
| 0.67 | 0.32 | (0.18) | – | (0.09) | (0.34) | 0.59 | – | 0.67 | 0.18 |
| 0.36 | 0.16 | (0.10) | – | (0.05) | (0.16) | 0.31 | – | 0.37 | 0.51 |
| – | – | – | – | – | – | – | – | – | – |
| – | – | – | – | – | – | – | – | – | – |

The four boxed columns in Table 6.31 highlight the predominantly nonoverlapping three-year correlations of monthly returns between the Lehman Brothers 7-Year Municipal Bond Index and four asset classes: (i) U.S. large-cap equities, as represented by the Standard & Poor's 500 Composite Index; (ii) intermediate-maturity U.S. Treasury Bonds, as represented by the U.S. Treasury 10-Year Note; (iii) real estate investment trusts, as represented by the NAREIT Index; and (iv) U.S. taxable

fixed-income securities, as represented by the Lehman Brothers Aggregate Bond index.

For the seven predominantly nonoverlapping three-year periods between 1988 through 1990 and 2002 through 2004, the correlations of monthly returns between the Lehman Brothers 7-Year Municipal Bond Index and the:

- **Standard & Poor's 500 Composite Index** ranged between −0.42 and 0.65;
- **U.S. Treasury 10-Year Note** ranged between 0.36 and 0.90;
- **NAREIT Index** ranged between −0.16 and 0.32; and
- **Lehman Brothers Aggregate Bond Index** ranged between 0.37 and 0.92.

Figure 6.24 graphically depicts the predominantly nonoverlapping three-year correlations of monthly returns between the Lehman Brothers 7-Year Municipal Bond Index and the Standard & Poor's 500 Composite Index, the U.S. Treasury 10-Year Note, the NAREIT Index, and the Lehman Brothers Aggregate Bond Index.

For additional observations on the predominantly nonoverlapping three-year correlations of monthly returns between the Lehman Brothers 7-Year Municipal Bond Index and unlisted securities, please refer to the table for the Nasdaq Composite Index.

**F I G U R E  6.24**

Intermediate-Maturity Tax-Exempt Bonds: Correlations of the Lehman Brothers 7-Year Municipal Bond Index

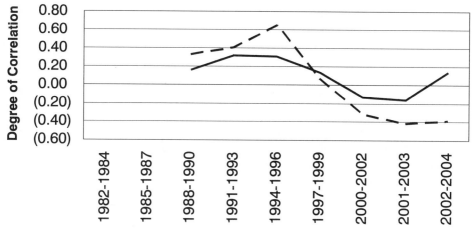

Selected Nonoverlapping 3-Year Time Periods

– – – S&P 500 Index
——— NAREIT Composite Index

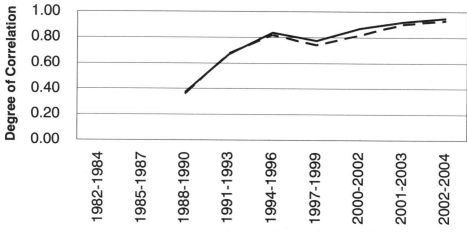

Selected Nonoverlapping 3-Year Time Periods

– – – U.S. Treasury 10-Year Note
——— Lehman Brothers Aggregate Bond Index

Source: The author.

**T A B L E   6.32**

Intermediate-Maturity U.S. Treasury Bonds: Correlations of the U.S. Treasury 10-Year Note[1, 2]

| U.S. Treasury 10-Year Note for 3-Year Periods from: | S&P 500 Composite Index | Nasdaq Composite Index | Wilshire 5000 Index | MSCI EAFE Net Index | MSCI Europe Free Net Index | MSCI Japan Net Index | Lehman Brothers 7-Year Municipal Bond Index |
|---|---|---|---|---|---|---|---|
|  | 1 | 2 | 3 | 4 | 5 | 6 | 7 |
| 1  2002–2004[2] | (0.45) | (0.50) | (0.45) | (0.33) | (0.38) | (0.01) | 0.93 |
| 2  2001–2003[2] | (0.54) | (0.50) | (0.55) | (0.41) | (0.42) | (0.19) | 0.90 |
| 3  2000–2002 | (0.49) | (0.40) | (0.49) | (0.38) | (0.42) | (0.09) | 0.82 |
| 4  1997–1999 | 0.08 | 0.04 | 0.04 | (0.18) | (0.16) | (0.13) | 0.74 |
| 5  1994–1996 | 0.62 | 0.20 | 0.51 | 0.10 | 0.32 | (0.10) | 0.82 |
| 6  1991–1993 | 0.39 | 0.17 | 0.34 | 0.30 | 0.33 | 0.24 | 0.67 |
| 7  1988–1990 | 0.60 | 0.46 | 0.58 | 0.20 | 0.22 | 0.17 | 0.36 |
| 8  1985–1987 | 0.12 | 0.04 | 0.11 | 0.19 | 0.31 | 0.12 | – |
| 9  1982–1984 | 0.40 | 0.32 | 0.38 | 0.15 | 0.25 | 0.07 | – |

[1]Nonoverlapping three-year correlations of monthly returns of the U.S. Treasury 10-Year Note with selected asset classes during nine three-year periods beginning with 1982–1984 and ending with 2002–2004.

[2]Strictly speaking, the years 2003–2005 represent the logical progression of nonoverlapping three-year periods which extends from 1982–1984 to 2000–2002; to furnish additional perspective, data have also been compiled for the 2001–2003 and 2002–2004 time periods.

Source: The author.

## Intermediate-Maturity U.S. Treasury Bonds

For the U.S. Treasury 10-Year Note for nine time periods, Table 6.32 displays the predominantly nonoverlapping three-year correlations of monthly returns with 14 other asset classes, beginning with the 1982 through 1984 triennium and ending with the 2002 through 2004 triennium.

| U.S. Treasury 10-Year Note | NAREIT Index | Nat'l Assn of Realtors Median Home Price | Venture Economics All Private Equity Fund Index | Handy & Harmon Spot Gold Price | Handy & Harmon Spot Silver Price | Lehman Brothers/ Bridgewater TIPS Index | Mei/Moses Fine Art Index | Lehman Brothers Aggregate Bond Index | HFRI Fund Weighted Composite Hedge Fund Index |
|---|---|---|---|---|---|---|---|---|---|
| 8 | 9 | 10 | 11 | 12 | 13 | 14 | 15 | 16 | 17 |
| 1.00 | 0.11 | (0.27) | – | 0.24 | (0.01) | 0.88 | – | 0.97 | (0.22) |
| 1.00 | (0.37) | (0.28) | – | 0.17 | (0.35) | 0.85 | – | 0.95 | (0.38) |
| 1.00 | (0.38) | (0.27) | – | 0.16 | (0.16) | 0.75 | – | 0.91 | (0.24) |
| 1.00 | 0.08 | (0.12) | – | 0.12 | (0.05) | 0.54 | – | 0.96 | (0.20) |
| 1.00 | 0.17 | 0.04 | – | (0.21) | (0.31) | 0.93 | – | 0.99 | 0.21 |
| 1.00 | 0.38 | (0.07) | – | (0.13) | (0.35) | 0.73 | – | 0.97 | 0.11 |
| 1.00 | 0.47 | 0.01 | – | (0.25) | (0.21) | 0.87 | – | 0.99 | 0.32 |
| 1.00 | 0.15 | 0.05 | – | (0.17) | (0.36) | 0.84 | – | 0.97 | – |
| 1.00 | 0.28 | (0.44) | – | 0.05 | 0.01 | 0.88 | – | 0.97 | – |

The four boxed columns in Table 6.32 highlight the predominantly nonoverlapping three-year correlations of monthly returns between the U.S. Treasury 10-Year Note and four asset classes: (i) U.S. large-cap equities, as represented by the Standard & Poor's 500 Composite Index; (ii) unlisted securities, as represented by the Nasdaq Composite Index; (iii) inflation-indexed securities, as represented by the Lehman Brothers/Bridgewater TIPS Index; and (iv) U.S. taxable

fixed-income securities, as represented by the Lehman Brothers Aggregate Bond Index.

For the nine predominantly nonoverlapping three-year periods between 1982 through 1984 and 2002 through 2004, the correlations of monthly returns between the U.S. Treasury 10-Year Note and the:

- ◆ **Standard & Poor's 500 Composite Index** ranged between −0.54 and 0.62;
- ◆ **Nasdaq Composite Index** ranged between −0.50 and 0.46;
- ◆ **Lehman Brothers/Bridgewater TIPS Index** ranged between 0.54 and 0.93.; and
- ◆ **Lehman Brothers Aggregate Bond Index** ranged between 0.91 and 0.99.

Figure 6.25 graphically depicts the predominantly nonoverlapping three-year correlations of monthly returns between the U.S. Treasury 10-Year Note and the Standard & Poor's 500 Composite Index, the Nasdaq Composite Index, the Lehman Brothers/ Bridgewater TIPS Index, and the Lehman Brothers Aggregate Bond Index.

For additional observations on the predominantly nonoverlapping three-year correlations of monthly returns between the U.S. Treasury 10-Year Note and other asset classes, please refer to the tables for the Wilshire 5000 Index, the MSCI Europe Free Net Index, the MSCI Japan Net Index, the Lehman Brothers 7-Year Municipal Bond Index, and the Lehman Brothers/Bridgewater TIPS Index.

Intermediate-Maturity U.S. Treasury Bonds: Correlations of the U.S. Treasury 10-Year Note

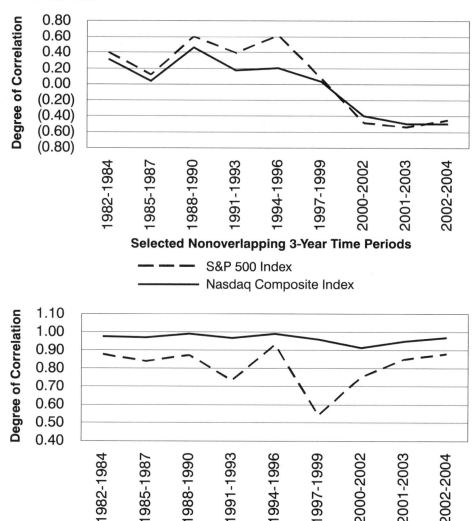

Source: The author.

**T A B L E  6.33**

Real Estate Investment Trusts: Correlations of the NAREIT Index[1, 2]

| NAREIT Index for 3-Year Periods from: | S&P 500 Composite Index | Nasdaq Composite Index | Wilshire 5000 Index | MSCI EAFE Net Index | MSCI Europe Free Net Index | MSCI Japan Net Index | Lehman Brothers 7-Year Municipal Bond Index |
|---|---|---|---|---|---|---|---|
|   | 1 | 2 | 3 | 4 | 5 | 6 | 7 |
| 1  2002–2004 [2] | 0.36 | 0.34 | 0.41 | 0.49 | 0.39 | 0.50 | 0.14 |
| 2  2001–2003 [2] | 0.43 | 0.38 | 0.47 | 0.55 | 0.50 | 0.49 | (0.16) |
| 3  2000–2002 | 0.19 | 0.04 | 0.19 | 0.28 | 0.29 | 0.11 | (0.13) |
| 4  1997–1999 | 0.51 | 0.40 | 0.56 | 0.34 | 0.44 | 0.04 | 0.14 |
| 5  1994–1996 | 0.24 | 0.21 | 0.28 | 0.19 | 0.25 | 0.00 | 0.31 |
| 6  1991–1993 | 0.43 | 0.56 | 0.49 | 0.24 | 0.19 | 0.25 | 0.32 |
| 7  1988–1990 | 0.74 | 0.84 | 0.80 | 0.23 | 0.39 | 0.10 | 0.16 |
| 8  1985–1987 | 0.74 | 0.79 | 0.77 | 0.52 | 0.62 | 0.27 | – |
| 9  1982–1984 | 0.63 | 0.60 | 0.62 | 0.46 | 0.55 | 0.32 | – |

[1]Nonoverlapping three-year correlations of monthly returns of the NAREIT Index with selected asset classes during nine three-year periods beginning with 1982–1984 and ending with 2002–2004.

[2]Strictly speaking, the years 2003–2005 represent the logical progression of nonoverlapping three-year periods which extends from 1982–1984 to 2000–2002; to furnish additional perspective, data have also been compiled for the 2001–2003 and 2002–2004 time periods.

Source: The author.

## Real Estate Investment Trusts

For the NAREIT Index for nine time periods, Table 6.33 displays the predominantly nonoverlapping three-year correlations of monthly returns with 14 other asset classes, beginning with the 1982 through 1984 triennium and ending with the 2002 through 2004 triennium.

| U.S. Treasury 10-Year Note | NAREIT Index | Nat'l Assn of Realtors Median Home Price | Venture Economics All Private Equity Fund Index | Handy & Harmon Spot Gold Price | Handy & Harmon Spot Silver Price | Lehman Brothers/ Bridgewater TIPS Index | Mei/Moses Fine Art Index | Lehman Brothers Aggregate Bond Index | HFRI Fund Weighted Composite Hedge Fund Index |
|---|---|---|---|---|---|---|---|---|---|
| 8 | 9 | 10 | 11 | 12 | 13 | 14 | 15 | 16 | 17 |
| 0.11 | 1.00 | 0.16 | – | 0.36 | 0.53 | 0.35 | – | 0.17 | 0.52 |
| (0.37) | 1.00 | 0.47 | – | 0.10 | 0.20 | (0.18) | – | (0.36) | 0.56 |
| (0.38) | 1.00 | 0.54 | – | (0.01) | 0.09 | (0.16) | – | (0.33) | 0.13 |
| 0.08 | 1.00 | 0.20 | – | 0.09 | 0.39 | 0.10 | – | 0.17 | 0.58 |
| 0.17 | 1.00 | 0.09 | – | (0.23) | (0.07) | 0.11 | – | 0.17 | 0.31 |
| 0.38 | 1.00 | 0.28 | – | (0.35) | (0.25) | 0.35 | – | 0.36 | 0.52 |
| 0.47 | 1.00 | 0.36 | – | (0.41) | (0.08) | 0.20 | – | 0.48 | 0.46 |
| 0.15 | 1.00 | 0.39 | – | (0.07) | 0.03 | 0.03 | – | 0.14 | – |
| 0.28 | 1.00 | (0.32) | – | 0.37 | 0.36 | 0.26 | – | 0.36 | – |

The four boxed columns in Table 6.33 highlight the predominantly nonoverlapping three-year correlations of monthly returns
between the NAREIT Index and four asset classes: (i) U.S. equities,
as represented by the Wilshire 5000 Index; (ii) residential real estate,
as represented by the National Association of Realtors Median
Home Price; (iii) inflation-indexed securities, as represented by the

Lehman Brothers/Bridgewater TIPS Index; and (iv) U.S. taxable fixed-income securities, as represented by the Lehman Brothers Aggregate Bond Index.

For the nine predominantly nonoverlapping three-year periods between 1982 through 1984 and 2002 through 2004, the correlations of monthly returns between the NAREIT Index and the:

- **Wilshire 5000 Index** ranged between 0.19 and 0.80;
- **National Association of Realtors Median Home Price** ranged between –0.32 and 0.54 during seven of the three-year periods;
- **Lehman Brothers/Bridgewater TIPS Index** ranged between –0.18 and 0.35; and
- **Lehman Brothers Aggregate Bond Index** ranged between –0.36 and 0.48.

Figure 6.26 graphically depicts the predominantly nonoverlapping three-year correlations of monthly returns between the NAREIT Index and the Wilshire 5000 Index, the National Association of Realtors Median Home Price, the Lehman Brothers/Bridgewater TIPS Index, and the Lehman Brothers Aggregate Bond Index.

For additional observations on the predominantly nonoverlapping three-year correlations of monthly returns between the NAREIT Index and other asset classes, please refer to the tables for the Standard & Poor's 500 Composite Index, the Lehman Brothers 7-Year Municipal Bond Index, the Handy & Harmon Spot Gold Price, and the HFRI Fund Weighted Composite Hedge Fund Index.

**F I G U R E  6.26**

Real Estate Investment Trusts: Correlations of the NAREIT Index

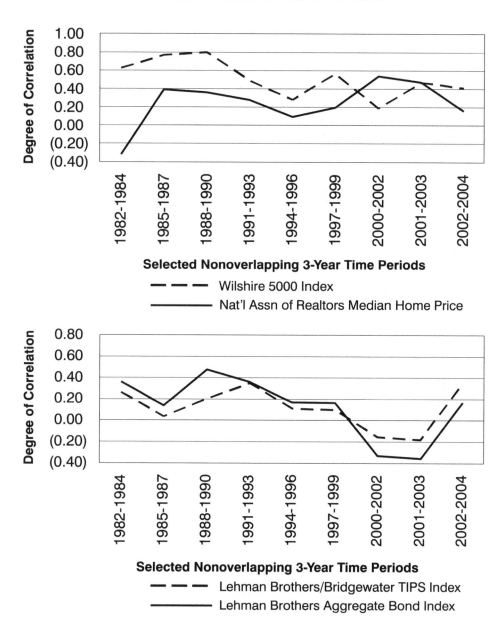

Source: The author.

**T A B L E  6.34**

Residential Real Estate: Correlations of the National Association of Realtors Median Home Price[1,2]

| National Association of Realtors Median Home Price for 3-Year Periods from: | S&P 500 Composite Index | Nasdaq Composite Index | Wilshire 5000 Index | MSCI EAFE Net Index | MSCI Europe Free Net Index | MSCI Japan Net Index | Lehman Brothers 7-Year Municipal Bond Index |
|---|---|---|---|---|---|---|---|
|  | 1 | 2 | 3 | 4 | 5 | 6 | 7 |
| 1  2002–2004 [2] | 0.16 | 0.12 | 0.16 | 0.22 | 0.19 | 0.27 | (0.35) |
| 2  2001–2003 [2] | 0.11 | 0.04 | 0.12 | 0.18 | 0.19 | 0.10 | (0.25) |
| 3  2000–2002 | 0.09 | 0.07 | 0.11 | 0.21 | 0.23 | 0.06 | (0.16) |
| 4  1997–1999 | 0.09 | 0.13 | 0.10 | 0.07 | 0.09 | 0.03 | (0.17) |
| 5  1994–1996 | (0.01) | (0.01) | 0.00 | 0.08 | 0.04 | 0.08 | 0.00 |
| 6  1991–1993 | 0.09 | 0.14 | 0.09 | (0.03) | (0.06) | 0.00 | (0.18) |
| 7  1988–1990 | 0.04 | 0.15 | 0.07 | (0.12) | (0.01) | (0.18) | (0.10) |
| 8  1985–1987 | 0.47 | 0.50 | 0.48 | 0.17 | 0.21 | 0.08 | – |
| 9  1982–1984 | (0.21) | (0.17) | (0.20) | (0.16) | (0.25) | (0.07) | – |

[1]Nonoverlapping three-year correlations of monthly returns of the National Association of Realtors Median Home Price with selected asset classes during nine three-year periods beginning with 1982–1984 and ending with 2002–2004.

[2]Strictly speaking, the years 2003–2005 represent the logical progression of nonoverlapping three-year periods which extends from 1982–1984 to 2000–2002; to furnish additional perspective, data have also been compiled for the 2001–2003 and 2002–2004 time periods.

Source: The author.

## Residential Real Estate

For the National Association of Realtors Median Home Price for nine time periods, Table 6.34 displays the predominantly nonoverlapping three-year correlations of monthly returns with 14 other asset classes, beginning with the 1982 through 1984 triennium and ending with the 2002 through 2004 triennium.

| U.S. Treasury 10-Year Note | NAREIT Index | Nat'l Assn of Realtors Median Home Price | Venture Economics All Private Equity Fund Index | Handy & Harmon Spot Gold Price | Handy & Harmon Spot Silver Price | Lehman Brothers/ Bridgewater TIPS Index | Mei/Moses Fine Art Index | Lehman Brothers Aggregate Bond Index | HFRI Fund Weighted Composite Hedge Fund Index |
|---|---|---|---|---|---|---|---|---|---|
| 8 | 9 | 10 | 11 | 12 | 13 | 14 | 15 | 16 | 17 |
| (0.27) | 0.16 | 1.00 | – | (0.09) | (0.01) | (0.24) | – | (0.28) | (0.01) |
| (0.28) | 0.47 | 1.00 | – | (0.26) | (0.02) | (0.29) | – | (0.32) | 0.07 |
| (0.27) | 0.54 | 1.00 | – | (0.13) | (0.04) | (0.22) | – | (0.29) | 0.07 |
| (0.12) | 0.20 | 1.00 | – | (0.36) | (0.19) | (0.13) | – | (0.10) | 0.16 |
| 0.04 | 0.09 | 1.00 | – | 0.08 | (0.08) | 0.03 | – | 0.01 | 0.15 |
| (0.07) | 0.28 | 1.00 | – | (0.21) | (0.04) | (0.19) | – | (0.07) | 0.17 |
| 0.01 | 0.36 | 1.00 | – | (0.05) | 0.25 | (0.08) | – | 0.02 | 0.26 |
| 0.05 | 0.39 | 1.00 | – | 0.07 | 0.16 | 0.08 | – | 0.07 | – |
| (0.44) | (0.32) | 1.00 | – | (0.08) | (0.19) | (0.32) | – | (0.46) | – |

The four boxed columns in Table 6.34 highlight the predominantly nonoverlapping three-year correlations of monthly returns between the National Association of Realtors Median Home Price and four asset classes: (i) U.S. large-cap equities, as represented by the Standard & Poor's 500 Composite Index; (ii) European equities, as represented by the MSCI Europe Free Net Index; (iii) real assets—precious metals—gold, as represented by the Handy & Harmon Spot Gold Price;

and (iv) U.S. taxable fixed-income securities, as represented by the Lehman Brothers Aggregate Bond Index.

For the nine predominantly nonoverlapping three-year periods between 1982 through 1984 and 2002 through 2004, the correlations of monthly returns between the National Association of Realtors Median Home Price and the:

- **Standard & Poor's 500 Composite Index** ranged between –0.21 and 0.47 during seven of the three-year periods;
- **MSCI Europe Free Net Index** ranged between –0.25 and 0.23 during seven of the three-year periods;
- **Handy & Harmon Spot Gold Price** ranged between –0.36 and 0.08 during seven of the three-year periods; and
- **Lehman Brothers Aggregate Bond Index** ranged between -0.46 and 0.07 during seven of the three-year periods.

Figure 6.27 graphically depicts the predominantly nonoverlapping three-year correlations of monthly returns between the National Association of Realtors Median Home Price and the Standard & Poor's 500 Composite Index, the MSCI Europe Free Net Index, the Handy & Harmon Spot Gold Price, and the Lehman Brothers Aggregate Bond Index.

For additional observations on the predominantly nonoverlapping three-year correlations of monthly returns between the National Association of Realtors Median Home Price and other asset classes, please refer to the tables for the NAREIT Index and the Handy & Harmon Spot Silver Price.

**F I G U R E   6.27**

Residential Real Estate: Correlations of the National Association of Realtors Median Home Price

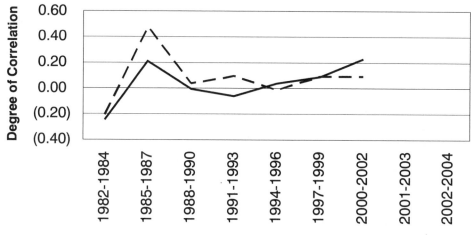

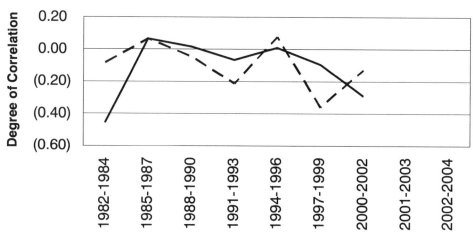

**T A B L E   6.35**

Real Assets—Precious Metals—Gold: Correlations of the Handy & Harmon Spot Gold Price[1, 2]

| Handy & Harmon Spot Gold Price for 3-Year Periods from: | S&P 500 Composite Index | Nasdaq Composite Index | Wilshire 5000 Index | MSCI EAFE Net Index | MSCI Europe Free Net Index | MSCI Japan Net Index | Lehman Brothers 7-Year Municipal Bond Index |
|---|---|---|---|---|---|---|---|
| | 1 | 2 | 3 | 4 | 5 | 6 | 7 |
| 1   2002–2004[2] | (0.02) | (0.05) | 0.02 | 0.16 | 0.05 | 0.37 | 0.23 |
| 2   2001–2003[2] | (0.11) | (0.20) | (0.10) | 0.03 | (0.02) | 0.22 | 0.17 |
| 3   2000–2002 | (0.24) | (0.06) | (0.15) | 0.00 | (0.08) | 0.21 | 0.16 |
| 4   1997–1999 | 0.04 | 0.14 | 0.07 | 0.23 | 0.11 | 0.33 | 0.03 |
| 5   1994–1996 | (0.28) | (0.20) | (0.27) | (0.13) | (0.26) | (0.02) | (0.24) |
| 6   1991–1993 | (0.28) | (0.29) | (0.28) | 0.09 | (0.11) | 0.13 | (0.09) |
| 7   1988–1990 | (0.44) | (0.46) | (0.45) | (0.06) | (0.15) | (0.04) | (0.05) |
| 8   1985–1987 | (0.31) | (0.28) | (0.30) | 0.19 | 0.08 | 0.19 | – |
| 9   1982–1984 | 0.46 | 0.37 | 0.45 | 0.22 | 0.20 | 0.19 | – |

[1]Nonoverlapping three-year correlations of monthly returns of Handy & Harmon Spot Gold Price with selected asset classes during nine three-year periods beginning with 1982–1984 and ending with 2002–2004.

[2]Strictly speaking, the years 2003–2005 represent the logical progression of nonoverlapping three-year periods which extends from 1982–1984 to 2000–2002; to furnish additional perspective, data have also been compiled for the 2001–2003 and 2002–2004 time periods.

Source: The author.

## Real Assets—Precious Metals—Gold

For the Handy & Harmon Spot Gold Price for nine time periods, Table 6.35 displays the predominantly nonoverlapping three-year correlations of monthly returns with 14 other asset classes, beginning with the 1982 through 1984 triennium and ending with the 2002 through 2004 triennium.

| U.S. Treasury 10-Year Note | NAREIT Index | Nat'l Assn of Realtors Median Home Price | Venture Economics All Private Equity Fund Index | Handy & Harmon Spot Gold Price | Handy & Harmon Spot Silver Price | Lehman Brothers/Bridgewater TIPS Index | Mei/Moses Fine Art Index | Lehman Brothers Aggregate Bond Index | HFRI Fund Weighted Composite Hedge Fund Index |
|---|---|---|---|---|---|---|---|---|---|
| 8 | 9 | 10 | 11 | 12 | 13 | 14 | 15 | 16 | 17 |
| 0.24 | 0.36 | (0.09) | – | 1.00 | 0.59 | 0.38 | – | 0.28 | 0.29 |
| 0.17 | 0.10 | (0.26) | – | 1.00 | 0.52 | 0.22 | – | 0.12 | 0.04 |
| 0.16 | (0.01) | (0.13) | – | 1.00 | 0.54 | 0.12 | – | 0.18 | 0.09 |
| 0.12 | 0.09 | (0.36) | – | 1.00 | 0.38 | 0.16 | – | 0.18 | 0.09 |
| (0.21) | (0.23) | 0.08 | – | 1.00 | 0.61 | (0.13) | – | (0.24) | (0.01) |
| (0.13) | (0.35) | (0.21) | – | 1.00 | 0.81 | (0.33) | – | (0.14) | 0.00 |
| (0.25) | (0.41) | (0.05) | – | 1.00 | 0.68 | (0.21) | – | (0.22) | (0.33) |
| (0.17) | (0.07) | 0.07 | – | 1.00 | 0.71 | (0.08) | – | (0.16) | – |
| 0.05 | 0.37 | (0.08) | – | 1.00 | 0.82 | 0.05 | – | 0.13 | – |

The four boxed columns in Table 6.35 highlight the predominantly nonoverlapping three-year correlations of monthly returns between the Handy & Harmon Spot Gold Price and four asset classes: (i) U.S. large-cap equities, as represented by the Standard & Poor's 500 Composite Index; (ii) real estate investment trusts, as represented by the NAREIT Index; (iii) inflation-indexed securities, as represented by the Lehman Brothers/Bridgewater TIPS Index; and (iv) U.S. taxable

fixed-income securities, as represented by the Lehman Brothers Aggregate Bond Index.

For the nine predominantly nonoverlapping three-year periods between 1982 through 1984 and 2002 through 2004, the correlations of monthly returns between the Handy & Harmon Spot Gold Price and the:

- **Standard & Poor's 500 Composite Index** ranged between –0.44 and 0.46;
- **NAREIT Index** ranged between –0.41 and 0.37;
- **Lehman Brothers/Bridgewater TIPS Index** ranged between –0.33 and 0.22; and
- **Lehman Brothers Aggregate Bond Index** ranged between –0.24 and 0.18.

Figure 6.28 graphically depicts the predominantly nonoverlapping three-year correlations of monthly returns between the Handy & Harmon Spot Gold Price and the Standard & Poor's 500 Composite Index, the NAREIT Index, the Lehman Brothers/ Bridgewater TIPS Index, and the Lehman Brothers Aggregate Bond Index.

For additional observations on the predominantly nonoverlapping three-year correlations of monthly returns between the Handy & Harmon Spot Gold Price and other asset classes, please refer to the tables for the Handy & Harmon Spot Silver Price, the Lehman Brothers/Bridgewater TIPS Index, and the HFRI Fund Weighted Composite Hedge Fund Index.

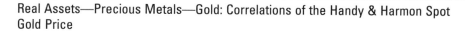

**F I G U R E  6.28**

Real Assets—Precious Metals—Gold: Correlations of the Handy & Harmon Spot Gold Price

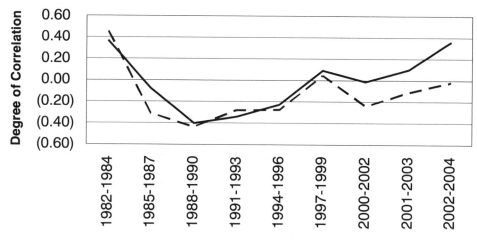

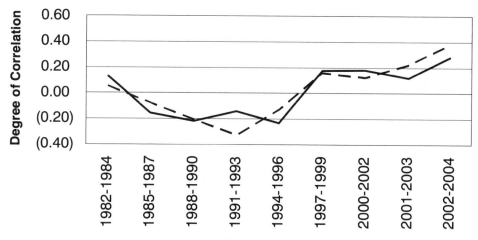

Source: The author.

**T A B L E  6.36**

Real Assets—Precious Metals—Silver: Correlations of the Handy & Harmon Spot Silver Price[1, 2]

| Handy & Harmon Spot Silver Price for 3-Year Periods from: | S&P 500 Composite Index | Nasdaq Composite Index | Wilshire 5000 Index | MSCI EAFE Net Index | MSCI Europe Free Net Index | MSCI Japan Net Index | Lehman Brothers 7-Year Municipal Bond Index |
|---|---|---|---|---|---|---|---|
| | 1 | 2 | 3 | 4 | 5 | 6 | 7 |
| 1  2002–2004[2] | 0.10 | 0.03 | 0.11 | 0.24 | 0.15 | 0.38 | (0.08) |
| 2  2001–2003[2] | 0.15 | 0.04 | 0.14 | 0.22 | 0.21 | 0.19 | (0.36) |
| 3  2000–2002 | 0.07 | (0.01) | 0.07 | 0.10 | 0.06 | 0.16 | (0.18) |
| 4  1997–1999 | 0.32 | 0.29 | 0.34 | 0.22 | 0.24 | 0.08 | (0.05) |
| 5  1994–1996 | (0.15) | (0.05) | (0.14) | (0.02) | (0.20) | 0.09 | (0.31) |
| 6  1991–1993 | (0.37) | (0.26) | (0.34) | 0.12 | (0.14) | 0.19 | (0.34) |
| 7  1988–1990 | (0.11) | (0.02) | (0.09) | 0.03 | (0.07) | 0.03 | (0.16) |
| 8  1985–1987 | 0.00 | (0.03) | 0.00 | 0.18 | 0.16 | 0.10 | – |
| 9  1982–1984 | 0.40 | 0.44 | 0.43 | 0.12 | 0.22 | 0.04 | – |

[1]Nonoverlapping three-year correlations of monthly returns of the Handy & Harmon Spot Silver Price with selected asset classes during nine three-year periods beginning with 1982–1984 and ending with 2002–2004.

[2]Strictly speaking, the years 2003–2005 represent the logical progression of nonoverlapping three-year periods which extends from 1982–1984 to 2000–2002; to furnish additional perspective, data have also been compiled for the 2001–2003 and 2002–2004 time periods.

Source: The author.

## Real Assets—Precious Metals—Silver

For the Handy & Harmon Spot Silver Price for nine time periods, Table 6.36 displays the predominantly nonoverlapping three-year correlations of monthly returns with 14 other asset classes, beginning with the 1982 through 1984 triennium and ending with the 2002 through 2004 triennium.

| U.S. Treasury 10-Year Note | NAREIT Index | Nat'l Assn of Realtors Median Home Price | Venture Economics All Private Equity Fund Index | Handy & Harmon Spot Gold Price | Handy & Harmon Spot Silver Price | Lehman Brothers/ Bridgewater TIPS Index | Mei/Moses Fine Art Index | Lehman Brothers Aggregate Bond Index | HFRI Fund Weighted Composite Hedge Fund Index |
|---|---|---|---|---|---|---|---|---|---|
| 8 | 9 | 10 | 11 | 12 | 13 | 14 | 15 | 16 | 17 |
| (0.01) | 0.53 | (0.01) | – | 0.59 | 1.00 | 0.12 | – | 0.05 | 0.23 |
| (0.35) | 0.20 | (0.02) | – | 0.52 | 1.00 | (0.31) | – | (0.34) | 0.16 |
| (0.16) | 0.09 | (0.04) | – | 0.54 | 1.00 | (0.11) | – | (0.15) | 0.05 |
| (0.05) | 0.39 | (0.19) | – | 0.38 | 1.00 | (0.01) | – | (0.05) | 0.32 |
| (0.31) | (0.07) | (0.08) | – | 0.61 | 1.00 | (0.24) | – | (0.31) | 0.08 |
| (0.35) | (0.25) | (0.04) | – | 0.81 | 1.00 | (0.50) | – | (0.35) | 0.12 |
| (0.21) | (0.08) | 0.25 | – | 0.68 | 1.00 | (0.30) | – | (0.17) | (0.01) |
| (0.36) | 0.03 | 0.16 | – | 0.71 | 1.00 | (0.23) | – | (0.36) | – |
| 0.01 | 0.36 | (0.19) | – | 0.82 | 1.00 | 0.00 | – | 0.09 | – |

The four boxed columns in Table 6.36 highlight the predominantly nonoverlapping three-year correlations of monthly returns between the Handy & Harmon Spot Silver Price and four asset classes: (i) U.S. equities, as represented by the Wilshire 5000 Index; (ii) residential real estate, as represented by the National Association of Realtors Median Home Price; (iii) real assets—precious metals—gold, as represented by the Handy & Harmon Spot Gold Price; and (iv) U.S. taxable

fixed-income securities, as represented by the Lehman Brothers Aggregate Bond Index.

For the nine predominantly nonoverlapping three-year periods between 1982 through 1984 and 2002 through 2004, the correlations of monthly returns between the Handy & Harmon Spot Silver Price and the:

- **Wilshire 5000 Index** ranged between –0.34 and 0.43;
- **National Association of Realtors Median Home Price** ranged between –0.19 and 0.25;
- **Handy & Harmon Spot Gold Price** ranged between 0.38 and 0.82; and
- **Lehman Brothers Aggregate Bond Index** ranged between –0.36 and 0.09.

Figure 6.29 graphically depicts the predominantly nonoverlapping three-year correlations of monthly returns between the Handy & Harmon Spot Silver Price and the Wilshire 5000 Index, the National Association of Realtors Median Home Price, the Handy & Harmon Spot Gold Price, and the Lehman Brothers Aggregate Bond Index.

**F I G U R E  6.29**

Real Assets—Precious Metals—Silver: Correlations of the Handy & Harmon Spot
Silver Price

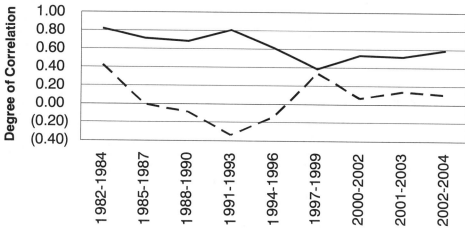

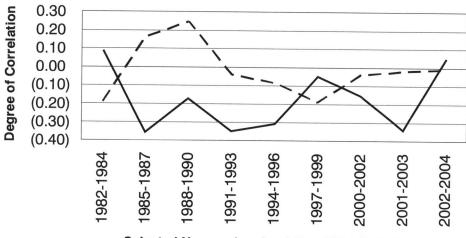

**T A B L E  6.37**

Inflation-Indexed Securities: Correlations of the Lehman Brothers/Bridgewater TIPS Index[1,2]

| Lehman Brothers/ Bridgewater TIPS Index for 3-Year Periods from: | S&P 500 Composite Index | Nasdaq Composite Index | Wilshire 5000 Index | MSCI EAFE Net Index | MSCI Europe Free Net Index | MSCI Japan Net Index | Lehman Brothers 7-Year Municipal Bond Index |
|---|---|---|---|---|---|---|---|
|  | 1 | 2 | 3 | 4 | 5 | 6 | 7 |
| 1   2002–2004 [2] | (0.26) | (0.30) | (0.24) | (0.11) | (0.19) | 0.17 | 0.85 |
| 2   2001–2003 [2] | (0.31) | (0.28) | (0.30) | (0.16) | (0.22) | 0.11 | 0.84 |
| 3   2000–2002 | (0.32) | (0.31) | (0.34) | (0.22) | (0.32) | 0.18 | 0.72 |
| 4   1997–1999 | 0.09 | 0.10 | 0.06 | (0.29) | (0.36) | (0.12) | 0.52 |
| 5   1994–1996 | 0.52 | 0.15 | 0.41 | (0.04) | 0.24 | (0.24) | 0.72 |
| 6   1991–1993 | 0.26 | 0.11 | 0.24 | 0.15 | 0.20 | 0.13 | 0.59 |
| 7   1988–1990 | 0.31 | 0.16 | 0.28 | 0.01 | 0.05 | 0.01 | 0.31 |
| 8   1985–1987 | 0.12 | 0.05 | 0.11 | 0.05 | 0.15 | 0.02 | – |
| 9   1982–1984 | 0.12 | 0.05 | 0.11 | 0.05 | 0.15 | 0.02 | – |

[1]Nonoverlapping three-year correlations of monthly returns of Lehman Brothers/Bridgewater TIPS Index with selected asset classes during nine three-year periods beginning with 1982–1984 and ending with 2002–2004.

[2]Strictly speaking, the years 2003–2005 represent the logical progression of nonoverlapping three-year periods which extends from 1982–1984 to 2000–2002; to furnish additional perspective, data have also been compiled for the 2001–2003 and 2002–2004 time periods.

Source: The author.

## Inflation-Indexed Securities

For the Lehman Brothers/Bridgewater TIPS Index for nine time periods, Table 6.37 displays the predominantly nonoverlapping three-year correlations of monthly returns with 14 other asset classes, beginning with the 1982 through 1984 triennium and ending with the 2002 through 2004 triennium.

| U.S. Treasury 10-Year Note | NAREIT Index | Nat'l Assn of Realtors Median Home Price | Venture Economics All Private Equity Fund Index | Handy & Harmon Spot Gold Price | Handy & Harmon Spot Silver Price | Lehman Brothers/Bridgewater TIPS Index | Mei/Moses Fine Art Index | Lehman Brothers Aggregate Bond Index | HFRI Fund Weighted Composite Hedge Fund Index |
|---|---|---|---|---|---|---|---|---|---|
| 8 | 9 | 10 | 11 | 12 | 13 | 14 | 15 | 16 | 17 |
| 0.88 | 0.35 | (0.24) | – | 0.38 | 0.12 | 1.00 | – | 0.88 | 0.03 |
| 0.85 | (0.18) | (0.29) | – | 0.22 | (0.31) | 1.00 | – | 0.86 | (0.08) |
| 0.75 | (0.16) | (0.22) | – | 0.12 | (0.11) | 1.00 | – | 0.76 | (0.14) |
| 0.54 | 0.10 | (0.13) | – | 0.16 | (0.01) | 1.00 | – | 0.57 | (0.09) |
| 0.93 | 0.11 | 0.03 | – | (0.13) | (0.24) | 1.00 | – | 0.92 | 0.17 |
| 0.73 | 0.35 | (0.19) | – | (0.33) | (0.50) | 1.00 | – | 0.64 | (0.07) |
| 0.87 | 0.20 | (0.08) | – | (0.21) | (0.30) | 1.00 | – | 0.86 | 0.04 |
| 0.84 | 0.03 | 0.08 | – | (0.08) | (0.23) | 1.00 | – | 0.86 | – |
| 0.84 | 0.03 | 0.08 | – | (0.08) | (0.23) | 1.00 | – | 0.86 | – |

The four boxed columns in Table 6.37 highlight the predominantly nonoverlapping three-year correlations of monthly returns between the Lehman Brothers/Bridgewater TIPS Index and four asset classes: (i) U.S. large-cap equities, as represented by the Standard & Poor's 500 Composite Index; (ii) intermediate-maturity U.S. Treasury Bonds, as represented by the U.S. Treasury 10-Year Note; (iii) real assets—precious metals—gold, as represented by the Handy & Harmon Spot Gold Prices; and (iv) U.S. taxable fixed-income securities, as represented by the Lehman Brothers Aggregate Bond Index.

For the nine predominantly nonoverlapping three-year periods between 1982 through 1984 and 2002 through 2004, the correlations of monthly returns between the Lehman Brothers/Bridgewater TIPS Index and the:

♦ **Standard & Poor's 500 Composite Index** ranged between –0.32 and 0.52;

♦ **U.S. Treasury 10-Year Note** ranged between 0.54 and 0.93;

♦ **Handy & Harmon Spot Gold Price** ranged between –0.33 and 0.22; and

♦ **Lehman Brothers Aggregate Bond Index** ranged between 0.57 and 0.92.

Figure 6.30 graphically depicts the predominantly nonoverlapping three-year correlations of monthly returns between the Lehman Brothers/Bridgewater TIPS Index and the Standard & Poor's 500 Composite Index, the U.S. Treasury 10-Year Note, the Handy & Harmon Spot Gold Price, and the Lehman Brothers Aggregate Bond Index.

For additional observations on the predominantly nonoverlapping three-year correlations of monthly returns between the Lehman Brothers/Bridgewater TIPS Index and other asset classes, please refer to the tables for the MSCI EAFE Net Index, the MSCI Japan Net Index, the NAREIT Index, and the Handy & Harmon Spot Gold Price.

**F I G U R E   6.30**

Inflation-Indexed Securities: Correlations of the Lehman Brothers/Bridgewater TIPS Index

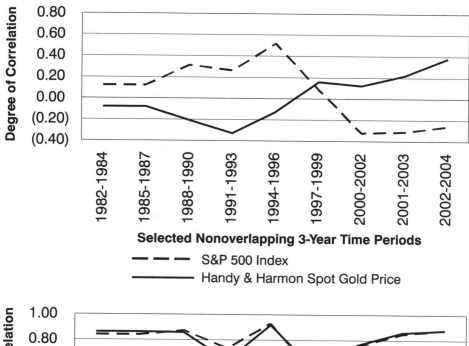

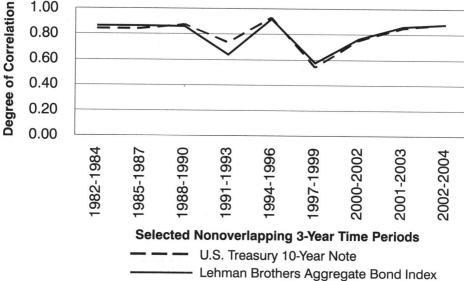

**T A B L E   6.38**

U.S. Taxable Fixed-Income Securities: Correlations of the Lehman Brothers
Aggregate Bond Index[1,2]

| Lehman Brothers Aggregate Bond Index for 3-Year Periods from: | S&P 500 Composite Index | Nasdaq Composite Index | Wilshire 5000 Index | MSCI EAFE Net Index | MSCI Europe Free Net Index | MSCI Japan Net Index | Lehman Brothers 7-Year Municipal Bond Index |
|---|---|---|---|---|---|---|---|
| | 1 | 2 | 3 | 4 | 5 | 6 | 7 |
| 1  2002–2004[2] | (0.34) | (0.43) | (0.34) | (0.21) | (0.26) | 0.03 | 0.95 |
| 2  2001–2003[2] | (0.41) | (0.39) | (0.42) | (0.29) | (0.29) | (0.15) | 0.92 |
| 3  2000–2002 | (0.33) | (0.19) | (0.30) | (0.20) | (0.24) | (0.01) | 0.87 |
| 4  1997–1999 | 0.19 | 0.12 | 0.15 | (0.10) | (0.06) | (0.11) | 0.77 |
| 5  1994–1996 | 0.62 | 0.23 | 0.52 | 0.12 | 0.35 | (0.09) | 0.83 |
| 6  1991–1993 | 0.41 | 0.18 | 0.36 | 0.38 | 0.40 | 0.31 | 0.67 |
| 7  1988–1990 | 0.61 | 0.47 | 0.59 | 0.22 | 0.24 | 0.18 | 0.37 |
| 8  1985–1987 | 0.15 | 0.07 | 0.14 | 0.13 | 0.29 | 0.03 | – |
| 9  1982–1984 | 0.46 | 0.38 | 0.45 | 0.15 | 0.28 | 0.05 | – |

[1]Nonoverlapping three-year correlations of monthly returns with selected asset classes during nine three-year periods beginning with 1982–1984 and ending with 2002–2004.

[2]Strictly speaking, the years 2003–2005 represent the logical progression of nonoverlapping three-year periods which extends from 1982–1984 to 2000–2002; to furnish additional perspective, data have also been compiled for the 2001–2003 and 2002–2004 time periods.

Source: The author.

## U.S. Taxable Fixed-Income Securities

For the Lehman Brothers Aggregate Bond Index for nine time periods,
Table 6.38 displays the predominantly nonoverlapping three-year correlations of monthly returns with 14 other asset classes, beginning with
the 1982 through 1984 triennium and ending with the 2002 through
2004 triennium.

| U.S. Treasury 10-Year Note | NAREIT Index | Nat'l Assn of Realtors Median Home Price | Venture Economics All Private Equity Fund Index | Handy & Harmon Spot Gold Price | Handy & Harmon Spot Silver Price | Lehman Brothers/ Bridgewater TIPS Index | Mei/Moses Fine Art Index | Lehman Brothers Aggregate Bond Index | HFRI Fund Weighted Composite Hedge Fund Index |
|---|---|---|---|---|---|---|---|---|---|
| 8 | 9 | 10 | 11 | 12 | 13 | 14 | 15 | 16 | 17 |
| 0.97 | 0.17 | (0.28) | – | 0.28 | 0.05 | 0.88 | – | 1.00 | (0.12) |
| 0.95 | (0.36) | (0.32) | – | 0.12 | (0.34) | 0.86 | – | 1.00 | (0.25) |
| 0.91 | (0.33) | (0.29) | – | 0.18 | (0.15) | 0.76 | – | 1.00 | (0.02) |
| 0.96 | 0.17 | (0.10) | – | 0.18 | (0.05) | 0.57 | – | 1.00 | (0.09) |
| 0.99 | 0.17 | 0.01 | – | (0.24) | (0.31) | 0.92 | – | 1.00 | 0.24 |
| 0.97 | 0.36 | (0.07) | – | (0.14) | (0.35) | 0.64 | – | 1.00 | 0.10 |
| 0.99 | 0.48 | 0.02 | – | (0.22) | (0.17) | 0.86 | – | 1.00 | 0.33 |
| 0.97 | 0.14 | 0.07 | – | (0.16) | (0.36) | 0.86 | – | 1.00 | – |
| 0.97 | 0.36 | (0.46) | – | 0.13 | 0.09 | 0.88 | – | 1.00 | – |

The four boxed columns in Table 6.38 highlight the predominantly nonoverlapping three-year correlations of monthly returns between the Lehman Brothers Aggregate Bond Index and four asset classes: (i) unlisted securities, as represented by the Nasdaq Composite Index; (ii) U.S. equities, as represented by the Wilshire 5000 Index; (iii) residential real estate, as represented by the National Association of Realtors

Median Home Price; and (iv) real assets—precious metals—silver, as represented by the Handy & Harmon Spot Silver Price.

For the nine predominantly nonoverlapping three-year periods between 1982 through 1984 and 2002 through 2004, the correlations of monthly returns between the Lehman Brothers Aggregate Bond Index and the:

- ◆ **Nasdaq Composite Index** ranged between –0.39 and 0.47 periods;
- ◆ **Wilshire 5000 Index** ranged between –0.42 and 0.59;
- ◆ **National Association of Realtors Median Home Price** ranged between –0.46 and 0.07; and
- ◆ **Handy & Harmon Spot Silver Price** ranged between –0.36 and 0.09.

Figure 6.31 graphically depicts the predominantly nonoverlapping three-year correlations of monthly returns between the Lehman Brothers Aggregate Bond Index and the Nasdaq Composite Index, the Wilshire 5000 Index, the National Association of Realtors Median Home Price, and the Handy & Harmon Spot Silver Price.

For additional observations on the predominantly nonoverlapping three-year correlations of monthly returns between the Lehman Brothers Aggregate Bond Index and other asset classes, please refer to the tables for the Standard & Poor's 500 Composite Index, the MSCI Europe Free Net Index, the MSCI Japan Net Index, the Lehman Brothers 7-Year Municipal Bond Index, the U.S. Treasury 10-Year Note, the NAREIT Index, the National Association of Realtors Median Home Price, the Handy & Harmon Spot Gold Price, and the Lehman Brothers/Bridgewater TIPS Index.

**F I G U R E   6.31**

U.S. Taxable Fixed-Income Securities: Correlations of the Lehman Brothers Aggregate Bond Index

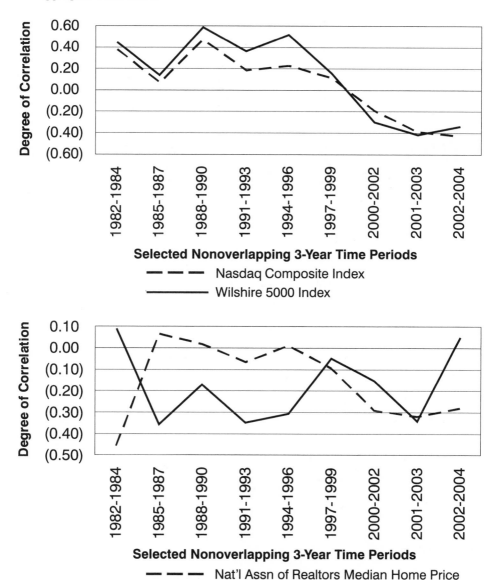

Source: The author.

T A B L E   6.39

Hedge Funds: Correlations of the HFRI Fund Weighted Composite Hedge
Fund Index[1, 2]

| HFRI Fund Weighted Composite Hedge Fund Index for 3-Year Periods from: | S&P 500 Composite Index | Nasdaq Composite Index | Wilshire 5000 Index | MSCI EAFE Net Index | MSCI Europe Free Net Index | MSCI Japan Net Index | Lehman Brothers 7-Year Municipal Bond Index |
|---|---|---|---|---|---|---|---|
| | 1 | 2 | 3 | 4 | 5 | 6 | 7 |
| 1   2002–2004 [2] | 0.80 | 0.79 | 0.84 | 0.84 | 0.77 | 0.54 | (0.14) |
| 2   2001–2003 [2] | 0.85 | 0.86 | 0.88 | 0.83 | 0.78 | 0.56 | (0.17) |
| 3   2000–2002 | 0.65 | 0.89 | 0.80 | 0.71 | 0.65 | 0.50 | 0.00 |
| 4   1997–1999 | 0.76 | 0.85 | 0.84 | 0.71 | 0.70 | 0.44 | (0.10) |
| 5   1994–1996 | 0.67 | 0.82 | 0.77 | 0.48 | 0.45 | 0.29 | 0.30 |
| 6   1991–1993 | 0.59 | 0.80 | 0.69 | 0.36 | 0.37 | 0.24 | 0.18 |
| 7   1988–1990 | 0.55 | 0.60 | 0.57 | 0.20 | 0.40 | 0.08 | 0.51 |
| 8   1985–1987 | – | – | – | – | – | – | – |
| 9   1982–1984 | – | – | – | – | – | – | – |

[1]Nonoverlapping three-year correlations of monthly returns of the HFRI Fund Weighted Composite Hedge Fund Index with selected asset classes during seven three-year periods beginning with 1988–1990 and ending with 2002–2004.

[2]Strictly speaking, the years 2003–2005 represent the logical progression of nonoverlapping three-year periods which extends from 1982–1984 to 2000–2002; to furnish additional perspective, data have also been compiled for the 2001–2003 and 2002–2004 time periods.

Source: The author.

## Hedge Funds

For the HFRI Fund Weighted Composite Hedge Fund Index for seven time periods, Table 6.39 displays the predominantly nonoverlapping three-year correlations of monthly returns with 14 other asset classes, beginning with the 1988 through 1990 triennium and ending with the 2002 through 2004 triennium.

| U.S. Treasury 10-Year Note | NAREIT Index | Nat'l Assn of Realtors Median Home Price | Venture Economics All Private Equity Fund Index | Handy & Harmon Spot Gold Price | Handy & Harmon Spot Silver Price | Lehman Brothers/Bridgewater TIPS Index | Mei/Moses Fine Art Index | Lehman Brothers Aggregate Bond Index | HFRI Fund Weighted Composite Hedge Fund Index |
|---|---|---|---|---|---|---|---|---|---|
| 8 | 9 | 10 | 11 | 12 | 13 | 14 | 15 | 16 | 17 |
| (0.22) | 0.52 | (0.01) | – | 0.29 | 0.23 | 0.03 | – | (0.12) | 1.00 |
| (0.38) | 0.56 | 0.07 | – | 0.04 | 0.16 | (0.08) | – | (0.25) | 1.00 |
| (0.24) | 0.13 | 0.07 | – | 0.09 | 0.05 | (0.14) | – | (0.02) | 1.00 |
| (0.20) | 0.58 | 0.16 | – | 0.09 | 0.32 | (0.09) | – | (0.09) | 1.00 |
| 0.21 | 0.31 | 0.15 | – | (0.01) | 0.08 | 0.17 | – | 0.24 | 1.00 |
| 0.11 | 0.52 | 0.17 | – | 0.00 | 0.12 | (0.07) | – | 0.10 | 1.00 |
| 0.32 | 0.46 | 0.26 | – | (0.33) | (0.01) | 0.04 | – | 0.33 | 1.00 |
| – | – | – | – | – | – | – | – | – | – |
| – | – | – | – | – | – | – | – | – | – |

The four boxed columns in Table 6.39 highlight the predominantly nonoverlapping three-year correlations of monthly returns between the HFRI Fund Weighted Composite Hedge Fund Index and four asset classes: (i) U.S. large-cap equities, as represented by the Standard & Poor's 500 Composite Index; (ii) real estate investment trusts, as represented by the NAREIT Index; (iii) real assets—precious metals—gold, as represented by the Handy & Harmon Spot Gold Price; and (iv) U.S. taxable fixed-income securities, as represented by the Lehman Brothers Aggregate Bond Index.

For the seven predominantly nonoverlapping three-year periods between 1988 through 1990 and 2002 through 2004, the correlations of monthly returns between the HFRI Fund Weighted Composite Hedge Fund Index and the:

- **Standard & Poor's 500 Composite Index** ranged between 0.55 and 0.85;
- **NAREIT Composite Index** ranged between 0.13 and 0.58;
- **Handy & Harmon Spot Gold Price** ranged between –0.33 and 0.09; and
- **Lehman Brothers Aggregate Bond Index** ranged between –0.25 and 0.33.

Figure 6.32 graphically depicts the predominantly nonoverlapping three-year correlations of monthly returns between the HFRI Fund Weighted Composite Hedge Fund Index and the Standard & Poor's 500 Composite Index, the NAREIT Index, the Handy & Harmon Spot Gold Price, and the Lehman Brothers Aggregate Bond Index.

Hedge Funds: Correlations of the HFRI Fund Weighted Composite Hedge
Fund Index

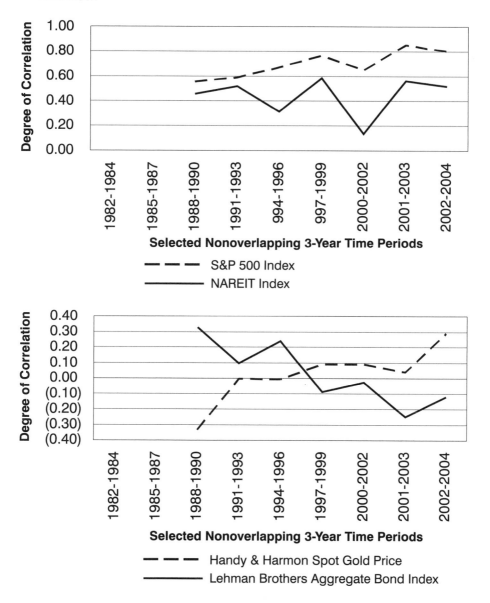

Source: The author.

S E C T I O N 4

# FINANCIAL MARKETS ANALYSIS AND INVESTMENT INSIGHTS

# CHAPTER 7

# RECOGNIZING CYCLICAL AND SECULAR TURNING POINTS

## OVERVIEW

One of the most important aspects of asset allocation and investment strategy is the ability to detect when conditions in the financial, economic, social, and political spheres are undergoing a major shift from favorable to unfavorable, or vice versa. Within the long span of many investors' lives, they are likely to encounter one or more periods of excessive bullishness or excessive bearishness for almost every asset class, and during such times, significant amounts of capital may be created or destroyed.

After placing financial-market turning points in an asset allocation context and distinguishing between the cyclical analysis and the secular analysis of forces affecting assets, this chapter discusses many of the fundamental, valuation, and psychological/technical/liquidity forces that could potentially indicate turning points as of the beginning of the new millennium. This chapter reviews potential *fundamental* factors such as: (i) deflationary forces; (ii) money-supply growth; (iii) the position of the Federal Reserve; (iv) leverage and consumption trends; (v) derivatives and other financial instruments; (vi) the balance of payments position of the U.S.; and (vii) demographics.

This chapter also considers potential positive or negative *valuation* factors such as: (i) U.S. equity valuations; (ii) the duration and divergence of U.S. equity returns; (iii) the U.S. pharmaceutical industry; (iv) Japan; and (v) gold. Potential psychological/technical/liquidity factors that are considered here include: (i) the central position of equities in Americans' mindspace; (ii) the ubiquity of equity; (iii) mania-like equity-market characteristics; (iv) high levels of annual equity turnover and merger and acquisition activity; and (v) the effective transformation of equities into other types of asset classes. The chapter concludes with the identification of selected asset bubble phenomena and questions to help investors identify signs of excess that may presage major shifts in the market climate for various kinds of assets.

## TURNING POINTS IN AN ASSET ALLOCATION CONTEXT

Many investors believe that long-term investment success depends on asset allocation, the timely balancing and blending of different asset classes to reduce risk and achieve targeted return objectives. Equally important, however, is knowing when to significantly overweight or underweight certain asset groups at the beginning or end of turning points that demarcate sustained movements in prices, economic growth rates, and asset market values that may last for up to a decade or more.

These turning points do not always follow the same pattern. For example, in some cases, a pronounced shift from high to much lower inflation, or from moderate inflation to disinflation or deflation, has been sparked by an unexpected event or policy measure that was immediately recognized as a sea change by a majority of investors. In other cases, the shift was subtle, obvious only in retrospect. Similarly, the turning point may be set in motion by one single factor, or by a combination of forces acting together.

Perhaps one of the twentieth century's greatest investors and asset allocators was Paul Cabot, manager of the Harvard University endowment for 17 years. He is credited with shifting Harvard's portfolio from a preponderance of bonds to a heavy emphasis on equities beginning in the late 1940s, in the face of a heavily pro-bond, anti-equities stance in financial markets and, for that matter, among many of the Trustees of Harvard College at the time. When asked about the requirements for success in investing, Mr. Cabot replied with quintessential Yankee brevity and directness: "You need only two things. First, you have to *get* the facts. Second, and much more difficult, you have to *face* the facts."

To face the facts, investors need to regularly step back from the daily, weekly, and quarterly information flow and ask themselves several key questions. These questions include: (i) how will a given asset class perform during the next two to five years or more? (ii) who is going to buy these assets at prices that will produce the projected investment returns, and what is going to motivate them to do so? and (iii) is the market overlooking extreme conditions that are sowing the seeds of radically different price behavior for these assets?

To answer these questions, investors need not only to be able to identify obvious things, such as patterns, linkages, the buildup of pressures, and cause-effect relationships, but also to spot subtle and hard-to-predict factors such as the degree of persistence of forces, the applicability of lessons learned in prior episodes, and the distinction between what changes or evolves in human nature and what remains truly constant and unchanging. Sometimes, it can take decades, or even a century, to revert to a mean. At other times, the mean changes, and prices never revert to the old mean.

Particularly in the advanced stages of major bull or bear markets, investors lose track of the successive order-of-magnitude differences between the difficulty of predicting, first, the *direction* of a price move; second, the *magnitude* of a price move; third, the associated degree of *variance* around a price move; and, fourth, and considerably more difficult, the *timing* of a price move. Rightly or wrongly, investment reputations, not to mention investment fortunes, have been created or destroyed based on the investor's skill (or luck) in predicting or totally missing when an old era is closing and a new one is about to dawn.

As of early 2000, the degree and duration of the U.S. equity market's advance since 1982 had led to two powerfully conflicting points of view about the future direction of equity prices. On the one hand, many investors and market strategists saw America as having entered a new era of high equity returns, propelled by a so-called New Paradigm of technological progress, quiescent inflation, low interest rates, high productivity, and not least, the apparent global triumph and spread of the American capitalistic model. This model included incentivization, shareholder activism, multinational penetration into the global arena, deregulation, flexible product and labor markets, corporate restructuring, free trade, rising living standards, innovation, and risk-taking. This group of bullish market participants viewed U.S. equities as a good short-term *speculation* and an excellent long-term *investment*; they viewed bonds at best as a passable short-term *investment* and more of a long-term *speculation*. A subgroup of these new-era, new-paradigm investors felt that even if they were incorrect, and equity prices moved downward, they would nevertheless be able to sell out at or near the peak of the equity market or protect themselves through the nimble use of hedging maneuvers such as selling stock index futures or purchasing put options.

On the other hand, a considerably smaller proportion of the investment population in early 2000 firmly sensed that the U.S. equity markets were nearing extreme points of valuation, euphoria, investor participation, and narrowness of equity price advances. This group believed that the extraordinarily high equity returns during the last five years of the 1982–2000 bull run heralded meaningfully lower, not higher, equity returns during the early years of the new century, particularly considering longer-term trends such as expanded price-earnings ratios and investors' degree of participation in the equity markets, low savings rates, high borrowing rates, overinvestment in many technology and telecommunications sectors, a high degree of U.S. dependence on non-U.S. capital inflows, wide income inequalities, and even such long-term factors as an erosion in the quality of the public elementary and high school educational infrastructure.

Regardless of any investor's own views at a given point in time, he or she should rigorously scan the horizon for signs of excess, that, appropriately interpreted, may indicate important and impending turning points in the returns a given asset class or a series of related asset classes may generate.

There was no lack of signs of topsy-turviness in the late 1999 and early 2000 investment climate. First, a growing body of evidence suggested that value-oriented investments were undervalued, while excessively high valuations in certain growth sectors were still prized. Second, in many instances, financial markets, not central banks, were considered by some observers to set monetary policy for nations, through the medium of market-determined currency values and interest rates. Third, many market participants believed that the outcome of the real economy was dependent on the financial sector, rather than financial sector outcomes reflecting underlying developments in the real economy. Fourth, variables that were once considered *linked* were seen to be *delinking*—such as the U.S. economy from the economies of large portions of the rest of the world, and annual price changes in the service sector from those in commodities or the manufacturing sector. Fifth, variables that were once considered *loosely linked* were seen to be *linking*—such as equity-market correlations around the globe, not to mention what was seen as an essentially circular and self-reinforcing connection between: (i) the equity market; (ii) the economy; and (iii) wealth-, income-, and leverage-driven consumer spending. Finally, many people believed that powerful new forces, including financial television, the Internet, equity mutual-fund flows, day trading, merger and takeover activity, and indexing had augmented or entirely supplanted the traditional market-influencing forces such as corporate profitability, earnings progress, balance sheet health, and growth in tangible book values.

## CYCLICAL ANALYSIS VERSUS SECULAR ANALYSIS

A critical element in recognizing financial turning points is the ability to differentiate between developments that are *short term*, or cyclical (from the Greek word *kyklos*, meaning "circle"), and those that are *long term*, or secular (from the Latin word *saecula*, meaning "age," or "epoch"). As asset markets get closer and closer to extreme points and potentially meaningful reversals, many investors perversely tend to focus on shorter-and-shorter-term indicators that are in fact cyclical in nature, while erroneously assigning secular significance to such trends and projecting them further and further out into the future.

In fact, in such circumstances, investors should more than ever attempt to bring long-term indicators within their analytical and reflective compass. This process is complicated by the fact that: (i) cyclical and secular indicators only very rarely all point in the same direction—at any given moment in time, some indicators will be flashing a positive signal, others negative; and (ii) cyclical and secular time periods often overlap with, and are in fact comprised of, one another.

The benefits to the investor of being right in his or her opinions and actions, and the costs of being wrong, will produce differing results, depending upon the time frame, magnitude, form, and sequencing of realized and unrealized investment outcomes. Table 7.1 presents a simplified version of the outcomes resulting from four combinations of potential short- and long-term scenarios.

For example, if the investor's short-term, cyclical options and actions (shown in Table 7.1) turned out to be correct, but his or her long-term, secular opinions and actions turned out to be incorrect, the investor's short-term success may be seriously vitiated or wiped out as long-term trends overtake short-term trends. Such results unfortunately proved to be the case for the shareholders of selected TMT (telecommunications, media, and technology) equities who saw their net

**T A B L E   7.1**

Outcomes of Selected Investment Opinions and Actions

| Short-Term, Cyclical Opinions and Actions | Long-Term, Secular Opinions and Actions | Outcomes |
| --- | --- | --- |
| Correct | Incorrect | The investor's transient, short-term success may be seriously vitiated or wiped out as long-term trends overtake short-term trends. |
| Incorrect | Incorrect | The investor may experience highly unfavorable and perhaps destructive investment results. |
| Incorrect | Correct | The investor may be able to survive, and eventually prosper, depending upon the form and amount of realized and unrealized losses versus gains. |
| Correct | Correct | The investor may compound investment capital at advantageous rates of return. |

Source: The Author.

worths rise significantly during the shorter-term (1995 through early 2000), only to decline precipitously in response to the onset of severely unformable conditions as the new millennium unfolded.

Keeping in mind the substantial overlaps between cyclical and secular developments, investors should attempt to monitor those areas that indicate *significant change at the margin*. Tables 7.2 and 7.3 contain a selected list of important cyclical and secular indicators.

It is important to note that the assignment of factors in Tables 7.2 and 7.3 to the "Fundamental," "Valuation," and "Psychological/Technical/Liquidity" headings, or to the "Cyclical" or "Secular" categories, is somewhat arbitrary and by no means fixed. For example, in the late stages of a bear market or the early stages of a bull market in equities, investors may very well rely on *classical valuation measures* (such as dividend yields, price-to-book ratios, and price/earnings multiples) as *short-term* guideposts, whereas in the later stages of a bull phase, these yardsticks may be totally downplayed as *cyclical* indicators and instead treated as *secular* indicators, or even ignored altogether. In such environments, investors may instead tend to focus on other kinds of model-based valuation measures, such as dividend discount models, the real earnings yield, and the anticipated equity risk premium. Investors should endeavor not to let themselves get too caught up in or fixated on one or two cyclical indicators to the exclusion of others, nor to ignore the subtle signals that secular measures emit.

## EXCESSES THAT POTENTIALLY INDICATE TURNING POINTS

To provide guidance to the main points in this chapter, this section summarizes the key conclusions about areas of excess that might have indicated major turning points around the beginning of the new millennium. Because of the degree of publicity and analytical commentary then devoted to: (i) America's position as the world's largest debtor nation, its continuing significant balance of payments deficit, and its financial dependence on foreign purchases of U.S. dollar denominated assets; and (ii) the year-2000 computing problem, these topics are not treated in detail here, even though each factor had the potential to set off a turning point. Similarly, this section gives no direct treatment to bolt-from-the-blue events such as health epidemics, natural disasters, acts of terrorism, social instability, or geopolitical developments involving countries and areas including China, Russia, North Korea, Latin America, Africa, or the Persian Gulf and Middle East.

### Fundamental Excesses Potentially Indicative of Turning Points as of Late 1999 and Early 2000

- ◆ **Deflationary forces** had been unleashed with some degree of severity in Japan and many other Asian countries; less severe, but no less serious, deflationary trends had been encountered in several European countries and in certain U.S. industrial sectors. It was a debatable question whether government leaders could identify and implement the correct mix of monetary, fiscal, currency, and regulatory policies to stimulate demand and reduce supply in a timely enough fashion to prevent deflationary price movements from leading to more widespread declines in prices and/or economic output.
- ◆ **Money-supply growth** in the U.S. had reached unsustainably high levels, which in many prior episodes preceded monetary-policy tightening to cool off the economy and reduce inflationary pressures. The effects of high money-growth rates had been dampened by the powerful deflationary forces in many sectors of the U.S. economy and overseas. Many market

**T A B L E  7.2**

Selected Cyclical and Short-Term Investment Indicators

| Fundamental | Valuation |
|---|---|
| • **Gross Domestic Product Change and Composition**<br>  - Consumer Employment, Confidence, Income, Consumption, and Savings<br>  - Business Output, Investment, and Purchasing Plans<br>  - Government Receipts and Expenditures<br>  - Imports and Exports<br><br>• **Corporate Profits**<br>  - Earnings Patterns, Estimates, and Revisions<br>  - Quality of Earnings<br><br>• **Short-Term and Long-Term Interest Rates**<br>  - Money-Supply Growth<br>  - Shape of the Yield Curve<br>  - Credit Spreads versus Benchmark Yields<br>  - Taxable/Tax-Exempt Yield Relationships<br><br>• **Price Level Changes**<br>  - Raw Materials<br>  - Employment Costs<br>  - Producer and Consumer Prices<br>  - Services<br><br>• **Currency Exchange Rates**<br>  - Current Account Balance<br>  - Balance of Payments<br>  - Inflation and Interest Rate Differentials<br>  - Investment and Other Capital Flows | • **Equity Valuation Models**<br>  - Dividend Discount Models<br>  - Inflation-Based P/E Models<br>  - Tactical Inflation-Based P/E Models<br>  - Forward Yield Gap Models<br><br>• **Real Earnings Yields**<br><br>• **Bond Valuation Models**<br>  - Fisher Inflation-Based Bond Models<br>  - Bond-Stock Yield Spreads<br><br>• **Anticipated Equity Risk Premiums**<br><br>• **Inflation and Interest Rate Differentials** |

Source: The author.

participants appeared unaware that past periods of excessive money-supply growth had generally not ended well for investors.

◆ **The position of the Federal Reserve** appeared to have undergone significant change by the late 1990s. On the one hand, financial markets seemed to expect the Fed to rescue a widening circle of financial sectors when they were in danger of failure, while allowing bubblelike conditions to continue. On the other hand, the financial markets also seemed to sense that they themselves were becoming much larger, and on occasions possibly more powerful, than the Fed.

### Psychological/Technical/Liquidity

- **Investor Cash Ratios**
- **Volatility and Standard Deviation**
- **Supply/Demand Relationships**
- **Gross and Net Mutual-Fund Flows**
- **Investor Cash Ratios**
- **Corporate Share Repurchases**
- **Gross and Net Equity Issuance**
- **Cash M&A Activity**
- **Investor Sentiment**
  - Market Vane Traders Sentiment
  - Investors Intelligence Insider
    Buy/Sell Ratio
  - Investors Intelligence Advisory
    Service Sentiment Ratio
- **Political/Electoral Effects**
- **Technical Measures**
  - Confirmation/Nonconfirmation of
    Price Indices
  - Percentage of Stocks above Their
    200-Day Moving Average
  - Daily Trading Volume
  - New Highs versus New Lows
  - Net Advances versus Declines
  - Breadth Ratios of Advancing to
    Declining Volume
  - Sector Rotation and Relative Sector
    Performance

◆ **Leverage and consumption** continued to reflect the multi-decade trend of increased borrowing relative to GDP by: (i) the federal government; (ii) nonfinancial entities including households; and especially, (iii) the financial sector. Due in part to the late 1990s surge in stock-market values, households' consumption outstripped their income growth. In the process, households' debt increased relative to their disposable income, and households reduced their personal saving rate to zero and below. Other sectors, including many parts of the banking and securities industries, had also moved towards higher levels of leverage. As later events came to show, such increased

**T A B L E  7.3**

Selected Long-Term Cyclical and Secular Investment Indicators

| Fundamental | Valuation |
| --- | --- |
| • Technological Progress, R&D Spending and Effectiveness<br>• Productivity Trends<br>• Investment and Infrastructure Spending<br>• Education, Health, and Security Spending and Effectiveness<br>• Tax Rates and Fiscal Policy<br>• Demographic Trends and Living Standards<br>• Environmental and Climatological Trends<br>• Long-Term Commodity Price Trends<br>• Long-Term Manufactured Goods Price Trends<br>• Global Supply/Demand Relationships<br>• Corporate Profitability and Profit Defensibility Trends<br>• Accounting Standards and Rule Changes<br>• Openness of World Markets<br>• Cross-Border Capital Flows<br>• Geopolitical Relationships<br>• Reserve Currency Relationships<br>• Monetary Policy | • Price/Earnings Ratios<br>• Price/Book Value Ratios<br>• Price/Cash Flow Ratios<br>• Price/Sales Ratios<br>• Market Price/Replacement Book Value Ratios ("Q"Ratios)<br>• Dividend Yields<br>• Market Capitalization/GDP Ratios<br><br>**Psychology/Technical/Liquidity**<br><br>• Merger and Acquisition Waves<br>• Industry Sector Performance<br>• Extreme Preferences (Manias) or Aversions<br>• Financial and Investment Leverage<br>• Societal Views toward Capital<br>• Popular Sentiment and Will<br>• Intergenerational Wealth Transfers |

Source: The author.

leverage increased financial risk and narrowed the margin of financial safety in the face of an economic downturn.

◆ **Derivatives** were burgeoning in total notional amounts outstanding, and substantially surpassed the aggregate global value of debt and equity securities, and even total global GDP. More than 70% of these derivatives were individually structured and traded over the counter between dealers rather than on a registered securities exchange. While these instruments were seen as tools for controlling risk as well as assuming risk, they had played a central role in several significant financial losses and systemic crises leading up to 2000. Derivatives were introducing elements of, and raising questions about, leverage, actual-versus-expected trading liquidity, transparency, complexity, counterparty creditworthiness, operational soundness, systemic risk, and international regulatory oversight.

◆ **Demographics** were widely viewed as a powerful additive influence on flows of funds to U.S. equities markets during the 1980s and 1990s, as the baby-boomer generation began to invest for retirement. No one knew whether or when, at some point early in the new century, investors might shift their focus to the implications of several profound issues, including: (i) who would buy the baby boomers' financial assets at the favorable prices they needed, to generate the favorable long-term returns being projected for them; (ii) the timing and pattern of projected net funds outflows from the U.S. Social Security Trust Fund and private pension plans; (iii) the sharply declining share of the world's population in developed countries versus developing countries; and (iv) significant declines in the working age population in many developed nations.

## Valuation Excesses Potentially Indicative of Turning Points as of Late 1999 and Early 2000

◆ **U.S. equity valuations** in the late 1990s were defended in many quarters as being justified by low inflation rates, low interest rates, low equity-risk premiums, and a variety of other model-based constructs. But in certain other circles, they were viewed as seriously and extraordinarily overvalued. This latter skepticism was based upon: (i) extraordinarily high valuations for many telecommunications- and Internet-related stocks, and to a somewhat lesser degree, for selected other pharmaceutical, consumer products, and technology companies. Skeptics also realized that price/earnings, price to book value, price to cash flow, dividend yield, market capitalization-to-GDP, and market capitalization-to-replacement value ratios for the Standard & Poor's 500 Index and certain other indices were at twice or more the level of their 50- to 70-year median values.

◆ **The duration and divergence of U.S. equity returns** exhibited extraordinary patterns through the 1980s and 1990s. Depending upon how one's definition of a market correction compares to that of an actual bear market, the Standard & Poor's 500 Index from October 1990 through early 2000 had risen the longest (more than 115 months) and the farthest (up more than 420%) of any bull market in the twentieth century, substantially exceeding the second-place holder, the great bull market of the Roaring 1920s. At the same time, the late 1990s were witnessing a possibly unprecedented degree of divergence in performance between: (i) the Standard & Poor's 500 Index and many broader-based indices such as the Value Line 1700, the NYSE Composite, and the Russell 2000; (ii) growth stocks and value stocks; and (iii) large-capitalization stocks and small-capitalization stocks. While neither the long duration nor the wide divergence of U.S. equity returns was sufficient in and of itself to reverse the trend in stock prices, to some observers, both developments appeared to indicate the buildup of market forces and the shift of many investors' thinking into potentially dangerous patterns of complacency and narrowness.

◆ **One non-telecommunications, non-Internet sector, the U.S. pharmaceutical industry,** carried very high historical valuations in the late 1990s on a price/earnings and price-to-sales basis, and accounted for a meaningful percentage of the total U.S. equity market capitalization. In part, supporters of these lofty valuations justified these prices based on the reliability, profitability, and high barriers to entry of the drug industry's income-generating capability. By early 2000, however, this high-margin, high P/E industry was facing: (i) the expiration of patent protection in the 2000 through 2005 period for several high-revenue drugs; (ii) increasing costs for drug marketing and promotion activity; and perhaps most seriously, (iii) early signs of impending downward pressure on drug prices from generic drug manufacturers and several other quarters.

◆ **Japan had experienced severe damage** to its equity and real estate markets, banking industry, and economy by the end of the second millennium. Questions remained about whether the essential conditions had yet been put in place to return Japan to economic and financial health. Some investors were carrying out thoughtful analysis of past and unfolding conditions in Japan in an attempt to furnish important lessons about Japan's boom-to-bust experience, its disinflationary/deflationary price

spiral, its decline into a liquidity trap, and successful and un-
successful ways of attempting to restructure and reinvigorate a
major developed economy such as Japan.

◆ **Gold price movements** tended to be virtually ignored for a
good part of the 1990s by mainstream investors who tradition-
ally believed a rise in the gold price indicated a return of *higher*
inflation and rising interest rates. In a world facing deflationary pressures, a small number of mainstream investors and
gold specialists began to examine whether *downward* movements in the price of gold might be a potential referent to
disinflationary or deflationary price, economic, and interest-rate trends.

## Psychological/Technical/Liquidity Excesses Potentially Indicative of Turning Points As of Late 1999 and Early 2000

◆ **The "equification of society"** is a phrase that some investors
began to use, to refer to pervasive equity investing in America
by the late 1990s. During such equification periods, the media
and popular conversation became immersed in stories of rapid
wealth accumulation, broadening access to successful speculation and investment techniques, and a belief in indefinitely
high and positive equity returns. Caution, risk awareness,
moderation, and financial conservatism tended to be significantly downplayed. Certain market sectors began to reflect
manialike characteristics, and the prices of a narrowing list of
highly popular stocks became increasingly detached from fun-
damental- or valuation-based considerations, and instead were
driven primarily by perception, psychology, liquidity flows,
and technical factors such as short-covering and the U.S. and
global equity underwriting calendar.

Some investors believed that an additional sign of excess was the
*simultaneous coexistence* of all or many of the areas of excess summarized here. Considered together, these areas of excess might very well
have increased the possibility that instability in any one area might
spread to and be reinforced by instability in another area.

The following sections illuminate in greater detail potential and
actual excesses that might help investors identify turning points, under
the same broad headings of "Fundamental," "Valuation," and "Psy-
chological/Technical/Liquidity" factors.

## FUNDAMENTAL EXCESSES THAT POTENTIALLY INDICATE TURNING POINTS

### Deflationary Forces

The last half of the 1990s and the years immediately following the turn of the new millennium witnessed a number of economic developments that caused investors to question whether significant parts of the world economy were entering a period of falling prices, or deflation. A fair amount of statistical and anecdotal evidence appeared to support this point of view. In the 11 European countries then comprising Euroland, headline consumer price inflation (excluding energy and food) in late 1998 and 1999 moved below 1% and core inflation declined to the 1.5% area. In Japan, the world's second largest economy, headline consumer prices fell by 0.3% in 1999, 0.7% in 2000, 0.7% in 2001, 0.9% in 2002, 0.3% in 2003, and was unchanged in 2004.

Price deflation causes investor anxiety because the potential for falling prices: (i) curtails demand, as household and business purchasers postpone their spending plans in anticipation of falling prices; (ii) dampens corporate sales, cash flow, debt service coverage, and earnings; (iii) causes a forced debt liquidation through default; and perhaps as a result, (iv) leads to lower stock prices. Certain supply/demand relationships and widely followed commodity price trends in early 1999 also indicated deflationary tendencies. For example, the price of gold, which had been viewed as a relatively reliable harbinger of long-term price trends and interest rates, fell to a 20-year low in April 1999. In the manufacturing sector, the 1999 worldwide automotive production capacity of 60 million vehicles was met by global demand for only 44 million vehicles. As of April 1999, the industrial commodities (excluding oil) price index, published by *The Economist* magazine since 1864, had fallen by more than 40% in real dollars since its 1995 cyclical high, and stood 80% below its level in 1845. Additionally, the Commodities Research Board Futures index of 30 industrial and agricultural commodities (excluding oil) moved to a 20-year low in early 1999, as Figure 7.1 illustrates.

The price of West Texas Intermediate crude oil appears in Figure 7.2.

Figure 7.2 shows that oil prices were giving off mixed signals, generally moving downward from late 1996 through early 1999 before moving upward in 2000 and 2001, and from 2002 through 2005.

Figure 7.3 shows the path of U.S. wholesale prices beginning in 1800.

F I G U R E   7.1

Commodities Research Bureau Futures Index

1967 1968 1970 1972 1973 1975 1977 1978 1980 1982 1983 1985 1987 1988 1990 1992 1993 1995 1997 1998 2000 2002 2003 2005

Past performance is not a guarantee of future results.

Source: Reuters-CRB Index (CCI).

To several analysts, any declining price trends during one or two decades were rendered more alarming when viewed in a multicentury context. As Figure 7.3 shows, since 1800, U.S. wholesale prices, after declining in three major waves (from the 1820s to 1840s, the 1860s to 1890s, and the 1920s to 1930s), began to break out of their mean-reverting long-wave pattern and progressed generally upward for the next four decades or so.

Close observation of the cyclical and secular movement of prices raises caveats about drawing widely applicable deflationary inferences purely from commodity and wholesale price data. First, commodity prices and wholesale prices may not indicate true underlying trends in an economy whose output is more than two-thirds in services, and well under one-third in agriculture, manufactured goods, and raw materials. The U.S. nonfarm labor force is even more heavily skewed toward services. Out of total year-end 2001 U.S. employment of 135.5 million people, 107 million worked in services, 25 million in

## F I G U R E  7.2

West Texas Intermediate Crude Oil Price Index

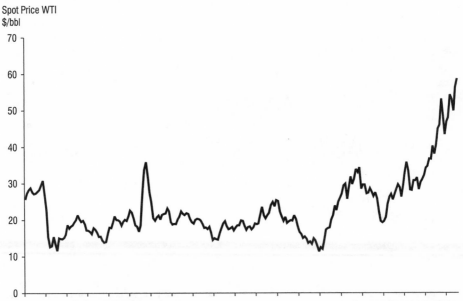

Past performance is not a guarantee of future results.

Source: Morgan Stanley Research.

mining, manufacturing, and construction, and 3.5 million in agriculture. Out of September 2005 total U.S. employment of 134.0 million people, 111.9 million worked in services, 22 million in mining, manufacturing, and construction, and 2.1 million in agriculture.

The price levels of commodities, manufactured goods, and services are influenced by several factors. These factors generally operate through their effects on supply and demand, as Table 7.4 summarizes.

For purposes of simplification, each of the factors influencing price levels is assumed in Table 7.4 to operate individually, with all of the other factors held constant. In reality, more than one factor can operate simultaneously on the price level of goods or services, so investors need to take into account the *net effect of multiple forces*. For example, the supply of a good or service may be falling, which would tend to increase its price level, but at the same time, the demand for that same good or service may be falling even more dramatically, lead-

**F I G U R E   7.3**

## U.S. Wholesale Prices and the Long Wave

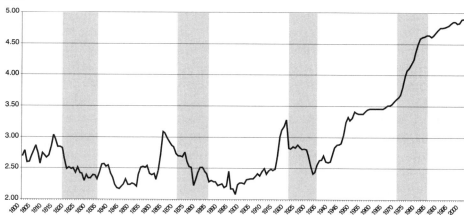

Notes:

Shaded areas denote long-wave downturns.

Past performance is not a guarantee of future results.

Source:  Bureau of Labor Statistics Wholesale Price Indices (1890-Present) and Warren and Pearson Wholesale Price Indices (1800-1890).

**T A B L E   7.4**

## Factors Influencing Economic Activity and Price Levels

| Factor | Effects Tending to *Reduce* Economic Activity and/or Price Levels | Effects Tending to *Increase* Economic Activity and/or Price Levels |
|---|---|---|
| Demand | Decreases | Increases |
| Supply | Increases | Decreases |
| Money Supply | Decreases | Increases |
| Money Velocity | Decreases | Increases |
| Interest Rates | Increases | Decreases |
| Productivity | Increases or Decreases | Decreases or Increases |
| Technological Progress | Increases or Decreases | Decreases or Increases |

Source: The author.

ing to an overall decrease in its price level. This latter force may be powerful enough to overwhelm the price-increasing effects of the reduction in supply. As a result, prices should fall, although not necessarily by as much as they might have in the absence of the supply reduction.

It is also important to note that money-supply, technology, and productivity factors tend to operate predictably only as long as an economy is operating within its normal patterns of supply/demand relationships. At times of extremely high or extremely low demand, however, these factors may exert diminished or even zero impact. For example, in an economy with sharply reduced demand and a severely diminished propensity to consume, increasing the supply of money, increasing the velocity of money, and/or reducing interest rates may not stimulate demand to any meaningful degree, a condition commonly known as a liquidity trap.

Deflationary forces were unleashed around the turn of the new millennium by a confluence of factors, some of which put downward pressure on prices through demand reduction, while others put downward pressure on prices through an increase in supply. Several, but not all, of these factors have been adapted from *Deflation,* by A. Gary Shilling (1998) and are set forth in Table 7.5.

While facing some or all of the demand-reducing and supply-increasing deflationary forces described in Table 7.5 in the early part of the twenty-first century, investors were considering: (i) whether any existing deflationary forces were merely cyclical (short term) in nature, or whether they might be secular (long term); (ii) whether or not deflation in commodity prices and some globally tradable goods would spread to wages and services; (iii) in what ways the developed industrial nations might feel the impact of replacing high-cost, high-income-earning labor with low-cost, low-income-earning labor in the "big emerging markets;" and (iv) what the effects of sustained deflation might be on central government policies and the real underlying economy. In addition, investors were pondering whether: (i) the general level of prices could *fall,* as they did in the U.S. by an annual average of 1.5% during 1871 through 1896, even as real economic output continued to *grow,* as it did by approximately 4.0% per annum from 1870 to 1896; or (ii) whether falling prices might accompany a period of contracting economic output and involuntary debt liquidation, also known as depression.

Neither central bankers, regulators, businesspeople, consumers, nor investors perfectly understand deflationary forces. Various degrees and types of deflation may exist in the prices of goods, commodities, or

**T A B L E   7.5**

Deflationary Forces at the Turn of the New Millennium

| Forces Tending to Reduce Prices by Reducing Demand | Forces Tending to Reduce Prices by Increasing Supply |
|---|---|
| • Reduced government expenditures and deficits were experienced in many developed nations. | • Deregulation and increased competition arose, due in part to the formation of transnational economic zones such as NAFTA and the European Union. |
| • A persistent anti-inflation policy bias was maintained by G-7 central banks, leading to high interest rates for an extended period. | • In several countries, public- and private-sector resources were shifted from defense-related activity to nondefense production. |
| • Demographic trends featured: (i) increasing numbers of retirees, with lower levels of income and spending growth; and (ii) increasing numbers of pre-retirees, with associated shifts from borrowing and spending to saving and investing. | • Competitive currency devaluations put more cheaper-priced goods into local and global markets. |
| • Lower levels of consumption and imports of commodities and other tradable goods resulted from economic difficulties in Japan, non-Japan Asia, and other emerging-market countries. | • The rise of market economies in the so-called Big Emerging Markets—including China, India, Indonesia, Brazil, Russia, Mexico, Nigeria, and Pakistan—was projected to add approximately 150 million new low-cost workers to the worldwide labor force each year through 2009. Projected increases in these workers' demand for goods and services were expected to be outweighed by the significant increased supply of low-cost labor that they represent (a "reverse Henry Ford effect"). |
| • Corporate restructuring led to employment layoffs, cost reduction pressure on suppliers, and a shift of manufacturing and some services to low-cost domestic and international sources. | |
| • Companies invested in information-technology resources to substitute capital for labor (e.g., ATM machines to replace bank tellers). | • Companies overinvested in productive capacity and in the buildup of facilities in low-cost regions around the world, especially in non-Japan Asia, Eastern Europe, and certain parts of Latin America. |
| | • Mass distribution techniques and the Internet were increasingly used for price discovery, corporate and governmental purchasing activity, and households' commercial and financial transactions. |

Source: *Deflation*, by A. Gary Schilling (1998), and the author.

services, and although some deflationary experiences accompany declining output, not all do. Deflation can impose a multiplicity of effects on employment, confidence, income, profitability, leverage, creditworthiness, demographic trends, consumption, savings, retirement, investment patterns, and asset markets of all types. In some way, the existence of *deflationary* forces in the late 1990s may be one of the reasons that traditional inflation-prediction methods were considered to be flawed, as the U.S. economy continued to grow and U.S. unemployment declined below its so-called natural level from 1996 to 1999, without leading to significant wage and price increases.

Similarly, the reality of and the potential for deflation have no doubt contributed to the contraction of the so-called inflation premium in interest rates. This inflation premium is measured as the differential between yields on conventional, coupon-bearing U.S. Treasury 10-year notes and their inflation-based counterparts—known as Treasury Inflation Protected Securities, or TIPS. From an average yield differential of approximately 360 basis points, this measure collapsed to around 60 basis points during the financial turmoil of July through October 1998 and partially recovered to roughly 150 basis points by April 1999. At this level, the TIPS/10-year U.S. Treasury notes spread indicated that fixed-income investors expected the U.S. Consumer Price Inflation rate to average less than 1.5% for the 10 years extending through 2009. Such a differential appeared too low for those economists expecting a pickup in inflation, but to other financial-market participants, this spread gave a powerful sign of the degree to which many investors were also factoring in the possibility of minimal inflation, or perhaps meaningful deflation, during some portions of the 2000 through 2010 decade.

It is important for investors to understand and closely monitor deflationary forces: how they start, what is and may be done about them, how long they are likely to prevail, and the strength of any countervailing inflationary forces. From the late 1940s through the mid 1990s in the U.S., during overexcited phases of classical economic cycles, the Federal Reserve increased interest rates to curtail excessive levels of *demand* relative to insufficient levels of *supply*. Such a policy response tended to work its restorative economic effects within a reasonably short time frame, generally 12 to 24 months. In the late 1990s, in Japan, in certain other parts of Asia, and in a number of other economies, excessive *supply* needed to be withdrawn to match insufficient *demand*. Recovery from generally deflationary conditions has not generally been accomplished as quickly as tempering an overheating inflationary economy, nor are the policy tools considered to be as efficacious. Reducing interest rates has not effectively decreased supply, nor has this measure always been potent enough to stimulate demand.

In short, it may be more difficult to extricate an economy from deflaionary than from inflationary conditions. Preventing modest deflationary trends from developing into a full-blown deflationary spiral depends on a number of factors, including: (i) the overall health of the domestic and global economy, including consumer and business expectations, spending patterns, and indebtedness; (ii) the stabilizing role of the government in the economy (in 1929, government expenditures represented 2.7% of the U.S. GDP, compared to approximately 31% as of 2004); (iii) the degree of room for and proclivity toward decisive action by regulators and other authorities; and (iv) the availability, rigor, efficacy, use, and reliability of fiscal and monetary policy tools at the disposal of the government and the central bank.

## Money-Supply Growth

If the presence of deflationary forces can be compared to an automobile fishtailing as it travels down an icy highway at high speed, the very high rates of U.S. real money supply growth in the 1997 through 1999 period could be likened to the driver of the vehicle *accelerating* in an attempt to *dampen* the fishtail oscillations. The maneuver may work, but it is dangerous and difficult to execute properly.

Because of their effects on economic activity, interest rates, and inflation, positive rates of change in the money supply have tended to offset and be offset by disinflationary or deflationary forces in several sectors of the global economy. Besides the rate of money-supply growth and monetary velocity, other measures of the degree of tightness or looseness of U.S. monetary policy include various kinds of monetary conditions indices, which incorporate short-term interest rates, bond yields and the trade-weighted exchange rate, and a financial conditions index, which is comprised of a monetary conditions index plus some gauge of equity prices. For example, for much of 1999, *monetary* conditions indices signaled neither monetary tightness nor looseness, while some *financial* conditions indices, reflecting the high level of equity valuations, indicated significant monetary ease.

The main monetary aggregates can be measured in several ways and do not always move in the same direction. Monetary growth rates can be affected by shifts in balances between various measures of the money supply, including: (i) M1, which is comprised primarily of currency plus demand deposits; (ii) M2, which primarily includes M1 plus small time deposits; (iii) M3, which primarily consists of M2 plus depository repo liabilities and large time deposits, retail money market funds, and savings deposits; and (iv) MZM (money at zero maturity), which primarily includes M2 minus small time deposits plus institutional money market funds. As the rate of change in the general price level fluctuates, the rate of growth in the nominal and the real money supply may also exhibit divergent patterns of growth. The growth rate of the *nominal* money supply is generally considered to be an important determinant of *price changes*, while the growth rate of the *real* money supply is felt to importantly influence *economic activity*.

During periods of low inflation, investors tend to focus on the behavior of the real money supply. As a very broad measure of transaction balances in the United States, MZM provides a comprehensive picture of changes in the money supply. Figure 7.4 tracks the 12-month smoothed percentage growth rate in real MZM.

As Figure 7.4 illustrates, the 12-month real growth rate of MZM in 1999 was slightly above 12%, the highest rate of growth since early 1987, and one of only three times in the previous 40 years that the money supply had grown this fast. At the same time, real M2 grew by 7%, the highest rate of growth since 1983, while real M3 grew by 9%, the highest rate of growth since 1972 to 1973.

**F I G U R E  7.4**

Real MZM Money Supply Growth

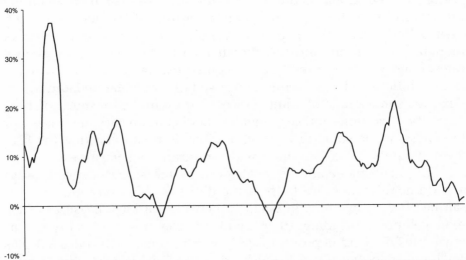

Past performance is not a guarantee of future results.

Source: Morgan Stanley Research.

Partly to supply monetary liquidity to stave off or avoid possible complications associated with the Y2K computer changeover, money-supply growth rates also were accelerating in many other major developed economics during 1999. For the aggregate G-7 countries—including the U.S., Canada, and the United Kingdom—plus the 11 countries of Euroland and excluding Japan, global broad money-supply growth accelerated from 6.2% in 1996 to 8.1% in early 1999. This liquidity growth substantially exceeded 1998 nominal GDP growth of 3.4% in these countries, allowing financial markets to recover from the Long Term Capital Management and Russian debt-default crisis conditions in the third quarter of 1998.

Historical experience has shown that high rates of money-supply growth: (i) are generally unsustainable for any protracted period of time; and (ii) often end badly, with accelerating rates of inflation either in the general price level, or in financial asset prices, which require an increase in interest rates, possibly producing a slowdown in economic activity and a downturn in financial markets to bring the inflation under control. Dramatic increases in the money supply are a potential source of investor concern because the general price level is also established by the velocity of money, and the quantity of money in circulation relative to: (i) the total amount of goods and services being supplied; and, to some degree, (ii) the total amount of financial assets.

Many investors consider the effects of changes in a country's *monetary velocity* to be almost as important as changes in its money supply. If a country's monetary velocity rises (or falls), a given supply of money is able to finance an increased (or decreased) volume of economic and financial transactions. When the general price level is steady or declining, the public appears to accept higher bank balances for a given level of economic and financial activity, leading to a lower velocity of money. When the general price level is increasing at a meaningful rate, individuals and businesses avoid holding excess money, which tends to produce a rise in monetary velocity.

## The Position of the Federal Reserve

Another highly significant potential turning point in the financial realm may stem from a shift in the roles the Federal Reserve System is asked to play, and second, in how the financial markets view the Fed. Since its founding in 1913, the Federal Reserve's role has evolved into that of: (i) promoter of full employment and price stability; (ii) lender of last resort to the U.S. banking system; (iii) defender of the external currency value of the U.S. dollar; and (iv) restorer of the nation's financial fabric when it becomes frayed due to excessive lending based on inflated collateral values.

In the three decades leading up to 2000, pervasive financial deregulation and sporadic but continuing financial reform swept through American—then through offshore-based, and, finally, through many non-U.S. indigenous—credit and capital markets. As a result, the financial markets had come to expect the Federal Reserve to monitor, be involved in the orderly workings of, and, if necessary, rescue a much wider array of global instruments, markets, trading methods, financial structures, and global financial linkages. Due in part to the widespread use, speed, volatility, and leverage of many transactions, the Fed increasingly became cast in the role of firefighter of any serious financial conflagration, almost without regard to its type or origin.

As such, in many instances, particularly in moments of indecision and uncertainty at times of financial turbulence, the Federal Reserve becomes a guide and informal leader of other capital markets participants, occasionally even of other central banks. Because of the increased scale, scope, and complexity of roles the Fed has at times been asked to play, the central bank has been forced to take account of the wider range of perils and implications of its policy actions. For example, owing to the precarious condition of the domestic and international capital markets in late 1998 and early 1999, the Fed was somewhat constrained in its ability to tighten monetary policy in the face of several signs of a financial asset bubble in the U.S., including: (i) evidence of "irrational exuberance" in U.S. equity markets (discussed later in this chapter); (ii) record levels of consumer credit as a percentage of disposable income; (iii) a negative household saving rate for the first time in 60 years; and (iv) 1994 through 1998 growth rates in consumer spending that were double the growth rates in consumer income. At the time, many investors felt that the Fed *should* have responded by tightening policy, but *didn't*.

The Federal Reserve-promoted bailout of the Long-Term Capital Markets hedge fund on September 23, 1998 presented almost a mirror image of these circumstances. In this case, in the views of many capital-markets participants, the Federal Reserve should *not* have responded, but *did*. This line of thinking held that: (i) global financial markets had effectively assumed many of the Fed's disciplinary, countercyclical, and policy roles ; and (ii) the Fed perhaps unnecessarily intervened to preserve a role for itself as a crisis-averter and activist participant in critical financial-market machinations and deliberations.

As the Federal Reserve has provided liquidity to the U.S. financial marketplace in the form of purchasing Treasury securities or lowering the target Fed Funds rate to stave off a crisis in a specific financial sector, in the opinion of many market participants it has sent a signal that it is prepared to act as a savior of, and lender of last resort to, an ever-broadening area. A partial list of these financial sectors is set forth in Table 7.6.

During many of the financial-sector crises highlighted in Table 7.6, when the Fed has finally come to the rescue during a financial crisis, one successful investment tactic has been to buy U.S. stocks and bonds. While such actions on the part of the Fed have had the positive effect of restoring investor confidence in the financial system, a byproduct of such bailouts may have been an exaggerated degree of *overconfidence* that the Federal Reserve will always be there to bail out beleaguered sectors that are in fact far removed from the core banking areas that were the Fed's original mandate to protect.

**T A B L E  7.6**

Federal Reserve Policy Easings to Help Rescue Financial Sectors

| Year | Entity in Financial Straits | Financial Sector Rescued |
|------|------------------------------|---------------------------|
| 1970 | Penn Central | Commercial Paper Market |
| 1974 | Franklin National Bank | Fed Funds Market |
| 1980 | Lenders to Hunt Brothers | Commodity Margin Lending |
| 1981 | Drysdale Government Securities | Repurchase Agreement Market |
| 1982 | Mexico, Brazil, Argentina | LDC Lending |
| 1984 | Penn Square Bank and Continental Illinois | Energy Lending |
| 1990 | Citicorp | Real Estate Lending |
| 1994 | Mexico | Latin America Emerging Market Debt |
| 1997 | Asian Countries | Asian Emerging Markets Debt |
| 1998 | Long-Term Capital Management | Hedge Fund Lending |
| 2001 | Federal Reserve Communication System | Fed Wire |
| 2001 | Bank of New York | Bilateral Net Settlement Arrangements |

Source: The author.

Perversely, the expectation that the Federal Reserve safety net will always be there may have encouraged many risk-seeking financial-market participants to take on greater risks than they might otherwise assume. The risk-assumption mentality generated by the cumulative effect of more than three decades of bailouts and rescues may in fact have pushed the financial system toward greater instability. Investors may thus come to assume *policy asymmetricality*: that central banks will rescue markets or market sectors when they are close to failing, but these same central banks will tend to pass up the opportunity to restrain markets when they develop bubblelike characteristics.

At the same time, investors may have become increasingly aware that often the financial markets take the lead in changing the level of short- or long-term interest rates, and currency-exchange rates, before the Fed intervenes as a policy action. One of the reasons is the enormous amount of daily trading volume in U.S. Treasury securities, U.S. Treasury options and futures, swaps, and foreign currency spot, forwards, options, and futures relative to the size of the Fed's own funds position and securities inventory. Furthermore, foreign central banks hold more U.S. Treasury securities (more than $1,982 billion as of 2004) than does the Federal Reserve System ($751 billion). As of year-end 2004, the Federal Reserve's total assets ($815 billion) were 45% below the total assets of America's largest financial enterprise, Citigroup ($1.48 trillion).

## Leverage and Consumption

As the U.S. economy has grown and evolved since the 1960s, the federal government, nonfinancial entities (including households), and the financial sector have increased the level of their borrowings relative to the gross domestic product. Table 7.7 details these borrowing trends.

As Table 7.7 shows, total U.S. debt has increased from 148% of GDP in the 1960s to 308% of GDP as of the end of third quarter 2005, with the greatest share of the increase coming from the financial sector. Paced in part by the burgeoning borrowing activity of the Federal Home Loan Mortgage Corporation and the Federal National Mortgage Association, the financial sector's credit-market debt outstanding rose from 6% of GDP in 1960 to 97% of GDP at the end of third quarter 2005.

While increased borrowing has allowed greater consumption and investment spending, such increased leverage also carries greater financial risks during an economic downturn. Such risks were brought to light in the dramatic increase in U.S. corporate bond defaults and large bankruptcy filings in 2001 and 2002.

## T A B L E  7.7

Credit Market Debt Outstanding

| Sector | As a Percentage of Gross Domestic Product | | | | | | |
|---|---|---|---|---|---|---|---|
| | 1960 | 1965 | 1970 | 1975 | 1980 | 1985 | 1990 |
| Federal Government | 45% | 36% | 29% | 27% | 26% | 38% | 43% |
| Nonfederal, Nonfinancial | 93% | 104% | 108% | 111% | 116% | 131% | 144% |
| Financial | 6% | 9% | 12% | 16% | 21% | 30% | 45% |
| Total | 148% | 154% | 154% | 160% | 170% | 205% | 237% |

| Sector | As a Percentage of Gross Domestic Product | | | | | | |
|---|---|---|---|---|---|---|---|
| | 1995 | 2000 | 2001 | 2002 | 2003 | 2004 | 3Q2005 |
| Federal Government | 49% | 34% | 33% | 35% | 37% | 37% | 36% |
| Nonfederal, Nonfinancial | 136% | 150% | 157% | 162% | 166% | 169% | 167% |
| Financial | 59% | 85% | 92% | 96% | 101% | 101% | 97% |
| Total | 250% | 277% | 289% | 299% | 309% | 313% | 308% |

Source: *Federal Reserve Bulletin, Z.1, Flow of Funds Accounts of the United States, Table L.1.*

In addition, for most of the 1990s, U.S. households' consumption growth outstripped their income gains. As Figure 7.5 depicts, this phenomenon was accompanied by a significant decline in the personal savings rate.

Figure 7.5 shows that the U.S. personal savings rate declined from around 8% in 1980, to 5% in 1992, to near zero from 1998 through 2004. This decline was offset in part by: (i) the greater sense of personal wealth generated by increasing residential real estate values and by the $4.5 trillion increase in the value of household equity holdings during 1994 through 1999; and (ii) steadily increasing levels of mortgage and consumer borrowing by households as a percentage of disposable income. Figure 7.6 shows the level of U.S. household liabilities as a percentage of disposable income.

Figure 7.6 shows that U.S. household liabilities increased from around 55 to 65% of disposable income in the 1960s, to around 70% in the mid 1980s, to around 119% in mid 2005.

Rising household debt may not give a complete picture of the health of individual consumers' finances. In searching for potential turning points and signs of financial excess, investors need to examine not only the *amounts* of leverage and indebtedness incurred by each sector, but also the *terms* of leverage, including interest rates, debt service and amortization schedules, penalty clauses, and other debt covenants such

**F I G U R E  7.5**

## U.S. Personal Savings Rate

Personal Savings Rate (%)

Past performance is not a guarantee of future results.

Source: Morgan Stanley Research.

as subordination and required financial ratios. To cite one example, the Federal Reserve Board *Survey of Consumer Finances* has reported that a widely used vehicle for consumer borrowing, credit cards, became much more widely distributed in the U.S. economy during the 1990s with riskier borrowers accounting for much of the increase.

In 1983, only 43% of U.S. households had a general-purpose credit card, but by 1995, that rose to 66%. Credit card chargeoffs—lenders' write-offs of bad credit card debt—rose to a 25-year high of 6% in 1997, versus an annual average of 3.5% during 1986 through 1990. At the same time, as the average cardholder profile shifted toward higher overall debt burdens and less-senior employment positions in more cyclically sensitive occupations, these cardholders' survey responses expressed a willingness to borrow greater amounts, and to borrow for generally riskier purposes.

**F I G U R E  7.6**

U.S. Household Liabilities as a Percentage of Disposable Income

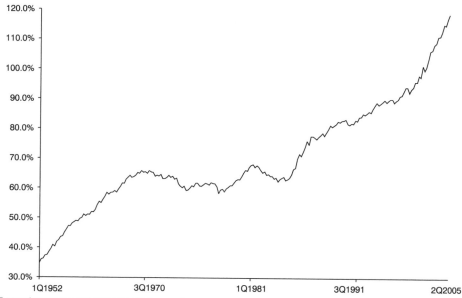

Past performance is not a guarantee of future results.
Source: Morgan Stanley Research.

From 1960 through 2000, while households, nonfinancial corporations, and the financial sector were increasing their indebtedness relative to GDP, within the financial category, the securities industry itself was increasing its leverage, as Table 7.8 shows.

Table 7.8 shows that New York Stock Exchange member firms' capital as a percent of assets moved from the 10 to 17% range (or a 6-to-10 times leverage factor) in the early 1970s, to the 5 to 6% range (or a 16-to-18 times leverage factor) in 2000 through 2003. Over this same time period, NYSE-member firms' total assets rose from $23.5 billion to $3.17 trillion, a 21% compound annual growth rate. Because the "capital" category in Table 7.8 includes not only equity capital, but also subordinated borrowings, the effective leverage factor for NYSE member firms dealing with the public is actually higher than the 2000 and 2001 range of 14 to 20 times leverage. As of 2004, subordinated liabilities of $77.431 billion were included in *total liabilities*. In 2003, subordinated liabilities of $66.694 billion were included in *total capital*.

**T A B L E  7.8**

Balance Sheet of NYSE Member Firms (in U.S.$ Millions)

| Year Ended December 31 | Assets | Liabilities | Capital | Capital As % of Assets |
|---|---|---|---|---|
| 1971 | $ 23,523 | $ 19,508 | $ 4,015 | 17% |
| 1972 | 29,174 | 24,784 | 4,390 | 15% |
| 1973 | 22,584 | 18,830 | 3,754 | 17% |
| 1974 | 22,202 | 18,814 | 3,388 | 15% |
| 1975 | 25,051 | 21,391 | 3,660 | 15% |
| 1976 | 38,181 | 34,268 | 3,913 | 10% |
| 1977 | 43,621 | 39,688 | 3,933 | 9% |
| 1978 | 53,902 | 49,512 | 4,390 | 8% |
| 1979 | 75,004 | 70,005 | 4,999 | 7% |
| 1980 | 102,242 | 95,407 | 6,835 | 7% |
| 1981 | 120,960 | 112,792 | 8,168 | 7% |
| 1982 | 172,141 | 161,362 | 10,779 | 6% |
| 1983 | 214,784 | 200,577 | 14,207 | 7% |
| 1984 | 275,463 | 258,615 | 16,848 | 6% |
| 1985 | 393,205 | 371,166 | 22,039 | 6% |
| 1986 | 452,541 | 422,431 | 30,110 | 7% |
| 1987 | 406,844 | 371,298 | 35,546 | 9% |
| 1988 | 484,879 | 445,851 | 39,028 | 8% |
| 1989 | 552,284 | 513,030 | 39,254 | 7% |
| 1990 | 550,440 | 514,599 | 35,841 | 6% |
| 1991 | 603,535 | 564,421 | 39,114 | 6% |
| 1992 | 744,957 | 701,440 | 43,517 | 6% |
| 1993 | 941,023 | 884,699 | 56,324 | 6% |
| 1994 | 848,706 | 791,857 | 56,849 | 7% |
| 1995 | 1,162,058 | 1,097,759 | 64,299 | 6% |
| 1996 | 1,359,754 | 1,289,014 | 70,740 | 5% |
| 1997 | 1,694,194 | 1,601,763 | 92,431 | 5% |
| 1998 | 1,750,077 | 1,644,423 | 105,654 | 6% |
| 1999 | 1,977,186 | 1,855,684 | 121,502 | 6% |
| 2000 | 2,344,278 | 2,202,802 | 141,476 | 6% |
| 2001 | 2,718,199 | 2,569,275 | 148,924 | 5% |
| 2002 | 2,647,372 | 2,502,799 | 144,573 | 5% |
| 2003 | 3,174,801 | 3,018,188 | 156,613 | 5% |
| 2004 | 3,841,156 | 3,745,007 | 96,149 | 3% |

Note: Prior to 2004, subordinated liabilities were included in total capital. In 2004, subordinated liabilities of $77.431 billion were included in the total liabilities. In 2003, subordinated liabilities of $66.694 billion were included in total capital.

Source: *NYSE Fact Book.*

In analyzing NYSE-member firms' balance sheets, it is also instructive to examine their income and expense experience. Table 7.9 displays income and expense data for NYSE-member firms from 1971 through 2004.

## T A B L E 7.9

Income and Expenses of NYSE Member Firms (U.S. $ Millions)

| Year Ended December 31 | Secs. Comm. As % of Revs. | Revenues | | | Pretax Profit Margin | Net Profit Before Taxes[1] | Estimated Net Profit After Taxes |
|---|---|---|---|---|---|---|---|
| | | From Securities Commissions | Total | Expenses | | | |
| 1971 | 54% | $ 3,124 | $ 5,807 | $ 4,662 | 20% | $ 1,145 | $ 915 |
| 1972 | 53% | 3,210 | 6,008 | 5,139 | 14% | 869 | 676 |
| 1973 | 55% | 2,663 | 4,816 | 4,740 | 2% | 76 | 43 |
| 1974 | 49% | 2,303 | 4,710 | 4,541 | 4% | 169 | 151 |
| 1975 | 50% | 2,949 | 5,927 | 5,116 | 14% | 811 | 415 |
| 1976 | 46% | 3,163 | 6,902 | 5,919 | 14% | 983 | 508 |
| 1977 | 42% | 2,809 | 6,730 | 6,314 | 6% | 416 | 188 |
| 1978 | 43% | 3,779 | 8,832 | 8,148 | 8% | 684 | 339 |
| 1979 | 36% | 4,012 | 11,264 | 10,164 | 10% | 1,100 | 557 |
| 1980 | 35% | 5,671 | 15,986 | 13,721 | 14% | 2,265 | 1,158 |
| 1981 | 27% | 5,346 | 19,805 | 17,666 | 11% | 2,139 | 1,086 |
| 1982 | 26% | 6,021 | 23,212 | 20,186 | 13% | 3,026 | 1,550 |
| 1983 | 28% | 8,348 | 29,542 | 25,732 | 13% | 3,810 | 1,959 |
| 1984 | 23% | 7,082 | 31,148 | 29,559 | 5% | 1,589 | 504 |
| 1985 | 21% | 8,249 | 38,739 | 34,593 | 11% | 4,146 | 2,112 |
| 1986 | 21% | 10,453 | 50,036 | 44,554 | 11% | 5,482 | 2,900 |
| 1987 | 25% | 12,621 | 50,675 | 49,587 | 2% | 1,088 | 653 |
| 1988 | 17% | 8,767 | 51,766 | 49,291 | 5% | 2,475 | 1,633 |
| 1989 | 17% | 10,152 | 59,537 | 57,695 | 3% | 1,842 | 1,216 |
| 1990 | 16% | 8,880 | 54,035 | 54,195 | (0.3%) | (160) | (106) |
| 1991 | 17% | 10,606 | 61,315 | 55,463 | 10% | 5,852 | 3,862 |
| 1992 | 18% | 11,583 | 62,834 | 56,652 | 10% | 6,182 | 4,080 |
| 1993 | 19% | 13,739 | 73,271 | 64,632 | 12% | 8,639 | 5,615 |
| 1994 | 19% | 13,510 | 71,369 | 70,203 | 2% | 1,166 | 758 |
| 1995 | 17% | 15,999 | 96,280 | 88,873 | 8% | 7,407 | 4,814 |
| 1996 | 15% | 18,400 | 120,254 | 108,979 | 9% | 11,275 | 7,329 |
| 1997 | 15% | 21,335 | 145,009 | 132,801 | 8% | 12,208 | 7,935 |
| 1998 | 14% | 24,144 | 170,114 | 160,385 | 6% | 9,729 | 6,324 |
| 1999 | 16% | 29,315 | 183,378 | 167,105 | 9% | 16,273 | 10,577 |
| 2000 | 14% | 33,686 | 245,202 | 224,188 | 9% | 21,014 | 13,657 |
| 2001 | 14% | 26,833 | 194,790 | 184,386 | 5% | 10,404 | 6,762 |
| 2002 | 19% | 27,571 | 148,676 | 141,727 | 5% | 6,949 | 4,517 |
| 2003 | 18% | 25,659 | 144,515 | 127,765 | 12% | 16,750 | 10,887 |
| 2004 | 17% | 26,386 | 160,249 | 146,531 | 9% | 13,718 | 8,917 |

[1]Before distribution to partners and federal and state corporate and personal taxes.
Source: *NYSE Fact Book.*

Table 7.9 shows a striking pattern about the income and expense record of New York Stock Exchange-member firms: the cyclicality of their pretax earnings (both in absolute terms and expressed as a percentage of revenues) against an apparent long-term backdrop of declining pretax margins. In only 4 of the 15 years from 1990 through 2004 did Wall Street earn double-digit pre-tax margins, compared with 6 of the prior 10 years, from 1980 through 1989. Partially reflecting the negotiated-commission era that began on May 1, 1975, commissions declined from 54 to 55% of NYSE-member firms' total revenues in the early 1970s to 14 to 16% of total revenues in the late 1990s.

Another striking observation is the extent of expense growth in the late 1990s. In 1993, NYSE-member firms earned $8.6 billion of pretax income on $73.3 billion of revenues. Looking at 1997 rather than 1998 (which included low profits or even losses for many firms in the third quarter), NYSE-member firms earned $12.2 billion of pre-tax income on $145.0 billion of revenues. Put another way, on the *incremental* $71.7 billion of revenues that NYSE-member firms were able to generate in 1997 versus 1993, they were able to earn *incremental* pre-tax profits of only $3.6 billion, a 5% incremental pretax margin in 1997 versus the 12% pretax margin experienced in 1993.

Related to debt and leverage is the ownership profile of publicly held U.S. Treasury securities by private investors. Table 7.10 shows the changing makeup of the ownership of U.S. Treasury bonds, notes, and bills from 1994 through the beginning of 2005.

From the beginning of 1994 to the beginning of 2005, the total dollar amount of U.S. Treasury securities outstanding increased $755.5 billion. In the same period, foreign and international investors—due to their forbearance, confidence in the U.S. economy, and a possible

**T A B L E  7.10**

Ownership Profile of Publicly Held U.S. Treasury Securities

| Ownership Category | Amounts in $ Billions | |
| --- | --- | --- |
| | 1994 | 2005 |
| Depository Institutions | $397.4 | $142.7 |
| U.S. Savings Bonds | 175.0 | 204.3 |
| Pension Funds | 344.2 | 298.3 |
| Insurance Companies | 233.4 | 151.5 |
| Mutual Funds | 212.8 | 261.9 |
| State and Local Governments | 443.4 | 407.0 |
| Foreign and International Investors | 661.1 | 1,982.2 |
| Other Investors | 632.5 | 407.4 |
| Total | $3,099.8 | $3,855.3 |

Source: *U.S. Treasury Bulletin.*

dearth of liquid investment alternatives—increased their U.S. Treasury holdings by more than $1,321.1 billion, nearly two times the growth in *total* securities outstanding. Partly because balance of payments considerations contribute to the foreign accumulation of dollar-denominated assets, the increase in foreign entities' Treasury holdings has made them by far the largest owner of U.S. Treasury securities. Foreign and international investors' share of publicly held U.S. Treasury securities increased from 21.3% in 1994 to 51.4% in 2005—more than twofold.

## Derivative Instruments

From the 1990s on through the turn of the century, the growth in annual trading volume and in notional amounts outstanding of financial derivative instruments added a substantial additional degree of leverage to the global financial system. Financial derivative instruments include futures, options, swaps, and related structures whose values are derived from the price of some underlying security, index, price, or another financial transaction. Although various forms of put and call options have appeared in the markets for goods and money since the days of the Roman Empire, the modern-era explosion in financial derivatives can be traced to the inception of currency futures trading on the International Money Market in Chicago in 1971, and the inauguration of the Chicago Board Options Exchange in 1973.

From their relatively modest beginnings, the amount of financial derivative instruments outstanding has grown to surpass the total value of all equities and fixed-income securities in the world, even substantially surpassing total world GDP. Table 7.11 shows the notional amounts of financial-derivative instruments outstanding from 1991 through 2004.

Table 7.11 shows that from 1992 through 2004, the notional amounts outstanding of *exchange-traded* financial-derivative instruments grew from $4.6 trillion to $46.6 trillion, of which $24.6 trillion, or 53%, represented exchange-traded interest-rate options. During the same time period, the notional amounts outstanding of *over-the-counter* financial-derivative instruments grew from $5.3 trillion to $181.1 trillion, of which $147.4 trillion, or 81%, represented over-the-counter interest-rate swaps. Taken together, the year-end total notional amounts outstanding of exchange-traded plus over-the-counter financial derivative instruments amounted to $240.5 trillion, more than six times as large as the total 2004 real world gross domestic product of

**T A B L E  7.11**

Selected Financial Derivative Instruments Outstanding

| Instruments | Notional Amounts Outstanding | | | | |
|---|---|---|---|---|---|
| | 1992 | 1993 | 1994 | 1995 | 1996 |
| | in Billions of U.S. Dollars | | | | |
| **Exchange-traded instruments** | **4,639.7** | **7,775.6** | **8,897.7** | **9,282.9** | **10,018.1** |
| Interest rate futures | 2,913.1 | 4,960.4 | 5,807.6 | 5,876.2 | 5,978.8 |
| Interest rate options | 1,385.4 | 2,362.4 | 2,623.6 | 2,741.8 | 3,277.8 |
| Currency futures | 26.5 | 34.7 | 40.4 | 33.8 | 37.7 |
| Currency options[1] | 71.1 | 75.6 | 55.6 | 120.4 | 133.1 |
| Stock market index futures | 79.8 | 110.0 | 127.7 | 172.4 | 195.8 |
| Stock market index options[1] | 163.8 | 232.5 | 242.8 | 338.3 | 394.9 |
| **Over-the-counter instruments[2]** | **5,345.7** | **8,474.5** | **11,303.2** | **17,712.6** | **25,453.1** |
| Interest rate swaps | 3,850.8 | 6,177.3 | 8,815.6 | 12,810.7 | 19,170.9 |
| Currency swaps[3] | 860.4 | 899.6 | 914.8 | 1,197.4 | 1,559.6 |
| Other interest rate-related derivatives[4] | 634.5 | 1397.6 | 1572.8 | 3704.5 | 4722.6 |

[1]Calls and puts.

[2]Data collected by ISDA only; the two sides of contracts between ISDA members are reported once only. Not included in this exhibit are Credit Default Swaps, which as of mid-2006 amounted to over $17 trillion in notional amounts outstanding.

[3]Adjusted for reporting of both currencies, including cross-country interest-rate swaps.

[4]Caps, collars, floors, and swaptions.

Source: *The Financial Times*, Futures Industry Association, selected futures and options exchanges, the International Swaps and Derivatives Association, and the Bank for International Settlements *Quarterly Review, September 2005:* Annex Tables 19 and 23A (*www.bis.org*).

approximately $35 trillion. The 10 largest participants in the over-the-counter financial derivatives market are involved as counterparties to an estimated 75% or more of the total over-the-counter notional amounts outstanding.

During the late 1990s a number of improvements were made to the reporting protocols, and, to a lesser degree, to the regulatory frameworks affecting financial-derivative instruments. Major participants' disclosure conventions include listing derivative assets' and liabilities'

| Notional Amounts Outstanding | | | | | | | |
|---|---|---|---|---|---|---|---|
| 1997 | 1998 | 1999 | 2000 | 2001 | 2002 | 2003 | 2004 |
| in Billions of U.S. Dollars | | | | | | | |
| **12,402.9** | **13,931.8** | **13,552.6** | **14,214.6** | **23,797.7** | **23,810.9** | **36,739.6** | **46,591.4** |
| 7,580.8 | 8,019.9 | 7,913.9 | 7,892.1 | 9,265.3 | 9,950.7 | 13,123.8 | 18,164.9 |
| 3,639.8 | 4,623.5 | 3,755.5 | 4,734.2 | 12,492.8 | 11,759.5 | 20,793.8 | 24,604.1 |
| 42.3 | 31.7 | 36.7 | 74.4 | 65.6 | 47.0 | 79.9 | 103.5 |
| 118.6 | 49.2 | 22.4 | 21.4 | 27.4 | 27.4 | 37.9 | 60.7 |
| 211.4 | 290.7 | 343.4 | 371.9 | 341.4 | 325.5 | 501.9 | 634.3 |
| 810.0 | 916.8 | 1,480.7 | 1,120.6 | 1,605.2 | 1,700.8 | 2,202.3 | 3,023.9 |
| **29,035.0** | **52,268.0** | **62,535.0** | **67,861.0** | **81,455.0** | **101,953.0** | **143,088.0** | **181,132.0** |
| 22,291.3 | 36,262.0 | 43,936.0 | 48,768.0 | 58,897.0 | 79,120.0 | 111,209.0 | 147,366.0 |
| 1,823.6 | 2,253.0 | 2,444.0 | 3,194.0 | 3,942.0 | 4,503.0 | 6,371.0 | 8,217.0 |
| 4920.1 | 13753 | 16155 | 15899 | 18616 | 18330 | 25508 | 25549 |

year-end and average fair values (the cost of replacing the derivative instruments), categorizing instruments by year of expected maturity and by counterparty credit rating, and describing intermediaries' risk management and control procedures.

Financial-derivative instruments can be relatively simple or highly complex in structure, and may be used for trading and investment purposes, as well as for asset and liability management. The creation of financial-derivative instruments has thus allowed a broad range of corporations, governments, and private investors to assume or lay off risk and thus alter their own risk profiles in the process.

What is not known for certain is the degree to which systemic risk has been increased or decreased by the widespread availability and use of financial-derivative instruments. In the late 1990s, a number of highly publicized financial losses, several of which exceeded one billion dollars, involved the authorized or unauthorized misuse of financial-derivative instruments, or the exposure of serious credit risk in the failure of a counterparty to perform according to the terms of its contract. A number of the more advanced financial derivative instruments tend to be difficult to understand, trade with any meaningful degree of liquidity, and value properly in a clear and straightforward fashion.

Many investors have expended significant amounts of money to buy or sell financial-derivative instruments for the purpose of hedging or buying insurance against adverse market moves. To date, the sellers of this financial-catastrophe insurance have generally been compensated at good odds and at good compensation levels. At the same time, numerous financial-markets participants disagree as to whether the risks of financial-derivative instruments have been properly priced.

## Demographics

Investment flows by members of the baby-boom generation in America represented one of the lynchpin sources of net new money into financial markets during the 1980s and 1990s. This population cohort, born between 1946 and 1964, began to set aside funds for retirement as they moved into their 40s, 50s, and early 60s. In numerical terms, the 45 to 64 age group grew from 54 million in 1996 to 71 million in 2005, faster than any other segment of the U.S. population.

While equity markets and the financial-services industry usually benefited from these powerful demographic trends, some observers began to raise questions about who might buy the financial assets accumulated by the baby boomers. Further questions have been raised about whether future buyers could possibly purchase such assets at prices that would provide favorable investment returns when the baby boomers begin converting their financial assets into cash to meet retirement living expenses. In fact, due to the changing U.S. population profile, the substantial net inflow of pension and retirement assets into defined-benefit and defined-contribution plans in the 1980s and 1990s has been projected to become a net outflow from 2015 on-

**T A B L E  7.12**

U.S. Population Distribution

| Age Bracket | Population Category | Percentage of Total U.S. Population | | Population Percentage Shift 2000–2050 |
| | | 2000 | 2050E | |
|---|---|---|---|---|
| 0–19 | Children | 29% | 26% | –3% |
| 20–64 | Employed | 59% | 53% | –6% |
| 65+ | Retirees | 12% | 21% | +9% |

Note: E = Estimate.

Source: U.S. Census Bureau, 2004, *www.Census.gov/ipc/www/usinterimproj.*

ward in the U.S. Social Security Trust Fund and from 2025 onward for all U.S. private pension plans.

Table 7.12 shows the distribution of the U.S. population by age groups in 2000 and in 2050.

Table 7.12 shows that from 2000 through 2050, the percentage of the total U.S. population that is represented by the 65-and-over age group is projected to *increase* by nine percentage points, from 12 to 21%, as the percentages represented by the 0-to-19 and 20-to-64 age groups are projected to decline by 3% and 6% respectively.

Although the reduced percentages of assets-accumulating individuals and the projected net outflow of Social Security and private-pension funds in the second and third decades of the twenty-first century are not of immediate concern to many investors, for other market participants these issues are expected to loom large at some point within the portfolio horizons and life expectancies of baby boomers who have been actively investing in U.S. equities in the 1980s and 1990s.

Another powerful demographic trend with important yet incompletely understood investment implications is the projected increase in world population in developing countries. The U.S. Census Bureau has forecasted that world population will grow from 6 billion in 1999 to 9 billion in 2044, with practically all of the net increase taking place in developing countries. As a consequence, the developed world's population share has been projected to decline as a percentage of the world's total population, from 20% in 1999 to 12.5% in 2044. Concurrent with these trends, the working-age population has been projected to decline sharply in the first half of the twenty-first century in Germany, Italy, Japan, and several other developed countries.

## VALUATION FORCES

### U.S. Equity Valuations

By the end of 1999 and early 2000, U.S. stock-market valuations appeared to be extremely overvalued, yet a number of major price indices and a selected number of industries and companies were confounding the skeptics and moving to new, previously unthinkable valuation levels. Such circumstances were exhibited again and again for several years in a row in the late 1990s in the U.S., and for several years in a row in the late 1980s in Japan. Many analysts and investment strategists argued that the U.S. equity valuations of the late 1990s were not extreme and were in fact justified, in view of low inflation rates, low interest rates, and a low equity risk premium.

Many investors consider the equity risk premium to be the difference between the return on a diversified equity portfolio and U.S. Treasury bills. From the 1920s to the 1990s, the equity risk premium averaged approximately 7.4%. In the late 1990s, several strategists and economists published views stating that equities appeared actually to be less risky than bonds, or lower, perhaps even zero. Judged on this basis, equities' valuations were deemed by no means extreme, and in the opinions of some commentators, were fairly valued or even undervalued on an absolute basis and relative to bonds.

Many of these optimistic investment practitioners—whose ranks were swelled by portfolio managers and analysts who had begun working in the investment industry after the onset of the 1982 U.S. bull market—relied to varying degrees on an array of valuation models. Chief among these valuation models were: (i) the so-called Fed model, which compares Wall Street's consensus forecast operating earnings for the next 12 months, divided by stock prices, with the yields on 10-year U.S. Treasury bonds; (ii) the Dividend Discount Model, developed in the 1930s and 1940s by the gifted economist John Burr Williams, which relies on projected earnings- and dividend-growth rates and an appropriate level of interest rates to capitalize this earnings stream; and (iii) various inflation-based valuation models, which compare the equity market price-earnings multiple with the underlying rate of inflation.

A steadily shrinking and perhaps beleaguered circle of market participants, most of whom had experienced the severe bear markets of 1970 and 1973 to 1974, and the hostile-to-financial-assets decade of the 1970s, held that the U.S. stock market was extraordinarily overvalued as of late 1999 and early 2000. This group believed that many of the model-based rationalizations of high equity prices were reminiscent of the methodologies used to justify ever higher price-earnings multiples and extreme overvaluation in the Japanese equity market in the late 1980s. This group of investors pointed out that for the S&P 500 companies, based on trailing 12 months' operating earnings, stock prices as of late 1999 were over 35 times earnings, more than double the 40-year historical median of 15 times earnings. Moreover, the P/E valuations were even higher after taking into account: (i) some portion of the dubiously excluded restructuring charges that were classified as nonrecurring; and (ii) options-related compensation costs, which many corporations elected not to include in their reported expenses. Including these two expense categories would have effectively *decreased* earnings and, for a given stock index price level, would therefore have significantly *increased* P/E ratios.

According to many classical valuation measures, in late 1999 and early 2000 the Standard & Poor's 500 Index was extremely overvalued, trading at more than twice its 50- to 70-year median levels. Besides price-earnings ratios, these measures include price to book value, price to cash flow, price to sales, and dividend yields. On the basis of the total market capitalization-to-GDP ratio, the U.S. equity market was seriously overvalued, at almost three times the 70-year median. Figure 7.7 shows the value of U.S. equities to GDP at selected cyclical peaks and troughs.

According to the data in Figure 7.7, the total market value of U.S. stocks reached an all-time high of over 200% of GDP in early 2000, surpassing both the 1929 peak level of 81% in the U.S. and the 1989 peak of 140% for the Japanese stock market relative to its GDP.

An alternative way of expressing the early equity market valuation rationality is to compare the market capitalizations of selected companies and industry sectors to other companies and industry sectors. Since many months in 1998 and 1999 witnessed soaring Internet stock values, a number companies exhibited outrageously high equity valuations, all the more absurd in light of these firms' meager revenues and significant operating losses. In many cases, these companies used their own inflated stock to acquire other Internet-related companies at equally ridiculous valuations.

For example, in April 1999, after the IPO of one company that offered customers the opportunity to name their own price for airplane tickets on the World Wide Web, its equity capitalization exceeded $10 billion, more than the equity capitalizations of Continental Airlines, Northwest Airlines, and United Airlines combined. With less than one year in business, this

**F I G U R E  7.7**

Ratio of Total U.S. Equity Capitalization to U.S. GDP

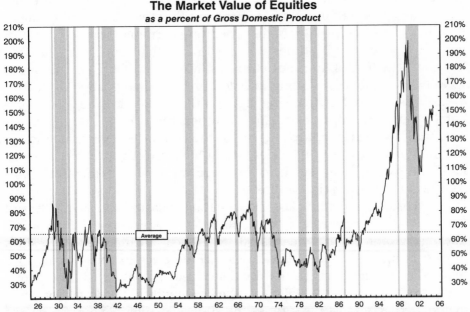

**The Market Value of Equities**
*as a percent of Gross Domestic Product*

Note: Shaded areas represent bear markets. Data after June 2005 is preliminary. The market value of equities includes the market value of the New York, American and Nasdaq Stock Exchanges

Source: The New York Stock Exchange; The American Stock Exchange; The National Association of Securities Dealers; The Bureau of Economic Analysis; Copyright © 2005 Crandall, Pierce & Company. All rights reserved.

Internet-based ticket service company lost $114 million selling $35 million worth of airplane tickets. In the process of comparing market capitalizations, it is helpful for investors to have some sense of the order-of-magnitude aggregate valuations placed on major sector and industry groupings. Table 7.13 shows the year-end 2004 equity-market capitalizations of each of the sector and Global Industry Classification Standard (GICS) groups in the $11.2 trillion Standard & Poor's 500 Index.

As of December 31, 2004, Table 7.13 shows that the sector with the largest capitalization was financials, with a year-end market capitalization of $2.21 trillion. Second was information technology ($1.72 trillion), followed by healthcare ($1.49 trillion).

Table 7.14 contains a useful valuation companion to the S&P sector and industry market capitalization data in Table 7.13.

## T A B L E  7.13

### Equity Market Capitalization for S&P 500 Sector and Industry Groups

| GICS[1] Sector | GICS Industry Group | Number of Companies | Total S&P Industry Equity Capitalization ($ millions) As of December 31, 2004 | % of Sector Market Cap | % of S&P 500 Market Cap |
|---|---|---|---|---|---|
| **Consumer Discretionary** | | **88** | **$1,265,349** | **100%** | **11%** |
| | Automobiles & Components | 9 | 73,668 | 5.8% | 1% |
| | Consumer Durables & Apparel | 22 | 147,356 | 11.6% | 1% |
| | Consumer Services | 13 | 187,891 | 14.8% | 2% |
| | Media | 16 | 410,962 | 32.5% | 4% |
| | Retailing | 28 | 445,472 | 35.2% | 4% |
| **Consumer Staples** | | **38** | **1,126,877** | **100%** | **10%** |
| | Food & Staples Retailing | 9 | 300,631 | 26.7% | 3% |
| | Food, Beverage & Tobacco | 22 | 549,898 | 48.8% | 5% |
| | Household & Personal Products | 7 | 276,348 | 24.5% | 2% |
| **Energy** | | **29** | **1,074,365** | **100%** | **10%** |
| | Energy | 29 | 1,074,382 | 100.0% | 10% |
| **Financials** | | **84** | **2,214,276** | **100%** | **20%** |
| | Banks | 28 | 802,347 | 36.2% | 7% |
| | Diversified Financials | 25 | 841,619 | 38.0% | 8% |
| | Insurance | 22 | 485,516 | 21.9% | 4% |
| | Real Estate | 9 | 84,793 | 3.8% | 1% |
| **Healthcare** | | **56** | **1,491,820** | **100%** | **13%** |
| | Health Care Equipment & Services | 36 | 572,425 | 38.4% | 5% |
| | Pharmaceuticals & Biotechnology | 20 | 919,503 | 61.6% | 8% |
| **Industrials** | | **53** | **1,228,418** | **100%** | **11%** |
| | Capital Goods | 35 | 968,847 | 78.9% | 9% |
| | Commercial Services & Supplies | 10 | 82,093 | 6.7% | 1% |
| | Transportation | 8 | 177,478 | 14.4% | 2% |
| **Information Technology** | | **78** | **1,729,921** | **100%** | **15%** |
| | Semiconductors & Equipment | 20 | 375,166 | 21.7% | 3% |
| | Software & Services | 26 | 599,706 | 34.7% | 5% |
| | Technology Hardware & Equipment | 32 | 755,049 | 43.6% | 7% |
| **Materials** | | **32** | **322,254** | **100%** | **3%** |
| | Materials | 32 | 322,254 | 100.0% | 3% |
| **Telecommunication Services** | | **9** | **349,157** | **100%** | **3%** |
| | Telecommunication Services | 9 | 349,157 | 100.0% | 3% |
| **Utilities** | | **33** | **388,095** | **100%** | **3%** |
| | Utilities | 33 | 388,095 | 100.0% | 3% |
| **S&P 500** | | **500** | **11,190,655** | | **100%** |

[1]Global Industry Classification Standard (GICS) is an industry classification system, developed by Standard & Poor's in collaboration with Morgan Stanley Capital International (MSCI).

Source: *Standard & Poor's, FactSet.* Last Updated: September 1, 2005.

Table 7.14 displays the after-tax net earnings performance of the 10 S&P industry groups, together with their more detailed subgroupings.

Particularly when viewed in conjunction with the industry market capitalizations in Table 7.13, the net profit data in Table 7.14 can help investors evaluate interindustry valuations in the context of aggregate profit performance. All the industries in Table 7.14 earned a combined $595 billion after taxes in 2004, up 29% from $459 billion in 2003 and

## T A B L E  7.14

### Aftertax Corporate Profits 2002 through 2004

| Industry Classification | After-tax Profits ($ millions)[1] | | |
| --- | --- | --- | --- |
| | 2002 | 2003 | 2004 |
| All-Industry Composite | 266,865.9 | 459,239.5 | 595,199.1 |
| Consumer Discretionary | 2,883.1 | 50,875.5 | 72,437.8 |
| **Automobiles & Components** | 4,638.3 | 5,335.2 | 9,019.2 |
| Auto Components | 1,868.0 | 704.8 | 591.3 |
| Automobiles | 2,770.3 | 4,630.4 | 8,427.9 |
| **Consumer Durables & Apparel** | 10,100.7 | 10,626.1 | 14,267.0 |
| Household Durables | 6,915.7 | 7,741.9 | 9,943.5 |
| Leisure Equipment & Products | 1,455.1 | 1,021.7 | 1,362.5 |
| Textiles, Apparel & Luxury Goods | 1,729.9 | 1,862.4 | 2,961.0 |
| **Hotels, Restaurants, & Leisure** | 5,080.4 | 6,054.9 | 9,637.8 |
| **Media** | (39,544.6) | 7,950.8 | 12,909.6 |
| **Retailing** | 22,608.4 | 20,908.5 | 26,604.2 |
| Distributors | 57.2 | 32.3 | 54.1 |
| Internet & Catalog Retail | 103.2 | 538.2 | 1,426.8 |
| Multiline Retail | 11,035.7 | 6,170.2 | 7,413.4 |
| Specialty Retail | 11,412.3 | 14,167.8 | 17,710.0 |
| Consumer Staples | 44,795.3 | 50,821.3 | 60,320.3 |
| **Food & Staples Retailing** | 5,552.7 | 13,740.5 | 15,180.4 |
| **Food, Beverage, & Tobacco** | 28,985.2 | 25,183.5 | 30,735.8 |
| Beverages | 6,871.6 | 7,531.4 | 7,834.4 |
| Food Products | 10,790.6 | 11,625.4 | 12,865.8 |
| Tobacco | 11,323.1 | 6,026.7 | 10,035.6 |
| **Household & Personal Products** | 10,257.4 | 11,897.3 | 14,404.1 |
| Household Products | 7,996.5 | 9,286.7 | 11,060.2 |
| Personal Products | 2,260.9 | 2,610.7 | 3,343.9 |
| Energy | 12,308.6 | 46,959.1 | 69,094.9 |
| Energy Equipment & Services | (4,030.1) | 1,808.3 | 2,905.5 |
| Oil & Gas | 16,338.7 | 45,150.9 | 66,189.5 |
| Financials | 1,07,243.4 | 1,39,815.8 | 1,60,078.3 |
| **Banks** | 52,612.1 | 66,575.0 | 57,735.1 |
| Commercial Banks | 52,612.1 | 48,890.9 | 48,661.0 |
| Thrifts & Mortgage Finance | NAV | 17,684.1 | 9,074.1 |
| **Diversified Financials** | 40,593.5 | 54,620.1 | 57,775.8 |
| Capital Markets | NAV | 26,559.6 | 23,779.8 |
| Consumer Finance | NAV | 8,545.7 | 10,815.7 |
| Diversified Financial Services | NAV | 19,514.8 | 23,180.3 |
| **Insurance** | 11,697.9 | 16,308.3 | 42,323.5 |
| **Real Estate** | 2,339.8 | 2,312.4 | 2,244.1 |
| Healthcare | 47,905.6 | 47,763.6 | 59,888.8 |
| **Healthcare Equipment & Services** | 13,610.4 | 17,583.2 | 20,919.8 |
| Healthcare Equipment & Supplies | 5,968.3 | 6,857.3 | 8,722.6 |
| Healthcare Providers & Services | 7,642.1 | 10,725.9 | 12,197.2 |

[1]Global Industry Classification Standard (GICS) is an industry classification system, developed by Standard & Poor's in collaboration with Morgan Stanley Capital International (MSCI).

Source: Standard & Poor's *FactSet,* using data as of September 1, 2005.

| Industry Classification | Aftertax Profits ($ millions)[1] | | |
|---|---|---|---|
|  | 2002 | 2003 | 2004 |
| **Pharmaceuticals & Biotechnology** | 34,295.2 | 30,180.3 | 38,969.0 |
| Biotechnology | (2,006.2) | 3,201.2 | 3,894.5 |
| Pharmaceuticals | 36,301.4 | 26,979.1 | 35,074.5 |
| Industrials | 36,891.5 | 49,902.6 | 57,469.5 |
| **Capital Goods** | 30,840.9 | 39,050.2 | 50,482.9 |
| Aerospace & Defense | 8,435.9 | 8,926.4 | 11,789.0 |
| Building Products | 672.0 | 682.9 | 800.6 |
| Construction & Engineering | 450.6 | 346.9 | 469.9 |
| Electrical Equipment | 2,087.1 | 2,088.4 | 2,787.2 |
| Industrial Conglomerates | 14,246.2 | 19,607.4 | 23,099.3 |
| Machinery | 4,583.2 | 6,953.2 | 10,780.4 |
| Trading Companies & Distributors | 366.0 | 444.9 | 756.5 |
| **Commercial Services & Supplies** | 8,268.0 | 5,138.1 | 6,923.1 |
| **Transportation** | (2,217.3) | 5,714.3 | 63.5 |
| Air Freight & Logistics | 4,402.8 | 3,981.1 | 5,053.3 |
| Airlines | (9,987.6) | (2,137.6) | (8,916.7) |
| Marine | 46.5 | 69.4 | 98.7 |
| Road & Rail | 3,321.0 | 3,801.4 | 3,828.2 |
| Information Technology | (12,048.2) | 38,494.0 | 68,667.8 |
| **Software & Services** | 9,699.2 | 18,771.7 | 24,170.5 |
| Internet Software & Services | (4,930.3) | (74.2) | 1,593.3 |
| IT Services | 2,349.0 | 5,349.4 | 6,268.2 |
| Software | 12,280.5 | 13,496.4 | 16,309.0 |
| **Semiconductors & Semiconductor Equip.** | (4,949.7) | 4,814.2 | 14,533.1 |
| **Technology Hardware & Equipment** | (21,747.4) | 14,908.0 | 29,964.2 |
| Communications Equipment | (14,946.5) | 5,815.8 | 9,823.3 |
| Computers & Peripherals | 3,706.7 | 13,092.0 | 17,846.2 |
| Electronic Equipment & Instruments | (5,862.1) | (4,359.8) | 1,518.7 |
| Office Electronics | 304.2 | 360.0 | 776.0 |
| Materials | 4,738.0 | 6,750.8 | 21,331.9 |
| Chemicals | 3,884.4 | 4,889.3 | 9,197.4 |
| Construction Materials | 586.8 | 374.0 | 922.1 |
| Containers & Packaging | 500.1 | (192.8) | 1,465.7 |
| Metals & Mining | (450.8) | 692.8 | 7,332.8 |
| Paper & Forest Products | 217.5 | 987.6 | 2,414.0 |
| Telecommunication Services | 12,837.0 | 15,612.4 | 9,585.1 |
| Diversified Telecommunication Services | 16,626.1 | 15,785.8 | 9,433.5 |
| Wireless Telecommunication Services | (3,789.1) | (173.4) | 151.7 |
| Utilities | 9,311.5 | 12,244.3 | 16,324.5 |
| Electric Utilities | 7,826.9 | 9,953.4 | 10,111.6 |
| Gas Utilities | 1,601.3 | 1,829.9 | 1,193.2 |
| Multiutilities & Unregulated Power | (116.6) | 461.0 | 5,019.7 |

compared with $266 billion in 2002. The leading 2004 industry earner was the energy industry ($69.1 billion, up from $12.3 billion in 2001), followed by diversified financials ($57.8 billion), and banks ($57.7 billion).

Coca-Cola provides a specific example of valuation-based analysis as of late 1999. With 52% of the global carbonated soft-drink market, Coca-Cola was widely admired, in some senses representing American business in the minds of many due to its extensive brand projection into the world at large. Coca-Cola was expected to produce 1999 revenues of $19.6 billion, generate a gross margin (sales less cost of goods sold) of 70%, and earn $3.6 billion after taxes. With a December 1999 market capitalization of $117 billion (down from $167 billion at year-end 1998), equity investors were valuing Coca-Cola at 33 times 1999 earnings.

Many investors felt that this was a rich multiple to pay for a company with slowing global unit case volume, a reduced rate of economic profit growth, large intercompany transfers with Coca-Cola Enterprises, and questions concerning the potential application of the Financial Accounting Standards Board's consolidation policy rule. On the other hand, Coke loyalists were of the mind that Coca-Cola represented outstanding long-term value, given its strong international competitive position, the company's powerful brand, its global bottling system, and its immense business opportunities in developing markets, China perhaps the most prominent among them.

Figure 7.8 outlines Coca-Cola's 35-year stock price and quarterly net earnings progress.

As the logarithmic depiction in Figure 7.8 illustrates, Coke's quarterly earnings had grown in a rising pattern for almost 30 years, with slight interruptions in 1974 and in 1987, before beginning to turn down in the middle of 1998. For a great part, but not all, of the 35-year span, Coca-Cola's stock price traced out a generally appealing pattern, divided into three phases. In the first phase, from 1966 through 1972–1973, Coke's stock price rose, sometimes at a rate exceeding the company's earnings growth rate. Then, in the midst of the 1973-to-1974 bear market in U.S. equities, Coke's stock price dropped almost 70 percent.

While this stock price decline was painful for Coke shareholders, equally painful was the fact that investors who purchased Coke shares in 1972 to 1973 had to wait *almost 13 years* to get even with their original purchase price. Sadly, some investors sold out at this point, an unfortunate investment decision in light of Coke's more than 20-fold price gain from 1985 through early 1998.

Investing capital successfully requires discipline, patience, fortitude, and insight. Coca-Cola equity investors most likely to be re-

## F I G U R E  7.8

Coca-Cola Company Stock Price Chart

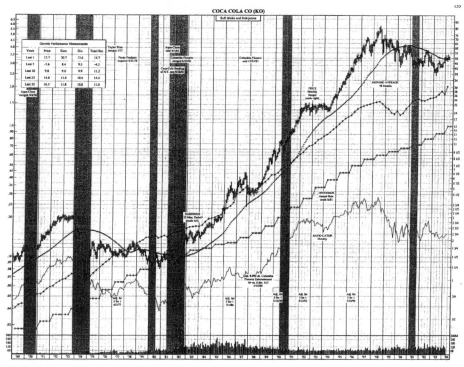

Note: Shaded areas indicate periods of U.S. economic recession.
Source: Securities Research Company.

warded are those who are willing and able to wait patiently for opportune valuations and judicious purchase times, to adopt and stick with a long-term view, to stay the course through varying extremes of valuation, and to evaluate Coca-Cola as a business enterprise rather than as a stock price. At the same time, investors need to pay heed at all times to the *valuations* of asset classes, industries, companies, and security types.

## Duration and Divergence of U.S. Equity Returns

◆ **Duration of Returns:** Viewed within an historical context, the 1980s and 1990s provided generous compound rates of return to investors in the U.S. equity markets. Three features stand out in the 1982 to 2000 bull market. First, bonds as well as stocks provided historically high rates of return during that time period: more than 11% compounded annually for 30-year U.S. Treasury bonds, and more than 17% compounded annually for the Standard & Poor's 500 Index. Second, perhaps reflecting the fact that the U.S. economy was in recession for only 8 of the 220 months from 1982 through 2000, the three bear-market episodes that began in the 1980s and 1990s were of short duration and relatively mild severity, lasting 9 months, four months, and four months, and declining 10.0%, 26.8%, and 14.8%, respectively. Third, the magnitude and duration of the 1982 through early 2000 upward move in the Standard & Poor's 500 Index was unprecedented in the twentieth century. Table 7.15 shows the duration in months and the associated percentage price change in the S&P 500 during major bull and bear market phases from 1929 through September 2005.

A review of the major bull and bear market experiences in the last seven decades of the twentieth century shows that the October 1990 through March 2000 upward move was by far the longest, lasting 113 months, and the strongest, with a 385.0% percentage gain. In the entire century, the closest any period came to this record was the advance culminating in late 1929—the beginning point of Table 7.15. In that upward move, lasting approximately 85 months, the index gained 380%.

Not all market observers agree on what constitutes a bear market. Some investment strategists define a *market correction* as a decline of 10% from cyclical peak price levels and an actual *bear market* as a decline of 20% from a cyclical peak, whereas more strict market interpreters also need to see minimum-duration times (e.g., the peak-to-bottom selloff must last at least three months) before officially terming such a decline a bear market. Regardless of these definitional distinctions, there is little disagreement about the magnitude and duration of the powerful advance in the Standard & Poor's 500 Index in the 1982 through 2000 period.

Past experience with long, powerful stock index price rises may furnish two additional insights worth heeding in connection not only with equities, but also with many other asset classes as well. First, major market upswings, once well under way, can endure a lot longer than justified by fundamental or valuation-based factors. Neither of these characteristics, in and of themselves, is sufficient to catalyze a sea change from an upward trend to a downward one. In the 1990 through 2000 advance and in other bull and bear market episodes, a number of

**T A B L E   7.15**

## Major Bear and Bull Markets, 1929–2005

| Dates | Duration, Months | S&P 500 Change, % | Dates | Duration, Months | S&P 500 Change, % |
|---|---|---|---|---|---|
| September 1929–June 1932 | 33 | –84.8 | January 1966–October 1966 | 9 | –17.3 |
| June 1932–February 1934 | 20 | 137.5 | October 1966–December 1968 | 26 | 38.1 |
| February 1934–March 1935 | 13 | –25.7 | December 1968–May 1970 | 17 | –28.6 |
| March 1935–February 1937 | 23 | 115.3 | May 1970–December 1972 | 18 | 55.2 |
| February 1937–April 1938 | 14 | –45.3 | December 1972–September 1974 | 21 | –46.6 |
| April 1938–October 1939 | 18 | 30.4 | September 1974–December 1976 | 27 | 53.8 |
| October 1939–April 1942 | 30 | –39.2 | December 1976–March 1978 | 15 | –15.1 |
| April 1942–May 1946 | 49 | 138.5 | March 1978–November 1980 | 32 | 52.0 |
| May 1946–June 1949 | 37 | –25.3 | November 1980–July 1982 | 20 | –19.0 |
| June 1949–January 1953 | 43 | 87.4 | July 1982–October 1983 | 15 | 53.3 |
| January 1953–September 1953 | 8 | –11.1 | October 1983–July 1984 | 9 | –10.0 |
| September 1953–July 1956 | 34 | 109.6 | July 1984–August 1987 | 37 | 118.0 |
| July 1956–December 1957 | 17 | –17.3 | August 1987–December 1987 | 4 | –26.8 |
| December 1957–July 1959 | 19 | 48.1 | December 1987–June 1990 | 30 | 49.6 |
| July 1959–October 1960 | 15 | –10.1 | June 1990–October 1990 | 4 | –14.8 |
| October 1960–December 1961 | 14 | 33.5 | October 1990–March 2000 | 113 | 385.0 |
| December 1961–October 1962 | 10 | –21.7 | March 2000–July 2002 | 28 | –39.6 |
| October 1962–January 1966 | 39 | 66.1 | March 2003–September 2005 | 30 | 51.1 |

▨ = Bear Market Phase          ☐ = Bull Market Phase

Past performance is not a guarantee of future results.

Sources: *Portfolio Management: Theory and Application*, by James L. Farrell, Jr., McGraw-Hill, 1996, Bloomberg L.P., and the author.

investment strategists have erred in predicting equity market downturns merely because of the then-current longevity and percentage gain of the stock market's upward phase.

Second, when the 10- or 15-year compound rates of return from owning equities reach high levels, they generally do not persist at these high levels for long periods of time. Instead, in the aftermath of multiyear high 10- or 15-year return experiences from investing in equities, stock ownership has generally offered only modest returns at best, or zero to neutral returns at worst. Based on the highly positive multiyear results from owning the S&P in the 1980s and 1990s, a small but growing number of investors began to temper their expectations for the years following the post-2000 period.

- ◆ **Divergence of Returns:** The latter years of the 1990s and early 2000 witnessed a four-pronged and widening gap between: (i) the Standard & Poor's 500 Index and broader market indices (such as the Value Line 1700 and the NYSE composite); (ii) large-capitalization stocks (such as those in the S&P 500 or the NASDAQ Index) and small-capitalization stocks (such as the Russell 2000 Index); (iii) growth-stock indices (such as the Russell 1000 Growth Index, or the S&P/Barra Growth index), and value-stock indices (such as the Russell 1000 Value Index, or the S&P/Barra Value Index); and (iv) between the very largest stocks in the S&P 500 and all the rest of the companies in the index.

The continuing and possibly unprecedented divergence in performance between the S&P 500 and NASDAQ indices on the one hand, and the NYSE Composite, Value Line 1700, and Russell 2000 indices on the other hand, became an increasingly worrisome sign of a narrower and narrower investor focus on a diminishing number of stocks that were effectively relegated to superstar, or "nifty-fifty" status. As further evidence of investors buying a limited number of stocks almost without regard to the prices, in the first quarter of 1999, just 21 stocks accounted for all of the S&P 500's gain. One-third of the 1999 first quarter's gain came from two stocks, Microsoft and America Online. Such a constriction in price leadership possibly indicated a lack of investor confidence in the broad market and was reminiscent of market price behavior near important market tops reached in 1929, 1968, and 1972–1973.

Figure 7.9 provides perspective on the relative price performance of small-cap stocks compared to large-cap stocks from January 1979 through September 2005.

With the Russell 2000 and the S&P 500 indices each indexed to the same starting point in January 1980, an *upward* slope to Figure 7.9 indicates relative *outperformance by the Russell 2000* (small-cap stocks) and a *downward* slope to the graph indicates relative *outperformance by the S&P 500* (large-cap stocks). With the exception of the 1980 to 1982 and the 1990 to 1994 periods, the S&P 500 (large-cap stocks) outperformed the Russell 2000 (small-cap stocks) virtually uninterrupted from 1994 through early 2000. One consequence of this unrelenting outperformance by the Standard & Poor's 500 Index was the inability of most equity mutual funds to beat the Standard & Poor's 500 Index. In 1998, 90% of U.S. domestic diversified equity funds failed to do so, underperforming the Standard & Poor's 500 Index return by 900 basis points, or 9%. In 1997, the average U.S. domestic equity fund underperformed the Standard & Poor's 500 Index by 2100 basis points, or 21%.

Figure 7.10 contains insight into the 25-year relative price performance of value stocks versus growth stocks.

**F I G U R E  7.9**

Russell 2000 Relative to S&P 500

(Indexed to Jan. 1980 = 100)

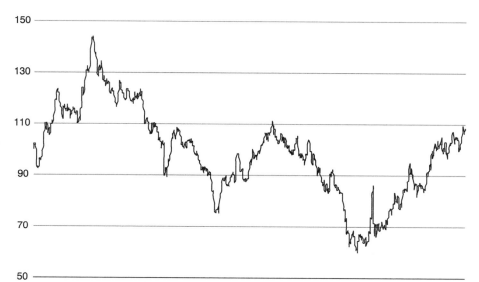

Past performance is not a guarantee of future results.

Source: Morgan Stanley Research.

With the Russell 1000 Value and the Russell 1000 Growth indices each indexed to the same starting point, an upward slope to Figure 7.10 indicates relative *outperformance by the Russell 1000 Value Index,* and a downward slope indicates relative *outperformance by the Russell 1000 Growth Index.* With several intervening periods of interruption, value stocks generally outperformed growth stocks from late 1980 through early 1988, and again in 1991 to 1993. In 1997, 1998, and 1999, however, growth stocks significantly outperformed value stocks. When assessing the growth-stock versus value-stock investment decision, investors generally assess several factors, including: (i) the price-earnings ratio relative to the earnings growth rate; (ii) forecast earnings growth; (iii) the *earnings surprise factor,* as evidenced by whether reporting companies' results exceed or fall short of consensus earnings estimates; (iv) the *earnings estimate revision factor,* as evidenced by whether analysts are revising their forecasts for

**F I G U R E  7.10**

Russell 1000 Value versus Russell 1000 Growth

(Indexed to Jan. 1980=100)

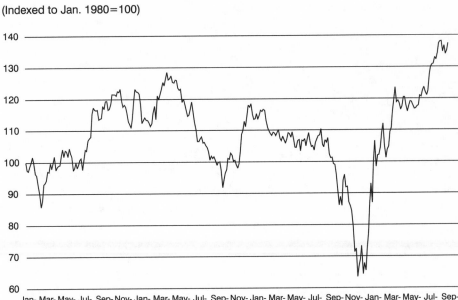

Past performance is not a guarantee of future results.

Source: Morgan Stanley Research.

companies' earnings upward or downward; and (v) the price-earnings ratio relative to past history and to existing market valuations.

The divergence between a limited number of highly prized companies and the large number of relatively neglected companies in the late 1990s was manifested in the wide disparity in S&P industry sector performance. Table 7.16 shows the one-, three-, and five-year returns ending December 31, 1998 of the main sectors of the Standard & Poor's 500 Index.

For the one-year period ending December 31, 1998, Table 7.16 shows that the two highest-performing S&P industry sectors were technology and healthcare, advancing 81% and 42%, respectively, versus 27% for the Standard & Poor's Index overall and declines of 3% and 7%, respectively for the two bottom-performing industry sectors, transportation and basic industries. This same performance disparity occurred during a longer time span. For the five-year period from 1994 through 1998, technology and healthcare *gained* 566% and 358%, respectively (that is, these two sectors almost septupled and quintupled),

**T A B L E  7.16**

Multiyear Price Performance of S&P 500 Sectors

| | Price Performance as of 12/31/98 | | |
|---|---|---|---|
| Sector | 5 Years 1994–1998 | 3 Years 1996–1998 | 1 Year 1998 |
| Technology | 566% | 302% | 81% |
| Healthcare | 358 | 149 | 42 |
| Consumer Nondurables | 154 | 125 | 37 |
| Utilities | 112 | 82 | 35 |
| Consumer Durables | 75 | 78 | 29 |
| S&P 500 | 164 | 100 | 27 |
| Capital Goods-Industrials | 155 | 86 | 12 |
| Energy | 81 | 70 | 11 |
| Financial | 215 | 119 | 11 |
| Consumer Noncyclicals | 169 | 72 | 10 |
| Transportation | 58 | 41 | (3) |
| Basic Industries | 36 | 17 | (7) |

Past performance is not a guarantee of future results.

Source: Morgan Stanley Research.

while the transportation and basic-industry sectors managed five-year gains of 58% and 36%, respectively.

## U.S. Pharmaceutical Stocks

At valuation levels prevailing as of December 31, 2001, the U.S. pharmaceutical industry represented a prime example of the valuation-related issues facing investors. With a 2001 year-end market capitalization of $1.2 trillion (within the overall S&P healthcare sector valuation of $1.5 trillion, representing approximately 11% of the value of the Standard & Poor's 500 Index), 2001 revenues of $229 billion, and 2001 net income of $40 billion, the industry as a whole was selling for 5.6 times revenues and fully 33 times trailing 12 months' profits. These lofty valuations were due in part to: (i) the profitability of the pharmaceutical industry (with 70 to 85% gross margins and 29% operating profit margins); (ii) the industry's prior track record of reliable profit growth; and (iii) high barriers to entry, stemming from the long lead times and substantial knowhow involved in managing the research and development process, U.S. Food and Drug Administration approval procedures, and a global marketing network.

Perhaps mindful of the flow of life-extending and lifestyle-quality-enhancing new drugs, as well as the fact that many drugs actually reduce overall healthcare costs by reducing hospitalization, the U.S. was virtually alone among developed nations in its lower relative degree of price controls on the drug market. In addition, in the mid 1990s, the U.S. Congress had effectively increased the net present value of new drugs by reducing by one and a half years the time needed to comply with the FDA drug approval process.

By the end of the 1990s, and in 2000 to 2001, despite the successful launch of several high-revenue drugs by individual companies, the U.S. pharmaceutical industry found itself facing: (i) the imminent run-off of 17-year patent protection on many of its more profitable drugs; (ii) a growing importance, competitiveness, and cost-intensity of drug marketing activity; and perhaps most serious, (iii) signs of impending downward pressure on drug prices from several important sectors of the drug-buying population.

One source of downward price pressure emanated from Medicaid (a means-tested, federal-state, healthcare-expense-matching program covering individuals under the age of 65) to meet or exceed the average 24% discount from normal selling prices that the U.S. Public Health Service, the U.S. Department of Defense, and the Veterans Administration paid. Health Maintenance Organizations (HMOs) were applying similar purchasing-power leverage to pharmaceutical companies, and as more and more individuals and families who formerly paid full prices joined HMOs, their aggregate leverage increased.

Another longer-term potential source of downward price pressure stemmed from the work of the National Bipartisan Commission on the Future of Medicare, which sought ways and means of sharing the costs of an unfunded Medicare liability—estimated at more than $18 trillion—between taxpayers, patients, and the healthcare industry. As of early 2002, Medicare reimbursed expenses for drugs only when they were administered as part of a patient's stay in the hospital. The U.S. government was expected in the short term to extend its policy of mandated drug-price discounts to Medicare payments, but the drug industry was more worried that both parties in Congress would continue to seek to curry voter favor by extending Medicare's coverage to a larger share of seniors' drug expenses.

As of 2002, seniors (the 65-and-over age cohort) represented *one-eighth* of the U.S. population, *one-quarter* of total U.S. voters, *one-third* of U.S. domestic pharmaceutical usage, and in part due to seniors' generally paying the full retail price for drugs out of their own pockets, perhaps as much as *one-half* of the pharmaceutical industry's total gross profits. The potential financial impact of U.S. seniors paying discounted rather than full prices for drugs was estimated to amount to $8 billion in reduced revenues and $6 billion or more in reduced aftertax profits, or 20% of the drug industry's total 2001 aftertax profits.

Figure 7.11 displays the indexed stock-price performance for the pharmaceutical industry and for local equity prices for the U.S., Europe, the U.K., and Japan, with the respective pharmaceutical and broad equity-market indices for all four areas set at a common base of 100 at the beginning of calendar year 1983.

What is immediately apparent in Figure 7.11 is the extraordinary rise in pharmaceutical equity prices in the U.S., Europe, and the U.K., both on an absolute basis and relative to the increase in the broad equity-market price indices in each of these three regions. Table 7.17 summarizes this phenomenon.

The dramatic stock-price performance of the pharmaceutical industry from 1983 through 2001 translates into pharmaceutical-industry equity indices that were more than 22 times their 1983 value in the U.S., 21 times their 1983 value in Europe, more than 17 times their 1983 value in the U.K., and just more than 2.5 times their 1983 value in Japan. Pharmaceutical stock prices declined significantly in all four regions from 1992 through 1994, due to politically driven proposals to restructure the U.S. healthcare industry, an important market not only for U.S. pharmaceutical companies, but also for their European, U.K., and Japanese counterparts. In fact, a large part of the powerful upward surge in pharmaceutical stock prices from 1983 through 2001 time frame was compressed into the 1994 through 2000 years.

In addition, a number of pharmaceutical companies were facing competitive pressures from generic drug manufacturers and a few companies had come under the critical scrutiny of the U.S. FDA for faulty manufacturing standards. Investors in U.S. pharmaceutical equities faced an extraordinarily profitable industry, representing approximately 11% of the total U.S. equity market capitalization, that had risen 23-fold in the 16 years from 1983 through the end of 2001, counterpoised against potential patent, pricing, and political pressures. Pharmaceutical-stock investors' fortunes, and possibly to some degree the direction of U.S. equity prices, highly depended on whether 40 times trailing earnings was an appropriate level to pay for U.S. pharmaceutical shares in such an environment.

F I G U R E   7.11

Pharmaceutical Sector Stock Price Performance

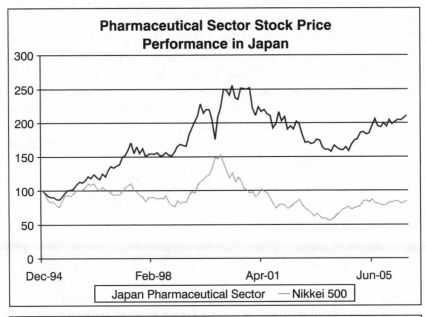

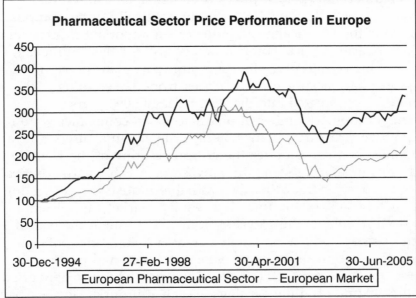

Source: Morgan Stanley Investment Research Department.

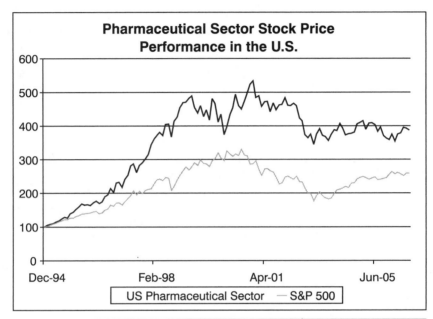

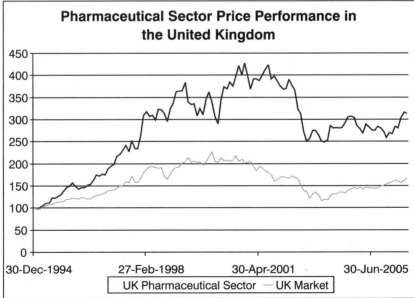

**T A B L E  7.17**

Comparative Pharmaceutical and Broad Equity Market Stock Price Performance, 1983–2001 (Indexed to a base of 100 on January 1, 1983)

| Region | Broad Equity Market | Compound Annual Growth Rate | Pharmaceutical Industry Equities | Compound Annual Growth Rate |
|---|---|---|---|---|
| United States | 790.1 | 11.5% | 2,208.7 | 17.7% |
| Europe | 809.7 | 11.6% | 2,095.1 | 17.4% |
| United Kingdom | 721.3 | 11.0% | 1,753.5 | 16.3% |
| Japan | 157.3 | 2.4% | 259.3 | 5.1% |

Comparative Pharmaceutical and Broad Equity Market Stock Price Performance, 1994–1H2005 (Indexed to a base of 100 on December 31, 1994)

| Region | Broad Equity Market | Compound Annual Growth Rate | Pharmaceutical Industry Equities | Compound Annual Growth Rate |
|---|---|---|---|---|
| United States | 259.4 | 9.5% | 386.2 | 13.7% |
| Europe | 220.3 | 7.8% | 334.2 | 12.2% |
| United Kingdom | 166.8 | 5.0% | 313.6 | 11.5% |
| Japan | 85.4 | −1.5% | 210.8 | 7.4% |

Past performance is not a guarantee of future results.

Source: Morgan Stanley Research.

## Japan

No discussion of valuation extremes that may potentially indicate turning points should omit consideration of Japan, both for the lessons gleaned from its extremely overvalued equity market in the late 1980s, as well as the painful aftermath of this overvaluation—including the multiyear damage to Japan's equity prices, real-estate values, and financial industry. In retrospect, many of the same features of the Japanese economic, financial, and social system that experts the world over adulated were later blamed for contributing to the country's severely straitened circumstances.

One of the prime examples of these core strengths-turned-into-flaws was the commonly held view of capital in Japan as just another factor of production that could be consumed much like labor or raw materials, rather than as an asset entitled to earn an appropriate rate of return. Perhaps related to this view was Japan's organization in many ways more as a planned economy than as a market-driven economy fully competitive in labor practices, distribution methods, and pricing regimes. The massive inflation, and then deflation, of Japan's financial and real asset bubble stemmed, in part, from: (i) an 8% annual rate of growth in monetary liquidity (defined as M-2 plus certificates of deposit) through most of the 1980s, culminating in 10-to-12% yearly growth rates in the latter years, followed by (ii) a sudden, sharp Bank of Japan-induced decrease in the monetary liquidity growth rate, beginning in 1990, and dropping to 0% annual growth by 1992. Two factors associated with the Japanese market's protracted demise included: (i) nonperforming bank loans, estimated at almost 30% of Japan's GDP at their peak in the aggregate, and (ii) a widespread loss of faith in the government's ability and willingness to bail out insolvent banks.

From the Nikkei 225 stock index's peak closing level of 38,916 on December 29, 1989, the index sank to below 10,000 in 2002 and to 7,607 in April 2003. For a period during this decline, from a level of 12,880 on October 9, 1998, the Nikkei 225 gained 30% by April 1999, to nearly 17,000, representing a 22% increase in yen terms. The October 1998 through April 1999 recovery was broad-based, with small-capitalization stocks also improving sharply. Reflecting investor sentiment that the Japanese banking system no longer represented a major threat to the health of the global financial system, bank stocks rose 50% and contributed one-third of the Nikkei's rise.

The equity market rally of early 1999 took place against a backdrop of gloomy economic developments and still-high valuations, and appeared to be driven by investor sentiment and liquidity flows more than by fundamental economic reform and rehabilitation. Despite a number of deteriorating fundamentals in the economy, non-Japanese investors provided much of the stock market recovery's 1998 through 1999 momentum, due to: (i) shifts in their significantly underweight-Japan asset allocations, for fear of missing out on a rally in Japanese equities; (ii) enthusiasm over the pickup in restructuring activity by Japanese corporations (including employee layoffs, cutbacks in new capital spending, the sale or closure of noncore businesses, and merger and acquisition activity, frequently involving non-Japanese buyers); (iii) signs of government recognition of the dangers of a financial meltdown, setting off a flurry of responses—the recapitalization of the banking system, the closure of several weak banks and the nationalization of two others, the establishment of a Financial Reconstruction Commission to oversee bank reform, and the tightening of bad debt reserve guidelines; (iv) accelerated stimulus by the public sector, through sizeable government spending programs and April 1999 cuts in personal income taxes, corporate taxes, and residential taxes; and (v) a growing awareness by non-Japanese investors of the wide performance differential that had persisted between Japan and other major equity markets in the late 1990s.

As of year-end 1998, although non-Japanese investors owned approximately 13% of the overall Japanese equity market, a much higher percentage of the freely traded supply of equities, and substantial percentages of many well-known Japanese corporations (for example, 45% of Sony, 23% of Kao Soap, and 23% of Takeda Chemical), their investment activity had in many cases not been a harbinger of higher stock prices. For example, from 1991 through 1998, non-Japanese investors invested a net $228 billion in Japanese equities, yet the Japanese market declined 35% during this period.

The Japanese economy remained in a precarious position during the 1999 through 2002 time frame, as Japan found that declining consumer spending and business spending were virtually unaffected by the lowest interest rates in several centuries. Ultimately, economic recovery in any nation depends on whether private demand turns upward, and many economic indicators from 1999 through 2002 in Japan, such as household spending and businesses' capital spending, were either very mixed or else not hopeful in this regard.

In light of numerous quarters of GDP contraction, large numbers of bankruptcies, low levels of corporate profitability, and Japanese consumers saving very high percentages (10 to 15%) of their income in 1999–2002, skeptical investors continued to question whether private sector demand was falling faster than public sector demand was rising. In such an environment, many potentially effective policy actions also carried harmful side effects that ran the risk of further weakening the economy.

For instance, many of the Japanese government's stimulative spending policies were intended to solidify the ruling party's political interests rather than hasten deregulation and promote deep-rooted corporate restructuring. Even the long-sought corporate cost-cutting and restructuring measures had negative consequences, including reduced capital outlays, worker layoffs, and cuts in overtime, bonuses, and wages, all of which encouraged consumers to reduce their spending. Partly as a result of increased corporate restructuring, Japanese unemployment rose to a 50-year record of 5.7% as of March 2002, to 3.79 million individuals. An additional perverse result of a positive development was grounded in concerns over a possible slackening of the necessary reformist zeal each time the Nikkei equity index was able to mount a sustained advance and the Japanese banking system was able to avoid a financial catastrophe.

For example, as of February 1999, the Topix Index of Japanese equity prices was trading at 173 times earnings, and if bank stocks were excluded, at 60 times earnings. Even after their 10-year decline, and amidst signs of a nascent rebound in early 1999, Japanese equities remained expensive compared to the U.S. equity market's 50-to-70-year median levels, on a price-earnings, price-to-book value, price-to-replacement value, and return-on-equity basis. For the latter measure, assuming that large Japanese companies' announced restructuring plans would turn out as successfully as anticipated, the return on equity of the Nikkei 225 companies was projected to increase from the 1998 level of 1.7% to only 6% to 7%, still well below the 18-to-20% average ROE for the S&P 500 in the late 1990s, much less the 10-to-12% average ROE for the S&P 500 prevailing in the early 1980s.

Various sporadic rallies in Japanese equity prices in 1999, 2000, 2001, and 2002 appeared to indicate an eventual positive turnaround in wealth levels, confidence, spending, and the economy, but several essential elements of a return to financial health remained in doubt. First, Japanese corporate managements had been perceived as fully capable of *not* following through on their announced cost-cutting and restructuring programs, and at many companies, it remained unclear exactly how important profitability and ROE ranked as criteria of management performance. Second, the Japanese government-led bank bailouts were not seen as reflecting the political will necessary to allow the bankruptcy or significant downsizing of weak borrowers; instead, bank bailouts were viewed as effectively keeping marginal, inefficient borrowers afloat. Third, the substantial levels of accumulated wealth and the high standard of living in Japan meant that people had not undergone anywhere near the degree of financial and social disruption experienced in many other parts of Asia or in the high-unemployment countries and industries in Europe. Japan's substantial wealth, its history, and its social mores may have inspired substantial levels of cautious, conservative aversion to risk and risk-taking, with a minuscule national venture capital industry and an innovation flow emanating primarily from large companies perhaps more than from individuals.

Fourth, a sustainable recovery in Japan depended on the writeoff of insupportable debts and the retirement of excess capacity, which required facing hard decisions about which companies' capacity should stay and which should be shuttered, possibly in favor of relocation to lower-cost areas such as China and other southeast Asian countries. Fifth, these decisions tended to be clouded by: (i) an inadequate legal infrastructure, and judicial-system bottlenecks relating to bankruptcy and creditors' rights; (ii) a small absolute number of bank regulators and accounting/auditing resources; and (iii) continuing intermittent episodes of apparent political progress, followed by what turned out to be political paralysis. Sixth, to offset the effects of its aging population, Japan's economic revitalization efforts were seen as needing to raise not only the *level* of productivity, but also the *growth rate* of productivity, by approximately 0.5% annually for a decade or more.

Finally, the process of bailing out the banks and attempting to reflate the Japanese economy were without significant costs. For example, some leading global debt-rating services downgraded the debt rating of Japan after total Japanese public-sector debt outstanding reached more than $6 trillion, exceeding 120% of GDP, up from 60% of GDP in 1993. To help pay for their stimulative policies, the Japanese authorities issued large amounts of Japanese-government bonds. Questions arose about whether significant acquisitions of JGBs would be carried out by: (i) the Trust Fund Bureau of the Ministry of Finance; and (ii) the Bank of Japan, via direct purchases through a controversial process known as monetization. Citing the likely unfavorable results of direct monetization, including higher bond yields, a weaker yen, and the lessening of incentives to reform, for quite some time in 1999 and 2000 the Bank of Japan resisted monetization. As a result, pressure was put on the capital markets and the private sector to absorb a large supply of government bonds to pay for economic recovery measures.

The speed of Japan's transformation proved to be gradual in the 1999-to-2002 period, with numerous disappointing retrenchments along the way due to: (i) the fact that cultures and mindsets change slowly and reluctantly; (ii) the number of years required to clean up the banks' bad loans; and (iii) the likely generation-long lingering resentment toward and mistrust of banks, securities brokerage firms, the investment process, and the non-Japanese financial industry. Although many observers have argued that a short, sharp shock (a "hard landing")—such as a withdrawal of government support for the equity, bank loan, and property markets—would have hastened the process of reform and recovery, others have believed that while this treatment might (or might not) be good for Japan, such a shock would have had substantial unfavorable repercussions for Japan, for Asia, and for the world economy as a whole.

At the opening of the twenty-first century, Japan faced several crucial choices and tradeoffs that were bound to affect the course of its economy and securities prices, not to mention those of many other developed countries. Figure 7.12 depicts these choices and tradeoffs.

As Figure 7.12 illustrates, for regulators and the Japanese central bank, a crucial tradeoff was whether to protect savings by shoring up the banking system, or to support stock prices. While these two alternatives may not be mutually exclusive, government officials and the monetary authority often have had to prioritize between these two asset categories. For Japanese corporations, a significant tradeoff has been between lifetime employment and corporate restructuring. For Japanese households, an important choice has been between saving for retirement versus current consumption. For the Japanese government and voting population, the choice has been between status quo politics and radical change.

In many financial respects, Japan and the United States in 1999 and early 2000 appeared to be virtual opposites of one another. Table 7.18 lists several of these comparisons.

Japanese households were savings- and cash-rich as of 1999 to 2000, with their $1.3 trillion in equity holdings worth only a fraction of their $11 trillion cash hoard. On the other hand, U.S. households' cash

**F I G U R E  7.12**

Crucial Tradeoffs and Choices Facing Japan

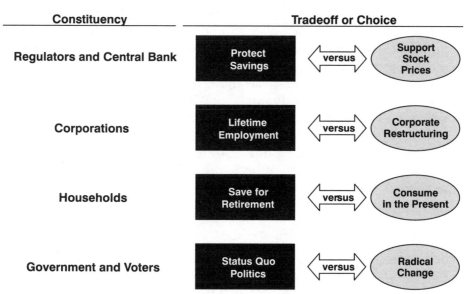

Source: The author.

**T A B L E 7.18**

Comparative Aspects of Selected Japanese and U.S. Financial Conditions

| | As of the Turn of the Millennium | |
| --- | --- | --- |
| | Japan | United States |
| Equity Markets | • A bear market lasting for more than 10 years. | • Record high levels for the Dow Jones Industrial Average, the Standard & Poor's 500 Index, and the NASDAQ Composite Index. |
| Personal Savings Rate | • At more than 14%, a 50-year cyclical high. | • Negative, for the first time in 60 years. |
| Current Account Balance of Payments | • In surplus, at more than 4.5% of GDP. | • In deficit, at more than 3.5% of GDP. |
| Households' Money Market Fund Balances, Savings Balances, and Time Deposits | • Approximately $11 trillion. | • Approximately $2.0 trillion. |
| Households' Domestic Publicly Traded Equity Holdings | • Approximately $1.3 trillion. | • Approximately $10 trillion. |

Source: The author.

balances amounted to only a fraction of their substantial equity holdings. On a national level, Japan's high personal savings rate, and its high current account balance of payments surplus, stood in stark contrast to America's negative personal savings rate and a substantial deficit in its current account balance of payments. The dollar balances accumulated by Japan, coupled with low Japanese domestic interest rates and high cash positions (i) contributed to meaningful flows of liquidity into the U.S.; (ii) allowed the U.S. government and other entities to borrow at more advantageous interest rates than otherwise possible; and thus (iii) made it less expensive than otherwise for U.S. households to borrow for the purposes of consumption spending and/or investing in U.S. equities. As these conditions persisted into 2002, an increasing number of observers felt that the positions of both Japan and the U.S. were unsustainable on a long-term basis.

## Gold

When considered in light of the centuries, even millennia, in which it has stood at the center of many nations' monetary and financial systems, gold occupied a somewhat neglected position in mainstream investors' thinking during the 1980s and 1990s. Through the ages, humankind has prized gold because of its beauty, rarity, resistance to physical corrosion, and the difficulty of quickly increasing its supply. Wars have been fought over gold, and wars have been stopped, temporarily suspended, or avoided through the payment of gold tribute.

Throughout its 1,100-year history, the Byzantine Empire, with Constantinople as its capital, maintained a monetary economy based on gold. Many historians ascribe the longevity of the Byzantine regime in part to the fiscal, monetary, and societal discipline coincident with its adherence to a gold standard. Its gold coin, weighing 4.5 grams and called the *bezant* (also known as the *solidus*, or *nomisma*) circulated freely within and outside the Empire for 645 years, from 324 to 969 A.D., and has been referred to as the U.S. dollar of the Middle Ages. Considering the relative lifespans of the U.S. dollar and the bezant, perhaps instead the U.S. dollar should be known as the bezant of the twentieth and twenty-first centuries.

In the U.S., the official price of gold was fixed at $20.67 per troy ounce (one troy ounce equals 1.0941 avoirdupois ounces) from the 1890s until 1934, and at $35.00 per ounce from 1934 until August 15, 1971. During this period, with some exceptions, foreign governments were *allowed* to convert their reserve holdings into gold at the $35.00 per ounce posted price, and U.S. citizens were *prohibited* from owning gold in most forms.

On August 15, 1971, and in a series of subsequent actions, U.S. President Richard M. Nixon and the U.S. authorities suspended gold convertibility by foreign central banks and allowed American citizens to buy and sell gold freely. During the 1970s, gold rose in price, making new highs in response to high inflation rates and geopolitical worries, catalyzed, among other things, by two major oil price increases by OPEC, the seizing of American hostages in the U.S. embassy in Iran, and the Soviet Union's invasion of Afghanistan.

After reaching an intraday high of $860 per ounce in January 1980, gold began to be marginalized by many investors, and, continuing in the 1990s, several central banks followed suit. As an indication of extreme thinking, gold had few supporters in 1999, 2000, 2001, and 2002. At the same time, the persistence and magnitude of the two-decade general downtrend in gold prices in and of itself was deemed an insufficient reason to turn bullish on gold as an investment and/or to consider gold's low price as a valuation excess that might potentially indicate a turning point—if not *upward*, then perhaps *downward*. As mentioned earlier in this chapter, in the section on deflationary forces, some investment strategists viewed gold's weak price behavior in the late 1990s and in the early years of the new millennium as a potential portent of a *decline* in the general price level and in inflation.

Figure 7.13 charts the gold price from 1975 through 2005.

The price of gold was essentially flat from late 1993 to late 1996, when it began a gradual and continuous downward move to a cyclical low below $260 per ounce in the second half of 1999. As of early 2006, gold had moved up in price and was trading above $550 per ounce. For gold to move *meaningfully* upward or downward in response to forces outside of normally operating supply-demand relationships, two factors have to be operating simultaneously: (i) an inflation/deflation and real interest-rate factor; and (ii) a geopolitical worry/geopolitical complacency factor. Without the first of these two factors in operation, the presence or absence of the second factor is of vastly reduced importance in providing direction to the gold price.

### F I G U R E  7.13

Gold Spot Price, U.S. Dollars per Ounce

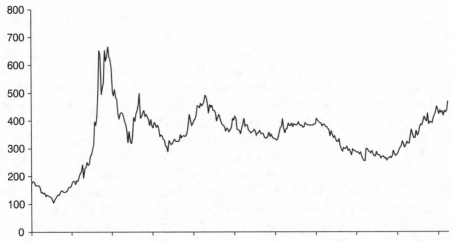

Past performance is not a guarantee of future results.

Source: Bloomberg Financial Markets.

**T A B L E  7.19**

## World Gold Supply and Demand (in Metric Tons)

| | 1995 | 1996 | 1997 | 1998 | 1999 | 2000 | 2001 | 2002 | 2003 | 2004 |
|---|---|---|---|---|---|---|---|---|---|---|
| **Supply** | | | | | | | | | | |
| Mine production | 2,291 | 2,375 | 2,493 | 2,542 | 2,574 | 2,591 | 2,621 | 2,589 | 2,593 | 2,494 |
| Official sector sales | 167 | 279 | 326 | 363 | 477 | 479 | 527 | 545 | 617 | 478 |
| Old gold scrap | 631 | 644 | 626 | 1,099 | 609 | 610 | 708 | 835 | 939 | 828 |
| Net producer hedging | 475 | 142 | 504 | 97 | 506 | – | – | – | – | – |
| Implied net disinvestment | 93 | 95 | 276 | – | – | 343 | 46 | – | – | 81 |
| | | | | | | | | | | |
| **Total Supply** | 3,657 | 3,535 | 4,225 | 4,102 | 4,166 | 4,023 | 3,902 | 3,969 | 4,149 | 3,851 |
| | | | | | | | | | | |
| **Demand** | | | | | | | | | | |
| Fabrication | | | | | | | | | | |
| Jewelry | 2,809 | 2,842 | 3,300 | 3,176 | 3,143 | 3,209 | 3,016 | 2,667 | 2,481 | 2,610 |
| Other | 502 | 485 | 562 | 567 | 593 | 557 | 474 | 480 | 512 | 553 |
| Total fabrication | 3,311 | 3,327 | 3,862 | 3,743 | 3,736 | 3,767 | 3,490 | 3,147 | 2,994 | 3,164 |
| Bar hoarding | 347 | 209 | 362 | 174 | 269 | 242 | 261 | 264 | 178 | 246 |
| Net producer hedging | – | – | – | – | – | 15 | 151 | 412 | 279 | 442 |
| Implied net investment | – | – | – | 185 | 161 | – | – | 146 | 699 | – |
| | | | | | | | | | | |
| **Total Demand** | 3,657 | 3,535 | 4,225 | 4,102 | 4,166 | 4,023 | 3,902 | 3,969 | 4,149 | 3,851 |
| | | | | | | | | | | |
| Average Gold price (London PM, U.S.$/oz) | $384.05 | $387.87 | $331.29 | $294.09 | $278.57 | $279.11 | $271.04 | $309.68 | $363.32 | $409.17 |

Past performance is not a guarantee of future results.

Note: Totals may not add due to independent rounding. Net producer hedging is the change in the physical market impact of mining companies' gold loans, forwards, and options positions. Implied net investment is the residual from combining all other data on gold supply/demand. As such, it captures the net physical impact of all transactions not covered by the other supply/demand variables.

Sources: Gold Survey 2005; Morgan Stanley Research.

Table 7.19 lists the chief sources of supply and demand for gold from 1995 through 2004 in metric tons. One metric ton is equivalent to 32,150.8 troy ounces, or 35,222.4 avoirdupois ounces.

On average from 1995 through 2004, the three largest sources of *supply* of gold were: (i) mine production, approximately 65%; (ii) the recycling of old gold scrap, approximately 16%; and (iii) official sector sales by central banks and supemational organizations, approximately 8%. During the same time period, the three largest sources of *demand* for gold were: (i) jewelry, approximately 75%; (ii) bar hoarding, approximately 8%; and (iii) electronics, approximately 6%.

Many long-term bulls on gold point out that the great inflation experienced by the world in the 1970s was partly traceable to: (i) the delinking of the U.S. dollar from its gold reserve anchor; (ii) the fact that since 1971, the U.S. dollar has been tied to nothing except itself; and (iii) the fact that the rest of the world lends money to the U.S. in a currency that the U.S. can create on its own and at negligible cost. Gold bulls argue that such a situation is ultimately untenable, and at some point, foreign holders of significant amounts of U.S. dollars will demand that these dollar balances once again be rendered convertible into gold. Gold skeptics agree that such a dramatic upward move in the price of gold relative to the then commonly accepted monetary tender of the realm has attended the close of several major empires in the course of history, but the gold doubters also point out that the upvaluation in the price of gold in many cases took 250 years or more beyond the originally predicted time frame to play out, a span of time still well beyond the investment horizons of even the most long-term of human investors.

## PSYCHOLOGICAL, TECHNICAL, AND LIQUIDITY FORCES

### The Equification of Society

♦ **The Central Position of Equities in Americans' Mindspace:**
Once in every several generations, the stimulation and rewards of speculating and investing in stocks reach such an advanced stage that many other aspects of society at large—economic, cultural, and social—appear to be dominated and consumed by what might be called an obsession with equity. During such an euphoric period, the media and popular conversation are filled with stories of rapid wealth creation, a broadening of access to successful speculation and investment techniques, and a belief that such conditions can continue indefinitely. The concepts of risk, caution, moderation, and financial conservatism are downplayed or ignored altogether.

The years 1997 through early 2000 exhibited many of these characteristics, while concurrently, the household sector built up a massive exposure to the U.S. stock market, both through direct purchases of stocks and mutual funds, indirect holdings in pension plans, and the wide use of stock options by many corporations as a component of compensation. During 1999, equities rose to a 50-year high of 25% of U.S. households' total assets, compared to a previous high of 23% in 1968 and a low of 8% in 1984. Table 7.20 shows the percentage of Americans directly owning equities at selected points in U.S. financial history.

**T A B L E  7.20**

Percentage of American Households Directly Owning Equity

| Year | Percentage of American Households Directly Owning Equity |
|------|----------------------------------------------------------|
| 1929 | 1.8% |
| 1951 | 4.0% |
| 1983 | 19.0% |
| 1989 | 32.5% |
| 1992 | 36.6% |
| 1995 | 41.0% |
| 1999 | 48.2% |
| 2002 | 49.5% |

Source: Investment Company Institute, Morgan Stanley Research.

Table 7.20 shows that from 1929, when only 1.8% of American households directly owned publicly traded equities, this percentage steadily rose, to 1983, when it reached 19.0%, to 36.6% in 1992, and, in a burst of enthusiasm for share ownership, to 48.2% in 1999, and to 49.5% in 2002. As for mutual funds, from 1991 through 1998, Americans invested more than $1.1 trillion of net new money in equity mutual funds. During this same period, the number of these mutual funds tripled, to 3,500 funds, and their year-end 1998 assets of $3.0 trillion represented 20% of the market value of all publicly traded stocks, up from 12% in 1994.

Partly as a consequence, the financial-services industry enjoyed boom profit years, with the industry's aftertax net earnings rising from $18.9 billion in 1996 to $25.1 billion in 1998, $40.4 billion in 1999, and $44.9 billion in 2000. (Table 7.15 displays these data, including the financial-services industry's 32% profit decline to $30.4 billion in 2001.) At this level of profits, in the late 1990s, the financial-services industry was the third most profitable industry in America in 1998, ranking behind banks ($37.3 billion) and cars and trucks ($25.7 billion), and ahead of drugs and research ($21.9 billion).

◆ **The Ubiquity of Equity:** Contributing to the heady financial atmosphere of 1997 through 1999 was the seeming pervasiveness of equity-market-related news. Cable and broadcast television viewers, newspaper and magazine readers, and pager, fax, e-mail, and online subscribers were deluged with earnings

forecasts, earnings preannouncements, earnings announcements, merger, acquisition, restructuring, and divestiture
news, press releases, and other corporate information, as well
as copious predictions about and commentary on the economy, interest rates, domestic and non-U.S. equity, bond, options, futures, and currency markets, asset allocation, and
investment strategy.

At times during the latter half of the 1990s, the media's fixation on
financial market information appeared to lead to a mediafication, or
sportsification, of the financial markets, with various financial-market
participants turned into celebrities, sports-event style reporting and
language, and even self-reflexive financial news features about the process of producing financial news stories profiling the effects of media
coverage on securities prices. One widely watched financial news
channel called its midday market update "The Halftime Report."

An indication of the increasing feverishness of trading activity
was the level of annual percent turnover on the New York Stock Exchange, defined as the total number of shares *traded* on the NYSE in a
given year as a percentage of the total number of shares *listed* on the
NYSE. Figure 7.14 contains a graph of annual percent turnover of
shares on the NYSE from 1921 through 2003.

As Figure 7.14 illustrates, annual NYSE turnover was relatively
quiescent during the 1950s (ranging between 12 and 23%) and the
1960s (between 12% and 24%), before increasing in the 1970s (between
16 and 28%), and rising even further in the 1980s (between 33% in 1981
and 73% in 1987). The 1990s and the period after the turn of the century
witnessed even higher rates of annual turnover, culminating in a
73-year high of 105% in 2002. Some market observers asserted that
NYSE annual turnover percentages understated the true degree of investor activity, since equally high rates of daily turnover in the
NASDAQ and listed options markets were not included.

The last time annual turnover on the NYSE exceeded 1998
through 2003 levels was in 1925 through 1929, when annual turnover
ranged between 84 and 132%. The total *annual* share volume peaked at
1.12 billion shares in 1929, a level that was below *one day's* peak 1999
NYSE trading volume. Annual trading volume fell more than 85%
from 1929, to 171 million shares in 1941 and 126 million shares in 1942,
and did not surpass the 1929 annual-share trading-volume peak until
*35 years later*, when 1.24 billion shares were traded in 1964.

**F I G U R E  7.14**

Annual Percent Turnover of NYSE Share Trading Volume

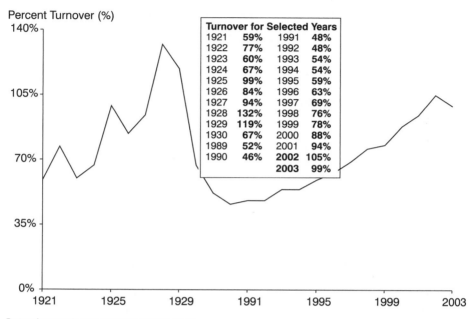

Past performance is not a guarantee of future results.
Source: Bloomberg Financial Markets.

Another sign of the ubiquity of equity was the dramatic rise in the number of NYSE market-data devices, including both price quotation and ticker display equipment. Table 7.21 shows the total number of operational NYSE market-data devices from 1980 through 2004.

As Table 7.21 shows, the total number of NYSE market-data devices grew from 67,574 as of year-end 1980 to 194,985 as of year-end 1990, a net gain of 127,411 devices, and from year-end 1990 to year-end 2004, increased from 194,985 to 422,343, a net gain of 227,358 devices.

Access to price quotes, information, research sources, financial advice, market comment, and online trading has become even more widespread with individuals' and companies' increasing use of the Internet. Two sources, Forrester Research and Gomez Advisors, estimated the number of online brokerage accounts at between 3.7 million and 7.5 million as of early 1999, with the former estimate including investors who used trading software packages and/or the World Wide Web to

**T A B L E   7.21**

NYSE Market Data Devices

| End of Year | Market Data Devices[1] |
|---|---|
| 1980 | 67,574 |
| 1981 | 80,059 |
| 1982 | 90,457 |
| 1983 | 114,358 |
| 1984 | 133,008 |
| 1985 | 142,613 |
| 1986 | 162,482 |
| 1987 | 195,570 |
| 1988 | 203,150 |
| 1989 | 200,830 |
| 1990 | 194,985 |
| 1991 | 193,239 |
| 1992 | 211,833 |
| 1993 | 237,838 |
| 1994 | 266,718 |
| 1995 | 276,061 |
| 1996 | 314,479 |
| 1997 | 351,237 |
| 1998 | 384,661 |
| 1999 | 419,113 |
| 2000 | 499,712 |
| 2001 | 471,659 |
| 2002 | 435,304 |
| 2003 | 402,152 |
| 2004 | 422,343 |

[1]Market data devices provide consolidated (network "A") last sale, bid-asked, and ticker display prices.
Source: *NYSE Fact Book.*

execute securities transactions and the latter estimate a more all-encompassing figure, comprising investors who had online access to information about their securities brokerage accounts.

◆ **Manialike Equity Market Characteristics:** Some distinguishing characteristics of advanced-state bull markets include: (i) investors hyperactively trading stocks on an intraday basis, with little regard for corporate fundamentals or valuations; (ii) buyers bidding up the prices of many companies in selected sectors to extremely overvalued levels; (iii) high daily trading volume and extraordinarily volatile stock-price movements; and occasionally, for the unwary, (iv) the potential for securities fraud. Many of these elements were present in energy stocks in 1980 through 1981, in biotechnology stocks in 1991 through 1992, and in the Internet and online brokerage-related stocks in 1998, 1999, and early 2000. During this time period, the market capitalization of the 96 Internet-related stocks tracked by Morgan Stanley rose from $120 billion in December 1998 to $400 billion only a few months later, in April 1999. In the corporate sector, many firms had to implement information technology protocols to prevent employees from day-trading and/or overly frequently checking the value of their securities portfolios—for some, as frequently as every 15 minutes—while on company time.

One highly telling view into the intersection of Internet stocks and chatroom-based electronic trading appeared in a page-one story in *The Wall Street Journal* of March 18, 1999, titled "Heard on the Net: CNET Cooks on Web Chatter, Until Word Comes to Get Out." In vivid detail, the article describes what nineteenth-century NYSE floor traders might have referred to as "ramping," or "bulling" a stock, what twentieth-century critics called stock-price manipulation, and what its supporters called momentum trading, transported into the cyberage, replete with its own language, syntax, and punctuation. While these speculative fires raged, securities and commodities industry regulators, the U.S. Congress, formal securities markets, registered broker-dealers and investment advisors, market-data vendors, online-trading services and crossing networks, and other market participants debated the purpose, form, and oversight responsibility of online trading and real-time investor chat rooms. In Congressional testimony in January 1999, Federal Reserve Chairman Alan Greenspan likened individual investors' speculation in Internet shares to the purchase of a lottery ticket, which could produce a total loss, or, at very long odds, a big payoff.

Exhibiting a pattern strikingly similar to the late stages of stock-market booms in the 1920s and 1960s, merger and acquisition activity soared from 1987 through 2004, as shown in Table 7.22.

Table 7.22 shows that the value of announced merger and acquisition transactions with a market value of $100 million or more rose from

**T A B L E  7.22**

Announced Merger and Acquisition Transactions

| Year | Dollar Amount (Billions)[1] | % U.S. Targets | % Non-U.S. Targets |
|------|------|------|------|
| 1987 | $301.9 | 70% | 30% |
| 1988 | 453.4 | 73% | 27% |
| 1989 | 481.0 | 55% | 45% |
| 1990 | 347.9 | 41% | 59% |
| 1991 | 249.8 | 39% | 61% |
| 1992 | 266.6 | 43% | 57% |
| 1993 | 344.6 | 56% | 44% |
| 1994 | 431.6 | 67% | 33% |
| 1995 | 806.1 | 57% | 43% |
| 1996 | 955.5 | 58% | 42% |
| 1997 | 1,451.5 | 56% | 44% |
| 1998 | 2,296.0 | 66% | 34% |
| 1999 | 3,046.9 | 48% | 52% |
| 2000 | 3,185.3 | 51% | 49% |
| 2001 | 1,523.0 | 46% | 54% |
| 2002 | 1,058.7 | 37% | 63% |
| 2003 | 1,223.7 | 42% | 58% |
| 2004 | 1,756.7 | 45% | 55% |

[1]Announced merger and acquisition transactions with an aggregate value of $100 million or more.
Source: Thomson Financial.

$301.9 billion in 1987 to $3.047 trillion in 1999 and $3.185 trillion in 2000, before plummeting 67% in 2002, to $1.059 trillion.

♦ **The Transformation of Equity Investing:** In 1999 and early 2000, as equities assumed a more important part of many Americans' lives and thinking, as news about equity investing became more broadly dispersed, and as stocks in certain industry sectors exhibited manialike characteristics, a growing number of investors believed that stocks no longer embodied the two chief characteristics of equities: (i) an ownership claim on a share of economic growth and the corporate value added by a business; and (ii) purchasing power protection through long-term compounding of returns.

Instead, many investors began to view equities in a different light, with equities transformed into other incarnations, including:

- **The Bankification of Equities:** In the late 1990s, many investors began to consider stocks as a valid repository for their short- and long-term savings balances, with the NYSE and NASDAQ effectively being thought of as America's national savings bank. It was unclear what proportion of these investors implicitly believed that the U.S. government would bail out the stock market and support equity prices in the event of a massive selloff.

- **The Commodification of Equities:** With many investors seeking to trade the market for short-term gain and increasingly uninformed about the fundamental characteristics of their stock holdings, external news, such as changes in the domestic and international sphere, political turmoil, and other macro-economic factors began to loom larger and larger in these participants' investment decisions, much in same fashion as commodity traders and speculators tended to view oil, currencies, and commodities.

- **The Bondification of Equities:** As many pharmaceutical, technology, and consumer-products companies reached extremely high price-earnings ratios in the late 1990s, the rationale for these valuations came more and more to be driven by the low interest rates used to discount their projected future earnings growth back to the present. In effect, high price-earnings stocks' valuations became increasingly a function of long-term interest rates, with interest-rate movements driving wide swings in the present value of these stocks—much like a zero- or low-coupon long-duration bond.

## ASSET BUBBLE PHENOMENA

After financial markets had produced high returns for a number of consecutive years, by early 2000, signs continued to emerge of increasingly stretched valuations and irrational investor psychology. Although it is extremely difficult to predict market tops and bottoms, it is no less difficult to identify when an asset bubble has formed. Nevertheless, several tell-tale indications, some of which had already been suspected or identified during 1996 through 2000, then later came to light amidst highly unfavorable circumstances and publicity during 2001 and 2002:

- **Widespread Wealth Creation:** Beginning in 1994, U.S. households' equity holdings appreciated by $5 trillion, reaching $9.3 trillion by the end of 2000. As part of this process, the number of U.S. households with a net worth of $1 million or more rose from 4 million households in 1990 to 8 million at the end of 1999.

- **Unrealistic Expectations:** Reflecting their positive experiences of the last half of the 1990s, investors' responses to several financial surveys indicated that: (i) they expected the returns from equity ownership to persist at annual rates of 15 to 20% or more for the indefinite future; (ii) the capital risks from equity ownership were viewed as being minimal; and (iii) asset diversification encompassing meaningful levels of cash, fixed-income securities, commodities, and other nonequity-like assets made little financial sense.

- **Investor Complacency:** By the late 1990s, many investors had concluded that the risks of being out of the equity markets far outweighed the risks of remaining virtually fully invested in equities; as a result, these investors became devoted to a "buy the dips" mentality, and felt similarly strongly that trying to identity major cyclical and even secular turning points in equities prices did not matter.

- **Financial Inadequacy:** As they observed venture capital, initial public offerings, and merger-and-acquisitions processes creating large new fortunes, a considerable number of well-off investors felt that their fortunes were not large enough. These feelings were often exaggerated as a result of significant perceived or actual disparities between the comparors' and comparees' ages, depth of business experience, absolute wealth levels, and the future growth prospects of the assets comprising their respective patrimonies.

- **Disrespect for Money:** In times such as the late 1990s, with substantial inflation of *financial assets*, a growing portion of investors exhibited some of the same signs of disrespect for the value of money that individuals tend to display during periods of high inflation of *goods and services*; in other words, the psychological benefits of *current* consumption appeared to out-weigh the benefits of *deferred* consumption, and in the process, individuals began to devalue the worth of money as a store of value compared with the utility of money as a medium of exchange.

◆ **Taxation Overawareness:** In virtually all economic conditions, many investors allow tax considerations to exert too strong an influence in their financial decision making, but this overawareness of tax factors in investing assumes an even larger role during late-stage bull markets as investors seek to keep as large a share as possible of their capital gains from falling into the coffers of the fiscal authorities.

◆ **Paper Riches, Purchasing-Power Poverty:** Due to lockup agreements, restrictions on sales by insiders and affiliates, and concerns about the signals that sales by corporate officers and directors might send to the financial marketplace, many individuals' equity wealth on paper could not readily be converted into spendable funds.

◆ **Aggressive and Creative Accounting and Financing Techniques:** Driven in part by a desire to increase their own company's revenues, earnings, image, and stock price, a considerable number of corporate executives took shortcuts, made use of excessively liberal or sometimes fraudulent revenue and expense recognition conventions, options-based incentive compensation and/or personal borrowing practices, and aggressive financing strategies involving bank debt, corporate bonds, derivatives, and the inappropriate issuance of equity or equity-linked securities.

As investors ponder the course of economic, financial, and social trends, and their likely effects on the fundamental, valuation, and psychological/technical/liquidity factors affecting asset values and security prices, they may formulate relevant questions that may provoke their thinking about a range of outcomes, from the likely to the barely possible. Several of these questions are set forth in Table 7.23.

By posing difficult-to-answer questions to others and to one's self, investors may be able to anticipate and take action in advance of significant downward or upward moves in asset prices. The questions in Table 7.24 are designed to help investors become more alert to signs of excess that may presage major shifts in the financial-market climate.

**T A B L E  7.23**

Questions to Consider

### Fundamental Questions

- **What factors could meaningfully arrest real economic growth,** leading to stagnation or an actual decline in economic output? What would be the likely extent and duration of such a slowdown or contraction? What would be the pattern of overall corporate profits, and specific industries' profits, under such circumstances?
- **What domestic or international events or policies could cause interest rates to rise or fall** in a major way from prevailing levels?
- **Are certain regions, economies, and industries facing an epoch of benign price deflation,** propelled by productivity growth, globalization, the Internet, global overcapacity, technological advances, and increasing supply? How narrow is the margin between benign price deflation and harmful price deflation, and what developments could shift deflation from the benign kind to the harmful kind?
- **What is the position of equities versus debt, U.S. versus non-U.S. securities, currency relationships, and privately versus publicly traded investments** in the event of a deflationary episode, or the reflationary policy actions taken to avoid such an outcome?

### Valuation Questions

- **What lessons can be learned about the shifting role of valuation-based disciplines in bear market episodes** in modern times in Japan in the 1990s, in non-Japan Asia between 1997 and 1999, and in the U.S. in 1973–1974 and in 2000–2002?
- After price/earnings ratios have experienced a meaningful multiyear expansion to historically high levels, **what factors would be necessary to sustain P/Es at such high levels,** and/or move them even higher, for an extended period of time?
- **Will the pattern of future equity bear market episodes fall: (i) more on equities than on bonds, or equally on both?** (ii) more on U.S. markets than on overseas markets, or equally on both? (iii) more on the S&P 500 than on the Russell 2000, or equally on both? (iv) more on growth stocks than on value stocks, or equally on both?
- For portfolio holding periods of 5 to 10 years or more, **is it preferable to invest in companies that appear to be relatively good value, based on low multiples of current earnings, or in companies that have exceptional growth potential, even if they appear expensive in valuation terms?**

### Psychological/ Technical/Liquidity

- **What forces and/or events could cause U.S. households to meaning fully reduce their exposure to equity investments?**
- How can the investor determine the minimum ongoing level of investment exposure to any given asset class? What is the investor's comfort zone of investment exposure in periods of rising, flat, or falling prices and overall returns for various asset classes?
- **What are the risks, rewards, appropriate parameters, and best implementation strategies of investment contrarianism?** What market forces and environments determine whether the investor should hold firm to principle and resist the crowd, and what market forces and environments dictate that the investor should not fight the crowd?

Source: The author.

# SECTION 5

# IMPLEMENTATION TACTICS AND STRATEGIES

# CHAPTER 8

# STRUCTURAL CONSIDERATIONS IN ASSET ALLOCATION

## OVERVIEW

An often-overlooked aspect of the asset allocation process concerns *the form and structure* in which the investor owns, controls, and ultimately disposes of his or her assets. *How* investors own and conserve assets should be as important as *what* assets they own, *what* risk management actions they take, and *what* overall investment strategy they pursue. These structural concerns are especially important in a technologically advanced world that places a premium on finding sound counsel, wise judgment, and prudent financial conduct. Many investors appear to be seeking greater *choice* through open financial services architecture, greater *convenience* through multiple access channels, and greater *control* over expenses through unbundling and ease of comparison pricing. In general, it is to the investor's benefit to have assets compound: (i) as long as possible; (ii) in as tax-advantaged a format as possible; and (iii) while keeping investment-related expenses as constrained as possible.

This chapter begins by tracking the evolutions in investors' financial thinking and action, from an initial focus on asset diversification within a single asset class, to asset allocation across several asset classes, to financial management encompassing multiple structural disciplines. Next, this chapter discusses the progression of investor objectives, including: (i) the creation and cultivation of wealth; (ii) the enhancement, preservation, and protection of wealth; and (iii) the deployment and distribution of wealth. The process, elements, and benefits of financial planning are also covered here.

Later, this chapter reviews the type, uses, and principal features of many of the most frequently utilized forms of personal trusts, including: charitable trusts; grantor-retained trusts; dynasty, Crummy, and life-insurance trusts; marital and credit-shelter trusts; and children's and special-needs trusts. This chapter also discusses the main forms of life insurance, including term insurance and permanent (cash-value) insurance, and immediate and deferred annuities. The chapter concludes with a survey of tax and liability-management issues of importance to investors.

It is important to keep in mind that any comments and guidelines contained in this chapter related to tax and legal matters are intended purely as background information. This book does not provide tax or other legal advice. Investors should consult with their own tax and legal advisors for any such advice.

## STRUCTURAL CONSIDERATIONS

In endeavoring to achieve their financial goals and build wealth, increasing numbers of investors have embraced a number of tax-advantaged and other structures, including traditional and rollover Individual Retirement Accounts (IRAs), 401(k) plans, 403(b) plans, 457 plans, SEP-IRA plans, Keogh Plans, deferred-compensation arrangements, fixed and variable annuities, custodial accounts under the Uniform Gifts to Minors Act (UGMA) or the Uniform Transfers to Minors Act (UTMA), Coverdell Education Savings Accounts (Educational IRAs), Series EE Savings Bonds, and state-sponsored college tuition savings programs (also known as Section 529 Plans). In addition, to achieve diversification and professional management, some individual investors have utilized so-called consulting or wrap accounts, which combine investor risk-and-return objective profiling and asset allocation with manager selection and monitoring. This process usually involves an asset-based fee.

Taxable investors have paid closer attention to the tax advantages of: (i) purchasing securities directly, or having their assets managed on a separate-account basis, rather than through mutual funds; (ii) investing in mutual funds with so-called high tax-efficiency ratings (the percentage of a mutual fund's total returns that it retains after taxes); and (iii) owning special tax-managed mutual funds, which seek to minimize fundholders' tax bills. Tax-managed funds' investment tactics, as well as those of tax-conscious separate-account managers and individual equity investors, include: (i) a low-turnover, long-term buy-and-hold approach to investment holdings; (ii) an orientation toward companies whose annual returns are mainly in the form of capital gains rather than dividends; and (iii) where appropriate, the offsetting of realized capital gains through the judicious realization of capital losses within the same tax year.

## Evolution of Investor Focus

As investors have become more aware of structural considerations in their asset allocation and investment activity, they have tended to embrace an important expansion in their financial thinking. This transformation follows in similar fashion the significant broadening of investors' range of view, from an emphasis purely on equity diversification, to a wider focus, encompassing asset allocation. Investors' enlarged scope of financial thinking and acting is depicted in Figure 8.1.

With the passage of time, many individual investors' focus tends to undergo a shift in emphasis. As investors make their first investments in an asset class such as equities and mutual funds, their primary focus tends to center on the proper degree of intra-asset class *concentration and diversification* in their portfolios. Within the equities asset class, industry and company groupings are a commonly utilized means of establishing and monitoring diversification parameters. Later, reflecting greater levels of accumulated and invested assets, investors may generally become more aware of inter-asset class *asset allocation* issues, including the proper proportion of U.S. versus non-U.S. securities, stocks versus bonds, and conventional assets versus alternative investments, with the last category including private equity, venture capital, real assets such as commodities, timber interests, oil and gas interests, precious metals, inflation-indexed securities, hedge funds, managed futures, and real estate. Even later, as assets build and the breadth of investors' considerations widens, individuals devote attention to a wider range of decisions. In addition to asset allocation and investment-strategy

## F I G U R E  8.1

### The Evolution of Investors' Financial Thinking and Action

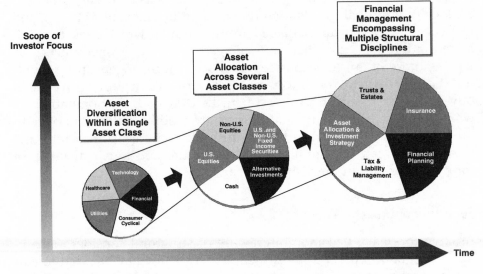

Source: The author.

concerns, *financial management* matters of interest include the use of personal trusts, insurance, financial planning (which may include retirement planning and education planning in addition to estate planning), and numerous forms of tax and liability management.

## Evolution of Investor Objectives

As assets grow, the principal objectives and concerns of investors in many cases may progress through a series of stages, as shown in Figure 8.2.

Figure 8.2 depicts the progression of investors' objectives and concerns at different stages of their financial lifetimes. In the first stage, when investors are building up their financial and nonfinancial assets, the *wealth-seeding stage*, their principal objectives center on the creation and cultivation of wealth. In the next stage, the *wealth-accumulation stage*, investors focus on the enhancement, preservation, and protection of wealth. In a still more-advanced stage, the *wealth-realization stage*, investors may turn their attention to the deployment and distribution of wealth during and after the investor's lifetime. To an increasing degree,

## The Progression of Investor Objectives

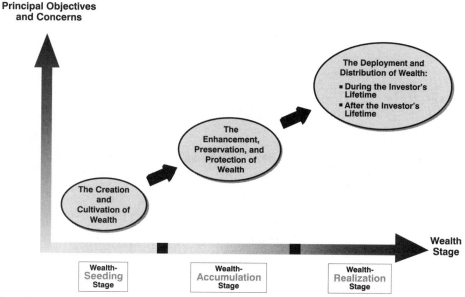

Source: The author.

the earlier in the progression between each of these three wealth stages the investor begins to think about financial-management issues, as well as the inter-asset class asset allocation and intraasset class diversification issues portrayed earlier in Figure 8.1, the greater the likelihood of understanding, anticipating, and potentially achieving such financial goals as efficiency, expense control, and enhanced wealth retention.

## FINANCIAL PLANNING

For investors along the entire wealth spectrum, financial planning can bring discipline, order, and rationality to thinking about and preparing for the future. Many of the key elements of financial planning are portrayed in Figure 8.3.

Figure 8.3 shows that financial planning refers to the process of: (i) collecting information about the investor's assets, liabilities, income, spending, and cash flow; (ii) integrating these data into a set of financial

**F I G U R E  8.3**

Elements of Financial Planning

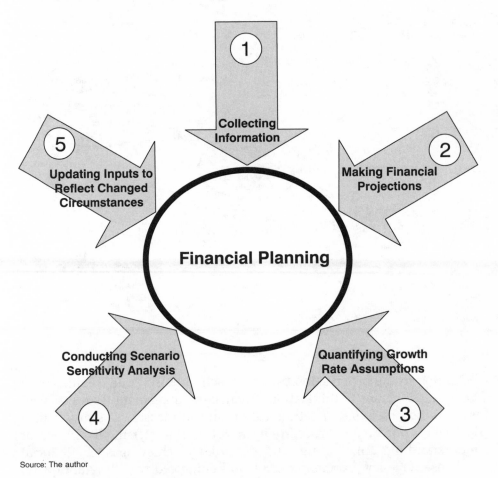

Source: The author

projections; (iii) making assumptions, and quantifying them, about growth rates in income, expenditures, cash flow, asset and liability values, and the tax environment; (iv) reviewing the originally projected outcomes and various what-if scenarios that may be affected by meaningful alterations in any of the key assumptions and forecasts; and (v) periodically updating the inputs and outputs of the financial plan to reflect changes in the investor's family and economic circumstances, the financial-market outlook, and tax realities.

## Importance of Financial Planning

Financial planning can help investors in several ways. First, financial planning can provide a structured framework for organizing and dealing with wealth in any of its three major embodiments: (i) as a significant *change in circumstances,* through such means as inheritance, the sale or public offering of an ownership position in a business, retirement with large sums in various forms as self-directed pension plans, awards from legal judgments, lottery winnings, or other sources; (ii) as a *projected accumulation of income flows versus expenditure flows* over a span of years; and (iii) as an *already existing, established fortune,* in any of several forms, including real estate, livestock, boats, aircraft, other real property, art, antiques, jewelry, collectibles, and various kinds of financial assets.

Second, financial planning can provide investors with a more comprehensive understanding of the role and effects of time in achieving established goals and objectives, such as funding educational expenses, effecting intergenerational wealth transfers, beginning to receive Social Security benefits and meeting retirement spending targets, and donating assets and/or income flows to philanthropic institutions.

A third benefit of financial planning derives from the array of information, choices, and decisions that surface before the investor. Financial planning leads the investor to consider key subjects such as: (i) the forms, amounts, vehicles, and beneficiaries of life, property, long-term care, medical, and disability-insurance coverage; (ii) the types, duration, conditions, and beneficiaries of various forms of personal trusts, private foundations, supporting organizations, and family limited partnerships; (iii) for business owners and/or the self-employed, succession, retirement planning, insurance, and funding buy-sell agreements; (iv) the size and timing of tax payments, including income, capital gains, estate, gift, property, and other taxes, at the local, state, federal, and in some cases, at the international level; (v) the use, timing, and structure of Qualified Domestic Relations Orders (QDROs), employer-furnished benefits, and pension and retirement-account inflows and outflows; (vi) the costs, conditions, magnitudes, and risks of borrowing and other forms of explicit and contingent liabilities; (vii) more organized document location and recordkeeping for such outlays as home-improvement costs, qualified child care, gifts, annual living expenses, tax deductions, and the purchase and sale of assets; and (viii) having an updated will and estate plan. These assessments provide the investor and his or her sources of financial and legal counsel with an integrated, consistent platform for making investment recommendations and decisions.

Two additional benefits of financial planning include: increased awareness of the potential need to make decisions that balance tradeoffs between various financial objectives; and the timely attention devoted to important monetary and personal issues well in advance of their reaching a critical state. Among the retirement planning Web sites available to investors are: *aarp.org; choosetosave.org; fidelity.com; finance.yahoo.com; financialengines.com; financialplan.about.com/cs/retirementplans; 401k.com; genworth.com, lifeevents.msn.com; ltsave.com; money.cnn.com/retirement; morningstar.com; mpower.com; napta.org; pfp.aicpa.org; psca.org; quicken.com; retirement-income.net; smartmoney.com; soa.org; ssa.gov; troweprice.com;* and *vanguard.com.*

## PERSONAL TRUSTS

When properly designed, managed, and kept updated, personal trusts can be a powerful tool to help: (i) reduce estate taxes, avoid capital-gains taxes, reduce family income taxes, and facilitate tax-advantaged gifts; (ii) transfer property to beneficiaries in a timely manner; (iii) control the management and distribution of assets placed in a given trust; (iv) avoid the probate process, with its associated expenses, public disclosure, and time delays; (v) carry out personal and financial activity in the event of incapacitation, through instruments such as a revocable living trust, power of attorney, healthcare proxy, and a living will; and (vi) protect assets against family disagreements and creditors' claims. As such, trusts often serve to prevent the unintended and hasty dissolution of assets that the investor has, in many cases, expended an intensive effort to build up during a significant period of his or her lifetime. For multiple-jurisdiction investors, offshore trusts may be used to protect, manage, and distribute assets.

### Importance of Personal Trusts

The basic concepts underlying personal trusts trace their origins to the practice of medieval knights leaving a portion or all of their property in the hands of a trustee to provide for family survivors and to care for assets during extended absences. The legal principles and procedures affecting personal trusts have thus evolved over decades, even centuries, and continue to evolve in legislatures and the courts. Among other factors, the structure of personal trusts often reflects: (i) the skill and knowledge of the investor's attorney who drafts the trust document; (ii) the imposition of appropriate standards of fiduciary responsibility and investment prudence on the designated trustee(s); (iii) the basic tenets of property law governing the form, duration, and conditionality of property disposition and use; (iv) federal, state, or local estate taxes, if applicable; (v) any relevant federal, state, or local gift taxes, which may have certain maximum lifetime donor or death exclusions; (vi) special factors, such as contemplation of death and generation-skipping rules; and (vii) the skill and capabilities of the trustee(s) chosen to administer and invest the trust.

Personal trusts can be divided into two groups: (i) *living trusts,* created during an individual's lifetime; and (ii) *testamentary trusts,* created under an individual's will and which take effect only upon his or her death. In addition, personal trusts can be: (i) *revocable trusts,* which allow individuals to transfer property to a trust, modify the terms of the trust, change the beneficiaries or the trustee of the trust, and even revoke the terms of the trust at any time while they are alive; or (ii) *irrevocable trusts,* which do not allow the terms of the trust to be changed nor its assets returned to the donor once the trust has been established. Individuals who use irrevocable trusts are generally willing to accept some loss of control of assets to take advantage of gift-tax exclusions and to avoid, reduce, or defer estate taxes.

Table 8.1 presents a selection of types and uses of personal trusts.

The brief descriptions of certain features, types, and uses of the trusts in Table 8.1—charitable trusts; grantor retained trusts; dynasty, Crummy, and life-insurance trusts; marital and credit-shelter trusts; and children's and special-needs trusts—are intended to suggest merely some, but by no means all, of the ways in which they can be and have been used by individuals in tax planning, estate planning, and charitable giving. Investors should consult their own attorney for specific advice in the proper uses of personal trusts within their estate or financial plan.

## LIFE INSURANCE AND ANNUITIES

Life insurance and annuities can be powerful financial tools that, appropriately understood and utilized, may provide significant tax and estate planning benefits. At the same time, both of these classes of instruments have some degree of complexity associated with them, and may yield less favorable economic results when used improperly.

**T A B L E  8.1**

## Selected Types and Uses of Personal Trusts

| *Charitable Trusts* | *Grantor Retained Trusts* | *Dynasty, Crummy, and Life Insurance Trusts* |
|---|---|---|
| **Charitable Remainder Trust (CRT)** | **Grantor Retained Annuity Trust (GRAT)** | **Dynasty Trust** |
| • Tax-exempt irrevocable trust.<br>• Highly appreciated assets may be sold by the trustee free of capital gains taxes.<br>• The beneficiary receives an annual payment, and the charity receives the assets at the end of the trust's term.<br>• Assets transferred to a CRT are entitled to a current-year tax deduction and reduce the donor's net estate. | • Payments from the trust assets go to designated recipients for a specified time period.<br>• Unlike a CRT, all assets eventually transfer to beneficiaries.<br>• The trust freezes the value of the assets for tax purposes at their worth when the trust is established.<br>• Securities or other assets that are likely to appreciate are often used to fund a GRAT.<br>• Can reduce estate taxes if the donor survives the term of the trust and if trust assets appreciate at a rate greater than IRS projections. | • An irrevocable trust designed to pass wealth to multiple generations while removing the assets from future estate and generation-skipping taxes.<br>• Dynasty trust provisions can be added to many kinds of trusts including credit shelter, Crummy, and life insurance trusts. |
| **Charitable Remainder Annuity Trust (CRAT)** | | **Crummy Trust** |
| • The annual payments from this CRT are equal to a fixed percentage of the trust assets when established. | | • An irrevocable trust designed to allow grantors to take advantage of the annual per-recipient gift tax exclusion.<br>• Most attractive to married couples with many beneficiaries. |
| **Charitable Remainder Unitrust (CRUT)** | **Grantor Retained Unitrust (GRUT)** | **Life Insurance Trust** |
| • The annual payments from this CRT are equal to a percentage of trust assets valued annually. | • Similar to a GRAT, except the annual payments are set as a fixed percentage of the year-end market value valued annually rather than as a fixed percentage of the initial market value at the time the trust was funded. | • A Crummy trust that purchases life insurance on the grantor's life. In a properly structured trust, the life insurance death benefit passes income and estate tax-free to the beneficiaries.<br>• Existing life insurance policies can be gifted to a life insurance trust in order to remove the death proceeds from the owner's estate. |
| **Net Income Makeup Charitable Remainder Unitrust (NIMCRUT)** | **Qualified Personal Residence Trust (QPRT)** | |
| • The annual payments from this CRT are equal to the lesser of the trust's net income or a percentage of assets valued annually. | • The trust holds title to the grantor's home or vacation home for a selected number of rent-free years, after which the trust terminates and the home is transferred to the beneficiaries.<br>• The grantor can continue to live in the home if rent is paid.<br>• A QPRT enables the grantor to make a gift of a valuable asset at a substantial discount in gift taxes. | |
| **Charitable Lead Trust (CLT)** | | |
| • Similar to a Charitable Remainder Trust, except the charity receives the annual income, and other individual beneficiaries receive the assets.<br>• The trust receives a charitable deduction each year for its distributions to charity. | | |

Source: The author.

| Marital and Credit Shelter Trusts | Children's and Special Needs Trusts |
|---|---|
| **Qualified Terminal Interest Property Trust (QTIP)** | **2503(b) Trust** |
| • Allows the grantor to provide lifetime income for his or her surviving spouse and control the ultimate distribution of the trust's assets for selected beneficiaries.<br>• Often used to ensure that if the surviving spouse remarries, he/she cannot disinherit the children from the first marriage. | • Trust income must be paid to the child and cannot be accumulated.<br>• Principal passes to the child at a future date specified in the trust.<br>• Often funded with gifts exempted from gift tax by the annual exclusion. |
| **Qualified Domestic Trust** | **2503(c) Trust** |
| • Gifts to the trust for a non-resident alien spouse qualify for the estate tax marital deduction and upon death of the NRA spouse, the assets go to other beneficiaries. | • Similar to the 2503(b) trust except that income may be accumulated.<br>• In return for this right, the child must have access to the principal when he/she reaches 21 years of age. |
| **Credit Shelter Trust** | **Special Needs Trust** |
| • Assets placed in this trust are usually equal to the applicable federal credit amount.<br>• Enables the trust grantor and his or her spouse to maximize the federal applicable exclusion available to each party.<br>• Upon the death of the surviving spouse, designated beneficiaries can continue to receive income payments or the trust's assets outright. | • Allows a disabled child or family member to receive financial support specifically earmarked to supplement, rather than supplant, government assistance programs.<br>• Properly utilized, the beneficiary can still qualify for SSI disability benefits. |

## Life Insurance

Life insurance is one of the many forms of insurance products, which, in the nonlife category, also include automobile, household, health, disability, and long-term care insurance. Each of these nonlife insurance products may fulfill important needs within an individual investor's overall financial planning. The forms and amounts of any insurance coverage should be evaluated in light of: (i) the individual's specific risk profile and financial circumstances; and (ii) product-specific characteristics such as coverage and benefit periods, deductibles and elimination periods, inflation provisions, and benefit triggers, among other features.

In its most basic form, life insurance involves a contractual relationship between the policyholder and an insurance company, in which the policyholder pays insurance premiums to the insurance company. In return, the insurance company agrees to pay the face value (also known as the maturity value, or death benefit) of the insurance policy to the designated beneficiary upon the death of the insured person. Among the various death benefit payout methods to the beneficiaries of life insurance policies are lump-sum payments, retained-asset accounts, lifetime-only annuities, joint-and-survivor annuities, period-certain annuities, and life with period-certain annuities.

Life insurance has many purposes, including: (i) serving as a source of liquidity for the payment of estate taxes upon the death of the insured, thus helping to keep intact all or a part of the insured's business, property, or investments; (ii) helping to pay funds to the insured's business sufficient to hire a replacement for him or her, and/or to meet any general business needs, following the death of the insured; (iii) replacing the income, royalties, or earnings stream that would be eliminated or reduced upon the death of the insured; and (iv) restoring and/or building wealth for surviving heirs of the insured. In view of these and other uses, life insurance can provide a sense of security to the policy beneficiaries, and peace of mind to the insured, that the beneficiaries' financial concerns will be assuaged after the death of the insured.

Life insurance also offers significant tax and liability management benefits. First, any increase in the cash value (investment) component of life insurance is not subject to income tax until the accumulated profit is withdrawn from the policy. Second, reflecting legislative awareness of the fact that life insurance is generally paid for in after-tax dollars, the cash value and death benefit of life insurance are not subject to income tax at death. Third, the insured is allowed to borrow against nearly the full cash value of the policy without incurring taxes. While the many life insurance companies offer a wide and at times bewildering array of life-insurance products, in essence, these products can be divided into two main categories: term insurance and permanent (cash value) insurance. Table 8.2 lists selected types and uses of life insurance.

*Term insurance* lasts for a specified period and generally has no cash buildup or investment component. The insured pays premiums that provide insurance coverage up until the end of the term, at which point the coverage ceases. Term insurance can be *annual renewable,* with premiums that keep rising each year, and *level-payment* term, in which the insured pays a fixed amount each year for the duration of his or her coverage. Renewal options, with various associated conditions, including medical examinations and higher premium levels, are a feature of many term insurance policies.

During the conversion period specified in the contract, the policy owner may convert the policy to permanent insurance without evidence of insurability. Term insurance pricing may be found on a number of Web sites, including *accuquote.com, consumerquote.com, instantquote.com, insure.com, insweb.com,* and *quicken.com.*

*Permanent (cash-value) insurance* combines the death benefit feature of conventional term insurance with a tax-deferred investment build-up feature. As with term insurance, the pricing of cash-value insurance depends upon the insured's age, gender, and health and any special features, fees, and terms contained in the policy. Investors should carefully scrutinize the composition and level of fees in cash-value insurance contracts, including: (i) sales charges and surrender charges; (ii) one-time and ongoing administrative fees; (iii) mortality charges, or the cost of insurance; (iv) state premium taxes; and (v) management fees on the assets in the investment portion of the contract. It is generally a good idea to draw upon the resources and expertise of an insurance professional to compare the terms, costs, and benefits of the wide variety of policies written by different life insurance companies.

The two principal types of permanent insurance are: (i) universal life insurance, in which the cash build-up portion of the policy is invested in and guaranteed by the insurance company's general investment account, and is subject to the claims of the insurance company's creditors, if the insurance company should experience financial difficulty; and (ii) *variable life insurance,* in which the death benefit is linked to the performance of an investment account and the insured can select

**T A B L E  8.2**

## Selected Types and Uses of Annuities and Life Insurance

| ANNUITIES | |
| --- | --- |
| **Immediate Annuities** | **Types of Deferred Annuities** |
| •After an initial upfront purchase, payments over time consist of a combination of principal and interest (or earnings, if a variable contract) based on expected mortality or for a fixed period. | **Fixed Annuity** |
|  | •Funds are invested in the general account[1] of the insurance company. •Interest rates are guaranteed for a stated period of time. |
| **Deferred Annuities** | |
| •Funds accumulate without tax until withdrawal or conversion to an immediate annuity. •Withdrawals from any deferred annuity are subject to ordinary income taxes up to the basis of the original investment. Withdrawals prior to age 59 1/2 are subject to a 10% IRS penalty under most circumstances. •The value of an annuity is also subject to surrender charges which decrease annually, normally during the first 6 to 8 years of the contract. •Any gains in contract value are subject to ordinary income taxes at death. | **Variable Annuity** |
|  | •Funds are invested in segregated accounts not generally subject to the claims of the company's creditors. Various investment combinations and options are available, including equity funds, bond funds, and cash management funds. Variable annuities are registered instruments subject to SEC rules and regulations. Investment changes can be made without taxation. |

[1]Investments in the insurance company's general account usually have the principal guaranteed by the company, and are subject to the claims of the insurance company's creditors.

Source: The author.

how the cash-value portion will be invested, separate from the insurance company's general investment account and thus separate from its creditors. Ratings of the financial strength of various life insurance companies may be found at *ambest.com, standardandpoors.com,* and *moodys.com.*

## LIFE INSURANCE

### Term Insurance

- Coverage is limited to the time period stated in the contract, e.g., 10 years, or to a specified age.
- Usually has a provision for conversion to permanent (cash value) life insurance.
- Right to convert may end prior to the end of the contract period.
- Conversion rights are often overlooked but are a major factor in the pricing of coverage.

*Major types of term insurance:*

#### Annual Renewable

- The premium increases on each policy anniversary date until the policy terminates.
- Some contracts are renewable to age 100, but become prohibitively expensive in later years.

#### Level Premium

- Premiums are fixed on a level basis, usually for 5-, 10-, 15-, or 20-year periods.
- Contracts are often renewable for one or two additional periods, but at a stepped-up rate.

#### Re-Entry Term

- Re-entry term is similar to annual renewable term, but is issued at more favorable rates that are conditional upon passing a medical exam each year or at the end of each stated period.

### Permanent (Cash Value) Life Insurance

#### General Comments

- The contract is for the life of the insured(s).
- Premiums over mortality and expense charges accumulate in a reserve fund as cash value, which accumulates free of income taxes.
- Cash value can be borrowed or surrendered, but gains upon surrender are subject to ordinary income tax.
- No income tax at death.

*Basic types of permanent insurance:*

#### Fixed Products

##### Whole Life (Participating)

- Level premiums for life, or some predetermined time period.
- Cash value is invested in the general account[1] of the insurance company.
- Excess interest and mortality gains are paid as dividends.
- Dividends can be re-invested and often in later years become high enough to pay the remainder of insurance premiums.
- The insured pays a fixed amount each year for the duration of coverage.

#### Universal Life

- Premiums are calculated on a level (target) annual basis, but may be skipped (resulting in lower cash values and earnings).
- Interest on policies is normally declared monthly, based on the company's general account investment performance.
- Premiums and interest increase the policy's cash account value.
- Premiums can be increased or decreased periodically.
- Mortality and expense charges decrease the cash account value.

#### Variable Products

##### Variable Life

- Similar to whole life and universal life except cash value is invested in separate accounts as in variable annuities.
- Available as single premium (SPVL), but then is subject to annuity rules for withdrawals or loans.

#### Other

##### Second-to-Die (Survivorship)

Individuals need to be aware of two additional features regarding life insurance. First, a life insurance contract can be considered a Modified Endowment Contract (MEC) under federal tax law if it is paid up via a single premium or a small number of premium payments. Withdrawals from the accumulated cash value, and/or loans against the cash value, of a MEC are fully taxable up to the amount of accumulated earnings in the contract. Usually, the insured needs to reach paid-up status no shorter than a certain number of years (determined by various complex calculation methodologies) to avoid having his or her life insurance policy classified as a MEC.

Second, the life insurance proceeds (the net death benefit) will be *included* in the insured's estate: (i) if the estate is named as the life insurance beneficiary; (ii) if the death benefit is earmarked through documents, such as a trust, to pay off a liability otherwise payable by the estate, including estate taxes; or (iii) if the insured holds at death or within three years of death the right to receive or control the economic benefits of the life insurance policy, its proceeds, or its cash value (known as *incidents of ownership*).

## Annuities

An annuity is defined as either a fixed and/or a variable stream of payments made at specified time intervals, in consideration of a stipulated premium paid either in prior installment payments or in a single payment. Annuities can be classified as either immediate or deferred. *Immediate annuities* are those that begin annuity payments currently or immediately. *Deferred annuities*, offered primarily by life insurance companies: (i) allow the tax-deferred compounding of the underlying investment, with a 10% IRS penalty for withdrawals of earnings before age 59 ½ (with exceptions for death, disability, and lifetime level payments); and (ii) may carry a death benefit, which reimburse an annuity owner's beneficiaries for the account value of the annuity contract should the annuity owner die during the term of the annuity.

*Fixed annuities* pay a set percentage of the investment, determined by yield levels prevailing at the time the annuity contract is purchased. *Variable annuities'* returns vary according to the annuity buyer's investment selections (known as subaccounts), such as equity funds, bond funds, and money market funds. Tax-free switching is allowed for variable annuity owners who wish to shift their investments from one subaccount to another. Table 8.2 lists some of the features of fixed and variable annuities.

Variable annuities' tax-deferred status has made them a popular investment vehicle for individual investors in certain time periods. In deciding whether to take advantage of annuities' tax-deferred compounding benefits, investors should analyze the potential tax savings offered by annuities compared with the various fees and restrictions placed on annuities. Annuities may carry *surrender charges*, which require investors to pay the insurer a percentage of their annuity investment if they decide to surrender the annuity, generally within the first 6 to 10 years of buying it. For a 7-year surrender charge structure, the surrender charge is usually 7% in the first year, declining by a percentage point each year to zero percent by the eighth year.

Sales expenses, or *loads,* can be either back-end or front-end, as with mutual funds, but these charges generally tend to be higher than sales charges on mutual funds. Annuities' relatively high expenses imply that their tax deferral benefits are worthwhile if the investor holds on to the annuity for a long enough time to defray the applicable surrender charges and other expenses. In short, the investor should investigate and quantify the trade-off between: (i) the deferral of capital gains and ordinary income taxes; and (ii) the annuity's surrender charges, other contract expenses, and any taxes and penalties imposed on early withdrawals.

Variable annuities often offer *enhanced death benefits* and, in some cases, living benefits. Most variable annuities guarantee a minimum death benefit equal to the account value or the original principal, whichever is higher. This basic death benefit is often supplemented by a guarantee that locks in the highest anniversary value and/or a 5% minimum annual increase. The guaranteed death benefit ensures heirs a minimum return regardless of financial-market performance.

Annuity owners can also enjoy *living benefits*. These benefits take the form of a guaranteed income base or an outright return of principal guarantee. The minimum income base is usually calculated using the highest anniversary value of fixed annual increase, similar to an enhanced death benefit. Living benefits protect the individual's future income from a severe market decline while preserving upside potential. Additional details concerning the structure and pricing of annuities may be found on Web sites such as *annuity.com, annuityadvantage.com, annuityshopper.com* and *iii.org/individuals/annuities.*

## TAX MANAGEMENT

Tax management refers to the importance of taking into account the federal, state, local, and international income, capital gains, withholding, estate, gift, and property tax implications of investment actions and investment structures. The Web sites of the Mutual Fund Education Alliance (*mfea.com*), the Chicago Board Options Exchange (*cboe.com*), and the Internal Revenue Service (*irs.gov*) contain numerous tax-law updates and other tax insights germane to investors. For example, investors should keep in mind the Alternative Minimum Tax (AMT), which makes sure that taxpayers pay a minimum level of federal income tax, without regard to how many credits, exclusions, and deductions they may be allowed to take. Each year, taxpayers who may be subject to the AMT carry out the following two steps: (i) they add back to ordinary income certain *deductions* (such as real estate taxes and state and local income taxes) and *preference items* (such as accelerated depreciation, passive losses from partnerships, and interest income from private activity municipal bonds issued after August 7, 1986); and (ii) they undertake a tax computation that is parallel to their normal tax calculation. If the AMT amount is less than or equal to the normal tax, the taxpayer pays only the normally computed tax, but if the AMT amount exceeds the normal tax, the taxpayer owes the Alternative Minimum Tax amount. Because the AMT exemption amounts are not indexed for inflation, with the passage of time, an increasing number of taxpayers have become subject to AMT taxation, particularly individuals with large families, who have exercised incentive stock options, or who live in high-tax states and thus claim large deductions from state and local taxes.

In addition to AMT considerations, investors' asset allocations, investment policies, and tax-management strategies should reflect some or all of the following tax-related decisions, among others:

◆ **Type of Security Owned:** (e.g., the interest income from U.S. government and certain federal agency securities is exempt from *state and local income taxes*, and the interest from most state and local government securities is exempt from *federal income taxes*).

◆ **Timing of Investment Actions:** (e.g., in periods of broad securities price appreciation, it may be advantageous for the investor to make Individual Retirement Account (IRA) contributions or charitable gifts of assets at the beginning, rather than at the end, of the investor's tax year);

◆ **Investment Tactics:** (e.g., assets held longer than a year and a day qualify for more favorable long-term capital gains tax rates than short-term capital gains, which are taxed at ordinary income tax rates; other tactics include making charitable contributions with highly appreciated capital assets, deferring income recognition into the next year and accelerating deductions into the current year, offsetting short-term capital gains with short-term capital losses, and identifying specific lots of securities when they are to be sold, rather than using a first-in, first-out (FIFO) cost basis);

- ◆ **Type of Account for Asset Ownership:** (e.g., certain amounts and/or types of assets might be more appropriately held in a child's account rather than a parent's, or in a conventional taxable account rather than in a tax-deferred IRA/Roth IRA account);

- ◆ **Donor-Advised Funds:** (e.g., a gift of cash or an appreciated asset may be donated with an immediate tax deduction to a donor-advised charitable fund, with the money distributed later at the donor's option to specifically designated charities. Three large funds include *charitablegift.org, vanguardcharitable.org,* and *schwabcharitable.org*; others include *calvertgiving.org,* with a focus on socially responsible investments, and *rotary.org/foundation/development/advisedfunds)*; and

- ◆ **Employer Securities:** (e.g., an investor contemplating a lump-sum distribution including employer securities might elect to apply the net unrealized appreciation rules, thus allowing capital-gains rather than ordinary-income tax treatment on the price appreciation of the employer securities; other measures may be taken to avoid triggering capital gains when an employee decides to exercise his or her incentive stock options).

It is worth reiterating that: (i) the tax code may change, and the tax-management stratagems briefly outlined here represent only a small subset of the full range of potential tax-management actions; (ii) investors should not ignore tax considerations in their financial management activities, nor they should allow taxes to become the primary driver of their investment actions, to the detriment of other factors; and (iii) investors should consult with their own tax and legal advisors for tax or other legal advice.

## LIABILITY MANAGEMENT

In the investor's quest to achieve his or her financial goals, liability management can be as important as asset management. The investor's liability-management decisions include the type, amount, cost, maturity, and terms of borrowings, as well as the tax-deductibility of various kinds of interest payments. It is important for investors to consult their tax advisors regarding the deductibility of interest before taking any tax-related borrowing actions, and to utilize appropriate personal or external resources to compare payment and amortization scenarios across various debt structures.

Three of the most common forms of borrowing by individuals include: (i) *margin borrowing,* with some or all of the investor's securities holdings used as collateral for the margin loans; (ii) *mortgage and home-equity loans* and lines of credit; and (iii) *credit card debt.* Borrowing may be undertaken for a variety of purposes, including: the desire to raise funds without liquidating assets; the purchase of a new home, the improvement of an existing home, or the refinancing of an already outstanding mortgage; to expand the investor's own business or to pay educational expenses; or to improve cash-flow management through debt consolidation.

For mortgage and home equity loans and lines of credit, the investor's choices encompass: (i) whether payments should be interest-plus-principal or interest only; (ii) the percentage of the asset's value to be financed; (iii) whether to have a fixed- or adjustable-rate loan, and if the latter, the index on which the rate is based, the interest-rate adjustment period, any interest-rate floor or ceiling options, and conversion features allowing a switch from adjustable to fixed rate; and (iv) the use of eligible securities as collateral in lieu of a cash down payment. *Reverse mortgages* allow established homeowners to tap into what might be substantial accumulated equity in their homes. In a reverse mortgage, the lender pays the homeowner a certain amount each month, with the principal and interest recouped when the home is sold at some point in the future.

Credit-card borrowings are another widely utilized source of debt financing by individuals. The interest paid on consumer borrowing debt is not tax deductible, but interest payments on home mortgages and/or home equity loans and home equity lines of credit generally are. Differentiating characteristics of credit card debt include interest rates, penalty charges, annual fees, cash rebates, discounts on goods and services purchased, expense management and tracking systems, and various kinds of point-reward programs based on the user's charge volume.

SECTION 6

# INFORMATION SOURCES

# C H A P T E R 9

# INFORMATION MANAGEMENT

## OVERVIEW

The Information Age has witnessed a dramatic expansion in the number and variety of information sources about asset allocation and investing, in the kinds of tools for accessing these sources, and even in the ways of thinking about learning and knowing. Increasingly, investors have come to want and expect to obtain information as quickly as possible, with high standards of accuracy and relevance. As a result, skill and proficiency in information management have become important, and in certain circumstances, critical success factors in asset allocation and investment management.

This chapter reviews methods of classifying information sources, strategies for building core knowledge versus staying informed, and pathways for and effective ways of managing information. This chapter also surveys the structure of the Internet and the World Wide Web, including portals, Web sites, Web-based tools, and the hierarchy of Internet search tools and information sources.

Many of the leading *media-based* information resources covered in this chapter include: books; business-school case studies; conference calls, chat rooms, and message boards; conferences, seminars, and workshops; corporations and industry organizations; educational institutions and research institutes; governmental and regulatory bodies; nonprint mass media; periodicals, newspapers and newsletters; professional and scholarly journals; professional organizations; Wall Street and the financial industry; Web-based tools; and Web sites and portals.

In addition, several *subject-based* information resources reviewed include: investing basics and fundamentals; asset allocation for individual and professional investors; individual-investor behavior; asset-class characteristics, returns, and risk; recognizing cyclical and secular turning points; spending versus reinvesting-income flows; comparative financial analysis; structural considerations in asset allocation; and asset allocation worksheets.

Information management, and the selection and use of information sources, are crucial success factors in asset allocation and investing. In view of the growing number of information sources, an ever-expanding supply of information, and ramifying delivery methods, investors need to be disciplined and innovative in how they obtain, apply, store, and retrieve information about asset allocation and investing. Investors can improve the chances of achieving favorable investment results if they can judiciously filter out superfluous information, know how and when to look for information, and learn to apply information effectively in real-world investment situations. When searching for information, it may be worthwhile to rapidly skim the figures and topics in this chapter, to be reminded of particularly relevant and useful sources, and to inspire investors to explore new pathways to knowledge.

## CLASSIFYING INFORMATION SOURCES

The proliferation of information sources and delivery channels underscores the need for care and diligence in their selection. For example, when properly used, the Internet offers swift and powerful means of locating the right information. On the other hand, using the Internet can also consume significant amounts of time and lead information-seeking investors down pathways that are inefficient and/or unreliable. The enormous quantity of Internet- and non-Internet-based information, coupled with investors' finite amounts of time to seek and obtain information, places a meaningful premium on efficiency and

**F I G U R E  9.1**

Methods of Classifying Information Sources

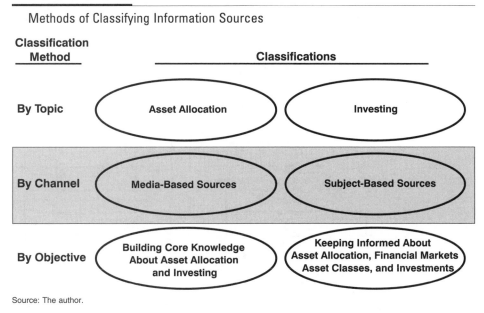

Source: The author.

discernment in the selection of regularly utilized sources, as well as resources employed in specific information searches.

The information sources surveyed in this chapter are by no means
all-inclusive, but have been chosen for their relevance, clarity, and utility. They address the disciplines of asset allocation and investment
management, grouped broadly by medium and by subject area. As far
as is practicable, selected sources focus on *building and adding core
knowledge* and/or *keeping the investor informed* about asset allocation, financial markets, asset classes, and specific investments. Figure 9.1 depicts these classification methods.

Information sources often do not fit neatly or intuitively into the
classification methods that appear in Figure 9.1—by topic, by channel,
and by objective. Many sources overlap more than one information
topic, channel, or objective. Over time, effective new information sources
may emerge, while others may decline in usefulness or fade away.

Figure 9.2 lists media- and subject-based information resources relating to asset allocation and investing that this chapter covers.

As Figure 9.2 outlines, *media-based* information resources on asset
allocation and investing include: books; business school case studies;
investor conference calls, chat rooms, and message boards; conferences,

**F I G U R E  9.2**

Selected Media- and Subject-Based Information Resources

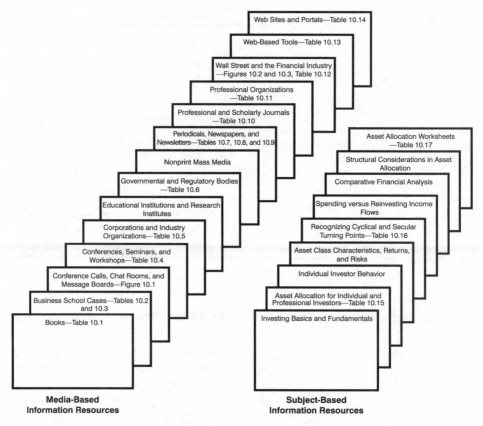

Media-Based
Information Resources

Subject-Based
Information Resources

Source: The author.

seminars, and workshops; corporations and industry organizations; educational institutions and research institutes; governmental and regulatory bodies; nonprint mass media, including satellite and cable TV, broadcast TV, radio, financial data purveyors, pagers and other wireless devices, and motion pictures; periodicals, newspapers, and newsletters; professional and scholarly journals; professional organizations; Wall Street and the financial industry; Web-based tools; and Web sites and portals.

*Subject-based* information resources on asset allocation and investing include: investing basics and fundamentals; asset allocation for individual and professional investors; individual investor behavior; asset class characteristics, returns, and risks; recognizing cyclical and secular turning points; spending versus reinvesting income flows; comparative financial analysis; structural considerations in asset allocation; and asset allocation worksheets.

Figure 9.3 shows the distinctions between *building the investor's core knowledge* about asset allocation and investing, and *keeping the investor informed* about asset allocation, financial markets, asset classes, and specific investments.

As Figure 9.3 shows, some sources—such as books, professional and scholarly journals, and research institutes—primarily focus on *building core knowledge.* Other sources—such as periodicals, newspapers, newsletters, radio and television, conference calls, and corporations—primarily focus on the *dissemination of information updates.* Finally, some sources—such as Wall Street and the financial industry, many Web sites and portals, and governments and regulatory

**F I G U R E  9.3**

Building Core Knowledge versus Keeping Informed

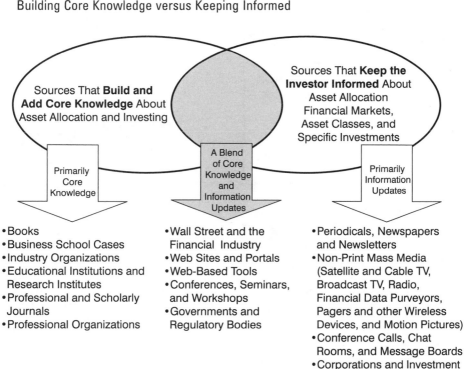

Source: The author.

bodies—furnish a *blend* of building core knowledge and providing information updates.

Given a discrete amount of time that investors can dedicate to investing activity, they make choices—either consciously or unwittingly—between acquiring core knowledge and keeping informed. Figure 9.4 contains a schematic representation of several of these tradeoffs.

The two boxes on the left side of Figure 9.4 show what happens when the investor tends to overemphasize *keeping informed,* denoted by Box ①, versus *acquiring core knowledge,* denoted by Box ②. In Box ①, the investor focuses more and more of his or her ongoing information-management activity on *keeping informed* about asset allocation, markets, asset classes, and investments, to the detriment of acquiring new core knowledge. As a result, the depth and the applicability of the investor's core knowledge erodes over time.

**F I G U R E 9.4**

Tradeoffs Between Acquiring Core Knowledge and Keeping Informed

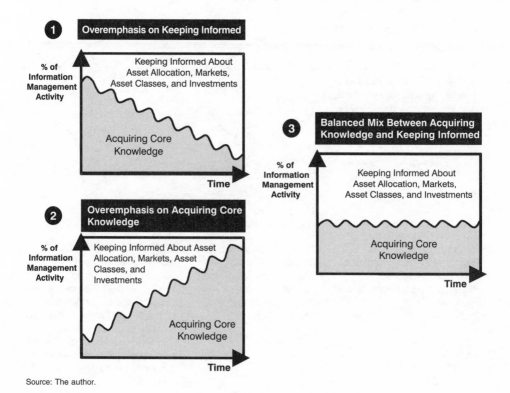

Source: The author.

In Box ②, the investor focuses an increasing share of his or her on-going information-management activity on *acquiring and building up his or her stock of core knowledge*, to the detriment of keeping informed about asset allocation, markets, asset classes, and investments. In such circumstances, the investor may develop or add to a substantial reserve of core knowledge, but in the process, he or she may place the asset allocation and/or specific investments at risk through neglect.

On the right side of Figure 9.4, Box ③ shows a *balanced, relatively steady mix* between acquiring core knowledge and keeping informed. In such a scenario, the investor devotes a roughly stable share of his or her information-management activity to acquiring and maintaining a currently applicable base of core knowledge. At the same time, the investor devotes an adequate portion of his or her effort to monitoring and keeping informed about asset allocation, markets, asset classes, and investments.

## STRATEGIES AND TACTICS FOR INFORMATION MANAGEMENT

Investors can greatly enhance their information management with good practices, described below:

- ◆ **Conduct Research Before Taking Action:** The investor's chances of success in asset allocation and investing may considerably improve if he or she takes the time to evaluate and thoroughly explore the relevant information sources *before* beginning the process of asset allocation and investing. Research and a modest amount of homework on asset allocation and investing can avoid many costly errors and mistakes.

- ◆ **Trust Human Instincts:** The role of technology—including personal computers, the Internet, and wireless devices—in information management often downplays or removes the amount of human reflection, consideration, intuition, and judgment that should factor into investors' decision making. It is hard to overstate the importance of in-person meetings, at which the perceptive investor can look his or her counterpart in the eye, observe body language, and take careful note of voice/gesture emphases and inflections.

- ◆ **Utilize Libraries:** Public libraries, libraries at educational institutions, and corporate libraries provide organized, relevant, and easily navigable resources. Many libraries often have publicly accessible high-speed Internet connections, and professional librarians who are highly skilled in research techniques and information management. The Online Computer Library Center, Inc. (*oclc.org*) is a library-oriented suite of resources designed to help libraries access knowledge through innovation and collaboration.

◆ **Prioritize and Customize Information Searches:** When looking for information, it helps to keep in mind the ultimate purpose and relative importance of the data, facts, and/or body of knowledge being sought. At times, the investor may seek to deepen his or her overall level of learning about and familiarity with a given subject, and at other times, the investor may only be looking for highly targeted and specific information. The investor's objectives will influence the number and type of sources consulted, the time devoted to the search, and the relative importance attributed to each source.

◆ **Manage and Stay on Top of the Information:** Investors should seek to remain in control of the information they need, rather than allowing the information to control them and their decision-making processes. There is no substitute for devoting time, effort, and good judgment to stepping back from the information, to see the forest for the trees.

◆ **Select Appropriate Media:** Identical information about asset allocation and investing is frequently accessible in several formats, ranging from physical attendance at a conference, to a live or recorded videoconference or Webcast of the conference, to transcripts of the conference proceedings via mail or courier service, via fax, or via the Internet. Figure 9.5 shows several pathways of obtaining information about asset allocation and investing.

Figure 9.5 shows that to an increasing degree, information may be accessed via *multiple channels*—from in person, to various forms of media, including satellite, cable, and broadcast TV, pagers and wireless devices—and in *more than one format*—from its originally produced version to its Web-based variant. Cost, ease of access, convenience, habit, and expediency often determine which channel and format the investor chooses.

◆ **Leverage Others' Efforts:** Efficient users of information about asset allocation and investing often develop creative ways to augment their own efforts by sharing knowledge with

## F I G U R E 9.5

Selected Pathways of Obtaining Information

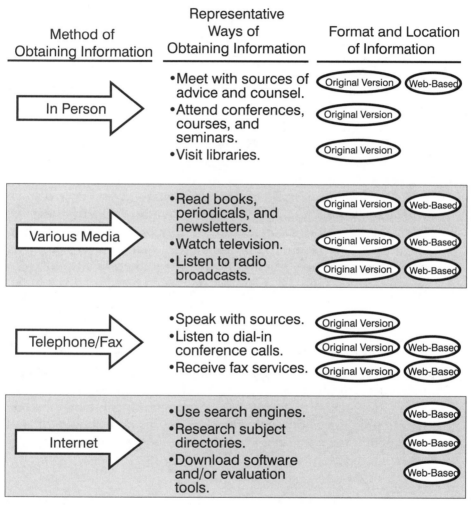

Source: The author.

friends, family members, professional colleagues, and counterparts who are employed by customers, suppliers, or even
competing organizations. For example, in such an arrange-
ment, one party may subscribe to certain publications while
another party subscribes to a different set of publications,

with each keeping the other informed about articles and subjects in their respective areas of interest. In some cases, businesspeople, lawyers, or professors may formally or informally engage a librarian to surveil a variety of sources on an ongoing basis for items of interest.

◆ **Respect Information Supply-and-Demand Relationships:** Investors may increase their chances of success in information management when they are aware of the level of their own demand for information relative to the supply of information they are seeking. Figure 9.6 displays four different information supply-demand relationships.

In general, when the investor has a *low* level of demand for information and the supply of information is also *low* (quadrant ③ in Figure 9.6), he or she may very well increase the chances of pursuing erroneous asset allocation or investment actions. Conversely, when the investor has a *high* level of demand for information and the supply of information is also *high* (quadrant ② in Figure 9.6), he or she may easily end up devoting too much time to information gathering and not enough time to analysis and action. When feasible, it is a good idea for the investor to maintain a realistic level of demand for information—not too high, and not too low—and to seek an appropriate supply of information. In Figure 9.6, this is depicted as the shaded circle in the middle of the four quadrants.

◆ **Be Mindful of Tax Treatment:** In many instances, expenses incurred to purchase books, periodicals, and other sources of information designed to generate investment income may be tax deductible. Investors with questions in this area should consult competent tax counsel and/or the relevant tax authorities in their jurisdiction.

## INFORMATION-MANAGEMENT CAVEATS

To optimize the investor's usage of information sources about asset allocation and investing, it is helpful to keep several reminders and cautions in mind:

◆ **It Is Impossible to Know Everything:** Once the investor has accepted the fact that it is humanly impossible to keep track of and know everything about asset allocation and investing, the need quickly becomes apparent for discipline, organization, prioritiza-

## F I G U R E 9.6

Information Supply-Demand Relationships

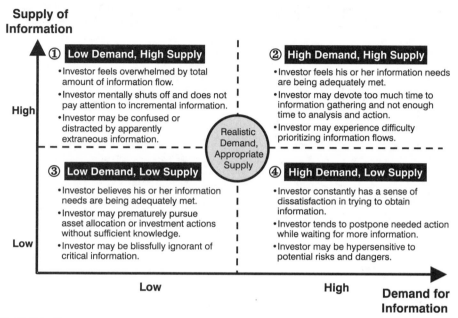

**Supply of Information**

① **Low Demand, High Supply**
- Investor feels overwhelmed by total amount of information flow.
- Investor mentally shuts off and does not pay attention to incremental information.
- Investor may be confused or distracted by apparently extraneous information.

② **High Demand, High Supply**
- Investor feels his or her information needs are being adequately met.
- Investor may devote too much time to information gathering and not enough time to analysis and action.
- Investor may experience difficulty prioritizing information flows.

*Realistic Demand, Appropriate Supply*

③ **Low Demand, Low Supply**
- Investor believes his or her information needs are being adequately met.
- Investor may prematurely pursue asset allocation or investment actions without sufficient knowledge.
- Investor may be blissfully ignorant of critical information.

④ **High Demand, Low Supply**
- Investor constantly has a sense of dissatisfaction in trying to obtain information.
- Investor tends to postpone needed action while waiting for more information.
- Investor may be hypersensitive to potential risks and dangers.

High — Low (Supply axis)
Low — High (Demand axis)

**Demand for Information**

Source: The author.

tion, and pruning information. Just as investors need to find their own *risk comfort level,* so too are they advised to seek out an *information comfort level* that reflects their resources, needs, vocational and avocational pursuits, level of interest, monetary and time constraints, experience, and other circumstances.

◆ **Information Does Not Equal Knowledge:** The purpose of searching for information about asset allocation and investing is to develop knowledge, and possibly to enhance the investor's wisdom and judgment about these disciplines. For information to contribute to knowledge, it needs to be relevant, timely, accurate, comprehensible, and ideally, in useful form.

◆ **Information Sources Possess Varying Degrees of Effectiveness:** The investor should relentlessly evaluate the quality, relevance, and effectiveness of each information source, keeping in mind that while some sources are effective, others are ineffective and highly marginal at best. Figure 9.7 portrays the

**F I G U R E 9.7**

Effective versus Ineffective Sources for Building Core Knowledge

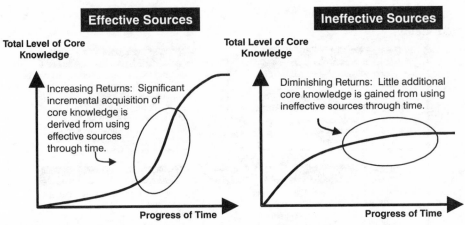

Source: The author.

results of using effective sources, as compared with ineffective sources, in *building core knowledge.*

The left half of Figure 9.7 shows how the use of effective information sources adds incremental core knowledge and enables the investor to build a significant store of core knowledge over time. The right half of Figure 9.7 paints a different picture, one in which the use of ineffective information sources adds little additional core knowledge about asset allocation and investing over time.

Figure 9.8 shows the effects over time of using effective sources, compared with ineffective sources, to keep informed about asset allocation, financial markets, asset classes, and specific investments.

The left half of Figure 9.8 depicts what happens when the use of effective information sources raises the investor's degree of being informed. The right half of Figure 9.8 shows that the more the investor uses ineffective sources, his or her degree of being informed rises at a slow rate and begins to stagnate, even at low levels.

◆ **Not All Investors Want the Same Level of Knowledge:** Some investors have a high degree of curiosity about, passion for, and interest in asset allocation and investing. As a result, they desire a high level of knowledge about these activities, and

## F I G U R E 9.8

Effective versus Ineffective Sources for Keeping Informed

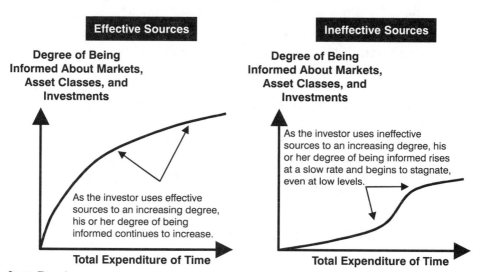

**Effective Sources**

Degree of Being
Informed About Markets,
Asset Classes, and
Investments

As the investor uses effective
sources to an increasing degree,
his or her degree of being
informed continues to increase.

**Total Expenditure of Time**

**Ineffective Sources**

Degree of Being
Informed About Markets,
Asset Classes, and
Investments

As the investor uses ineffective
sources to an increasing degree, his
or her degree of being informed rises
at a slow rate and begins to stagnate,
even at low levels.

**Total Expenditure of Time**

Source: The author.

they seek a sufficient quantity and quality of information sources to satisfy their wants. At the other end of the spectrum, owing in part to differences in interest, demands on their available time, personal characteristics, and other factors, some investors prefer a lower information flow about asset allocation and investing. Below a certain information level, it may be prudent for such investors to seek out professional talent who can carry out these activities on the investor's behalf.

◆ **There Are Many Ways to Store and Retrieve Information:** In evaluating and using information sources, it is a good idea to remember that one person's way of *organizing, storing, searching for, and retrieving* information may be different from another person's. As a consequence, prior to using a given information source, the investor should strive to develop an overall perspective on and sense of its organization, contents, dates of creation and/or updating, and storage, disposal, and retrieval procedures.

◆ **Searching for Information Is an Art as Well as a Science:** At times, the most relevant and useful information is located in a swift and straightforward manner. On other occasions, the most appropriate and effective information is not easy to find. Under such circumstances, it would be wise to keep in mind the roles of luck, guessing, serendipity, perseverance, and creativity as the investor searches for needed information.

◆ **Information Needs to Be Ratified by Time:** Some information about asset allocation and investing is highly perishable and quickly outdated; some information is timeless, in that its usefulness, truth, and applicability endure for long periods of time; and some information may possess highly perishable and highly enduring aspects simultaneously. For these reasons, investors need to recognize, and take special precautions about, the current and likely future relevance of each information source consulted.

## INTERNET-BASED INFORMATION SOURCES

From its origins in the late 1960s as a US government- and military-sponsored system of linking computers, the Internet has burgeoned in succeeding decades, to a computer network comprised of thousands of networks around the world. The Internet's growth has been spurred by: (i) the development of the World Wide Web (www) by Tim Berners-Lee in 1990-1991, allowing one interface to access virtually all of the different computer and communications protocol types on the Internet; (ii) the invention of an enhanced Internet browser, called Mosaic, by Marc Andreesen in 1993, which allows various kinds of search engines to roam across the World Wide Web and locate information according to parameters the Internet user specifies; and (iii) the first official-specification release, in 1995, of Hypertext Markup Language (HTML), which allows programmers, document creators, Web site designers, and others to place tags within a document that permit user-selectable links or connections to other documents in a variety of formats including text, graphics, sound, images, databases, radio and television broadcasts, multimedia presentations, and several forms of interactive collaboration in real time.

Figure 9.9 shows several of the most frequently used features of the Internet that apply to the investor's search for appropriate information sources. (Unless otherwise noted, all Internet addresses mentioned are preceded by the keystrokes *http://www.;* thus, for example, this book refers to the more formal *http://www.google.com* in its shorthand form, as *google.com.*)

**F I G U R E 9.9**

Internet-Based Information Sources About Asset Allocation and Investing

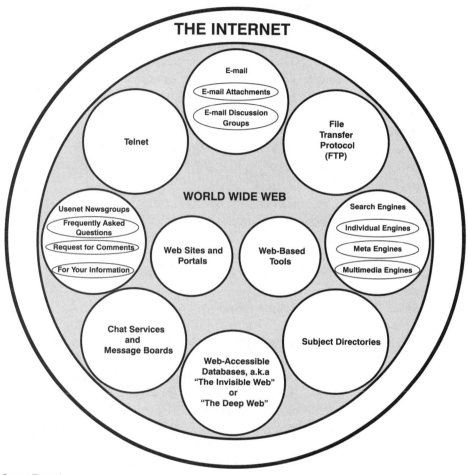

Several of the leading types of Internet-based information sources depicted in Figure 9.9 are described below:

- ◆ **E-Mail:** allows investors to send electronic mail messages—for example, in the form of queries for information from sources about asset allocation and investing—to any other user of e-mail with a mailbox address on the Internet. The power and desirability of using e-mail messaging expanded considerably with the development of the **e-mail attachments** capability. This feature allows users to attach a wide variety of file types (such as Microsoft Excel spreadsheets or Microsoft Word documents) to e-mail messages sent via the Internet.

- **E-Mail Discussion Groups:** conduct ongoing discussions on the Web in topic-centered groups notified by e-mail according to instructions in a software program known as a *listserv*. Investors wishing to participate in one or more e-mail discussion groups devoted to relevant topics relating to asset allocation and investing must first send their e-mail address to the appropriate computer-based subscription management program known as a *listserver*. Web sites such as *majordomo.com*, and *liszt.com* contain a searchable collection of e-mail discussion groups.

- **File Transfer Protocol (FTP)**: is now commonly embedded in most Web browser programs, to allow investors to transfer the contents of entire files from Internet host computers to their personal computers. FTP sites contain software, graphical, text, and numerical information, downloadable multimedia files, and other resources. FTP files can be retrieved via *download.com, ftpfind.com,* and *shareware.com.*

    Investors with a **Telnet** program configured to their Web browser and installed on their local computer can dial up the address and, sometimes, a specific terminal number on a remote computer. This gives them the ability to log onto the remote computer and use the computer as if they were actually sitting in front of the remote computer itself. In this fashion, investors can search library catalogs and use online databases to find targeted information about asset allocation and investing.

- **Search Engines:** are computer programs that search some subset of the documents on the Web for information on a given topic and then apply certain specified algorithms to query the index of information gathered by the program. **Individual search engines** use their own program, commonly referred to by such names as a spider, a crawler, a wanderer, or a robot, to amass a searchable index. This index is usually: (i) populated based on the user's specifications as to such search criteria as words, phrases, dates, and Web address (domain) locations; and then (ii) ranked according to the search engine's proprietary relevancy rules such as frequency of mention in the underlying document, concept,

popularity, type of site, or links from other pages ranked high by
the search engine. Some widely used individual search engines
include *altavista.com, alltheweb.com, askjeeves.com, excite.com,
google.com, hotbot.com, msn.search, northernlight.com, teoma.com,* and
*yahoo.com.* Guides to search engines and search-engine collections
can be found at *beaucoup.com, search.aol.com, searchengineguide.com,
completeplanet.com, websearch.about.com,* and *searchenginewatch.com.*
(For a comprehensive list of search engines, *searchenginewatch.com*
lists and rates their attributes.)

◆ **Meta Search Engines**: also known as parallel, mega, or
multithreaded search engines, search multiple individual
search engines simultaneously. Many users prefer meta search
engines that remove duplicate underlying documents collected
from more than one search engine and present a combined index in a single list ranked according to relevancy. To do this,
several successful meta search engines often allow the user to
specify a time limit for the total search or to limit the total
number of results retrieved per engine. Some widely used
meta search engines include *c4.com, clusty.com, ixquick.com,
kartoo.com, mamma.com, metacrawler.com, pandia.com, dogpile.com,
profusion.com, surfwax.com, vivisimo.com,* and *webcrawler.com.*

◆ **Multimedia Search Engines:** offer searches of some combination of radio, audio, video, maps, photographs, artworks, car-
toons, sounds, sound effects, architecture, prints, and
illustrations. Several noteworthy multi-media search engines
include: *images.google.com, corbis.com, multimedia.lycos.com,
picsearch.com, photodude.com, thepicturecollection.com, speechbot.re-
search.compaq.com,* and *ditto.com.* Documents that are published
in Adobe's portable document format (PDF) may be searched
via *adobe.com.* In addition, a number of search-engine services
will track Web sites for new information that matches targeted
search terms at periodic intervals that the user specifies.
Among others, these services include *karnak.com.*

It appears reasonable to assert that traditional search
engines may have access to less than 10 percent of the available content on the Web, based on Yahoo's statement early in
the New Millennium that there are possibly up to 100 billion
Web pages, and Google's statement around the same time
that they had indexed 8.8 billion pages. Many investors do
not fully utilize many of the strengths of search engines,

either because they choose a search engine poorly, have a suboptimal search strategy, or both. A large number of search engines use the principles of Boolean logic (developed by the British mathematician George Boole, who lived from 1815 to 1864), but these search engines often use Boolean logic in vastly different ways. To greatly increase the power, focus, and speed of their services, investors should familiarize themselves with, or seek the advice of someone adept in, the logic, syntax, basic and advanced search options, case sensitivity, quotation marks, truncation conventions, popularity and link ranking, proximity operations, and concept clustering capabilities of the various types and brands of search engines. Some offerings have subject directories (described below) embedded alongside or shared with the search engine, and in other instances, a standalone subject directory may produce results superior to those of a search engine. A short amount of time devoted to learning about search engines can save the investor considerable time and effort in searching for information.

♦ **Usenet Newsgroups:** number in the thousands and are organized to exchange articles, comments, and messages centered upon a variety of business, investing, academic, computer-related, and other subjects. Usenet administrators manage each Usenet news service, and make topical postings available to specific Usenet newsgroups or central computers. This information is accessible for reading by Usenet members who have so-called newsreader programs, such as the Messenger program included with the Netscape Communicator package, which allows entry to a Usenet bulletin board. A service called *jumpcity.com* provides an annotated subject directory with links to any Usenet newsgroups associated with a given subject. Usenet newsgroups can also be searched by, among other tools, search engines such as *altavista.com, groups.google.com, hotbot.com, newsfeeds.com, newsville.com, profusion.com,* and *tile.net.*

A number of Usenet newsgroups have collected current and/or previous postings into groups of entries that may be of interest to members. **Frequently asked questions,** or **FAQs,** list answers to the most commonly posed inquiries about the Usenet newsgroup's specific topic. The Internet FAQ consortium has brought together a collection of FAQ information at *faqs.org*. **Request for comments (RFC)** and **for your information (FYI)** postings also often contain highly technical information that group members can peruse.

◆ **Subject Directories:** provide investors and other Internet users with a list of selected links to specific search areas. *Academic and professional subject directories* usually serve the needs of the academic and professional community, and are set up and maintained by experts and/or librarians in the fields covered by a specific directory. Several respected examples include: *academicinfo.net; infomine.ucr.edu,* maintained by the University of California school system; *clearinghouse.net,* consisting of the Argus Clearinghouse's rated guides to Internet-based subject collections; *vlib.org; ipl.org;* and *lii.org,* an annotated subject directory known as the Librarian's Index to the Internet.

Some *business or commercial portals that function as subject directories* are usually advertising-supported and generally focus on topics that academic and professional subject directories do not commonly address. Other prominent examples of business or commercial subject directories include: *excite.com,* consisting of a searchable, annotated listing of Web sites; *about.com,* whose topical directories have been assembled by subject specialists; and *financialfind.com.*

Subject directories vary substantially in their degree of selectivity, and frequently resemble the output of an Internet search engine, with the distinction that the links to sources in directories have been usually culled, assembled, annotated, and/or recommended by experts. In some cases, subject directories are packaged together with a search engine, allowing the user to: (i) search the directory on a standalone basis; or (ii) combine a directory search with the results from the search engine's traversal over the World Wide Web. Examples include: LookSmart, primarily a human-compiled directory of Web sites, whose tab for Articles is lauded for the access it provides to content from thousands of periodicals; *directory.google.com,* which allows the user to scan the valuable information compiled by the open directory; RDN, Resource Directory Network at *rdn.ac.uk,* the U.K.'s free national gateway to Internet resources for the learning, teaching, and research communities; and *search.msn.com.*

◆ **Web-Accessible Databases:** are usually highly specialized databases that cannot be located easily with most of the conventional search engines. For this reason, Web-accessible databases are sometimes also known as "The Invisible Web" or "The Deep Web." Armed with the right tools, investors can comb through Web-accessible databases to find targeted information that they otherwise might not have obtained. CyberAge Books has published a book about Web-accessible databases called *The Invisible Web*, by Gary Price.

One of the best ways to discover Web-accessible databases is to explore sites that gather searchable databases on the Web such as *profusion.com's* "The Invisible Web" listing of more than 10,000 databases; *searchiq.com's* topical directory of searchable databases; George Washington University's list of free online databases at *gwis2.circ.gwu.edu*; and *thebighub.com*, which contains topic-based search methods for Web-accessible databases and other specialty search engines.

◆ **Chat Services and Message Boards:** provide a means for investors to communicate with each other on a real-time basis. When equipped with an Internet Relay Chat (IRC) software program, investors can exchange messages with each other on a variety of channels devoted to specific subjects. Further information about the IRC service can be found at *irc.com*. Several Web sites let subscribers take part in chat room conversations about asset allocation and investing, as well as a wide range of other subjects, some frivolous and superficial, others substantive and profound. Some widely used sponsors of topical chat services include the Microsoft Network (*msn.com*), America Online (*aol.com*), the Motley Fool (*fool.com*), and Yahoo! Chat (*yahoo.com*).

Several of the most widely used message boards provide a great volume of information, some of which is penetrating and insightful, some of which is redundant and of questionable value. The *companysleuth.com* service allows investors to search the most widely used message boards for postings about companies the investor is interested in following. Among scores of message board sites, three of the most popular include *siliconinvestor.com*, *ragingbull.com*, and *finance.yahoo.com*.

◆ **Web Sites, Portals, and Web-Based Tools:** are often indistinguishable from one another, because portals are, in fact, Web sites themselves and contain links to their own and/or other Web sites and Web-based tools due to a high degree of similarity, overlap, and definitional indistinctness between Web sites and Web-based tools (which are also Web sites, strictly speaking). Figure 9.10 presents selected types of Internet portals, Web sites, and Web-based tools.

The distinction is somewhat artificial between the Web sites and the Web-based tools shown in Figure 9.10. Generally speaking, Internet-based resources that *advise, teach, inform, and execute transactions* appear under the category of Web sites, and the Internet-based resources that perform an *analytical, charting, evaluational, or management function* for the investor appear under the heading of Web-based tools.

Figure 9.10 also shows several ways investors can access portals, Web sites, and Web-based tools. For reasons of habit or preference, many investors access one or more of the popular portals first, and then click on links to that portal's own areas and sections of specific interest, shown as the central portion of Figure 9.10. Alternatively, an investor may proceed to a specific Web site or a specific Web-based tool, either directly or through links embedded within a portal. Some portal-based, continuously updated lists of the most popular search terms are the Yahoo Buzz Index, at *buzz.yahoo.com*, the Lycos Top 50, at *50.lycos.com*, Dogpile Search Spy at *dogpile.com*, MSN Search Insider at *imagine-msn.com/insider*, and Google Zeitgeist at *google.com*. Yahoo News also publishes the most frequently forwarded content and the most viewed content in general and specific topic areas, including finance, at *dailynews.yahoo.com*.

Figure 9.10 shows that some of the functions and services relating to asset allocation and investing that are available on specific Web sites include, but are not limited to, offerings in broad categories: advice sources; calendar-based releases; educational materials; filings and announcements; news; research; and securities brokerage. Similarly, some of the functions and services relating to asset allocation and investing available as Web-based tools include offerings in the broad categories of: analytics; chart services; portfolio management updates; software programs; technology reviews; and wealth management packages.

In approaching information sources about asset allocation and investing, investors would do well to consider Web sites and Web-based tools together. In many cases, a given address on the Web may simultaneously contain certain information listed under Web sites in Figure 9.10, with other resources listed under *Web-based tools*.

## F I G U R E 9.10

Selected Internet Portals, Web Sites, and Web-Based Tools

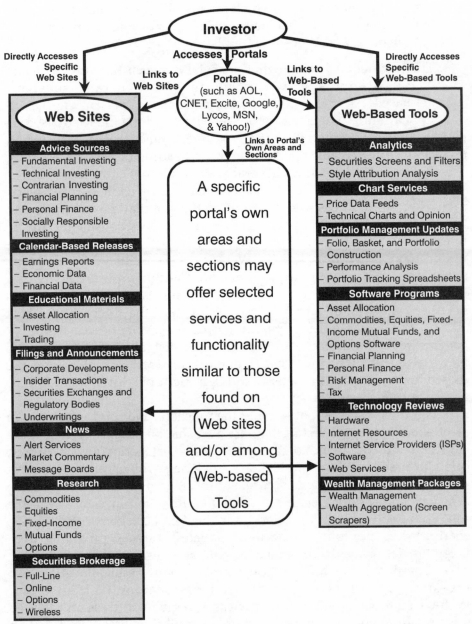

Source: The author.

Common examples might include educational materials or advice sources with software programs and securities brokerage services with analytics, chart services, or portfolio management updates. Specific information sources and Web addresses for the various categories in Figure 9.10 are discussed later in Chapter 10.

## OPTIMIZING INTERNET-BASED INFORMATION SOURCES

For many investors, the Internet consists primarily of three things: e-mail; chat rooms; and basic search engines. With a modest investment of time, reflection, and curiosity, investors may avail themselves of several other powerful features of the Internet that will vastly improve, if not optimize, the quality of their quest for an accurate, efficient, effective, and timely flow of information about asset allocation and investing. The following paragraphs offer a number of suggestions for optimizing the investor's access to and use of Internet-based information sources.

- ◆ **Gain Familiarity with the Full Extent of Internet-Based Information Sources:** Within the World Wide Web, at least 10 types of resources will broaden and deepen investors' core knowledge and the degree to which they are informed about asset allocation and investing. As Figure 9.9 previously showed, these resources include: e-mail services in various formats; telnet; file transfer protocol; usenet newsgroups; several kinds of search engines; chat services and message boards; subject directories; Web-accessible databases; Web sites and portals; and Web-based tools.

- ◆ **Blend Net-Based with Non-Net-Based Information Sources:** Information management can be enhanced when the investor views Internet-based and non-Internet-based sources not in isolation from each other, but instead, as part of a continuous spectrum. Investors can reduce errors and duplication—and devote more attention to asset allocation and investing—by utilizing information from either of these two broad spheres to reinforce, check, or fill in gaps from the other sphere; errors and duplication of effort can thus be substantially minimized.

- ◆ **Remember Subject Directories and Web-Accessible Databases:** Many subject directories and Web-accessible databases reflect highly targeted, evaluative input by their creators or administrators. As such, they can be a powerful adjunct to, or in some cases, a more effective tool than, a conventional search engine for locating information.

◆ **Recognize the Hierarchical Structure of Internet-Based Information Sources:** Figure 9.11 shows several levels in a hierarchy of Internet-based information sources, and Web site addresses for representative information sources within each level.

The most basic level—level ⑤ in Figure 9.11— includes information sources themselves, which the investor may turn to because he or she believes the information can be found on a specific Web site. Level ④ represents information sources, such as portals, which contain or link to sites that may contain the information that the investor wants. Level ③ depicts information sources that regularly evaluate and often rank other sources (Level ⑤) as well as portals (Level ④). Level ② shows search engines, subject directories, and Web-accessible databases, some of which may provide leads to independently located information, or to the information sources in Level ⑤ or in Level ④. Level ① refers to guides to search engines, to search engine collections, and to searching the Internet as a research tool. In effect, these information sources can help the investor evaluate and locate search engines and related tools on the Internet.

◆ **Respect the Changing Nature of the Internet:** Internet-based information changes over time. Web sites, information storage and retrieval technologies, the contents and organization of databases and subject directories, and search engines change. Some resources adapt, keep pace with, or even lead change, while other resources—highly relevant and current in the recent past—may or may not become outmoded. Investors need to ask themselves about the current usefulness and applicability of any Internet-based information sources on which they rely.

◆ **Appreciate the Capabilities and Shortcomings of Search Engines:** To many Internet-using investors, most search engines appear similar. As a result, the vast majority of these investors' searches, conducted over millions of pages on the Web, produce very large numbers of hits, often from unevaluated sources of highly uneven quality. In fact, a significant number of search engines have differentiating characteristics that can dramatically in-

## F I G U R E  9.11

Hierarchy of Internet-Based Information Sources

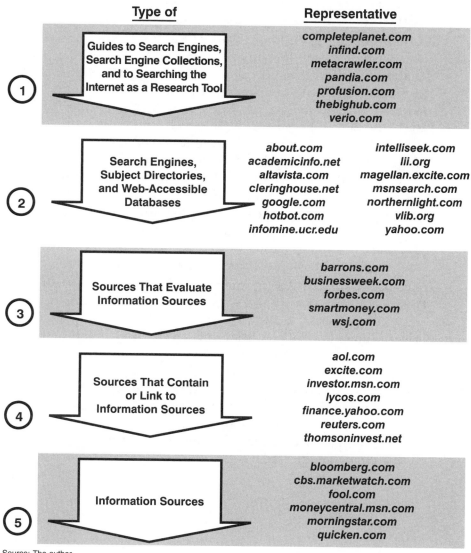

**Type of** — **Representative**

1. Guides to Search Engines, Search Engine Collections, and to Searching the Internet as a Research Tool
   - completeplanet.com
   - infind.com
   - metacrawler.com
   - pandia.com
   - profusion.com
   - thebighub.com
   - verio.com

2. Search Engines, Subject Directories, and Web-Accessible Databases
   - about.com
   - academicinfo.net
   - altavista.com
   - cleringhouse.net
   - google.com
   - hotbot.com
   - infomine.ucr.edu
   - intelliseek.com
   - lii.org
   - magellan.excite.com
   - msnsearch.com
   - northernlight.com
   - vlib.org
   - yahoo.com

3. Sources That Evaluate Information Sources
   - barrons.com
   - businessweek.com
   - forbes.com
   - smartmoney.com
   - wsj.com

4. Sources That Contain or Link to Information Sources
   - aol.com
   - excite.com
   - investor.msn.com
   - lycos.com
   - finance.yahoo.com
   - reuters.com
   - thomsoninvest.net

5. Information Sources
   - bloomberg.com
   - cbs.marketwatch.com
   - fool.com
   - moneycentral.msn.com
   - morningstar.com
   - quicken.com

Source: The author.

fluence the power, speed, accuracy, and effectiveness of an information search. Some search engines search the full text of underlying information, while others search only the title and a brief description of the underlying information. Search engines have differing search territories, search algorithms, syntax logic, sensitivity to lower- and upper-case letters or to phrases, and field-recognition rules. In general, most of the popular search engines cannot retrieve password-protected material or the contents of subject directories and Web-accessible databases.

◆ **Comprehend the Fundamentals of Search Techniques:** Investors wishing to conduct a narrow, specialized search for information on asset allocation and investing may choose a different search engine from one that might have been used in a broad, open-ended search. Some search engines have basic and advanced search features; some also offer the investor the option to search further within the retrieved results. Newer search engines, and updated versions of old search engines, sort information by relevancy (for example, the presence of terms in the title, the number of times and how close to the beginning the terms appear in the document, and other properties). Other investor-selected search attributes include: popularity; linking frequency to other sites; top- and second-level domain name; directory name; and file name.

◆ **Evaluate Carefully All Internet-Based Information Sources:** Investors must rigorously and unfailingly judge the source, accuracy, completeness, sponsorship, potential biases, and point of view of any information retrieved from the Web. A substantial proportion of the material on the Web is self-submitted and self-published, with little or no editing or independent review as to style, organization, or content, attribution of quoted or excerpted materials, and other characteristics. When using Internet-based information sources, or any other information sources for that matter, a word to the wise is worth repeating: *caveat lector* ("let the reader beware").

# CHAPTER 10

# SOURCES OF INFORMATION

## MEDIA-BASED INFORMATION SOURCES

Investors in search of reliable, effective information sources about asset allocation and investing may find what they want in a variety of media, ranging from books to periodicals to Web sites, as well as many other types of sources that are reviewed in the following sections. A number of sources may be classified in more than one place. For instance, a book on investing in real estate may be listed here in: (i) the *media-based* section on *books*, if it is of reasonably broad coverage and interest; or (ii) in the *subject-based* section on *asset-class characteristics*, if it primarily describes the specific attributes of real estate as an asset class. As another example, books *about* specific media (e.g., a book about conference calls and message boards) may be classified in that media section rather than in the books section. Investors should think about the most likely locations for the information they seek, and then rapidly survey the sources in these and other information classification sections.

## Books

Since the invention of the movable-type printing press by Johannes Gutenberg in 1450, through the electronic era, books have remained a convenient, cogent, and highly portable means of gathering information together for easy and repeated access. Books are widely available through: public and private libraries; specialty, local, and national chain bookstores; and online book ordering services (often with readers' comments and reviews), such as *amazon.com, barnesandnoble.com,* and *borders.com.*

Figure 10.1 lists notable books on asset allocation and investing, grouped into subcategories on: asset allocation; how to invest and getting started in investing; investment classics; human elements in investing; reference sources and definitions; historical perspective; and investment insights.

The books listed in Table 10.1 provide nonoverlapping sources of reasonably high quality and enduring value. Not every book will fit into each investor's needs on each occasion in the same way. With the passage of time, some of these books may be issued in a subsequent edition, some may go out of print in hardback and be reissued in paperback, and some of them may go out of print altogether. In the latter case, the investor should: (i) turn to a local library to check the book out; (ii) borrow it through an interlibrary loan; or (iii) locate the book on one of the online used book sites, such as *powells.com, alibris.com,* or *usedbookfind.com.* Other sources of used books include *abcbooks.com* and *half.com.* Barton Biggs's essay, "Best Books," in the June 9, 1992, issue of Morgan Stanley's *Investment Perspectives* offers an annotated listing of leading investment books.

## Business School Case Studies

A rich, up-to-date, and frequently overlooked source of information about asset allocation and investing can be found in the case studies and background notes prepared by many leading graduate schools of business. Their Web sites usually contain lists, summaries, or complete copies of potentially relevant cases. Table 10.2 lists business schools and their Web sites.

Some of the business schools listed in Table 10.2 that offer active case-writing and case-development programs include those at Harvard Business School, Columbia Business School, London Business School, Stanford Business School, the University of Michigan Business School,

## T A B L E  10.1

### Selected Books on Asset Allocation and Investing

**How to Invest/Getting Started in Investing**

*The Wall Street Journal Guide to Understanding Money and Investing*, by Kenneth M. Morris and Alan M. Siegel. Fundamentals of finance and investments, clearly explained and illustrated.

*Bull's Eye Investing: Targeting Real Returns in a Smoke and Mirrors Market,* by John Mauldin. Examines six major ways to look at the stock market.

*The Motley Fool Investment Guide*, by David and Tom Gardner. The practical details of common-sense investing.

*The Irwin Guide to Using the Wall Street Journal,* by Michael B. Lehmann. How to use the *Journal* to make informed business and investing decisions.

*The Only Investment Guide You'll Ever Need*, by Andrew P. Tobias. Pragmatic advice for many phases of the money realm.

*How to Buy Stocks*, by Louis Engel and Brendan Boyd. A basic description of equities for the beginning investor.

*Investment Management: Portfolio Diversification, Risk, and Timing—Fact and Fiction*, by Robert L. Hagin. Handbook for investors seeking superior results.

*The Complete Bond Book*, by David M. Darst. An introductory guide to investing in fixed-income securities.

*The Motley Fool Investment Guide for Teens,* by David and Tom Gardner. For young people seeking to master the fundamentals of investment.

*E-Books From the Wall Street Journal,* by the reporters and editors of the *Wall Street Journal.* Selected articles from *Wall Street Journal* Special Reports.

*Online Investing: Become a Successful Internet Investor,* by the reporters and editors of *wsj.com.* What it takes to get started in investing online.

*Equity Portfolio Management*, by Frank J. Fabozzi. Equity management styles, models, and analytical techniques.

*Investing Online for Dummies*, by Kathleen Sindell. How to invest online.

*Invest Like the Best: Using Your Computer to Unlock the Secrets of the Top Money Managers,* by James O'Shaughnessy. Sound and practical guidance to investing.

*Stock Investing for Dummies,* by Paul Mladjenovic. A good starting point for those interested in investing.

*Unconventional Success: A Fundamental Approach to Personal Investment,* by David Swensen. Shows individual investors how to manage their assets.

*What Works on Wall Street: A Guide to the Best-Performing Investment Strategies of All Time,* by James O'Shaughnessy. No-nonsense guidance to the investment process.

**Asset Allocation**

*The Art of Asset Allocation,* by David M. Darst. A comprehensive discussion of the mechanics, underpinnings, tools, principles, and pathways of asset allocation and investment strategy.

*Mastering the Art of Asset Allocation,* by David M. Darst. An examination of the subtleties and inner workings of asset allocation through in-depth study of leading university endowments, compound interest, and returns correlations, among other topics.

*Asset Allocation: Balancing Financial Risk,* by Roger C. Gibson. Selecting an appropriate mix of asset classes by understanding how investments interact with one another in a portfolio.

*Pioneering Portfolio Management: An Unconventional Approach to Institutional Investment,* by David F. Swensen. Strategic and tactical aspects of asset allocation.

*Active Asset Allocation: State-of-the-Art Portfolio Policies, Strategies, and Tactics,* ed. by Robert D. Arnott and Frank J. Fabozzi. The risk, rewards, and many dimensions of active asset allocation.

*Global Asset Allocation: Techniques for Optimizing Portfolio Management,* ed. by Jess Lederman and Robert A. Klein. Twenty essays on the qualitative and quantitative aspects of asset allocation.

**Investment Classics**

*The Intelligent Investor: A Book of Practical Counsel,* by Benjamin Graham. Underlying principles of equity investing.

Continued

**T A B L E  10.1 (Continued)**

## Selected Books on Asset Allocation and Investing

**Investment Classics (Continued)**

*The Essays of Warren Buffett,* ed. by Lawrence A. Cunningham. Principles of valuation and how markets work.

*Common Stocks and Uncommon Profits,* by Philip A. Fisher. Metrics for valuing and selecting sound long-term equity investments.

*The Art of Speculation,* by Phillip L. Carret. Timeless insights into the art and science of investing.

*The Battle for Investment Survival,* by Gerald M. Loeb. How a bear market affects investors and their modus operandi.

*A Random Walk Down Wall Street,* by Burton G. Malkiel. Perceptive teaching and wise counsel about the investment arena.

*Investment Policy,* by Charles D. Ellis. Thinking about and setting investment policy.

*Stocks for the Long Run,* by Jeremy J. Siegel. Pragmatic and historical arguments for investing in equities over a period of decades.

*Irrational Exuberance,* by Robert J. Schiller. An economic, psychological, demographic, sociological, historical, and behavioral analysis of equity market levels.

*Inside the Yield Book: New Tools for Bond Market Strategy,* by Sidney Homer and Martin L. Leibowitz. Essential bond wisdom.

*Capital Ideas,* by Peter L. Bernstein. Histories of the ideas that have shaped modern finance.

*Contrarian Investment Strategy,* by David Dreman. A classic work on investment contrarianism.

*Classics: Volumes I and II,* ed. by Charles D. Ellis. Contains many of the seminal essays on investment management.

*Extraordinary Popular Delusions and the Madness of Crowds,* by Charles Mackay. Periodic financial derangements of the masses.

*The Investor's Anthology: Original Ideas from the Industry's Greatest Minds,* ed. by Charles D. Ellis with James A. Vertin. A collection of concise commentaries on the art and practical realities of investments.

**Human Elements in Investing**

*Hedgehogging,* by Barton M. Biggs. Insight into human traits in the hedge fund realm.

*The Money Game,* by Adam Smith. Insights into colorful types of investor psychologies.

*Groupthink,* by Irving L. Janis. The complexities and pitfalls inherent in group decision making.

*Markets, Mobs, & Mayhem,* by Robert Menschel. A modern look at the madness of crowds.

*Supermoney,* by Adam Smith. Humorous and profound observations on financial markets.

*The Coming Generational Storm,* by Laurence Kotlikoff and Scott Burns. An analysis of America's approaching demographic time bomb.

*The Roaring 80s,* by Adam Smith. Lessons from a special decade.

*The Money Masters,* by John Train. Profiles of successful investors and speculators.

*Reminiscences of a Stock Operator,* by Edwin Lefèvre. Mistakes, lessons, and successes in the mind of a legendary equities trader.

*Where Are the Customers' Yachts?: A Good Hard Look at Wall Street,* by Fred Schwed, Jr. An examination of the foibles and fallibilities of the financial arena.

*Liars' Poker,* by Michael Lewis. Witty observations from the training program of a Wall Street firm in heady times.

*Den of Thieves,* by James B. Stewart. Excesses of the incipient junk-bond era.

*The New Money Masters,* by John Train. Additional profiles of successful investors and speculators.

*Confusión de Confusiones,* by Joseph P. de la Vega. The essentials and mistakes of options speculation in 17th century Amsterdam.

*Barron's Finance and Investment Handbook,* by John Downes and Jordan E. Goodman. Reference source and a how-to guide to reading the financial press.

*The Economist Guide to Economic Indicators,* by the Economist Newspaper Ltd. Making sense of economics and the economy.

*The Wisdom of Crowds,* by James Surowiecki. A fun and timely take on the upside of the herd instinct.

*Dictionary of Finance and Investment Terms,* by John Downes and Jordan E. Goodman. Explanations of over 5,000 terms.

Continued

## Human Elements in Investing (Continued)

*The Complete Words of Wall Street,* by Allan H. Pessin and Joseph A. Ross. A comprehensive collection of definitions and examples from the securities industry.

*Every Investor's Guide to Wall Street Words,* by David L. Scott. Terms, illustrative case histories, charts, and graphs of use to beginners and professionals.

*Stocks Bonds Options Futures,* by the staff of the New York Institute of Finance. The fundamentals of investments and their markets.

*Stock Options: An Authoritative Guide to Incentive and Nonqualified Stock Options,* by Robert R. Pastore. The essentials of personal options.

*The Bond Buyer's Primer,* by Sidney Homer. Twenty-one timeless and witty lessons applicable to all kinds of investor.

*The Handbook of the Bond and Money Markets,* by David M. Darst. An analysis of fixed-income securities types, investor behavior, and investment strategies.

## Historical Perspective

*The Trouble With Prosperity: A Contrarian's Tale of Boom, Bust and Speculation,* by James Grant. Cautionary lessons from folly in financial history.

*The Go-Go Years: The Drama and Crashing Finale of Wall Street's Bullish 60s,* by John Brooks. Portraits of the people, companies, and atmosphere of a boom era.

*The Great Crash, 1929,* by John K. Galbraith. The causes and consequences of the stock market crash of 1929.

*When Genius Failed,* by Roger Lowenstein. The rise, fall, and rescue of long-term capital management.

*A History of Interest Rates, 2000 B.C. to the Present,* by Sidney Homer. An epic recounting of financial history.

*Against the Gods: The Remarkable Story of Risk,* by Peter L. Bernstein. A comprehensive study of human efforts to understand risk.

*Devil Take the Hindmost,* by Edward Chancellor. The sociology of manias and their aftermaths.

*Panic on Wall Street,* by Robert Sobel. The definitive study of American panics.

*Manias, Panics, and Crashes: A History of Financial Crises,* by Charles P. Kindleberger. The components of distress in financial markets since 1618.

*Lessons from the Greatest Stock Traders of All Time,* by John Boik. Focuses on the Babe Ruths of investing.

*Origins of the Crash: The Great Bubble and Its Undoing.* Tech companies in the 1990s.

*The Funny Money Game,* by Andrew Tobias. A 1973 classic about the rise and fall of National Student Marketing.

*The Stock Market Crash—and After,* by Irving Fisher. The events and spirit that led to the October 1929 stock market crash.

*The Crash and Its Aftermath: A History of Securities Markets in the United States, 1929–1933,* by Barrie A. Wigmore. Profound scholarship into the Depression era.

*Lombard Street: A Description of the Money Market,* by Walter Bagehot. The personalities, sociology, and workings of the British financial system in the mid-19th century.

*The Myths of Inflation and Investing,* by Steven Leuthold. An important reference work.

*The Big Board,* by Robert Sobel. The lore, legends, and history of many of Wall Street's renowned operators and events.

*Securities Markets in the 1980s,* by Barrie A. Wigmore. Thorough scholarship into a decade of change.

*Who's Afraid of Adam Smith? How the Market Got Its Soul,* by Peter J. Dougherty. The relevance of Adam Smith's *Theory of Moral Sentiments.*

## Investment Insights

*Against the Gods:The Remarkable Story of Risk,* by Peter L. Bernstein. Measuring and controlling risk.

*Dean LeBaron's Treasury of Investment Wisdom,* by Dean LeBaron and Romesh Vaitilingham. How investment thinking has been deepened and enriched in modern times.

*The Buffetology Workbook,* by Mary Buffett and David Clark. Value investing the Warren Buffett way.

*How Technical Analysis Works,* by Bruce M. Kamich. Introduction to the art of reading price charts.

*How to Think Like Benjamin Graham and Invest Like Warren Buffett,* by Lawrence A. Cunningham. Useful facts, tools, and approaches to analyze the value of any business.

Continued

**T A B L E  10.1 (Concluded)**

## Selected Books on Asset Allocation and Investing

**Investment Insights** (Continued)

*Margin of Safety: Risk-Averse Value Investing Strategies for the Thoughtful Investor,* by Seth A. Klarman. An intelligent, candid discussion of value investing.

*Mastering Risk,* by James Pickford. Overview of the important concepts of risk management.

*One Up on Wall Street: How to Use What You Already Know to Make Money in the Market,* by Peter Lynch with John Rothchild. Principles of self-reliance in investing.

*The Alchemy of Finance,* by George Soros. Deep commentary on reflexivity.

*Stock Market Wizards: Interviews with America's Top Stock Traders*, by Jack D. Schwager. Lessons from successful equity traders.

*The Market Gurus*, by John Reese and Tod Glassman. Market insights through investment leaders who have made a difference.

*The (Mis)behavior of Markets,* by Benoit Mandelbrot and Richard Hudson. The basic assumptions as to how the market works don't always hold up.

*The New Financial Order: Risk in the Twenty-First Century,* by Robert J. Shiller. Using modern information technology to temper risks.

*The Portable Financial Analyst: What Practitioners Need to Know,* by Mark Kritzman. Risk as an inescapable feature of investing.

*The Power of Gold: The History of an Obsession,* by Peter L. Bernstein. Gold's influence on the evolution of monetary systems and trade from early civilization to present day.

*Tomorrow's Gold: Asia's Age of Discovery,* by Marc Faber. Charts how old investor trends developed and how new patterns might emerge.

*Trade Like a Hedge Fund,* by James Altucher. Highlights 20 successful uncorrelated strategies and techniques for trading the markets.

*24 Essential Lessons for Investment Success: Learn the Most Important Investment Techniques from the Founder of Investor's Business Daily,* by William J. O'Neil. Short-term trading and technical chart-reading tips.

*Winning the Loser's Game: Timeless Strategies for Successful Investing,* by Charles D. Ellis. Wise counsel for long-term equity investing.

*Value Investing: From Graham to Buffett and Beyond,* by Bruce Greenwald et. al. An introduction to value investment principles.

*What Works on Wall Street,* by James P. O'Shaughnessy. An analysis of the successes and failures of various investment strategies.

*Investment Biker,* by Jim Rogers. Frank views on international markets and economies.

*Quality of Earnings: The Investor's Guide to How Much Money a Company Is Really Making,* by Thornton L. O'Glove with Robert Sobel. Deep understanding of financial statements.

*Valuegrowth Investing, by* Glen Arnold. Examines philosophies and investing techniques used by some of the world's best investors.

*The Management of Investment Decisions,* by Don Trone. Insights into the investment process.

*The Wall Street Journal Guide to Planning your Financial Future,* by Kenneth M. Morris et. al. A survey of issues relating to retirement planning.

*John Bogle on Investing,* by John C. Bogle. Observations by a value guru on 50 years of investing.

*Financial Shenanigans,* by Howard Schilit. Commentary on accounting legerdemain, by the founder of the Center for Financial Research and Analysis.

*Essential Stock Picking Strategies,* by Daniel A. Strachman. Interviews with and lessons from portfolio managers.

Source: The author.

Northwestern Business School (Kellogg), and the NYU Salomon Center for Research in Financial Institutions and Markets within NYU's Stern School of Business. Table 10.3 contains a small number of Harvard Business School cases dealing with the subject of asset allocation.

**T A B L E  10.2**

Selected Graduate Business Schools and Their Web Sites

| Business School | Web Site |
|---|---|
| Babson College (Olin) | babson.edu |
| Boston College (Carroll) | bc.edu |
| Carnegie Mellon | gsia.cmu.edu |
| Columbia Business School | columbia.edu/cu/business |
| Cornell University (Johnson) | johnson.cornell.edu |
| Dartmouth College (Tuck) | dartmouth.edu/tuck/ |
| Duke University (Fuqua) | fuqua.duke.edu |
| Emory University | goizueta.emory.edu |
| Georgetown University (McDonough) | mba.georgetown.edu |
| Harvard Business School | hbs.edu |
| Indiana University (Kelley) | kelly.iupui.edu |
| INSEAD Business School | insead.fr/mba/ |
| London Business School | london.edu |
| MIT Sloan School | mitsloan.mit.edu |
| New York University (Stern) | stern.nyu.edu |
| Northwestern Business School (Kellogg) | kellogg.nwu.edu |
| Purdue University (Krannert) | mgmt.purdue.edu/programs/masters |
| Stanford Graduate School of Business | gsb.stanford.edu |
| UNC—Chapel Hill (Kenan-Flagler) | kenanflagler.unc.edu |
| University of California—Berkeley (Haas) | haas.berkeley.edu |
| University of California at Los Angeles (Anderson) | anderson.ucla.edu |
| University of Chicago GSB | gsb.uchicago.edu |
| University of Maryland (Smith) | umd.edu |
| University of Michigan | bus.umich.edu/prostudents/mba |
| University of Pennsylvania (Wharton) | wharton.upenn.edu |
| University of Rochester (Simon) | simon.rochester.edu |
| University of St. Gallen | unisg.ch |
| University of Texas—Austin (McCombs) | bus.utexas.edu |
| University of Virginia (Darden) | darden.edu |
| University of Western Ontario (Ivey) | uwo.ca/grad |
| Vanderbilt University (Owen) | mba.vanderbilt.edu |
| Washington University (Olin) | olin.wustl.edu/prospective |
| Yale University School of Management | mba.yale.edu |

Source: The author.

## Conference Calls, Chat Rooms, and Message Boards

To keep track of current developments and the future outlook of their existing holdings and potential investments, an increasing number of investors are accessing live conference calls via toll-free telephone connections or audiotape replays and Webcasts (broadcasts over the World Wide Web) of conference calls. Many of these conference calls

**T A B L E 10.3**

Selected Harvard Business School Cases on Asset Allocation

| Business School Case | Topic |
| --- | --- |
| The Harvard Management Company (1994) | Strategic asset allocation and absolute return investments |
| The Harvard Management Company and Inflation-Protected Bonds | Inflation-protected bonds in the asset allocation of investors |
| Brinson Partners | The evolution and role of asset allocation as a discipline |
| Yale University Investments Office | Alternative investments in the asset allocation of a long-term investor |
| Yale University Investments Office (2000) | The proper proportion of alternative assets in a portfolio |
| The IBET Pension Fund | Real estate in the asset allocation of long-term investors |
| Long-Term Capital Management, L.P. (A) (B) (C) (D) | Complex trading strategies using sophisticated models |

Source: The author.

with the investment community and the news media are held by companies, and in some cases, by Wall Street research, economics, and strategy sources, during the so-called earnings season, consisting of the six weeks after the end of each fiscal or calendar quarter. During such periods, several thousand companies release their financial results as required by the U.S. Securities and Exchange Commission (SEC). Some companies also hold mid-quarter conference calls to provide new earnings guidance or to confirm earlier forecasts.

In October 2000, the SEC also broadened individual investors' access to corporate earnings releases and corporate earnings estimates through the promulgation of Regulation FD. This rule, also known as Fair Disclosure, prohibits companies from releasing corporate information selectively to professional securities analysts and institutional asset managers, and requires companies to make such information available simultaneously to the broad public.

Conference calls have several advantages and some drawbacks as a source of information about asset allocation and investing. On the positive side, investors are able to hear with their own ears and make judgments about the tone of voice, inflections, and relative emphases of the speakers in such forums. In addition, they may judge the quality and observe the substance and tenor of securities analysts' and other call participants' questions and answers. On the other side of the ledger, conference calls can be lengthy and sometimes overly management-slanted or tedious. In addition, the investor needs to evaluate the information presented in the conference call, not in isolation, but in concert with other information sources, and with the same degree of care and screening that he or she should apply to any information source, written or verbal.

To access conference calls over the Web, many investors will need first to install RealPlayer software, which they can download free of charge from *real.com*. Among the commonly accessed conference call Web sites are: (i) *bestcalls.com;* (ii) *ccbn.com;* (iii) *earnings.com;* (iv) *streetevents.com;* (v) *vcall.com;* and (vi) portal-type sources such as *biz.yahoo.com/cc* and the *Wall Street Journal's* Web site, *wsj.com*. The conference-call related features on these and several other Web sites may include: (i) calendar listings and e-mail notification services for upcoming scheduled conference calls for subjects, companies, and in some cases, the conference calls of specified companies' competitors; (ii) access numbers and dial-in pass codes for investors who wish to participate in the conference calls directly rather than via a Webcast; and (iii) listings of annual shareholder meetings, investor conferences, special announcements, and other events of interest to investors.

Chat rooms and message boards represent a highly empowering, yet potentially undisciplined, means for investors to receive, seek out, and share information, to express opinions, and to sift through and listen to the opinions of others. Figure 10.1 outlines the subtle distinctions between chat rooms, message boards, e-mail discussion groups, and usegroups.

Figure 10.1 shows that chat rooms and message boards usually involve a *two-way* flow of information to and from the investor, while e-mail discussion groups (in which information automatically flows to the investor) and usegroups (in which the investor has to take action to retrieve centrally posted information) usually involve a *one-way* flow of information to or from the investor. Many investors use the terms chat rooms and message boards interchangeably, and these two services do in fact possess many similar characteristics.

The distinctions between chat rooms and message boards primarily center on the timing of the posting and retrieval of information. In *chat rooms*, information and/or opinions are shared and exchanged in real-time by investors and other investors in large group forums, on a bilateral basis, or on a limited multilateral basis. In *message boards*,

**F I G U R E 10.1**

Selected Investor-Involved Information Sources

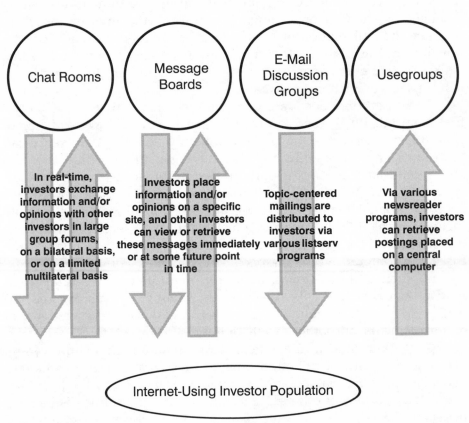

Source: The author.

information and/or opinions may be placed on a specific site, and investors can view or retrieve these messages immediately or at some future point in time. In addition, chat rooms devoted to asset allocation- and investing-related topics may at times take on a more free-form and broader-ranging array of viewpoints, whereas message boards may remain more tightly focused on a specific company, asset class, investment style, or another relatively delineated theme.

Owing to the frequently unaffiliated status of the authors of postings on chat rooms and message boards, these information sources often contain candid opinions and factual material that may not otherwise be encountered. At the same time, postings on chat rooms and message boards may be highly biased, slanted, partially or wholly incorrect, or even fraudulent. As a result of these dichotomous attributes of chat rooms and message board postings, investors would do well always to keep in mind the possibility that a given piece of information found in one of these media may be of high value, low value, or negative value. Some message boards allow users to filter out certain identified authors, to block spam messages, to report abusive postings, and to rate the messages of other users.

Among other places, chat rooms and/or message boards can be found on *aol.com, msn.com, finance.yahoo.com, fool.com, ragingbull.com, siliconinvestor.com,* and *vectorvest.com.* Many of these sites have hundreds, if not thousands, of chat rooms or message boards. For some topics, one Web site may capture the preponderance of investors' comments and inquiry flow, and for other topics, an entirely different Web site may have a dominant share of the traffic. These facts of life pose a formidable, but not insurmountable, challenge to investors seeking the most information-rich resource for their inquiries on asset allocation and investing.

## CONFERENCES, SEMINARS, AND WORKSHOPS

Conferences, seminars, and workshops offer investors the opportunity to broaden and deepen their knowledge about asset allocation and investing, to hear and potentially meet experts in the field, and not insignificantly, to interact with other attendees at such sessions. Many conferences', seminars', and workshops' sponsors have their own Web sites containing: copies of material distributed at the meetings; slide presentations, papers, and/or transcripts of the proceedings; lists of participants and presenters; and feedback from previous sessions. The drawbacks of attending such forums may include the expenditure of time, money, and possibly travel distance to take part, as well as the fact that not all of the content may be relevant or appropriately pitched to the investor's needs.

Many of the most valuable conferences, seminars, and workshops are sponsored by some of the other media-based information sources discussed in this chapter, including corporations, industry organizations, educational institutions, governments and regulatory bodies, nonprint mass media, periodicals, newspapers, and newsletters, professional and scholarly journals, professional organizations, and Wall Street and the financial industry. Details about and listings of many, but by no means all, of the conferences, seminars, and workshops sponsored by these and other sources may be found at *financial-conferences.com, globalinvestor.com,* and *finance.yahoo.com.* Table 10.4 lists a limited number of selected additional sponsors of conferences, seminars, and workshops.

The list of conferences, seminars, and workshops in Table 10.4 represents only a small fraction of such offerings about asset allocation and investing. Interested investors can explore various comprehensive listings of these sources to find forums that focus on their needs.

## CORPORATIONS AND INDIVIDUAL INVESTOR ORGANIZATIONS

Corporations and individual investor organizations can often provide investors with a substantial amount of practical and useful information about asset allocation and investing. Investors may generally write, call or email a company's Office of the Secretary to obtain copies of a company's annual report, recent press releases, selected analysts' reports on the company (not available in all cases), and certain other informative documents (such as its annual Form 10-K and its quarterly Form 10-Q), which most publicly held companies are required to file with the SEC. Other convenient means of obtaining many participating companies' annual reports are through the Public Register's Annual Report Service (*prars.com*), the *Wall Street Journal* (*wsj.com*), or *Barron's* (*barrons.com*).

Details about no-load stocks (a means of purchasing stock directly from corporations), contact information, and downloadable order forms can be found at *netstockdirect.com.* Many public companies also offer dividend reinvestment plans (DRIPs), which allow investors to purchase stock directly from the company, or to plow back the dividends they receive on an existing stockholding into the company's shares. Additional information about DRIP plans can be located at *dripinvestor.com* and/or in the book, *Buying Stocks Without a Broker*, by Charles Carlson.

Individual investor organizations offer much helpful information about asset allocation and investing, particularly for beginning investors. Table 10.5 contains a selected list of organizations focusing on the needs of the individual investor.

The Web sites listed in Table 10.5 address the information needs of individual investors, retired persons, family offices, mutual fund investors, and investment clubs. Investment clubs can help individuals learn about the fundamentals of investing.

## T A B L E 10.4

### Selected Sources of Conferences, Seminars, and Workshops

| Web Site Name | Comments |
|---|---|
| bloomberg.com | A geographically dispersed series of seminars run by Bloomberg LLC, on topics ranging from operating Bloomberg equipment to asset allocation and investing in various kinds of securities. |
| cboe.com/rmc | Conferences on risk management, sponsored by the Chicago Board Options Exchange. |
| fame.ch | Workshops on global asset allocation, risk assessment, and related topics, sponsored by the International Center for Financial Asset Management and Engineering (FAME). |
| grantspub.com | Thoughtful and provocative conferences sponsored by *Grant's Interest Rate Observer* magazine, addressing issues ranging from credit quality to investing in specific asset classes. |
| ibbotson.com | Basic and advanced asset allocation workshops conducted by Ibbotson Inc., as well as customized and computer-based training services. |
| iiconferences.com | Conferences sponsored by *Institutional Investor* magazine and related publications on topics of interest to institutional investors, and often, to individual investors as well. |
| investools.com | Provider of workshops and individual training sessions. |
| opalgroup.net | Conferences on a variety of investment topics organized by the Opal Financial Group. |
| snlcenter.com | Advanced training programs sponsored by the SNL Center for Financial Education. |
| wharton.upenn.edu | Public presentation of new and ongoing research by the faculty in the Financial Institutions Center and other disciplines within the Wharton School at the University of Pennsylvania. |
| windowsfs.com | Conferences offered in conjunction with financial services partners focusing on the delivery of advice and consultation for development of wealth management strategies. |

Source: The author.

A useful introductory Web site about investment clubs is *iclubcentral.com;* a listing of investment clubs services is located at *businessjeeves.com;* a geographic directory of investment clubs can be found at *investorguide.com;* investment club administration software is contained on *ouriclub.com;* and an interesting specific investment club Web

**T A B L E 10.5**

Selected Individual Investor Organizations

| Web Site Name | Comments |
|---|---|
| aaii.org | Sponsored by the American Association of Individual Investors, a national membership organization founded in 1951, that provides basic educational materials and other resources about equity investing, mutual funds, portfolio management, and retirement planning. |
| aarp.com | Practical, reliable advice on many investing-related topics from the American Association of Retired Persons (AARP). |
| better-investing.org | Investment information and educational tools provided by the National Association of Investors Corporation (NAIC) for more than 50 years to investment clubs and individual investors of all knowledge levels, to help them become successful long-term investors. More than 70% of the NAIC's 650,000 members are women. |
| cfraonline.com | An independent financial research organization, the Center for Financial Research and Analysis, concentrating on companies that employ unusual or aggressive accounting practices to mask operational problems. |
| familyoffice.com | Topics of interest relating to the establishment and ongoing management of family offices, sponsored by the Family Office Exchange, Inc. (FOX). |
| ici.org | Information on mutual fund investing from the Investment Company Institute, a leading mutual fund industry trade association. |
| memberlink.net | Resources oriented toward the needs of individual investors, administered by the Institute for Private Investors. |
| mfea.com | Fundamental information about most types of mutual funds from the Mutual Fund Education Alliance, a trade group for no-load (no sales charges) mutual funds. |
| sia.com | An innovative education-based Web site accessible either directly or via a pop-up screen on SIA member firms' own Web sites. |
| wfic.org | Investor education programs to individuals and investment clubs around the world, sponsored by the World Federation of Investors, founded in 1960. |

Source: The author.

site is *chickslayingnesteggs.com*. The book, *Starting and Running a Profitable Investment Club*, by Thomas O'Hara, *et al.* spells out the basics of organizing an investment club. Investors can broaden and deepen their knowledge about asset allocation and investing by exploring the course offerings, case studies (described earlier in the "business case studies" section), reading materials, basic and advanced learning programs, and publications of accredited and for-profit educational institutions and research institutes. Accredited educational institutions, including colleges, junior colleges, community colleges, graduate schools, institutes, and universities may offer one or more avenues to learning. These information sources include: (i) courses at the undergraduate, graduate, or extension school level; (ii) continuing and executive education programs; (iii) seminars and learning modules; (iv) full-fledged degree programs; and (v) university presses. Links to the catalogs of more than 130 university presses in the U.S. and abroad may be found at *aaupnet.edu*.

## EDUCATIONAL INSTITUTIONS AND RESEARCH INSTITUTES

Investors can find a listing of geographically proximate educational institutions through one of the search engines described in this chapter or on *usnews.com*. Investors may decide to attend classes in person, or where permitted, to pursue studies on a distance-learning basis, either through correspondence courses or over the Internet. In the latter case, educational institutions and intermediary firms may make courses available through interactive video-enabled conferencing systems. These systems use Internet Protocols that allow the delivery of broadcast-quality transmissions through digital subscriber lines (DSLs), T-1 lines, asynchronous transfer mode (ATM), cable modems, wi-fi, or satellite transmission. Some Internet-based continuing education programs with selected courses of potential interest to investors include the University of Maryland (*umuc.edu*), Columbia Video Network (*ci.columbia.edu*), Duke Global Executive (*fuqua.duke.edu*), the University of Texas-Dallas (*utdallas.edu*), The Stanford Center for Professional Development (*scpd.stanford.edu*), the University of Northern Colorado Online (*unconline.edu*), and the University of Phoenix Online (*uopxonline.com*).

For-profit learning and corporate training companies include Apollo Group (*apollogrp.com*), Bell & Howell Company (*bellhowell.com*), Career Education Corporation (*careered.com*), Corpedia (*corpedia.com*), convergys (*convergys.com*), Education Management (*edumgt.com*), Learning Tree International (*learningtree.com*), SkillSoft (*skillsoft.com*), Unext (*unext.com*), and XtremeLearning (*xtremelearning.com*).

Video conferencing companies include Avistar Communications (*avistar.com*), Clear One Communications (*clearone.com*), and Polycom, Inc.

(*polycom.com*). At any given point in time, only some of these firms may have offerings relating to asset allocation and investing.

Two entities that offer multi-lesson interactive education courses about asset allocation and investing include Dow Jones University (*dju.com*) and Motley Fool's Investing Online Seminar Series (*fool.com/school*). Both of these offerings permit the investor to ask questions and share ideas in special chat sessions with the instructor and other course participants. Investors may work through the course materials and complete assigned exercises at their own pace, within a multiple-week time frame for each course. To advance industry standards for the performance of fiduciary audits, the Center for Fiduciary Standards at the University of Pittsburgh (*pitt.edu*) offers training programs and research publications.

## GOVERNMENTAL AND REGULATORY BODIES

Investors can find a wealth of useful information relating to asset allocation and investing among the annual reports, special reports, monthly or quarterly publications, annual fact books, and conference proceedings of governmental and regulatory organizations. Regulatory filings (available via *freeedgar.com*), such as companies' 10-K or 10-Q reports and investment advisors' ADV Forms that must be filed with the SEC, also contain important and relevant insights. These materials may generally be downloaded and/or ordered in hard-copy form via the organization's Web site, either for free or a nominal charge. Alternatively, investors may be able to print the desired information directly from the government's or the regulatory body's Web server.

Table 10.6 contains a list of selected governmental and regulatory bodies.

Many regulatory bodies, stock, options, and futures exchanges, foreign central banks, and supranational organizations produce monthly, quarterly, semiannual, or annual publications, data, reports, filings, and analyses that can add considerable value to the investor's process of thinking about and executing asset allocation and investment policy.

## NONPRINT MASS MEDIA

Nonprint mass media provide investors with effective means of keeping informed about financial markets, and to a lesser degree, of building or adding to core knowledge about asset allocation and investing. Nonprint

**T A B L E  10.6**

Selected Governmental and Regulatory Bodies

| Governmental or Regulatory Body | Web Site |
| --- | --- |
| **Federal Reserve Bank** | |
| Federal Reserve System | *federalreserve.gov* |
| Federal Reserve System Online | *federalreserveonline.org* |
| Federal Reserve Bank of Atlanta | *frbatlantafed.org* |
| Federal Reserve Bank of Boston | *bos.frb.org* |
| Federal Reserve Bank of Chicago | *frbchi.org* |
| Federal Reserve Bank of Cleveland | *clev.frb.org* |
| Federal Reserve Bank of Dallas | *dallasfed.org* |
| Federal Reserve Bank of Kansas City | *kc.frb.org* |
| Federal Reserve Bank of Minneapolis | *minneapolisfed.org* |
| Federal Reserve Bank of New York | *ny.frb.org* |
| Federal Reserve Bank of Philadelphia | *phil.frb.org* |
| Federal Reserve Bank of Richmond | *rich.frb.org* |
| Federal Reserve Bank of San Francisco | *frbsf.org* |
| Federal Reserve Bank of St. Louis | *stlouisfed.org* |
| **Governmental and Regulatory Bodies** | |
| U.S. Department of the Treasury | *ustreas.gov* |
| U.S. Department of Commerce | *doc.gov* |
| U.S. Department of Labor | *dol.gov* |
| U.S. Government Printing Office | *gpo.gov* |
| U.S. Securities and Exchange Commission | *sec.gov* |
| Commodity Futures Trading Commission | *cftc.gov* |
| Federal Deposit Insurance Corp. | *fdic.gov* |
| National Association of Securities Dealers | *nasd.com* |
| National Futures Association | *nfa.futures.org* |
| Securities Industry Association | *sia.com* |
| **Stock, Options, and Futures Exchanges** | |
| New York Stock Exchange | *nyse.com* |
| Nasdaq | *nasdaq.com* |
| American Stock Exchange | *amex.com* |
| Arizona Stock Exchange | *azx.com* |
| Boston Stock Exchange | *bostonstock.com* |
| Chicago Board of Trade | *cbot.com* |
| Chicago Board Options Exchange | *cboe.com* |
| Chicago Mercantile Exchange | *cme.com* |
| Coffee Sugar and Cocoa Exchange | *csce.com* |
| Kansas City Board of Trade | *kcbt.com* |
| New York Mercantile Exchange | *nymex.com* |
| New York Cotton Exchange | *nyce.com* |
| Philadelphia Stock Exchange | *phlx.com* |

Continued

**T A B L E  10.6 (Concluded)**

Selected Governmental and Regulatory Bodies

| Non-U.S. Central Banks | |
|---|---|
| Bank of England | *bankofengland.co.uk* |
| Bank of China | *bank-of-china.com* |
| Bank of Japan | *boj.or.jp/en* |
| European Central Bank | *ecb.int* |

| Supranational Organizations | |
|---|---|
| Bank for International Settlements | *bis.org* |
| International Monetary Fund | *imf.org* |
| World Bank | *worldbank.org* |

Source: The author.

mass media include satellite and cable television, broadcast television, radio, satellite radio, financial data purveyors, pagers and other wireless devices, and motion pictures. A partial listing of these sources can be found under "Internet Broadcasts" on *yahoo.com*.

Financial programming carried over satellite, cable, and broadcast radio and television channels that focus on these topics, can be found on *bloomberg.com, marketwatch.com, clearstation.com, moneycentral.msn.com, cnn.com, cnnfn.com, foxnews.com/business*, and *msnbc.com*. Specific scheduled shows that address topics relating to asset allocation and investing include "WealthTrack with Consuelo Mack" (*wealthtrack.com*), "Wall Street Week" (*pbs.org/wsw*), and "Moneywise with Kelvin Boston" (*pbs.org/moneywise*).

Financial radio programming can also furnish insights on subjects germane to asset allocation and investing. The schedules and content of special and regularly scheduled radio programs, can be located on *bloomberg.com, clearchannel.com, coxradio.com, emmis.com*, and *infinity.com*. Specific radio shows include "Money Talk," hosted by Bob Brinker (*bobbrinker.com*), "Money Matters" (*moneymatters. garygoldberg.com*), "ON24" (*on24.com*), "High Noon on Wall Street" (*msnbc.com*), "The Motley Fool Radio Show" (*fool.com*), and "MG and the StockDoctor" (*stockdr.com*). Additional nonprint mass media sources include: (i) financial-data purveyors such as Bloomberg (*bloomberg.com*), Reuters (*reuters.com*), and Thomson Financial (*thomson.com/financial*); (ii) financial pager and wireless services, such as *informpage.com*, and (iii) movies that treat financial subjects, including *Boiler Room, Wall Street, Trading Places, Rogue Trader, Barbarians at the Gate,* and *Bonfire of the Vanities.*

## PERIODICALS, NEWSPAPERS, AND NEWSLETTERS

Periodicals, newspapers, and newsletters help investors keep informed about news developments and changing market conditions that affect the spheres of asset allocation and investing. In addition, these publications often contain the insights and commentary of experienced journalists and investment professionals, practical guidance for investors, and useful tools that can be applied to asset allocation and investing tactics and strategies. Several publications, such as *Forbes, Fortune, Business Week, The Economist, Smart Money, Worth, Barron's,* the *New York Times,* the *Financial Times,* and the *Wall Street Journal,* produce special issues or reports on a quarterly, semiannual, or annual basis, addressing subjects such as: mutual-fund performance reviews; surveys of past results and the investment outlook for a broad range of specific asset classes; and investing, personal-finance, or retirement-planning guides. Each quarter on its "Economic and Financial Indicators" page, *The Economist* publishes a summary of the asset allocation recommendations of several financial services firms, providing a breakdown of holdings by instrument, by geographical region, and by currency.

Annotated lists of popular periodicals, magazines, newspapers, and newsletters can be found on *finance.yahoo.com, investorama.com,* and *financial-freebies.com.* These lists also contain a number of highly focused publications addressing: (i) Canadian, British, Japanese, Latin American, Asian, and emerging-markets investments; (ii) foreign-exchange, commodities, options, and futures markets; (iii) mutual funds; (iv) hedge funds; and (v) other alternative-investment vehicles such as private equity, venture capital, and real estate. A survey of one experienced investor's reading strategy is contained in "Caveat Lector," by Barton M. Biggs, in the October 10, 1994 issue of Morgan Stanley's *Investment Perspectives.*

Many of the publications listed in this section, such as the *Wall Street Journal,* the *New York Times,* and *Barron's,* are available online as well as in hard-copy format; some newer publications are available only online; and some publications have one or more sibling publications that may be of specialized interest to certain investors. In cases in which the investor is not familiar with the publication, it is a good idea to review several recent issues at a library or newsstand, or to request trial review copies or a trial subscription from the publisher.

**T A B L E  10.7**

Selected Periodicals and Magazines

| Periodical/Magazine | Web Site |
| --- | --- |
| Active Trader Magazine | activetradermag.com |
| Bank Credit Analyst | bcapub.com |
| Bloomberg Markets | bloomberg.com/media/markets |
| Bloomberg Money | bloomberg.com/media/ukmoney |
| Business Week | businessweek.com |
| Dow Jones Asset Management | dowjones.com |
| Economist | economist.com |
| Forbes | forbes.com |
| Fortune | fortune.com |
| Funding Post | fundingpost.com |
| Global Investor | global-investor.com |
| Grant's Interest Rate Observer | grantspub.com |
| Harvard Business Review | hbsp.harvard.edu/products/hbr |
| Hedge Fund Magazine | thehfa.org |
| Institutional Investor | iiplatinum.com |
| Investment Dealer's Digest | sdponline.com/product/banking |
| Investment Advisor | investmentadvisor.com |
| Kiplinger's Personal Finance | kiplinger.com/magazine |
| Money | money.com |
| Morningstar | morningstar.com |
| Online Investor | theonlineinvestor.com |
| Outstanding Investor Digest | oid.com |
| Pensions and Investments | pionline.com |
| Red Herring | redherring.com |
| Reuters | reuters.com |
| Smart Money | smartmoney.com |
| The Street | thestreet.com |
| Thought Spotlight Magazine | jpmorgan.com |
| Value Line Investment Survey | valueline.com |
| Venturewire | venturewire.com |
| Wired | wired.com |
| Worth | worth.com |

Source: The author.

Table 10.7 lists selected periodicals and magazines.

The periodicals and magazines in Table 10.7 range from moderately priced, general interest publications targeted at a broad cross-section of the investing public, to specialized offerings with high subscription prices aimed at a narrower audience whose full-time professional responsibilities are focused on asset allocation and/or investing. Several even more specialized magazines are described below in the section on professional and scholarly journals.

## Newspapers

Newspapers deliver a regular stream of news and financial markets coverage, editorial opinion, and special surveys and reports. Several newspapers publish regular reviews of various firms' asset allocation frameworks and investment recommendations. Table 10.8 contains a listing of selected nationally and internationally oriented newspapers of interest to investors.

In addition to nationally and internationally oriented newspapers shown in Table 10.8, many award-winning newspapers provide reporting and regular features of value to investors. These newspapers include the *Los Angeles Times*, the *Chicago Tribune*, the *San Francisco Chronicle*, the *Boston Globe*, the *Boston Herald*, the *Philadelphia Enquirer*, the *Atlanta Constitution*, the *New York Post*, the *Miami Herald*, the *St. Louis Post-Dispatch*, the *Nashville Tennessean*, the *Denver Post*, the *Minneapolis Star-Tribune*, the *Seattle Times*, the *Houston Chronicle*, the *Dallas Morning News*, the *Detroit Free Press*, the *Sacramento Bee*, the *New Orleans Times-Picayune*, the *Toronto Globe and Mail*, and the *Montreal Gazette*. A Web site maintained by Dow Jones, *factiva.com*, can help investors find answers to business and financial questions in an archive of more than 6,000 U.S. and international newspapers and other publications.

**T A B L E  10.8**

Selected Newspapers

| Newspaper | Web Site |
| --- | --- |
| *Barron's* | *barrons.com* |
| *Financial Times* | *ft.com* |
| *Investment News* | *investmentnews.com* |
| *Investor's Business Daily* | *investors.com* |
| *The New York Times* | *nytimes.com* |
| *San Jose Mercury News* | *mercurynews.com* |
| *USA Today* | *usatoday.com* |
| *The Wall Street Journal* | *wsj.com* |
| *The Washington Post* | *washingtonpost.com* |

Source: The author.

## Newsletters

Newsletters occupy a special and important niche within the universe of information sources about asset allocation and investing. As independent sources of fact and commentary, newsletters often supply fundamental and/or technical insights about overall market trends and developments in specific asset classes, mutual fund and hedge fund categories, market sectors, and market subsectors. Table 10.9 lists selected newsletters.

It is worth repeating that hundreds, even thousands, of publications such as the selected newsletters listed in Table 10.9 are vying for the investor's attention. To evaluate the efficacy of a specific newsletter, investors would be wise to request copies of back issues and/or a free or low-cost trial subscription. In an annual survey published early in each calendar year, *Forbes* magazine (*forbes.com*) analyzes the performance of many leading market newsletters in up-market environments and in

**T A B L E  10.9**

Selected Newsletters

| Newsletter | Web Site |
| --- | --- |
| Alternative Investment Managers Association Newsletter | *aima.org* |
| Better Investing | *betterinvestingnewsroom.org* |
| Capitol Analysts Network | *capitolanalysts.com* |
| Dines Letter | *dinesletter.com* |
| Economics Strategy and Portfolio Newsletter | *peterlbernsteininc.com* |
| Felix Kloman's Risk Reports | *riskreports.com* |
| Fidelity Independent Advisor | *investools.com* |
| Fidelity Insight | *fidelityinsight.com* |
| Fidelity Investor | *fidelityinvestor.com* |
| Fidelity Monitor | *fidelitymonitor.com* |
| The Gilder Report | *gildertech.com* |
| Gloom Boom and Doom Report | *gloomboomdoom.com* |
| The Investment Fund for Foundations | *tiff.org* |
| Investor Insight | *investorinsight.com* |
| Kiplinger's Report | *kiplinger.com* |
| No-Load Fund Investor Newsletter | *financialnewsletters.com/* |
| Private Asset Manager | *iiwealthmanagement.com* |
| Property and Portfolio Research | *ppr-research.com* |
| Retired Investor | *retiredinvestor.com* |
| Wall Street Letter | *wallstreetletter.com* |

Source: The author.

down-market environments. Two other evaluative sources of information about newsletters are: (i) *Hulbert Financial Digest* (*hulbert.com*), which provides ratings of investment newsletters and the portfolios they recommend; and (ii) Financial Newsletter Network (*financialnewsletters.com*), which publishes a guide to financial and investing newsletters.

## Professional and Scholarly Journals

Professional and scholarly journals in large part serve to advance the intellectual frontiers about asset allocation and/or investing. These journals often contain groundbreaking, advanced, and mathematically rich discussions of the theoretical underpinning of financial and investment topics. In view of their high subscription prices and the deep and rigorous treatment of their subject matter, professional and scholarly journals are primarily utilized by academics and a number of investment professionals.

Table 10.10 contains a listing of professional and scholarly journals.

### T  A  B  L  E  10.10

Selected Professional and Scholarly Journals

| Journal | Web Site |
|---|---|
| **Professional Journals** | |
| *Financial Analysts Journal* | *aimrpubs.org* |
| *The Journal of Alternative Investments* | *iijournals.com* |
| *The Journal of Derivatives* | *iijournals.com* |
| *The Journal of Financial Planning* | *jounalfp.net* |
| *The Journal of Fixed-Income* | *iijournals.com* |
| *The Journal of Investing* | *investmentresearch.org* |
| *The Journal of Accountancy* | *aicpa.org/pubs/index.htm* |
| *The Journal of Portfolio Management* | *iijournals.com* |
| *The Journal of Private Equity* | *iijournals.com* |
| *The Journal of Private Portfolio Management* | *iijournals.com* |
| *The Journal of Psychology and Financial Markets* | *investmentresearch.org* |
| *The Journal of Risk Finance* | *iijournals.com* |
| *The Journal of Wealth Management* | *iijournals.com* |
| *Emerging Markets Quarterly* | *investmentresearch.org* |
| **Scholarly Journals** | |
| *The Journal of Business* | *journals.uchicago.edu* |
| *The Journal of Finance* | *afajof.org* |
| *The Journal of Financial Economics* | *jfe.rochester.edu* |
| *The Review of Economics and Statistics* | *mitpress.mit.edu* |

Source: The author.

As a general rule, the *professional journals* listed in Table 10.10 tend to contain information primarily of relevance to professional investors, investment strategists, economists, securities research analysts, and some individual investors, whereas the *scholarly journals* tend to contain information primarily of relevance to teachers, researchers, and advanced-level students within the academic community. There may be considerable overlap and useful knowledge sharing for interested practitioners between each of these two types of journals. In many cases, full-length or abridged versions of articles appearing in professional and scholarly journals may be reprinted in one or more of the publications listed earlier in this chapter in the section about periodicals, newspapers, and newsletters.

## Professional Organizations

Professional organizations create, maintain, and disseminate a significant amount of information of value to investors seeking solid and reliable resources about asset allocation and investing. Many professional organizations publish research studies, reading lists, teaching materials, and in some cases, course modules that can lead to certification of professional attainment. Table 10.11 lists selected professional organizations.

In general, professional organizations such as the ones in Table 10.11 fit into three broad categories:

- **Certification, Accreditation, and Educational Organizations:** establish and maintain specific standards of knowledge, ethical behavior, and professional conduct. Representative organizations include the CFA Institute, which confers the Chartered Financial Analyst (CFA) certification, the Certified Financial Planner Board of Standards (the CFP certification), the American Institute of Certified Public Accountants (the CPA designation), the Institute for Certified Investment Management Consultants (the CIMC designation), and the Investment Management Consultants Association, which confers the Certified Investment Management Analyst (CIMA) certification.

- **Associative Organizations:** share information among members and with the public, and represent the common interests of their membership vis-à-vis lawmakers, competing industries, suppliers, customers, and creditors. Representative organiza-

**T A B L E  10.11**

Selected Professional Organizations

| Organization | Web Site |
|---|---|
| **Certification, Accreditation, and Educational Organizations** | |
| Alternative Investment Management Association | *aima.org* |
| American Institute of Certified Public Accountants | *aicpa.org* |
| Certified Financial Planner Board of Standards, Inc. | *cfp-board.org* |
| Chartered Financial Analyst CFA Institute | *cfa.institute.org* |
| Institute for Certified Investment Management Consultants | *icimc.org* |
| Investment Counsel Association | *investmentadviser.org* |
| Investment Management Consultants Association | *imca.org* |
| National Association of Personal Financial Advisors | *napfa.com* |
| **Associative Organizations** | |
| American Bankers Association | *aba.com* |
| Closed-End Fund Association | *closedendfundforum.com* |
| Family Office Exchange | *familyoffice.com* |
| Financial Planning Association | *fpanet.org* |
| Global Association of Risk Professionals | *garp.com* |
| Hedge Fund Association | *thehfa.org* |
| Institute for Private Investors | *memberlink.net* |
| Investment Company Institute | *ici.org* |
| Managed Funds Association | *mfainfo.org* |
| National Association of Investment Professionals | *naip.com* |
| National Association of Variable Annuities | *navanet.org* |
| National Venture Capital Association | *nvca.org* |
| New York Society of Security Analysts | *nyssa.org* |
| Securities Industry Association | *sia.com* |
| The VIP Forum | *thevipforum.com* |
| **Community-Type Organizations** | |
| Association of Small Foundations | *smallfoundations.org* |
| The Commonfund | *commonfund.org* |
| Council on Foundations | *cof.org* |
| Emerging Markets Traders Association | *emta.org* |
| The Investment Fund for Foundations | *tiff.org* |
| The Philanthropy Roundtable | *philanthropyroundtable.org* |

Source: The author.

tions include the Institute for Private Investors, the Family Office Exchange, the VIP Forum, and the National Association of Investment Professionals.

◆ **Community-Type Organizations:** pool resources, share best practices, and provide access to ideas and tools. Representative organizations include the Council on Foundations, the Investment Fund for Foundations, the Common Fund, the Emerging Markets Creditors Association, and the Philanthropy Roundtable.

## Wall Street and the Financial Industry

The words "Wall Street" have come to describe not only the half-mile-long thoroughfare in lower Manhattan that runs from Broadway to the East River, but also LaSalle Street in Chicago, Montgomery Street in San Francisco, and more recently, the widely diffused urban, suburban, and occasionally even rural sites where investors and the diverse parts of the financial industry interact and ply their trade. Distinctions between different sectors of the financial industry have blurred considerably in modern times, and key participants in the industry have opted to pursue sometimes highly divergent strategies. Some entities focus narrowly but deeply on one or more specialized areas of activity, while others aim to thrive in a broad range of activities and disciplines across many sectors and in many global markets.

Figure 10.2 shows a number of the sectors that comprise Wall Street and the financial industry.

The sectors depicted in Figure 10.2 are by no means complete. They have been selected primarily for their relevance and usefulness as information sources about asset allocation and investing. Other areas of financial activity that are engaged in by the firms in these sectors, such as securities underwriting, corporate lending, and mergers and acquisitions, are not referred to in any great detail here. In the exhibit, the many sectors of the financial industry are represented by a ring of overlapping circles that affect, and are affected by, not only their neighbors, but also by virtually all of the other finance sectors. This high degree of multiple involvement and interdependence is represented by the hexagonal figure in the center of the figure, which depicts the mutual relationships that occur between each sector and practically all of the other sectors.

As a result, investors should keep in mind that many of the information sources listed under one category in Figure 10.2 could very well be listed simultaneously in several of the categories. For example, some large financial services firms, such as Citigroup, JP Morgan Chase, and BancAmerica Securities, conduct business as investment banks, commercial banks, securities brokers, trust companies, and online brokers (sometimes through an affiliate or a wholly owned subsidiary). Similarly, almost all of the sectors in Figure 10.2, not merely the considerably abbreviated list of the firms classified within the research category, publish research in one form or another. Some of the information about asset allocation and investing that is produced by Wall

Selected Sectors Within Wall Street and the Financial Industry

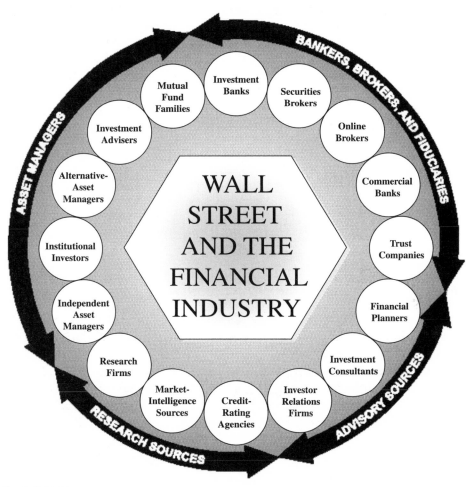

Source: The author.

Street and the financial industry is available primarily to clients of a specific originating firm, while other information may be much more widely accessible through a variety of channels, including some of the Web sites and Web-based tools described more fully below.

In broad terms, the asset allocation and investing services side of Wall Street and the financial industry may be grouped into four categories: (i) bankers, brokers, and fiduciaries; (ii) asset managers; (iii)

**F I G U R E  10.3**

Selected Asset Allocation and Investing Services of Wall Street and the
Financial Industry

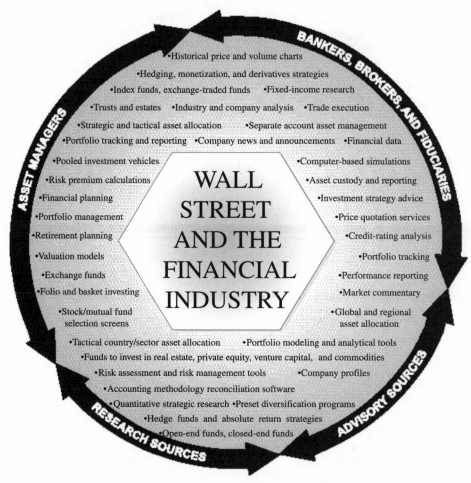

Source: The author.

research sources; and (iv) advisory sources. Figure 10.3 shows several
of the publications and services produced by the key sectors within
these four categories.

Because many of the services and publications in the asset allocation and investing realm are produced by more than one, and in some
cases, all four of these broad categories, they are shown together in Figure 10.3. A purely representative, but by no means exhaustive, listing

of these publications and services includes: (i) macro- and microcommentary, analysis, advice, and planning assistance; (ii) asset allocation and asset management services and products; (iii) software-based modeling, simulations, and analytical tools; (iv) financial data and price quotation services for indices and specific investments across the full gamut of asset classes; (v) trade execution, hedging, monetization, reporting, and custody services; and (vi) extended study programs, courses, seminars, and workshops for the training and development of employees and, occasionally, clients and/or the public at large.

Table 10.12 lists selected participants in Wall Street and the financial industry.

**T A B L E  10.12**

Selected Participants in Wall Street and the Financial Industry

| Entity | Web Site |
|---|---|
| **Investment Banks and Commercial Banks** | |
| Bank of America | *bankofamerica.com* |
| Bear Stearns | *bearstearns.com* |
| Citigroup | *citigroup.com* |
| Credit Suisse | *credit-suisse.com* |
| Deutsche Banc Securities | *alexbrown.db.com* |
| Goldman Sachs | *gs.com* |
| JP Morgan Chase | *jpmorganchase.com* |
| Lehman Brothers | *lehman.com* |
| Merrill Lynch | *ml.com* |
| Morgan Stanley | *morganstanley.com* |
| UBS | *ibb.ubs.com* |
| | *wellsfargo.com* |
| **Securities Brokers** | |
| AG Edwards | *agedwards.com* |
| Edward Jones | *edwardjones.com* |
| Prudential Securities | *prudential.com* |
| | *piperjaffray.com* |
| **Online Brokers** | |
| Ameritrade | *ameritrade.com* |
| Charles Schwab | *schwab.com* |
| E-Trade | *etrade.com* |
| Fidelity | *powerstreet.com* |
| Harris Direct | *harrisdirect.com* |
| Interactive Brokers | *interactivebrokers.com* |
| Terra Nova | *terranovaonline.com* |
| Merrill Lynch Direct | *mldirect.com* |
| | *tdwaterhouse.com* |

Continued

**T A B L E  10.12 (Continued)**

Selected Participants in Wall Street and the Financial Industry

| Entity | Web Site |
|---|---|
| **Trust Companies** | |
| Bessemer Trust | *bvp.com* |
| Fiduciary Trust | *fiduciary-trust.com* |
| Morgan Stanley Trust | *morganstanley.com* |
| Northern Trust | *ntrs.com* |
| Trust Company of the West | *tcw.com* |
| U.S. Trust | *ustrust.com* |
| Wilmington Trust | *wilmingtontrust.com* |
| **Mutual Fund Families** | |
| AIM | *aimfunds.com* |
| Alliance Capital | *alliancecapital.com* |
| American Century | *americancentury.com* |
| Delaware Investments | *delawarefunds.com* |
| Deutsche Asset Management | *deutsche-funds.com* |
| Dreyfus | *dreyfus.com* |
| Evergreen | *evergreeninvestments.com* |
| Federated | *federatedinvestors.com* |
| Fidelity Investments | *fidelity.com* |
| Franklin Templeton | *franklintempleton.com* |
| Gabelli | *gabelli.com* |
| Goldman Sachs Asset Management | *gs.com* |
| Invesco | *invesco.com* |
| Janus | *janus.com* |
| JP Morgan | *jpmorganfunds.com* |
| Lazard | *lazardnet.com* |
| Legg Mason | *leggmason.com/funds* |
| Loomis Sayles | *loomissayles.com* |
| MFS | *mfs.com* |
| Merrill Lynch Asset Management | *ml.com* |
| Morgan Stanley Investment Management | *morganstanley.com/im* |
| Nuveen | *nuveen.com* |
| Oppenheimer | *oppenheimerfunds.com* |
| PIMCO | *allianzinvestors.com* |
| Putnam Investments | *putnam.com* |
| Schwab | *schwab.com/funds* |
| T. Rowe Price | *troweprice.com* |
| TCW | *tcw.com* |
| UBS Paine Webber | *ubs.com* |
| Value Line | *vlfunds.com* |
| Van Kampen | *vankampen.com* |
| The Vanguard Group | *vanguard.com* |
| Washington Mutual | *wmgroupoffunds.com* |
| Wells Fargo | *wellsfargoadvantagefunds.com* |
| Wellington Management | *wellmanage.com* |

| Entity | Web Site |
|--------|----------|
| **Investment Advisors** | |
| American Express | *americanexpress.com* |
| Brown Brothers Harriman | *bbh.com* |
| Eaton Vance | *eatonvance.com* |
| Foliofn] | *foliofn.com* |
| Lord Abbett | *lordabbett.com* |
| Neuberger Berman | *nb.com* |
| Stein Roe and Farnham | *steinroe.com* |
| Scudder Kemper | *scudder.com* |
| Tweedy Browne | *tweedy.com* |
| Waddell Reed | *waddell.com* |
| **Alternative Asset Managers** | |
| Clayton, Dubilier & Rice | *cdr-inc.com* |
| KKR | *kkr.com* |
| Kleiner Perkins Caufield & Byers | *kpcb.com* |
| Pequot Capital | *pequotcap.com* |
| Perry Capital | *perrycap.com* |
| Sequoia Capital | *sequoiacap.com* |
| Texas Pacific Group Venture Capital | *tpgvc.com* |
| Tudor Investment | *tudorventures.com* |
| **Institutional Investors** | |
| Bill & Melinda Gates Foundation | *gatesfoundation.org* |
| California Public Employees Retirement System | *calpers.ca.gov* |
| Capital Group Companies | *capgroup.com* |
| The Commonfund | *commonfund.com* |
| Ford Foundation | *fordfound.org* |
| New York State Teachers' Retirement System | *nystrs.org* |
| Paul Allen Foundation | *pgafamilyfoundation.com* |
| Rockefeller Foundation | *rockfound.org* |
| TIAA-CREF | *tiaa-cref.org* |
| **Independent Asset Managers** | |
| Hoisington Investment Management | *hoisingtonmgt.com* |
| Off Wall Street Consulting Goup | *offwallstreet.com* |
| Thomas J. Herzfeld Advisors | *herzfeld.com* |
| **Financial Planners** | |
| Ayco Consulting Group | *ayco.com* |
| Direct Advice | *directadvice.com* |
| U.S. Social Security Administration | *ssa.gov* |
| **Investment Consultants** | |
| Barra | *barra.com* |
| Callan Associates | *callan.com* |
| Cambridge Associates | *cambridgeassociates.com* |
| Cerulli Associates | *cerulli.com* |
| Evaluation Associates | *eval-assoc.com* |
| Frank Russell Company | *russell.com* |
| Hewitt Investment Group | *hewittinvest.com* |

Continued

**T A B L E 10.12 (Concluded)**

## Selected Participants in Wall Street and the Financial Industry

| Entity | Web Site |
|---|---|
| **Investment Consultants (Cont.)** | |
| SEI | *seic.com* |
| Style Research (UK) | *styleresearch.com* |
| Wilshire Associates/Trust Universe Comparison Service (TUCS) | *wilshire.com* |
| Windermere Investment Associates | *windinvest.com* |
| **Investor Relations Firms** | |
| Burson-Marsteller | *bm.com* |
| Business Wire | *businesswire.com* |
| CFO News | *cfonews.com* |
| Financial Relations Board | *frbinc.com* |
| Hill and Knowlton | *hillandknowlton.com* |
| National Investor Relations Institute | *niri.org* |
| PR Newswire | *prnewswire.com* |
| Ruder Finn | *ruderfinn.com* |
| **Credit-Rating Agencies** | |
| Dun & Bradstreet | *dnb.com* |
| Fitch | *fitchibca.com* |
| Moody's Investors Services | *moodys.com* |
| Standard & Poor's | *standardandpoors.com* |
| **Market Intelligence Sources** | |
| AOL Personal Finance | *money.aol.com* |
| Briefing.com | *briefing.com* |
| Fly on the Wall | *theflyonthewall.com* |
| Kiplinger | *kiplinger.com/personalfinance* |
| Morningstar | *morningstar.com* |
| MSN Money | *moneycentral.msn.com* |
| Mutual Fund Education Alliance | *mfea.com* |
| Quicken | *quicken.com* |
| Quote | *quote.com* |
| Reuters Money Network | *money.net* |
| Securities Research Company | *stockmarket.co.nz* |
| Wall Street Journal | *wsj.com* |
| Yahoo! | *finance.yahoo.com* |
| **Research Firms** | |
| Buyside | *buyside.com* |
| Earnings Whispers | *earningswhispers.com* |
| Hoover's | *hoovers.com* |
| Ibbotson | *ibbotson.com* |
| IBD Research (*Investor's Business Daily*) | *investors.com* |
| Leuthold Group | *leutholdgroup.com* |
| Motley Fool | *fool.com* |
| Sectorbase | *sectorbase.com* |

| Entity | Web Site |
|--------|----------|
| **Research Firms (Cont.)** | |
| Telescan Financial Services | *telescan.com* |
| Thomson First Call | *thomson.com* |
| Thomson I/B/E/S | *rimes.com/ibes.xmp* |
| ValueLine | *valueline.com* |
| VectorVest | *vectorvest.com* |
| Zacks Analyst Watch | *zacks.com* |

Source: The author.

Investment banks, securities brokers, online brokers, commercial banks, and trust companies are prolific sources of information about most phases of asset allocation and investing. In addition, these entities are primary conduits for investors to carry out the functions of trade execution, hedging, monetization, reporting, and custody for their investments.

Mutual funds, investment advisers, alternative-investment managers, institutional investors, and independent asset managers have published a considerable quantity of material on the asset allocation and investment management process. Many of these firms have constructively added to the publicly available store of knowledge about the long-term merits of various investment styles, disciplines, and methodologies in conventional as well as alternative asset classes.

Financial planners, investment consultants, and investor-relations firms often play an important advisory role to investors seeking advice about asset allocation and investing. A comprehensive listing of financial planners and registered investment advisors may be found at *dmoz.org*. Operating in many cases from an independent vantage point, these firms disseminate publications, generally impartial advice, and frequently customized opinions that can shed light on crucial issues relating to investment performance analysis, short-term tactics, and long-term strategy.

Credit-rating agencies, market-intelligence sources, and specialist research firms offer a number of valuable tools to aid the investor in: (i) screening, ranking, and selecting specific types of investments ranging from stocks to bonds to mutual funds and other instruments; (ii) obtaining consensus earnings estimates, price quotations, company profiles, or credit information; and (iii) tapping into insightful and often highly candid research reports, notes, and opinions, sometimes from mainstream financial and investing services organizations, and sometimes in highly prescient writing from unaffiliated sources.

## Web-Based Tools

Web-based tools are generally considered to be Internet-based resources that perform an analytical, charting, evaluational, or management function for the investor. Web-based tools, usually
software-driven, may be distinguished from portals and Web sites. Table 10.13 contains a listing of selected Web-based tools applicable to asset allocation and investing.

**T A B L E   10.13**

Selected Web-Based Tools Applicable to Asset Allocation and Investing

| Entity | Web Site |
| --- | --- |
| **Analytics** | |
| *Securities Screens and Filters* | |
| FactSet Research Systems, Inc. | *factset.com* |
| MarketScreen | *marketscreen.com* |
| StockWiz Pro 2000 | *stockwiz.com* |
| Tradeworx | *tradeworx.com* |
| *Style Attribution Analysis* | |
| FactSet Research Systems, Inc. | *factset.com* |
| Frontier Analytics | *frontieranalytics.com* |
| Quantix | *quantix.com* |
| **Chart Services** | |
| *Price Data Feeds* | |
| eSignal | *esignal.com* |
| Prophet Charts | *prophetfinance.com* |
| *Technical Charts and Opinion* | |
| ClearStation | *clearstation.com* |
| Dorsey Wright & Associates | *dorseywright.com* |
| Equis | *equis.com* |
| MarketClub | *marketclub.com* |
| MetaStock | *metastock.com* |
| OmniTrader | *omnitrader.com* |
| Trendsetter Software | *trendsoft.com* |
| **Portfolio Management Updates** | |
| *Folio, Basket, and Portfolio Construction* | |
| Advisory World | *advisoryworld.com* |
| Barra | *barra.com* |
| Dean LeBaron | *deanlebaron.com* |
| FactSet Research Systems, Inc. | *factset.com* |
| Foliofn | *foliofn.com* |
| InvestWare | *iclub.com/investware_welcome.asp* |
| Marketocracy | *marketocracy.com* |
| *Performance Analysis* | |
| RiskGrades | *riskgrades.com* |
| Winnav | *winnav.com* |
| Wilshire Associates | *wilshire.com* |

| Entity | Web Site |
|---|---|
| *Portfolio Tracking Spreadsheets* | |
| GainsKeeper | *gainskeeper.com* |
| Investment Technologies | *invest-tech.com* |
| Stock-Trak | *stocktrak.com* |
| Trade Logic | *tradelogic.com* |
| **Software Programs** | |
| *Asset Allocation* | |
| Advisory World | *advisoryworld.com* |
| Frontier Analytics | *online.sungard.com/frontier* |
| Ibbotson Associates | *ibbotson.com* |
| Morningstar Principia Pro | *morningstar.com* |
| Northfield Information Services | *northinfo.com* |
| Quantec Ltd. | *quantec.com* |
| Vestek Systems | *vestek.com* |
| *Commodities, Equities, Fixed-Income, Mutual* | |
| *Funds, and Options Software* | |
| Bureau of the Public Debt | *publicdebt.treas.gov* |
| Bonds Online | *bondsonline.com* |
| Covered Call | *coveredcalls.com* |
| FactSet Research Systems, Inc. | *factset.com* |
| Fund Manager | *fundmanager.com* |
| Investing in Bonds | *investinginbonds.com* |
| Investorama | *iclub.com* |
| IVolatility | *ivolatility.com* |
| MarketStream | *uniserv.com* |
| Microhedge | *microhedge.com* |
| Option Find | *optionfind.com* |
| Option Monitor | *optionmonitor.com* |
| Option Searcher | *optionsearcher.com* |
| Option Wizard | *option-wizard.com* |
| Write Call | *writecall.com* |
| Yahoo! Finance Bond Center | *bonds.yahoo.com* |
| *Financial Planning* | |
| AccuQuote | *accuquote.com* |
| American Academy of Estate Planning | *estateplanforyou.com* |
| Deloitte & Touche Online | *deloitte.com* |
| Direct Advice | *directadvice.com* |
| Estate Planning Links | *estateplanninglinks.com* |
| Financial Engines | *financialengines.com* |
| Financeware | *financialplanauditors.com* |
| My CFO | *mycfo.com* |
| mPower | *mpower.com* |
| National Network of Estate Planning | *netplanning.com* |
| Nolo Press | *nolo.com* |
| Portfolio X-Ray | *morningstar.com* |
| QuickQuote | *quickquote.com* |
| Quicken 401k Advisor | *quicken.com* |
| *Personal Finance* | |
| AdviceAmerica | *adviceamerica.com* |
| American Express | *americanexpress.com* |

Continued

**T A B L E  10.13 (Concluded)**

Selected Web-Based Tools Applicable to Asset Allocation and Investing

| Entity | Web Site |
|---|---|
| **Software Programs** (*Cont.*) | |
| *Personal Finance* (*Cont.*) | |
| Citibank Online | *citibankonline.com* |
| Central Personal Finance Manager | *fncentral.com* |
| Pay Pal | *paypal.com* |
| *Risk Management* | |
| Investment Technologies | *invest-tech.com* |
| mPower/Morningstar | *mpower.com* |
| *Tax* | |
| 1040.com | *1040.com* |
| 2nd Story Software | *taxact.com* |
| Fairmark Press Tax Guide for Investors | *fairmark.com* |
| Internal Revenue Service | *irs.gov* |
| H.D. Vest | *hdvest.com* |
| H&R Block | *hrblock.com* |
| National Association of Tax Practitioners | *natptax.com* |
| Quicken Turbotax | *quicken.com* |
| Tax and Accounting Sites Directory | *taxsites.com* |
| Tax Prophet | *taxprophet.com* |
| TaxAct | *taxact.com* |
| **Technology Reviews** | |
| *Hardware* | |
| CNET.com | *cnet.com* |
| *Internet Resources* | |
| CNET Help | *help.com* |
| Citrix Online | *citrixonline.com* |
| Del.icio.us | *del.icio.us* |
| Digg.com | *digg.com* |
| IDG | *idg.net* |
| *Internet Service Providers (ISPs)* | |
| internet.com Corporation | *internet.com* |
| *Software* | |
| INVESTORSoftware | *investorsoftware.com* |
| *Web Services* | |
| WebHelp | *webhelp.com* |
| **Wealth Management Packages** | |
| *Wealth Management* | |
| Asset Management | *assetmanagement.com* |
| EnvestNet | *envestnet.com* |
| VIP Private Capital | *vipprivatecapital.com* |
| *Wealth Aggregation (Screen Scrapers)* | |
| Citi.com | *myciti.com* |
| Financial Navigator | *financialnavigator.com* |
| My CFO | *mycfo.com* |
| Yodlee | *yodlee.com* |

Source: The author.

The listing of Web-based tools applicable to asset allocation and investing in Table 10.13 is by no means complete and is subject to change with the passage of time due to the initiation, closing, mergers, and consolidations of sites. A comprehensive listing of Web sites prepared by David Montgomery and Robert S. Levitt, "Investment Research on the Internet," may be found at *ibbotson.com* or at *netmind.com*. Some of the tools that are classified under one of the headings in Table 10.13 may have features that might also lead to their classification under another heading. In general, the Web-based tools listed fall under the heading that captures their primary use and functionality.

Securities screens and filters help investors sort through current and historical data to organize and rank securities, industry groups, and mutual funds according to certain specified criteria. Some securities screens and filters provide periodic updates and alerts, and others allow the investor to import and export data to and from spreadsheets. Style attribution analysis tools allow the investor to decompose and examine the sources of contribution to the overall investment performance of a portfolio. Some of these tools also contain features that utilize fundamental and/or quantitative criteria to determine: (i) the intrinsic worth of specific investments in the portfolio; (ii) the degree of fair, over- or undervaluation of whole portfolios or individual investments; and (iii) the suitability of a given portfolio or asset allocation versus the investor's specified objectives.

Price data feeds show real-time or delayed securities price quotations in one or more formats, ranging from tables or matrices to charts. These data feeds may usually be organized and grouped alphabetically, by industry, or according to other preferences an investor chooses. Technical charts and opinion services show historical prices and sometimes trading volume data. Some packages provide commentary on the price patterns shown in the graphs. Many charting services allow the investor a high degree of flexibility in selecting the time frame and price parameters for displaying the charts.

Folio, basket, and portfolio construction tools allow investors to create optimal projected portfolios, or in some cases, baskets or folios (groups of a limited number of securities selected by the investor to meet specific investment goals). These simulated portfolio, basket, and folio construction packages may be based on capital market expectations, historical results, risk tolerance, transaction costs, hedging decisions, and investment policy constraints. Some services have built-in monitoring capabilities that send alerts to pagers, cell phones, or other wireless devices if portfolio values rise or fall by specified amounts. Performance analysis packages utilize back-testing methods and statistical principles to analyze the returns, risk, variance, correlation, and other measures of selected portfolios, indices, and specific investments. Some performance analysis tools calculate several types of moving averages and give buy or sell signals to the investor according to certain preselected criteria. Portfolio-tracking spreadsheets are relatively straightforward devices that compute the individual and aggregate values, as well as other measures such as marginability and available buying power, of lists of securities or portfolios.

Asset allocation software programs may offer one or more capabilities, including: (i) investor-risk profiling, portfolio optimization, cash-flow forecasting, rebalancing analysis, historical back-testing, and rebalancing features; (ii) the creation and analysis of multiclass, multistructure portfolios of stocks, bonds, cash, mutual funds, hedge funds, and various kinds of alternative investments; and (iii) parameter-selection criteria incorporating normal and skewed returns objectives, downside risk, standard deviation, time horizons, cash flow and distribution targets, tax considerations, and asset mix/portfolio diversification constraints.

Commodities, equities, fixed-income, mutual funds, and options software refers to the wide variety of specialized Web-based tools that has been created to help investors focus on individual sectors of the financial markets. Many of these packages offer analytical tools, commentary, trading tactics and investment strategies, frequently asked questions, and calculations of fair values and historical and implied volatilities. The *iclub.com* site has a directory of financial software sites on the Web, with more than 15,000 links organized into more than 250 categories.

Financial-planning Web-based tools help investors set goals, enter personal and risk tolerance characteristics, select asset allocation mixes and investment strategies, and obtain advice related to financial planning, life insurance, estate planning, trusts, education planning, and retirement planning. Many of these Web-based tools provide: (i) definitions and fundamental knowledge to help the investor work with professional planners; (ii) links to specialists; (iii) projected tax-liability calculations, sample wills, online insurance application forms and quote-collection engines; and in some cases (iv) Monte Carlo simulators, which generate thousands of chance scenarios to produce probable outcomes of simulations involving a number of random variables.

Personal finance tools can help investors manage money inflows and outflows, pay bills, budget expenditures, and use the resultant information as a basis for constructing a financial plan. By linking directly to the investor's checking account or credit card provider, personal finance services allow users to send funds via e-mail.

Risk-management tools allow investors to complete risk-assessment questionnaires to identify risk-tolerance levels and accordingly, to map out appropriate investment strategies. Some risk-management packages permit investors to enter the details of specific portfolios to see how they would have fared in previous bear market episodes. Tax Web-based tools contain federal- and state-tax information, forms, instructions, online tax-filing packages, and tax strategies. When using these tools, it is always wise for the investor to seek out advice from competent professional counsel and/or the tax authorities themselves.

Web-based tools are widely available to give the investor technology reviews of hardware, Internet resources, Internet service providers, software, and Web services. These tools contain technical and pricing reviews, usage hints and instructions, and comprehensive directories of IT service-provider firms' resources, technical support, tutorials, training, skills development modules, discussion forums, and expert advice, both for average users and Internet industry and Internet technology professionals.

Wealth-management packages are intended to help investors, particularly those with sizeable, dispersed, and/or complex holdings, keep track of and adjust the composition of their overall fortune. Wealth-aggregation Web-based tools, also known as screen scrapers, pull together online financial data from various accounts, including banking, retirement, mutual fund, securities brokerage, credit card, airline frequent-flyer programs, and other types of asset- and liability-based accounts. These packages thus allow investors to view what they own and what they owe from an aggregated, and thus more informed and organized, perspective.

## Web Sites and Portals

Web sites, and the portals which lead to them, are Internet-based resources that advise, teach, inform, and execute transactions. Figure 9.10 in Chapter 9 shows how Web sites may be distinguished from portals and Web-based tools. Table 10.14 lists selected Web sites and portals applicable to asset allocation and investing.

The Web sites and portals in Table 10.14 have been selected based on their quality and applicability to investors' overall asset allocation and investing needs. This listing of Web sites and portals is by no means complete, and many of these sites could easily be classified under more than one of the categories in the table. Investors should keep in mind that Web-based tools and Web sites and portals in Tables 10.13

**T A B L E  10.14**

Selected Web Sites and Portals Applicable to Asset Allocation and Investing

| Entity | Web Site |
|---|---|
| **Advice Sources** | |
| *Fundamental Investing* | |
| Find Articles | findarticles.com |
| Fundadvice | fundadvice.com |
| Internet Investing | internetnews.com/stocks |
| I Club Central | iclub.com |
| *Technical Investing* | |
| Big Charts | bigcharts.com |
| ChartFilter | chartfilter.com |
| Clearstation | clearstation.com |
| Outercurve Finance | diginexus.com |
| StockCharts | stockcharts.com |
| StockTables | stocktables.com |
| Wall Street City | tscn.com |
| *Contrarian Investing* | |
| Contrarian Investing | contrarianinvesting.com |
| Fall Street | fallstreet.com |
| Fiend Bear | fiendbear.com |
| Prudent Bear | prudentbear.com |
| *Financial Planning* | |
| mPower/Morningstar | mpower.com |
| Financial Engines | financialengines.com |
| Quicken Retirement Planner | quicken.com |
| T. Rowe Price Retirement | troweprice.com |
| Vanguard Retirement Resource Center | vanguard.com |
| *Personal Finance* | |
| CheckFree | checkfree.com |
| Gomez Research | gomez.com |
| Morningstar Retirement Planner | morningstar.com |
| Paytrust | pmb.paytrust.com |
| PayTrust | paytrust.com |
| RefDesk | refdesk.com |
| Status Factory | statusfactory.com |
| *Socially Responsible Investing* | |
| Calvert Group | calvert.com |
| Citizens Funds | efund.com |
| Domini Social Investments | domini.com |
| Ethical Investment Research Service | eiris.org |
| Good Money Home Page | goodmoney.com |
| Green Money Journal | greenmoney.com |
| Social Investment Forum | socialinvest.org |
| **Calendar-Based Releases** | |
| *Earnings Reports* | |
| Annual Report Gallery | reportgallery.com |
| Beartopia | beartopia.net |
| Lycos Network | lycos.com |
| Shareholder Direct | shareholder.com |

| Entity | Web Site |
|---|---|
| StockZ | *stockz.com* |
| WhisperNumber.com | *whispernumber.com* |
| *Economic Data* | |
| Factiva | *factiva.com* |
| FreeLunch | *freelunch.com* |
| RefDesk | *refdesk.com* |
| SmartEconomist | *smarteconomist.com* |
| *Financial Data* | |
| Factiva | *factiva.com* |
| MSN Money Central | *moneycentral.msn.com* |
| Smart Money | *smartmoney.com* |

**Educational Materials**

*Asset Allocation*

| | |
|---|---|
| About Mutual Funds Asset Allocation | *mutualfunds.about.com* |
| Efficient Frontier | *efficientfrontier.com* |
| Ibbotson Associates | *ibbotson.com* |
| RunMoney | *runmoney.com* |

*Investing*

| | |
|---|---|
| Bloomberg Institute | *bloomberg.com* |
| China Online | *chinaonline.com* |
| Excite | *excite.com* |
| Find Articles | *findarticles.com* |
| Morningstar | *morningstar.com* |
| Motley Fool | *fool.com* |
| MSN Money Central | *moneycentral.msn.com* |
| Smart Money | *smartmoney.com* |
| World News | *worldnews.com* |
| Zacks Advisor | *zacksadvisor.com* |

*Trading*

| | |
|---|---|
| A Trader's Financial Resource Guide | *marshallnet.com* |
| EquiTrend | *equitrend.com* |
| GuruFocus | *gurufocus.com* |
| Intrade | *intrade.com* |
| Investors Alley | *investorsalley.com* |
| MarketWatch | *marketwatch.com* |
| StreetInsider | *streetinsider.com* |
| TimerTrac | *timertrac.com* |
| Winstock Pro | *winstocksw.com* |

**Filings and Announcements**

*Corporate Governance and  Developments*

| | |
|---|---|
| Beartopia | *beartopia.net* |
| CEO Express | *ceoexpress.com* |
| Corporate Governance | *corpgov.net* |
| Corporate Information | *corporateinformation.com* |
| Corporate Library LLC | *thecorporatelibrary.com* |
| Encycogov.com | *encycogov.com* |
| Institutional Shareholder Services | *finance.yahoo.com* |
| RefDesk | *refdesk.com* |
| Reuters MoneyNet | *money.net* |
| ShareholderProposals.com | *shareholderproposals.com* |

Continued

**T A B L E  10.14 (Continued)**

Selected Web Sites and Portals Applicable to Asset Allocation and Investing

| Entity | Web Site |
|---|---|
| **Filings and Announcements (*Cont.*)** | |
| *Corporate Governance and Developments (Cont.)* | |
| Standard & Poor's | *governance.standardandpoors.com* |
| Thomson Financial | *thomsonfinancial.net* |
| *Insider Transactions* | |
| 10K Wizard | *10kwizard.com* |
| InsiderScore | *insiderscore.com* |
| NetSteering | *netsteering.com* |
| *Securities Exchanges and Regulatory Bodies* | |
| Edgar Online | *edgar-online.com* |
| Free Edgar | *freeedgar.com* |
| SEC Forms Descriptions | *sec.gov* |
| *Underwritings* | |
| 123Jump | *123jump.com/ipo* |
| Alert-IPO! | *qualisteam.com* |
| Edgar Online IPO | *ipoportal.edgar-online.com* |
| Hoover's IPO Central | *hoovers.com/global/ipoc* |
| IPO Monitor | *ipomonitor.com* |
| IPO Home | *ipohome.com* |
| Yahoo! IPOs | *biz.yahoo.com/ipo* |
| **News** | |
| *Alert Services* | |
| Equity Alert | *equityalert.com* |
| FeedDemon | *feeddemon.com* |
| Find Articles | *findarticles.com* |
| Google News Alerts | *google.com/alerts* |
| NewzCrawler | *newzcrawler.com* |
| NewsInABox | *newsinabox.com* |
| Personal Stock Monitor | *dtlink.com* |
| Quote Watch | *quoteino.com* |
| Smart Money | *smartmoney.com* |
| Wall Street City | *tscn.com* |
| *Market Commentary* | |
| CNN/Money | *money.cnn.com* |
| Earnings Whispers | *earningswhispers.com* |
| Excite | *excite.com* |
| Investors Alley | *investorsalley.com* |
| Morningstar | *morningstar.com* |
| MSN Money | *moneycentral.msn.com* |
| Opinion Journal | *opinionjournal.com* |
| The Street | *thestreet.com* |
| Street IQ | *streetiq.com* |
| Topix | *topix.net* |
| Yahoo! Finance | *finance.yahoo.com* |
| *Blogs/Search Engines for Blogs* | |
| AAO Weblog | *accountingobserver.com* |
| Big Picture | *bigpicture.typepad.com* |

| Entity | Web Site |
|---|---|
| BloginWallStreet | *bloginwallstreet.com* |
| Bloglines | *bloglines.com* |
| Blog Maverick | *blogmaverick.com* |
| Briefing.com | *briefing.com* |
| Capital Spectator | *capitalspectator.com* |
| China Stock Blog | *chinastockblog.com* |
| DayPop | *daypop.com* |
| ETF Investor | *etfinvestor.com* |
| Feedster | *feedster.com* |
| Global View | *globalview.com* |
| IceRocket | *icerocket.com* |
| Infectious Greed | *paul.kedrosky.com* |
| Internet Stock Blog | *nternetstockblog.com* |
| J Curve | *jurveton.blogspot.com* |
| Monty's Bluff | *montysbluff.com* |
| Random Roger's Big Picture | *randomroger.blogspot.com* |
| Schaeffer's Research Daily Market Blog | *schaeffersresearch.com* |
| Seeking Alpha | *seekingalpha.com* |
| Technorati | *technorati.com* |
| ThinkEquity Partners | *thinkequity.com* |
| TraderMike | *tradermike.net* |
| Trader Wizard | *traderwizard.com* |
| Undollar Digest | *undollars.com* |
| *Message Boards* | |
| Beartopia | *beartopia.net* |
| ClearStation | *clearstation.com* |
| MotleyFool | *motleyfool.com* |
| Raging Bull | *ragingbull.com* |
| Silicon Investor | *siliconinvestor.com* |

**Research**

*Commodities*

| | |
|---|---|
| Barchart.com | *barchart.com* |
| The Bullion Desk | *thebulliondesk.com* |
| Chicago Mercantile Exchange | *cme.com* |
| Chicago Board of Trade | *cbot.com* |
| Commodity Trading World | *acommodity.com* |
| Daily Futures | *dailyfutures.com* |
| Futures Guide | *futuresguide.com* |
| Futures Industry Institute | *fiafii.org* |
| Futures Knowledge | *futuresknowledge.com* |
| Futures Net | *futures.net* |
| Futures pc quote | *pcquote.com* |
| Goldseek | *markets.goldseek.com* |
| Grant's Pass Futures & Options | *gpfo.com* |
| INO | *ino.com* |
| Kitco | *kitco.com* |
| Le Metropole Café | *lemetropolecafe.com* |
| MineSet, Jim Sinclair | *jsmineset.com* |
| Mineweb | *mineweb.com* |
| Reuters | *reuters.com* |

Continued

**T A B L E  10.14** (Concluded)

Selected Web Sites and Portals Applicable to Asset Allocation and Investing

| Entity | Web Site |
|---|---|
| **Research (*Cont.*)** | |
| *Equities* | |
| ADR | *adr.com* |
| BigCharts | *bigcharts.com* |
| Doh | *doh.com* |
| European Investor | *europeaninvestor.com* |
| Investment Trivia | *investmenttrivia.com* |
| Motley Fool | *fool.com* |
| Small Cap Center | *smallcapcenter.com* |
| Stock Market Trivia | *stockmarkettrivia.com* |
| WISI | *wisi.com* |
| World News | *worldnews.com* |
| Yahoo! Finance | *finance.yahoo.com* |
| Zacks Advisor | *zacksadvisor.com* |

Source: The author.

and 10.14 and elsewhere in this chapter may disappear, and a considerable number of newly created and repackaged Web sites and portals are likely to be added to the Internet, with the passage of time.

Many Web sites and several of the functions listed separately in Table 10.14 are linked through portals. A number of publications carry helpful textual reviews of Web-based tools, Web sites, and portals, including *Forbes* (in its periodic "Best of the Web" issues), *Business Week* (in its periodic "Our Guide to Online Investing" issues), *Barron's* (in its "Electronic Investor" and "Best Internet Sites" series), and the *Wall Street Journal* (in its "Online Investing" reports).

Fundamental-investing Web sites and portals help investors evaluate the intrinsic value of different kinds of investments according to various time-honored fundamental and valuation criteria. The Web sites and portals listed under "Technical Investing" focus on price and trading-volume patterns, money and liquidity flows, and a number of psychological factors that attempt to help predict the subsequent direction and magnitude of securities prices. Many of these Web sites and portals present such information in the form of graphs and charts. Contrarian-investing Web sites and portals provide information and opinions that lean against the prevailing investment wisdom. During extended bull market phases, such sites may offer bearish commentary and perspective, and during protracted bear market cycles, such sites may publish bullish opinions.

Financial-planning Web sites and portals provide information about the process of self-evaluation, goal setting, and returns projection to predict potential outcomes for capital balances, inflows, and out-flows during the course of an investor's lifetime. Many of these sources, especially when used in conjunction with the financial-planning software programs listed in Table 10.13, can help investors weigh tradeoffs and examine the effects of varying assumptions on: retirement planning; insurance, trusts, and estate planning; education planning; and, not least, tax planning. The personal finance Web sites and portals listed in Table 10.14 should also be viewed in combination with the personal finance software programs cited in Table 10.13. These resources offer education and advice about budgeting, keeping track of income flows, paying bills, and managing the assets and liabilities sides of an investor's balance sheet. Socially responsible investing Web sites and portals help investors locate assets and asset managers that reflect and/or take account of social, ecological, environmental, and other factors.

Earnings-reports Web sites and portals keep abreast of companies' periodic earnings announcements. In addition to the sources listed in Table 10.14, a variety of other portals and Web sites can render this information easily accessible to the investor. Several economic- and financial-data Web sites and portals contain historical and newly released information about changes in various countries' economies and their respective subsectors, corporate profits, price levels, consumer, business, and investor psychology, capital market conditions, interest rates, exchange rates, monetary and fiscal policy, and international trade and capital flows. Often, these data are also presented in graphical form.

Asset allocation Web sites and portals contain information and guidance about the process of: (i) deciding on the proper mix of stocks versus bonds, domestic versus nondomestic securities and conventional versus alternative assets; (ii) choosing an appropriate risk level; and (iii) determining the right rebalancing strategy. A significant amount of related information is contained in the Web-based tools on asset allocation listed in Table 10.13. A great many Web sites and portals offer education and advice on trading and investing. These resources range from the simple to the complex, from the superficial to the profound, and from the highly relevant to the esoteric. Investors should visit a number of these Web sites and portals, as well as the resources listed under commodities, equities, fixed-income, mutual funds, and options software in Table 10.13, to locate sites that match their specific needs, preferences, and circumstances.

Corporate-developments Web sites and portals allow investors to keep track of fundamental business and earnings developments, earnings reports, and other news releases. Investors will want to choose the number and configuration of news providers, whether to utilize free or for-payment services, and how frequently and in what format they wish to receive this information. Insider-transactions Web sites and portals monitor publicly disclosed purchases and sales of a corporation's securities by its directors, officers, and major shareholders. In many cases, such information may indicate how those closest to a firm's business activities feel about that company's prospects. Securities exchanges and regulatory bodies' Web sites and portals provide highly useful documents in which most publicly traded companies must describe their main business activities, disclose the financial results of their operations, and publish income statements, balance sheets, summaries of cash flow, and related footnotes. Underwritings Web sites and portals detail upcoming and past public offerings, including filing prices, the number and form of the securities offered, the lead manager(s) of the transaction, and other information.

Many of the alert-services Web sites and portals send some form of electronic or wireless signal to investors to signify news, the reaching of a specific price target, or other information. Similarly, a large number of market-commentary Web sites and portals provide reporting, opinions, and predictions relating to investment strategy, investment behavior, and the likely course of financial asset prices. The capabilities of message boards, accessible through many of the leading financial portals, depicted in Figure 10.1, are also described more fully in earlier in this chapter (please see "Conference Calls, Chat Rooms, and Message Boards").

Equities, fixed-income, commodities, mutual funds, and options research Web sites and portals contain a voluminous amount of information, a good part of which is figuratively uncensored and independently produced. As a result, investors gain access to a fair degree of candor, even if at the cost of potentially extreme and/or erroneous opinions. Some sites are free, while others charge a subscription fee. Investors would do well to test several sites to find one or more to their liking.

Full-line, online, options, and wireless brokerage Web sites and portals offer a wide range of services, pricing structures and discount schedules, technology features, margin lending facilities, conditions for accessing research and underwritings, and the degree of service-level contact with investment representatives and/or call centers. The borders between these four types of securities brokerage firms have become less distinct, with several full-line brokers also offering online, options, and wireless brokerage.

## SUBJECT-BASED INFORMATION SOURCES

### Investing Basics and Fundamentals

Many useful information sources about investing basics and fundamentals were mentioned in earlier sections of this chapter on: (i) books; (ii) periodicals, newspapers, and newsletters; (iii) Wall Street and the financial industry; (iv) Web-based tools; and (v) Web sites and portals. Several kinds of additional resources, many of which are regularly updated or replaced by improved versions, that can be of significant value about investing basics and fundamentals, include: (i) regular features, periodic special surveys, signed columns, and specific articles in newspapers and magazines; (ii) educational writings published as standalone pamphlets, as part of the communications and literature of investment management, brokerage, research, and advisory firms; and (iii) portions of financial firms' Web sites. A small and purely representative sampling of such sources is described here.

Several newspapers and magazines publish columns about asset allocation, the selection of specific investments, financial market prognostications, the use of fundamental and technical measures of market valuation, common pitfalls to avoid, and how to develop and refine an overall philosophy of and approach to investing. Among these sources are: (i) "Getting Going," by Jonathan R. Clements in the *Wall Street Journal*; (ii) "Strategies," by Mark Hulbert, "Business Analysis," by Floyd Norris, "Market Insight," by Kenneth L. Gilpin, "Portfolios, Etc.," by Jonathan Fuerbringer, and "Market Watch," by Gretchen Morgenson, in the *New York Times*; (iii) "Investor's Corner," by Nancy Gondo, in *Investor's Business Daily*; (iv) "The Long View," by Philip Coggan, and the series of *"Financial Times* Surveys" in the *Financial Times*; (v) "The Bottom Line," by James J. Cramer, in *New York*; (vi) "Investing," by James K. Glassman, in the *Washington Post*; (vii) "The

Trader," by Michael Santoli, in *Barron's*; and (viii) "The Financial Page," by James Surowiecki, in *The New Yorker*. Earlier writings in these columns may usually be retrieved in the archives found on each publication's Web site.

The annual and quarterly reports, marketing literature, and other communications of many firms in Wall Street and the financial industry can furnish much useful information about investing basics and fundamentals. Table 10.12 lists some of these sources. For example, the annual report and other publications of the Commonfund, a cooperative not-for-profit investment organization that manages money for more than 1,500 colleges and universities, addresses topics relating to investment basics and the fundamentals of asset allocation and conventional investment vehicles, alternative investments, and absolute-return strategies.

Other helpful resources include the annual reports of the investment offices of Yale University, Stanford University, Notre Dame, MIT, the University of Texas, and Harvard University, each of which contains reviews of the investment activities of the universities' respective investment arms. These reports usually discuss several topics germane to asset allocation and include each university's strategic asset allocation.

Many of the other organizations in Table 10.12, as well as specific entities within these broad categories, such as individual mutual funds, publish copious amounts of valuable material relevant to investors seeking to build their overall knowledge base. A representative example is *What Has Worked in Investing*, a 42-page booklet published by the investment advisory firm Tweedy, Browne Company L.P. This survey describes studies of more than 40 investment approaches and characteristics associated with exceptional investment returns over time.

As part of their overall investor education initiatives, several leading mutual-fund evaluation services also provide information about investing basics and fundamentals, including such topics as investing for the long-term, risk-reward tradeoffs, types, objectives, and descriptions of mutual funds, and the pros and cons of market timing. Some Web sites of these firms are: *fidelity.com; moneycentral.msn.com; standardandpoors.com; schwab.com; quicken.com; morningstar.net;* and *smartmoney.com*. Articles and features accompanying the quarterly mutual fund performance reviews published in *Barron's, Business Week, Forbes,* the *New York Times,* and the *Wall Street Journal* contain additional insights.

Some larger mutual-fund management families offer asset allocation funds, also known as strategic advisor funds, which provide a range of asset allocation strategies to meet different investors' goals, philosophies, and risk tolerances. Such funds usually invest in the underlying portfolios of several mutual funds managed by the same investment management company. The prospectuses of these asset allocation or strategic advisor funds contain clear and straightforward information on the practice of asset allocation. An analysis of the total and disaggregated investment performance of 19 asset allocation mutual funds from 1983 through 1990 is contained in "How Well Do Asset Allocation Mutual Fund Managers Allocate Assets?" by Anthony Chan and Carl R. Chen in the Spring 1992 issue of the *Journal of Portfolio Management*.

A number of Web sites supply tools and insights about investing basics and fundamentals for beginning, intermediate, and advanced investors, in some cases for children, and occasionally, for professional investors. Besides educational essays and articles, these Web sites include: searchable dictionaries and glossaries of financial and investment terms; online tutorials, interactive workshops and learning modules; key life-event planning and financial calculators; risk-assessment profiles; short seminars and full-length courses; question-and-answer sessions; and links to other Web sites. Financial basics, mutual-fund fundamentals, and how-to guides to investing are contained on: *fool.com, investment.com, vanguard.com, askmerrill.com,* and *citigroup.com,* among other sites. Additional guidance on the basics of stocks, bonds, mutual funds, options, and other investments can be found on *investopedia.com* and *investorguide.com*. Several organizations that have Web sites devoted to investor basics and fundamentals include the General Electric Center for Financial Learning, at *ftknowledge.com,* the Women's Institute for Financial Education, at *wife.org,* and the National Endowment for Financial Education, at *nefe.org*.

## Asset Allocation for Individual and Professional Investors

Individual and professional investors can avail themselves of a wide variety of resources dedicated to the theory and practice of asset allocation, ranging from articles, to monographs and books, to Web sites and other tools. While the body of literature on asset allocation is sizeable and growing, selected sources on asset allocation for institutional investors may also be of relevance.

One of the most widely quoted (and occasionally misquoted) writings on asset allocation is "Determinants of Portfolio Performance," by

Gary P. Brinson, Brian D. Singer, and Gilbert L. Beebower, which appeared in the July-August 1986 issue of *Financial Analysts Journal*. This article asserts that 93.6% of the variation of a portfolio's investment returns is explained by its asset allocation policy. A subsequent article by the same authors, in the May-June 1991 issue of *Financial Analysts Journal*, "Determinants of Portfolio Performance II: An Update," extended the authors' original performance-attribution framework to account for actual and synthetic cash holdings within asset classes.

The conclusions and methodology of these studies were challenged in "The Asset Allocation Hoax," by William W. Jahnke, which appeared in the February 1997 issue of the *Journal of Financial Planning*. Several aspects of this debate are discussed in: (i) "The Importance of Asset Allocation," by John Nuttall, which can be found on *crosswinds.net*; (ii) "Asset Allocation: The Debate Continues," by W. Webb, in the January 1998 issue of *Registered Representative* magazine; (iii) "Asset Allocation: Revisiting the Debate," by Amy C. Arnott, in the September 1997 issue of *Morningstar Mutual Funds*; (iv) "An Asset Allocation Debate," by Harold Evensky, William Jahnke, and Roland Surz; and (v) "The 93.6% Question of Financial Advisors," by Meir Stratman, the latter two articles appearing in the Spring 2000 issue of the *Journal of Investing*.

Ibbotson Research has published several insightful studies about asset allocation on *ibbotson.com*. These articles include: (i) "The Role of Asset Allocation in Portfolio Management," by Scott L. Lummer and Mark W. Riepe; (ii) "Asset Allocation Models Using the Markowitz Approach," by Paul D. Kaplan; (iii) "Does Asset Allocation Policy Explain 40%, 90%, or 100% of Performance?" by Roger G. Ibbotson and Paul D. Kaplan; and (iv) "Taming Your Optimizer: A Guide through the Pitfalls of Mean-Variance Optimization," by Scott L. Lummer, Mark W. Riepe, and Lawrence B. Siegel.

Several additional helpful articles on asset allocation include: (i) "Asset Allocation for Private Investors," by Robert Apelfeld and Jean L. P. Brunel, and "After-Tax Asset Allocation and the Diversification of Concentrated Low Cost-Basis Holdings: A Case Study," by Nancy L. Jacob, in the Spring 1998 issue of the *Journal of Private Portfolio Management*; (ii) "Managing Asset Classes," by James H. Scott, Jr., in the January-February 1994 issue of *Financial Analysts Journal*; (iii) "Apples, Oranges, and Asset Allocation," by Carolyn T. Geer in the September 18, 2000 issue of *Fortune*; (iv) "A Mouse Can Allocate Your Assets," by Peter Kafka, in the December 27, 1999 issue of *Forbes*; (v) "Asset Allocation, Portfolio Optimization: Better Risk Adjusted Performance?" by

Gerald Butrimovitz, in the August 1999 issue of the *Journal of Financial Planning*; (vi) "Are Investors Over-Invested in Equities?" by Fernando Diaz, on the Barclay Group Research Web site at *barclaygrp.com*; (vii) "In Asset Allocation, Think Location, Location, Location," by Mark Hulbert, in the December 17, 2000 issue of the *New York Times*; and (viii) "A 93.6% Solution? No, Asset Allocation Isn't Everything, But It Has an Impact," by Jonathan Clements in the October 7, 1997 issue of the *Wall Street Journal*.

Several books that shed light on the subject of asset allocation are listed alphabetically in Table 10.15.

The books shown in Table 10.15 are in addition to the books listed earlier in Table 10.1 and contain insights about asset allocation principles, the risks and rewards of asset allocation, and many important details surrounding the asset allocation process. The applicability and effectiveness of these books may vary greatly depending on the investor's background, interest level, financial needs, intellectual curiosity, degree of reliance upon and contact with sources of advice, and other circumstances. As a result, it is a good idea to first look at a book of potential interest in the library or bookstore, or to order the book from an online bookseller for examination and review. Among the small but growing number of books on asset allocation for individuals that have been published directly on the Internet is *Investment Strategies for the 21st Century*, by Frank Armstrong, locatable at *fee-only-advisor.com*.

## Individual Investor Behavior

In many cases, the asset allocation and investing needs of individuals are similar to those of professional investors. Both groups seek to achieve favorable short-term and long-term investment results, while keeping various measures of portfolio risk to a minimum. At the same time, most individual investors face several issues that may be of a different level of concern to professional investors, including: (i) income taxes, capital-gains taxes, and other levies; (ii) retirement planning and tax-deferred retirement accounts; and (iii) the degree of aversion to risk of loss. Two reports published annually on the composition and dynamics of the individual investors' marketplace are *The Future of Money Management in America*, by Bernstein Research (*bernstein.com*), and *World Wealth Report*, by Gemini Consulting (*geminiconsulting.net*). The *tax efficiency* of an investment expresses the investor's after-tax return from an investment as a percentage of his or her pre-tax return. Writings that address this subject include: "Measuring and Evaluating Portfolio

## T A B L E 10.15

### Selected Books on Asset Allocation for Individual and Professional Investors

**Reference Sources and Definitions**

*The Art of Asset Allocation,* by David M. Darst. A comprehensive discussion of the mechanics, underpinnings, tools, principles, and pathways of asset allocation and investment strategy.

*Mastering the Art of Asset Allocation,* by David M. Darst. An in-depth examination of the inner workings of asset allocation, with a discussion of leading university endowments, compound interest, multiperiod rates of return, and the role of correlations,

*Asset Allocation in a Changing World,* by the CFA Institute. Essays on the principles and practices of asset allocation.

*Asset Management for Endowments and Foundations,* by William Schneider with Robert Dimeo and D. Robinson Cluck. Specialized asset allocation techniques.

*Asset Allocation Techniques and Financial Market Timing,* by Carroll D. Aby, Jr. and Donald E. Vaughn. Technical analysis applied to asset allocation.

*Diversify: The Investor's Guide to Asset Allocation Strategies,* by Gerald W. Perritt and Alan Lavine. A review of various asset allocation methods.

*Dynamic Asset Allocations: Strategies for the Stock, Bond and Money Markets,* by David A. Hammer. An introduction to several of the traditional and contemporary models used in making asset allocation decisions.

*Getting Started in Asset Allocation,* by Bill Bresnan and Eric Gelb. Introductory guidance and advice on the asset allocation process and asset allocation techniques.

*Global Tactical Asset Allocation: Theory and Practice,* by Robert H. Brown and William A. R. Goodsall. Insights into asset allocation rebalancing.

*The Intelligent Asset Allocator: How to Build Your Portfolio to Maximize Returns and Minimize Risk,* by William J. Bernstein. Asset allocation guidelines.

*Investment Alchemy: An Investor's Guide to Asset Allocation,* by Guy E. Baker and Rick Jensen. A no-nonsense discussion of investment strategies.

*Investment Counseling for Private Clients,* by the CFA Institute. Determining and constructing optimal after-tax asset allocations.

*Investment Policy and the Asset Allocation Process,* by the Investment Management Consultants Association Staff. Basic applications of asset allocation.

*Market Neutral: State-of-the-Art Strategies for Every Market Environment,* edited by Jess Lederman and Robert A. Klein. Eleven perspectives on market neutral investing.

*The New Money Management: A Framework for Asset Allocation,* by Ralph Vince. How to obtain optimal synergy among the components of a portfolio.

*The New Science of Asset Allocation,* by Warren E. Bitters. A survey of contemporary thinking about asset allocation.

*Risk Is a Four-Letter Word: The Asset Allocation Approach to Investing,* by George Hartman. A pithy discourse on selected asset allocation principles.

*Simple Asset Allocation Strategies,* by Roger C. Gibson. Insights on assessing the investor's time horizon and determining the correct portfolio balance.

*Strategic Asset Allocation,* by John Y. Campbell and Luis M. Viceira. Theoretical and empirical results relating to the choice of portfolio assets for retirement savings.

Source: The author.

Performance After Taxes," in the Winter 1998 issue of the *Journal of Portfolio Management*; "Ranking Mutual Funds on an After-Tax Basis," in Publication 344 of the Stanford University Center for Economic Policy Research; and "Is Your Alpha Big Enough to Cover Its Taxes?" in the Spring 1993 issue of the *Journal of Portfolio Management*.

Resources related to retirement planning and tax-deferred retirement accounts are available via many of the financial planning Web-based tools in Table 10.13 and the financial planning Web sites and portals in Table 10.14. Additional helpful writings on these subjects are contained on the Morningstar Web site, *morningstar.com*. For non-U.S. individual investors, Credit Suisse (*credit-suisse.com*), HSBC (*hsbc.com*), and Union Bank of Switzerland (*ubs.com*) offer a wide variety of resources germane to international tax planning, retirement planning, and risk management.

Risk analysis and risk management are crucial aspects of individual investors' asset allocation and investing activity. Several services offer information and tools to help quantify and control risk, including: (i) RiskMetrics (*riskmetrics.com*), a venture originally co-owned by JP Morgan Chase and Reuters and later spun off, whose RiskGrades product measures the relative price volatility of specific securities or portfolios of securities versus that of a widely diversified global basket of equities; (ii) Contingency Analysis (*contingencyanalysis.com*), which covers such subjects as value-at-risk (VAR), leverage, diversification, derivative instruments, risk measures, and risk visualization; (iii) the Global Association of Risk Professionals (*garp.com*), which has a large number of notes, monographs, and readers' commentaries on a wide range of risk-related topics; (iv) Byg Publishing's (*bygpub.com*) comprehensive and well-explained collection of risk calculators; (v) the Forecaster service developed by Financial Engines and accessible at Money.com's site (*money.cnn.com*); (vi) the Portfolio Monitor Beta, correlation, return/risk ratio, and other services of Trade Trek (*tradetrek.com*); (vii) FinPortfolio's (*finportfolio.com*) portfolio analysis capability, including risk-adjusted return analysis, VAR analysis, and market exposure; and (viii) the projections and risk matrix tools found at *derivatives.com*.

Additional useful resources can be found in: (i) the 10-part series on the many different forms of risk, called "Mastering Risk," published by the *Financial Times* (*ft.com*) in April-June 2000; (ii) Leah Modigliani's writings on the Modigliani-Modigliani ($M^2$) risk measure, on the Morgan Stanley Web site (*morganstanley.com*); and (iii) the October 2000 issue of the *Federal Reserve Bank of New York Economic Policy Review* (*ny.frb.org*), in which Leslie Rahl of Capital Market Risk Advisors enumerates and describes 48 different kinds of risks facing participants in the financial realm. *Seeing Tomorrow: Rewriting the Rules of Risk,* by Ron S. Dembo and Andrew Freeman, draws upon the fields of psychology and quantitative analysis to help investors gauge risk and choose actions when the outcomes are uncertain.

Advanced software to help individual investors in the asset allocation process includes: (i) Power Optimizer, developed by Allied Financial Software (*software@software4advisors.com*), which can produce historic return and risk calculations and optimized portfolios for a wide array of financial asset types; and (ii) Wilshire Horizon, developed by Wilshire Associates (*wilshire.com*), incorporating individual and multiple asset class constraints and downside risk optimization options.

Writings that discuss the mutual influence of asset allocation and individual investor behavior include: (i) "The Importance of Asset Allocation," by William Jahnke, and "Global Asset Allocation: Philosophy, Process, and Performance," by Roger G. Ibbotson and Charles H. Wang, in the Spring 2000 issue of the *Journal of Investing*; (ii) "A Simple Model for Lifetime Asset Allocation," by Bernard Scherer and Thomas Ebertz, and "The Incidence and Impact of Losses from Stocks and Bonds," by Charles P. Jones and Jack W. Wilson, in the Summer 1998 issue of the *Journal of Private Portfolio Management*; and (iii) *Investment Counseling for Private Clients (1998)*, published by the CFA Institute (*cfainstitute.org*).

## Asset Class Characteristics, Returns, and Risk

To gain an appreciation of the role that different asset classes can play in asset allocation and investing, it is useful to have some sense of their liquidity, quality, diversification, correlation, taxation, investment returns, and risk characteristics. Some of these issues are addressed in the CFA Institute (*cfainstitute.org*) publications, *Asset Allocation in a Changing World* (1998) and *The Future of Investment Management* (1998). Another means of working toward this knowledge is to refer to the Investment Universe section of the Asset Allocation Worksheets in Chapter 9 of *The Art of Asset Allocation*. An additional source of perspective on the components of the compound annual performance of several major asset classes for each year during various short, intermediate, and long periods of time is in *Stocks, Bonds, Bills and Inflation,* updated and published each year by Ibbotson Associates (*ibbotson.com*). Annual investment flows into and out of the major asset classes by the major categories of institutional and individual investors are quantified in the Flow of Fund Accounts published by the Federal Reserve System (*federalreserve.gov*).

Several thorough and helpful resources on equity and fixed-income investing can be found in the CFA Institute (*cfainstitute.org*) publications, *Equity Research and Valuation Techniques* (1998), *Investing in Small-Cap and Microcap Securities* (1997), *Investment Styles, Market Anomalies, and Global Stock Selection* (1999), and *Global Bond Management* (1997). Many of the Web sites and portals devoted to equities and fixed-income securities in Table 10.14 contain illuminating information about the characteristics, returns, and risk attributes of these two asset classes. Additional sites that contain investment-performance databases and calculators of correlation, beta, alpha, and other measures for 300 asset classes, ranging from equity indices, currency indices, and exchange rates, to mutual funds, specific stocks, variable annuities, and closed-end funds, include: (i) the LaPorte Asset Allocation System (*laportesoft.com*); (ii) the Wilson Analytics programs (*wilsonweb.com*); (iii) the ScanData package (*scandata.com*); and (iv) the Ibbotson EnCorr and Analyst software systems (*ibbotson.com*). One methodology, and the rationale for projecting future returns for several mainstream asset classes, is contained in "Predictions of the Past and Forecasts for the Future, 1976–2025," by Roger G. Ibbotson (*ibbotson.com*).

Tutorials, news and commentary, definitions, and statistics covering a database of more than 20,000 fixed-income securities are contained on the BondResources Web site (*bondresources.com*), and the BondEdge Web site (*bondedge.com*). The tradeoff between risk and return in various portfolio mixes of stocks and bonds is discussed in "Asset Allocators, Cautious on Stocks, Pile into Bonds," in the June 3, 1997 issue of the *Wall Street Journal*, and "Bonds Let You Sleep at Night but at a Price," in the September 8, 1998 issue of the *Wall Street Journal*. The characteristics of Convertible Bonds are reviewed in "Convertible Bonds as an Asset Class: 1957–1992," by Scott L. Lummer and Mark W. Riepe, in the September 1993 issue of the *Journal of Fixed-Income*.

Much helpful information on non-U.S. securities in developed and emerging markets can be found on *adr.com, globalinvestor.com, ft.com, bradynet.com,* and *securities.com*. Each week, *The Economist* magazine (*economist.com*) publishes a set of detailed financial indicators for developed markets and emerging-market indicators for emerging markets. Further insights into some of the nuances of investing in non-U.S. securities are contained in the CFA Institute publications,

*Currency Risk in International Portfolios* (1999), *Managing Currency Risk* (1997), and *The International Equity Commitment* (1998), as well as "Hedging Your Bets? Look Homeward, Investor," by Jonathan Fuerbringer, in the February 4, 2001 issue of the *New York Times*.

Broadly defined, alternative asset classes include commodities, oil, gas, and timber interests, real estate, venture capital, private equity, inflation-indexed securities, art, hedge funds, and various forms of hedge fund funds of funds. Although sometimes more volatile than conventional asset classes on an individual basis, the judicious use of alternative assets may lower portfolio risk, raise the level of expected returns, and create more efficient portfolios. The 1998 CFA Institute publication, *Alternative Investing* offers a sound overview of nontraditional investing. Other follow-up articles falling under the alternative investing topic include: *Hedge Fund Management* (2002*); Integrating Hedge Funds into a Private Wealth Strategy* (2004); *Challenges and Innovation in Hedge Fund Management* (2004); and, *Dimensions in Private Equity* (March 2005).

Several helpful sources on commodity investments include: (i) "Investing in Commodities," by Daniel J. Nash, in the February 2001 issue of *Global Equity and Derivative Markets*, available at *morganstanley.com*; (ii) "Investing in Global Hard Assets: A Diversification Tool for Portfolios," by Gary Baierl, Robert Cummisford, and Mark W. Riepe, published in April 1999 by Ibbotson Research (*ibbotson.com*); and (iii) "GSCI Collateralized Futures as a Hedging and Diversification Tool for Institutional Portfolios: An Update," by Paul D. Kaplan and Scott L. Lummer, in the Winter 1998 issue of the *Journal of Investing* (*investmentresearch.org*).

Due to the fact that their investment performance is more closely correlated with the value of their underlying properties than with other asset classes, real estate can help create more efficient asset allocations. Public and private real estate as an asset class is analyzed by Owen Thomas and Russell Platt on pages 19–27 of the *Alternative Asset Class Conference Proceedings* published by Morgan Stanley and Miller Anderson & Sherrerd (*morganstanley.com*) in December 1996, and by Ted Bigman on pages 6–8 of the Summer 1999 *Issues of Interest* published by Morgan Stanley Investment Management (*morganstanley.com*). A useful book on real estate is *The Unofficial Guide to Real Estate Investing*, by Spencer Strauss and Martin J. Stone.

Beginning in the last several decades of the twentieth century, venture capital and private equity have emerged as important sectors of the alternative-investments asset class. Heightened investor interest due to periods of high if volatile returns, larger amounts of available funds, a greater degree of specialization of fund strategies, and an increasing portion of venture capital and private equity investment flows outside the United States have characterized both of these asset groupings. While each area may have some degree of overlap with the other, venture capital and private equity are usually considered to have distinct fields of focus. Venture-capital investing in companies encompasses: the *idea stage*, usually funded by angel investors; the *prototype stage*, which may attract seed capital; and the *expansion stage*, in which an enterprise may raise funds to move to *later-stage development*, often a precursor to going public or being acquired by another company.

Private-equity investing tends to focus on industries facing structural change, innovation opportunities, or combination potential. Private-equity investment activity spans a broad spectrum and includes management buyouts, leveraged buyouts (LBOs), turnaround situations, mezzanine or bridge financing, and distressed investment strategies.

An analysis of the investment returns, standard deviations, and correlations of 148 venture capital funds tracked by Venture Economics Investor Services (*ventureeconomics.com*) is set forth in "Venture Capital and Its Role in Strategic Asset Allocation," by Gary T. Baierl, Peng Chen, and Paul D. Kaplan, published in June 2000 by Ibbotson Research (*ibbotson.com*). A thorough overview of the issuers, investors, intermediaries, returns, and reference sources in the venture-capital and private-equity arena is contained in "The Economics of the Private Equity Market," by George W. Fenn, Nellie Liang, and Stephen Prowse in the January 1996 issue of the *Federal Reserve Bulletin* (*federalreserve.gov*).

Other useful sources for tracking developments in the private-equity and venture-capital markets are the quarterly and annual reports to investors of the private-equity and venture-capital partnerships and funds of funds managed by the leading investment banks and alternative investment firms who are active in this field. A listing of many of these firms is published in the various directories produced by Asset Alternatives Inc. (*assetnews.com*). Asset Alternatives also sponsors conferences and publishes several newsletters relating to the venture capital and private equity field, as well as *Private Equity Partnerships Terms and Conditions* and *Private Equity Funds-of-Funds: State of the Market*. Early-stage investing is described in *Angel Investing: Matching Startup Funds with Startup Companies*, by Robert J. Robinson and Mark Van

Osnabrugge, and investors can learn more about the private-securities investing marketplace on the Off-Road Capital Web site, *offroadcapital.com*.

Just as private-equity and venture-capital investors seek to exploit value and pricing inefficiencies in *direct investment activity*, hedge funds and related alternative-investment managers seek to take advantage of value and pricing inefficiencies in *portfolio or securities investment activity*. Many hedge funds are highly specialized, while others pursue a suite of approaches, within one or more of the following areas: (i) *relative value or convergence strategies*, involving convertible-bond arbitrage, capital-structure arbitrage, mortgage-securities arbitrage, or other forms of fixed-income arbitrage; (ii) *event-driven strategies*, involving merger arbitrage, corporate restructuring and stub creation, distressed securities, orphan securities, or post-bankruptcy investing; (iii) *long-short or hedging strategies*, involving statistical arbitrage or an emphasis on specific equity or fixed-income sectors; (iv) *managed futures strategies* carried out by Commodity Trading Advisors (CTAs); and (v) *selection- or timing-based strategies*, involving global macrotactical asset allocation, the use of multiple strategy models, or specialized equity selection techniques.

Research reports produced by Wall Street firms about hedge funds include: (i) "Understanding of the Sources of Hedge Fund Returns," by Thomas Schneeweis, Vassilis Karavas, Rae DuBose, and Madanda Machayya, published in July 2005 by Ursa Capital (*ursacapital.com*); (ii) "Why Hedge Funds Make Sense," by Michael W. Peskin, Satish I. Anjilvel, Michael S. Urias, and Bryan E. Boudreau, in the November 2000 issue of the Morgan Stanley Quantitative Strategies publication *Global Equity and Derivative Markets (morganstanley.com)*; (iii) "The Benefits of Hedge Funds" and "Understanding Hedge Fund Performance," by Thomas Schneeweis and George Martin, published in August 2000 and November 2001 respectively, by Lehman Brothers Global Prime Brokerage Group (*lehman.com*); and (iv) "Hedge Funds Demystified," published in the July 1998 issue of *Pension and Endowment Forum*, by Goldman Sachs (*gs.com*) and Financial Risk Management Ltd. (*frm.uk.com*). Other insightful writings on hedge funds have appeared in several Morgan Stanley *Investment Perspectives* publications, authored by Barton M. Biggs (in the August 14, 2000 and June 27, 2001 issues); Byron R. Wien (in the February 28, 1994, February 11, 1998, June 19, 2003, November 17, 2004, and June 2, 2005 issues); and Leah Modigliani (in the December 12, 1997, September 23, 1999, and December 21, 1999 issues).

Information as to specific hedge funds, hedge-fund funds of funds managers, investment styles, and investment performance can be found on the Web sites of the Hennessee Group LLC (*hennesseegroup.com*), the HedgeWorld Portal (*hedgeworld.com*), Credit-Suisse/Tremont Advisers (*csfb.com*), VAN Hedge Fund Advisors (*vanhedge.com*), TASS Investment Research Ltd. (*tremont.com*), MAR Hedge (*marhedge.com*), Hedge Fund Alert (*hfalert.com*), and Hedge Fund Net (*hedgefund.net*). Listings of selected hedge funds' specific investment holdings can be found on the Web sites of PlusFunds (*plusfunds.com*), and Measurisk (*measurisk.com*). The methodology and index policy for the hedge fund indices that have been created by CSFB/Tremont and by Morgan Stanley Capital International (MSCI) for specific segments of the hedge fund industry are locatable at *credit-suisse.com, tremont.com,* and *msci.com,* respectively.

Several monographs and books provide further guidance for approaching hedge funds, including: (i) *All About Hedge Funds* by Robert Jaeger, published in 2002 by McGraw-Hill; (ii) "The Impact of Leverage on Hedge Fund Risk and Return," by Thomas Schneeweis, George Martin, Hossein Kazemi, and Vassillis Karavas, published in 2005 in the *Journal of Alternative Investments,* Volume 7, Number 4; (iii) *Sound Practices for Hedge Fund Managers,* published in February 2000 by Caxton Corporation, Kingdon Capital Management, LLC, Moore Capital Management, Inc., Soros Fund Management LLC, and Tudor Investment Corporation (*tudorventures.com*); (iv) *Hedge Funds, Leverage and the Lessons of Long-Term Capital Management,* published in April 1999 by the President's Working Group on Financial Markets; (v) *The Case for Hedge Funds,* published in 1999 by Credit-Suisse/Tremont Advisers, Inc. (*credit-suisse.com*) and TASS Investment Research Ltd. (*tremont.com*); (vi) *Structuring Hedge Funds,* published in November 1998 by Skadden, Arps, Slate, Meagher & Flom LLP (*sasmf.com*); (vii) *Hedge Funds: Investment and Portfolio Strategies for the Institutional Investor,* edited by Jess Lederman with Robert A. Klein; (viii) *Fundamentals of Hedge Fund Investing: A Professional Investor's Guide,* by William J. Crerend and Robert A. Jaeger; and (ix) *The Hedge Fund Handbook: A Definitive Guide for Analyzing and Evaluating Alternative Investments,* by Stefano Lavinio.

## Recognizing Cyclical and Secular Turning Points

To recognize cyclical and secular turning points in the economy, financial markets, or specific asset classes, investors need to marshal not only a substantial number of the information resources described throughout this chapter, but also a high degree of vigilance, patience, reflection, insight, selective filtering, and, depending on the circumstances, some appropriate blend of optimism and skepticism. In effect, investors are attempting to see the forest for the trees—to assess the degree of deviation from normal market conditions, to anticipate what catalysts might precipitate change, to recognize whether and how short- and long-term forces might reinforce or offset one another, and to discern the establishment or cessation of short-, medium-, and long-term trends. These are difficult but not impossible challenges, provided that investors can: (i) exercise good judgment; (ii) distinguish valid signals from mere noise; (iii) distill information down to its essence; and not least, (iv) maintain emotional control.

Table 10.16 contains a highly abbreviated listing of indicators of cyclical and secular turning points, organized according to fundamental factors, valuation factors, and psychological/technical/liquidity factors.

By monitoring the developments shown in Table 10.16, investors should be able to gain at least some general sense as to important economic, spending, saving, investment, social, monetary, fiscal, political, and investing trends. The aim is to be watchful and perceptive, but not prone to reading too much nor too little into one or a small number of indicators.

In some ways, investors seek to spot patterns, to keep track of persistent and underlying themes, and to identify meaningful change taking place at the margin. The chances of achieving such aims can be increased with the assistance of many resources, possibly emanating directly from the Internet, possibly from Wall Street and the financial industry, and very possibly from independent sources, including the investors' own instincts. In such circumstances, it may also help for investors to be mindful of new understandings and relevant applications from the fields of science, psychology, sociology, and even anthropology. Without being flip or superficial, it might also be worthwhile for to pay some *appropriate* (not too much, not too little) attention to currents in popular culture for the effects they *might* have on the selected indicators in Table 10.16 and financial asset prices.

Many of the governmental and regulatory bodies listed in Table 10.6 publish thoughtful, unbiased studies of intermediate- and long-term trends. Of particular value are the periodic bulletins published by the 12 Regional Federal Reserve Banks and by the Federal Reserve System in Washington. Also helpful are the studies and monographs published by the Bank of England (*bankofengland.co.uk*), the European Central Bank (*ecb.int*), the Bank for International Settle-

## T A B L E  10.16

Selected Indicators of Cyclical and Secular Turning Points

| Source | Developments to Monitor |
| --- | --- |
| **Fundamental Factors** | |
| Bureau of Economic Analysis | National statistics such as GDP |
| Economic Policy Institute | Commentary on socioeconomic issues |
| Federal Reserve Board | Interest rates and money supply growth |
| FedStats | Info from every bureau of the U.S. government |
| U.S. Department of Labor | Employment and unemployment trends |
| U.S. Department of Commerce | Economic growth trends |
| U.S. Department of Labor | Consumer and producer price indices |
| National Income Accounts | Corporate profitability trends |
| U.S. Congress | Taxation and spending policies |
| CNN, FOX, ABC, CBS, NBC, Bloomberg | Degree of geopolitical stability |
| World Currency Markets | Degree of exchange rate stability |
| **Valuation Factors** | |
| S&P, Dow-Jones | Expansion or contraction in P/E multiples |
| S&P, Dow-Jones | Expansion or contraction in P/B ratios |
| Chicago Board Options Exchange | Volatility indices |
| **Psychological/Technical/Liquidity Factors** | |
| Opinion Polls and Investor Surveys | Consumer and investor confidence |
| Opinion Polls and Investor Surveys | General sentiment toward capitalism, risk-taking, regime stability, and the future |
| Investment Company Institute, Lipper Inc., Strategic Insight, Market Trim Tabs | Equity mutual fund flows |
| Financial Accounting Standards Board | Spirit and letter of financial probity |
| Securities Data Corporation | Supply of Securities Underwritings |

Source: The author.

ments (*bis.org*), the International Monetary Fund (*imf.org*), and the World Bank (*worldbank.org*).

Other periodicals that can provide perspective on long-term trends include the *Bank Credit Analyst* (*bcapub.com*), *Grant's Interest Rate Observer* (*grantspub.com*), the special surveys of *The Economist* (*economist.com*), the *Harvard Business Review* (*hbsp.harvard.edu*), *Foreign Affairs Quarterly* (*foreignaffairs.org*), and *Wired* (*wired.com*). Newsletters in the same vein include *Capitol Analysts Network* (*capitolanalysts.com*), *The Richebächer Letter* (*investmentrarities.com*), and *The Gilder Report* (*gildertech.com*).

Many of the books listed earlier in Table 10.1 can provide long-term perspective on the identification of cyclical and secular turning points. Three of the most important are: (i) *The Essays of Warren*

*Buffett*, edited by Lawrence A. Cunningham; (ii) *Stocks for the Long Run*, 2d ed., by Jeremy J. Siegel; and (iii) *Irrational Exuberance*, 2d ed., by Robert J. Shiller. Two insightful articles by the latter authors are: (i) "Big-Cap Tech Stocks Are a Sucker Bet," by Jeremy J. Siegel, in the March 14, 2000 *Wall Street Journal*; and (ii) "Why Did the Nikkei Crash?" by Robert J. Shiller, Fumiko Kon-Ya, and Yoshiro Tsutsui, in the February 1996 issue of the *Review of Economics and Statistics*. Books that address the uses and abuses of financial derivatives include: (i) *When Genius Failed: The Rise and Fall of Long-Term Capital Management*, by Roger Lowenstein; (ii) *Big Bets Gone Bad: Derivatives and Bankruptcy in Orange County*, by Philippe Jorion and Robert Roper; and (iii) *The Collapse of Barings*, by Stephen Fay.

## Spending versus Reinvesting Income Flows

The question of spending versus reinvesting income flows is intricately bound up with notions of compounding returns, the reinvestment of bond coupons, and the reinvestment of equity dividends. Such topics are also linked to an investor's time horizon, tax status, reinvestment rates and opportunities, and not least, his or her spending behavior. Spending versus reinvesting is one of the most crucial aspects of the entire asset allocation and investing process. Yet a great number of participants in the financial markets, ranging from investors to issuers to intermediaries, are unaware or only faintly aware of the importance of this subject, how to measure its effects on realized portfolio performance, and where to obtain further information.

One of the earliest and most lucid books of the modern era on the power and mathematics of simple and compound interest, the time value of money, and the fundamentals of reinvesting versus spending income flows is the classic work, *Inside the Yield Book: New Tools for Bond Market Strategy*, by Sidney Homer and Martin L. Leibowitz. The basics of simple and compound interest, including the future value and present value of a single sum and a stream of payments, often referred to as an annuity, are contained in *Investment Science*, by David G. Luenberger, and in *The Desktop Guide to Money, Time, Interest, and Yields*, by Charles J. Woelfel. The latter book also discusses many special applications of compound interest and annuities.

A clearly explained and diagrammed discussion of the compounding of investment returns, applicable to bonds, equities, and virtually all asset classes, appear as in pages 5–27 of *Yield Curve Analysis: The Fundamentals of Risk and Return*, by Livingston G. Douglas. Pages 74 and 75 of this book cogently explain the concept of *realized compound yield,* which effectively adjusts the quoted rate of return of an investment for: (i) the actually realized returns on any interim cash flows generated by the investment; and (ii) the actually realized sale price of the investment, if disposed of prior to its maturity or scheduled holding period. Pages 237–286 of *Yield Curve Analysis* delve more deeply into the three components of total return (price return; coupon or dividend return; and reinvestment return), and give extensive treatment to several factors, such as time horizon, which determine the relative importance of reinvestment return.

Pages 325–337 of *The Corporate Bond Market,* by Richard S. Wilson and Frank J. Fabozzi, describe an investment concept known as *horizon analysis,* which allows investors to analyze the performance of an investment based on different return scenarios for reinvestment rates and for ranges of realized future investment values. A set of straightforward calculations of realized compound yield, also known as effective yield, holding-period yield, or horizon return, is set forth on pages 45–53 of *Bond Markets: Analysis and Strategies,* by Frank J. Fabozzi and T. Dessa Fabozzi. Another helpful resource, *Investment Manager's Handbook,* edited by Sumner B. Levine, contains, on pages 324–338, a clear discussion of the concept and practice of *immunization* as a way to reduce or eliminate reinvestment risk.

The importance of formulating an endowment spending policy, and how such a policy interacts with dividend and interest reinvestment, are treated in: (i) "Endowment Spending Policy," by Stephen T. Golding and Lucy S. G. Momjian; and (ii) "Transcript of the May 1998 Conference Call on Spending Policies for Endowments and Foundations," published by Morgan Stanley Investment Management (*morganstanley.com*). Profound insights into the importance of dividend reinvestment to the achievement of equity returns over the long term are contained in the annual edition of *Stocks, Bonds, Bills and Inflation,* published by Ibbotson Associates. For the major data series from 1926 to the present on large-company stocks (based on the Standard & Poor's Composite Index), long-term government bonds, and intermediate-term government bonds, the book supplies detailed breakdowns of the contribution to total investment return provided by capital-appreciation return, income return, and by, dividend-reinvestment return. Dividend-reinvestment return is the return from investing any dividends received by the investor into the same asset class in subsequent months within each year. The significant long-term contribution of dividend reinvestment to the total capital growth brought about by investment in equities is also helpfully displayed in charts and tables. Information sources on dividend-reinvestment plans (DRIPs) are described earlier in this chapter, in the section on corporations and individual investor organizations.

Warren E. Buffett, in *The Essays of Warren Buffett*, edited by Prof. Lawrence A. Cunningham, proves to be an extremely articulate proponent of reinvesting, or plowing back, the earnings from a portfolio or direct investment into the investment itself, provided that the plowback can be achieved at attractive rates of return. Due to the toll exacted each year by the tax authorities on dividend payments, Buffett prefers that companies that are attractive businesses reinvest as much of their earnings as possible in their own capital base, allowing the highly positive effects of compounding to run their course.

## Comparative Financial Analysis

Comparative financial analysis refers to the process of: (i) selecting which financial data are appropriate, reliable indicators of the value of an investment; (ii) combining or making adjustments to these data to facilitate comparison across similar investments; and (iii) collecting and organizing such information through various time periods. Comparative financial analysis can be carried out on a wide range of U.S. and non-U.S. equity and debt securities, mutual funds, hedge funds, separate investment accounts, real estate, inflation-indexed securities, commodities, art, and private- equity and venture-capital investments. For purposes of efficiency, many of the examples and sources described in this chapter involve equity and debt securities, yet some version of these techniques and tools may also apply in one form or another to other asset classes.

Investors generally devote time and energy to comparative financial analysis for several reasons, including: (i) to gauge the relative merits and real-world performance of an investment, relative to its peers or to other types or categories of investments; (ii) to identify more clearly and efficiently any signs of financial improvement or deterioration, perhaps gaining some understanding of the causes of such change; and (iii) to glean deeper understanding, insight, and perspective from careful scrutiny of data in close proximity to each other.

Several books describe in some detail the rationale for and process of comparative financial analysis. *Graham and Dodd's Security Analysis*, by Sidney Cottle, Roger F. Murray, and Frank E. Block, provides guidance on how to calculate per share ratios, price ratios, profitability ratios, growth ratios, stability ratios, payout ratios, credit ratios, and other important ratios. These calculations are placed in a broader context of how to approach financial-statement examination, fixed-income security analysis, and the valuation of equity securities and contingent claims.

*Investment Analysis and Portfolio Management,* by Jerome B. Cohen and Edward D. Zinbarg, develops a framework for equity and fixed-income security analysis, using traditional methodologies and newer techniques. Volume II of *The Financial Analyst's Handbook,* edited by Sumner B. Levine, contains an overview of analytical processes, followed by sector-specific analyses and commentary on more than 25 industries. Useful perspective on the extent and limitations of many accounting conventions in assessing corporate health can be found in *Quality of Earnings: The Investor's Guide to How Much Money a Company Is Really Making,* by Thorton L. O'Glove and Robert Sobel. Harvard Business School (*hbs.edu*) has published another helpful resource for comparative financial analysis, *Business Analysis and Valuation Using Financial Statistics.*

The equity and fixed-income research departments of a number of investment banks, commercial banks, securities brokers, and independent firms have produced much work of fine quality on accounting, valuation, and comparative financial analysis. To cite one example, Trevor S. Harris and his colleagues at Morgan Stanley (*morganstanley.com*) have created accounting standardization tools (called ModelWare) and have written extensively on accounting, valuation, and tax policy, as well as a series of detailed earnings-monitor measures that can help investors assess the sustainability of a company's financial health. Morgan Stanley has also published *Apples-to-Apples,* a thorough and wide-ranging series of industry-based reports designed to assist investors in comparing the financial condition of companies around the world.

Early each year, *Forbes* magazine publishes its "Platinum 400" list, drawn from a universe of more than 1,300 U.S. and non-U.S. companies with at least $1 billion in annual sales. After eliminating companies that do not meet certain financial performance criteria, *Forbes* then classifies the remaining companies into 23 broad industry groupings. These top 400 companies are helpfully displayed together, facilitating comparisons of return on capital, growth in sales and earnings per share, sales, net income, operating margin, profit margin, and the ratio of debt to total capital.

Many financial data sources offer specialized ways of displaying financial information. Which ones an investor decides to employ will usually depend on his or her preferences and how the data are going to

be used. ValueLine (*valueline.com*) publishes one-page information
sheets on most leading U.S. and some non-U.S. companies. These
sheets are replete with more than 20 historical and projected measures
of financial performance, augmented by charts, textual commentary,
and attractiveness ranking criteria. On the Web site of the SEC (*sec.gov*),
the investor can review, select, and print out a company's and its officers' most recent filings with the SEC. For a given company,
SmartMoney (*smartmoney.com*) can display more than 25 key measures,
including five-year sales and earnings growth, forward P/E ratio, net
profit margins, price/sales, price/book, return on equity, return on assets, and other indicators.

   After an investor selects a company, *Forbes* (*forbes.com*) calculates
more than 45 measures, not easily found elsewhere, including beta,
gross margin, revenues per employee, receivables inventory and asset
turnover, interest coverage, and other indicators of financial performance. These measures are then shown alongside similar measures for
the industry and sector in which the company operates. On an adjacent
part of its Web site, *Forbes* also displays more than 50 valuation criteria,
and indicators as to earnings, securities price, performance, technical
condition, debt risk, trading volume, balance sheet strength, and other
financial barometers.

   Validea (*validea.com*) rates individual securities according to various
investment-style criteria, including price-earnings/growth, value, momentum, contrarian, growth, price/sales, and other disciplines. In addition, Validea provides: (i) general commentary on the appropriate uses
of, normal and exceptional levels for, and how specific measures stack
up for companies selected by the investor; and (ii) certain valuation criteria such as price-earnings/growth ratio, sales and P/E ratio, inven-
tory-to-sales ratio, earnings per share growth rate, and total debt/equity
ratio, among others. FactSet (*factset.com*) provides a cross-section of valuation, profitability, and financial data that allows investors to generate
comparative financial indicators on a domestic and global basis.

   Through a variety of helpful links, the BusinessWeek Online
(*businessweek.com*) Web site brings together: (i) fundamental company
information; (ii) analyses such as Zacks earnings estimates, the
ProSearch criteria report, comparative data for similar companies, and
several technical indicators; and (iii) quarterly and annual statements
of earnings, income, and cash flows. For specific companies, Business-
Week Online furnishes profitability, valuation, and financial strength
ratios, growth statistics, and selected income statement and balance

sheet items compared to the company's industry and S&P 500 aggregate data. Standard & Poor's stock reports (*standardandpoors.com*) provides reports on U.S. public companies including key market statistics. Reuters (*reuters.com*) shows a company's RiskGrade ratios, a dynamic benchmark for measuring financial risk. Fortune (*fortune.com*) has current and historic data on America's largest companies.

Among other information, Yahoo!Finance (*biz.yahoo.com*) shows the time and date of sources of news information (and links to those sources) on companies selected by the investor, as well as reported insiders' transactions in the company's securities during the previous 12 months. Bloomberg (*bloomberg.com*) has earnings estimates, charting capabilities, and other useful information on stocks, and a significant amount of analytical perspective, descriptive material, and other data on: corporate, U.S. Treasury, government agency, municipal, and convertible bonds; currencies; and commodities. For a large population of companies, (firms with total sales exceeding $3 million or employees numbering greater than 50), Dun & Bradstreet's Million Dollar Database (*dnbmdd.com*) furnishes search functions and financial information, comprehensive lists of corporate affiliates' and subsidiaries' Web sites, and executives' biographies. Hoover's Online (*hoovers.com*) contains crisp, multiyear presentations of companies' income statement and balance sheet data, including gross profit margin, operating margin, and net profit margin figures. MSN MoneyCentral (*moneycentral.msn.com*) has charts, price quotes, analyst information, recent news, and stock-screening capabilities.

Reference USA (*referenceusa.com*) provides credit ratings, business lines, and other data, accessible in a wide variety of search categories, on more than 11 million U.S. businesses. For more than 500,000 companies, Lexis-Nexis (*lexis-nexis.com*) allows investors to enter the name or ticker symbol of a company, and then pulls together a snapshot of the company, related news articles, management information, pertinent legal cases, and trademarks and patents.

Primark (*primark.co.uk*) provides scanned images of the financial statements of 21,000 international companies, and financial documents and SEC filings for more than 9,000 U.S. companies. FIS Online (*fisonline.com*) furnishes extensive profiles of more than 10,000 U.S. companies and more than 10,000 international companies, with search facilities to create lists of companies according to parameters such as financial ratios and other criteria. Perfect Information (*perfectinformation.com*) allows access to an electronic library of U.K. and European companies' reports and accounts, merger and acquisition filings, shareholder letters, and bond and stock offering prospectuses.

## Structural Considerations in Asset Allocation

Structural considerations in asset allocation and investing refer to the range of issues relating to how investors hold, build, protect, and disburse wealth in all its forms. Structural considerations involve important activities such as financial planning, personal trusts, estate planning, insurance planning, retirement planning, education planning, philanthropic planning, personal finance and liability management, and tax planning.

Many leading firms in the accounting, asset management, securities brokerage, and financial advice and education fields offer up-to-date advice relating to several key structural considerations in asset allocation and investing, and a number of these firms' Web sites should be consulted to learn more about structural considerations. In the accounting community, resources can be located at, among other Web sites, KPMG (*kpmg.com*), Deloitte & Touche (*deloitte.com*), Pricewaterhouse Coopers (*pwcglobal.com*), and Ernst & Young (*ey.com*). In the asset management and securities brokerage fields, investors may wish to explore, among other Web sites, Fidelity (*fidelity.com*), Alliance Capital (*alliancecapital.com*), Vanguard (*vanguard.com*), Charles Schwab (*schwab.com*), T. Rowe Price (*troweprice.com*), Merrill Lynch (*ml.com*), Morgan Stanley (*morganstanley.com*), JP Morgan Chase (*jpmorganchase.com*), and Citigroup (*citigroup.com*).

In the financial advice and education field, several savings, retirement, education, and other calculators, personal-finance assessment questions, glossaries, risk-management modules, instructional materials, forms, brochures, fee lists, and other tools may be found at, among other Web sites, Motley Fool (*fool.com*), SmartMoney (*smartmoney.com*), Quicken (quicken.com), MSN Money Central (*moneycentral.msn.com*), and Financial Engines (*financialengines.com*). Yahoo! (*finance.yahoo.com*) has lists of articles, software, and links to other Web sites in most of the topical areas germane to structural considerations. Essays and articles on the structural aspects of asset allocation and investing can also be found in many of the periodicals and magazines (Table 10.6), newspapers (Table 10.8), and newsletters (Table 10.9) listed in this chapter.

- ◆ **Financial planning** resources help investors think about and construct a more organized framework for dealing with

wealth in all its forms. Investors with a reasonably complete
financial plan will usually be able to address a wide range of
issues, including retirement, philanthropy, trusts, estate planning, education, and tax and liability management. Direct
Advice (*directadvice.com*) offers an online financial planning
service that allows investors to participate in an online inter-
view, create a financial plan, and make adjustments to their
plan over time. Other useful financial planning resources can be
accessed at FinPlan (*finplan.com*), Financeware (*financeware.com*),
Leadfusion (*leadfusion.com*), and Financial Engines
(*financialengines.com*).

◆ **Retirement planning** relates to the timing and structure
   of pension and retirement-account inflows and outflows,
   and may also encompass deferred-compensation plans,
   nonqualified employee-stock options, and individual and
   corporate retirement accounts. An additional resource that
   many investors may wish to consult is the U.S. Social Security
   Administration (*ssa.gov*).

◆ **Personal trusts,** when properly established and administered,
   can be an extremely important means of transferring and pro-
   tecting property. Investors may access some of the resources
   described in Chapter 8 and at the beginning of this section to
   acquire information about various kinds of revocable and irrevocable trusts, including charitable trusts, grantor-retained
   trusts, dynasty trusts, life-insurance trusts, children's-needs
   trusts, special-needs trusts, marital trusts, credit-shelter trusts,
   and other trusts. In dealing with trusts, it is important for investors to consult qualified counsel for advice on matters such
   as the application of personal trusts within an estate or financial plan.

   AAAdir Directory (*aaadir.com*) has a directory of banks
   and trust companies that are active in the trust field. Informa-
   tion about estate attorneys can be found on the Web site of the
   National Academy of Elder Law Attorneys (*naela.org*) and the
   American College of Trust and Estate Counsel (*actec.org*).
   Many trust companies, including Bessemer Trust (*bvp.com*),
   Fiduciary Trust (*fiduciarytrust.com*), Morgan Stanley Trust
   (*morganstanley.com*), Merrill Lynch Trust (*ml.com*), Northern
   Trust (*ntrs.com*), Trust Company of the West (*tcw.com*), U.S.
   Trust (*ustrust.com*), and My CFO (*mycfo.com*), offer trust

consulting and planning services to help investors integrate trust structures with their asset allocation, investing, and tax strategies. A helpful source of advice to beneficiaries of trusts is Heirs Inc. (*heirs.net*).

◆ **Estate planning,** which encompasses such issues as wills, dealing with probate, and gift and estate taxation, often involves or is otherwise closely connected to personal trusts. Several of the previously mentioned Web sites, such as Charles Schwab (*schwab.com*), have a number of helpful features, including estate-planning educational services, an estate-tax and probate calculator, and resources for surviving spouses, inheritors, and estate executors. Many of these firms also offer insights about living wills, durable powers of attorney, record keeping, and the proper titling of assets. Estate-planning Web sites may include investor questionnaires, charts, graphs, tables, and scenario and case studies. Savewealth (*savewealth.com*) provides information designed to prepare individuals to work with counsel to plan their estate, including multiple links to a variety of research sources on estate planning. Deloitte & Touche Online (*deloitte.com*) offers estate-planning strategies and checklists, descriptions of estate-planning documents, comparative estate-tax calculations under different scenarios, and helpful guidance on how to discuss estate planning with attorneys and family members. Prudential Insurance (*prudential.com*) and Phoenix Wealth Management (*phoenixwm.phl.com*) provide information on how various forms of life insurance can be utilized in an estate plan, estate-planning actions of special relevance to small business owners, and a series of questions to help investors determine whether and when an estate plan needs updating.

◆ **Philanthropic planning** involves strategies to effect the donation of assets and/or income flows to charitable, religious, educational, cultural, artistic, environmental, social, community, and other causes. *The Chronicle of Philanthropy* (*philanthropy.com*) publishes articles and other information about philanthropic activity, and the National Center for Family Philanthropy (*ncfp.org*) provides written materials, frequently asked questions, conferences, workshops, descriptions of agencies and groups involved in philanthropy, and advice on philanthropic planning strategies. In recent years, donor-advised

funds have become an increasingly utilized means of contributing to philanthropic organizations. Similar to community
foundations, donor-advised funds offer an immediate tax deduction for donations, charge a small fee for asset administration, and offer donors the choice, over time, of where to
donate the funds. Among the firms offering donor-advised
funds are Fidelity (*fidelity.com*), Schwab (*schwab.com*), T. Rowe
Price (*troweprice.com*), and Vanguard (*vanguard.com*).

◆ **Insurance planning** describes the process of evaluating and
selecting the terms, amounts, forms, and vehicles of insurance,
including life, health, home, renter, auto, boat, flood, business,
liability, Medicare, long-term care, and disability insurance.
InsWeb (*insweb.com*) allows investors to obtain multiple offerings and price quotes from leading insurance companies, articles from insurance industry, regulatory, and consumer
groups, and to utilize tools and calculators to help make insurance decisions. Useful information from the buyer's perspective on the interplay between life insurance, retirement, estate
taxes, and investing is contained on the Web site of Life Insurance Boot Camp (*lifeinsurancebootcamp.com*).

Allstate Insurance (*allstate.com*), Northwestern Mutual
(*nmfn.com*), The Hartford (*thehartford.com*), Metropolitan Life
Insurance Company (*metlife.com*), and MSN MoneyCentral
(*moneycentral.msn.com*) have personal-insurance questionnaires
that will suggest specific types and amounts of life insurance
coverage that investors may need. Progressive Insurance (*pro-
gressive.com*) enables the purchase of certain types of insurance
via the Internet and a secure online storage capability for the
investor to save personal information.

Variable annuities, which are essentially portfolios of various types of mutual funds combined with several key features
of insurance, allow an investor's assets to compound on a
tax-deferred basis. Educational information about variable annuities can be obtained from the National Association of Variable Annuities (*navanet.org*), the Variable Annuity Research
and Data Service, also known as VARDS (*vards.com*), and leading variable annuity asset managers, among which are Nation-
wide Financial Services (*nationwide.com*); Lincoln Financial
Group (*lfg.com*); and Hartford Financial (*thehartford.com*). Selected low-cost annuity contracts can be found at
*annuitynet.com,* as well as on the Web sites of Vanguard

(*vanguard.com*), Teachers Insurance Annuity Association–College Retirement Equities Fund (*tiaacref.org*), Schwab (*schwab.com*), and Fidelity (*fidelity.com*).

- **Education planning** refers to the process of projecting capital flows, investment rates of return, current and future education costs, and tax rates to pay for major educational expenses. Many of the financial-planning resources described above contain informative modules and calculators that focus on education-related investment structures, including education IRAs, Uniform Gifts to Minors Act (UGMA), and Uniform Transfers to Minors Act (UTMA) programs, minors trusts, IRS Section 529 plans, zero-coupon college investment plans, and tax-free zero-coupon-laddered municipal portfolios. Among other helpful resources on education planning are: (i) The Motley Fool's (*fool.com*) "Paying for College," a 13-section guide for saving, financial aid, loans, scholarships, and related subjects; (ii) the College Savings Plan Network (*collegesavings.org*); (iii) Intuit's (*intuit.com*) question-and-answer program on education IRAs; (iv) "College Savings 101" on the *Forbes* Web site at (*forbes.com*); (v) the *U.S. News and World Report* (*usnews.com*) "College Planner," a series of six worksheets designed to help organize the process of evaluating, selecting, applying to, and paying for a college or university; and (vi) the Yahoo! (*yahoo.com*) list of resources relating to education savings plans.

- **Liability management** may also include personal finance (paying bills and banking) and involves the terms and amounts of credit card debt, margin loans, home-equity loans, mortgages, and other forms of borrowing. Quicken (*quicken.com*) and Microsoft Money (*moneycentral.com*) allow investors to securely pay all their bills online and also offer numerous other features that tie together many aspects of the asset allocation, investing, and financial-planning process. *You Have More than You Think: The Foolish Guide to Personal Finance,* by David Gardner and Tom Gardner, contains pragmatic advice on personal financial management.

- **Tax planning and management** addresses the size and timing of tax payments, including income, capital-gains, estate, gift, property, and other taxes to the federal, state, local, and occasionally, international fiscal authorities. Deloitte & Touche (*deloitte.com*), T. Rowe Price (*troweprice.com*), About

*(about.com)*, Tax Planet *(taxplanet.com)*, Leadfusion *(leadfusion.com)*, Ernst & Young *(ey.com)*, Quicken Turbo Tax *(quicken.com)*, Pricewaterhouse Coopers *(pwcglobal.com)*, H&R Block *(hrblock.com)*, SmartMoney *(smartmoney.com)*, KPMG *(kpmg.com)*, SmartLeaf *(smartleaf.com)*, and Vanguard University *(vanguard.com)* provide some or all of the following capabilities: (i) articles, references, and notes describing tax strategies, tax laws, and tax rulings; (ii) worksheets, calendars, and charts to help investors complete their tax filings; (iii) access to tax message boards and/or online tax advisors; (iv) tax calculators, tax-efficiency calculators, and explanations of how to calculate estimated taxes owed; and (v) the tax impact of potential buy, sell, or hold investment decisions. Other topics addressed include tax audits, the Alternative Minimum Tax (AMT), Individual Retirement Accounts (IRAs), Social Security and payroll taxes, partnership taxation, and online filing procedures.

The National Bureau of Economic Research *(nber.org)* has published a study, "Do After-Tax Returns Affect Mutual Fund Inflows?" by Daniel Bergstresser and James Poterba, which indicates that many mutual fund investors do in fact pay attention to funds' after-tax investment performance. Effective April 16, 2001, the SEC mandated that equity and fixed-income mutual funds had to include after-tax results for the past 1-, 5-, and 10-Year periods in the fund's prospectus, with after-tax returns presented in a standardized format to facilitate performance comparisons across funds. Each year, Motley Fool *(fool.com)* publishes an updated version of *The Motley Fool Investment Tax Guide: Smart Tax Strategies for Investors,* which contains a number of helpful suggestions and techniques that take account of taxes in the investment realm.

## Asset Allocation Worksheets

Asset allocation worksheets allow investors to evaluate specific blends of assets that are generated based on an investor's own profile and needs. Table 10.17 displays several of the worksheet featured on selected Web sites containing asset allocation worksheets.

To a large degree, the asset allocation worksheets listed in Table 10.17 rely on some number of inputs, supplied by the investor, to suggest asset allocations that attempt to meet specified goals. Among other

**T A B L E  10.17**

Selected Asset Allocation Worksheets

| Provider | Web Site | Representative Features |
|----------|----------|------------------------|
| Bank of America | *bankofamerica.com* | Detailed retirement planner and explanation of asset allocation concepts. |
| Fidelity | *fidelity.com* | Target asset mix for investment goals appropriate to investor profile. |
| Quicken | *quicken.com* | Linkages between investor characteristics, strategy, and retirement planner action plan. |
| MarketWatch | *marketwatch.com* | Five asset allocation models to match investor's risk parameters. |
| Van Kampen | *vankampen.com* | Average annual returns of several hypothetical portfolios. |
| Vanguard | *vanguard.com* | Introduction to and quiz on asset allocation, investor questionnaire, and suggested asset allocation. |

Source: The author.

factors, the inputs include personal information such as the investor's age and retirement age, investment experience, number and ages of dependents, income level, living expenses, expected life events, tax rates, projected rates of return for various asset classes, capital contributions and withdrawals, annual income required from the portfolio, investment goals, investment mentality, and willingness to rebalance the portfolio.

To develop suggested allocations of assets, many of the asset allocation calculation engines rely upon long-term average rates of return for the major asset classes. When actual results deviate from these long-term averages for any meaningful length of time, the investor's experience may vary greatly from the results anticipated by the asset allocation planning models. To take account of this fact, and to test outcomes for variances in the timing of returns, some firms use Monte Carlo simulation techniques, which generate hundreds or thousands of possible outcomes. In this way, investors can assess the odds of reaching a particular outcome and adjust their investing, saving, and spending practices accordingly. Background information on Monte Carlo simulations can be found at *palisade.com* and *analycorp.com,* and financial projections using Monte Carlo methods can be accessed at the Web sites of Decisioneering (*decisioneering.com*), Financial Engines (*financialengines.com*), and T. Rowe Price (*troweprice.com*).

# INDEX

# Praise for *Mastering the Art of Asset Allocation*

*"The big secret on Wall Street, whether it be stock selections by the major portfolio managers or my own Lightning Round on 'Mad Money,' is that asset allocation is the bedrock underlying all decisions. Not until David Darst's excellent treatise have we gotten the intellectual underpinnings behind the secret. Leave it to David to put it all in plain English so we can understand this, the single most important aspect of successful investing."*

> **–JIM CRAMER,** Markets Commentator, TheStreet.com; Host of CNBC's "Mad Money with Jim Cramer"

*"David Darst is one of the great students of asset allocation. His book is stuffed with fascinating insights."*

> **–BARTON M. BIGGS,** Managing Partner, Traxis Partners; Founder, Morgan Stanley Investment Management; Author of *Hedgehogging*

*"Inadequate diversification has ruined many an investor. In this book, David Darst demonstrates with clean and easy rules how individuals can invest like the pros and reduce their risk while earning generous returns."*

> **–BURTON G. MALKIEL,** Chemical Bank Chairman's Professor of Economics, Princeton University; Author of *A Random Walk Down Wall Street*

*"This book is a powerful piece of work. Unlike the typical get-rich-easy stuff that only misleads and harms readers, Darst deals authoritatively, comprehensively, and lucidly with the single most important and complex decision any investor has to make—and keep on making: asset allocation. Every investor should—no, must—read this book."*

> **–PETER L. BERNSTEIN,** Peter L. Bernstein, Inc.

*"David Darst is the king of asset allocation . . . Mastering the Art of Asset Allocation is just a treasure trove of great information."*

–**CONSUELO MACK,** Anchor and Managing Editor of "Consuelo Mack **WealthTrack**;" former Anchor of "The Wall Street Journal Report" and "Louis Rukeyser's Wall Street"

*"David Darst can mine deep veins of financial data and come up with a masterful strategy of asset allocation—how much should go where. He carries his learning lightly, and it is his talent to make the complex look easy. And who else could bring Baron Rothchild's famous axiom about timing so brilliantly up to date: 'Buy on CNN, sell on CNBC.' Makes perfect sense."*

–**JERRY GOODMAN,** Founding Editor of *Institutional Investor Magazine;* Co-founder of *New York Magazine;* Host and Editor in Chief of the Emmy Award-winning PBS television show "Adam Smith's Money World;" Author of *Supermoney* and *The Money Game*

*"If you want a rigorous, realistic, fact-filled guide to the best thinking about asset allocation, David Darst has it all in this one great guide-book."*

–**CHARLEY D. ELLIS,** The Partners of '63; Former Director and Founder, Greenwich Associates; Author of *Capital: The Story of Long-Term Investment* and *Winning the Loser's Game*

*". . . Some of the best opportunities for creating value lie not in stock-picking but in financial-asset diversification skill. . . . David Darst unlocks these asset allocation secrets in this lucid, easy-to-grasp presentation that should be a valued and well-thumbed resource for any savvy investor!"*

–**SAMUEL L. HAYES, III,** Jacob H. Schiff Professor of Investment Banking, Emeritus, Harvard Business School; Chair of the Investment Committee at Swarthmore College